CRUISING GUIDE TO
WESTERN FLORIDA

CRUISING GUIDE TO
WESTERN
FLORIDA

FIFTH EDITION

By Claiborne S. Young

PELICAN PUBLISHING COMPANY
GRETNA 2000

Maps by Carol Deakin and Kerry Horne
Cover photograph by author
Text photographs by author and first mate, unless otherwise indicated

ISBN 1-56554-737-3
ISSN 1097-8038

Information in this guidebook is based on authoritative data available at the time of printing. Prices and hours of operation of businesses listed are subject to change without notice. Readers are asked to take this into account when consulting this guide.

Printed in the United States of America

Published by Pelican Publishing Company, Inc.
1000 Burmaster, Gretna, Louisiana 70053

This book is dedicated

to my good friend,

frequent research assistant,

father-in-law,

and companion

for many watery miles,

Earle S. ("Bud") Williams.

Contents

Acknowledgments

First and foremost I want to thank my first-rate first mate, Karen Ann, without whose help as an experienced navigator, photographer, research assistant, and partner in life this book would not have been possible. I would also like to extend a warm thanks to my mother for all her encouragement and stories of Florida in the old days.

A very special thanks is extended to my research assistant, Earle ("Bud") Williams, to whom this book is dedicated. Thanks also to my other tireless research assistants, Bob Horne, Andy Lightbourne, and Kerry Horne. Without their many selfless hours spent with this writer during on-the-water research, this book would have been ever so much more difficult.

I would like to gratefully acknowledge the invaluable assistance of Mike and George McCreary, founders and co-owners of Caliber Yachts in Clearwater, Florida. For many years, the two brothers have faithfully taken care of my boats and vehicles while research for this book's various editions has been in progress. Mike and George are turning out some of the finest quality sailcraft on the water today.

A very special thanks goes to Walter Stilley, Andy Egeressy, and all the other members of Boater's Action and Information League (BAIL) for allowing me to specify their organization's suggested anchorages.

My warmest and most personal appreciation is extended to Morgan Stinemetz, cruising writer extraordinaire and sailing columnist for the *Sarasota Herald,* and to Doran Cushing, publisher of *Southwinds* magazine. Both of these fine friends have been tireless in their efforts to help with my research and to promote my guides. I will be owing them favors for the next millennium.

A very special acknowledgment is paid to Ed Beckhorn and G. Gale Vinson of Marco Island. Ed and Gale are very active in the Marco Power Squadron and U.S. Coast Guard Auxiliary. They have done much to keep this writer informed about even the smallest change on the waters lying about Marco Island and the Ten Thousand Islands. If info like theirs was available for all the waters I cover, this job would be a snap!

I would additionally like to recognize the contributions of Kerry Horne and Ms. Carol Deakin, who provided the wonderful maps throughout this guide.

I gratefully acknowledge the assistance of the many dockmasters and marina managers throughout Western Florida who gave so much of their time and wisdom to me during my research. While they are too numerous to mention, their input was invaluable.

Finally, I would like to thank Dr. Milburn Calhoun, Nancy Calhoun, Kathleen Calhoun Nettleton, Nina Kooij, Tracey Clements, and the rest of the staff at Pelican Publishing Company. It has been a genuine pleasure to once again work with the "Pelican Bunch," and I hope our relationship will continue for many years to come.

Introduction

It has been said of Florida's western coastline that the good Lord cursed it with shallow water but then, in His wisdom, blessed the land with great beauty. This old saw is entirely apt. There is really no better summary of these memorable waters' cruising characteristics. While, to be sure, there is almost always a channel to which mariners can look for decent depths, soundings of 5 to 6 feet are considered quite respectable in Western Florida, where they might be looked at askance along the Sunshine State's eastern coastline. But, for those cruisers who find their way past the shoals and shallows, the shores that open out before them are some of the most unforgettable they will ever experience.

The vast stretches of Western Florida that have been spared the plundering hand of modern development can only be described as idyllic. I have only to close my eyes for a few moments to bring to mind the almost eerie beauty of the Little Shark River, with its tangled cypress shores reflected against brown waters and set amidst an almost palpable silence. The wide expanse of the Ten Thousand Islands, with their myriad anchorages and almost secret backwater recesses, calls to mind the adventurous outdoor yearnings in all of us. Consider for a moment the lovely waters of Pine Island Sound, with its old, stilted fishing houses that recall the days when salty men worked long and hard to harvest a life from the sea. Or you might want to reflect for a moment on serene Gasparilla Island with its dreamlike inn, named for an infamous buccaneer whose story seems so much larger than life. Then there are the legendary man-killing turtles of the Myakka River and the almost shocking elegance of the Ringling estate overlooking Sarasota Bay. Still not convinced? Well, how about the singing ghosts of Manatee River and the incredible edifice of the Sunshine Skyway Bridge, spanning the entrance to Tampa Bay. And, lest we forget, there is the natural splendor of the Big Bend rivers, with names like Withlacoochee, Steinahatchee, and Suwannee drawn from another time. While, tragically, we must acknowledge that portions of the Western Florida coastline have fallen to the bulldozer and the blight of high-rise condominiums, there is still so much that is fair and beautiful.

Cruising captains can rejoice in the many paths open to them in Western Florida which slip quietly from the hustle and bustle of mainstream, modern life and into the quiet and rewarding recesses of natural splendor. My explorations and chronicling of the waters set about Western Florida make up one of the most rewarding undertakings in my writing career. I sincerely hope that each and every one of you will have the same opportunity to experience the wonders of this storied coastline. Let's weigh anchor and get started.

The geography of Western Florida's coast is varied and sometimes complicated. Southwestern Florida lacks a protected inland waterway and pleasure craft voyaging up the coast are relegated to the open waters of the Gulf of Mexico. Moving south to north, as we will throughout this guide, mariners cruising up from Marathon will be awed by the wild beauty of Cape Sable, the southwesternmost point of mainland Florida. This land is part of the Everglades National Park and safe from man-made changes. Two ports of call, the Park Service village of Flamingo and the anchorages along the Little Shark and Shark rivers, are well worth every cruiser's attention.

North of Cape Sable, skippers can explore the myriad backwaters and anchorages of the Ten Thousand Islands. This wild region is also little developed and offers a fascinating overview of the Everglades' coastal ecology. Everglades City is the only developed port of call in this region.

Captains cruising north of the islands to the city of Naples have two choices. You can continue your offshore voyage around the Cape Romano shoals or cut inside via a well-buoyed inland route. This latter passage features many cruising possibilities, but it is not a part of the official Western Florida ICW and depths can be a bit thin from time to time.

Naples offers good marina and repair yard facilities, but it's back to the open Gulf when time comes to head north again. With fair breezes or humming engine, you will soon arrive at the port of Fort Myers Beach and, a bit further along, San Carlos Bay and the southerly genesis of the Western Florida ICW. Here cruisers can turn aside on the combined path of the Caloosahatchee River and the Okeechobee Waterway to visit the old port town of Fort Myers before beginning their northward trek up the ICW.

The ICW soon introduces visiting cruisers to the fascinating waters of Pine Island Sound, with its rich history and enough potential havens for weeks of exploration. You will not want to miss Cabbage Key and Gasparilla Island.

A wide body of water known as Charlotte Harbor cuts northwest from the northerly headwaters of Pine Island Sound and leads intrepid cruisers to the town of Punta Gorda and two streams of note, the Myakka and Peace rivers. A detour away from the ICW to cruise up Charlotte Harbor and its feeder rivers can be more than rewarding, particularly for sailors.

The Western Florida ICW darts north again through Lemon Bay and several sheltered landcuts on its way to Venice, one of the friendliest coastal communities in Western Florida. Another trek to the north lands pleasure craft at the southerly beginnings of this coastline's most developed region. The city of Sarasota overlooks a bay of the same name along this stretch of the Waterway and offers full facilities for visiting yachtsmen.

Soon the Waterway skips past charming Anna Maria Island on its way to sprawling Tampa Bay. Cruisers new to Florida's west coast will probably have to exercise considerable self-control to keep from gasping as the broad mouth of Tampa Bay opens out before them for the first time. The Sunshine Skyway Bridge spanning the bay's mouth is one of the most impressive structures that this writer has ever witnessed.

Tampa Bay is the largest body of inland water along the Western Florida coastline. Its waters provide ready access to the marine facilities at Tampa and, in particular, the fortunate city of St. Petersburg.

The Manatee River, an important auxiliary water on southeastern Tampa Bay, leads cruisers by the hundreds to the Bradenton city waterfront. Here the prolific marina facilities are supplemented by one of the most fascinating live aquatic displays that you will ever enjoy.

North of the great bay, the ICW passes through one of the most intensely developed stretches of coastline that I have ever explored. The westerly reaches of St. Petersburg combine with the teeming city of Clearwater and a host of beachside communities to form an almost unbroken chain of development. The Waterway runs through a dredged passage between heavily populated barrier islands to the west and the built-up mainland to the east.

North of Clearwater, development begins to slow its frenzied pace a bit. The village of Dunedin is a delightful port of call with out-of-this-world dining possibilities.

Finally, the Western Florida ICW ends hard by the beautifully natural shores of Anclote Key. A quick cruise up nearby Anclote River will bring fortunate cruisers to the colorful town of Tarpon Springs, with its strong Greek flavor and fascinating sponge markets.

Now it's once again back to the open waters of the Gulf as mariners pass through the northernmost reaches of Western Florida on their way to the Panhandle. Look at any map of Florida and you will quickly understand why this region is called the Big Bend. While shallow water is everywhere in evidence, the various rivers along the way offer some of the most beautifully natural cruising in all of Florida. The Withlacoochee and Suwannee rivers are absolute "must-stop" ports of call in this region.

Finally, our quick travelogue comes to an end at the snow-white lighthouse marking the entrance to the St. Marks River. This "Panhandle river" offers good marina facilities and yet another beautiful shoreline, not to mention a historic site of particular interest.

Now captains and crew must turn west on the deep and clear waters of the Florida Panhandle. A few more miles will bring you to St. George Sound, bounteous Dog Island, the charming village of Carrabelle, and, perhaps most importantly, the easterly tip of the Northern Gulf ICW. For more information on this region and the inland and offshore waters west to New Orleans, please consult this writer's *Cruising Guide to the Northern Gulf Coast.*

The history of Western Florida is dotted with colorful figures and happenings like shells on a beach. It is my belief that no one can enjoy his or her cruise as he or she should without an appreciation of the heritage of the lands and waters through which he or she is traveling. For this reason, I have included a good smattering of Western Florida history throughout this guide. Wherever possible, the interested reader is referred to sources of additional information.

Weather along Western Florida is very different from what might be expected by cruisers from more northerly climes. Springs are warm to downright hot, and often humid, with relatively frequent thunderstorms. Nevertheless, this season is considered one of the best cruising times in the region. In the absence of any major storms, there is usually just enough wind for a good sail, and many days are clear and sparkling. Of course, cold fronts and other weather systems can mar this pattern of good weather, but most mariners will find spring cruising along the Western Florida coastline to be a genuine delight.

The long, hot, humid summers can leave cruisers used to cooler climates breathless from the heat. From June through September, and sometimes well into October, there are many days of calm air. Sweltering sailcraft are forced to plod along under auxiliary power. As if that weren't problem enough, frequent afternoon thunderstorms can, and often do, get violent. St. Petersburg and Tampa Bay bear the unenviable moniker of "Lightning Capital of the World." Truly, summer cruising along Western Florida should be planned with a ready ear to the latest weather forecast and radar report. No matter what the weather folks say though, if a dark cloud comes over the horizon, abandon everything and race for the nearest shelter.

The weather during the autumn months of October through December would be a serious contender with the spring season as the best cruising time on the Western Florida coast, but for the minor issue of hurricanes. The season for these great storms stretches from August through November. Any student of the region's history can readily tell you of the many, many hurricanes that have battered Florida's Gulf Coast in years past. If the weather service detects one of these giants heading your way, hole up until all that sound and fury has passed. These things are not to be taken lightly.

Winters in Western Florida are short and sweet, and are usually finished by March at the latest. Rarely does any part of the coastline experience freezing temperatures, except for the occasional exception along the northerly portion of the Big Bend. Strong northerly winds are part and parcel of the Western Florida winters and cruising skippers should be alert for these strong blows. If such winds persist for several days, they can sometimes lower water levels in north-to-south-lying bodies of water below charted levels.

In this guide I have endeavored to include all the information captains may need to take full advantage of Western Florida's tremendous cruising potential. I have paid particular attention to anchorages, marina facilities, and danger areas. All navigational information necessary for a successful cruise has been included, and these data have been split apart in their own sections and screened in gray for ready identification.

Each body of water has been personally visited for the very latest depth information. However, remember that bottom configurations do change. Dockside depths at marinas and inlets seem to be particularly subject to rapid variation. The cruising navigator should *always* be equipped with the latest charts and "Notice to Mariners" before leaving the dock.

The sketch maps presented in the body of this text are designed to locate anchorages and facilities and give the reader a general knowledge of the coastline. They are *not* intended for navigation.

This guide is not a navigational primer and it assumes that you have a working knowledge of piloting and coastal navigation. If you don't you should acquire these skills before tackling the coastal waters.

The waters set about the western coastline of the Sunshine State have a wide variety of navigational characteristics. As a general rule, cruisers can expect far shallower depths than those found in Eastern Florida or on the Panhandle. This exacting nature of Western Florida's waters frequently calls for careful navigation with a close watch on the sounder. Powercraft, in particular, should not be in so great a hurry to reach their intended port of call that they spend the better part of a day contemplating the value of good coastal navigation from the vantage point of a sandbar.

Tidal currents often flow swiftly along the inland waters of Western Florida. All mariners should be alert for the side-setting effects of wind and current. Sailcraft, particularly when cruising under auxiliary power, and single-engine trawlers should be especially mindful of the quickly moving waters when traversing the many narrow channels so typical of this coastline.

As development has gone forward in Western Florida, many homes, modest and palatial, have been built along the banks of the ICW. Some of these have their own private docks. In order to prevent having their boats rocked and their lawns sprayed with salt water by each passing vessel, residents have petitioned for and been granted "minimum wake" and "no wake" speed restrictions in ever increasing numbers during the last several years. I have tried to detail the major "no wake" areas, but be warned: new regulations are being put into effect constantly. These regulated zones can slow your cruise considerably, particularly if you pilot a planing-hull powercraft. Be sure to allow plenty of time in your cruising itinerary to avoid frustration.

With the increasing development have also come bridges with restricted opening hours. While, again, this is not as large a problem here as on Florida's east coast, sailcraft must contend with a host of regulated spans. Plan your hours around the opening times to avoid long delays. If you are forced to wait, be wary of the strong tidal currents that are often found on these waters. Stay alert and study the movements of any other vessels which might be waiting for the bridge.

Last but not least, with increasing development have come some rules this writer would prefer to describe in far saltier terms than gentility permits here. Between Naples and Clearwater, cruisers may find that anchorage is locally restricted to a 72-, 48-, or even 24-hour period. These perplexing regulations are inconsistent, in flux, and undergoing a strong challenge by local boating groups. Check with the marinas for the latest word.

One cruising advocate group that is making a real difference in the Western Florida anchorage struggle is BAIL (Boater's Action and Information League). This Sarasota-based organization has convinced the Florida state government to sanction a group of anchorages stretching from Marco Island to Tampa Bay. While these "BAIL-suggested" havens are most definitely *not* meant to preclude the possibility of dropping the hook elsewhere, cruisers can be reasonably sure of spending an uninterrupted evening in a BAIL anchorage. Within the body of this guide, I will point out and clearly identify all BAIL-suggested anchorages.

Unfortunately, several local municipalities have seen fit to regulate BAIL anchorages within their corporate limits. Apparently, the BAIL anchorage program remains a voluntary issue with local governments. We consider this an unfortunate development. These new restrictions will be identified in the body of this guide, but, at the current time, there is nothing (except good sense) to keep other local authorities from imposing similar restrictions. As with virtually all other anchorages in Western Florida located within the confines of urbanized regions, cruisers must now enter even BAIL anchorages expecting the possibility of being asked to move on within a 72-hour (or less) time period.

All navigators should have a well-functioning depth sounder on board before leaving the dock. This is one of the most basic safety instruments in any captain's arsenal of aids. The cruiser who does not take this elementary precaution is asking for trouble. An accurate knotmeter/log is another instrument that will prove quite useful. It is often just as important to know how far you have gone as to know what course you are following.

The modern miracle of satellite-controlled GPS (Global Positioning System), particularly when interfaced with a laptop computer loaded with the latest digitized nautical charts, is yet another powerful navigational aid. GPS is more important when navigating the waters of Western Florida than on any other coastline that this writer has ever reviewed. With the lack of a protected, well-marked intracoastal waterway from Cape Sable to Fort Myers, and similar cruising conditions to the north along the Big Bend, a GPS suddenly becomes an invaluable, almost necessary tool that many navigators will not want to live without.

Western Florida skippers will find it most advantageous to keep the current chart and a pair of good binoculars in the cockpit or on the fly-bridge at all times. With these aids on hand, problems can be quickly resolved before you have a close encounter of the grounding kind.

In this guide, lighted daybeacons are always called "flashing daybeacons." I believe this is a more descriptive term than the officially correct designation "light," or the more colloquial expression "flasher." Also, to avoid confusion, daybeacons without lights are always referred to as "unlighted daybeacons." Similarly, lighted buoys are called "flashing buoys."

So there you have it, with all its beauty, splendor, and warts too. The coastline of Western Florida from Cape Sable to the Florida Panhandle is indeed special. Cruisers of every taste and persuasion will certainly find something that strikes their fancy. It has been my privilege to help introduce these unforgettable waters to you. I sincerely hope that soon you will have the chance to experience them for yourself. Bathed by a benevolent sun and washed by the warm Gulf waters, the Sunshine State's western coastline waits to greet you. Good luck and good cruising!

CRUISING GUIDE TO
WESTERN
FLORIDA

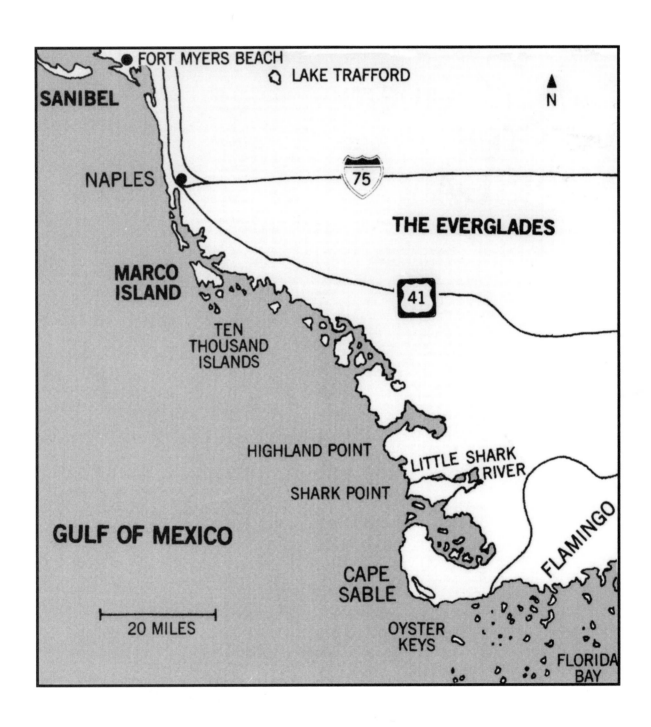

CHAPTER 1

Flamingo to Fort Myers Beach

If ever there was a single section of coastline that is a microcosm for the entire Western Florida seashore, it is most certainly that often lonely stretch of sand and vegetation between Cape Sable and Fort Myers Beach. Florida's southwesternmost coastline is a collection of varied cruising grounds that strike this writer as lands (and waters) of incredible contrasts.

Take, for instance, the almost completely undeveloped lands lying about Cape Sable, the southwestern tip of mainland Florida. This region is an integral part of the Everglades National Park and is almost completely free from human development. The waters lapping against these beautifully natural shores are almost universally shallow. There are but two ports of call to which cruising captains can look for overnight safety and security. Not to be overlooked, one of these stops comprises what may well be the most beautiful anchorage in all of Florida. While there are significant differences between the two coastlines, the waters about Cape Sable strikingly remind this writer of Western Florida's Big Bend, north of Anclote Key and Tarpon Springs. Here, too, shallow water lies abundantly about little-disturbed shores, and only a few rivers provide deep enough entrance depths to be considered by cruisers. Also, like the Big Bend, behind Cape Sable there is no protected Intracoastal Waterway maintained by the Army Corps of Engineers and to which mariners can look for safe passage. North from Cape Sable to Marco Island (at least), both pleasure and commercial craft must ply the Gulf of Mexico's open waters while cruising north or south along the Western Florida coastline.

Above Plover Key and Lostmans River, the coastline changes radically. Suddenly skippers and crew are plunged into that fascinating portion of Western Florida known, appropriately enough, as the Ten Thousand Islands. The name says it all. There are probably ten thousand islands, or keys, at least, between Lostmans River and Marco Island. Exploration possibilities boggle the mind. The presence of but one readily accessible marina south of Marco Island and the relative lack of navigational aids, coupled with the ever-present shallow water, calls for a spirit of adventure and a well-supplied vessel.

I cannot cruise the Ten Thousand Islands without musing back to my wanderings among the sparsely developed islands of Pine Island Sound, north of Fort Myers and the Caloosahatchee River. Both regions have a siren's song that speaks to the very core of the true explorer who relishes the notion that every puff of air or turn of the screw takes him or her a bit farther from civilization.

Captains cruising north through the Ten Thousand Islands must make a fundamental choice. You can continue offshore past the monumental Cape Romano shoals, or come inside these shallows and follow a marked and charted channel past Marco Island to the city of Naples.

Here again, the coastline, chameleonlike, takes on an entirely new character. Whether you cruise to Naples via its inland waterway (not a part of the official Western Florida ICW) or enter through the city's excellent inlet, Gordon Pass, you will find a teeming waterfront crowded with docks and shopping facilities.

Another offshore run will bring northbound cruisers to the community of Fort Myers Beach on Estero Island. The shores of this once historic island are now fringed with a beachside honky-tonk of cheap shops and motels. On a happier note, a host of marinas and a fine anchorage wait to greet the visiting cruiser.

Who could visit Naples or Estero Island and not come away feeling the kinship between this city and the shores of the ICW lying about St. Petersburg, Sarasota, and Clearwater? All of these communities represent highly developed Florida and offer a myriad of services for all cruising craft.

Finally, a quick run up the Gulf from Estero will bring mariners to the southern mouth of San Carlos Bay and the official genesis of the Western Florida ICW. This latter section will be covered in the second chapter of this guide but, for now, let's push on to the exciting cruising possibilities of southwestern Florida.

Charts   Cruising navigators will need a whole bevy of NOAA charts for complete coverage of the waters from Flamingo to Naples.

11451—useful chart for approaching Cape Sable and Flamingo from the Florida Keys and points south

11433—principal chart for the Cape Sable and Flamingo region; cruisers planning to enter the marina at Flamingo will require this cartographical aid; also provides excellent detail of the Little Shark and Shark rivers' entrances and interior reaches

11431—large-coverage chart covering the southwestern Florida coastline from Cape Sable to the Ten Thousand Islands; this chart shows some offshore aids to navigation not pictured on the larger scale, more detailed inshore charts; most captains voyaging north along the coastline will want to have this chart

11432—a detailed chart picturing the coastline from the Little Shark River to Lostmans River that is really much more important to small craft running the Everglades National Park Wilderness Waterway than to skippers of sailboats or large powercraft; it still might be useful to provide a more detailed look at geographic reference points as you move north along the coast; skippers with electronic navigation aboard may be able to get by with 11431 only

11430—important large-scale, detailed chart that covers all waters from Lostmans River and the Ten Thousand Islands to Naples and Wiggins Pass, including the inland Marco Island to Naples waterway; this one is a must

11429—small-scale, offshore chart covering the waters from the Ten Thousand Islands to a point north of Naples

11427—provides detailed navigational information for all inland and near-shore waters between Wiggins Pass and Fort Myers; this chart is needed by all cruisers planning to visit Fort Myers Beach, Fort Myers, or the southerly genesis of the Western Florida ICW

11426—another of those general, large-coverage offshore charts, this one detailing the waters from south of San Carlos Bay and Fort Myers to Charlotte Harbor; this chart does provide the only coverage of Charlotte Harbor, which is addressed in chapter 2

Bridges

Goodland/Highway 92 Bridge—crosses Marco Island-Naples waterway and Big Marco River north of unlighted daybeacon #12—Fixed—55 feet

Marco Island (Highway 951)/Juge S. S. Jolley Bridge—crosses Marco Island-Naples water-way and Big Marco River west of unlighted daybeacon #26—Fixed—55 feet

Fort Myers Beach Bridge—crosses Matanzas Pass/Fort Myers Beach channel east-southeast of unlighted daybeacon #13—Fixed—65 feet

Flamingo to Lostmans River

One fine summer morning in early August of 1992, my fearless research assistant, Kerry Horne, and this writer headed out early in the morning from the marina at Flamingo, bound for the entrance to Little Shark River. As we rounded the three points of Cape Sable, we were amply rewarded for our early departure. To see the lovely white sand beaches back dropped by the mysterious cypress, brooding pines, and tall hardwoods was a very special experience indeed. Kerry described the Gulf's waters as akin to "color-tinted photographs of the Caribbean." We turned to each other and observed almost at the same moment that very few people, even frequent cruisers along Western Florida's coastline, had ever laid eyes on this magnificent sight.

In reflecting on this observation since that August morning, this writer has come to understand why so few take advantage of such a unique cruising opportunity. Skippers heading south to the Keys, or even those northbound from Marathon, are very likely to ride offshore and head for Naples or Fort Myers Beach. With only one marina (which requires a long passage off the direct north-south track to reach its docks) and a single anchorage, navigators studying chart 11433 might be excused for thinking that there is little to call them closer to shore.

What a mistake! In spite of their scarcity, the two ports of call in the Cape Sable region are worthy of attention from every single mariner cruising south of Everglades City and Marco Island.

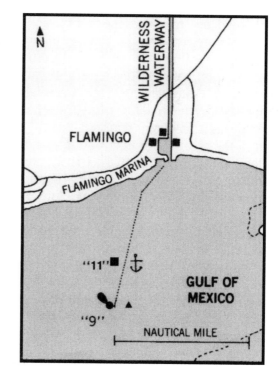

Flamingo

Flamingo was once one of the wildest frontier towns in all of Florida. Sadly, nothing is now left of the Flamingo of yesteryear. Today, visiting cruisers will find only a lodge, marina, and restaurant operated by a U.S. Park Service concessionaire.

It is a run of better than 12 nautical miles from the waters off the "East Cape" section of Cape Sable through the northerly waters of Florida Bay to the southerly dockage basin of Flamingo Lodge and Marina. Minimum depths on the entrance channel are about 4½ to 5 feet (found near unlighted daybeacon #16). Typically, soundings range from 5 to 9 feet. Boats drawing less than 4 feet should not have any problems. If you need more water, wait for a higher tide before attempting the passage.

Flamingo Marina has a rather unique situation. There are two dockage basins at this facility that are separated by a concrete floodgate. The harbor north of the gate is used by small craft engaged in cruising the so-called Wilderness Waterway through Everglades National Park. This shallow passage leads the adventurous small-craft skipper through the heart of the great sea of trees and grass north of Flamingo to Everglades City. The waterway is only appropriate for very small (18 feet or less), outboard-powered craft and thus will not be further discussed in this guide. The marina at Flamingo maintains a hoist that can actually lift smaller powercraft over the concrete barrier and deposit them safely in the waters to the north or south. This lift is not heavy enough for larger vessels, but, as mentioned, that point is mostly moot anyway.

Of more interest to cruising-size craft is the sheltered dockage basin on the bay side of the marina, just north of unlighted daybeacon #18. Here you will find fixed wooden piers where transients may dock in 4½- to 6-foot dockside depths. Water and 30-amp power connections are available. Gasoline and diesel can be purchased at a fuel dock just south of the concrete floodgate, where you will also discover a waste pump-out service. Shoreside showers and a laundromat are at hand beside the full-line variety and ship's store. For those wanting to take a break from the live-aboard routine, the adjacent lodge is quite convenient. The restaurant in the complex is not open during the summer months, but you can still get pizza and sandwiches at the bar, which is in operation year round.

Flamingo Marina (941) 695-3101
    http://www.flamingolodge.com

Approach depth—4½-9 feet
Dockside depth—4½-6 feet
Accepts transients—yes
Fixed wooden piers—yes
Dockside power connections—up to 30 amp
Dockside water connections—yes
Waste pump-out—yes
Showers—yes
Laundromat—yes
Gasoline—yes
Diesel fuel—yes
Ship's and variety store—yes
Restaurant—on site

Flamingo makes an ideal base of operations for those wanting to explore Everglades National Park. Check at the lodge office concerning information about tram tours for those who arrive by water and lack landside automobile transportation. These sorts of excursions are usually offered, except during certain times of the summer. Call ahead of time to see if the park trams are operating.

We cannot leave Flamingo without a word about the mosquitoes. As a boy growing up on the North Carolina coast, I used to think the Carolinas had a mosquito problem. Boy, I did not know anything. I have never seen such bloodthirsty mosquitoes as those in the Florida Everglades. At times they swarm so thickly that it seems as if everything (and everyone) will be completely covered within a few minutes by frenzied, buzzing, biting insects the size of condors. They practically carried us off during the night and early morning while we were docked at Flamingo. According to Park Service employees, the mosquitoes are at their worst between May and November. They really seem to come out after a rain. The more rain, the more mosquitoes. It should also be noted that calm conditions seem to encourage the little beasts. On a calm summer night, or early in the morning, after a heavy rainfall it could be a battle for your life.

The Everglades' mosquitoes are not only a problem in Flamingo. The same conditions can be expected on Shark River and throughout the Ten Thousand Islands. The locals swear by a body lotion produced by the Avon cosmetic company called Skin-So-Soft. While it is most certainly not an insect repellent, apparently mosquitoes hate the taste of this fragrant, perfumy liquid and will not bite if you have slopped the oily concoction on your skin. By all accounts, I would have a large bottle of Skin-So-Soft on board before anchoring or tying up to the docks anywhere between Cape Sable and Marco Island.

Flamingo History In his fascinating book, *True Tales of the Everglades*, Stuart McIver comments about Flamingo's roots:

> When the settlers at the tip of Cape Sable established a post office in 1893, they were told they had to give their settlement a name. . . . They considered "End of the World." Instead,

they picked a romantic, exotic name for their own personal hell-hole. They called it Flamingo. . . . In the 1890s flocks of the spectacular tropical birds were commonly seen in the Cape Sable area . . . so the name made sense. So did "End of the World," since the Cape at that time was an isolated society populated mostly by people who were running away from something—the law, civilization, or maybe their wives.

This short, quaint description tells all, and the term "hell-hole" seems particularly appropriate in view of the climate and the mosquitoes. In those early days the few residents of Flamingo made a living fishing, cultivating sugarcane, and distilling more than a few quarts of moonshine.

Apparently mosquitoes were at least as big a problem then as they are now. Each house was equipped with a room fronting the outdoors that was called a "loser." Before anyone entered a house, they were supposed to beat away or "lose" their mosquitoes with a palmetto branch in the little room.

In 1901, Flamingo received one of its most prominent early citizens, Steve Roberts. Uncle Steve, as he came to be called, migrated south from Gainesville, Florida, with "cattle rustling" rumors snapping at his heels. He raised a big family which eventually became the most prominent in the tiny settlement.

In 1908 the village's sugarcane was beset by a horde of hungry rats. Desperate to save their one cash crop, Uncle Steve's son Gene took a boat to Key West, where he advertised, "Will pay 10 cents Apiece for Every Cat." It wasn't long before he had a boat full of snarling, fighting felines. It must have been a long, trying trip back to Flamingo, but the effort was worth it. In no time at all the new swamp cats had routed out almost every rat within miles.

However, the real fame of Flamingo lies not in fishing, sugarcane, or even rats, but in the wholesale slaughter of the exotic birds which lived in the Everglades and the high-ground "hammocks" near the village. At the turn of the century, a truly unfortunate trend in fashions resulted in the stylish practice of decorating women's hats with colorful bird feathers or plumes. The demand rose so quickly that hunters in the Everglades soon could make more money than they had ever dreamed of before. At one point, egret feathers were selling for $32 an ounce, more than the price of gold at the time. The mass killings drove many of the Everglades' winged species to the brink of extinction after only a few years.

Finally, the state of Florida came to the rescue and outlawed the killing of birds for their plumage in 1901. For several years thereafter, it was a battle between the local game wardens and the plume hunters, but finally this sad trend in fashions crept into the pages of history.

In 1922 a road was pushed through the Everglades from Miami to Flamingo. Surprisingly enough, this artery of commerce was the death knell of the tiny community. As Stuart McIver comments in his other, equally fascinating book, *Glimpses of South Florida History,* "People had found a way to get out." Many of the original homes were destroyed in the great hurricane of 1926 and the rest rotted away, with not a trace remaining today.

Flamingo Legend

It was during that tense period when plume hunting had been outlawed but before the fashion went out of style, that the "National Association of Audubon Societies" hired a group of wardens to enforce the new state law. Several of these heroic individuals operated out of Flamingo, and one of the most famous was Guy Bradley.

On July 8, 1905, the sounds of distant gunfire were heard over Florida Bay. Guy walked out of his front door and sighted a schooner in the distance that he recognized as the boat of Capt. Walter Smith. He had already arrested Smith twice before for plume hunting, and the gunfire left little doubt about the captain's present activities.

The intrepid warden got his gun and began rowing his small dinghy across Florida Bay. It was a trip from which he would never return. His body was found soon afterward. Guy Bradley had become the first warden to die in the defense of Florida's native bird population.

Captain Smith fled to Miami, where he managed to successfully avoid indictment through political connections. Nevertheless, the warden's sacrifice was not to be in vain. As a direct result of the anger engendered by Guy Bradley's death, new legislation was passed in both Tallahassee and Washington which was to end the plume trade within a few years once and for all.

Guy Bradley was buried on the tip of Cape Sable, and a deeply grateful Audubon Society erected a plaque over his grave. In 1960 Hurricane Donna washed the grave away, but the brave warden and his untimely but honorable death have not been forgotten. Today a notable monument has been erected to Guy Bradley's memory at the Flamingo Visitor's Center.

Flamingo and Cape Sable Anchorages

A few boats occasionally anchor in the waters off Cape Sable during fair weather. None of the havens described below is particularly sheltered, and they should not be employed if there is a hint of foul weather in the forecast.

Captains wanting to anchor off Flamingo, rather than tie up at the marina docks, might consider doing so in the 4- and 5-foot waters east of unlighted daybeacon #11. Don't stray too far from the marked channel, or depths may deteriorate further.

In light winds, cruisers may consider anchoring in the charted 7- and 8-foot waters northwest and southeast of Middle Cape. Anchor abeam of the cape's westerly tip, either to the north or south. Do not attempt to make a closer approach to the beach except by dinghy, as depths rise quickly.

Middle Cape is surrounded by a beautiful white sand beach backed by tall trees that look as if they have not known the hand of man since time immemorial. You explorer types might try dinghying ashore through the surf for an unforgettable visit. Just don't forget about the mosquitoes if the winds are calm.

Little Shark River and Shark River Anchorages

The marked entrance into the westerly mouth of Little Shark River lies some 11 nautical miles north of Middle Cape. Out of the hundreds and hundreds of anchorages that this writer has visited and reviewed, the memory of Shark River will always remain with me as one of the most beautiful and awe-inspiring of the lot. The dark waters rolling by with their strong tidal currents fitfully reflect the heavily wooded shores. Though it is well within the confines of Everglades National Park, visitors to Shark River will not see the "river of grass" for which the region is so famous. Closer to the coast, the Everglades supports deep woods of cypress, pine, and a few hardwoods. The river's primeval shoreline looks as if it has

Little Shark River entrance

been undisturbed since the days when the Timucuan Indians poled their canoes along the stream, many hundreds of years before the first European touched the Florida shoreline. Anchoring in these rarified confines and watching the Evening Star unhindered in the clear coastal airs can quickly lead to a substantial dropping of the blood pressure. Of course, on calm nights, part of that lower reading may be courtesy of a few million mosquitoes draining you dry, but, hey, nothing's perfect.

At the time of this writing, minimum low-water depths of 5½ feet can be expected in the marked entrance channel. Care must be taken to hold to these soundings at the stream's western mouth. First-time visitors should be *sure* to read the navigational account of Little

Anchored on Little Shark River

Shark River presented in the next section of this chapter *before* undertaking their first entry into the stream.

East of Little Shark River's entrance, depths improve markedly, typically to better than 8 feet. While there are a few unmarked shoals to watch out for, careful cruisers piloting craft as large as 45 feet can find their way into the confines of (Big) Shark River, a few miles to the east and north. This delightful passage currently features minimum 6-foot depths.

A complete compendium of all the places that cruising craft might anchor on the Little Shark and Shark rivers would make up a small pamphlet of its own. While a number of potential havens are outlined below, this list is by no means exhaustive. Captains with wanderlust running hot in their veins can pilot their vessels to literally dozens and dozens of overnight stopovers.

One concern when anchoring on either of the Shark rivers or their adjoining streams is the strong tidal currents that plague these waters. On-site experiments with our own hook suggest that the holding ground is good. Nevertheless, this is one spot where you had really better take a good, long look once the anchor is down to be sure you aren't dragging before popping open a cool one (define it as you wish) to begin the evening's relaxation.

For those who want an early start the next morning, the Little Shark River offers an anchorage just east of its entrance. The charted cove northwest of unlighted daybeacon #4 offers first-rate protection and depths of 5½ to 6 feet. Shallow water protrudes much farther out from the back (northwestern shores) of the cove than is indicated on chart 11433. For best depths, anchor just inside the cove's southeastern mouth, on the center of its southwest-to-northeast axis. Protection is superb and the deeply wooded shores mentioned above are very much in the picture. Boats up to 48 feet should not have any problems with swinging room.

Notwithstanding all of this first anchorage's good qualities, I feel that bodies of water like the two Shark rivers deserve a little further upstream exploration. Believe me, you won't be sorry for the additional time spent cruising on this incredibly beautiful river.

The next anchorage (moving to the east) that you might consider is found on the river's southeasterly offshoot at unlighted daybeacon #69. Good depths of 9 feet are carried to a position 100 yards north of the point where

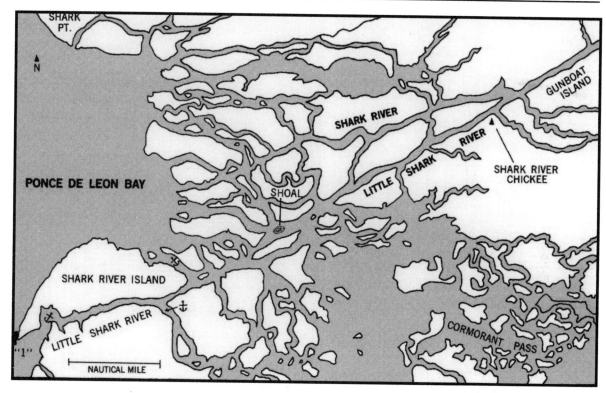

the stream splits into two southerly branches. Again, protection is superb and the shores are all one could ask for. Captains piloting boats larger than 40 feet might feel a bit cramped.

The main branch of the Little Shark River cuts northeast from unlighted daybeacon #69. Unmarked shoals become somewhat more frequent, but are still easily handled by careful cruisers. The fork of the Little Shark River that cuts back to the northwest, west of unlighted daybeacon #68, and leads eventually to Ponce de Leon Bay is yet another super overnight stop in most winds for all but the very largest boats. Depths run from 6 to 9 feet and the shoreline is, if possible, even more magnificent. Strong westerly and northwesterly winds could blow straight into the stream from the bay and raise a chop, but otherwise this anchorage is also well sheltered. Don't attempt to follow the stream out into Ponce de Leon Bay, where there are a host of unmarked shoals. Drop your hook well southeast of the entrance into the bay.

The marked channel in the Little Shark River cuts southeast at unlighted daybeacon #64 and eventually joins up with the Everglades Wilderness Waterway. Larger pleasurecraft should avoid cruising past #64.

It is still feasible to cut into the northerly branch of the Little Shark River just before reaching #64. After skirting around a few charted shoals, you can work your way either into the upper reaches of the Little Shark River, or through one of the deep, north-south, connecting streams into the Shark River. For those who really want a good look at the region, consider a round trip, cutting north on one of the two connecting streams

Little Shark River shoreline

southwest of charted Shark Cutoff, then east-northeast on the main body of the Shark River to the waters abeam of charted Gunboat Island. You can then retrace your steps to charted "Marker 6" and follow the upper reaches of the Little Shark River back to the stream's entrance channel. This is a magnificent trip for powerboats, albeit a bit lengthy for the sailing brethren. In any case, you don't have to undertake the entire loop. Even a portion of the passage is well worthwhile. Cruisers can anchor almost anywhere along the upper reaches of the Shark or Little Shark rivers. Just be sure that the anchor is well down and show a nighttime anchor light.

Don't attempt to follow the Shark River above Gunboat Island. Depths finally begin to deteriorate northeast of this point.

FLAMINGO TO LOSTMANS RIVER NAVIGATION

The first thing to understand about navigating the waters of extreme southwesterly Florida is the lack of any protected Intracoastal Waterway. This means that all north-to-south cruising must be accomplished by braving the waters of the open Gulf of Mexico. While this is far from a daunting prospect in fair weather, or even for sailcraft in moderate breezes, the Gulf has been known to get its dander up on more than one occasion. Smaller cruising craft, in particular, *must* take the latest weather forecast into account before venturing out on these wide waters.

The second thing to remember is the almost universal shallowness of the southwestern Florida coastline. This shoally character makes for a very long cruise between stops. Except for Flamingo and the Little Shark River, captains bound north from Marathon and the Florida Keys must cruise a good 36 nautical miles from East Cape (the southernmost of Cape Sable's three points) to the first available anchorage (shallow-draft only) at New Turkey Key. It's yet another run of better than 13 nautical miles from a position abeam of New Turkey Key to Indian Key. This isle marks the channel leading to Everglades City, the only port of call with readily accessible marina facilities in the Ten Thousand Islands region. It doesn't take a rocket scientist to understand that it's going to be a lengthy cruise from Cape Sable to Everglades City. Powerboats must be sure to have sufficient fuel aboard, and all pleasurecraft should make appropriate preparations for covering such a distance without the possibility of putting into a nearby harbor.

Entrance into Flamingo Employing either DR (dead-reckoning) navigation, a Loran, or GPS, work your way to a point south and west of East Cape. Use your binoculars to pick out unlighted daybeacon #1A, south of East Cape, and flashing daybeacon #2, 1.6 nautical miles farther to the south. For best depths, set course to come abeam of and pass #2 by about 1 nautical mile to the aid's northerly side. This wide gap will help you avoid the charted 5-foot depths north of #2.

From flashing daybeacon #2, the channel is reasonably straightforward, though there are wide gaps between the various aids to navigation along the way. Be sure to have compass courses pre-plotted, and faithfully follow them as you work your way along.

Pass unlighted daybeacons #6 and #8 to their northerly sides (as you would expect from the good old "red, right, returning" rule). Shallow water lies south of these aids.

At flashing daybeacon #9, the channel turns sharply north and cuts through a dredged passage into Flamingo Marina's southerly dockage basin. This is the shallowest portion of the passage to Flamingo. Expect some 5-foot (possibly 4½ at extreme low water) depths abeam of unlighted daybeacon #16. If you should decide to anchor east of unlighted daybeacon #11, ease your way about 50 yards due east from #11. Drop the hook before proceeding any farther. To the east, soundings rise to 4-foot levels or less. At unlighted daybeacon #16, the channel swings a bit to starboard, then cuts back north at unlighted daybeacon #18. The harbor's entrance will then be obvious dead ahead. As you cruise into the creek, the marina docks will come abeam to port.

North to Little Shark River Cruising the gap between East Cape and Little Shark River is actually surprisingly simple in good weather. If you stay within sight of shore, both Middle and Northwest capes are quite obvious. Flashing daybeacon #4 off Northwest Cape is also valuable in determining your position.

Look at either chart 11431 or 11433 for a moment and note the "Marker" symbols. These are actually on-the-water signs that denote the boundary of Everglades National Park. You can keep up with your position by ticking these off as you go along. Thus, with the plentiful landmarks and other points of reference, even Loran and GPS-less boats should be able to find their way to Northwest Cape in good weather.

On the other hand, local cruisers have warned this writer that the "Everglades National Park" signs, mentioned above, are a real navigational hazard at night. Apparently they lack any of the reflector tape that usually allows easy detection of aids to navigation with a searchlight. Watch out for these potential obstructions if your passage through these waters takes place after sunset.

The situation changes radically north of this cape. No readily recognizable landmarks grace the shoreline between Northwest Cape and the entrance to the Shark River. There are no aids to navigation either, except for the park boundary markers. Just to make matters a bit more

interesting, flashing daybeacon #1, at the western mouth of Little Shark River, is very hard to spot from the water. The 16-foot daybeacon blends right in with the tall trees along Shark River Island.

I can only recommend using your binoculars and good dead-reckoning navigation, plus a GPS, to find your way to flashing daybeacon #1. It's not always an easy process, but the reward more than justifies the effort.

The Little Shark River & the Shark River The Little Shark River's entrance channel is the shallowest and most critical part of the entire passage throughout the region. Come abeam of and pass both flashing daybeacon #1 and unlighted daybeacon #3 by some 50 yards to their southeast and southerly sides. Don't get closer to the aids. The channel seems to be shoaling on its northwesterly side. By keeping off the markers, you can currently maintain minimum 5½-foot depths.

After leaving #3 behind, the river soon cuts to the north. Good depths spread out in a broad band along the centerline for some distance upstream.

If you drop the hook on the cove northwest of unlighted daybeacon #4, remember to anchor on the outer portion of the cove's mouth. Farther to the northwest, depths shelve upward with surprising rapidity at the rear of the cove.

You can easily turn into the mid-width of the river fork branching southeast from unlighted daybeacon #69. Just be sure to halt your forward progress at least 100 yards short of the split in the stream.

Cruisers seeking the more upstream anchorages and the (Big) Shark River should cut northeast at #69. As you emerge from this connector stream into the wider water west of unlighted daybeacon #68, you will go through one stretch of 6-foot depths. Unlighted daybeacon #68 marks the first real shoal you need to worry with in the Little Shark River. If you are entering the anchorage northwest of #68, favor the stream's southwesterly shores to avoid the shallows. Cruising craft continuing upstream should pass #68 to its southerly side.

You can continue to follow the buoyed route to unlighted daybeacon #64. Discontinue following the markers at this point. To the east and south, the marked cut leads to the Wilderness Waterway and depths deteriorate. Those lucky captains and crew continuing on to the Shark River should probably employ the deep feeder stream just west and north of #64.

As you approach the wider waters to the northeast, the trickiest section of the passage to the Shark River will be encountered. Notice the large patch of 4-foot shoals pictured clearly on chart 11433, bounding the stream's center. To avoid this hazard, round the point, cut east, and favor the southern shores heavily until you are well past the shoal. You may then take your choice of the two north-to-south feeder streams (and enter the Shark River), or continue to track your way up the Little Shark River until intersecting the Shark River near charted "Marker 6."

On-site research did not reveal any depth problems in passing south of the island which sits at the confluence of the Little Shark and Shark rivers. Simply hold to the mid-width scrupulously as you pass the island. Good depths continue upstream to Gunboat Island. This guide's coverage of the Shark River ends at this point.

On to the Ten Thousand Islands   North of the Little Shark River entrance, passing cruisers must continue on the open waters of the Gulf. This is an area where boats with GPS have a definite advantage. Some of the charted aids to navigation are actually founded in rather shallow water and the prudent mariner will pass well west of these markers. It's always possible to miss a beacon under these circumstances, and without a good dead-reckoning track or an electronic means to fix your position, it could be a white-knuckle cruise.

Shallow water is waiting to trap you on the various rivers or coves indenting the shoreline between the Little Shark River and Pavilion Key (near flashing daybeacon #10). All are quite shallow. Even Ponce de Leon Bay, just north of the Little Shark River, is riddled with unmarked shoals.

North of Lostmans River and flashing daybeacon #8, it's time to make a very basic decision. If you plan to explore the Ten Thousand Islands, or follow the inland route via Marco Island to Naples, set your course to pass east of the long, long Cape Romano shoals. Eventually, you should come abeam of flashing daybeacon #10 well to its westerly quarter. Pavilion Key heralds your entrance into the Ten Thousand Islands region. Some great cruising is just ahead.

Navigators following the offshore route should set course to pass several miles west of the Cape Romano shoals. An unnumbered 18-foot flashing daybeacon marks the southerly reaches of these shallows.

Ten Thousand Islands

At the turn of the century . . . the Ten Thousand Islands, a bewildering maze of mangroves, gave cover to fugitives, derelicts and a few harmless hermits. The seven unwritten laws of that wild country, an early account says, were:

1. Suspect every man
2. Ask no questions
3. Settle your own quarrels
4. Never steal from an islander
5. Stick by him, even if you do not know him
6. Shoot quick, when your secret is in danger
7. Cover your kill

Well, since those days, the settlements in the Ten Thousand Islands have acquired a far more savory reputation. However, the rugged American individualism symbolized in this rough credo (recounted in Stuart McIver's *Glimpses of South Florida History*) is still very much part and parcel of this region where wild, untamed land is the rule, not the exception.

As we explore the Ten Thousand Islands together in the pages that follow, you will hear a few of the stories which have filtered out of the islands through the years. It's not hard to imagine how the rugged and often colorful pioneers in this land of water and islands engendered a folklore which is as rich as swampland muck, although the occasional outsider has added a bit of spice here and there as well. No less a personage than John James Audubon spent some time here while performing his early studies of birds and their habits.

And speaking of birds, those who go gently will have the opportunity to observe a bounty of winged wildlife in the islands. Great egrets, great blue herons, roseate spoonbills, wood storks, and better than a hundred other varieties of birds may be spotted as you cruise along. Practically the entire Ten Thousand Islands are within the confines of Everglades National Park. As such, these small bodies of land are some of the most prolific and varied bird sanctuaries in the United States.

Cruisers who prefer to tie up to the piers of a full-service marina with every amenity will most likely want to lay on the throttles or crank out the jib a bit more and head directly for Marco Island or Naples. But those mariners whose eyes get dreamy while contemplating the idea of backwater cruising where few have been before them will find a wealth of rewards in cruising the Ten Thousand Islands.

The Ten Thousand Island region begins north of Lostmans River and runs to Coon Key Light. Here cruisers following the inside route can enter a sheltered passage running north to Marco Island and Naples. After exploring the Ten Thousand Islands, those captains following the outside route will have to duck back out into the Gulf well south of the Cape Romano shoals before continuing their northward trek.

Shallow water is very much commonplace in the islands. Cruisers must take extra care to stay off the bottom while trying to navigate the various anchorages and channels cutting this way and that around the islets. This process is made ever so much more difficult due to the relative lack of navigational aids. What may look quite obvious on the chart can be almost irrecognizable on the water. If you've been lucky enough to visit a particular anchorage previously, and locked the location into your GPS's memory, so much the better. Otherwise, you are in for some exacting coastal navigation.

This is most certainly one portion of the

Western Florida coastline where those fortunate cruisers who have a GPS aboard, interfaced with a laptop computer (loaded with the digitized NOAA nautical charts and appropriate navigational software such as NavTrek Solo), have a distinct advantage. Personally, we make it a point to have this wonderful marvel of electronic navigation aboard whenever we are cruising these waters.

With this navigational complexity in mind, the anchorages outlined below have been chosen for their relative proximity to some recognizable geographic or on-the-water point of reference. Thus, the list is by no means even close to complete. Those who simply must drop the hook where none have gone before, and are willing to risk finding the bottom, will discover many an additional overnight stop to explore and savor.

Marina facilities in the Ten Thousand Islands are meager. One old inn welcomes transient cruisers at the village of Everglades City. Good food, lodging, and supplies (not to mention good sightseeing) are close at hand, and the inn now offers full fueling services. The only other marina in this region now has such a shallow entrance channel that we can no longer recommend it at all for cruising-size vessels.

The Rod and Gun Club in Everglades City is now the only realistic marina alternative for cruising vessels in the entire Ten Thousand Island region. Better be sure those tanks are topped off and your vessel is in top condition before taking the plunge.

I cannot close without making plain my personal affection for the Ten Thousand Islands. This writer knows of no other cruising ground that offers so many gunkholes and fascinating opportunities to explore far from the remotest confines of civilization. It's truly not for everyone, but the rugged call of the islands is a song that will be hard for many to ignore.

New Turkey Key

Our first anchorage in the Ten Thousand Islands will certainly not go down in history as the easiest to find. You must also travel through some definite 4-foot low-water depths to reach the haven in question. Obviously, this anchorage is restricted to those vessels drawing 3½ feet (or preferably less), with skippers who are confident in their navigational skills and who pilot boats 40 feet or smaller.

A cruise of some 5 nautical miles to the north-northwest of flashing daybeacon #8 (west of Lostmans River) will bring you abeam of Plover and North Plover keys. These twin islands, along with a third body of land, Buzzard Key, protrude fairly far out from shore and are somewhat recognizable to the careful navigator. While none of these isles offers more than light-air anchorage, a better haven awaits just to the north.

Another 1.5 nautical miles will bring you abeam of Turkey and New Turkey keys to the east-northeast. These islands tend to blend in with the shoreline and you will have to do some yeoman's work with your binoculars to make the correct identification. After accomplishing this demanding deed, you can follow the wide band of charted 4- and 5-foot waters to the 6- and 8-foot depths off the eastern side of New Turkey Key. The tent symbol on chart 11430 denotes this island as an Everglades National Park campground, but we saw no evidence of this facility from the water. The shores exhibit the usual, thickly wooded growth so characteristic of these islands.

Protection is quite good from eastern and western winds, but minimal in blows from the north or south. In any case, this is most assuredly not a foul-weather hidey hole. Better-sheltered spots are found just to the north.

Pavilion Key

Captains should choose to anchor off the southwestern shores of Pavilion Key only during times of light airs. Depths run 4 to 6 feet and there is little in the way of shelter for all save easterly breezes. I mention Pavilion Key not so much as a potential anchorage, but as a landmark and a historical location. In cruising north into the Ten Thousand Islands, Pavilion Key is quite prominent and it is visible for several miles. As such, it can serve as an invaluable navigational point of reference.

Pavilion Key History   In 1904 the Burnham Clam factory began operating near Caxambas Pass, on the southern shores of Marco Island. A goodly portion of the clam beds that fed the hungry plant lay off Pavilion Key. In those days clams were gathered by hand, and it was back-breaking work.

Some time after 1911 Capt. Bill Collier developed the "clam dredge" at Marco which allowed clams to be harvested from deeper waters. While it led to a temporary boom for local clammers, the vast beds lying about Pavilion Key were exhausted after only a few years.

Lumber Key

One of the most beautiful anchorages in all the Ten Thousand Islands is found off the northwestern banks of Lumber Key. Using Pavilion Key as a navigational reference, along with your binoculars, you must be careful to identify this isle from its fellows. At first, we were confused by Rabbit Key. From the water, the two islands appear to be almost joined together.

We sounded depths of mostly 6 feet while carefully cruising up the strand of deeper water northwest of the two keys. Low-tide depths of 4 feet are possible, so this anchorage is again restricted to vessels drawing 3½ feet or less. There is good protection from southern and southeasterly winds, but the anchorage is wide open to northern, northwestern, and westerly blows.

The shores of Lumber Key are fringed with a white sand beach and beg to be explored by dinghy. In the right wind and weather, this will surely be one of the most delightful spots you will ever find to swing on the hook.

Jack Daniels Key

By the time you come abeam of Jack Daniels Key, Indian Key Pass and the marked channel to Everglades City are only 1.5 nautical miles to the northwest. You can use flashing daybeacon #1, just southwest of Indian Key, as a point of reference to help locate both of the anchorages reviewed below.

Study chart 11430 for a moment and note the unnamed, round island sitting south of

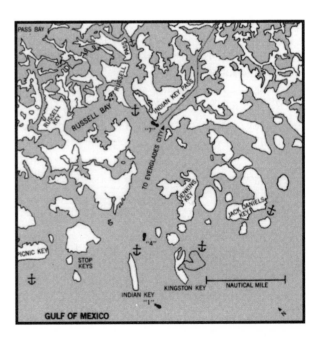

Jack Daniels Key. While some shoals abut the little isle's shoreline, a band of minimum 5-foot water rings the land mass. It is quite possible to approach from the southwest side of the island through minimum 5-foot depths. You can then work your way around the southeastern quarter of the island and drop the hook off its northeastern corner. I would be uncomfortable trying this maneuver with a vessel larger than 40 feet. This spot is well sheltered from all but southerly and southeasterly winds. Small craft that draw 3 feet or less can probably circumnavigate the little island if they so desire. Vessels that need more water should probably stick to the track outlined above.

Kingston Key

One of the navigationally simplest anchorages south of Indian Key Pass is found on the charted 7-foot waters lying off the eastern shores of Kingston Key. Using flashing daybeacon #1 as a reference to help identify Kingston Key, it then becomes an elementary matter to follow the deep water around the isle's southern and southeastern shores to the good water off the relatively straight eastern banks. Minimum entrance depths seem to be 6 feet, and you can drop the hook in 7-foot soundings. These waters should accommodate vessels drawing 5½ feet. As usual, the scenery is all any naturalist could hope for, and you'll be sad to say you're on your way.

Indian Key Pass and the Channel to Everglades City

Indian Key may just be the most important of all the Ten Thousand Islands, and not just because John James Audubon once camped on its shores while drawing and studying the region's native birds. Indian Key sits astride

one of the two marked passages in the Ten Thousand Islands. This channel offers not only two superb anchorages, but reliable access to the Barron River and the village of Everglades City. This community is the only modern-day town to survive in the entire region.

Returning our attention to Indian Key for a moment, the island plays host to yet another of the official Everglades National Park campgrounds. Of more interest to cruisers, the most popular anchorage between Lostmans River and Marco Island lies just northeast of the isle. Here, a long sandspit, not really shown on chart 11430, runs well northeast of the island proper. This bar is partially covered at high water, so be wary.

Boats of almost any size can anchor southeast of the sandspit, off Indian Key's northeasterly tip, in 6 to 10 feet of water. We have never had occasion to visit this anchorage

Anchored off Indian Key

without finding several fellow pleasurecraft swinging tranquilly on the hook. Shelter is more than adequate for all but particularly strong northeasterly winds, which would blow straight down Indian Pass channel. To say that the anchorage is attractive would be akin to saying the same of, oh, Michelle Pfeiffer. It would be all too easy to linger here for days on end while simply soaking up the ambiance. A dinghy trip to the all-natural shores of Indian Key is a must. It would also be a good time to break out the mask, snorkel, and fins. The waters about Indian Key are well worth an underwater exploration.

The only real disadvantage to this haven comes in the form of early morning passages by the numerous commercial fishing craft operating out of nearby Everglades City. These boats sometimes come roaring out of the channel hard by Indian Key quite early in the morning. Fellow cruisers have told this writer of being awakened as early as 3:30 A.M. by these noisy vessels.

Captains can alternately follow the charted tongue of deep water northwest of Indian Key. However, as this passage does not lead to any really sheltered spots, and depths eventually poop out as Gaskin Bay is approached, it makes sense to follow the marked passage southeast of the key.

Indian Key Pass maintains minimum 6-foot depths all the way to the Everglades City waterfront. There is one tricky spot near unlighted daybeacon #3 off Indian Key where it would be possible to briefly wander into 4 feet of water, but cautious mariners can avoid this trouble spot. During the past several years, shoaling used to be noted between unlighted daybeacon #10 and unlighted day-beacon #13, but a recent on-the-water check showed that this difficulty, at least for the

moment, seems to have been removed either by dredging or natural water movement.

Bird watching while cruising along Indian Key Pass is absolutely magnificent. With any luck you will observe many of the species that originally drew John James Audubon to the region.

Southwest of flashing daybeacon #7, Russell Pass opens into the northern flank of the Indian Key-Everglades City channel. This sidewater offers yet another first-rate overnight anchorage. Cruisers must avoid a shoal at the pass's entrance, but you can quickly bypass this hazard and drop the hook in from 7 to as much as 18 feet of water. Larger vessels can anchor in the patch of charted 8- to 18-foot depths just north of the entrance. There's enough swinging room for the *QEII*.

Better protection is acquired as the stream curves to the northeast. Visiting cruisers can anchor in the 7- to 14-foot waters of the pass just short of the large, shallow cove cutting into the southeasterly banks. This anchorage's shelter is the finest imaginable.

If you're looking for a real hurricane hole, continue following Russell Pass to the northeast until you are 200 yards southwest of the charted split in the stream. Here, amidst 6 to 7 feet of water, visiting cruisers can play bridge comfortably while the winds howl overhead. This latter haven has a feeling of rare isolation, and it is highly recommended by this writer.

Returning our attention to the main Indian Key-Everglades City channel, this passage continues to track its well-outlined way to the northeast across a dredged cut through Chokoloskee Bay. Northeast of unlighted day-beacon #30, a channel runs in from the southeast. This cut serves the Everglades National Park Visitor's Center found near the

Chokoloskee causeway. There are no services for private pleasurecraft at the Park Service facility and visiting cruisers are advised to avoid this cut.

Before going on to discuss the Barron River and Everglades City, let us pause a moment for a word about Chokoloskee Island. Consult chart 11430 and you will notice that Chokoloskee Island is today joined to Everglades City by a long causeway. It was not always so. Once Chokoloskee was one of the most isolated settlements in Florida. This tiny village produced some of the most colorful figures and stories in the history of the Sunshine State. We shall meet a few of these characters and hear bits of their tales in our discussion of Everglades City and Chokoloskee Island history below. Unfortunately, the accurate 2- and 3-foot soundings noted on chart 11430 in Chokoloskee Bay make it off limits for most cruising-size vessels. Even Sandfly Pass, which still serves the island's shallow-draft fishing craft, is much too tricky and uncertain for any but the local captains. If possible, try to find land transportation from Everglades City that will allow you to visit the island and its fascinating Ted Smallwood Store Museum. If only for its isolation in these days of mass transportation, the island is well worth your time.

Northeast of unlighted daybeacon #32, the marked channel cuts into the mouth of the Barron River. Soon the development set about Everglades City will become apparent on the starboard shore. The already brisk tidal current picks up even more. Be ready for the quickly moving waters.

Everglades City

Today, Everglades City is a quiet community which still looks to the bounty of its waters for much of its livelihood. Commercial fishing boats line the city waterfront row upon row. They speak eloquently of that American spirit of individualism which seems to be fading all too quickly into the fabric of the past.

Tourism is coming very slowly to Everglades City. The non-fishing residents of the community depend upon the visitors to the Everglades National Park Visitor's Center, just to the south, for their livelihood. A few low-level modern apartments and condos have been built, but the town still looks much the same as it did fifty years ago. Be sure to take a stroll through the center of the village and observe the old, whitewashed city hall. A tall telephone microwave tower reaches skyward in the traffic circle. It is the town's only ready link with the outside world. Barron Collier's "laundry building" still stands between the Rod and Gun Club and the microwave tower. The Everglades City Museum recently opened in this historic structure and a stop here is highly recommended.

A visit to Everglades City and Chokoloskee always seems to have an ethereal, unreal quality, at least to this writer. It's almost as if you have found an old novel about southern Florida and turned to a yellowed picture of a village as it was in those days. If you come looking for nightlife or a glitzy restaurant, forget it. But if you seek a glimpse at an almost vanished speck of Americana, then spare no effort to visit Everglades City.

North of unlighted daybeacon #41, the old river takes a jog to starboard. After rounding the turn, the cool, white exterior of the historic Rod and Gun Club will be obvious, also to starboard. This historic structure was built during the time when Barron Collier brought prominence to Everglades City as a sporting and timbering center. Today, the old inn maintains a long, fixed wooden face pier fronting

Everglades City Hall

directly onto the Barron River. Dockside depths are a good 6 to 8 feet. Power and water connections are available and gasoline and diesel fuel can be purchased. However, the water flowing from the dockside connections is not potable. You will have to acquire drinking water elsewhere. Currently, the Rod and Gun Club boasts the only diesel fuel readily available for pleasurecraft in all of the Ten Thousand Islands. Sailcraft with diesel auxiliaries, take note! The Rod and Gun Club offers a single, clean shower for its transient patrons, and a laundromat can be reached via a one-block walk.

The inn no longer rents out its rooms in the main building, but landside accommodations are available at several cabins spread about the grounds. The on-site restaurant is located just off the beautifully paneled lobby, with its huge stuffed marlin and billiard table. Neither the lobby nor the restaurant is air-conditioned, a concern during the summer and early fall months.

Those dining at the Rod and Gun Club's restaurant have the option of taking their meals on a screened porch overlooking the water. In fair, cooler weather this is a wonderful setting. We found the food acceptable, even if not really worth writing home about.

For all the Rod and Gun Club's character, I would personally just as soon beg, borrow, or steal a ride to the Oyster House Restaurant (941-695-2073), just across the street from the entrance to the Everglades Visitor's Center. It

Rod and Gun Club, Everglades City

would be quite a walk from the inn's docks, but I think you would be well rewarded for the effort. At the Oyster House you have many choices, but two are clearly outstanding. The seafood platter is legendary and is highly recommended by this writer. You simply will not find better fried shrimp, scallops, fish, or deviled crab anywhere in Florida. For the more adventurous palate, there is the Everglades platter, which features alligator meat and frog legs. *Bon appétit!*

Another good dining spot is the Oar House Restaurant (941-695-3535), located within a three-block walk of the Rod and Gun Club. While we have not yet had the good fortune to sample the fare here for ourselves, several locals have recommended this restaurant (par-ticularly for breakfast). There are few better endorsements for any dining choice.

Rod and Gun Club (941) 695-2101

Approach depth—6-10 feet
Dockside depth—6-8 feet
Accepts transients—yes
Fixed wooden dock—yes
Dockside power connections—20 and 50 amp only
Dockside water connections—yes (nonpotable water)
Showers—yes (one)
Laundromat—within 1 block
Gasoline—yes
Diesel fuel—yes
Restaurant—on site

The Barron River channel continues

marked and deep for quite some distance above the Rod and Gun Club. Most of the waterfront is lined by private docks serving commercial fishing craft. Just before you reach a low-level, fixed bridge, the Barron River Marina (941-695-3591) overlooks the southeastern banks. This facility is mostly a small-craft marina, and cruising-size vessels would probably do better to berth at the old club.

Everglades City Festival

Come the first weekend in February every year, the usually modest population of Everglades City explodes temporarily by some 70,000 hungry souls. This can only mean that it's once again time for the Everglades City Annual Seafood Festival. The downtown district is covered with local craftsmen and more than a few booths serving the best and freshest in local seafood. Visitors will also have the opportunity to learn more about this community's rich heritage. If you happen to be cruising in the water off Indian Key during early February, don't miss this festival! You'll be ever so glad to have made the extra effort.

For more information, call the Everglades City Chamber of Commerce at (941) 695-3941.

Everglades City History During the mid-1800s, the body of water we know today as the Barron River was called Potato Creek. Local lore suggests that the Indians living along the stream grew potatoes there during the Seminole Indian Wars.

Sometime during (what the locals call) the "War of Northern Aggression," John Weeks began a vegetable-farming operation near Cape Sable. Following the war's close, Weeks moved north to Potato Creek and settled down for a short period of time.

It was not to be long before William Smith Allen, the first permanent white settler in what was to become Everglades City, arrived. Smith was a "Connecticut Yankee" who moved to Key West, along with others who were loyal to the Union, at the beginning of the Civil War. Following an abortive experiment in the cultivation of castor beans on Sanibel Island, Allen was on his way back to Key West when he put in at Potato Creek for fresh water. He was so impressed with the fertility of the land that he bought out Weeks' holdings and returned to settle on the land shortly thereafter.

Allen built a house set atop stilts on the present-day site of the Rod and Gun Club. He owned all of the land presently occupied by Everglades City from 1873 to 1889. Following this period, he returned to Key West and died shortly thereafter.

Sometime in 1881, George Shorter and his son, George Jr., arrived in Everglades (as it was then known) and began cultivating eggplants, cucumbers, and tomatoes. Following the death of the senior Shorter, George Jr. began growing sugarcane. He eventually purchased all of William Allen's holdings for a mere eight hundred dollars and vastly expanded the cultivation of his cane.

Shorter took over Allen's old house and proceeded to hold sway over the struggling community until his death in 1922. During that long reign, Allen established a post office in the small village which took the name of Everglade. The name was finally changed to Everglades in 1923, and later to Everglades City.

As the years went past, George Shorter, Jr., expanded his family home and began to take on boarders and sportsmen who came to Everglades for the magnificent hunting and fishing. As Dr. Charlton W. Tebeau writes in his informative *The Story of the Chokoloskee Bay Country*, "The Shorter House set a lavish table with all the products of that country in abundance. This was the foundation of the modern Rod and Gun Club, always famous for its cuisine. In 1898 he (Shorter) planted the great Madeira tree now growing in front of the Club."

In 1893, Everglade got its first school, only to have it demolished by a hurricane a scant year later. A new school was built and the Reverend George W. Gatewood came to Everglade soon thereafter to establish the first church.

In 1922 a man came to Everglade who was destined to change the small town forever. Barron G. Collier had made a fortune in the manufacture of New York trolley cars. He purchased nearly a million acres of land from the Southern States Land and Timber Company, including most of the swamps and hammocks set about Everglade. He also bought up Frank Shorter's holdings and set up his headquarters in Everglades. After the bright lights of Broadway, one can only assume that Collier was ready for a quieter, although not less energetic, life.

A new county was created around Everglades and named for Barron Collier. With the coming of the Tamiami Trail in 1928, linking Everglades City to Miami, Collier began logging operations in earnest. He purchased a small railway that ran from Everglades City to Deep Lake Hammock. The original engine of this tiny railroad was a modified Model T Ford. Never one to mess about, Collier changed all that over the next decade. Tons and tons of pine logs were hauled out of Deep Lake Hammock and transported by rail to Everglades City. There, they were transshipped by water to points north.

Under Barron Collier's management, the town of Everglades City became a timbering center. The local economy boomed. To better serve his shipping operation, Collier persuaded the state of Florida to dredge the entrance to what soon came to be known as the Barron River (the former Potato Creek). Soon fishermen throughout the region began delivering their catch to the village's shores.

Sport hunting and fishing grew to be even more important. The Rod and Gun Club was built during this period, and it became known to sportsmen throughout the United States as one of the hot spots for hunting and fishing in all of Florida.

In these all-too-modern times, Barron Collier's timbering empire is but a distant memory. There is only the Rod and Gun Club to remind visitors of those days of glory. It is to the good fortune of all that the clash of a diesel truck's gears are still a rarity in Everglades City. The modern-day wanderer may yet stroll through the quiet lanes of a village that has changed little in the last sixty years. I'm sure Barron Collier, the man who fled New York for the serenity of the Everglades, would be pleased.

Chokoloskee Island History Chokoloskee Island is connected to Everglades City not only by a causeway, but by its rugged history as well. As Stuart McIver astutely comments in *Glimpses of South Florida History*, "The (Chokoloskee) island is less than 150 acres in size—yet it has seen more than its share of individualists over the years." Indeed, neither this writer nor anyone else could have said it better.

Chokoloskee Island saw its first permanent white settler arrive in the person of Capt. Dick Turner sometime around 1870. Captain Turner had been a scout during the tragic Seminole Wars and had perhaps visited and admired the island before settling there.

In 1886 the man who was to become known as the "Sage of Chokoloskee" arrived to settle on the island. C. G. McKinney founded the settlement's first store and its first post office. He became widely known over the years as a newspaper columnist. Under his pen mosquitoes became "swamp angels" and moonshine was "low-bush lightning." In 1924 he wrote:

> Our schoolteacher . . . is going to give up her school today, it is too much for her nerves. She had a trying time here. . . . Maybe we don't need any school—we all know enough anyway. They seem to learn to chew tobacco, curse and drink booze at an early age and think their education is complete when they have these necessities ground into their topknots.

Maybe things haven't changed as much since those days as we think!

During the 1890s Ted Smallwood settled on Chokoloskee and set up what would become the island's largest retail business. Smallwood's store sat directly on Chokoloskee Bay and he soon dredged a deep-water channel to its docks. The entrepreneur invited both Indian and white settlers to visit his establishment.

In 1924 a hurricane blew the store off its foundation. Mr. Smallwood had his fill of that and raised the entire structure up on stilts. He ran this Chokoloskee Island version of the classic American country store until his death in 1943. His daughter, Thelma, continued the operation until her death in the early 1980s. The store still stands today and has been wonderfully restored as a museum by a collection of dedicated, local volunteers. Chief among this group is Mr. Smallwood's granddaughter, Ms. Lynn Smallwood McMillian. Visitors are now welcome after paying a modest entrance fee. The store's interior has been transformed once again into a close copy of what it looked like in Ted Smallwood's day. Some of the original merchandise still adorns the shelves. Old wooden boxes, antique washing machines, classic tools, and a wide assortment of other odds and ends recalling bygone days are on display. An on-site gift shop offers books and other literature concerning the region's history.

The third Saturday in March of every year is Seminole Day at the old Ted Smallwood store. Members of the local Seminole tribe share with visitors a celebration of their Native American history, culture, and music.

Even though there is no ready waterborne access for cruising-size craft, I highly recommend a visit to the Ted Smallwood Store Museum. Sometimes, transportation can be arranged through the Rod and Gun Club, or you might try giving the museum a call at (941) 695-2989. However you get there, the museum is a joy for any who are interested in old-time Americana.

Smallwood's store also figured prominently in an event that forms the central theme of Peter Matthiesen's book *Killing Mr. Watson.* By 1900 a host of small settlements had taken root in the mangroves near Everglade (Everglades City) and Chokoloskee Island. Some of these were established by families, but others were the abodes of less savory characters who seemed to appear from nowhere. One of these latter mini-communities was known as the "Watson Place."

The principal inhabitant, Ed Watson, was known as a friendly enough man, if you did not cross him. He took up farming on the banks of the Chatham River, south of Chokoloskee. It was rumored that he paid his help little and some of the workers mysteriously disappeared around payday.

By 1910 Watson had gathered together a somewhat more permanent group of five individuals on his farm, including a woman called Hannah Smith (also known as "Big Six"), a man known as Leslie Cox, and an unidentified black man. It was during the fall of 1910 that a group of clammers from Chokoloskee found Big Six's body in a nearby swamp. Within a few days, the old black man showed up at Chokoloskee muttering about murders at the Watson Place. Soon Watson himself arrived, claiming that Cox had committed the murder.

The islanders were not convinced by Watson's story and asked the sheriff to investigate. For whatever reason, the officer delayed and Watson set out on his own, supposedly to hunt for Cox.

Within a month Watson motored back up to the Chokoloskee waterfront right in front of Smallwood's store, claiming to all who would listen that he had killed Cox. He produced the latter's hat as proof. Some of the islanders who were standing around in front of the store agreed to travel back to the Watson Place and inspect the body, but others more skeptical of Watson insisted that he first be disarmed.

According to one account, Watson became so enraged that he tried to discharge his shotgun into the assembled crowd. Both shells, apparently soaked during a recent storm, misfired. Most of the group on the docks were also carrying guns and they opened up on Watson as a man. The would-be farmer and could-be murderer fell to the dock, pierced by several dozen bullets, and his secrets died with him.

Picnic Key Anchorage

When winds are not blowing from the west or southwest, the 4- and 5-foot waters nestled between the arms of Tiger and Stop keys, southwest of Picnic Key, make a good anchorage for boats drawing 3½ feet or less. The shores of Picnic Key are girded by a beautiful white sand beach and are well worth breaking out the dinghy.

Faka Union River and Canal Channel and Port of the Islands Marina

Unlighted daybeacon #3 off Gomez Point marks the southwesterly genesis of the marked channel leading northeast to the Faka Union River. The marked channel southeast of Panther Key cuts a winding path generally northeast for 4 nautical miles to the mouth of Faka Union River. This body of water leads, in turn, to the arrow-straight Faka Union Canal. Another run of 2.8 nautical miles up the canal leads you to Port of the Islands Marina flanking the northerly shores of the west-side cove just south of the U.S. 41-Tamiami Trail fixed bridge.

Within the past several years, this channel has shoaled severely as it begins its approach to the Faka Union River. We have heard numerous accounts of cruising craft (even those of the smaller powercraft variety) finding the bottom smack in the middle of this so-called channel. Our own on-site observations lead us to believe that low-water soundings are now considerably less than 3 feet in places. With this information in hand, we no longer recommend a visit to Faka Union Canal or Port of the Islands Marina for cruising-size craft.

If you should choose to ignore this advice, we strongly suggest that you time your entry and egress during high water. Even at high water, this cut is no longer suitable for boats drawing more than 4 feet.

As if the shoaling described above were not problem enough, tidal currents flow through the Faka River and its canal with a fierceness that this writer has seldom before witnessed. If the tide is on the ebb, it could take considerably longer to reach Port of the Islands than you might think.

A late-breaking report, received just as this account is going to press, suggests the Faka Union Canal approach channel has now been taken over by Collier County. Within the next several years, it is likely that this channel will be improved, at least to some extent. We'll keep you informed on the latest developments in our *Salty Southeast* newsletter.

It should also be noted that all of the Faka Union River and the adjoining canal are idle-speed, no-wake zones. This speed restriction is designed to protect the considerable colony of manatees that live in the area waters. We actually saw a manatee while cruising along the canal, so the restrictions are for real and quite necessary.

Port of the Islands Marina (941-394-3101) has, to be blunt, been an indifferently managed facility for some years. Now, we are happy to report that new owners have taken over, and many improvements are on the drawing board. However, until and if this marina's approach channel via Faka Union River and Canal is dredged, we cannot recommend a visit to this facility. With this stricture in mind, we will not offer any further review of Port of the Islands at this time.

TEN THOUSAND ISLANDS NAVIGATION

If it weren't for the lack of navigational markers, the abundance of shallow water, and the difficulty of telling one of the Ten Thousand Islands from the other, navigation of the waters between New Turkey Key and the Coon Key Light would be a snap.

Yes, gentle reader, that is truly tongue-in-cheek. There is perhaps no other portion of the Western Florida coastline that offers as much of a navigational challenge as the Ten Thousand Islands do. Take your time—in fact, take all the time that may be necessary to carefully identify important landmarks before plunging ahead. Maintain an eagle eye on the sounder, and if you are lucky enough to be equipped with Loran or GPS, make full use of these navigational wonders. The extra effort you make to avoid turning "bow" to "plow" will be more than justified by the opportunities for backwater discovery in this land that time has seemingly forgotten.

New Turkey Key Anchorage Strangely enough, New Turkey Key can be difficult to identify from the water without the benefit of careful navigation and/or electronic positioning equipment. From a position abeam of flashing daybeacon #8 off Lostmans River (which should be passed *well* to its western side), a cruise of some 5 nautical miles will bring you abeam of Plover and North Plover keys. These two islands sit fairly far out from shore and are recognizable. Be sure to stay well to the west of the twin islands, as they are surrounded by shoal water for the most part. Continue paralleling the coastline as you cruise northwest for another 1.5 nautical miles. This should bring you abeam of New Turkey Key, which will appear to be the isle farthest from shore in the immediate area. Set a course to approach New Turkey Key by some .2 nautical miles to the south of the isle's southwestern tip. As you work your way carefully to the east, begin curving your course to the north after coming abeam of the key's northeast-to-southwest axis. Use your sounder to follow the correctly charted 6- and 8-foot depths until you are between the island's northeasterly tip and the unnamed key to the east.

Drop your hook here. *Don't* attempt to cruise north past the tip of New Turkey Key. Depths immediately rise to 3½ feet or less.

On to Pavilion Key   Pavilion Key, west of Duck Rock, is an important body of land for navigational purposes. The key is quite prominent due to its position relatively far from the mainland. Throw in flashing daybeacon #10, lying off the islet's southwesterly tip, and it's not hard to imagine why this island and its daybeacon can serve as one of the most identifiable navigational reference points between Lostmans River and Coon Key Light.

From a position abeam of #10, many skippers will set course for Indian Key and flashing daybeacon #1. While you might also choose to cruise to flashing daybeacon #1K, well to the southwest of Indian Key, this would seem to be a useless trek, adding several miles to your sojourn.

Before going on to detail the passage from Indian Key to Everglades City, let's pause for a moment to review the anchorages between Pavilion and Indian keys.

Lumber Key Anchorage   From flashing daybeacon #10 off Pavilion Key, use either

DR (dead-reckoning) navigation or a GPS to work your way around to a point well southwest of the charted channel northwest of Lumber and Rabbit keys. Keep a close watch on your sounder as you work your way northeast along the broad tongue of deep water, northwest of the two isles. On the water, Rabbit and Lumber keys will appear to be almost joined together by an interconnecting sandspit. Lumber Key will appear as the larger of the two.

Drop the hook northwest of Lumber Key as you come abeam of the island's center. You may be able to spot a small creek cutting into the island, which will help you identify this anchorage.

If you should decide to visit Lumber Key, go in by dinghy. A band of shoals abuts the island's shoreline. Be sure to scrupulously avoid the shallow bay between Lumber and Rabbit keys. Depths on this errant body of water run from ½ to 3 feet. On-site research failed to disclose the charted "pile" marking the split in the channel northeast of the just-described anchorage. Captains are strictly advised to anchor southwest of this fork!

Jack Daniels Key   It would probably be best to acquire flashing daybeacon #1 off Indian Key before attempting to enter either the anchorage adjacent to Kingston Key or the one adjacent to Jack Daniels Key. Using #1, it is a relatively simple matter to identify the Kingston isle. You should then set a course to pass this body of land by at least 300 yards to its southwesterly side before turning northeast into the anchorage. Stay well off Kingston Key and be sure to pass south of the charted marshy shoal southwest of Jack Daniels.

As you approach Jack Daniels, use your binoculars to help pick out the unnamed island south of the key. Cruise around the smaller island's southeasterly shores, keeping some 100 yards off the beach. Be on guard against the charted tongue of 3-foot water to the east.

Drop your anchor once abeam of the small island's northeastern tip. Here you will be nestled between the unnamed isle and Jack Daniels Key to the north.

Only very nervy skippers should attempt to continue a circumnavigation of the small island to the west and south. Shoals extend off the little island for about 50 yards on this section of the channel.

Kingston Key Anchorage   Again, using flashing daybeacon #1 off Indian Key, cruise around Kingston Key's southwestern reaches, keeping several hundred yards off the beach. Turn slowly to the northeast and pass the key's southeasterly tip by at least 200 yards to your port side.

You can then bend your course yet again, this time to the north-northwest, and come abeam of the key's easterly shoreline by about 75 yards to your port side. Don't slip farther to the east, as depths climb to 4 feet or less. Drop the hook before cruising any farther to the northwest. While small craft can circumnavigate Kingston Key, depths run to 4 feet and the passage is really a little too confining for cruising-size vessels.

Indian Key Pass Channel and Anchorages
All navigators should be aware of the difficulty in spotting flashing daybeacon #1, the southwesternmost aid to navigation on the marked channel off Indian Key. This very important beacon blends right in with the trees on Indian Key and can be exceedingly hard to spot, even with binoculars. Take your time and be sure to identify this aid correctly before attempting to enter the channel.

After finding #1, pass the beacon fairly close to its southeasterly side and set course to come abeam of and pass unlighted daybeacon #3 to its immediate southeasterly side. Try not to wander to the southeast between #1 and #3 or you might find the charted patch of 4-foot waters. Of course, you don't want to stray too close to Indian Key's southeasterly shoreline either.

During our last visit to Indian Key, we tried several times to find this charted 4-foot shoal, but even with the aid of the GPS interfaced with a laptop computer and digitized charts, it never appeared on our sounder. Just to be safe, though, watch out for it anyway.

Once abeam of #3, point to come abeam of flashing daybeacon #4 to its westerly quarter. As you approach #4, watch to the west and, at mid or low tide, you can spot the long (partially uncharted) sandspit running northeast from Indian Key.

Even if the tide is high and you can't find the spit, cruise west from #4 to a point at least 50 yards southeast of Indian Key's spit. If this sounds somewhat confusing, study the sketch map depicting these waters on page 34. You can then drop the hook in about as secure a spot as you are likely to find in the Ten Thousand Islands. If the mosquitoes and weather cooperate, your first chosen task might just be a quick breaking out of the dinghy and a trip ashore to visit Indian Key.

It is quite possible to cross to the northeast side of the Indian Key sandspit and circumnavigate the island in 6-foot minimum depths. However, since we have already found our way to the best anchorage adjacent to the key, and the southeasterly passage is marked, most cruisers will probably choose to forego this excursion.

Indian Key Pass remains broad and deep well upstream of unlighted daybeacon #6. Come abeam of this aid to its northwesterly side and continue on, pointing to come abeam of and pass flashing daybeacon #7 to its southeasterly quarter. Just before reaching #7, another excellent anchorage opportunity beckons from the north.

Successful entry into Russell Pass is complicated by the large, charted shoal thrusting into the westerly reaches of the pass's southern entrance. This hazard is easily avoided by favoring the eastern third of the entrance.

You must also take care not to approach the shoreline too closely just north of flashing daybeacon #7. A thin, but nevertheless treacherous band of shallows flanks this point.

Soon, good depths open out almost from shore to shore on Russell Pass. You need only stay within shouting distance of the centerline for good depths all the way to the split in the channel, well to the northeast at the charted "Mangrove."

Everglades City and the Barron River East of flashing daybeacon #7, the well-marked channel follows a dredged route through the various isles to the mouth of the Barron River. Tidal currents pick up markedly and are a real concern for sailcraft and single-screw trawlers. Be sure to watch over your stern as well as the course ahead to quickly note any lateral slippage.

At unlighted daybeacon #10, the cut runs hard by the southern banks and soon passes through a sharp turn to the northeast heralded by unlighted daybeacon #11. As mentioned earlier, there used to be a shoaling problem between #10 and unlighted daybeacon #13. For the moment, these shallows seem to have disappeared, but they could always reappear. Stick to the cut's mid-width between #10 and its turn to the northeast marked by unlighted daybeacons #11, #11A, and flashing daybeacon #12.

A new no-wake manatee zone stretches from the gap between unlighted daybeacon #27 and flashing daybeacon #28 to unlighted daybeacon #32. Even then, upstream of #32, you will quickly approach the Everglades City waterfront and a host of private docks. The best plan is simply to proceed at idle speed on the entire channel northeast of #27 and #28.

The channel passes between two small, rock-filled islands at unlighted daybeacons #29 and #30. Long before reaching #29 and #30, you will spot the tall telephone microwave tower which graces the town circle in Everglades City. This antenna will be the first visible evidence that you are approaching this unique community.

Northeast of unlighted daybeacon #30, the marked channel leading southeast to the Everglades National Park Visitor's Center and Chokoloskee Bay flows into the main cut. Ignore unlighted daybeacons #1 and #2, the northwesternmost aids on this side channel, and continue straight ahead, pointing to come abeam of unlighted daybeacon #32 to your starboard side.

Unlighted daybeacon #32 marks the entrance to the Barron River. Slow down as you cruise into the river. The entire stretch between the stream's mouth and the fixed bridge well upstream is an idle-speed, no-wake zone.

At flashing daybeacon #33 the channel takes a hard jog to starboard. Soon you will pass unlighted daybeacon #34 to your starboard side. Look to port and you will sight the Ten Thousand Islands' Outward Bound program headquarters. As a cruiser, you're already enjoying many of the benefits that are provided by this organization for its participants.

Continue following the markers upstream on the Barron River. The docks of the Rod and Gun Club will come abeam to starboard after rounding the turn past unlighted daybeacon #41. Farther to the north, the river's southern and southeastern banks are lined with an interesting collection of commercial fishing vessels and their attendant wharves. Eventually, the river's track is pinched by a 12-foot fixed bridge near the charted designation "Dupont."

Picnic Key Anchorage   Well, I know it's getting repetitive to say it, but, again, make use of good old flashing daybeacon #1 off Indian Key to identify Stop Keys to the north-northwest. Pleasurecraft that can stand some 4-foot depths can cruise into the broad swath of 4- and 5-foot waters fronting the southwestern shores of Picnic Key, sheltered between the arms of Tiger and Stop keys.

Take the greatest care to avoid the charted tongue of 1- and 2-foot waters jutting to the west from Stop Keys. On-site research revealed that this shoal has built out farther than is shown on the "current" edition of chart 11430. In fact, we had plenty of time to contemplate the cuts in the NOAA charting budget while trying to push our grounded craft off this sandbar.

Drop anchor at least 50 yards off Picnic Key's white sand beach. Slop on the Skin-So-Soft, blow up the old dinghy, and head ashore for some great exploration.

Faka Union River and Canal Channel   As if you weren't tired of hearing me say this, unlighted daybeacons #3 and #4, off Panther Key, are quite hard to spot from the water. Just to make matters a bit more interesting, there are no convenient geographic references nearby, either. Use your best and brightest binoculars, along with good DR or electronic navigation, to find the aids.

As mentioned repeatedly above, the Faka Union River and Canal channel has now shoaled badly as it begins its approach to the Faka Union Canal northeast of unlighted daybeacon #19. We have had reports of even small powercraft finding the bottom at low water. Our on-site readings confirm MLW soundings of 3 feet or less in spots.

Adding insult to injury, many of the charted aids to navigation are now in poor condition and some are missing entirely.

With these problems in mind, we no longer recommend this channel for any cruising-size craft if and until the cut is dredged by the new owners of Port of the Islands Marina. As such, we will offer no further details of this passage here. If, in the future, the channel is improved, we will resume describing this cut in detail.

On to Coon Key Light   Mariners choosing to run the inside route past Marco Island to Naples should set course for the unnum-

bered 22-foot flashing daybeacon south-southeast of Coon Key. Depths on these waters can occasionally run to as little as 4 feet, but at most tides you can expect at least 4½ to 5 feet of water. This is the shallowest portion of the entire passage to Naples.

For best depths, come abeam of the Coon Key Light by at least 100 yards to its north-easterly side. You can then set course to the north-northwest and enter the waterway.

Coon Key to Naples

A marked inland channel leads north from Coon Key, past Marco Island and Capri Pass, to the city of Naples and its fine inlet. In recent years, this passage has been much maligned and sailors, in particular, have abandoned it in favor of an offshore passage to Gordon Pass (Naples' inlet). For boats that draw 4 feet or less (and are not in a hurry), this strategy may just be a mistake. While not a part of the official Western Florida ICW, the Marco Island-Naples channel, or waterway, as we shall dub it, now maintains minimum 5-foot depths along most of its length. This passage features excellent protection from inclement weather, adequate anchorages, and good, if widely spaced, facilities. There are a few tricky spots, but if you are looking for something other than an offshore passage, the Marco Island cut is the only game in town.

The one exception to the 5-foot minimum rule on the Marco Island-Naples waterway is found at the passage's southerly entrance, near Coon Key Light. Here you may occasionally find dead low-water depths of as little as 4

feet. Boats needing 4½ to 5 feet can wait for a higher tide and run the entire route in safety.

It is also quite possible for cruisers to sail offshore to Capri Pass inlet, just north of Marco Island, and enter the inside passage through this seaward cut. This route avoids the shallower southern reaches of the water-way, but still allows mariners to visit the facilities on Marco Island, and then cruise north to Naples. This half-outside, half-inside cruising plan is an excellent alternative for boats draw-ing between 4½ and 5½ feet. With a little cau-tion, captains who pilot vessels of this draft can cruise inside to Naples with no problems, whereas if they tried to cruise north on the inland passage from Coon Key Light, the unhappy sound of the keel dragging bottom might just be heard.

Unfortunately, the state of Florida has re-cently seen fit to establish a whole series of extremely confusing "manatee no-wake zones" on portions of the Marco Island-Naples waterway. Some of these zones are in effect only at certain times of the day and year, and the various beginnings and endings of the restricted waters seem haphazard. As one local cruiser told this writer, "we had no idea that manatees could read the clock, the calendar, and a nautical chart." So, whatever we cruisers may think of them, these slow-speed restrictions are now a fact of life on the Marco Island-Naples waterway. Be sure to figure the delays that will be caused by these regulated waters into your cruising plans.

The Marco Island-Naples waterway begins at Coon Key Pass, skirts past the fascinating village of Goodland, and then runs down the Big Marco River past Sanctuary Sound and into East Marco Bay. Good, recently expanded facilities are available to mariners cruising along this stretch in Goodland and on Factory Bay.

Well-marked Capri Pass cuts into the Western Florida shoreline north of Marco Island. This inlet holds minimum 6- to 8-foot depths but there is now one significant shoal to avoid. As always with seaward passages, these conditions are subject to rapid change. Barring any future alterations, pleasurecraft of most sizes and drafts can run Capri Pass with only the usual difficulties in passing between the ocean and inland waters.

North from Capri Pass, the waterway leading north to Naples cuts in behind several other shallow inlets. Cruisers will find a super anchorage near one of these cuts.

Most depths between Capri Pass and Naples run 6 feet or better. There is but one spot where the sounder may dip to 5-5½ foot readings.

North of Dollar Bay, the Marco Island-Naples cut intersects Gordon Pass, which serves the city of Naples. Our research showed the inlet to be well marked, currently deep, and reasonably easy to run.

Additionally, a wonderful anchorage is found just off the inlet channel.

North of Gordon Pass, the marked route follows a dead-end passage through Naples Bay to the Gordon River and the city of Naples. This teeming tourist city has been rebuilding its waterfront over the last several years, and the results are quite impressive. A fine city facility and two yacht clubs wait to greet the weary cruiser. One of the finest waterside shopping complexes in Western Florida graces the city waterfront and, if that's not enough for you, what may just be the best independent marine store in all of Florida guards the easterly fork of the Gordon River.

The Gordon River passage dead ends at the Naples waterfront, at least for cruising-size craft. Both branches of the river are pinched off by low-level fixed bridges, but the upstream reaches are quite shallow anyway. Northbound vessels must retrace their steps to Gordon Inlet and cruise offshore to Fort Myers Beach and Estero Island.

The cruising possibilities between Coon Key and Naples are varied and almost too numerous to number. Let's push right on and detail the many gunkholes and ports of call along the way.

Caxambas Pass Channel

The long approach channel to Caxambas Inlet cuts west from the unnumbered 22-foot Coon Key Light. Depths of 5 to 6 feet are held on this cut east of unlighted daybeacon #6, north of Dickmans Island. The channel has shoaled between unlighted daybeacons #8 and #19, where low-water depths as thin as 3 feet can now be expected. This portion of the channel is known locally as "the picket line." Cruising craft drawing 3 feet or better must confine their explorations to the waters east of #6.

The marked approach to Caxambas Pass has also shoaled badly between charted unlighted daybeacon #19 and unlighted daybeacon #8. Tentative plans are in the works to define a new channel south of the current channel in this region, but unless these plans come to fruition, visiting cruisers are strictly advised to limit their explorations to the waters west of "the picket line."

The Caxambas Pass channel is not completely without merit, however. West of unlighted daybeacon #1 (west of Ramsey Key), skippers can anchor in depths of 7 to 10 feet, sheltered between Helen Key to the south and Horrs Island to the north. This spot is well sheltered from all but gale-force winds.

At unlighted daybeacon #19, west of Pass Key, a marked channel cuts east to Barfield Bay. This shallow passage leads to the private docks of an exclusive development on Horrs Island. There are no facilities for visiting cruisers.

Coon Key Pass Anchorage

Back on Coon Key Pass and the principal Marco Island-Naples route, captains may consider dropping the hook with fair winds in the lee of the small, unnamed island east of Neal Key and west-northwest of unlighted daybeacon #2. Depths of 10+ feet run to within 20 yards of the island's easterly shoreline. There should be enough elbow room for most pleasurecraft. As an additional bonus, the anchorage affords a super view of Gullivan Bay's magnificent waters to the south. You can also dinghy ashore to nearby Coon Key, which is graced with a lovely white sand beach.

Obviously, this is not a heavy-weather anchorage. Winds over 10 knots from any quarter save the west would make for a rocking evening. In calm conditions though, you simply could not choose a more beautiful setting to while away a few hours in the cockpit with a cool one in hand.

Tripod Key-Sugar Bay Anchorage

Mariners will find an important anchorage on the charted 5-foot offshoot leading to Sugar Bay, east of unlighted daybeacon #3. This would be a great spot for captains cruising south in craft as large as 50 feet to wait out bad weather before venturing out onto the open waters of the Ten Thousand Islands. Even northbound cruisers arriving late in the day could make use of this haven before starting north the next morning. This sidewater is well protected and has minimum depths of 5 to 6 feet. The surrounding shores are completely undeveloped and make for a real feeling of isolation.

Surprisingly enough, and contrary to soundings indicated on chart 11430, minimum 5-foot depths, with many readings in the 8- to 12-foot range, continue upstream to a point some 100 yards southwest of Sugar Bay. Be sure to anchor well short of the bay itself as these waters are quite shoal. In heavy weather, skippers may choose to anchor in the more protected upper portion of the approach stream (southwest of Sugar Bay) for best shelter. With fair breezes in the offing, it's a simple matter to drop the hook only 100 yards or so northeast of the main channel.

Goodland and Associated Facilities

The very special village of Goodland sits perched on the outcropping of land north and west of unlighted daybeacon #6 (on Coon Key Pass). Goodland is actually an extension of Marco Island, but it's light years different in character. Amidst all the dense development on Marco, this village survives as a rugged commercial and small-craft fishing center

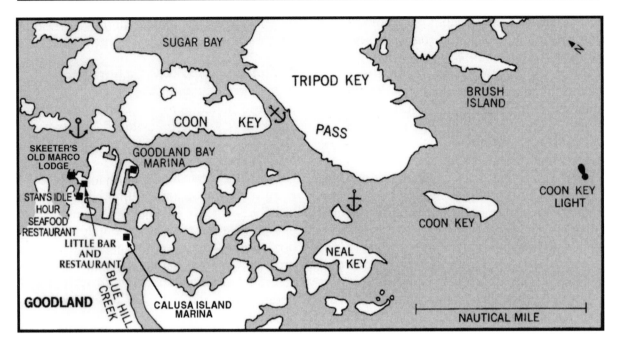

where the residents are still far more interested in what's biting than in what's happening on Wall Street. A small museum in the village recalls the island's early occupation by the Timucuan and Caloosa Indians.

Numbers to know in Goodland Island include:

A-OK Taxi—941-394-1113
Patron Transportation—941-394-6179
Yellow Cab—941-659-0800
Avis Rental Cars—941-481-1511
Hertz Rent A Car—941-927-8929

Goodland is noted for its superb seafood restaurants. While they may lack what some might term sophistication, the food is clearly all anyone could ask for and the atmosphere is often festive. This writer was privileged to sample the bountiful fare in the Little Bar and Restaurant and Skeeter's Old Marco Lodge. Both these dining spots served, without a

doubt, some of the finest seafood that this writer has ever enjoyed in Western Florida.

Two marinas serve pleasureboats in Goodland. These highly competent, often crowded, and superfriendly marinas sit at a very strategic point. Much like the anchorage described above, cruisers can wait out bad weather here for the trip south or rest from their journeys through the Ten Thousand Islands, with the added benefits of full power and water connections.

Goodland Bay Marina is located west of unlighted daybeacon #6. The dry-storage operation fronts directly onto the island's southern shores, but the principal dockage basin is located in the sheltered *T*-shaped cove just to the west.

Goodland Bay accepts transients for overnight dockage and offers berths at fixed and floating wooden piers with all power and water connections. Overnighters are usually accommodated at the floating piers. Transient space is often at a premium here, so call ahead of time to check on slip availability.

Depths at most of the marina's docks run at least 6 feet, while MLW entrance soundings are in the 5½- to 6-foot range. Some shallower soundings are found at the rear slips, but these are reserved for the exclusive use of small, shallow-draft powercraft. Gasoline (but no longer diesel fuel) is readily available, as are waste pump-out services and full mechanical repairs for both gasoline and diesel engines. An on-site 35-ton travelift readily facilitates haul-outs and full below-waterline repairs. There is also an on-site ship's/variety/tackle store as well as extensive dry stack storage for smaller powercraft.

The marina also maintains a first-rate breakfast and lunch restaurant. The fried grouper sandwich is absolutely wonderful.

Goodland Bay Marina (941) 394-2797

Approach depth—5½ to 8 feet
Dockside depth—6 feet
Accepts transients—yes
Fixed and floating wooden piers—yes
Dockside power connections—30 and 50 amp
Dockside water connections—yes
Waste pump-out—yes
Gasoline—yes
Mechanical repairs—yes
Below-waterline repairs—yes
Ship's and variety store—yes
Restaurant—on site, several others nearby

Access to Goodland's second pleasurecraft facility, Calusa Island Marina, is gained by traversing the marked entrance channel to Goodland Bay Marina and then continuing to follow the waters of charted Blue Hill Creek as they sweep to the west. First-timers should be sure to read the navigational account of this channel before attempting entry.

Newly minted Calusa Island Marina actually has two dockage basins. Most resident and visiting craft are accommodated at a series of floating wooden and concrete decked piers that fronts directly onto the waters of Blue Hill Creek and features 6-foot dockside depths. A long fixed wooden face pier and the marina's fuel dock are discovered on a second harbor lining the shores of the sheltered offshoot striking north to the charted "R. Mast." Low-water depths in this harbor can run as thin as 4½ feet.

One of the marina's resident cruisers has warned this writer against using the inner harbor piers because of the long climb necessary to reach the dock at low tide. On the other hand, no one could ask for a more sheltered spot to ride out really heavy weather.

Transients are accepted at Calusa Island Marina, but some of the resident captains have warned us that the marina owner is pushing hard to sell his slips on a permanent basis. It seems likely that space for visitors may become a bit tight at some point in the future. Call ahead of time to check on berth availability.

Most slips at Calusa Island feature full power, water, cable television, and telephone hook-ups. Waste pump-out service is available as are adequate showers and an on-site laundromat. Gasoline and diesel fuel can be purchased at the inner basin fuel dock, and mechanical repairs can sometimes be arranged through independent technicians.

Calusa Island offers full haul-out, below-waterline repair services. The yard's 50-ton travelift can handle most pleasurecraft.

Rounding out the marina's services are an on-site ship's and variety store as well as dry stack storage for smaller powercraft. Unfortunately, there is little in the way of provisions nearby. The closest supermarket is a good five miles away, so be sure your galley is stocked.

All in all, we were impressed with Calusa Island Marina, and are glad that its new slips augment Goodland's transient space. As far as we are concerned, any night spent in Goodland is a good night.

Calusa Island Marina (941) 394-3668

Approach depth—5½ to 8 feet
Dockside depth—6 feet MLW (outer docks)
4½-5 feet MLW (inner harbor)
Accepts transients—yes
Fixed and floating wooden piers—yes
Floating concrete piers—yes
Dockside power connections—30 and 50 amp
Dockside water connections—yes

Waste pump-out—yes
Showers—yes
Laundromat—yes
Gasoline—yes
Diesel fuel—yes
Mechanical repairs—yes (independent technicians)
Below-waterline repairs—yes
Ship's and variety store—yes
Restaurant—several nearby

All three of Goodland's principal restaurants are accessible directly from the ICW, although two sport low-tide entrance and dockside depths of only 3½ feet. The fixed, wooden slips of Skeeter's Old Marco Lodge (941-642-7227) will be readily visible along the southerly flank of the Marco Island-Naples waterway principal channel between

Skeeter's Old Marco Lodge, Goodland

unlighted daybeacons #8 and #10. Craft as large as 35 feet should find a place to moor comfortably while dining. No overnight services are available. Depths alongside run around 5 to 6 feet at low tide.

This dining spot has had a fortunate change of ownership during the last several years. The fresh management has spent a considerable sum of change refurbishing both the restaurant's interior and its menu. During a recent lunch here with Marco Island's two foremost cruising experts, Ed Beckhorn and Gale Vinson, we were all very impressed with our seafood soup and entrees. This writer is now pleased to give this new dining choice in Goodland his enthusiastic approval.

Captains piloting vessels that can stand some low-tide depths of 3½ feet can opt for either a truly first-class or another funky dining experience in Goodland. The small canal, just west of Skeeter's docks, leads south past a host of local fishing craft to two restaurants of note.

First up is the Little Bar and Restaurant (941-394-5663). This dining spot overlooks the creek's southeasterly banks and it has three small slips (3- to 3½-foot low-water depths) that should be just large enough for 28 footers.

Need more depth? Consider a stay at nearby Goodland Bay or Calusa Island marinas. It's only a short walk from either dockage basin to the Little Bar or Stan's (see below).

No matter how you get to the Little Bar, the food is wonderful. This is where many of the locals on Marco go back time and time again for seafood. The menu is surprisingly extensive and sophisticated, but the good old fried oysters simply cannot be beat.

Stan's Idle Hour Restaurant (941-394-3041) guards the terminus of the creek. The welcome is about as warm as it gets, and the food is acceptable. Outside (as well as inside) dining is available and there is often nightly entertainment during the fall, winter, and

Stan's Idle Hour Restaurant, Goodland

spring months. Stan's can be the setting for some real down-home, raucous parties from time to time. The crowds on Sunday are legendary!

Several fixed, wooden slips adjoining Stan's can accommodate boats as large as 28-30 feet, although most are really meant for smaller craft. Approach and dockside depths run to 3½ feet at low tide. Be sure to take this skimpy water into account when planning a visit to Stan's.

Goodland Bay Anchorage

Visiting captains sometimes choose to anchor in the charted patch of deeper waters northeast of unlighted daybeacon #7. Depths did not prove to be as deep as shown on the chart. Our sounder (plus the tide tables) indicated low-water depths of 5 to 6 feet. There's enough swinging room for vessels up to 45 feet in length, and good protection from eastern, southeastern, and western winds. Nevertheless, this is not a foul-weather hidey-hole. Consider the anchorage described above off Tripod Key and Sugar Bay for really heavy weather. The islands to the east, northeast, and southeast are in their natural state, while the Goodland waterfront lies just to the west. It would be only a quick dinghy trip from this anchorage to reach Skeeter's Old Marco Lodge, the Little Bar and Restaurant, or Stan's Idle Hour Restaurant (see above).

Big Marco River

From Goodland, the Marco Island-Naples channel cuts first north and then northwest through the Big Marco River. The channel passes under the Goodland fixed bridge north of unlighted daybeacon #12. Immediately north of this span, a marked channel cuts west to Moran's Barge Restaurant, Marina and

Motel (941-642-1920). This cut holds 4½-foot low-water depths. The on-site restaurant is surprisingly sophisticated, even if definitely pricey. The motel also seems to be a fine place to spend a night with dry ground under your feet. Unfortunately, the management of Moran's has firmly informed this writer that no transient space is available. So, unless you want to take a long dinghy ride, all the Moran's facilities are probably best bypassed by cruising-size craft.

Between unlighted daybeacons #16 and #17, the river's track is deep almost from shore to shore. While there is most certainly some tidal current, the river offers more than enough protection and swinging room for overnight anchorage by most sizes of pleasurecraft. This stretch of the channel is mostly free from commercial traffic, but you should still anchor well away from the mid-width and show a bright anchor light just in case some fishing craft happens along during the night.

Northwest of unlighted daybeacon #24, the channel runs past Sanctuary Sound. This portion of the passage is subject to shoaling and navigation becomes more than slightly tricky. Be *sure* to read the navigational account of the Marco Island channel presented later in this chapter before running this stretch for the first time.

East Marco Bay Anchorage

East of the Marco Island (Highway 951)/ Jude S. S. Jolley Bridge, chart 11430 correctly notes a broad stretch of deep water running towards Three Island Cove and Addison Bay. While you can find minimum 5-foot depths for .5 nautical miles east of the bridge, the channel is surrounded by unmarked shoals and shelter is minimal. Frankly, there are far, far better resting spots to the north and south, but if night should be fast approaching and winds are light, you could use this haven for immediate shelter.

Marco Island & Associated Facilities

Marco Island was once considered the northernmost of the Ten Thousand Islands. Well, it doesn't seem that way any longer. It now looks as if some unwanted corner of Fort Lauderdale or Clearwater has been dropped from the sky upon this body of land. To say that portions of Marco are intensely developed falls short of the mark. High- and low-rise condominiums dot the landscape, set beside far more attractive single-dwelling neighborhoods that sprawl like grains of sand on a beach. To find all of this so close to the natural world of the Ten Thousand Islands and the mostly undeveloped passage south from Naples is a real shock.

By the way, if you find yourself on or near Marco Island and in need of outboard or I/O repairs, you're in luck. Call Mike Polly at Intercoastal Marine (754 E Elkcam Street, 941-642-0067).

Numbers to know on Marco Island include:

A-OK Taxi—941-394-1113
Patron Transportation—941-394-6179
Yellow Cab—941-659-0800
Avis Rental Cars—941-481-1511
Enterprise Rent-A-Car—941-642-4488
Hertz Rent A Car—941-927-8929

Marco Island's newest pleasurecraft facility graces the waterway's southwesterly banks, immediately west of the high-rise, fixed Marco Island bridge (itself west of unlighted daybeacon #26). Marco Island Yacht and Sailing Club is a sumptuous development, set amidst an ultrasheltered harbor and beautifully manicured

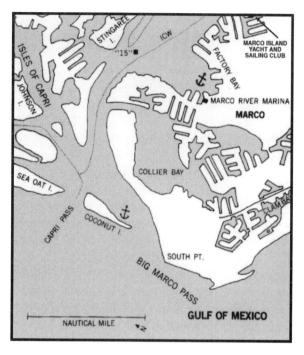

grounds. A large, luxurious clubhouse overlooks the dockage basin's northwesterly tip and is prominently visible from the water. This is primarily a members-only club, but fortunately the management has wisely chosen to accept visiting cruisers with a maximum stay of two nights.

Dockage is afforded at the latest version of concrete decked, floating piers, featuring 30-50-amp power, freshwater, and cable television connections. A few slips have 100-amp hook-ups as well. Depths alongside run to some 6 feet or better at low water.

A single shoreside shower is open to visitors, but it's a long walk to this facility at the harbor's northwesterly tip (near the large clubhouse). Waste pump-out service is available, but you will have to look elsewhere for fuel. Transient visitors are allowed to satisfy their appetite at the club's memorable dining room one night. Otherwise, those cruisers not wishing to prepare a meal aboard will probably want to call a taxi and visit one of the many restaurants on Marco Island or Goodland.

It's a hefty walk of some five blocks to a supermarket and Eckerd Drugs. Ask the friendly dockmaster or any of his staff for directions. Many will probably want to take a taxi rather than undertake this prodigious hike (check above for taxi numbers).

In spite of the time limit put on your stay, Marco Island Yacht and Sailing Club deserves every cruiser's consideration. If you seek a fully appointed marina with all the amenities of a stopover in Fort Lauderdale, this is the spot.

Marco Island Yacht & Sailing Club (941) 642-2531
    http://www.marcoislandyachtclub.com/

Approach depth—6-10 feet
Dockside depth—6+ feet
Accepts transients—yes (two-night stay maximum)
Floating concrete piers—yes
Dockside power connections—30, 50, and some 100 amp
Dockside water connections—yes
Waste pump-out—yes
Showers—yes (one)
Restaurant—one on site and several accessible by taxi

Marco Island's other first-class marina is found on the southerly banks of Factory Bay, south-southwest of unlighted daybeacon #15. Though you would probably never know it from looking at chart 11430, two channels actually serve the bay. The easternmost of the two passages (marked by three red unlighted daybeacons) cuts through the bay's waters and leads to Marco River Marina. Entrance depths range from 6 to 8 feet, while you will find 7 to 8 feet of water at the well-sheltered

docks. Transients are eagerly accepted for overnight or temporary dockage at (mostly) fixed wooden piers sporting every conceivable power and water connection.

Complete mechanical and haul-out services (using either of two travelifts rated at 15- and 35-ton capacities, respectively) are readily available. If you need it fixed, this is the place to be.

Gasoline, diesel fuel, and waste pump-out services are on hand, as is a very impressive, full-line ship's, clothing, and variety store, plus a large parts department. Adequate, partially climate controlled shoreside showers are available and a laundromat is located some two miles away from the harbor. Smaller powercraft will find plentiful dry stack storage.

Cruisers needing to restock their larders will find a supermarket and large drugstore within a half- to three-quarter-mile walk. If this is a bit too much of a hike, call one of the taxi services listed above.

The on-site Jack's Lookout Restaurant (941-394-5944) serves sandwiches, hamburgers, and hot dogs. For more substantive fare, several other restaurants, including the Windjammer (941-643-6880) and Snook Inn (941-394-3313), are within walking distance. These two restaurants will also provide complimentary transportation and a free drink to all patrons of Marco River Marina. If you are looking for a large, full-service marina, Marco River is certainly one of the best bets on the island waters.

Marco River Marina (941) 394-2502
    http://www.marcoriver.com

Approach depth—6-10 feet
Dockside depth—7-8 feet
Accepts transients—yes
Fixed wooden pier and slips—yes
Dockside power connections—up to 50 amp

Dockside water connections—yes
Waste pump-out—yes
Showers—yes
Laundromat—two miles away
Gasoline—yes
Diesel fuel—yes
Mechanical repairs—full service
Below-waterline repairs—full service
Ship's and variety store—yes (large)
Restaurant—one on site and several more
  nearby

Moving south to north along Western Florida's coastline, our first BAIL-suggested anchorage is found on the southern shores of Factory Bay, southwest of unlighted daybeacon #6, and a bit southeast of the entrance to Marco River Marina. Minimum 5½-foot depths hold to within 100 yards of a shoreline that is overlooked by dense high-rise condo development. This is not the spot to be caught in strong northern or northeasterly winds, but it does feature good shelter when the fickle breezes are blowing from other quarters.

A second marina used to flank Factory Bay's western shoreline. The old Factory Bay Marina is now closed and is rapidly being replaced by a high-rise condominium.

Coconut Island Anchorage (BAIL-Suggested)

West of flashing daybeacon #14, the Marco Island-Naples waterway runs quickly on to an important intersection with Big Marco Pass and Capri Pass. Big Marco Pass is impassable by all but smaller, very shallow draft local powercraft. Capri Pass is quite a different story.

Coconut Island sits squarely at the confluence of the two inlets. Depths ranging from 7 to 9 feet are held off the island's eastern and southeastern shores, south of flashing daybeacon #9. This used to be a very popular spot for weekenders to anchor during good weather

and it is still a BAIL-suggested anchorage. In spite of the island's erosion problems (see below), visiting cruisers may consider dropping the hook here when winds do not exceed 10 knots. Anchor off the island's southern or southeasterly shores.

Protection is certainly not sufficient for heavy weather and this writer would be hesitant to try and jockey a boat larger than 48 feet into this refuge. If there is any mention of possible thunderstorms in the forecast, you should seek overnight shelter elsewhere.

Cruisers who haven't visited Coconut Island lately are in for quite a shock. As a part of its program to remove non-native trees and plants from the Florida environment, the state has removed all the Australian pines from Coconut Island. With the trees gone, erosion has been decimating this isle at an alarming pace. The charted spit that used to comprise the island's southerly tier has now disappeared entirely. It may not be many more years before all of Coconut Island vanishes, and its anchorage will only be a distant memory.

Capri Pass

Capri Pass is the only safe inlet for cruising-size craft between Coon Key Light and Gordon Pass. This inlet currently holds minimum 6- to 8-foot depths and is well marked. Cruisers who have not run this pass for the last several years may be surprised by some new shoaling and at least one aid to navigation has been moved to accommodate this influx of shallows. Be sure to read the navigational section on Capri Pass later in this chapter to avoid a nasty ambush.

As mentioned earlier, boats drawing a bit too much for comfortable passage through Coon Key Pass and the Big Marco River can run offshore to Capri Pass and then put in to the deeper section of the Marco Island-Naples waterway. You can then either turn south to take advantage of the marina facilities on Marco Island, or north to Gordon Pass and Naples along the protected inside passage.

Johnson Bay Anchorage

North of Capri Pass, the inland channel to Naples skirts through a dredged cut in Johnson Bay. Cruisers will find an anchorage near unlighted daybeacon #14 for boats up to 40 feet. The charted deep water west-northwest of #14 makes a good spot to spend the night if winds do not exceed 20 knots. Depths of 8 to 12 feet hold to within 75 yards of the western banks. You will be subject to the wake of all passing vessels, but otherwise protection is pretty good. Don't forget to show an anchor light.

The current configuration of the deep water adjacent to this anchorage is now different than that pictured on the present edition of chart 11430. Read the navigational account of this anchorage in the next section before visiting this haven.

Little Marco Island Anchorage (BAIL-Suggested)

North of unlighted daybeacon #29, the waterway to Naples enters a superbly sheltered landcut that extends north to Dollar Bay. At unlighted daybeacon #33, the main passage intersects a deep channel running back south beside Little Marco Island to Hurricane Pass (also known as Little Marco Pass). The southern two-thirds of the creek leading to Hurricane Pass can serve as a near ideal heavy-weather anchorage. While there are a few unmarked shoals to avoid, the cautious skipper should be able to hold minimum 6½- to 7-foot low-water depths north of the stream's intersection with Hurricane Pass.

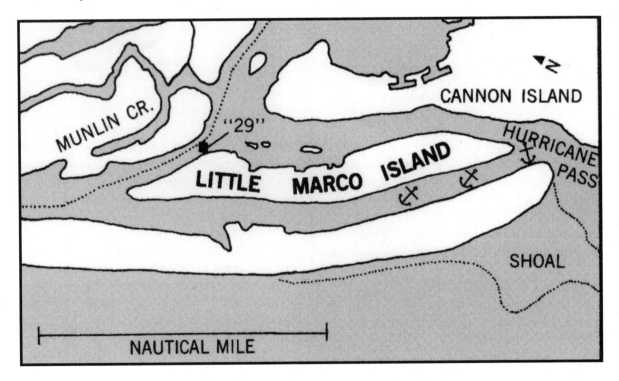

Until recently, cruisers could watch for a large stand of Australian pines overlooking the westerly banks, and drop the hook abeam of this delightful foliage in 8 to 10 feet of water. These pines have now been removed (as at Coconut Island—see above) by the state of Florida. Now, your best bet is to watch the sounder. As soon as depths impove to 8 feet or better, select any likely spot to drop the hook.

The Little Marco Island channel eventually swings south to Hurricane Pass. While chart 11430 would suggest shoal water on the interior portion of the inlet, on-site research revealed a very different situation. As a matter of fact, the southern tip of the peninsula lining the channel's western flank is undoubtedly one of the most popular stopovers for local weekend (smaller) powercraft.

During our last visit to the pass, it looked as if all of Florida had their small powerboats pulled up onto the beaches. Pleasurecraft of almost any size can anchor off the point in minimum 7-foot depths. Protection is fair from all but southern and southwesterly winds, but insufficient for strong blows. For my money, I would choose the interior anchorage sandwiched between the beach and Little Marco Island every time.

Cruising craft should not attempt to run Hurricane or Little Marco passes, no matter what the size or draft of their vessel might be. While we observed a few local outboarders running the inlet, unmarked shoals are rife and there are absolutely no markers on the pass.

Rookery Bay Anchorage

Take a look at the current edition of chart 11430 and note the charted 5-foot offshoot leading to shallow Rookery Bay, opposite unlighted daybeacon #47. Boats up to 38 feet can drop anchor in 5 to 8 feet of water on the westernmost hundred yards of this passage. Protection is wonderful and should be sufficient for anything short of a hurricane. Rookery Bay itself is quite shallow and is part of a huge wildlife refuge. Exploration by dinghy would be worthwhile. If you do visit the bay, go quietly and don't disturb any nesting birds.

Gordon Pass Inlet

Immediately north of unlighted daybeacon #73, the markings on the Marco Island-Naples waterway come to an end. To the north, a set of beacons leads to Naples, while the well-outlined path to Gordon Pass inlet cuts to the west. Gordon Inlet offers just about everything any mariner might ever hope for from a pass. The channel is clearly outlined by numerous aids to navigation and features minimum 10-foot depths. There is even a super anchorage on the cut's interior reaches. If you want more than that from an inlet, then you are hard to please.

Gordon Pass Anchorage (BAIL-Suggested)

North of unlighted daybeacon #12 on Gordon Pass, minimum depths of 5 feet can be held through the mid-width of the charted channel that leads to a series of canals lined by sumptuous homes. This passage allows ready access to a most fortunate anchorage. Cruisers can safely wait for fair breezes before venturing out Gordon Pass, or those who arrive late in the day from points offshore can spend the night in peace and security before heading up to Naples or down to Marco Island the next morning.

While it would otherwise be possible for a boat of any size to anchor in the first bay-like area north of the entrance, chart 11430 designates these waters as a cable area. Heed this warning unless the notion of a high-voltage anchor appeals.

Instead, cut east on the first offshoot to starboard, north of the entrance. You can then cruise through minimum 9-foot depths until the stream turns again to the north. Here the waters open out into another wide bay with excellent 7- to 9-foot depths. There is enough room for a small ocean freighter to swing easily on the hook, and there is immaculate protection from all winds. It is not an exaggeration to contend that you should be safe in any blow under 50 knots. The surrounding shores are heavily lined by some of the most expensive private homes that you are likely to see in all of Western Florida. *Be sure* to foster good relations between cruisers and property owners by *not* trespassing on any of this very private property.

Port Royal Anchorage

North of Gordon Pass, it's as if someone has flipped a light switch connected with residential development. Gone are the undeveloped shores to the south. Passing cruisers are now engulfed in a mass of palatial homes, beginning first on the western banks. This development is the harbinger of the city of Naples to the north. Before visiting with this fascinating city, we need to review one anchorage, a repair yard, and a marina that lie between Gordon Inlet and the principal Naples waterfront.

North of unlighted daybeacon #21, a 5½- to 7-foot channel cuts into the western banks and leads to a *Y*-shaped series of canals. There are two unmarked shoals to avoid at the entrance, but good coastal navigators should be able to make it through with the usual caution.

Once the pesky entrance is left behind, there are at least three spots where pleasure-craft can drop the hook in peace and security. The first refuge is found abeam of the toe of charted 7-foot water cutting to the southwest. You can drop the Danforth (or the plow) into waters of 6½ to 7 feet of depth with excellent protection from inclement weather.

During a really heavy blow, it is quite feasible to ease down into the southwesterly off-shoot a bit for even more shelter. As is the case with all three of these anchorages, the shoreline is covered with affluent private homes.

The next potential anchorage is discovered south of the split in the canal. Here the waters broaden out enough to give plenty of swinging room, but there is still good shelter. Depths run from 6 to 7 feet. To my mind, this is an even better spot than the first anchorage described above. There is a bit more protection and it's still quite close to the main channel.

Just about any captain could find what he might be looking for in the way of superior anchorage in these first two havens, but for those who like to explore, you may also follow the westerly branch of the canal until it broadens out into a lake-like area (where it dead ends). Skippers will find good depths ranging from 7 to 10 feet and the splendid protection so characteristic of this entire region.

Southpointe Yacht Club

South of unlighted daybeacon #22, one marina graces the eastern shores of the Naples channel. Southpointe Yacht Club (941-774-6392) is part of a large condo and townhouse development.

Mariners visiting Southpointe must enter through a strangely marked entrance (*be sure* to read the navigational account on the marina later in this chapter) and then cruise up a long canal to reach the super-protected harbor. Minimum low-water entrance depths run from 6 to 7 feet, while excellent soundings of 8 to 9 feet are exhibited dockside.

Unfortunately, Southpointe Yacht Club no longer accepts transients or live-aboards. Cruisers must now bypass this facility unless they are lucky enough to own property in the development.

Royal Yacht Services

At unlighted daybeacon #25, a short hop north of the just discussed Port Royal anchorage, a marked channel strikes off to the north-northeast. This shallow cut leads to Royal Yacht Services (941-775-0117). With the demise of Turner Marine (see below), this is one of the few repair yards left in Naples that caters to pleasurecraft.

On the other hand, let it be known loud and clear that the only word to describe this yard's approach channel is "shallow." Depths are all but nil at low tide, and even at high water, you can't count on any more than 5 feet. Clearly, this facility is limited to boats drawing less than 5 feet, and even then, most vessels must time their entrance and egress for high tide.

If you successfully traverse the entrance cut, you will find a friendly repair yard offering full below-waterline, haul-out repairs courtesy of a 60-ton travelift. Complete mechanical servicing for both diesel and gasoline power plants is also available. Some do-it-yourself work is still allowed here—a real rarity in modern-day Florida.

Always assuming you can negotiate the tricky entrance channel, we recommend this facility to our fellow cruisers. Wise captains will call ahead to check on the latest depths and the time of high tide.

Naples

No one without seriously impaired vision would ever characterize Naples as a village. It is a genuine city in every sense of the word—and yet, this writer could not help but gain the impression that life was just a bit slower here and less frenzied than that of Fort Lauderdale or even Clearwater. To be succinct, we found Naples to be a delightful vacation and tourist city with ample services for cruisers and a long list of shopping, motel, and restaurant facilities. Mariners who have not visited this fair town heretofore are in for a genuinely pleasing experience.

Naples is famous for its long city pier (on the Gulfside beach) and its fabulous sunsets over the Gulf. The *T*-shaped pier was originally built in 1888 and extends 600 feet out into the Gulf. In spite of having to be rebuilt following a hurricane in 1910, a fire in 1922, and a hurricane in 1960, this venerable structure survives intact.

During our time in Naples we were privileged to observe one of the city's famous late-day displays of natural pyrotechnics. I can truthfully tell you that these spectacular sunsets are *not* just a creation of the local Chamber of Commerce. Another point of interest in Naples is the Palm Cottage Museum (137 12th Avenue South, 941-261-8164). Palm Cottage has been preserved to appear just as it did upon its construction in 1895 when Naples was just a quiet fishing village. The old homeplace is one of the last surviving tabbie homes in southwest Florida.

What is tabbie, you may ask? For those of you who don't know, tabbie was an early building material used in coastal sections of the southeast United States. It was formed by burning limestone and shells together. The secret of its making has now been lost.

Cruisers will need a taxi or rental car to visit Palm Cottage. It is a bit too far for walking from the city waterfront.

Cruisers lucky enough to tie up in Naples between May 3 and 19 will find themselves smack in the middle of the Tropicool Fest. This celebration of art exhibits, concerts, food, and sporting events is becoming larger and larger with each new season.

Numbers to know in Naples include:

Airport Taxi—941-768-5400
Beach and Island Cab—941-263-8402
Yellow Cab—941-659-0800
Avis Rental Cars—941-643-0900
Budget Rent A Car—941-643-2212
Hertz Rent A Car—941-643-1515
Boat/U S Marine Center—941-774-3233
West Marine—941-793-7722
Chamber of Commerce—941-774-3233
Naples Visitors Center—941-262-6141

Naples Anchorages & Facilities

North of flashing daybeacon #34, cruisers will observe most of Naples' marinas along the western shores. North of flashing daybeacon #40, the waters split at the mouth of the Gordon River. Tidal currents are absolutely fierce along this stretch. Some additional facilities are found on the deeper westerly branch. With care, boats drawing 4 feet, or preferably less, can enter the easterly fork and visit with one of the most impressive ship's and nautical stores anywhere. Both forks of the Gordon River are soon blocked by low-level fixed bridges. Passage above the bridges is not recommended for cruising-size craft and is not further commented upon in this guide.

As we shall see in the account below, Naples offers much in the way of services for

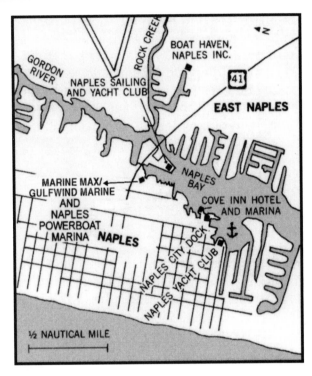

visiting cruisers. The city marina, in particular, is quite friendly to transients. However, transient slips have recently become more scarce. Wise captains should now be sure to make advance reservations rather than arrive late in the day only to find no room at the inn.

We begin our trek along the Naples waterfront at unlighted daybeacon #35. West of #35, cruisers will find Naples Yacht Club, the southernmost of two side-by-side facilities on Crayton Cove. This yacht club is one of two such organizations in the Naples region. Entrance depths run between 7 and 13 feet. Most of the slips have 7 to 8 feet of water, with a few 6-foot soundings on the inner piers.

Members of accredited yacht clubs with reciprocal agreements are accepted for transient dockage *only* with advance arrangements. Be sure to call well ahead of time to work out your dockage needs. The club dockmaster is on duty daily from 8 A.M. to 4:30 P.M. Berths are provided at fixed wooden piers with full power and water connections. Gasoline and diesel fuel are available to members and club guests only. Showers and ice are available in the clubhouse. The club also features a swimming pool at which accredited guests are welcome. The dining room serves lunch and dinner daily, but reservations are requested. Coat and tie are required after 6 P.M.

Naples Yacht Club (941) 262-6647 (clubhouse)
262-7301 (dockmaster)

Approach depth—7-13 feet
Dockside depth—6 to 8 feet
Accepts transients—members of clubs with reciprocal agreements *only* with advance arrangements
Fixed wooden piers—yes
Dockside power connections—30 and 50 amp
Dockside water connections—yes
Showers—yes

Gasoline—yes (members and club guests only)
Diesel fuel—yes (members and club guests only)
Restaurant—on site

A BAIL-approved anchorage used to lie between the Naples Yacht Club entrance channel and the Naples City Dock, northwest of unlighted daybeacon #35. Recently, the city of Naples has installed a free (though there may be a charge in the future) eight-buoy mooring field on these waters. The assistant city dockmaster has informed this writer that while anchorage is not strictly prohibited here, it is now "discouraged." According to her account, this new stricture was put in place due to the problem of anchored boats dragging on the soft silt bottom and injuring nearby vessels. After I checked with several local cruisers, this account seems to be confirmed. So, with reluctance, we will give this mooring field our tacit approval, but not without a sigh at the loss of another unrestricted anchorage.

Naples mooring field

As you enter the mooring field, a sign warns all captains to check in with the city dockmaster. Skippers who have not already arranged for a mooring buoy ahead of time may want to make their first stop at the outermost face (fuel dock) of the Naples City Dock to sign up with the dockmaster and get their mooring buoy assignment.

Within the mooring field, low-water depths of 6 to 8 feet can be expected. Shelter is quite good from all but fresh northeasterly breezes. The surrounding shores are, as you would expect, heavily developed.

The Naples City Dock is found just north of the Naples Yacht Club and to the west of unlighted daybeacon #36. This is a fine city facility that gladly accepts transients at fixed wooden piers with water and power connections up to 50 amps. Good entrance depths of 7 to 12 feet are complemented by similar dockside soundings. Just as you would expect, the deeper slips are found on the outer docks. Gasoline and diesel fuel are dispensed at the outermost section of the fixed, wooden, *T*-shaped pier. Fuel prices are some of the best in the region. The marina's showers have now been remodeled and feature full climate control. The on-site laundromat is covered but open to the weather on one side. Free waste pump-out service is available as well.

Over and above these dry statistics, we have found the harbormaster and his staff at the Naples City Dock to be superfriendly and unusually helpful, always ready to go that extra mile to meet the needs of visiting cruisers. They even provide free bikes to facilitate a quick tour of the nearby Naples shopping district. That's

Naples City Dock

going above and beyond the ordinary in our estimation.

Naples City Dock (941) 434-4693
   http://www.naplescitydock.com

Approach depth—7-12 feet
Dockside depth—7-12 feet
Accepts transients—yes
Fixed wooden piers—yes
Dockside power connections—30 and 50 amp
Dockside water connections—yes
Waste pump-out—yes
Showers—yes
Laundromat—yes
Gasoline—yes
Diesel fuel—yes

Ship's store—nearby
Restaurant—on site

An interesting complex of shops and restaurants is found just behind the city docks. The Dock at Crayton Cove Restaurant (941-263-9940) sits just north of the city pier. This fine eatery features open-air dining and some of the most delectable cold seafood salads that you will ever enjoy. In season, the stone crab claws are nothing to sneeze at either. Just watch out for the price of imported beer. Crayton Cove has its own small, *C*-shaped docks to which small powercraft are free to moor. Dockside depths run 5 to 6 feet.

Dock at Crayton Cove Restaurant, Naples

Now, as if all that were not enough, there is a whole series of shops located behind the restaurant. One of these, the Naples Ship's Store (830 12th Avenue South, 941-649-0899), will be of great interest to visiting and resident cruisers alike. This well-managed establishment features an extensive selection of nautical gear, clothing, and marine publications. Take a few moments to browse the teeming shelves. Anyone interested in things nautical will find more than a little to engage him. Tell Eric we sent you!

Napoli on the Bay Restaurant (941-649-7337) sits just beside the Naples Ship's Store. This firm boasts super pizza and other Italian delicacies, as well as scoop ice cream.

Cruisers seeking fresh fruit will want to set a course for Crayton Cove Gourmet and Fruit Shipper (800 12th Avenue South, 941-262-4362), a few doors up from Napoli on the Bay. This is a great place to restock the galley with a few specialty items.

Those whose tastes run to French-style cuisine will want to make every effort to check out the Bleu Provence (1234 8th Street South, 941-261-8239), just across the street from Crayton Cove Gourmet. We have not had a chance to sample the fare here, but judging from this restaurant's popularity, the food must be spectacular. Be sure to call for reservations on weekends to avoid long waits.

Italian-style cookery is not forgotten either. Michelangelo Ristorante (755 13th Avenue, 941-643-6177), diagonally across the street from Crayton Cove Gourmet, serves wonderful pasta.

Visiting cruisers up for a five-block walk (or a short bicycle or taxi ride) can visit another couture-style Naples shopping district. Stroll west on 12th Avenue. Eventually you will come to 3rd Street. An elegant collection of specialty shops, art galleries, and sophisticated restaurants stretches along this byway for several blocks.

In this latter category, Tommy Bahamas Tropical Cafe (1220 3rd Street South, 941-643-6889) is clearly one of the most popular, with plentiful outdoor seating. Anyone up for a visit to jolly old England should be sure to check out the Old Naples Pub (255 13th Avenue South, 941-649-8200). Superb Continental-style dining is readily available at Campiello Restaurant (1177 3rd Street South, 941-435-1166). Try to get a table in the delightful courtyard.

One of the most tempting dining spots, at least to our palates, is the Terra Grill (1300 3rd Street South, 941-262-5500). Check it out!

Turning now to Naples' other on-the-water facilities, the docks of Cove Inn Hotel & Marina (941-262-7161) lie immediately north of the city pier and share the same cove. As its name implies, this facility features a large hotel with a line of docks out back. All of the facility's slips are privately owned and no transient dockage is currently available.

On the other hand, the small coffee shop in the Cove Inn Hotel may just serve the best breakfast in Naples. It's a quick walk of only two blocks from the Naples City Dock to this notable dining spot, so if you're up for some great eggs or scrumptious hot cakes, give this restaurant your immediate attention.

Just north of the Cove Inn, passing cruisers will note the Naples Coast Guard Auxiliary headquarters on the western banks. There are no facilities at the clubhouse for visiting craft, but it's a comfort to know that the squadron is on the job in Naples.

A large cove indents the western banks above the Coast Guard Auxiliary headquarters. There is a local launching ramp for small craft here, but depths of as little as 3 feet render this water inappropriate for anchorage by larger vessels.

Old Naples Seaport (941 434-8548) lines the banks west of flashing daybeacon #40. The marina docks are overlooked by a large, enclosed dining and retail complex. In the past, transients were sometimes accepted at this facility, but all the available slips have now been permanently sold. There are no longer any services for visiting cruisers.

For many years, resident and transient cruisers alike looked forward to a visit with Turner Marine of Naples north of unlighted daybeacon #39. Recently, this property has been purchased as a first step in developing an extensive complex of condos, docks, and marina facilities that will be known as the Naples Boat Club. The old Turner Marine buildings, docks, and repair yard will be demolished to make way for the new construction. The new owners seem to be extremely friendly and have informed this writer that facilities will almost certainly be available for visiting cruisers upon completion of their extensive project. However, as construction is just getting under way at this time, we will not be able to comment intelligently about just what the future Naples Boat Club will or won't have in the way of marine services until the next edition of this guide. In the meantime, watch out for all the new construction, and please send us a report on what you find here to opcom@netpath.net.

Naples Sailing & Yacht Club maintains a floating breakwater-enclosed harbor on the point of land separating the two branches of the Gordon River. This club is glad to accept members of other yacht clubs with reciprocal privileges for overnight or temporary dockage.

Berths are cheerfully provided at both fixed and floating docks with full power and water connections. Low-tide dockside depths range from 4½ to 6 feet. The club's dockmaster is in attendance daily from 8:00 A.M. until 4:00 P.M. Call ahead to make advance arrangements if you plan to arrive at any other time. Showers are available in the clubhouse.

The on-site dining room is open for lunch and dinner Tuesday through Saturday, and there is also a Sunday midday brunch. Reservations are requested but not required. A host of other restaurants are close at hand, including the famed Kelly's Fish House.

This writer could not help but be impressed by the friendliness of this organization during his brief contact with the club membership. It is highly recommended.

Naples Sailing & Yacht Club (941) 774-0424
(941) 774-2649 (dockmaster)

Approach depth—6 feet
Dockside depth—4½-6 feet
Accepts transients—members of other yacht
    clubs with reciprocal privileges
Fixed and floating docks—yes
Dockside power connections—30 and 50 amp
Dockside water connections—yes
Showers—yes
Restaurant—on site and several others nearby

Turning our attention now to the deeper, western branch of the Gordon River, passing cruisers will first come upon a stream making its way in from the western banks which serves both Marine Max/Gulfwind Marine and the Naples Powerboat Marina (941-261-8878). This latter facility maintains a host of covered slips set back in a protected L-shaped cove. All dockage is strictly reserved for resident craft and signs warn against entry into the slips by visiting boats.

Marine Max/Gulfwind Marine (941-262-6137) is a full-service repair facility offering complete mechanical and below-waterline, haul-out repairs. The yard's travelift is rated at 70 tons. You will spot Marine Max/Gulfwind Marine's docks to starboard as you enter the westerly stream. This firm is part of an excellent chain that we will meet throughout our remaining journey north along the Sunshine State's western coastline. This location caters particularly to the needs of larger pleasure-craft. All wet-slip dockage is reserved for service customers.

Opposite Marine Max/Gulfwind Marine, visiting cruisers will spy Bay Marina (941-992-2601). This tiny facility offers some wet-slip dockage for smaller resident powercraft,

as well as recently expanded dry stack storage. Depths alongside run to 4½ feet. No services are available for transients.

Continuing up the west-side branch, the western shores are flanked by a portion of the so-called Tin City shopping center. This complex series of gift shops, restaurants, and retail businesses of all descriptions are grouped under (you guessed it) tin-roofed buildings. One of the largest of these structures fronts directly onto the water.

On the eastern shore, a series of private docks line the banks above Bay Marina. Next up is Port of Call Boat Rentals, with no services for transients.

Immediately south of the fixed bridge, Kelly's Fish House (941-774-0494) lines the

Kelly's Fish House, Naples

eastern banks. While the available dockage is taken up by the restaurant's own fishing vessels, visiting cruisers should make every effort to visit this outstanding dining spot. Locals and this writer agree that Kelly's serves the finest fried (and a few broiled items) seafood in Naples, bar none. The restaurant is within walking distance of Boat Haven Marine.

Let us now turn our attention for a moment to the easterly branch of the Gordon River below the fixed bridges. The water is much shallower on this fork than on its western counterpart. Low-tide depths of 4 to 4½ feet are not uncommon. Only boats drawing less than 4 feet should attempt to visit the facilities along this stream.

There is really only one reason to visit the eastern branch. Boat Haven Marine Supply features a bevy of mostly covered (though some are left open for sailboats) slips on the last charted offshoot making off from the eastern banks, south of the fixed bridge. This marina accepts transients at its fixed wooden piers with water and 20-amp, 120-volt (only) power connections. Mechanical repairs are readily available and smaller vessels can be hauled for below-waterline servicing by way of an overhead crane with a 5-ton capacity or an 8-ton forklift. Gasoline, but no diesel fuel, can be purchased dockside and visiting cruisers can make use of shoreside showers.

Boat Haven's real attraction is its marine and ship's store perched just behind the dockage complex. Of all the hundreds of nautical stores that this writer has ever visited, I have never seen a finer such operation. Whether you are seeking the latest in foul-weather gear, that certain size stainless screw, or even

the most up-to-date charts and nautical publications, you can believe me when I say that you need look no further. Not only is the selection truly vast, but the store is neat, well laid out, and extremely organized—a real rarity with ship's stores. In short, *don't miss it!*

The's Waterfront Cafe (941-775-8115) is now located immediately adjacent to Boat Haven. The's offers superb seafood and seafood salads. One fine, cool January day, we had the opportunity to dine here at an outside table overlooking the water. The food was good and the scenery was enough to inspire us to begin searching for more permanent Naples dockage.

Boat Haven, Naples Inc. (941) 774-0339

Approach depth—4-4½ feet (low-water)
Dockside depth—4-4½ feet (low-water)
Accepts transients—yes
Fixed wooden slips—yes (many covered)
Dockside power connections—20-amp, 110-volt only
Dockside water connections—yes
Showers—yes
Gasoline—yes
Mechanical repairs—yes
Below-waterline repairs—yes (smaller vessels)
Ship's store—yes (*Wow!*)
Restaurant—on site and several nearby

North of the entrance to Boat Haven, The's Waterfront Cafe maintains a dock fronting the eastern banks. Even though you may see a large trimaran docked here, do not attempt to moor at these piers. On-site inspection revealed depths of less than 3 feet.

North of The's, the passage is soon spanned by a low-level fixed bridge. This guide's coverage of the Gordon River ends at this point.

COON KEY TO NAPLES NAVIGATION

Cruising captains voyaging north from the Ten Thousand Islands to Naples have three different routes to choose from. Sailors, in particular, might decide to skirt south of the Cape Romano shoals and follow the open waters of the Gulf north to Gordon Pass. While this route serves up nothing in the way of protection, there are certainly no depth problems.

A second alternative is to split your passage between the offshore and inland routes. Those choosing this alternative can cruise offshore to a point just north of Marco Island and then come inside via mostly deep and well-marked Capri Pass. You can then turn briefly south to visit Marco Island's marinas, or cruise north through minimum 5½-foot depths (with typical depths from 6 to 10 feet) all the way to Gordon Pass and Naples. Obviously this passage has some of the best of both worlds and should be a serious consideration, particularly for sailors.

This writer's personal favorite, though, is the full inside channel from Coon Key Light, past Marco Island, and then on to Naples. In spite of its problems, there is a backwater feeling to the waterway south of Marco Island which will appeal to the heart of any true cruiser.

Skippers setting out upon the Marco Island-Naples waterway from Coon Key must contend with the possibility of encountering a few low-tide depths of 4½ feet. Only boats drawing 4 feet or less can cruise this waterway with absolute safety. On a rising tide, you might consider taking a boat needing 4½ or even 5 feet of water

through the passage, but this is a bit risky. A few portions of the waterway south of Marco Island are not really as well marked as they should be, and the channel is subject to shoaling.

Let me also once again mention the complex manatee no-wake zones that have now been set up along the Marco Island-Naples waterway. Be *sure* to read the various signs along the way, even if you have to use your binoculars to make out the small print. You won't believe how the speed limits change back and forth at certain times of the day and certain months of the year.

Whatever route you choose, this is a pleasant section of the Western Florida coastline. With the exception of the heavy development on portions of Marco Island, most of the coastline, both inside and outside, is undeveloped. Good coastal navigation must be practiced on all three passages, so stay alert and don't concentrate so much on the scenery that you become a fixed part of it.

The Offshore Route Any cruiser worth his or her salt knows that it's not a very swift idea to undertake a 25-nautical-mile offshore passage if foul weather is in the offing. If you decide to cruise offshore to Capri Pass or Naples (Gordon Pass), it would be very wise to wait for fair breezes before undertaking the passage.

Study chart 11429 and note the miles and miles of shoals extending south from Cape Romano. Boats that try to cut this corner obviously do so at their own peril. For safety's sake, you should set your course to pass south of the unnumbered 18-foot flashing daybeacon marking the shoal's southerly limits. Continue cruising west from the 18-foot daybeacon for another 4 nautical miles or so before making your turn to the north. This maneuver will assure a safe passage past the shoals.

For the next 18 nautical miles you're on your own. There are no aids to navigation between the unnumbered 18-foot flashing daybeacon and flashing daybeacon #2 (currently charted as flashing buoy #2) off Capri Pass. Fortunately, except in the vicinity of Big Marco Pass, good depths run reasonably close to the Gulf beaches. This relatively deep water allows navigators to keep the shoreline in sight during daylight and fair weather as they work their way north. Nevertheless, all mariners should follow careful compass courses on this long run and maintain an accurate dead-reckoning track. Of course, a Loran or GPS would be most helpful as well. Be sure that you are *at least 1.5 nautical miles offshore* as you approach Big Marco Pass, at the northern end of Marco Island. Extensive shoals run well west from this unusable passage.

East of flashing daybeacon #2, you can now switch to chart 11430 for a more detailed picture of the pass. Further navigational information on Capri Pass will be presented in our review of the Marco Island-Naples waterway.

It's another cruise of slightly better than 7 nautical miles from #2 to a new, much larger flashing daybeacon #1 (currently charted as flashing buoy #1) off Gordon Pass. Again, you can follow the shoreline. In the absence of strong winds, this is a

relatively simple and quite delightful passage. From #1, it's a straight shot east into the inlet's interior reaches. Don't drift too far to the north. A partially submerged jetty extends for several hundred yards out into the Gulf from the pass's northwestern point. For more information, consult the navigational account of Gordon Pass presented later in this chapter as a part of the inland route's coverage.

Caxambas Pass Channel   Returning now to Coon Key Light, east of Cape Romano, let us turn our attention briefly to the channel leading first northwest and then west to Caxambas Pass. Remember that depths of 5 to 6 feet are held only as far west as unlighted daybeacon #6. West of #6, the channel turns briefly north and runs through a shoal-ravaged section with low-water soundings of 3 feet or less. Obviously, cruising-size craft should halt their forward progress well east of #6.

Also, as noted earlier in this chapter, extensive shoaling has taken place west of unlighted daybeacon #19, in and around the waters denoted by unlighted daybeacons #8 and #10. Unless a new channel is marked at some future point by the county authorities, these shallows are even more reason for visiting cruisers to confine their explorations to the waters east of #6.

To enter the channel, set course from Coon Key Light to come abeam of unlighted daybeacon #2, well south of Neal Key, to its immediate northeasterly side. Do not drift to the south as you approach #2. Chart 11430 correctly forecasts depths of 1 to 3 feet in that quarter.

Continue on by pointing to pass unlighted daybeacon #4 fairly close to its northerly quarter. Northwest of #4, deep water spreads out in a broader passage.

Note that marker colors now reverse for no good reason that I can see. Point to come abeam of unlighted daybeacon #1 to its immediate northeasterly quarter.

At #1, the channel swings around the northeasterly tip of Helen Key and plunges west. Between #1 and unlighted daybeacon #3, cruisers will find the best place to drop the hook.

Coon Key Pass   Let us now return to a review of the principal Marco Island-Naples waterway via Coon Key Pass. One of the shallowest portions of this passage is found between Coon Key Light and Coon Key. Despite the 4-foot soundings on chart 11430, we did not find any low-water readings of less than 5 feet in this area. Boats drawing more than 4 feet should, nevertheless, proceed with the greatest caution and probably wait for a rising tide.

From Coon Key Light, set a northerly course to pass the easterly shores of Coon Key by some 200 yards off your port side. Point to eventually come abeam of and pass unlighted daybeacon #2 by about 100 yards to its westerly quarter. By the time you are abeam of Coon Key's white sand enshrouded, northerly tip, good depths of 6 feet or better will return and be with you for some time.

As you approach #2, be mindful of the shallower water running off Coon Key's northerly tip. North of #2, you may choose to throw out the anchor just east of the

small, unnamed island east of Neal Key. Good depths run to within an amazing 20 yards of the island's eastern shoreline.

To continue on the main channel, set course to come abeam of and pass unlighted daybeacon #3 to its easterly side. Just before reaching #3, a superb anchorage possibility opens out to the east.

Tripod Key-Sugar Bay Anchorage   Enter the broad stream leading northeast to Sugar Bay on its centerline. Drop the hook well short (southwest) of Sugar Bay. This body of water is quite shoal and should only be entered by dinghy.

On Coon Key Pass   North of unlighted daybeacon #4, Coon Key Pass skirts around the point of land occupied by the village of Goodland. On-site research did reveal the charted 3-foot depths immediately adjacent to unlighted daybeacon #6. Happily, we sounded nothing less than 5 feet by staying at least 25 yards west of #6. As you pass #6, the dry stack storage building associated with Goodland Bay Marina will be visible to the west.

Goodland Bay and Calusa Island Marinas
To access both these marina facilities, continue on the main channel past unlighted daybeacon #6 until you are some 50 yards short of Goodland's southeasterly point. Cut sharply to the west and favor the northerly shores heavily as you work your way along. You will spy several pilings outlining the southerly side of the channel, with arrow pointers atop the piles indicating that they should be passed to their (the

pilings') northern sides. Stay at least 40 yards north of these aids to navigation for best depths.

Soon you will pass the dry stack storage and a few floating docks to starboard. This is *not* the principal Goodland Bay Marina dockage area. Continue cruising west and the charted *T*-shaped cove will open out to the north. Enter on the mid-width. The marina docks and buildings will be sighted on the cove's easterly banks.

To continue on to Calusa Island Marina, bypass the northerly turn into Goodland Bay. Cruise west on the waters of Blue Hill Creek, favoring the northerly shoreline. Soon you will round a point with a private, fixed wooden dock, backed by a sumptuous homeplace. Hug the outer edge of the private dock for best depths.

Continue favoring the northerly banks, and soon you will spot Calusa Island's outer dockage basin lining the creek's northerly banks. Be *sure* to hug the outer face of these piers as you cruise to your assigned slip. Even a small jog to the south may well land you in 4 feet of water.

The entrance into Calusa Island's inner harbor basin will open out to the north, just as you sight the outer docks ahead. Here you will find the fuel dock, but remember that low-water soundings can run as skinny as 4½ to 5 feet. Captains piloting vessels drawing better than 4½ feet would do well to fuel up at mid- or high tide.

On the Coon Key Channel North of unlighted daybeacon #6, slow-speed regulations are in effect to unlighted daybeacon #10, with an associated no-wake zone run-

ning from #10 to unlighted beacon #15. At unlighted daybeacon #7, the channel turns sharply west and skirts the southerly reaches of otherwise shallow Goodland Bay.

Goodland Bay Anchorage To make good your entry into the tongue of deeper waters northeast of unlighted daybeacon #7, abandon the main channel as you come abeam of #7 on it easterly side. Work your way carefully to the north for some 25 yards, and then cut to the northeast. Drop the hook as soon as you are clear of the channel and any fellow cruisers that you might find in this haven. Farther to the northeast, depths deteriorate quickly.

On to Big Marco River Watch the southern shores as you cruise west between unlighted daybeacons #8 and #10. The slips associated with Skeeter's Old Marco Lodge will be readily visible along the banks.

Captains seeking to visit Stan's Idle Hour Restaurant and the Little Bar and Restaurant should cut into the mid-width of the southward running canal, immediately west of Skeeter's. Follow the canal's centerline to its southern terminus. Stan's will be spotted on the southeastern corner of the stream's southerly tip. Remember, low-water soundings in this small stream run as little as 3½ feet. If you need more depth, consider a stop at nearby Goodland Bay Marina.

Don't slip to the north as you approach unlighted daybeacon #8. A huge patch of shallows flanks the channel in this quarter.

North of unlighted daybeacon #12, the waterway meets up with the 55-foot fixed

Goodland bridge. Immediately north of this span, a marked and charted channel cuts sharply west to Moran's Barge Marina. Enter on the mid-width and expect low-water soundings of some 4½ feet. Remember, no transient dockage is available, but if you can find an empty slip in which to tie off temporarily, the on-site restaurant is interesting.

Chart 11430 pictures an offshoot of 7-foot water just north of the bridge on the eastern banks. Our research showed that this small sidewater has almost shoaled in entirely. It is still possible to barely get off the main channel, should you be desperate to drop the hook, but you cannot cruise more than 25 yards or so to the east before depths begin to rise.

Unlighted daybeacon #15 introduces visiting cruisers to Big Marco River, running first north and then northwest to unlighted daybeacon #17. This portion of the stream is deep almost from bank to bank and is well sheltered. If you should decide to drop the hook here, ease your way off the main channel and remember to show an anchor light.

West of unlighted daybeacon #20, the channel cuts south of a small island even though chart 11430 would suggest that the best water runs north of this isle. Our soundings showed up nothing less than 5 feet through the buoyed section, however, so keep the faith with the marked passage.

Be sure to stick to the marked channel between unlighted daybeacon #20 and unlighted daybeacon #21. Shoal water waits to greet the unwary outside the buoyed cut.

By the time you approach unlighted daybeacon #24 to its southerly side, the high-rise development on Marco Island will be glaring at you in the distance. Hold on for a minute—there is still one trouble spot to negotiate.

Perhaps the shallowest and trickiest portion of the entire run from Coon Key Pass to Capri Pass is found between unlighted daybeacon #25 and the fixed, 55-foot Marco Island (Highway 951)/Jude S. S. Jolley Bridge. This portion of the channel calls for the greatest caution.

From #25, you *must* set course to come abeam of unlighted daybeacon #26 to its immediate *southwesterly* side. On the water, this looks all wrong. You will be headed away from the bridge's very visible pass-through and you will be tempted to adjust course to the north. *Don't do it!* This maneuver will land you in 2 to 3 feet of water.

Just to make matters a bit more complicated, it's a fairly lengthy run of almost 1 nautical mile between #25 and #26. My best advice is to run a careful compass (or GPS) course and monitor your depth sounder continuously. After coming abeam of #26 hard by its southwesterly quarter, you should curl around the aid and cruise northeast until coming abeam of the bridge's central pass-through. Cut northwest to pass under the bridge.

The mostly unmarked (but reasonably easy to follow) entrance to shiny new Marco Island Yacht and Sailing Club strikes to the southwest, between the northwestern face of the Marco Island/Jude S. S. Jolley Bridge and the charted powerlines crossing the main channel farther to the northwest.

Look for the canal that allows entrance to the harbor, and cut directly in from the main channel towards the canal's mid-width. Along the way, you will spot two signs north of your course that warn of a shoal impinging on this flank of the approach cut. Obviously it would not bode well to slip to the north. Once into the canal, the marina and yacht club will be quite visible to port.

Marco Island & Factory Bay Anchorage (BAIL-Suggested)   North and west of the Marco Island/Jude S. S. Jolley Bridge, the color configuration for aids to navigation reverses. Northbound craft should now pass red beacons to port and green markers to starboard. This scheme holds as far as Capri Pass, and actually continues out to sea on the inlet.

A wide swath of deep water opens out past the 55-foot fixed bridge. You should not have any difficulty in cruising to a point abeam of Factory Bay, which is southwest of the main channel. Remember that Factory Bay is served by two channels. Most cruisers will want to contend with the easterly (or central) passage only, as it leads to the bay's principal marina and a BAIL-suggested anchorage. The pleasurecraft facility that used to flank Factory Bay's westerly channel is now out of business.

Captains cruising north on the waterway will first come upon the well-marked cut leading through the bay's easterly (or central) section. The three red unlighted daybeacons outlining this cut make a cruise down this channel to Marco River Marina a snap. Be sure to pass unlighted daybeacons #2, #4, and #6 to your starboard side.

Cruisers looking to drop the hook in the BAIL-suggested anchorage along the southern shores of Factory Bay should depart the marked central channel abeam of unlighted daybeacon #6. Ease your way a bit to the south, feeling your way along with the sounder. Drop the hook before approaching to within less than 100 yards of the heavily developed banks.

The second channel skirts along Factory Bay's western banks and calls for a bit more caution. Should you choose to ignore our advice, and explore this cut, abandon the main channel some 50 yards northwest of unlighted daybeacon #15 and cut to the south. Watch for the first aid to navigation on the westerly cut, unlighted daybeacon #1. Pass this marker fairly close to your port side. From #1, use your binoculars to pick out the westerly channel's next aid to navigation, unlighted daybeacon #3. Between #1 and #3, you will most likely spy a whole series of piles and signs east of your course line. All these structures mark a large shoal running along the midsection of Factory Bay. Stay well away from these markers and point to pass #3 to your port side.

From #3 point to come abeam of #5, also to your port side.

Capri Pass and Coconut Island Anchorage (BAIL-Suggested)   West of Factory Bay deep water opens out almost from bank to bank on the Marco Island-Naples waterway, moving towards Big Marco and Capri passes.

North and west of unlighted daybeacon #15, power cruisers will have to contend with yet another manatee no-wake zone until reaching unlighted daybeacon #11. To me, this regulated zone seems especially ludicrous, as the waters are wide and the currents move swiftly—seemingly not a good place for manatees to hang out. Oh well, who understands the Florida Department of Natural Resources anyway?

West of flashing daybeacon #14, passing cruisers may note a small channel cutting south into Collier Bay. We cruised through this cut and found no facilities nor room for anchorage. Collier Bay itself is quite shallow, with depths less than 3 feet as the norm.

As with all inlets, bottom configurations are subject to change on Capri Pass, and aids to navigation are often moved to follow the shifting sands. Don't be too surprised to find a somewhat different configuration of markers by the time you visit than the one outlined below.

Southwest of unlighted daybeacon #11, the northerly shores drop away. The channel continues southwest towards Coconut Island, skirting a long shoal building west from the north-side point of land. Set course to eventually come abeam of flashing daybeacon #9 to its fairly immediate southerly side. At this point, the channel cuts sharply to the north-northwest.

You may also choose to anchor abeam of Coconut Island near #9. Cut south-southwest from #9 and anchor off the isle's southeasterly or southerly banks.

Cruisers approaching Capri Pass from the Gulf's open waters will be pleased to learn that charted flashing buoy #2 (the westernmost aid to navigation on the Capri Pass channel) has recently been replaced by 16-foot, multidolphin flashing daybeacon #2.

This new marker is far easier to spot than the old floating buoy.

Big Marco Pass is quite shoal and changeable. Even small powercraft might want to think long and hard before attempting this perilous inlet.

To continue north along the Marco Island-Naples waterway to Capri Pass, cut north-northwest from flashing daybeacon #9 and pass to the west of unlighted junction daybeacon #C. The main body of Capri Pass will then lie to the west, while the channel to Naples cuts to the northeast.

Capri Pass is well marked and reasonably easy to follow. From #C, pass to the south of unlighted daybeacon #7 and continue out to sea keeping (as you would expect) green markers to your starboard side and red beacons to port. Just be *sure* to stay *inside* the marked passage. Shoal water waits to greet your keel both south and north of the channel.

Cruisers entering Capri Pass from the Gulf of Mexico must be sure to pass to the west of #C if they are turning south-southeast to Marco Island.

Waterway to Naples   Mariners continuing north to Naples and Gordon Pass must now contend with some shallows flanking the channel running inland from Capri Pass. Shoaling on the channel's northern tier prompted the Coast Guard to relocate unlighted daybeacon #1 farther to the south several years ago. This scheme of aids to navigation still seems to have solved the problem, but be on the alert for new intrusions of shallow water as you pass through this tricky passage.

Be sure to pass unlighted daybeacon #C to its northwesterly side to avoid the long tongue of charted shallow water east and northeast of this aid. Only then should you swing to the northeast and point to pass unlighted daybeacon #1 to its southeastern quarter. Take your time and watch the sounder carefully during this difficult passage between #C and #1.

After rounding the turn at unlighted daybeacon #C, the color configuration of the local aids to navigation changes yet again. From Capri Pass to the intersection with the Gordon Pass channel, northbound captains should pass green aids to their port side and take red markers to starboard.

As you make the turn from #C, you may spy a few weekend boats pulled up onto the beach inside Cannon Channel, north of unlighted daybeacon #7. Cruising boats should not attempt to enter this offshoot. Depths run less than 4 feet.

After passing between #2A and #3, the Naples waterway channel takes a sharp jog to the north and enters a more sheltered passage. A marked, but currently uncharted, local channel makes off to the northeast from #2A into the "Isles of Capri." Visiting cruisers should probably ignore this cut and follow the principal Marco Island-Naples waterway channel by pointing to pass unlighted daybeacon #5 to its easterly side. Between #5 and #12, favor the western shore slightly, just as the markers would indicate, to avoid the correctly charted band of shallows flanking the eastern banks.

From #12, the channel turns east and follows a dredged cut through the lower reaches of shallow Johnson Bay. Stick strictly to the marked channel throughout this stretch.

Johnson Bay Anchorage   To visit this haven, come abeam of unlighted daybeacon #14 and then cut directly in towards the northwestern banks. Drop the hook before approaching to within less than 75 yards of shore. Do not drift to the south towards unlighted daybeacon #13. In spite of what chart 11430 would lead you to believe, some shoaling has apparently occurred near #13.

On to Little Marco Island   The Naples waterway leaves Johnson Bay near unlighted daybeacon #25. Don't be tempted to try the tiny charted offshoot of deeper water north of #25. Shoaling has reduced the depth in this sidewater to 3 feet or less. At unlighted daybeacon #27, the waters running inland from Hurricane Pass briefly intersect the Naples waterway. This passage is now very shoal. Even small powercraft will find the bottom if they stray onto these waters.

Unlighted daybeacon #28A heralds a turn to the northwest through a dredged cut. Pay close attention to the markers as you pass out into the waters north of Little Marco Island. A long shoal is building out from this island's northerly tip. Pass between unlighted daybeacons #33 and #34, favoring #34 slightly.

Little Marco Island Channel & Anchorage (BAIL-Suggested)   To enter this lovely sidewater, be sure you are at least 50 yards north of unlighted daybeacon #34. Enter the side channel by favoring the western shores. Continue favoring the western banks as you cruise downstream for the next .5 nautical miles to avoid the correctly charted shallows abutting the eastern shoreline. South of this point, good depths open out almost from shore to shore. Pick any likely spot to drop the hook.

If you should decide to continue on to Hurricane Pass, hold to the mid-width until you intersect the wide waters to the south. If you are really brave, you can partially round the westside point, keeping some 25 yards or so off the beach. I would seriously suggest discontinuing your explorations once abeam of this point. To the south and west, depths are uncertain at best.

Rookery Bay Anchorage   The charted off-shoot leading to Rookery Bay is located abeam of unlighted daybeacon #47. Enter on the centerline and drop the hook before proceeding more than 75 yards upstream. Visit Rookery Bay strictly by dinghy.

On the Naples Channel   North of unlighted daybeacon #47, the waterway leading north to Naples and Gordon Pass enters a sheltered landcut for some 2.3 nautical miles. Another no-wake, manatee zone holds sway on the waters between #47 and unlighted daybeacon #52. Slow down and enjoy the sights.

After passing unlighted daybeacons #64 and #65, the channel passes out into shallow Dollar Bay. Again, stay to the marked passage and you should not have any difficulty.

North of unlighted daybeacon #71, the Naples waterway rushes on towards an intersection with Gordon Pass and the marked channel running north through Naples Bay. Watch for shoaling and additional markers at this intersection. At the current time, you should pass unlighted daybeacon #73 to its fairly immediate easterly side. Then, look for unlighted junction daybeacon #G. If you are cruising north, pass this aid to its easterly quarter and come abeam of flashing daybeacon #20 to its westerly quarter. Just north of #G, you can easily turn west into the Gordon Pass channel.

Gordon Pass   Be sure to pass to the north of unlighted junction daybeacon #G when making your initial approach to Gordon Pass. After coming abeam of #G, point to initially pass unlighted daybeacon #18 to its northerly side and continue seaward by passing all red markers to your port side and all green beacons to starboard. At unlighted daybeacon #10, an idle-speed, no-wake zone begins and stretches west to unlighted daybeacon #7A.

At flashing daybeacon #9, the channel takes a temporary turn to the south and then curves back sharply to the west at unlighted daybeacon #7A. Between #7A and the next aid to navigation, unlighted daybeacon #7, a dramatic shoal encroaches on the northern side of the Gordon Pass channel. Be sure to stay south of #7A and #7. Follow the remaining markers out to sea. For best depths, don't cut either north or south from the inlet channel until you reach flashing buoy #1, the outermost marker on this passage. Some shallow water lies south, and particularly north, of the cut's outer reaches between unlighted daybeacon #7 and flashing daybeacon #1.

Cruisers approaching Gordon Pass from the Gulf will discover that charted flashing buoy #1 (the westernmost aid to navigation on the Gordon Pass channel) has recently been replaced by a 16-foot, multidolphin flashing daybeacon. This new marker is far easier to spot than the old floating buoy.

Gordon Pass Anchorage (BAIL-Suggested) To enter the excellent anchorage making into the northern shores of the Gordon Inlet channel, depart the main cut directly abeam of unlighted daybeacon #12 and cruise north-northwest into the mid-width of the canal's mouth. Follow the centerline as the main branch of the canal turns to the east and then opens out to the north.

On the Naples Channel North of Gordon Pass, the numbering scheme on the aids to navigation lining the channel to Naples changes one last time (in order to keep pace with the configuration of marker numbers on Gordon Pass), but the color configuration remains the same. North of unlighted daybeacon #21, cruisers will find a good anchorage to the west and a private marina to the east.

Port Royal Anchorage North of unlighted daybeacon #21, identify the canal entrance cutting into the western banks. Enter the mouth by favoring the southerly banks. This maneuver will help you to avoid the charted patch of 3-foot shallows to the north.

Once past the bothersome entrance, all you need to do is stay just slightly off any of the banks for good depths all the way to the upstream limits on both arms of the canal.

Southpointe Yacht Club Two privately maintained aids to navigation associated with Southpointe Yacht Club will be spotted east of the main channel just north of unlighted daybeacon #21. To enter the marina, pass between unlighted daybeacon #2 and an unnumbered warning beacon (to your port side). You will find this to be a strange maneuver, as these aids will point you south of the entrance canal. Be assured, however, that a shoal guards the mid-width of the canal's entrance. After cruising between the two aids, work your way carefully to the northeast and enter the canal. Yes, I know this sounds strange, but an on-site check and a conversation with the marina dockmaster confirmed that this is the correct procedure.

On to Naples As you pass between flashing daybeacon #24 and unlighted daybeacon #25, you will spy the marked channel cutting north-northeast to Royal Yacht Services. Remember that low-tide depths are nil, and even at high water, depths run only about 5 feet. Good luck!

North of flashing daybeacon #27, you will pass out into the main body of Naples Bay. Tidal currents begin to pick up and reach a crescendo as you approach the Gordon River.

After passing between unlighted daybeacon #33 and flashing daybeacon #32, cruisers should slow to idle speed. No-wake regulations are in effect for all the waters of Naples Bay and Gordon River north of #33 and #32.

North of unlighted daybeacon #33, Crayton Cove opens out on the western banks. Continue following the main channel and pass between unlighted daybeacon #35 and flashing daybeacon #34. You can then cut west to the Naples Yacht Club, and the adjacent mooring field.

The Naples Yacht Club and the adjacent city mooring field have their own combined marked entry channel outlined by small unlighted daybeacons. When leaving the main channel to visit either facility, pass (you guessed it) green markers to your vessel's port side and take red beacons to starboard. Cruisers intent on a visit to the mooring field can cut to the north and pick up a buoy immediately after passing west of unlighted daybeacon #4.

Visitors to the Naples City Dock should turn northwest after passing between #34 and #35 and head for the outer fuel dock. Here you will find the dockmaster's office and your slip assignment.

To continue cruising north to the Tin City shopping center, set course to pass just west of unlighted daybeacon #36. Between #36 and unlighted daybeacon #39, unlighted daybeacon #38 denotes the channel's easterly edge. Pass #38 to its westerly side.

Cruisers plying the waters north of #38 may note a small, marked channel striking north-northwest. This cut serves Old Naples Seaport, but as no services are now available at this facility for visitors, most mariners will wisely bypass this cut.

North of flashing daybeacon #40, you will spy the enclosed harbor of Naples Sailing and Yacht Club bordering the point between the two branches of the Gordon River. To reach Marine Max/Gulfwind Marine and the Tin City shopping area, cut into the mid-width of the west-side fork. Be prepared for some of the strongest tidal currents that you have ever seen. Marine Max/Gulfwind Marine will come up first on the western shores, followed by the Tin City complex. Kelly's Fish House lines the eastern shore.

Boats entering the eastern fork of the Gordon River should pass just south of the Naples Sailing and Yacht Club docks, north of flashing daybeacon #40. While you may see local small craft entering and exiting this fork via a straighter course, trust me when I say that you can hold best depths by following the above maneuver.

Once on the eastern fork, hold to the middle until the entrance to Boat Haven Marine Supply opens out from the eastern shore. Farther upstream, the shallow docks of The's Waterfront Cafe line the eastern banks, while a series of private condo berths guard the western shoreline. Soon the river is spanned by a low-level fixed bridge, and this guide's coverage of the Gordon River ends at this point.

Gordon Pass to Fort Myers Beach

North of Naples there is no inland passage leading to Fort Myers Beach and San Carlos Bay, gateway to the official Western Florida ICW. Mariners must by necessity cruise off-shore through the Gulf's open waters. In fair weather, this can be a truly enjoyable pas-sage, particularly for sailcraft. If winds exceed 20 knots and the all-too-usual summer thun-derstorms are present, it could be a very dif-ferent story.

South of San Carlos Bay there are really only two ports of call that might interest cruis-ing captains, and one of these is marginal. In times past, some boats used to take shelter in Doctors Pass, about 5 miles north of Gordon Pass. Unfortunately, this channel is subject to periodic shoaling. A local group known as the Save the Bays Association is working with the city of Naples to keep the channel open. We wish the association well in its efforts, but until the channel is completely stabilized, we still suggest visiting cruisers consider this channel a bit risky.

Wiggins Pass, 12 nautical miles above Gordon Pass, is a more realistic alternative. At the time of this writing, shoaling has lowered minimum entrance depths to a bare 4 feet, but maintenance dredging was scheduled a short time ago. One marina on the inlet's interior waters does offer a few transient services, and a developing high-rise condo with yacht club may take some visitors from time to time.

The teeming resort community of Fort Myers Beach on Estero Island represents a very differ-ent sort of port. An offshore run of 12.7 nauti-cal miles north of Wiggins Pass will lead cruising craft to Matanzas Pass. This inlet, immediately north of Estero, is a deep and reli-able channel that pleasurecraft of all de-scriptions can use with confidence. The inlet leads, in turn, to a whole series of channels east and northeast of the island. No fewer than ten marinas and boatyards, plus one super anchorage, are adjacent to Fort Myers Beach.

Wild-eyed captains may even consider fol-lowing the marked but ill-charted track south-east to Big Carlos Pass. While there are some 4- to 5-foot low-tide depths along the way, there is also one good marina and a few remote anchorages.

So let's push on to explore these last waters south of the Western Florida ICW. With any luck at all, we should find more than a little to interest us along the way.

Wiggins Pass
The first thing to understand about Wiggins Pass is that the entrance channel is mercurial. At the time of this writing, depths on the inlet's entrance channel have shoaled to a scant 4 feet at low tide. Maintenance dredg-ing to 12-foot MLW soundings was recently scheduled for completion, but the bottom may (and probably will) have changed again by the time of your arrival. Smart captains will give Marco River Marina-Wiggins Pass Division a quick call on the VHF to check on present conditions before attempting to enter the inlet.

After negotiating the entrance, depths im-prove to 6 feet or better. One passage cuts off to the south along the course of the Cocohatchee River, but this stream leads only to some private docks grouped around a development near the charted 25-foot fixed bridge. Visiting cruisers should continue on to

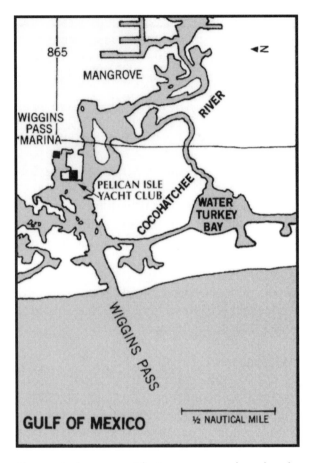

the east along a cut between several undeveloped mangrove islands. Soon you will spot the passage to Marco River Marina-Wiggins Pass Division off to port. This marina is located on the eastern tip of the charted offshoot designated as facility #45 on chart 11427.

The same good people we met in our discussion of Marco River Marina, earlier in this chapter, own and manage this facility. Unfortunately, there is very little in the way of transient dockage here. The wet-slip space is quite limited and while, occasionally, visitors who pilot boats 38 feet and smaller can tie up for the night, there is nothing in the way of dockside power and water connections.

On the plus side, this marina does offer gasoline, diesel fuel, and a soon-to-be-expanded ship's and variety store. Full mechanical repairs are offered and boats can be hauled out by way of a new 35-ton travelift. Extensive dry stack storage is available for smaller power craft.

A mammoth high-rise condo and marina complex known as Pelican Isle Yacht Club looms over the southern point of land flanking the approach channel to Marco River Marina. A meager two of the club's many slips are kept open for visitors with appropriate reciprocity agreements through the Register of American Yacht Clubs. If you should have the necessary affiliation and space is available (be *sure* to call before your arrival), you will find berths at both fixed and floating wooden decked piers featuring all power and water connections. The harbor is well sheltered from inclement weather. Depths alongside run 6 feet or better. Some shoreside showers are available as well.

Pelican Island Yacht Club (941) 566-1606

Approach depth—6+ feet (if dredging completed)
Dockside depths—6 feet
Accepts transients—limited
Fixed and floating wooden piers—yes
Dockside power connections—30 and 50 amp
Dockside water connections—yes
Showers—yes

In times past this writer recommended anchorage on the waters west of the charted, 14-foot fixed bridge. Both banks are now lined so heavily with private docks that it is impractical to spend an evening here swinging on the hook.

Big Carlos Pass

Big Carlos Pass cuts between the southeastern tip of Estero Island and Black Island. Don't even think about trying this seaward cut. It is completely unmarked and shoals flank the so-called channel from every quarter. Again, as at Doctors Pass, local small-craft skippers may tell you that they use Big Carlos all the time. Just remember, they don't have your size or draft, and it's a lot easier for them to extricate themselves from the bottom.

Matanzas Pass

Matanzas Pass Inlet cuts in from the southeastern foot of San Carlos Bay and runs behind Estero Island. This passage holds minimum depths of 9 feet, with most soundings being much deeper. It is a relatively simple matter to follow this well-defined channel southeast to the 65-foot fixed bridge connecting Estero with San Carlos Island. A host of facilities associated with Fort Myers Beach line both banks east and west of the fixed span.

Alternate Channel

A charted and well-buoyed channel cuts east from flashing daybeacon #9 on the Matanzas Pass channel and leads to one facility on the sheltered waters northwest of the 6-foot fixed bridge connecting the mainland with San Carlos Island. Minimum depths are 5½ feet, but the interior portion of the channel can be confusing for first-timers. Be sure to read the navigational account presented in the next section of this chapter before your first visit.

Eventually, the principal fork of the alternate channel cuts to the southeast and flows under a low-level fixed bridge. Another channel leads cruisers from the bridge into Hurricane Bay. As all but the smallest of boats will enter the Hurricane Bay cut from the east, this passage will be covered in connection with the Fort Myers Beach section.

Just before reaching the low-level span, skippers can cut north and take advantage of Hurricane Bay Marine (941-466-8898). This somewhat small, but obviously well equipped facility offers complete mechanical repairs for both gasoline- and diesel-powered craft, plus haul-outs courtesy of a 25-ton travelift. This is perhaps the smallest of the several full-service boatyards in Fort Myers Beach.

Fort Myers Beach

The community of Fort Myers Beach sits on one of the most intensely developed strips of land in Western Florida. Quite frankly, not all of this development can be accurately described as attractive. Strip-type shopping centers line both sides of the main road. While some are becoming, obviously well managed operations, others look as if they are about to collapse. During the winter tourist season, visitors to Fort Myers Beach can be counted in the thousands. During our last visit in August, the beach was, shall we say, jumping.

While Fort Myers Beach may not be all that the naturalistically inclined among us might ask for, there is no denying its wonderful pleasurecraft facilities and its popularity among the cruising crowd. Sailboats from far and wide regularly take advantage of the large, well-sheltered anchorage adjacent to the town waterfront. Bolstered by no fewer than ten marinas and boatyards, visiting cruisers have a plateful of choices.

Mariners in need of supplies should be able to find whatever they might desire at Fort Myers Beach. While it may be a bit of a walk (or you might bum a ride with a friendly local), groceries, personal items, and marine supplies are all available within a mile or so of the waterfront.

Hurricane Bay Marine, Fort Myers Beach

Numbers to know in Fort Myers Beach include:

Apple Taxi—941-482-1200
Locomotion Taxi—941-463-4111
Royal Palm Transportation—941-765-6669
Avis Rental Cars—941-768-2121
Budget Rent A Car—941-765-0480
Enterprise Rent-A-Car—941-275-3393
Chamber of Commerce—941-454-7500

The Koreshans of Estero Island

In 1894 one of the strangest religious groups in the long and varied history of Florida came south to settle along the shores of Estero Island. Dr. Cyrus Read Teed, a Chicago physician, developed a cosmology known as Koreshan Unity. He was described by a contemporary as "an undersized, smooth-shaven man whose brown, restless eyes glow and burn like live coals." Dr. Teed contended that the universe was a hollow sphere with a circumference of 25,000 miles. Mankind lived on the interior portion of the shell that comprised the universe's limits, and the sun was at the center.

Along with 200 of his followers, Teed arrived on Estero Island in 1894 and founded "New Jerusalem." He planned a city of eight million inhabitants with streets 400 feet wide.

In 1896 Dr. Teed presented a demonstration south of the Naples Pier. He conducted what were described as "geodetic surveys," which, he claimed, proved his theory that the earth was concave-shaped. As Stuart McIver comments in *Glimpses of South Florida History*, "His survey . . . convinced his followers, who already believed. Outsiders were unimpressed."

Members of the Koreshan sect were required to sign over all their worldly goods to the community. Neither coffee, tea, nor alcohol was permitted. In an even more bizarre twist, Dr. Teed insisted on total celibacy among the commune's members. Men and women were housed in separate dormitories. Like the earlier Shakers, no one ever seemed to address the question of how the community was supposed to continue into the next generation.

By all accounts the Koreshans became highly competent farmers and bakers. For a time they published an agricultural newspaper known as *The American Eagle*. Copies are now rare collector's items.

In spite of his declaration that he was immortal, Dr. Teed died suddenly in 1908. His faithful followers kept watch over his body for a week, convinced he would rise from the dead. Finally, the county authorities insisted that he be buried. As Stuart McIver again comments, "So Teed's body was placed in a bathtub and sealed in a brick-and-concrete tomb at the east end of Estero Island. In 1921, a hurricane washed his tomb away." Oh, how the mighty have fallen!

After Dr. Teed's death, the Koreshan community broke up. The last four members deeded the remaining property to the state of Florida as a historical site in 1961. Three of the original buildings have been preserved, including the "planetary court," art hall, and bakery. The site is now open to the public daily from 9 A.M. to 4 P.M. Guided tours are conducted at 10:30 A.M. and 2:30 P.M. You will need motorized land transportation to access this attraction from the Fort Myers Beach marinas.

Fort Myers Beach Facilities and Anchorage (BAIL-Suggested)

Moving west to east, the first Fort Myers Beach facility that you will encounter on the southern shoreline is Moss Marine (south of unlighted daybeacon #13). Big changes have taken place at this facility since the last edition of this guide.

A large gambling ship now makes its home at Moss Marine, and, during our last visit, the parking lot was filled to overflowing with the floating casino's patrons. It is this writer's opinion that much of the focus at Moss Marine has shifted towards the gambling business.

Additionally, Moss Marine no longer offers anything in the way of repair services for pleasurecraft. Check out our reviews of Olsen Marine Service and, particularly, Gulf Marine Ways and Supply below if you need repairs.

Moss Marine still accepts transients at fixed wooden piers with water and up to 50-amp power connections. Gasoline and diesel fuel are available, as are shoreside showers and waste pump-out service. A laundromat is located within a two-block walk. The marina's forklift is now used exclusively for the facility's dry stack storage. There is also a ship's and variety store on the premises, and a host of good seafood restaurants is within walking distance.

Moss Marine (941) 463-6137

Approach depth—8 feet (minimum)
Dockside depth—7-10 feet
Accepts transients—yes
Fixed wooden piers—yes
Dockside power connections—30 and 50 amp
Dockside water connections—yes
Waste pump-out—yes
Showers—yes
Gasoline—yes
Diesel fuel—yes
Ship's and variety store—yes
Restaurant—several nearby

Snug Harbor Restaurant (941-463-8077) guards the southern banks just east of Moss

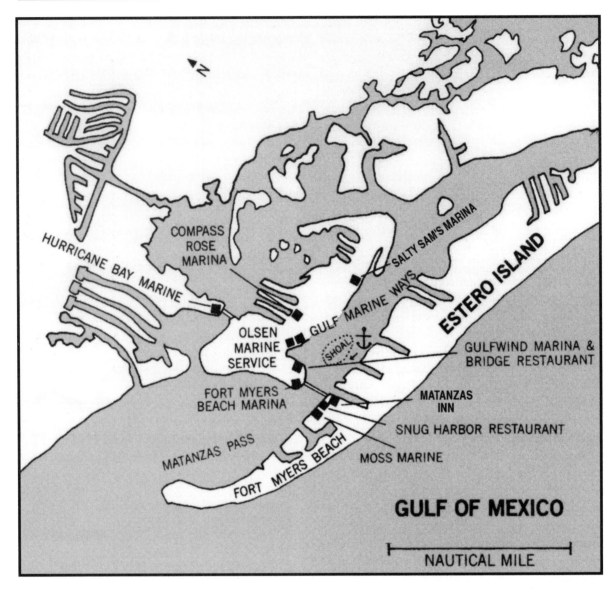

Marine. While no docking is allowed next to the restaurant itself, the facility does maintain a *T*-shaped pier on the southern banks, just short of the bridge. Restaurant patrons are free to moor to this pier in depths of 5½ to 8 feet. It might even be possible to negotiate an overnight stay, but the dock lacks power and water connections.

Fort Myers Beach Marina occupies the northern banks opposite the Snug Harbor docks (still west of the bridge). This ultra-friendly facility welcomes not only transients but live-aboards as well, a true rarity in the present-day Florida marine community. Berths are cheerfully provided at modern, fixed wooden piers with all power, water,

Fort Myers Beach high-rise bridge

cable television, and telephone connections. Depths at the outer slips are an impressive 8 to 20 feet, dropping to about 6 feet at the inner berths. A fuel dock fronting onto the main channel offers both gasoline and diesel fuel. Waste pump-out service is available at the fuel pier.

Shoreside, visiting cruisers will find showers and a full-line ship's and variety store. Full mechanical repairs are featured for both gasoline and diesel engines. While the marina does not have a travelift or railway, smaller boats can be hauled out with the forklift that usually serves the facility's dry stack storage customers. A host of dining spots is within an easy step, including the notable Bridge Restaurant (see below). For breakfast or lunch though, we heartily recommend that you check out Kristine's Island Cafe (751 Fisherman's Wharf, 941-465-8988), a scant block and a half from the docks. The cuisine can accurately be described as "down home," but, trust us, it doesn't get better than this.

This writer found Fort Myers Beach Marina to be an unusually friendly establishment ready to go that extra mile to meet any and all needs of visiting cruisers. It is highly recommended.

Fort Myers Beach Marina (941) 463-9552
http://www.yamahausa.com/Dealers/
ftmyers/ftmyers.htm

Approach depth—8 feet (minimum)
Dockside depth—6-20 feet
Accepts transients—yes
Fixed wooden piers—yes
Dockside power connections—30 and 50 amp
Dockside water connections—yes

Waste pump-out—yes
Showers—yes
Gasoline—yes
Diesel fuel—yes
Mechanical repairs—yes
Ship's store—yes
Restaurant—many nearby

East of the 65-foot fixed bridge, the mid-width of the wide waters stretching to the east plays host to a large shoal. Deep channels run north and south of these shallows. First-time visitors who aren't aware of the centerline shoal can be confused by the markers.

Immediately east of the fixed span, Matanzas Inn (941-463-9258) offers a single, fixed wooden pier along the southern shore. The dockage is managed by an on-site charter agency (941-463-4166). Three to five slips are usually open for the use of transients. The piers have 30-amp power and freshwater connections. Depths vary widely, ranging from 8 to 12 feet at the outer docks to 5 to 6 feet nearer shore. A laundromat is available to transients at the adjacent motel. This would also be a convenient spot to take a break from the liveaboard routine if you have recently braved one too many waves. The on-site restaurant serves superb seafood, particularly of the broiled variety.

Considering the limited number of available transient slips, advance reservations would be an excellent precaution.

Matanzas Inn Dock (941) 463-4166

Approach depth—8 feet (minimum)
Dockside depth—5-12 feet
Accepts transients—yes (3 to 5 slips usually
    open for transients)
Fixed wooden pier—yes
Dockside power connections—30 amp
Dockside water connections - yes
Laundromat—yes
Restaurant—on site

Moving east of the 65-foot fixed bridge, deep water runs along the southern banks in a fairly broad band. The stretch between unlighted daybeacons #14 and #26 is a very popular, BAIL-suggested anchorage for both sailcraft and powerboats. Depths range from 7 to 12 feet, with the deeper soundings to the west. Protection is excellent and anchored visitors should be able to play a round or two of cards in peace as long as winds don't exceed forty knots. Skippers will find plenty of swinging room, unless the anchorage happens to be very crowded, and then larger vessels may be a bit cramped. Should you encounter this state of affairs, try a Bahamian-style mooring to minimize your swinging room.

Courtesy of a local cruising enthusiast, dinghy dockage is available along the anchorage's southerly shores at a private pier. Look for a snow-white house with a short, fixed wooden pier stretching out from a green lawn. You will probably spy several other dinghies already tied to this structure. All the owner asks is that visiting cruisers complete his informal registration process. Wow, what a service! We salute him for his thoughtfulness.

The markers can be confusing along this stretch for newcomers. This, coupled with the proximity of the large shoal occupying the center of the bay, means it would be more than slightly prudent to consult the navigational account of Fort Myers Beach (below) before entering Matanzas Pass.

The well-marked channel flanking the northern banks, east of the 65-foot bridge, maintains minimum depths of 8 feet, with typical soundings of 10 to 12 feet. As you enter this cut at unlighted daybeacon #14, picturesque Dixie Fish Company will be spotted to port as you cruise north. There are no facilities for pleasurecraft at Dixie, but diplomatic

Dixie Fish Company, Fort Myers Beach

cruisers might be able to purchase some of the freshest seafood to prepare aboard.

A quick jog north on the channel will bring you abeam of Gulf Star Marina and the Bridge Restaurant (941-765-0050). Gulf Star (941-765-1956) is in the dry stack storage business for smaller powercraft. No regular transient services other than gasoline are available. The marina does have one *L*-shaped dock fronting onto its shoreside facilities, and patrons of the Bridge Restaurant are free to tie up while dining. During the winter tourist season, much of this dock is occupied by a large tour boat. Dockage space is a bit skimpy during these periods.

Near unlighted daybeacon #16, the channel swings sharply to the east. As you are passing through this turn, Olsen Marine Service (941-463-6750) will come abeam on the northern banks. This yard offers full mechanical and below-waterline, haul-out repairs. According to a conversation with the yard personnel, all wet-slip dockage is now occupied by resident craft and service customers. The yard's travelift is rated at 37 tons.

The monstrous travelift belonging to Gulf Marine Ways and Supply boatyard (941-463-6166) will become quite apparent as you come abeam of unlighted daybeacon #18.

This writer has seldom before beheld such a mammoth lift. It is rated at 150 tons. This may just be one of the only yards in the country that could haul the infamous *Trump Princess*. Gulf Marine specializes in repairs to large pleasurecraft. If you are lucky enough to own a boat larger than 45 feet and it is in need of repairs, this is clearly the place to be between Cape Sable and St. Petersburg!

Salty Sam's Marina (formerly Palm Grove Marina) is found on the northern banks, northeast of unlighted daybeacon #24. Visiting cruisers can be well assured of a warm welcome at this extrafriendly and knowledgeable marina.

New ownership took over at this facility in 1999, and the large gambling ship that once resided here is now happily only a memory. Once again, the emphasis has been placed on serving cruisers and pleasurecraft of all descriptions.

Current plans call for the addition of a 300-berth dry stack facility, followed by a complete renovation of the main building and the on-site showers. A tiki bar, serving a full line of seafood entrees, will be built on the marina grounds during the fall of 2000. Quite obviously, good things are in the offing at Salty Sam's, and we invite our fellow cruisers to check it out!

Transient berths are cheerfully provided at first-rate, all-floating (wooden decked) docks. Depths at most of the marina's piers range from 9 to 10 feet, but a few slips near the eastern end of the complex have only 6 to 7 feet of water. Water and power connections up to 50 amp are at hand, as are gasoline, diesel fuel, and waste pump-out services.

As mentioned above, the shower building is set for renovation, but the existing units are adequate, and the marina's laundromat is already refurbished. As if that's not enough, visitors will discover a full-line, on-site ship's and variety store, complete with a welcome paperback exchange library in the store. Mechanical repairs are available for gasoline and diesel engines, and boats up to 27 feet can be hauled via a forklift. It's a pleasant walk of a few blocks back down the road to the Bridge Restaurant or Kristine's Island Cafe (see above).

Salty Sam's Marina (941) 463-7333
   http://www.saltysamsmarina.com

Approach depth—8-11 feet
Dockside depth—9-10 feet (mostly)
Accepts transients—yes
Floating wooden docks—yes
Dockside power connections—30 and 50 amp
Dockside water connections—yes
Waste pump-out—yes
Showers—yes
Laundromat—yes
Gasoline—yes
Diesel fuel—yes
Mechanical repairs—yes
Below-waterline repairs—haul-out up to 27 feet
   with forklift
Ship's and variety store—yes
Restaurant—several nearby

Hurricane Bay Channel and Facilities

East of unlighted daybeacon #24, the marked channel follows the northeastern shores of Estero Island and continues on to the east and southeast. At unlighted junction daybeacon #A, the channel leading to Hurricane Bay opens to the northeast. This cut is reasonably well marked with small, privately maintained daybeacons and it is fairly easy to follow during daylight.

Minimum depths of 5 feet are held moving first northeast and then northwest on the Hurricane Bay passage as far as the canal serving Compass Rose Marina. A few low-water soundings as shallow as 4½ feet are encountered between the marina canal and the low-level fixed bridge.

Compass Rose Marina sits perched on the southern headwaters of the canal that makes into the northern shores of San Carlos Island, south of unlighted daybeacon #24. This facility is one of the best live-aboard marinas in all of western Florida, but no temporary transient dockage is available. That's due to the fact that there is a long, long waiting list of live-aboards who want to take up residence at Compass Rose.

This marina provides many services for its patrons, including a wonderful cruiser's lounge and paperback exchange library. Most every day you will find a "community lunch" in progress midday at the marina lounge. The feeling of community is tangible.

Compass Rose berths are set amid fixed wooden piers with water and 30-amp power connections. Typical depths alongside run 6 to 7 feet. Adequate showers and a laundromat are found on the premises. Waste pump-out is also available.

All cruisers can count on full mechanical and below-waterline, haul-out repairs at Compass Rose. Compass Rose seems to specialize in repairs to sailcraft, judging from the number of sailing vessels in its slips. The yard's travelift is rated at 40 tons. Gasoline (but no diesel fuel) can be purchased, but the on-site ship's store has been pretty well phased out.

Compass Rose Marina (941) 463-2400

Approach depth—5-8 feet
Dockside depth—6-7 feet
Fixed wooden slips—yes
Dockside power connections—30 amp

Dockside water connections—yes
Waste pump-out—yes
Gasoline—yes
Mechanical repairs—yes
Below-waterline repairs—yes

West of the Compass Rose Canal, Channelmark Waterfront Restaurant (19001 San Carlos Boulevard, 941-463-9127) features dockage for its patrons on the southern flank of the low-level, fixed bridge. While you must traverse some 4½-foot depths to reach the restaurant, pierside depths are in the 5- to 8-foot range. No overnight accommodations are available.

Channel to Big Carlos Pass

There are two schools of thought about the marked channel leading southeast from Fort Myers Beach, past the northeastern shores of Estero Island, to Big Carlos Pass. On the one hand, local powerboaters and pontoon boats use this cut regularly without mishap. On the other, visiting cruisers should know that they must contend with a few patches of 4- to 4½-foot depths in the winding, often confusing channel. To this writer's way of thinking, the channel is clearly only for boats under 36 feet in length, drawing less than 4 feet, and piloted by captains with wanderlust in their souls and hair on their chests (women included).

For those who brave the passage, there are some potential rewards. Mid-Island Marina guards the banks of Estero Island, southwest of unlighted daybeacon #29. This friendly firm is located, as its name implies, at about the midpoint of the island's southeast-to-northwest axis. While the marina is glad to accept transients for overnight or temporary dockage at its modern, fixed wooden piers (with all power and water connections), the management has informed this writer that few have hitherto made it this far. Dockside depths are a very respectable 7 to 8 feet. Another plus is that the shallowest portion of the channel to Big Carlos Pass seems to lie southeast of the marina. It should be possible to traverse the cut from Fort Myers Beach to this marina with minimum depths of 5 feet.

Mid-Island offers full services, including gasoline, diesel fuel, and mechanical and haul-out repairs (35-ton travelift), plus a ship's and variety store. The nearby Mucky Duck Restaurant (2500 Estero Boulevard, 941-463-5519—no, I didn't make up that name) is famous locally, and well worth your time.

Mid-Island Marina (941) 765-4371

Approach depth—5-8 feet
Dockside depth—7-8 feet
Accepts transients—yes
Dockside power connections—30 and 50 amp
Dockside water connections—yes
Gasoline—yes
Diesel fuel—yes
Mechanical repairs—yes
Below-waterline repairs—yes
Ship's and variety store—yes
Restaurant—nearby

Southeast of Mid-Island Marina, the channel twists and winds its way to the waters northeast of Big Carlos Pass. The cut can be confusing and low-water depths occasionally drop to 4½ feet.

As mentioned earlier, Big Carlos Pass is completely unmarked and surrounded by shoal water. While the interior portion of the inlet north of the bascule bridge is deep, this would be a terribly exposed spot to anchor and the tidal currents are expectedly swift.

It is possible for those who simply must anchor where none have gone before to follow a few markers into the correctly charted deeper waters northeast of Black Island (itself southeast of Big Carlos Inlet). The best spot to drop the hook is found abeam of the first small offshoot, which runs to the southwest. While this small stream is quite shallow, the channel east and northeast of the creek is broad and should provide enough swinging room for any vessel, even a large one, brave enough to make it this far. Protection is good to fair and the shoreline is undeveloped. In fact, it is part of a park. Those few who find their way to this haven will have the satisfaction of knowing that they have successfully navigated waters that have known little else but small fishing skiffs for many years.

GORDON PASS TO FORT MYERS BEACH NAVIGATION

Captains accustomed to mostly inland cruising along sheltered waterways may be a bit daunted by cruising offshore to Matanzas Pass and Estero Island, or possibly Wiggins Pass. Sailors used to offshore passages will hardly be bothered.

With winds under 15 knots, almost all mariners will find the cruise north along the Gulf to be pleasant. In foul weather, all but larger sailcraft should deeply consider staying in port and putting on another pot of coffee.

As with the outside route north from Cape Romano to Gordon Pass, there are no offshore aids to navigation with which skippers can tick off their progress. Again, though, good depths run to within a mile of the shoreline. It's reasonably easy to follow the coast and duck in at the appropriate spot.

Those of you who hunger for a little inland cruising with gunkholes aplenty nearby, hang on a bit longer. Just to the north, the official Western Florida ICW begins and the siren's song of Pine Island Sound calls to the explorers among us. Just be sure to get through this last offshore route safely, and then you'll be ready for the exciting waters ahead.

Gordon Pass to Wiggins Pass It is a run of some 12 nautical miles from flashing daybeacon #1, at the western terminus of the Gordon Pass Channel, to Wiggins Pass. As discussed above, there are no aids to navigation along the way, except the few markers associated with shallow Doctors Pass, but you can follow the beaches, staying at least 1 nautical mile offshore. Keep a good dead-reckoning or GPS track. Don't mistake the markers of shallow Doctors Pass for Wiggins Pass.

Use your binoculars to pick out daybeacon #WP, the westernmost aid to navigation on the Wiggins Pass channel. Even if you don't plan to put into the pass, this beacon can serve to fix your position.

Wiggins Pass As reported earlier in this chapter, the outer portion of Wiggins Pass has currently shoaled to low-water depths of 4 feet, but maintenance dredging set for March of 2000 should have been completed by the time you read this account. As the aids to navigation will undoubtedly be changed following this channel improvement, it makes no sense to review the cur-

rent configuration of daybeacons within these pages.

Please remember that even after dredging, this is one of those channels that seems to silt in just about as fast as the Army Corps of Engineers can pump out the sand. Wise mariners will give Marco River Marina-Wiggins Pass Division a call (by telephone or VHF) well before their arrival to check on the latest conditions.

After passing through the outer, shoal-prone section of the channel, cruisers will spot the southeastward-running course of the Cocohatchee River, marked by a pair of daybeacons, as they near green, unlighted daybeacon #11. This sidewater is not suggested for visitors. Instead, continue dead ahead between the mangrove islands.

Soon you will spy a whole series of teeming docks on the port shores. If you wish to visit Marco River Marina-Wiggins Pass Division or Pelican Isle Yacht Club, follow this shore on around into the sheltered cove to the northeast.

Please remember that this writer no longer recommends anchoring on the waters west of the charted 14-foot fixed bridge. One look at all the vessels berthed on both sides of this channel will tell you in short order the reason for this change of heart.

On to Matanzas Pass It's a run of 12.7 nautical miles north from Wiggins Pass to Matanzas Pass, at the northwestern tip of Estero Island. Keep at least a mile offshore as you pass Wiggins, to avoid the shoals running off the inlet's northerly flank.

Increase your offshore clearance to at least 1.5 nautical miles as you cruise past

Big Carlos Pass. This maneuver will serve to avoid the considerable offshore shoals surrounding the seaward side of this errant cut.

Use your best DR skills or electronic navigation to locate the unnumbered 40-foot flashing daybeacon, west-southwest of the Estero Island microwave tower. This is the southernmost aid marking the broad passage of deep water between the incredibly long shoals running southeast from Point Ybel on Sanibel Island, and a second set of shallows abutting the western shores of Estero Island. By all means, stay northeast of the 40-foot flashing daybeacon, unlighted daybeacon #3, and flashing daybeacon #5. West and southwest of these markers, you could wander into the Point Ybel shoals.

From a position abeam of the unnumbered 40-foot flashing daybeacon, cruise directly between the next two pairs of beacons. These markers are located better than 1 nautical mile apart. It might be a good idea to follow a compass course through this section of the channel.

As you come between flashing daybeacons #5 and #6, it's decision time. You can either continue on into San Carlos Bay to the north-northwest, or swing sharply northeast into the Matanzas Pass channel.

Flashing daybeacon #1 is the westernmost aid in the Matanzas cut. Anybody who remembers his or her good old "red, right, returning" rule will know to pass #1 to his or her port side when making his or her way into the inlet.

East of #1, tidal currents pick up, as expected, but the channel is well marked and reasonably simple to follow in good weather. At the time of this writing, charted unlighted daybeacons #5 and #6 have been replaced by floating buoys. You may or may not find these aids still in their present form at the time of your arrival. Whether it is an unlighted buoy or an unlighted daybeacon, #6 marks the northwestern point of Estero Island. Give this aid a wide berth, as the adjacent point seems to be building outward.

At flashing daybeacon #7, the channel begins a hairpin curve to the south-southeast. Be sure to come abeam of flashing daybeacon #9 to its southwesterly side. At #9, an alternate channel makes off to the east.

Alternate Channel Remember that the alternate channel leading from #9 leads only to a marine repair yard lacking any transient dockage. If you are not looking for repairs at Hurricane Bay Marine, it would be better to continue cruising upstream on the main cut.

If you do run the alternate channel, depart the inlet passage at flashing daybeacon #9. Immediately you are faced with a choice. The principal alternate channel runs to the east, while a second, uncharted but marked cut makes off to the east-northeast. Choose the starboard (easternmost cut), and enter this channel by cruising between unlighted daybeacons #1 and #2.

Follow the prolific markers to the east into the mouth of the canal off the northwesterly end of San Carlos Island. As you pass into the canal, watch for a marked channel running to the north. Ignore this cut—it leads to a series of private docks associated with area homes and a condo complex.

Continue up the main canal, holding to the center as you approach the low-level fixed bridge. Hurricane Bay Marine occupies the land off the northwestern corner of the bridge. *Don't cut the corner* when approaching this boatyard. Instead, continue almost up to the fixed bridge, and turn north when the docks come abeam to your port side. Shallow water is located just west of the yard's docks. To avoid this shallow patch, hug the boatyard's piers as you turn to the north. Do not attempt to cruise north up the offshoot past the boatyard. Very shallow water is quickly encountered.

On to Fort Myers Beach   A slow-speed, no-wake zone begins at flashing daybeacon #10 and remains in effect throughout the waters surrounding Fort Myers Beach. All vessels should slow to idle speed.

Continue following the markers as they lead you along the deep water abutting the northern and northeastern banks of Estero Island. As you approach unlighted daybeacon #13, Moss Marine will come abeam on the southern banks, followed by Snug Harbor Restaurant. Fort Myers Beach Marina will come abeam to the north, just short of the fixed bridge.

Fort Myers Beach Waters & Anchorage (BAIL-Suggested)   The 65-foot fixed bridge heralds your entrance into the waters lying about the resort community of Fort Myers. As you pass under the bridge, it might be a good time to virtually stop and sort out the markers. They can be quite confusing for first-timers.

It's best to think of the channel east of the fixed bridge as an irregular circle built around an oval-shaped shoal, occupying the middle of the bay. Unlighted daybeacon #14 is a key aid, marking the southwestern foot of the shoal. If you plan to follow the channel skirting along the northerly shore, cut northeast soon after passing through the bridge, and pass #14 to its westerly side. At unlighted daybeacon #16, the channel begins a turn to the east, paralleling the northern shore. The remainder of the channel is marked by red beacons, which should all be passed to your starboard side.

You will first pass the Bridge Restaurant and Gulf Star Marina, followed by Olsen Marine Service and Gulf Marine Ways and Supply. Salty Sam's Marina will be spotted north-northeast of unlighted daybeacon #24.

Unlighted daybeacon #24 marks the intersection of the cut running along the northerly banks with the channel skirting the southerly shore. Let us now turn our attention to this passage.

As you pass under the 65-foot fixed bridge, you will undoubtedly see a host of anchored vessels dead ahead. These craft occupy the deep water, BAIL-suggested anchorage along the southerly banks, south of the mid-width shoal. To enter this channel safely, pass unlighted daybeacon #14 to its *southerly* side. Yes, I know this seems wrong by the color, but trust me, this is the way to do it.

As you cruise east, continue favoring the southerly shore. Unlighted daybeacon #26 marks the easterly reaches of this southside channel. Pass #26 also to its *southerly* side and continue cruising east. Leave #24 well to your port side.

The channel remains well marked east and southeast of #24. Cruisers wanting to visit Compass Rose Marina should continue following the markers, passing red beacons to your starboard side and green markers to port, until encountering unlighted junction daybeacon #A. Cut to the northeast and pass #A to your starboard side as you enter the Hurricane Bay Channel.

Hurricane Bay Channel   Captains and crew bound northeast and then northwest on the Hurricane Bay Channel should pass red beacons to their (the cruiser's) starboard side and take green markers to port.

The cut skirts first to the northeast, passing around the easterly tip of San Carlos Island, and then turns northwest. The canal cutting south to Compass Rose Marina comes up just west of unlighted daybeacon #24.

A 6-foot fixed bridge spans the water just west of unlighted daybeacon #28. All but very small craft will be forced to retrace their steps to the east.

Channel to Big Carlos Pass   It would take page upon page upon page to even begin to describe all the twists and turns in the marked passage leading to Big Carlos Pass, and the markers would probably be different by the time you arrive anyway. Suffice it to say that the channel can be confusing and as shallow as 4½ feet in places. Passage in the dark would be nothing short of a nightmare. Southeastbound vessels should take red beacons to their (the cruiser's) starboard side and green markers to port.

At unlighted daybeacon #12, a no-wake zone begins and stretches southeast for 2 miles. Mid-Island Marina is found abeam of unlighted daybeacon #29 on these waters.

The portion of the channel between Fort Myers Beach and Mid-Island Marina is certainly the deeper part of this cut. Boats drawing 4 feet or less should be able to reach the marina with proper caution. Southeast of this facility, the channel is far more winding and treacherous.

The southeasterly running passage eventually encounters Big Carlos Pass near unlighted daybeacon #68. I suggest that you continue straight across the inlet, pointing for the northeasterly corner of Black Island. You will spot a high-rise Days Inn on the northwestern shores of Black Island, near the inlet bridge.

Watch for unlighted daybeacon #2 off Black Island. Pass this beacon by some 15 yards to your starboard side. Continue following the shores of Black Island to the east and southeast. Several more red markers help you keep to the good water.

Eventually, you will spy the first offshoot cutting to the southwest, south-southeast of unlighted daybeacon #10. You can recognize this little sidewater by its low-level, fixed bridge. Anchor abeam of this stream, but don't try to enter the creek. It is quite shoal.

CHAPTER 2

Fort Myers to Gasparilla Island

While researching the various marinas and boatyards around Fort Myers, I came across the story of a couple from Vermont who chartered a sailboat at nearby Burnt Store Marina, and set out for a week's cruise of Pine Island Sound. The charter operator told the cruising duo to give him a call on the VHF if they encountered any problems. After six days or so, the charterer had not heard a peep and decided to give the couple a call. His radio broadcast found them sitting in a snug anchorage alongside Chino Island. When he inquired about when they were going to come home, the captain replied, "We are home." Within a few months husband and wife had moved their own boat to Fort Myers and were happily living aboard.

Now, while it would certainly be a bit of an exaggeration to claim that every cruiser who explores Pine Island Sound, Charlotte Harbor, the Caloosahatchee River, and Fort Myers decides to move there, this little tale does serve to point out the incredible appeal these waters have for mariners. You could literally spend weeks exploring Pine Island Sound alone and still not exhaust all the possibilities. Secluded anchorages, good marinas, historic inns with fabulous dining, deserted, white sand beaches, beautiful state parks . . . well, the list could go on and on, but perhaps you are beginning to get the idea. There is perhaps no other portion of the Western Florida coastline that combines, in such delightful measure, the fortunate qualities of ready accessibility and fabulous, often unpopulated cruising grounds as does the stretch between the Caloosahatchee River and Gasparilla Island! Get ready for a genuine cruising treat!

Cruising captains arriving from points south will be pleased to learn that the official genesis of the Western Florida ICW begins near the mouth of the Caloosahatchee and runs north from San Carlos Bay through Pine Island Sound. Skippers may also alternately choose to cruise up the Caloosahatchee to Fort Myers. This river boasts a host of fine marinas and several anchorages.

Before continuing our geography lesson, let us pause for a moment to note that the Caloosahatchee is the westerly genesis of the Okeechobee Waterway. This most useful route allows cruisers ready, prompt, and enjoyable access between the Sunshine State's eastern and western coastlines (for boats that can clear one 49-foot bridge). For additional information, please consult this writer's *Cruising Guide to Eastern Florida,* a quite pleasant and totally comprehensive work that can, like this book, be had at your local bookstore for a mere fraction of its true value.

From San Carlos Bay, the ICW flows north and northwest into enchanting Pine Island Sound. As already alluded to above, this water body is a Mecca for cruising craft, with a siren's call that may require lashing yourself to the mast.

The western reaches of Pine Island Sound are bordered by a series of barrier islands which all have their own unique appeal. Sanibel, Captiva, Cayo Costa, Cabbage Key and, most particularly, Gasparilla Island are ports of call that are well known and loved by every cruiser plying Western Florida's coastal waters.

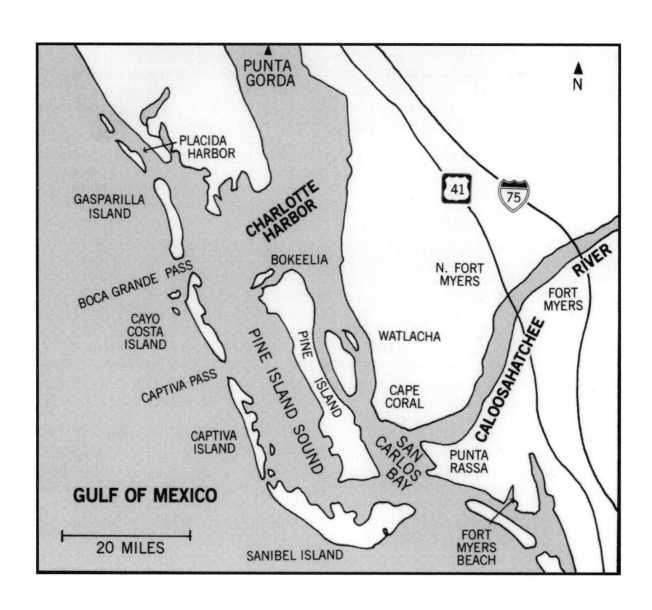

The northwestern arm of these waters is known as Gasparilla Sound. The ICW cuts briefly through the sound before rushing beyond this chapter's coverage at the long Gasparilla Island causeway bridge.

North of Pine Island Sound, the vast bay known as Charlotte Harbor opens out to the northeast. Abandoned by the ICW, the harbor offers many miles of good cruising grounds, with excellent facilities available at the old port town of Punta Gorda. Charlotte Harbor's two feeder streams, the Myakka and Peace rivers, offer additional opportunities for gunkholing and overnight anchorage.

Northbound skippers and crew must bid a fond goodbye to this region of delightful waters north of Gasparilla Island as the ICW enters Placida Harbor. This writer would be willing to wager that even with all the fine waters to the north, many dyed-in-the-wool cruisers will look back with a glance of sad longing in their eyes.

Charts Navigators must purchase three NOAA charts for a complete picture of all the waters between Fort Myers Beach and Gasparilla Island, including Charlotte Harbor. **11427**—a most important chart; provides complete coverage of the approaches to San Carlos Bay, the Caloosahatchee River to Fort Myers, Pine Island Sound, and the ICW's southerly section
11425—large-scale, detailed chart that picks up the Western Florida ICW at Boca Grande Pass, just south of Gasparilla Island, and runs north all the way to Tampa Bay; another must for anyone traveling this section of the coastline
11426—a general chart good for showing the offshore entrances to San Carlos Bay and Pine Island Sound; its principal use, however, is its coverage of the upper reaches of Charlotte Harbor, including the Myakka and Peace rivers

Bridges
Sanibel Island Causeway Bridge, southwestern span—crosses Sanibel Island channel northwest of Point Ybel and flashing daybeacon #2—Fixed—26 feet
Sanibel Island Causeway, eastern span—crosses San Carlos Bay channel leading north from the Gulf to mile 0 of Western Florida ICW, and western mouth of Caloosahatchee—Bascule—26 feet (closed)—opens on the hour and every 15 minutes thereafter 7:00 A.M. to 7:00 P.M.; at other times of day opens on demand
Pine Island/Matlacha Pass Bridge—crosses Matlacha Pass channel north of unlighted daybeacon #55—Bascule—9 feet (closed)

—opens on demand 8:00 A.M. to 7:00 P.M.; closed overnight
Cape Coral Bridge—crosses Caloosahatchee at standard mile 142 of Okeechobee Waterway, northeast of flashing daybeacon #70—Fixed—55 feet
Mid-Point Bridge—crosses Caloosahatchee at standard mile 138 of Okeechobee Waterway, northeast of unlighted daybeacon #62—Fixed—55 feet
Caloosahatchee/Highway 41 Bypass Bridge—crosses Caloosahatchee at standard mile 135 of Okeechobee Waterway, east-northeast of flashing daybeacon #49—Fixed—55 feet

Edison Memorial Bridge—crosses Caloosahatchee at standard mile 134.5, west of unlighted daybeacon #41—Fixed—56 feet—incorrectly charted on 11427, it actually forms a Y and appears to be two separate bridges

Boca Grande Bayou Bridge—crosses Boca Grande Bayou (and canal), north of Gasparilla Island basin anchorage—Fixed—13 feet

Boca Grande Causeway Bridge—crosses ICW at standard mile 34.5, northwest of unlighted daybacon #21—Swing bridge—9 feet (closed)—January through May, opens on the hour and every 15 minutes thereafter 10:00 A.M. to 5:00 P.M.; at other times of day and year opens on demand

Myakka River/El Jobean Bridge—crosses Myakka River at charted location of El Jobean—Fixed—24 feet

Live Oak Point/Punta Gorda (Highway 41) Twin Bridges—cross foot of Peace River northeast of unlighted daybeacon #4 near Punta Gorda waterfront—Fixed—45 feet

Peace River/Interstate 95 Twin Bridges—cross Peace River east of unlighted daybeacon #12—Fixed—45 feet

San Carlos Bay

The wide, sometimes shallow inner reaches of San Carlos Bay introduce cruising skippers to the southerly beginnings of the Western Florida ICW and the mouth of the Caloosahatchee River highway to Fort Myers and the Okeechobee Waterway. This interior section of the bay is enclosed by Sanibel Island to the west and southwest, and the Florida mainland to the east. A very long shoal, discussed in the last chapter, stretches southeast from Point Ybel on Sanibel Island. There is a smaller but still worrisome patch of shallows southeast of Punta Rassa on the mainland side, while the mid-width of the bay above the Sanibel Island bridge is rife with shoals. Fortunately, there are deep, marked passages around all these hazards.

Entry from the Gulf of Mexico

Once by the long shoal stretching southeast from Point Ybel on Sanibel Island (see preceding chapter), there are actually two viable channels that powercraft can use when entering San Carlos Bay. The westerly passage, paralleling the southeasterly reaches of Sanibel Island, is deep and reasonably well marked, but it does pass under a fixed bridge with only 26 feet of vertical clearance. Obviously, for most sailcraft this route is not a viable option. Happily for cruisers, Sanibel Island's one full-service marina is found southeast of this span and is accessible to all types of pleasurecraft.

Many pleasurecraft, particularly sailcraft, will choose the primary entrance into San Carlos Bay by way of the marked channel skirting the southwesterly reaches of Punta Rassa. This passage passes under a bascule bridge and soon leads to both the mouth of the Caloosahatchee and the southerly entrance to the Western Florida ICW. Along the way, there are at least two anchorages worthy of consideration.

Let us now turn our attention to the Sanibel Island channel, and then return to a review of the principal Punta Rassa Cut.

Sanibel Island

Even though a goodly portion of Sanibel

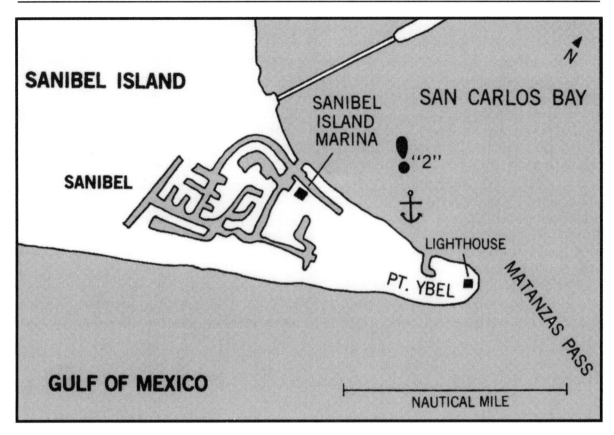

Island actually fronts onto Pine Island Sound, as opposed to San Carlos Bay, the island's one full-service pleasureboating facility is found in the latter region. We will therefore take a moment to review its history and characteristics here.

Strong archeological evidence suggests that Sanibel Island was occupied by Caloosa Indians long before the first white man ever gazed upon its shores. The highly organized Caloosa culture survived through the 1700s, but by 1801 the Indians had been decimated by disease, slave traders, and other hostile tribes.

Historical rumors link Sanibel with the pirates that operated along the Western Florida coastline during the early 1800s. Jose Gaspar was the most famous of these buccaneers. It is said that he stopped at Sanibel from time to time. Who knows—maybe a portion of his treasure still lies in the island's soil, waiting for some enterprising young explorer to come along with shovel and pail.

In 1833, a New York investment company established the town of "Sanybel" near the island's southerly tip. This was a short-lived community and within a few years all the settlers had left the island.

In 1884 construction began on a lighthouse to mark the eastern tip of Sanibel. This aid to navigation was needed by the numerous cattle transports voyaging to and from nearby Punta Rassa. The light's foundation was actually pre-built in New York and shipped by water to Sanibel. Within a mile of the island, the transport ship sank, but most of the structure was eventually salvaged. New parts were manufactured to replace those that were lost, and the light shone out over San Carlos Bay within a few months thereafter.

The Sanibel Lighthouse remains in operation to the present day. A park has been built around the old light, and the original keeper's quarters have been preserved. Visitors with automobile transportation will find parking within a few hundred yards of the lighthouse. Cruising craft can anchor behind Point Ybel and dinghy ashore in fair weather (only). However you get there, be sure to take the

Sanibel Island Lighthouse

opportunity to visit this old sentinel which speaks so eloquently of those rugged, uniquely American days of men and tall ships that will never come again.

Sanibel Island was opened for homesteading in 1888. Within a few years a successful agricultural community had been established in the "Wulfert area." The first schoolhouse was built in 1892 at a cost of $75.

In 1894 the Bailey family opened a general store under the name of the Sanibel Packing Company. This family firm has survived for almost a hundred years and today is doing business as "Bailey's General Store" (2477 Perwinkle Way, 941-472-4648).

The great hurricanes of 1921, and particularly 1926, all but wiped out the farmers on Sanibel. Shortly after this latter storm, regular ferry service was established with the mainland, allowing the island to be visited by more and more tourists.

This trend toward tourism was forever established as the island's future when a bridge was built from Punta Rassa to Sanibel in 1964. Since that time a portion of the island has been intensely developed, while other regions have been set aside as all-natural areas. Sanibel was incorporated as a city in 1974 and community leaders have striven to protect their island from overpopulation through strict zoning regulation. These efforts have met with some success, though it must be said that gunkholers seeking a remote island paradise may find a bit too much hustle and bustle for their tastes.

The largest and most accessible undeveloped portion of Sanibel Island is the 5,000-acre J. N. ("Ding") Darling National Wildlife Refuge. The sanctuary is named for Mr. J. N. Darling, a famous political cartoonist who served as head of the U.S. Biological Survey.

Under his supervision at least 330 wildlife refuges were established across the country.

Today, visitors to the Ding Darling refuge can take a quiet five-mile drive through the grounds and observe many of the birds and other wildlife which thrive in the region. There is also a visitor's center which gives a fascinating overview of the island's ecological character.

Two other island attractions are worth every visitor's attention. The Sanibel Island Visitor's Center (1159 Causeway Road) sits just to the right of the main highway, a short distance west of the Punta Rassa bridge. Here newcomers can pick up all sorts of information about the island, its facilities, and attractions. The Visitor's Center can be accessed via a long walk from Sanibel Island Marina (see below).

Visiting cruisers will probably need ground transportation to reach the Island Historical Museum (950 Dunlop Road, 941-472-4648). The charming island home that houses the museum is made from hard Florida pine and peppered with "Cracker furniture." Beaded woodwork, bronze water fixtures, and large, old, glass windows add to the appeal and allow visitors to gain a sure impression of how the early islanders lived. The museum is open from 10 A.M. to 4 P.M., Thursday and Saturday.

Sanibel Island is the site of many festivals and annual events. One of the most notable is the Sanibel Shell Fair, usually held in early March. The fair is centered around a colorful shell exhibit competition. Needless to say, there are a host of other activities in which sporting competitions and food figure prominently.

Speaking of the Shell Fair, we would be remiss in our review of Sanibel if we left without mentioning the fabulous shell hunting for which the island is so famous. Because of the way Sanibel thrusts out into the Gulf, every new tide brings fresh treasures to the island's exposed beaches. Many a cruiser has dinghied ashore day after day to search for these colorful offerings from the sea.

So there you have it—the collection of the historic and the latter-day spirit that makes up modern Sanibel Island. While it is undoubtedly the most developed part of Pine Island Sound, many of Sanibel's charms most assuredly endure.

Numbers to know on Sanibel Island include:

Airport Shuttle—941-472-0007
Apple Taxi—941-482-1200
Sanibel Taxi—941-472-4160
Enterprise Rent-A-Car—941-454-0770
Sanibel Island Visitor's Center—
   941-472-1080

Point Ybel Anchorage

For many years, this writer, BAIL, and any number of other cruising authors have recommended anchoring in the shelter of Point Ybel, southeast of flashing daybeacon #2. Recently, however, several boats have dragged anchor while taking shelter in this haven during foul weather. These unfortunate craft have ended up stuck on the bridge just to the northwest. Severe damage to the vessels and the bridge has been the unhappy result. For this reason, cruisers should be *sure* to anchor behind Point Ybel *only* where there is not even a hint of windy weather. The local authorities enforce a 48-hour anchorage limit on these waters due to the above described difficulties.

Clearly, this anchorage's bad reputation must come from poor bottom-holding conditions. Conversely, the cove is fairly well sheltered, courtesy of Point Ybel to the east, which cuts out far enough to give good protection when winds are blowing from this quarter. The body of the island renders excellent shelter when winds are blowing from the south or southwest. The anchorage is completely open to blows across the bay from the north. Impressive depths of 17 feet or better run to within 100 to 150 yards of the southern banks.

Due to the poor holding ground and ever-present, strong tidal currents, those captains who do choose to anchor here would be wise to put out two anchors and to be very, very sure they are well set before heading below.

The anchorage's shoreline is dotted with luxurious development which makes for interesting viewing from the water. You can see the upper portion of the Point Ybel Lighthouse peeping over the tall pines to the east.

Sanibel Island Marina

Southwest of flashing daybeacon #2, a single pair of daybeacons marks the entrance into Sanibel Island Marina. As you cruise between unlighted daybeacon #2 and unlighted daybeacon #1, the canal leading to the marina will be spotted dead ahead. This cut holds 5- to 7-foot depths. The marina flanks the canal's southerly face.

This friendly and very accommodating facility gladly accepts transients and offers protected dockage at fixed wooden piers featuring

Sanibel Island Marina

water and good power connections. The piers appear to be relatively new and are quite nice. In the mornings, the cheerful staff delivers muffins and the local newspaper to all guest craft. How's that for great service? The fuel dock fronts onto the canal, but most of the dockage is found in a cove-like basin just to the south. Minimum dockside depths run around 5½ feet, but many slips in the harbor boast 6 to 8 feet of water. Gasoline and diesel fuel are readily available, as are adequate, non-climate controlled shoreside showers and a laundromat. The marina offers full mechanical repairs for both gasoline and diesel power plants. The on-site ship's and variety store is worth every visitor's perusal.

Immediately behind the docks, famished cruisers will find the famous Granma-Dot's Restaurant (941-472-8138). Named for a woman who fell in love with cruising Pine Island Sound, this famous dining spot features open-air dining and marvelous Western Florida seafood. The fried grouper sandwiches have to be experienced to be believed. To be succinct, don't miss it!

Sanibel Island Marina (941) 472-2723
   http://www.swfl.com/sanibel/index.html

Approach depth—5-7 feet
Dockside depth— 5 ½-8 feet
Accepts transients—yes
Fixed wooden piers—yes
Dockside power connections—30 and 50 amp
Dockside water connections—yes
Laundromat—yes
Gasoline—yes
Diesel fuel—yes
Mechanical repairs—yes
Ship's and variety store—yes
Restaurant—on site

Tarpon Bay Channel

Northwest of the 26-foot (vertical clearance)

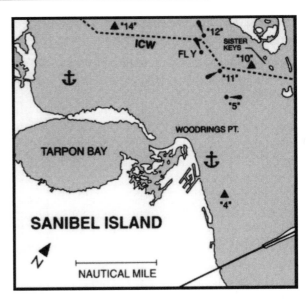

section of the Sanibel Island bridge, passing cruisers may note a pile-marked channel cutting southwest (well northwest of unlighted daybeacon #4) to shallow Tarpon Bay. In spite of the "7 ft rep 1987" notation on chart 11427, this passage is quite shoal and fit only for dinghies and large to mid-size wading birds. A few captains occasionally choose to anchor in the deeper waters of the main channel during fair weather and dinghy into Tarpon Bay through this cut. However, it would be far more convenient for cruising-size craft to berth at Sanibel Island Marina. You can then rent bikes easily enough at the marina or several other commissaries to visit the remainder of the island, including the Ding Darling wildlife refuge to the north.

Dixie Beach Anchorage (BAIL-Suggested)

In fair weather and light winds, some boats occasionally anchor off charted Dixie Beach, flanking the southwesterly shoreline between unlighted daybeacon #4 and flashing daybeacon #5. Depths of 8 feet or better stretch to within 200 yards (only) of shore. Care must be exercised to avoid the charted 2- and 3-foot shallows lying to the northwest. This haven offers some protection from southern and southwesterly winds that don't exceed 10 knots, but it is wide open to breezes from all other directions. Obviously, this is *not* a foul weather hidey-hole. The surrounding shore is peppered with moderate, but not unattractive residential development.

Like the anchorage behind Point Ybel (see above), the holding ground adjacent to Dixie Beach is suspect. Be sure your hook is well set, and check for dragging periodically. Again, in a like vein to the Point Ybel haven, the Sanibel Island city government imposes a 48-hour-stay limit for this anchorage.

Punta Rassa Anchorage

Let us now return our attention to the principal entrance into San Carlos Bay, southwest of charted Punta Rassa. Cruisers can anchor in the charted deep water northeast of #8. You must avoid the long tongue of shallows north and east of #8, but with careful navigation, minimum depths of 6 to 7 feet can be held to within 250 yards of the northeasterly banks. Closer to shore soundings rise to 4- and 5-foot levels. Protection is good from northern and eastern breezes, but nil when winds are blowing from the south or west. This is not a heavy-weather anchorage and should not be used if a stormy forecast is in the offing. The immediate shoreline is delightfully in its natural state, but several tall, high-rise condo buildings at Punta Rassa are visible to the northwest.

Punta Rassa

The bascule bridge stretching from the high-rise Jimmy Connors tennis complex at old Punta Rassa to Sanibel Island serves as a

landmark for what was one of the most unexpectedly important ports of call in early Florida. Following the conclusion of that dark conflict known as the War Between the States, semi-wild cattle wandered the marshes and hammocks of North Central Florida. Some were strays that had wandered off from ranches, while others had escaped from both Confederate and Union troops during the war.

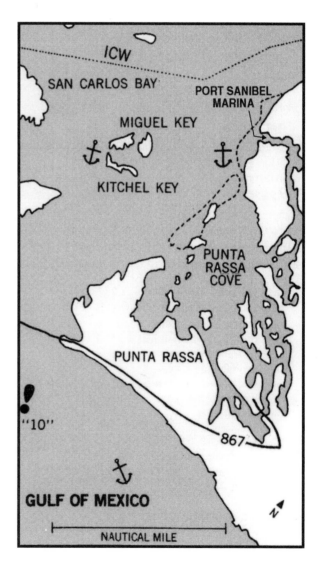

A few enterprising individuals began rounding up these beasts and forming small cattle ranches. As a fortunate coincidence, it was just about this same time that Spanish authorities came to Florida from nearby Cuba searching for a ready source of beef. The Spaniards set up headquarters at the tiny village of Punta Rassa, and offered gold coins for every cow delivered. Soon cattle drives were in progress all across Northern Central Florida, headed for Punta Rassa. The bewildered owners of the small ranches suddenly found more hard money in their pockets than they had expected to see during their entire life. They bought clothes, guns, and furniture before heading home to begin the process anew.

These Florida cowboys used long, rawhide whips to keep the cattle together. All accounts agree that they could pop and crack the whips with an explosion of sound that would subdue even the most reluctant steer. As the years went by, these cowboys became known as "Florida Crackers." Though this term was later used to describe poor farmers throughout the South, it had its origins with the Florida cattle drivers who traveled to and from Punta Rassa.

With the coming of Cuban independence, the trade at Punta Rassa dried up, though cattle raising has remained a part of Central Florida's economy to the present day. If you would like to learn more about the Florida cowboys, Patrick D. Smith's wonderful novel, *A Land Remembered*, is highly recommended. It is a "must read" for anyone interested in Floridian history.

Meanwhile, a prominent citizen of the small coastal village, George Shultz by name, had begun a business that presaged modern-day Punta Rassa. Shultz took over an old army barracks that was sitting practically out over the water and proceeded to open a hotel that drew the likes of no less than Pres. Grover Cleveland, Thomas Edison, the Duke of Sutherland, and John Jamison, the famous distiller of Irish whiskey. The clever operator and promoter ran off the snakes and rats and set up a fine restaurant. He did little else to improve his building, however, and the old walls remained unpainted. According to Stuart McIver, writing in *Glimpses of South Florida History,* "Instead of deriding him for not painting the place, Shultz's guests praised him for not tampering with its primitive charms. Instead of calling the hotel run-down, they called it unique." In this writer's opinion, whatever the modern-day promoters of the Jimmy Connors Tennis Center may have up their sleeves, they have nothing on Mr. Shultz. The unique hotel burned in 1906 and is now but a distant memory.

Kitchel-Miguel Key Anchorage

North of the Punta Rassa-Sanibel Island span, chart 11427 correctly notes a channel of deep water cutting northwest from the main channel (near unlighted daybeacon #11) to the southwesterly tip of Kitchel and Miguel keys. This route is unmarked and navigationally challenging and there is certainly some danger of slipping into the surrounding shoals, but good navigation and cautious cruising may bring you through minimum 7-foot depths to an anchorage just off the southwestern point of the two keys. Boats up to 36 feet should have ample room. The two keys, as well as the other nearby islands, are completely undeveloped mangroves. This natural character produces a feeling of enjoyable isolation which is altogether welcome.

On the water, Kitchel and Miguel keys appear as one solid mass of land and trees, very different from the nebulous structure pictured on chart 11427. Don't be fooled by this contradiction.

This is not a good anchorage for riding out a heavy blow. The two islands provide shelter to the east and northeast, and Big Island and Fisherman Key give some protection to the south and west. Nevertheless, winds over 15 knots, particularly from the northwest or southeast, clearly call for a different plan.

Punta Rassa Cove Anchorage (BAIL-Suggested)

Some cruisers occasionally anchor in the deep water east of the gap between flashing daybeacons #13 and #14, bordering on the western reaches of shallow Punta Rassa Cove. Clearly this is a fair-weather refuge at best. It is open to all but easterly winds and is regularly scoured by the strong tidal currents present throughout this entire area. Minimum 6-foot depths are held to within 150 yards of the eastern banks.

Port Sanibel Marina

East of unlighted daybeacon #11, a 5½-foot marked channel cuts through the otherwise shallow waters of Punta Rassa Cove to a large, well-sheltered facility that goes under the moniker of Port Sanibel Marina. Even though this facility's Web site lists transient dockage among the marina's services, the office manager firmly informed this writer that all slip space is currently filled. She went on to say that cruising visitors can usually be accommodated only during off-season (summer) when some of the resident craft have vacated their usual space. Be sure to call ahead to find out if any transient berths are indeed available before betting too heavily on a night spent at this facility.

Should you find space at Port Sanibel, your craft will be berthed at fixed wooden piers in

about as sheltered a harbor as you are ever likely to find. Full power and water connections, waste pump-out, plus full fueling services (gasoline and diesel fuel) are available. Depths alongside run 6+ feet.

Shoreside, both showers and a laundromat are available. The on-site Lighthouse Restaurant is ever so handy.

So, if you can find space, give Port Sanibel a look. Unfortunately, most visiting cruisers will find it necessary to just keep cruising on by.

Port Sanibel Marina (941) 472-8443
    http://www.marinafinder.com/cgi-bin/mari nafinder/marinashow?14

Approach depth—5½ feet MLW
Dockside depth—6+ feet
Accepts transients—very limited
Fixed wooden piers—yes
Dockside power connections—30 and 50 amp
Dockside water connections—yes
Waste pump-out—yes
Showers—yes
Laundromat—yes
Gasoline—yes
Diesel fuel—yes
Restaurant—on site

Major Intersection

North of flashing daybeacon #14 and unlighted daybeacon #15, the northward-running channel through San Carlos Bay runs headlong into a very crucial intersection. Mile 0 of the Western Florida ICW is found at unlighted can buoy #1. The Waterway runs west-southwest from this point across the so-called miserable mile until it begins to turn north at flashing daybeacon #11 into the southerly reaches of Pine Island Sound.

To the northeast, flashing daybeacon #101 marks the beginning of the Caloosahatchee River channel and the Okeechobee Waterway. We will first briefly review the initial section of the ICW and then follow the Caloosahatchee to Fort Myers in a separate section.

The Miserable Mile

For a Waterway that can boast of so many delightful sights and cruisable waters, the Western Florida ICW's beginning is far from auspicious. The problem stems from the north-to-south set of the prevailing tidal currents which regularly boil out of Pine Island Sound, Matlacha Pass, and the Caloosahatchee River. This initial portion of the ICW runs east to west, thereby ensuring that currents run *across* the Waterway. This 90-degree current can lead to rapid shoaling of the Waterway channel. While the Corps of Engineers can usually be relied upon to keep the passage open, it's a good idea to hold strictly to the middle of the channel. This is not the sort of place to test the ICW's limits.

In addition to the shoaling problems comes the real possibility of lateral leeway. All pleasure vessels, not just sailcraft and single-screw trawlers, must keep just as vigilant a watch over their sterns as on the course ahead to quickly note any slippage. Failure to follow this commonsense practice can quickly result in a call to Sea Tow.

Fortunately, the miserable mile is very well marked and most captains will come through with nothing worse than tense shoulders. Markers are frequently added, taken away, and shifted, so don't be surprised to find a different configuration of aids to navigation than those pictured on chart 11427 or discussed in the navigational account below.

Picnic Island Anchorage

Believe it or else, there is actually a fair-weather anchorage available to boaters along the miserable mile. Study chart 11427 for a moment and note Picnic Island, southeast of unlighted daybeacon #8. The charted deep water east and northeast of the island makes a good anchorage in light airs or when winds are blowing from the southwest. Good depths of 12 feet hold to within 50 yards or so of the island's northeastern shores. Don't attempt to circumnavigate the island. There is very shoal water to the south and west.

Picnic Island is completely in its natural state, with white, sandy beaches backed by scrub growth and a few smaller trees. It is apparently a popular weekend destination for local cruisers. During a research trip several years ago, we spotted a party in progress amidst a remote broadcast by a local radio station.

SAN CARLOS BAY NAVIGATION

Navigation of the various San Carlos Bay channels would be pretty simple stuff if it were not for the all-too-pervasive tidal currents. Even so, most skippers need only be on guard against excessive leeway and follow elementary compass courses between the various aids to navigation.

Entry from Gulf of Mexico After avoiding the long shoal stretching southeast from Point Ybel (see preceding chapter), point to come abeam of flashing daybeacon #8 to its southwesterly side. Once abeam of #8 you can explore the anchorage to the northeast, follow the Sanibel

Island channel to the southwest, or cut up the main San Carlos Bay passage to the northwest.

Punta Rassa Anchorage To enter the anchorage southeast of Punta Rassa, sweep widely around flashing daybeacon #8 to the southeast. This maneuver will help to avoid the large, charted tongue of shallows running southeast from Punta Rassa. Once you are within some 300 to 400 yards of the northeastern banks, begin feeling your way carefully to the northwest with your sounder. Minimum depths of 6 to 7 feet extend for almost .7 nautical miles to the northwest. If soundings rise above 6 feet, you have gone too far. Retreat a bit to the southeast for better depths. Good water runs to within 250 yards of the northeastern shoreline, short of the charted shallows to the northwest.

Sanibel Island Channel Remember that the upper reaches of the Sanibel Island channel are spanned by a fixed bridge with 26 feet of vertical clearance. Cruisers can visit the island's only full-service marina and one anchorage without having to pass through this span.

From flashing daybeacon #8, set a careful compass course to come abeam of flashing daybeacon #2, northwest of Point Ybel, by some 100 yards to its southerly side. It's a fairly lengthy run of 1.5 nautical miles between #8 and #2. Stay on course and watch for leeway.

Ignore unlighted daybeacon #1, which you may sight northwest of your track when cruising between #8 and #2. This aid marks an old center channel in San Carlos Bay that is now shoal and dangerous.

Point Ybel Anchorage (BAIL-Suggested)
As you approach flashing daybeacon #2, the anchorage adjacent to the shores of Sanibel Island will come abeam to the south. Simply cruise in behind (to the west of) the shelter of Point Ybel, which you will recognize courtesy of its tall Australian pines, and drop the hook within 100 yards of the shoreline. This anchorage is subject to strong tidal currents and exhibits poor holding ground. A second anchor might be a wise precaution. Be sure the hook(s) are well set before going below to begin cooking that Florida lobster for dinner.

Sanibel Island Marina Once abeam of flashing daybeacon #2, point directly for the southernmost pass-through of the long Sanibel Island bridge, which you will sight dead ahead. Soon you will come abeam of the entrance to Sanibel Island Marina to the south.

Watch the southern shore for a single pair of daybeacons, unlighted #1 and #2. Continue cruising on the main channel until the gap between these aids is directly abeam to the south. Then turn sharply south and pass between #1 and #2 into the mouth of the canal dead ahead.

As you cruise through the connecting canal, favor the westerly (starboard) banks. A shoal seems to be building out from the canal's easterly flank.

Soon additional canals will open out to port and starboard. Ignore these side streams and continue straight ahead. You will soon spy the marina's fuel docks to port.

On the Sanibel Channel Northwest of flashing daybeacon #2, the wide Sanibel Island channel soon meets the 26-foot fixed, southernmost span of the bridge connecting Punta Rassa and the island. Cruise through the bridge and point to pass unlighted daybeacon #3 to its northeasterly side. Use your binoculars to pick out unlighted daybeacon #4 ahead. As you would expect, pass this aid to its southwesterly quarter.

It's a cruise of another 1.2 nautical miles or so before you reach the next aid on the Sanibel channel, flashing daybeacon #5. Fortunately, the passage remains wide and mostly deep. Be sure to pass #5 by at least 50 yards to its northeasterly side. This beacon marks a shoal building into the channel from the southwest.

Dixie Beach Anchorage (BAIL-Suggested) To make good your entry into the open anchorage lying southwest of the gap between unlighted daybeacon #4 and flashing daybeacon #5, point for the deeper waters just northwest of the charted local canals immediately southeast of Dixie Beach. Don't approach the canals themselves as they are rather shallow. Also, take extra care to avoid the correctly charted, broad tongue of shoal water stretching north-northeast from Woodrings Point. Remember, this anchorage is only recommended in fair weather and light breezes.

On to the ICW From #5 it's a quick run to intersect the ICW at flashing daybeacon #11. At #11 the Waterway cuts west and northwest into the southerly foot of Pine Island Sound.

Main San Carlos Bay Channel Let us now return to flashing daybeacon #8, southeast of Punta Rassa, where our discussion of the Sanibel Island channel began. The principal bay channel continues straight ahead from #8 until eventually reaching flashing daybeacon #10.

Once abeam of #10, you may spot unlighted daybeacon #3 well west of your course. Do not attempt to cruise toward this aid—it is founded in shoal water.

Instead, turn north from #10 and point for the easternmost, bascule section of the long Sanibel Island bridge. Be mindful of the correctly charted shallows to the east between #10 and the bridge.

The Punta Rassa span (of the Sanibel Island bridge) has a closed vertical clearance of 26 feet. Cruisers whose craft can't clear this height must contend with a restrictive opening schedule. This span opens on the hour and every 15 minutes thereafter from 7:00 A.M. to 7:00 P.M., seven days a week. At all other times of the day, the bridge opens on demand.

On the Bay Channel North of the Punta Rassa-Sanibel Island span, the tall towers of the Jimmy Connors Tennis Center will be sighted to the east. The channel bends farther to the north at this point and skirts the eastern shores along a broad band of deep water. Point to pass unlighted daybeacon #11 to its easterly quarter. Just before reaching #11, boaters may choose to anchor abeam of Miguel and Kitchel keys to the northwest.

Kitchel-Miguel Key Anchorage   Here's a novel way to find the deep-water channel leading to the anchorage southwest of Kitchel and Miguel keys. Look at the five high-rise buildings along the Punta Rassa shoreline. Note the center and largest of the structures. If you align your stern with this building and set course for a point just southwest of the twin keys, you will hopefully be in good water all the way. Of course, more buildings could go up in the future in the Punta Rassa complex, so take these instructions with a grain of salt.

In any case, depart the main channel well south of unlighted daybeacon #11 to avoid the charted shoal building south from the aid. You can then follow the channel past the northeastern tip of Fisherman Key until coming abeam of Miguel and Kitchel keys (which will appear as one solid land mass) by some 30 yards to your starboard side.

Don't attempt to cruise farther to the northwest. Very shallow water guards the approaches to the ICW northwest of the twin keys.

Punta Rassa Cove Anchorage (BAIL-Suggested)   Simply cruise northeast from the gap between flashing daybeacons #13 and #14 towards the shoreline. Drop the hook before approaching to within less than 150 yards of the banks. Don't attempt to enter charted Shell Creek. It may look good, but on-site research revealed that depths quickly rise to less than 3 feet near its southwestern mouth.

On to the Intersection   North of flashing daybeacon #13, point to pass between flashing daybeacon #14 and unlighted daybeacon #15. After passing #15, powercraft should slow down and all boats should proceed with caution. The intersections with the ICW and the Caloosahatchee channel are just ahead.

Watch for flashing daybeacon #101, to the northeast, and unlighted can buoy #1 to the northwest. Cruise directly between these markers.

Now you must choose whether to cut northeast into the Caloosahatchee River, or west-southwest to follow the Waterway.

On the Miserable Mile   Pass unlighted can buoy #1 to its fairly immediate northwesterly side and continue cruising to the west-southwest to follow the Waterway. Northbound craft should pass all red markers to their (the cruiser's) starboard sides and take green beacons to their port. Watch for strong currents sweeping across the channel and be ready for leeway corrections.

Just before coming abeam of unlighted daybeacon #8 to its northwesterly side, passing cruisers may spy unlighted daybeacon #1 to the northwest. This is the first aid on the Matlacha Pass channel, which is reviewed later in this chapter.

Captains may also choose to cruise to the anchorage off Picnic Island between unlighted can buoy #7 and unlighted daybeacon #8.

Picnic Island Anchorage   Simply depart the Waterway about halfway between unlighted can buoy #7 and unlighted daybeacon #8, and cruise carefully towards the northeastern banks of Picnic Island. Drop the hook within 50 yards (no closer) of the shoreline and break out the old dinghy.

Remember, this is *not* a foul-weather anchorage. If a thunderstorm appears along the horizon, better head for more secure shelter.

On the ICW At unlighted daybeacon #10, the "miserable mile" ends as the ICW comes under the shelter of Pine Island to the northwest. Flashing daybeacon #11 introduces the northbound ICW cruiser to the southern reaches of Pine Island Sound.

We will now turn our attention to a brief discussion of Matlacha Pass, followed by a more extensive review of the Caloosahatchee River to Fort Myers. Continued coverage of the Western Florida ICW will resume in the Pine Island subsection, later in this chapter.

Matlacha Pass

Many captains traversing the so-called miserable mile have probably looked at the markers running northwest from unlighted daybeacon #1 and wondered about the charted passage east of Pine Island known as Matlacha Pass. Due to a lack of reliable information, few have heretofore been willing to try this cut. Below you will find the details needed to explore this little-frequented passage, but let it be known that the channel is *only* appropriate for craft drawing 4 feet or less and that can clear a *32-foot power line!*

Matlacha Pass cuts through the broad but mostly shallow body of water that separates the Florida mainland from Pine Island. This island has long been the refuge of commercial fishermen and small villages. While some modern development is beginning to be evidenced on Pine Island, it is still for the most part delightfully devoid of tourists and intensive land use.

The pass channel is a winding, twisting route that has some low-water depths of as little as 4½ to 5 feet. Typical soundings range from 6 to as much as 15 feet. The cut must be navigated with extreme caution. Nighttime passage is strictly not recommended.

There are no real facilities for cruising vessels on Matlacha Pass, and there are only two good anchorages. In spite of these shortcomings, those skippers who pilot shallow-draft vessels and hunger for waters where they are not likely to have any neighbors may just find that Matlacha Pass fits their cruising plans nicely.

Pine Island History In 1513 Pine Island was visited by none other than Ponce de Leon, the founder of St. Augustine. By this time, he had probably given up on the fountain of youth and was exploring Western Florida in the hopes of founding a Spanish outpost on the western shores of the Florida peninsula. The explorer left a stone marker behind, and was killed nearby soon afterward in an attack by hostile Indians. Speculation persists that had Ponce lived, another St. Augustine might have arisen near the shores of Pine Island.

Givney Key Anchorage

Matlacha Pass's first anchorage, moving south to north, is found southeast of Givney Key in the charted deep water north-northeast of unlighted daybeacon #3. The haven is located conveniently near the "miserable mile" portion of the Western Florida ICW and well south of the annoying 32-foot power lines. This fortunate position renders the refuge accessible to most pleasurecraft of either the sail or powered persuasion that draw 5 feet or less.

Minimum depths of 6 feet are held between #3 and a position 250 yards southeast of Givney Key, assuming you can follow the broad but completely unmarked channel. The key gives good protection from northerly winds, while Pine Island to the west and the mainland to the northeast provide some shelter when it's blowing from either of these quarters. The anchorage is wide open to southerly blows.

This is clearly not a foul-weather stop. On the other hand, if fair breezes are in the forecast, it is a lovely overnight refuge. The undeveloped shores of Givney Island to the northwest are hard to stay away from. The Pine Island banks to the west are also delightfully in their natural state. During our first cruise of Matlacha Pass almost a decade ago, we observed a 30-foot sailboat tucked snugly for the night in this anchorage. If the weather cooperates, why not take this opportunity to experience a night in the clear coastal airs without a hint of civilization in sight?

Pine Island Bridge & Anchorage (BAIL-Suggested)

North of unlighted daybeacon #55, the Matlacha Pass channel ducks under a 9-foot (closed vertical clearance) bascule bridge that links Pine Island with the mainland. This span is known locally as "the fishingest bridge in the world." Chances are that passing cruisers will spot a host of anglers fishing from the span at any time of the day or night.

A few low-key docks are found on either side of this bridge. A small restaurant fronts the channel on its southwestern banks, just southeast of the span. While it would not appear to be standard operating procedure, one thirty-footer could probably tie to the pier in 5- to 6-foot depths. On the opposite shore, a small gift and novelty shop has a dock boasting 9 feet of water. Besides a public launching ramp, these are really the only facilities along this portion of Pine Island for all but small powercraft.

It is possible to anchor just east of the main channel, immediately south of the bridge in 6½ to 10 feet of water. This haven is BAIL-suggested. Protection is good from all but particularly strong southern and southeasterly blows. Once the hook is down, the diplomatic cruisers among us should be able to dinghy ashore and find a place to tie off temporarily. Two restaurants and some low-key, convenience-type variety stores are within walking distance.

The 56-foot charted power line immediately north of the bridge has been raised to 75 feet of vertical clearance. Now, sailors cruising south from Pine Island Sound can take advantage of the anchorage described above without having to contend with the 35-foot power line to the south, or the more tortuous southerly portion of the Matlacha Pass channel.

MATLACHA PASS NAVIGATION

Matlacha Pass winds, twists, and squirms its way north from San Carlos Bay to Charlotte Harbor and Pine Island Sound. Remember that a few soundings show waters as thin as 4½ to 5 feet (though typically depths are much better), and the passage is spanned at one point by a 32-foot power line. Only maneuverable vessels drawing 4 feet or less should attempt this passage.

Waters outside of the marked channel have consistent depths of 3 feet or less. This is most assuredly *not* the place to go exploring off the buoyed track.

The southerly reaches of the pass are best navigated using chart 11427. This cartographical aid's minute detail makes for much easier identification of the cut's winding path. North of unlighted daybeacon #25, you must switch to chart 11426. Unfortunately, no larger-scale chart covers the northerly section of Matlacha Pass.

Leaving the "Miserable Mile" Continue cruising west-southwest on the Waterway channel until you are some 100 yards to the east-northeast of unlighted daybeacon #8. Watch to the northwest for unlighted daybeacon #1. This is the first aid on the Matlacha Pass channel and it closely borders the Waterway passage. Cut off the ICW and pass #1 fairly close to its northeastern side. Then, set a new course to come abeam of unlighted daybeacon #2 to your starboard side (its southwesterly quarter). From this point on, cruisers northbound on Matlacha Pass should take all red beacons to their (the cruisers') starboard side and pass all green markers to port. This rule holds true on the pass all the way north to unlighted daybeacon #95, off Pine Island's northern tip, bordering the southern reaches of Charlotte Harbor.

Givney Key Anchorage For best depths, leave the main channel immediately after passing unlighted daybeacon #3. Point directly for the center of Givney Key, which you will spot well to the north. Drop the hook before approaching to less than 250 yards of the small key. Closer in, depths rise above 5 feet. Do your explorations by dinghy. Retrace your track back to #3 when departing the anchorage.

On Matlacha Pass It would take more pages than I can count to try and delineate every twist and turn of the Matlacha Pass channel. A few of the more obvious bends are described below, but be ready for quick course changes at all times, and watch over your stern for leeway.

Between unlighted daybeacons #3 and #4, the channel takes a hard jog to the west. Set course to pass unlighted daybeacon #5 to your port side and continue on, pointing to pass between unlighted daybeacons #6 and #7. This is one of the shallowest stretches of Matlacha Pass. Be ready for some 5-foot depths.

Adjust course sharply north after passing between #6 and #7 and point to come abeam of and pass unlighted daybeacon #8 to your fairly immediate starboard side.

At unlighted daybeacon #17, northbound skippers must follow a hairpin to port, followed by another turn to starboard at unlighted daybeacon #18.

Watch the western shores at unlighted daybeacon #24 and you will catch sight of Masters Lodge on the Pine Island shoreline. No services are available for cruising craft, but the buildings make for an interesting view from the water.

North of unlighted daybeacon #29, the channel greets an overhead power line with a measly **32 feet** of vertical clearance. Sailcraft—take note of this very real hazard!

Northbound mariners will sight the Pine Island-Matlacha Pass Bridge after passing unlighted daybeacon #55. This span has a closed vertical clearance of 9 feet. It opens on demand from 8:00 A.M. to 7:00 P.M., but is closed entirely during the evening and nighttime hours.

To anchor (BAIL-suggested) south of the bridge, simply ease your way off the channel a bit to the east and drop the hook. Be sure to show an anchor light!

The 56-foot charted power line immediately north of the bridge has been raised to 75 feet of vertical clearance.

North of the bridge, the two shorelines exhibit even less development and are absolutely beautiful. Minimum depths of 7½ feet continue on to the end of the pass, with most soundings being much deeper.

At unlighted daybeacon #79 the Matlacha Pass channel begins a lazy turn to the west, skirting the northern tip of Pine Island. The passage ends at unlighted daybeacon #95, north of Bokeelia Island, which is an off-shoot of its larger sister, Pine Island.

A marked and charted channel continues south down the easterly reaches of Pine Island Sound. This route will be reviewed in the discussion of Pine Island Sound presented later in this chapter. For now, we need only note that marker colors reverse after leaving the Matlacha Pass route and entering the southbound channel.

Caloosahatchee River to Fort Myers

Few Western Florida rivers can lay claim to as delightful a port of call as the Caloosahatchee has in Fort Myers. Many captains cruising the Western Florida coastline may want to take a day or two out of their schedules to experience the delights of this colorful city, with its excellent marina (and yacht club) facilities, a beautifully restored downtown business district, and more than its share of historic attractions.

Of course, the Caloosahatchee (which translates to "river of the Caloosa") also serves

as the westernmost link in the exciting Okeechobee Waterway. This reliable route not only provides ready access between Florida's two coastlines, it also allows cruisers to experience the "other Florida" of cowboy ranches, small villages, and mighty lakes. Sadly, we can only explore a small portion of this enticing route in this guide. East of Fort Myers, please consult my *Cruising Guide to Eastern Florida* for a minutely detailed account of the Okeechobee Waterway.

The Caloosahatchee below (west of) Fort

Myers offers a few anchorages and good marina facilities. At least one of these anchor-down spots is sufficient for heavy weather.

The banks of the Caloosahatchee range the full gamut from very heavy, high-rise type development to all-natural stretches. The cruising is certainly not dull from a visual perspective.

All in all, this writer heartily recommends a cruise up the Caloosahatchee to Fort Myers. In fair weather, it's a delightful sojourn, and a night or two spent in Thomas Edison's adopted city is sure to yield cruising memories to be cherished for many years to come.

Shell Point Anchorage (Okeechobee Standard Mile 148)

Boats drawing less than 5 feet and in need of immediate anchorage might consider the charted deep water on the cove east and south of flashing daybeacon #96. You must avoid several unmarked shoals, but it is possible to get off the main channel and drop the anchor in some 5 to 6 feet of water near the cove's mouth. Farther to the south, water levels rise to 4 feet or less in spite of the soundings shown on 11427. Protection is fairly good from southern and southeasterly winds, but the anchorage is wide open to blows from any other direction. This is not a poor-weather haven. The surrounding shores are in their natural state and are quite attractive.

Tarpon Point Marina & Glover Bight Anchorage (BAIL-Suggested) (Okeechobee Standard Mile 146.5)

A marked channel leads cruisers from unlighted daybeacon #92 (currently charted as unlighted nun buoy #92) past Cattle Dock Point and finally to a first-class marina on the charted offshoot making into the northwestern

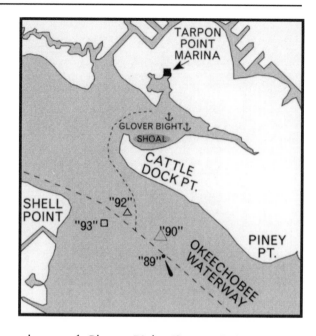

shores of Glover Bight. Tarpon Point Marina features ultramodern, fixed wooden docks and slips in a very well protected harbor. Transients are accepted at berths with all power and water connections. Minimum entrance depths are 7 feet, with typical soundings ranging up to 15 feet. Dockside, visiting cruisers will find at least 7½ to 12 feet of water. We did sound some 6½-foot depths directly against the seawall, but almost all of the marina's other 175 slips have much better water.

Fully climate controlled, spotless showers and a waste pump-out service are both readily available. Gasoline and diesel fuel can be purchased at a separate fuel pier near the marina's entrance. Seacoast Yacht Charters (941-540-8050), which we shall hear far more about in our chapter 5 discussion of the Anclote River, maintains an office on the premises. A Boat/U S towboat now makes its home at Tarpon Point as well. About the only services you will not find at Tarpon Point are a laundromat, repairs, and a restaurant.

Tarpon Point Marina

Tarpon Point Marina (941) 549-4900

Approach depth—7-15 feet
**Dockside depth—7½-12 feet (many slips much
    deeper)**
Accepts transients—yes
Fixed wooden piers—yes
Dockside power connections—30 and 50 amp
Dockside water connections—yes
Waste pump-out—yes
Showers—yes
Gasoline—yes
Diesel fuel—yes

The charted channel traversing Glover Bight continues west past the marina and eventually leads to a series of canals, mostly lined by private homes. There are no facilities nor enough anchor room for visiting cruisers on these waters.

On the other hand, mariners may well choose to anchor on the northeasterly reaches of Glover Bight, northeast of unlighted daybeacon #9. Depths of 7 to 14 feet extend to within 200 yards of the rear of the cove, but there is an unmarked shoal to the southeast that must be avoided. There is good shelter from all but strong southwesterly blows. The surrounding shores are delightfully undeveloped.

St. Charles Yacht Club (Okeechobee Standard Mile 146)

A new, well-appointed yacht club guards the Caloosahatchee's southerly banks between flashing daybeacon #89 and unlighted daybeacon #86. The club's basin is designated as facility #16A on chart 11427.

St. Charles Yacht Club is glad to welcome guests from other yacht clubs with the appropriate reciprocal agreements. The well-marked entrance cut carries at least 6 feet of water, and visitors will discover 6½- to 7-foot dockside soundings.

All berths are provided at new, fixed wooden piers featuring fresh water and 30-50-amp power hookups. Gasoline, diesel fuel, and waste pump-out services are available for members and official club guests only. Showers and a full laundromat are on hand shoreside in the clubhouse.

The club dockmaster is on duty 8:00 A.M. to 5:00 P.M., seven days a week. He suggests that visitors make advance arrangements by telephone. Call 941-466-4935.

Lunch is served in the club dining room 11:30 to 2:30 Tuesday through Saturday, and the evening meal is available between 6:00 and 8:30 Wednesday through Saturday. There are no other restaurants within easy walking distance.

On the other hand, cruisers with the fever to purchase something can hike one mile to the Sanbel Factory Outlets center. Here you will find 55 shops waiting to take your money. Just be sure it's a real bargain before you lay out the cold cash.

All in all, we were very impressed with St. Charles Yacht Club. Its location is very advantageous for those with the appropriate reciprocity agreements who don't want to stray as far upstream as Fort Myers. We suggest that you give these good folks a look-see.

St. Charles Yacht Club (941) 466-2007
Approach depth—6 feet MLW
Dockside depth—6½-7 feet MLW
Accepts transients—members of other yacht clubs with reciprocal privileges only
Fixed wooden piers—yes
Dockside power connections—30 and 50 amp
Dockside water connections—yes
Waste pump-out—members and offical guests only
Showers—yes
Laundromat—yes
Gasoline—members and offical guests only
Diesel fuel—members and official guests only
Restaurant—club dining room on site

Bimini Basin Anchorage (BAIL-Suggested) (Okeechobee Standard Mile 145)

East of unlighted daybeacon #83, a well-marked channel maintaining 6-foot depths leads into the northern banks. By easing west-southwest along this shoreline, you can find your way to the charted northward running canal that eventually leads to a large bay-like body of water charted as Bimini Basin on 11427. Depths hold in the 6- to 8-foot region all the way into this super-protected anchorage. This is a great spot to ride out really foul weather while listening to the wind howl overhead. The surrounding shores are guarded by a dense collection of residential, and some high-rise, development.

In the last edition of this guide, I warned fellow cruisers that the city of Cape Coral was running cruisers away from Bimini Basin. We are now pleased to report that Cape Coral has officially recognized these waters as an anchorage, and stays up to 15 days are allowed.

There is the opportunity to dinghy ashore in this anchorage. Use your binoculars to pick out a city park along the northeasterly shoreline. You can temporarily moor your dinghy adjacent to this park while hiking a short distance to a convenience store, bank, bakery, hardware, or grocery store. Ask any local for directions.

Cape Coral Yacht Basin (Okeechobee Standard Mile 144)

Another excellent marina is found north-northwest of unlighted daybeacon #78 in a sheltered canal and dockage basin behind Redfish Point. City-owned Cape Coral Yacht Basin has minimum entrance depths of 5½ to 8 feet, with 5½ to 10 feet of water dockside. The entrance channel can be a bit confusing for first-time visitors, but a little explanation courtesy of the navigational data presented in the next section of this chapter should see you through.

The friendly dockmaster gladly accepts transients at fixed wooden piers with water

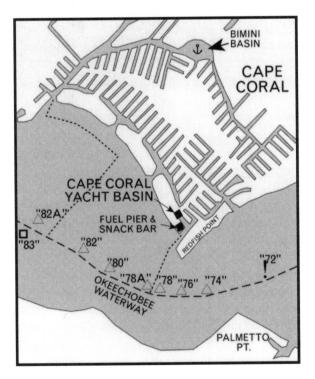

connections and power connections up to 50 amps. There are usually 6 to 10 slips open for transients. Given this limitation, advance reservations would be a wise precaution. Showers, a laundromat, and waste pump-out service are available. The city of Cape Coral leases out a fuel dock (gasoline and diesel fuel) alongside a small open-air snack bar that flanks the western side of the canal leading from the river to the dockage basin.

This city marina is set within the boundaries of a delightful city park. For a nominal fee visitors can make use of tennis courts and a large, heated swimming pool.

Cruisers can hike nine lo-o-ong blocks or, better yet, make use of the marina's free bike rentals or the city bus service to access a Publix supermarket, Eckerd Drugs, and liquor store in the main Cape Coral business district astride Cape Coral Parkway. You can also take a taxi (see below).

In this same business district, hungry visitors should make every effort to find their way to Mr. C's Restaurant (850 W Lafayette, 941-542-2001) or Sal's Just Pizza (910 Cape Coral Parkway, 941-540-7373). Both of these dining spots have been recommended to this writer by the city dockmaster.

Clearly the Cape Coral Yacht Basin has a lot to offer, particularly for a municipal facility. You can scarcely do better anywhere on this portion of the Caloosahatchee. Tell Paul we sent you!

Cape Coral Yacht Basin (941) 574-0809

Approach depth—5½-8 feet
Dockside depth— 5½-10 feet
Accepts transients—yes
Fixed wooden piers—yes
Dockside power connections—30 and 50 amp
Dockside water connections—yes
Waste pump-out—yes

Cape Coral Yacht Basin

Showers—yes
Laundromat—yes
Gasoline—yes
Diesel fuel—yes
Restaurant—long walk, medium bike ride, or
quick taxi away

Numbers to know in Cape Coral include:

Lou's Taxi—941-549-5272
Yellow Cab—941-495-3200
Avis Rental Cars—941-484-2227
Cape Coral Rent-a-Car—941-542-2025
Chamber of Commerce—941-549-6900

Gulf Harbour Yacht & Country Club (Okeechobee Standard Mile 143.5)

A glittering marina, condo complex, and golf club known as Gulf Harbour Yacht & Country Club overlooks the Caloosahatchee's southeasterly shoreline between unlighted daybeacon #74 and flashing daybeacon #73. The facility's well-marked entrance channel carries 6½- to 8-foot depths at MLW, and the passage is denoted by a tall, square "lighthouse," which displays a white light at night.

While transients are still welcome at Gulf Harbour, cruising visitors are now accepted on a space-available basis. This facility has become so popular that there is a waiting list for slip space. Call ahead of time to check on transient dockage availability.

Gulf Harbour's dockage basin has been dredged out behind a barrier island that separates the harbor from the main body of the Caloosahatchee. This arrangement affords excellent protection from foul weather for all vessels moored in this marina. The mainland shores are overlooked by a vast array of medium-rise condos.

All berths at Gulf Harbour feature fresh water and 30-, 50-, and 100-amp power hookups as well as telephone and cable television connections. Depths alongside run some 6½ feet at MLW. Each and every slip boasts its own waste pump-out connection. How's that for "full service"?

Both gasoline and diesel fuel are available at a fueling pier located in the heart of the dockage complex. Light mechanical servicing can be arranged through local, independent technicians by the friendly dockmaster and his staff.

First-class showers and a full laundromat are available shoreside in their own building overlooking the harbor. The dockmaster's office doubles as an extensive ship's and variety store.

One on-site restaurant, Johnny Brown's (941-433-5111), is easily accessible from the dockage basin. A long taxi ride into Fort Myers will be necessary to reach any additional dining choices (see below).

After paying a fee, visiting cruisers can take advantage of the marina's on-site swimming pool, exercise room, aerobics room, tennis courts, and golf course (all on a space-available basis).

Gulf Harbour also boasts its own charter operation. Vacation Yachts, Inc. (800-971-0101),

is a quickly growing operation that currently specializes in both multihull and monohull sailcraft. We were struck by the eager management's obvious commitment to providing the best-maintained craft possible to their clients. We suggest that you give Vacation Yachts a long, hard look when next your plans call for chartering a sailcraft in the Fort Myers region.

If you are looking for a bustling, full-service, high-energy marina along the length of the Caloosahatchee River, and dockage space happens to be available, your search is ended. Set your course for Gulf Harbour, and you will not be disappointed.

Gulf Harbour Yacht & Country Club (941) 437-0881

Approach depth—6½-8 feet (low water)
Dockside depth—6½ feet (low water)
Accepts transients—space-available basis (call ahead of time to check)
Concrete floating docks—yes
Dockside power connections—30, 50, and 100 amp
Dockside water connections—yes
Waste pump-out—yes (at every slip)
Showers—yes
Laundromat—yes
Gasoline—yes
Diesel fuel—yes
Mechanical repairs—yes (light repairs—independent technicians)
Ship's and variety store—yes
Restaurant—on site

Deep Lagoon Marina (Okeechobee Standard Mile 143.5)

Cruisers seeking entry to Deep Lagoon can break off from the main river channel between flashing daybeacons #73 and #72 and follow a rather confusing channel east and then south into the interior reaches of Deep Lagoon.

Since 1964, this body of water has played

host to a small pleasurecraft dockage facility and repair yard known as Deep Lagoon Marina. Now, the same good folks that we met at Naples who are redeveloping Turner Marine have taken over this property and are preparing to initiate a huge construction project. The resulting condo and marina complex will be known as Deep Lagoon Boat Club. The building process is slated to stretch over the next couple of years.

When complete, Deep Lagoon Boat Club will reportedly boast plentiful wet slip dockage (including spaces for transient visitors), a ship's store, full fuel dock, and "service center." The new owners have also advised this writer that there will be "over 60,000 square feet of marine-related retail, meeting rooms and offices, laundry and bathhouse facilities, pools, and social rooms."

Sounds impressive! We will report to you on Deep Lagoon Boat Club's progress in the next edition of our guide and in our on-line newsletter, *The Salty Southeast*. In the meantime, call 941-454-2628 for more information.

Until the eventual completion of Deep Lagoon Boat Club, there is little reason to enter the like-named body of water, unless you just want to explore or check out the progress of construction. If you do decide to visit the lagoon, expect entrance depths of 6 to 8 feet in the marked channel.

The Landings Yacht Club (Okeechobee Standard Mile 142.5)

The charted channel southeast of flashing daybeacon #70 serves the private dockage basin of The Landings Yacht Club (941-481-7181). This facility is associated with a huge condo development and does not accept visiting craft for dockage. The adjacent ship's (and variety) store and fuel dock (gas and

diesel fuel) are open to the public. Entrance depths run around 6 feet with 5- to 6-foot soundings dockside.

Cape Coral

Northeast of flashing daybeacon #70, captains and crew cruising up the Caloosahatchee will soon exchange greetings with the Cape Coral Bridge. Forty years ago, there was not even a small village at the modern-day site of Cape Coral. Today, the community numbers 48,000 citizens, making it the largest city on the Caloosahatchee. As you might have guessed, Cape Coral is the product of a development company which promoted the town as a "planned city" beginning in 1954.

In the fascinating book *The Rivers of Florida* (edited by Del and Marty Marth), George Lane, Jr., recalls the days before the coming of Cape Coral as seen through the eyes of an old fisherman: ". . . the fish once were so thick that you could nearly walk across their backs in the river. . . . Downriver (opposite Cape Coral) we'd see redfish feeding, and it would look like a hundred square yards of fish tails in the air." Sadly, those days are gone in the wake of rampant development.

Whiskey Creek Anchorage (Okeechobee Standard Mile 140)

Captains piloting boats less than 36 feet in length and drawing 4 feet or less will find an obscure anchorage on Whiskey Creek, southeast of unlighted daybeacon #66. While the channel is well marked with small, unlighted daybeacons, depths run as thin as 4½ feet.

Eventually, the stream takes a sharp swing to starboard and is soon crossed by a low-level, fixed bridge. Between the starboard turn and the bridge, visiting cruisers can anchor in 4½ feet of water amidst fairly numerous, but quite seemly private homes on both shores. Protection is excellent from all winds and should be sufficient for anything short of a full gale. The skimpy swinging room may call for a Bahamian mooring or even a stern anchor.

Paradise Yacht Club (Okeechobee Standard Mile 137)

Captains will discover Paradise Yacht Club (formerly Harbour Village Marina) along the Caloosahatchee's westerly banks, in the sheltered harbor to the west-northwest of unlighted daybeacon #58. This marina is now a 100 percent live-aboard facility with a waiting list. Transients are no longer accepted, only because there is no more space at the inn. If berths should become available anytime in the future, visiting cruisers will be gladly accommodated.

There are not many marinas left in all of Florida friendly to live-aboards, much less a facility that is populated almost exclusively with cruisers of this ilk. If you are seeking a good spot to spend a life on the water, get your name on the waiting list here right away. You could scarcely make a better choice than Paradise Yacht Club.

The yacht club's docks are composed of first-class, fixed wooden piers with good power and water connections. Minimum entrance depths now run in the 5-foot range, with some 5½ to 7 feet of water at dockside. Paradise no longer has a fuel dock, so gas up elsewhere. The marina features clean, non-climate controlled showers, a laundromat (with paperback exchange library—also not air-conditioned), and waste pump-out services. The only restaurant within walking distance is open for breakfast and lunch only. Of course, you could always take a taxi into nearby Cape Coral for your evening repast.

Through a special arrangement, patrons of Paradise Yacht Club may make use of a refreshing swimming pool and several tennis courts just across the street at Lockmoor Country Club. This is yet another great advantage for live-aboards berthing at this facility.

It's unfortunate that slip-space limitations will keep many cruisers from experiencing the delights of Paradise Yacht Club. On the other hand, if you are looking for a marina in which to live aboard for an extended period of time, this is "the" place in the Fort Myers, Caloosahatchee region.

Paradise Yacht Club (941) 997-1603

Approach depth—5 feet
Dockside depth—5½-7 feet
Accepts transients—limited—space-available basis
Fixed wooden piers—yes
Dockside power connections—30 and 50 amp
Dockside water connections—yes
Waste pump-out—yes
Showers—yes
Laundromat—yes

Caloosa Isle Marina (Okeechobee Standard Mile 136.5)

Caloosa Isle Marina, yet another of the Caloosahatchee, Fort Myers facilities, is found at the western terminus of the charted channel west of (32-foot) flashing daybeacon #C. Mechanical repairs for both diesel and gasoline engines and haul-outs via a 30-ton travelift are available.

Caloosa Isle is known for having a decent selection of parts at its ship's and variety store. A few transient berths may be available at the facility's fixed, wooden piers, but the number of wet slips is very limited. Advance reservations would be a very good idea indeed. Full power and water connections are found at each berth. Entrance depths run a meager 4 to 5 feet with 4-foot low-water dockside depths. Obviously, dockage at Caloosa Isle is pretty much confined to shallow-draft vessels. Gasoline is readily available, as is dry storage for smaller powercraft. The on-site Shucker's and Company Crabhouse (941-995-7001) is now open for all three meals of the day, and it seems popular with the local crowd.

Caloosa Isle Marina (941) 656-1700

Approach depth—4-5 feet
Dockside depth—4 feet
Accepts transients—limited
Fixed wooden piers—yes
Dockside power connections—30 and 50 amp
Dockside water connections—yes
Showers—yes
Laundromat—yes
Gasoline—yes

Mechanical repairs—yes
Below-waterline repairs—yes
Ship's and variety store—yes
Restaurant—on site

Royal Palm Yacht Club (Okeechobee Standard Mile 135.5)

The channel leading to the breakwater-enclosed harbor of Royal Palm Yacht Club cuts southeast between flashing daybeacon #54 and unlighted daybeacon #52. Good entrance depths of 7-8 feet lead to an occluded entrance marked by arrows painted on the breakwater. Inside the harbor, cruisers will find depths of 6 to 7 feet at fixed wooden slips (some set against the concrete breakwater). Members of other yacht clubs with reciprocal privileges are gladly accepted for guest dockage. The dockmaster is on duty from 8:00 A.M. to 3:00 P.M., Tuesday through Sunday. The

Royal Palm Yacht Club, Fort Myers

club's slips feature both 30- and 50-amp power connections, as well as water connections. Shoreside visitors will discover good showers in the clubhouse. Lunch and dinner are served in the main dining room Tuesday through Sunday. A convenience store is located two blocks to the north on McGregor Boulevard. The Fort Myers contingent of the notable Chart House Restaurant (2024 W First Street, 941-332-1881) can be reached by a three-block walk.

This writer gained the swift and sure impression that Royal Palm is a very active club that is quite friendly to visiting cruisers from other clubs. If you are lucky enough to have the appropriate credentials, then by all means give this facility your most serious consideration.

Royal Palm Yacht Club (941) 334-2176
   http://www.royal-palm-yacht-club.org/

Approach depth—7-8 feet
Dockside depth—6-7 feet
Accepts transients—members of other yacht
   clubs with reciprocal privileges only
Fixed wooden piers—yes
Dockside power connections—30 and 50 amp
Dockside water connections—yes
Showers—yes
Restaurant—on site and nearby

Marina Town Yacht Club (Okeechobee Standard Mile 135.5)

The long, charted channel leading northwest from unlighted daybeacon #52 to Hancock Creek serves one of the finest facilities on the Caloosahatchee. Marina Town Yacht Club eagerly accepts transients at fixed wooden piers and slips set against a concrete seawall with water connections and power connections up to 100 amps! Currently only two slips are kept open full time for transients, but the dockmaster has informed this writer that three of four other resident boats are almost always absent, and visitors can be accommodated in these berths as well. Call ahead of time to check on berth availability.

Marina Town's harbor is very well protected and would be a good place to ride out heavy weather before venturing out into the open Gulf. Minimum entrance and dockside depths run around 5 feet, with many soundings ranging from 6 to 8 feet. Good (non-climate controlled) showers and an on-site laundromat are readily available, as is a waste pump-out facility. Mechanical repairs of both the gas and diesel varieties are readily available on-site by way of Gulf Coast Yacht Services (941-997-8822). This firm also maintains a small ship's store in the complex just behind the docks. Still not enough for you? Well, let's throw in a cooling swimming pool and tennis courts. Several supermarkets, drugstores, and motels are all within a three-block walk.

OK, so now you want to stay awhile. You're in luck. Surprisingly enough, Marina Town caters to live-aboards, which is an all-too-occasional rarity along the present-day Western Florida coastline.

When it comes time to slake a healthy appetite, Marina Town features not one, but two dockside restaurants. Mariners Inn Restaurant (941-997-8300) changed hands in 1999, and the new owners seem intent on raising this dining spot from its former mediocrity. Sneaker's Restaurant (941-997-7110) is located in the building adjacent to Mariners Inn. While we have not yet had a chance to dine here, the knowledgeable dockmaster has assured us that it provides a worthy alternative.

Cruisers intent on chartering a sail or powercraft to explore the Western Florida coastline can do themselves a big favor by

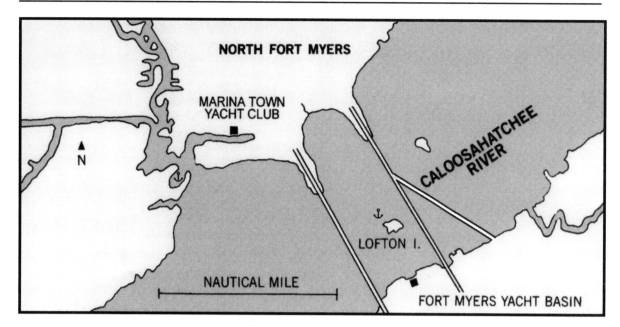

contacting Southwest Florida Yachts (800-262-7939), based at Marina Town Yacht Club. The firm's power charter fleet is found at this facility. A sailcraft fleet is maintained at Burnt Store Marina on Charlotte Harbor (see below). Tell Captains Vic or Barb that we sent you.

Marina Town Yacht Club (941) 997-2767

Approach depth—5-8 feet
Dockside depth—5-6 feet
Accepts transients—yes
Fixed wooden slips—yes
Dockside power connections—up to 100 amp
Dockside water connections—yes
Waste pump-out—yes
Showers—yes
Laundromat—yes
Mechanical repairs—yes
Ship's store—yes
Restaurant—2 on site

Hancock Creek Anchorage (Okeechobee Standard Mile 135.5)

Skippers piloting boats 34 feet and smaller, which draw 4½ feet (or preferably a little less), can track their way to a small but very secure anchorage on Hancock Creek, within shouting distance of Marina Town. At unlighted daybeacon #26, the Marina Town approach channel swings sharply to the north. Cruisers looking to anchor off can instead swing to the south-southwest and enter the small, charted cove indenting Hancock Creek's southerly banks. Low-water depths do run as thin as 5 feet, and swinging room is somewhat limited. On the other hand, you won't find better shelter anywhere. A few private homes overlook the rear section of the cove, but their lush green lawns stretching down to the water only add to this haven's appeal.

The best place to anchor is found on the rear (southwesterly) third of the cove's length. There is a bit more swinging room here than at the creek's entrance. If you can fit the somewhat stringent size and draft requirements, this is a great place to spend the evening.

Centennial Harbour Marina (Okeechobee Standard Mile 135.5)

The enclosed, well-protected dockage basin of Fort Myers' newest pleasurecraft facility guards the Caloosahatchee's southeasterly banks, southeast of flashing daybeacon #49. Centennial Harbour Marina opened for business in 1999 with a whole raft of ultra-modern, concrete decked floating piers. Even more slips are slated for the future.

The marina's scantily marked entrance channel carries 7 to 8 feet of water, while soundings of 6½ to 8 feet are typical in the breakwater-enclosed dockage basin. Transients are eagerly accepted, as well as large cruising groups. Full power and water connections are readily available dockside, as is waste pump-out service. Diesel fuel delivery can be arranged by way of a shoreside fuel truck for vessels requiring a goodly amount of petrol in the tank.

Climate-controlled showers and a full laundromat are located in the dockmaster's building just behind the dockage basin. Here you will also find a small variety store and a most welcome e-mail hookup. On-line cruisers, and that's now most of us, will be ever so glad of this feature. The Chart House Restaurant mentioned above is located immediately adjacent to this marina, while Shooters Waterfront Cafe (2220 W First Street, 941-334-2727) is a scant two blocks away. The entire Fort Myers business district is easily accessible by foot or a very quick taxi ride.

There can be no argument that Centennial Harbour is a wonderful addition to the Fort Myers cruising scene. With its plentiful dockage combined with the municipal marina's prodigious wet slip space (see below), transient space in and near downtown Fort Myers is now quite impressive indeed.

Centennial Harbour Marina (941) 461-0775
Approach depth—7-8 feet
Dockside depth—6½-8 feet
Accepts transients—yes
Floating concrete piers—yes
Dockside power connections—30 and 50 amp
Dockside water connections—yes
Waste pump-out—yes
Showers—yes
Laundromat—yes
Variety store—small
Restaurant—next door and several nearby

Fort Myers Yacht Basin (Okeechobee Standard Mile 135)

Three bridges span the Caloosahatchee northeast of the Marina Town channel. Well, at least on the water it looks like three bridges. Contrary to its depiction on chart 11427, the easternmost "Edison Memorial Bridge" actually forms a Y pattern from the middle of the river to its southeasterly terminus. To captains and crew sighting the spans from their cockpits or flybridges, the Edison span appears to be two separate bridges. Coupled with the more downstream Caloosahatchee/Highway 41 Bypass Bridge, there are now, for all practical purposes, "three" bridges crossing the combined paths of the Caloosahatchee and the Okeechobee Waterway in downtown Fort Myers.

Fort Myers Yacht Basin guards the southeasterly banks between the first and second (moving west to east) river bridges. The marina actually encompasses two protected dockage basins, as well as a long face dock fronting directly onto the river. This facility features 276 slips. While extensive space is always reserved for transients, advance reservations might be a wise course of action.

Visitors will find just about every type of dockage imaginable. Some slips are composed

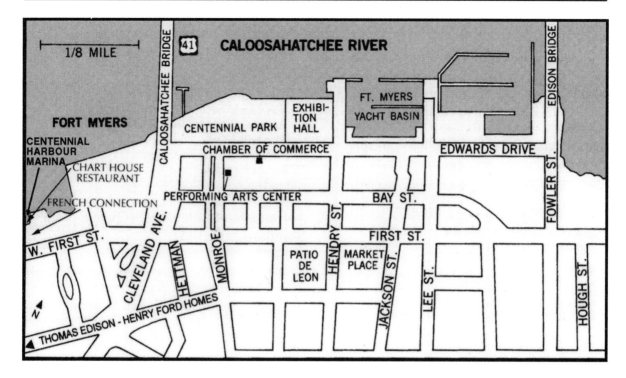

of wooden pilings set out from the concrete breakwater, while the eastern basin features a set of concrete floating docks reserved for smaller craft. All are absolutely first rate berths with 30-, 50-, and now some 100-amp power and water connections. While especially large pleasurecraft sometimes have to be moored to the outer face dock, the two breakwater-enclosed basins provide better protection and are much to be preferred. Dockside depths in the east basin run about 7 feet, with soundings of 6 to 7 feet encountered in the west-side harbor. The outer face dock boasts at least 10 feet of water.

The marina ship's store, dockmaster's office, air-conditioned showers, clean bathrooms, laundromat, and boat brokerage occupy a good-sized building set between the two dockage basins. The ship's store at Fort Myers Yacht Basin (941-334-6446) is now privately leased and well stocked with not only nautical but convenience-store-type food items as well.

Gasoline (both 89 and 93 octane grades available) and diesel fuel can be purchased at a fuel pier on the Caloosahatchee immediately in front of the dockmaster's building (between the two dockage basins). Free waste pump-out is also offered.

Visitors to Fort Myers Yacht Basin will find themselves a short step from the many attractions of downtown Fort Myers (see discussion below). A host of hotels, car rental agencies, grocery stores, and other shoreside businesses of all descriptions are a short stroll or taxi ride away.

The huge Amtel Towers overlooks the marina and offers "world-class dining." A branch of the redoubtable Chart House restaurant chain (2024 W First Street, 941-332-1881) is also within walking distance, as is the French Connection (2288 First Street, 941-332-4443), both recommended by the local marina staff. Shooters Waterfront Cafe (2220 W First Street, 941-334-2727) is close by too. There is no longer a downtown grocery store accessible by foot, but you can easily take a taxi to and from one of the local supermarkets.

Fort Myers Yacht Basin (941) 334-8271

Approach depth—8-10 feet
Dockside depth—10 feet (fuel and face dock)
           7 feet (east basin)
           6-7 feet (west basin)
Accepts transients—yes
Fixed wooden and concrete docks—yes
Floating concrete docks—yes

Fort Myers Yacht Basin

Dockside power connections—up to 100 amp
Dockside water connections—yes
Waste pump-out—yes
Showers—yes
Laundromat—yes
Gasoline—yes
Diesel fuel—yes
Mechanical repairs—arranged through local
    independent contractors
Ship's and variety store—yes
Restaurant—many nearby

Lofton Island Anchorage (Okeechobee Standard Mile 135)

We are happy to report that the city of Fort Myers has recently begun to welcome cruisers at an officially sanctioned city anchorage behind charted Lofton Island. This small body of land lies along the charted channel's northerly flank, opposite Fort Myers Yacht Basin.

The only real problem about entering the Lofton Island haven lies in the incorrect charting of the Edison Memorial Bridge, as discussed above. To hold good entrance depths of 7½ feet or better, captains should favor the westerly face of the west-side Edison span. Unfortunately this portion of the bridge remains uncharted on 11427. On the water, though, it's fairly obvious. Be sure to read the navigational account of this anchorage presented below before attempting first-time entry.

After traversing its unmarked entrance cut, cruising craft can curl around behind (north and northwest of) Lofton Island on the broad, correctly charted patch of 7- and 8-foot waters. For maximum shelter, drop anchor as the body of Lofton Island comes abeam to the south. Stay at least 50 yards off the isle's shoreline.

Lofton Island anchorage, Fort Myers

Protection is good from southerly blows, courtesy of the lee afforded by Lofton Island, and there is some shelter to the north from the mainland shores. This is most certainly, however, *not* a foul-weather hideyhole. Nevertheless, when winds aren't too ornery, this is a good spot to spend the evening, and it has the distinct advantage of being within shouting distance of downtown Fort Myers.

Downtown Fort Myers

Numbers to know in Fort Myers include:

Bluebird Cab—941-275-8294

Preferred Taxi—941-334-0000
Yellow Cab of Fort Myers—941-334-9999
Yellow Cab—941-332-1055
Avis Rental Cars—941-768-2022
Budget Rent A Car—941-765-0480
Hertz Rent A Car—941-768-3100
Boat/U S Marine Center—941-481-7447
E&B Marine—941-275-5939
West Marine—941-275-6077
Chamber of Commerce—941-332-3624

Within the last decade Fort Myers has done a magnificent job renovating its downtown waterfront. Where once old wharves and crumbling warehouses stood, cruising visitors will now find a lovely green park, an arts center, a convention complex, and the local Chamber of Commerce. All of these attractions are located within walking distance of the city marina on Edwards Drive. You might also take the time to stroll down First Street through the main downtown business district. It will soon be obvious that business is returning to this section of the city.

One cannot visit Fort Myers without getting the deep impression of a warm welcome and a general air of friendliness. It's no secret among my friends that Fort Myers is one of this writer's favorite cities in Western Florida. I hope you too will have the opportunity to make the acquaintance of this unique town that Thomas Edison adopted.

Fort Myers History Fort Myers was established along the banks of the Caloosahatchee after the Seminole Indian wars in 1850. It was abandoned shortly thereafter, but again saw service during the Civil War. With the river serving as a ready source of transportation and commerce, the village of Fort Myers began growing about 1868, and the town was finally incorporated in 1911.

Beginning in the late 1800s Fort Myers played host to three giants of American science and industry. Thomas Alva Edison, perhaps America's greatest scientist, came south to the city by the Caloosahatchee searching for a healthful winter climate. He fell in love with Fort Myers and returned every winter for the rest of his days.

The energetic scientist soon bought a lot by the river and began to design his winter residence. The house was built in sections in Fairfield, Maine. The various components were then transported by two sailing schooners to Fort Myers, where they were assembled in 1886. This was one of the first prefabricated homes in the United States.

An extensive laboratory was added so that Edison could continue his scientific work while in residence. A swimming pool was built, braced with native bamboo rather than the usual steel rods. It was filled by an artesian well that was 1,100 feet deep.

Before long Edison managed to convince his friends Henry Ford and Harvey Firestone to share his winter quarters in Fort Myers. Ford eventually built a home next door to Edison, and the two remained fast friends until the great scientist's death.

While wintering in Fort Myers, Edison dreamed up the notion of manufacturing synthetic rubber from Florida's native goldenrod weed. With the financial backing of both Ford and Firestone, Edison managed to produce a new strain of the weed which grew to an astonishing 14 feet in height. History suggests that these experiments led to the modern-day production of synthetic rubber, without which automobile transportation would be impractical at best.

Thomas Edison loved tropical plants and was interested in the by-products that might be derived from them. Over the years he established an elaborate botanical garden at his Fort Myers home containing more than 1,000 plants from around the world. In one instance he planted a 2-inch (diameter) banyan tree that Harvey Firestone brought him from India. That same tree survives to this day and the circumference of its trunk has increased to 400 feet.

Edison loved automobiles. Henry Ford presented a gift to his neighbor in 1907 of a prototype Model T Ford. For the next twenty years, Ford had his engineers add the latest updates to the car every twelve months. Edison refused to part with the original model for a newer version.

Today, both the Thomas Edison and Henry Ford homes (2350 McGregor Boulevard, 941-334-3614) have been preserved and are open to the public. The scientist's homeplace has been left just as it was upon Edison's death. The rooms are filled with memorabilia, including the phonographs, brass lamps, and car-bon-filament light bulbs designed by Edison himself. The old laboratory is still intact and immensely impressive. A collection of antique cars is also on display, including Edison's 1908 Cadillac Opera Coupe, prototype Model T Ford, and a 1936 Brewster limousine.

All cruising and landlubber visitors to Fort Myers should make every effort to tour these two historic homes for themselves. They are open from 9:00 A.M. to 4:00 P.M. weekdays, and Sunday afternoons as well.

CALOOSAHATCHEE RIVER NAVIGATION

Navigation of the Caloosahatchee can certainly not be described as the proverbial piece of cake. Unlike many Floridian rivers, shoal water is rife on the Caloosahatchee, often abutting the marked channel. Cruising navigators, particularly those visiting this stream for the first time, must proceed with due caution and deliberation. Keep chart 11427 and the information contained in this account handy at all times to quickly resolve any confusion. Maintain a closer than usual watch on the sounder, and you should catch sight of the soaring towers of Fort Myers with good water still under your keel.

It would serve little purpose to outline every single shoal near the river's main channel in the account below. It would require page after page, and you can certainly read chart 11427 as well as this writer. We will therefore only review those waters of critical concern and the instances where my on-site research showed the chart to be in error.

Sidewaters along the Caloosahatchee are usually well marked. Even so, the channels often wind and intersect other cuts. Care is again called for when navigating the various gunkholes along the way.

The prolific markers denoting the river's various side channels can give rise to unexpected difficulties when cruising the main body of the Caloosahatchee. It's often all too easy to mistake some of the markers on these alternate cuts for those stretched along the main channel. Have your binoculars ready to help sort out any confusion.

While we are discussing side channels, it should be noted that a majority of the charted cuts appearing on chart 11427 serve only private docks in residential neighborhoods. Most of these passages are only of the most minimal interest to visiting cruisers.

Well, let's push on up the Caloosahatchee's appealing path to Fort Myers. There are more than a few sights for us to enjoy along the way.

Entry into the Caloosahatchee River
Come abeam of flashing daybeacon #101 at the river's mouth to its northwesterly

side. Cut to the northeast and point to come abeam of and pass unlighted daybeacon #99 to its northwesterly side. From this point on, skippers cruising upstream (eastbound) on the Caloosahatchee should take all green markers to their (the cruisers') starboard side and all red beacons to port.

From #101 to #99, captains can make use of the charted range. The forward marker is found north of #99. Westbound mariners can also use a similar range anchored with flashing daybeacon #96 as its forward marker.

At #99 passing cruisers should take note of an idle-speed, no-wake zone which extends upstream for 1.4 miles. This restriction comes to an end near flashing daybeacon #89. The regulation is apparently in place to protect manatees, though the speed limit signs lack the usual manatee designations. There are certainly no docks or private property on these waters to worry with.

Northeast of unlighted daybeacon #99, the river channel is flanked by two long islands to the northwest and the Punta Rassa mainland to the southeast. This is a sheltered portion of the Waterway, but the channel is narrow and currents can run quite swiftly. Stay alert and watch for leeway.

East of flashing daybeacon #96, the river's first anchorage opportunity, albeit a limited one, will come abeam to the southeast.

Shell Point Anchorage   Entry into the anchorage west of Shell Point is complicated by the unmarked (but charted) underwater rock flanking the westerly side of the entrance and the tongue of 1-foot water to

the east. To avoid these treacherous hazards, continue cruising upstream (east) past flashing daybeacon #96 on the main river channel for some 200 yards. Then cut sharply to the south and cruise into the mouth of the cove. Be sure to drop the hook at the cove's entrance. Farther to the south, depths rise markedly.

On the Caloosahatchee River   East of flashing daybeacon #96, the river channel cuts a bit to the south and heads past unlighted daybeacon #94 near Shell Point. East of #94, a whole collection of markers impinges upon the main cut. The daybeacons ranging to the south serve local craft, while the marked channel cutting northwest into Glover Bight, past Cattle Dock Point, serves a first-class marina and a BAIL anchorage.

Cruisers following the main river channel should point to pass unlighted daybeacons #93A and #93 to their northerly sides. Past #93, use your binoculars to pick out the low-lying, unlighted nun buoy #92 well ahead. This aid marks a sunken wreck. Favor the southerly side of the channel when passing #92.

Tarpon Point Marina & Glover Bight Anchorage (BAIL-Suggested)   Be sure to pass unlighted daybeacon #92 (currently charted as unlighted nun buoy #92) when cruising east before turning into the Glover Bight channel. Turn hard to the northwest and point to pass the channel's first aid, unlighted daybeacon #1, to port. From this point on, follow the old, faithful red, right, returning rule into the marina.

Continue on, pointing to pass unlighted daybeacon #2 to starboard. This portion of the track will bring you pretty close to the shores of Cattle Dock Point. Don't worry—good depths seem to run quite close to this shoreline.

The entire Glover Bight channel is now a minimum-wake zone. Power captains should slow to non-planing speed all the way in to the marina docks.

Continue following the markers outlining the winding channel until you are abeam of unlighted daybeacon #9. At this point, break off from the marked track and set course to the north-northeast for the marina entrance, which will be spied dead ahead. As you cruise into the marina, watch to your starboard side for the fuel dock. The marina office is located at the rear of the harbor.

To anchor on the northeasterly waters of Glover Bight, depart the marina entrance channel once abeam of unlighted daybeacon #9. Work your way carefully to the northeast, favoring the northwesterly shores slightly. This maneuver will serve to avoid the correctly charted shallows abutting the southeasterly shoreline. Be sure to drop the hook before cruising to within less than 200 yards of the cove's northeasterly tip.

The charted markers continue past Glover Bight hard by the northern shoreline into a series of canals. There are no facilities, and there really isn't even room to anchor on these small streams. Those intrepid explorers who just have to see it all should be sure to follow the starboard cut at the first *T*-intersection in the canals. The port branch is quite shoal.

St. Charles Yacht Club Channel   The partially charted channel leading to the protected St. Charles Yacht Club dockage basin breaks off to the south about halfway between flashing daybeacon #89 and unlighted daybeacon #86. A sign at the northern head of this passage identifies the channel as the St. Charles Yacht Club cut. There are actually far more markers outlining this channel than are depicted on the latest edition of chart 11427. The presence of these numerous aids renders navigation of this cut a snap. Just pass all red markers to your starboard side and take green, odd-numbered beacons to port. What could be simpler?

Eventually the channel will swing sharply to starboard as you enter the inner basin. Soon the yacht club's docks will come abeam to port.

On the Caloosahatchee River   East of flashing daybeacon #89, the river channel bypasses two shoals flanking both sides of the cut by passing south of unlighted daybeacon #86 and north of unlighted #85. The channel running to the north abeam of #86 is one of the local cuts servicing resident craft.

Bimini Basin Anchorage (BAIL-Suggested) To visit the sheltered, BAIL-suggested anchorage in Bimini Basin, break off from the main Caloosahatchee channel east of unlighted daybeacon #83 and follow the marked (and charted) channel to the north-northwest. As you would expect, take all red beacons to your starboard side and green markers to port. After passing the last of the south-to-north markers, you will approach the northerly banks and sight a broad entrance to a series of canals. This is *not* the route to Bimini Basin.

Instead, turn to the west (don't cut this corner too sharply) and keeping the charted, unlighted red daybeacons off your port side, work your way around the shore until coming abeam of unlighted daybeacon #16. You should then cut north into the canal that is (almost) abeam of this aid.

Continue following the main canal, ignoring all the various side branches, until the main stream turns slightly to the north, northeast. At this point the canal splits in a Y intersection. Follow the northeasterly branch to the basin.

Study chart 11427 for a moment and these seemingly complex maneuvers will seem far clearer. Drop the hook anywhere you choose in the basin. Do not attempt to land anywhere except along the shores of the public park.

On the Caloosahatchee River The Caloosahatchee channel between #86 and flashing daybeacon #72 is rife with shoals abutting the channel. Chart 11427 even warns of "Rocks" near unlighted daybeacon #84. This writer didn't try to find them, but conversations with local captains indicate they are indeed down there. Slow down and be absolutely sure of the proper course before cruising ahead.

A charted range south of unlighted daybeacon #78 may help navigators keep to the channel, which runs south of unlighted daybeacon #80. At #80, the channel turns ever so slightly to the north.

Between unlighted daybeacons #80 and #78, unlighted daybeacon #78A has been placed along the channel's northwesterly edge. Be sure to pass #78A to its fairly immediate southeasterly side. Don't stray too far to the southeast or you could wander into the charted shallows south of #78.

Be sure to come abeam of and pass unlighted daybeacon #78 to its immediate southeasterly side. As chart 11427 correctly forecasts, 3- and 4-foot water flanks the southeastern side of the channel between the forward range marker and #78.

Cape Coral Yacht Basin Enter Cape Coral Yacht Basin by abandoning the river channel some 25 to 50 yards southwest of unlighted daybeacon #78. Set course for the mid-width of the canal west of Redfish Point. Along the way you will pass between unlighted daybeacons #1 and #2, then between #3 and #4. After you leave #3 and #4 in your wake, the long Cape Coral fishing pier will come abeam to port. At this point marked channels serving local docks cut to the east and west. Ignore these cuts and cruise into the mid-width of the canal dead ahead.

As you enter the canal, the fuel dock will come abeam to port, followed by the main harbor farther upstream in the charted, squared-off cove also to port.

On the Caloosahatchee River Flashing daybeacon #73 denotes the channel's southeastern edge between unlighted daybeacon #74 and flashing daybeacon #72. This aid to navigation marks the charted tongue of 4-foot shallows abutting the channel. Obviously, you should pass northwest of #73.

Watch for the charted 2-foot shoal southeast of flashing daybeacon #72. Be sure to pass #72 close by its southeasterly side. Cruisers may choose to enter the channel leading to Deep Lagoon short of #72.

Gulf Harbour Yacht & Country Club   The marked entrance channel leading to the Gulf Harbour dockage basin cuts southeast between unlighted daybeacon #74 and flashing daybeacon #73. Use your binoculars to pick out the outermost channel markers, flashing daybeacons #1 and #2. Should you have any trouble (and you probably won't) locating this channel, look for a tall, beige, square-towered "lighthouse" towering over the southeastern shoreline. This tower guards the harbor entrance's southwesterly flank and displays a white light at night.

Set a course from the main river channel, designed to cruise directly between #1 and #2. After leaving these markers in your wake, pick out unlighted daybeacons #3 and #4 ahead. As you pass between #3 and #4, your course will lead you between the arms of twin stone breakwaters. Soon this track will pass into a sheltered harbor behind a barrier island. A long series of small, red unlighted daybeacons denotes a shelf of shallow water jutting out for a short distance from the southeast shore of the barrier island. Pass all these aids to navigation by at least 10 yards to your starboard side.

Continue cruising into the heart of the basin. The dockmaster's office overlooks the harbor's southeasterly shores in the middle of the complex.

Deep Lagoon   This channel is complicated by the presence of several local side cuts which do not appear on the current edition of chart 11427. To enter, break off from the Caloosahatchee some 300 yards southwest of flashing daybeacon #72. Set course to pass between the westernmost aids on the Deep Lagoon channel, unlighted daybeacons #1 and #2. Continue cruising straight ahead. Soon you will spot a small channel cutting off to starboard. Ignore this local passage and maintain your course to the east.

After cruising a bit farther into the stream's mouth, watch for a red and green junction daybeacon. Channels radiate out to port and starboard, as well as straight ahead, from this aid. To reach the future site of Deep Lagoon Boat Club, pass the junction daybeacon to your port side and cut sharply into the starboard-side (southward-running) channel. A group of mostly uncharted aids will bring you abeam of the new complex.

On the Caloosahatchee River   The main river channel begins its approach to the Cape Coral fixed bridge northeast of flashing daybeacon #72. As you cruise to flashing daybeacon #70, the marked channel to The Landings will be passed southeast of your course, while a host of local channels may be spied to the northwest.

The Cape Coral span has a vertical clearance of 55 feet. Sailcraft that need more height must forego visiting Fort Myers and cruising the remainder of the Okeechobee Waterway (which, incidentally, has one bridge east of Lake

Okeechobee with a vertical clearance of only 49 feet).

Northeast of the Cape Coral bridge, the channel remains straightforward, with nothing but local cuts flanking the river as far as unlighted daybeacon #68. From this aid, captains who pilot vessels drawing 4 feet or less may choose to enter and anchor in Whiskey Creek on the southeastern shore.

Whiskey Creek Anchorage   Set course from unlighted daybeacon #68 to pass between the outermost set of markers on the Whiskey Creek channel, unlighted daybeacons #1 and #2. This entire cut is an idle-speed manatee zone. All craft should proceed strictly at slow speed.

After passing the last red daybeacon to your starboard side (did you remember "red, right, returning"?), the creek cuts sharply to starboard. You will spy the charted, low-level fixed bridge dead ahead. Anchor on the mid-width between the starboard turn and the bridge.

On the Caloosahatchee River   Shallow water flanks the main channel to the northwest between unlighted daybeacons #68 and #64. East and northeast of this point, good water opens out on both sides of the passage for the most part to unlighted daybeacon #60.

The Caloosahatchee's newest, fixed high-rise bridge spans the river northeast of unlighted daybeacon #62. This span has a vertical clearance of 55 feet.

Cruisers choosing to visit Paradise Yacht Club can depart the main channel at unlighted daybeacon #58 and follow the marina's markers to the western banks. The harbor entrance lies immediately northwest of the innermost markers, unlighted daybeacons #18 and #19.

North-northeast of unlighted daybeacon #60, shallow water abuts a goodly portion of the river channel's westerly flank. Watch for leeway. You can use the charted range (both of its markers are charted as "#C") to help avoid the shallows.

Cruisers heading for Caloosa Isle Marina should leave the river channel south of the 32-foot, flashing daybeacon #C and set course for the outer markers. Once in between these prolific aids, favor the southerly side of the marked cut. This channel seems to be shoaling on its northern and northeasterly sides.

At flashing daybeacon #54, the main river channel begins to bend around to the northeast and heads on towards the Caloosahatchee fixed bridge. Short of the span, cruisers can access Royal Palm Yacht Club by the easy-to-follow channel cutting southeast, visit Marina Town to the northwest, or check out the new Centennial Harbour Marina guarding the southeasterly banks at flashing daybeacon #49.

Marina Town Yacht Club & Hancock Creek   The southeasternmost markers on the Marina Town-Hancock Creek channel sit close by the Caloosahatchee channel's northwestern flank, just northeast of unlighted daybeacon #52. The multitude of markers will carry you safely across the charted bar and in towards the northwestern banks. Close to shore, the channel takes a hard jog to starboard and eventually leads into the interior reaches of Hancock Creek.

To make good your entry into Marina Town Yacht Club, continue following the marked cut and watch for a broad offshoot cutting off to the north at unlighted daybeacons #25 and #26. Enter this stream by passing between #25 and #26. Continue along its mid-width as the canal flows through a sharp turn to the east. The marina docks will soon be obvious on the port-side shore.

Cruisers who choose to anchor in the small cove south-southwest of unlighted daybeacons #25 and #26 should depart the marked channel before passing between these two markers. Instead, cut sharply to the south-southwest and enter the mid-line of the small cove that you will sight dead ahead. For maximum swinging room, continue on the centerline into the rear third of the cove's waters. Remember, depths can run as thin as 5 feet in this anchorage.

Centennial Harbour Marina The break-water-enclosed dockage basin of Centennial Harbour Marina guards the Caloosahatchee's southeasterly banks between flashing daybeacon #49 and the Caloosahatchee fixed bridge. The basin's entrance is found along its upstream (northeasterly) side. The wet slips currently available line the southwesterly portion of the harbor.

On to Fort Myers East- and westbound skippers alike should take great care while cruising along the channel southwest of the Caloosahatchee fixed bridge. Shallow water abuts the cut on its northwestern side, and it's pretty doggone easy to confuse the markers on the Marina Town passage with the main channel's aids to navigation. *Be sure* to come abeam of and pass unlighted daybeacon #52 to its southeasterly side and continue on straight to the bridge's central pass-through, favoring the southeastern side of the channel. Along the way, pass flashing daybeacon #49 to its fairly immediate northwesterly side.

As you approach this fixed span, slow down. Numerous signs warn that the entire stretch between the three Fort Myers bridges is an idle-speed, no-wake zone. The Florida Marine Patrol is known for its vigilance on these waters. All vessels should proceed strictly at slow speed.

The Caloosahatchee/Highway 41 Bypass fixed bridge has a vertical clearance of 55 feet. After leaving the span behind, you will observe a cool, airy park on the southeastern shores, followed by the Fort Myers Yacht Basin.

Fort Myers Bridge Confusion As mentioned earlier in this chapter, navigation of the Fort Myers waterfront has been confused by the incorrect charting of the Edison Memorial Bridge. This span crosses the Caloosahatchee a short jog east-northeast of Fort Myers Yacht Basin.

If you were flying above this bridge in a helicopter, it would be quickly apparent that the span now forms an almost perfect Y. As the bridge crosses the river from northwest to southeast, it splits about halfway across the river, and by the time the divergent spans reach the southeasterly banks, they are far enough apart to actually appear to be two separate spans. So, as stated earlier, there are actually three bridges across the main Caloosahatchee channel adjacent to the downtown Fort Myers waterfront. Both spans of the Edison bridge are fixed structures and feature 56 feet of vertical clearance.

All this would not be a real problem, except that the charting folks at NOAA have not yet caught on to this bridge arrangement. The latest edition of chart 11427 still depicts the Edison bridge as a single span. Actually, the chart is picturing only the easternmost of the two Edison bridges. Sighhh, when will NOAA get on the ball?

This chapter's coverage of the Caloosahatchee ends at the Edison bridges. A continuing account of the upper Caloosahatchee and the Okeechobee Waterway can be found in my *Cruising Guide to Eastern Florida*.

Lofton Island Anchorage The mischarting of the Edison bridge is a real problem for those making use of the city-sanctioned anchorage behind Lofton Island. For best depths, cruisers should depart the main river channel immediately west of the uncharted, westerly span of the Edison bridge. Cruise to the north-northwest, keeping the bridge about 25 yards off your starboard side. Shallower water lies off Lofton Island's easterly shoreline, so best depths can be maintained by heavily favoring the bridge's westerly face. Similarly, soundings off the western shores of Lofton Island are quite thin.

Eventually, after tracking your way north-northwest just off the Edison bridge's westerly face, you will come abeam of the correctly charted, broad ribbon of deeper water that stretches to the southwest. Turn to port and follow these good depths to a point some 50 yards off Lofton Island's northerly banks. Here you will find plenty of room to anchor. Chances are that you will already find several fellow craft ensconced in this haven.

Pine Island Sound

If it weren't for the difference in the color and depth of the water, and the lack of island vegetation and stilted houses along the shores, this writer could almost think of a cruise through Pine Island Sound as a sojourn amidst the northern Abaco chain in the Bahamas. Even with all the obvious differences, there is that same feel of adventure mixed with myriad gunkholing and anchorage possibilities. As the story of our cruising couple at the beginning of this chapter points out, it's an easy place to wander off and forget that the rest of the world is out there. In short, Pine Island Sound comprises some of the most wonderful cruising grounds in Western Florida.

Pine Island Sound's southern reaches are bordered to the west by the long body of Sanibel Island. This isle was reviewed in the first section of this chapter. To the east, the lightly developed shores of Pine Island are a delight, as well as a reminder of a colorful past.

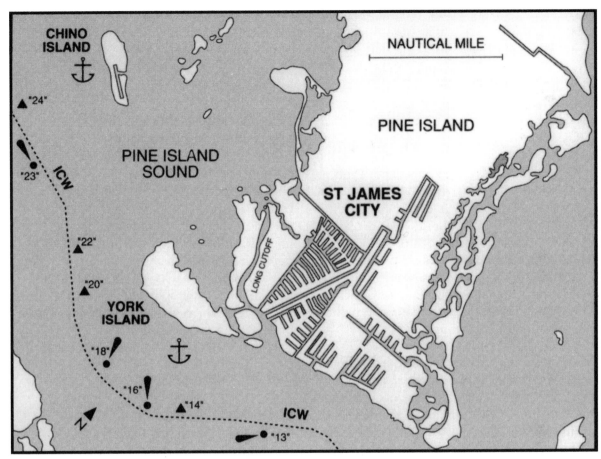

North of Sanibel, Captiva and North Captiva islands offer marina facilities and a few possible overnight anchorages. The various passes between these islands are unmarked and tricky for strangers.

Cayo Costa is completely in its natural state and will be preserved in the foreseeable future as a state park. Cruisers should make every effort to visit this wonderland of white sand beaches, lush scrub growth, and maritime forests. There are at least two good anchorages along its length and the fabulous inn at Cabbage Key is also within striking distance.

In addition to these larger bodies of land, Pine Island Sound is peppered with many smaller islands. The majority (though not all) of these islets are wildlife preserves and landing is not permitted. Many species of birds use these small islands as nesting grounds. The hundreds of birds and dozens of species present are truly magnificent. The National Park Service requests that cruising craft stay at least 50 yards offshore from these protected beaches. It's just possible that a closer approach could scare nesting birds violently out of their nests, possibly causing injury to their young.

Feel free to look from a safer distance, however. Have your binoculars ready! Pine Island Sound is a Mecca for bird watchers by all accounts.

We will now rejoin the Western Florida ICW where we left it at the western terminus of the "miserable mile" earlier in this chapter. The Waterway darts north through the heart of Pine Island Sound, past deep and reliable Boca Grande inlet, before flowing north into the upper reaches of Pine Island Sound, which is known appropriately enough as Gasparilla Sound. This body of water is bordered to the west by wonderful Gasparilla Island. With its beautiful Victorian inn, two lighthouses, quaint downtown, and a plenitude of wonderful restaurants, this isle should be on every cruiser's list of must-stop ports of call.

The ICW takes its leave of Gasparilla Sound at the long bridge and causeway connecting the Florida mainland to Gasparilla Island. Continued coverage of the Waterway will be presented in the next chapter.

St. James City Channel (Standard Mile 4)

St. James City is a residential community with a strong fishing flair that occupies the southern tip of Pine Island. A channel leads northwest from the ICW's flashing daybeacon #13 to an intricate series of canals serving St. James City and southern Pine Island. On-site research reveals that this passage has low-water depths as thin as 4 feet.

York Island Anchorage (BAIL-Suggested) (Standard Mile 5)

In northwestern or northerly breezes, cruising captains can anchor in minimum 7-foot depths off the southern shores of York Island, well northwest of the ICW's flashing daybeacon #13. Good water runs to within 100 yards of the all-natural banks. This anchorage is quite open to winds blowing from any other quarter. Unless light airs or northerly winds are definitely in the forecast, it would be better to consider the haven described below.

Be sure to anchor well east of the Waterway's unlighted daybeacon #20. This aid marks the southwesterly tip of a prohibited sea-grass flat. Anchoring on these waters is a real no-no.

Ding Darling Anchorage (BAIL-Suggested) (Standard Mile 5.5)

The wide and mostly deep cove south of flashing daybeacon #16 is an absolutely enchanting anchorage for any size pleasurecraft. The shores are part of the J. N. ("Ding") Darling National Wildlife Refuge and are magnificently in their natural state. Good depths of 5½ to mostly 6 feet run to within 200 yards of the banks. Protection is excellent from all but northerly winds. This is a superior anchorage which this writer highly recommends to his fellow cruisers.

Unfortunately, the local government on adjacent Sanibel Island now limits stays in this anchorage to 48 hours. Go figure.

Chino Island Anchorage (BAIL-Suggested) (Standard Mile 8)

Northeast of unlighted daybeacon #24, visiting cruisers can carry a good 7½ to 8 feet of water to within 50 yards of the Chino Island shoreline. During our on-the-water research, we observed several large sailcraft anchored in the lee of this isle. The anchorage is well protected from northern and northeasterly blows, but wide open to breezes blowing from any other direction. The island's shores are completely undeveloped and are enshrouded with thick growth resembling mangrove. Chino Island is privately owned, and landing by dinghy is not permitted. If the weather forecast is cooperative, this is yet another in the long list of wonderful overnight stops on Pine Island Sound.

Wulfert Channel

An indifferently marked, dead-end channel runs west from flashing daybeacon #26 to Wulfert Channel and a tiny, now-closed inlet that used to be called Blind Pass. As this channel is shallow, and now, with the inlet's closing, leads pretty much nowhere, captains should probably avoid this cut entirely.

Captiva Island

Captiva Island sits directly north of Sanibel and is joined to the latter body of land by a fixed highway bridge. In many ways, Captiva is a carbon copy of Sanibel, except that it lacks large wildlife refuges and is, for the most part, a bit less crowded.

Captiva is five miles in length but seldom more than a half-mile wide. In earlier times, Captiva served as a "lime plantation." In this sort of agricultural enterprise, plants are grown in the rich limestone (hence the name) soil. The original owner, a man named Chadwick, planted hundreds of palm trees under which modern visitors still enjoy a pleasant shade. The great hurricane of 1926 blew so much salt water over the island that the land was "ruined for agriculture."

By 1938 tourists had begun arriving by mailboat and the island has been developed as a resort colony ever since. Today, the South Seas Plantation development occupies 330 acres on Captiva's northern tip.

Roosevelt Channel Facilities & Anchorage (BAIL-Suggested) (Standard Mile 13)

Minimum depths of 5 feet lead from unlighted daybeacon #38 down a surprisingly well outlined passage into Roosevelt channel, running between Captiva Island and Buck Key. Two marinas and one BAIL-suggested anchorage serving Captiva Island are both found

along this passage. Moving north to south, the first, Jensen's Twin Palms Marina (941-472-5800), lies off unlighted daybeacon #13. This is a strictly small-craft, albeit super-friendly, facility that offers only gasoline and a bait and tackle store. Low-water depths at the fuel dock run 6 feet or so.

Between Jensen's and Tween Waters, veteran Western Florida cruisers will miss the small wooden pier that used to be associated with Timmy's Nook Restaurant. This long-time local favorite was closed in 1995, and a new, modern restaurant called the Green Flash (941-472-1370) now occupies this spot. The Green Flash has its own fixed wooden pier with soundings alongside of 5 feet or better. There should be enough room for vessels as large as 36 feet. We have not had the opportunity to review the bill of fare at this dining attraction. Please let us know your experiences by e-mailing us at opcom@netpath.net.

The larger Tween Waters Marina is found a good distance to the south on the Captiva Island shoreline. This facility is associated with a large motel and three on-site restaurants. The marina accepts transients, but space is somewhat limited at its one wooden, fixed pier. Mean low-water dockside soundings are

Green Flash restaurant, Captiva Island

some 6 feet on the dock's outer face while the inner side has soundings around 5 feet. Full power and water connections are supplemented by gasoline, diesel fuel, free waste pump-out service, and a variety store. We are pleased to report that Tween Waters' older showers have now been replaced by modern, fully climate controlled units. They are an immense improvement. There are now three laundromats on the premises as well. Mechanical repairs can sometimes be arranged through independent contractors.

Tween Waters Motel features a host of recently refurbished rooms, tennis courts, and a swimming pool with a newly remodeled bar. A public beach is found just across the street. If you need a day or two off the water with solid ground under your feet, this resort is very convenient.

When it comes time to satisfy the old appetite, I highly suggest the on-site Old Captiva House restaurant. Housed in a "conchlike" building recalling the Florida of yesteryear, it delights diners with baked grouper and other seafood entrees.

> **Tween Waters Marina (941) 472-5161**
>   **http://www.tween-**
>   **waters.com/images/marina_new_1.htm**
>
> **Approach depth—6 feet (minimum)**
> **Dockside depth—5-6 feet (MLW)**
> **Accepts transients—yes**
> **Fixed wooden pier—yes**
> **Dockside power connections—30 and 50 amp**
> **Dockside water connections—yes**
> **Waste pump-out—yes**
> **Showers—yes**
> **Laundromat—yes**
> **Gasoline—yes**
> **Diesel fuel—yes**
> **Variety store—yes**
> **Restaurant and snack bar—three on site (plus**
>   **one bar)**

A popular, BAIL-suggested anchorage is found just off the eastern side of the Roosevelt Channel between unlighted daybeacons #14 and #15 (abeam of Tween Waters Marina). Depths vary widely in this anchorage, ranging from as little as 5 to as much as 14 feet of water. Shelter is not adequate for heavy weather and the anchorage is wide open to northern and northeasterly blows. The shores of Captiva Island display moderate to heavy residential and condo development, while Buck Key to the east is completely in its natural state.

South Seas Plantation Marina (Standard Mile 13.5)

One of the finest marinas in all of Western Florida is found near the western foot of the marked and charted channel running west from flashing daybeacon #39. South Seas Plantation Marina is part of a huge condo and private home development near the northern tip of Captiva Island. The facility offers very protected dockage for transient and resident craft alike at both fixed wooden and concrete piers in the charted basin south and west of unlighted daybeacon #10.

The South Seas Plantation entrance channel has been remarked and shifted over the last several years. It is now a more or less straight route, with but a slight dogleg at unlighted daybeacon #13. Low-water depths seem to run at least 6 feet, with many deeper soundings. The ultrasheltered dockage basin has typical soundings of 6 to 8 feet, but a few of the innermost slips carry only 5 feet of water.

Full power and water connections (including a few 100-amp services) are readily available at each berth. The docks also have cable TV and telephone hookups. The marina maintains spotless, climate-controlled bathrooms

South Seas Plantation Marina, Captiva Island

and showers, plus a full laundromat. There is also an extensive on-site ship's and variety store with an extensive deli. Gasoline, diesel fuel, and free waste pump-out service are offered as well.

Transients can enjoy a cooling dip at the swimming pool a short stroll away or a rousing game of tennis at any of several nearby courts. If golf is more your thing, there is a PGA-certified nine-hole course in the complex, and visiting cruisers are welcome to use it.

When it's time for dinner, you have three restaurants to choose from. This writer can confidently recommend the King's Crown, a "formal gourmet restaurant." Better dig out your last clean shirt for this one. Those wanting a more informal atmosphere will find the freshest of seafood and (optional) open air dining at Captain Al's to be delightful. Free trolley service is provided throughout the spacious South Seas Plantation complex, and you might use this novel method of transportation to visit Chadwick Restaurant, some 1½ miles from the docks. Captain Al's and King's Crown can be reached through the main South Seas switchboard, while Chadwick can be direct dialed at 941-472-7575.

Many cruisers with a sweet tooth (like this writer) frequent Uncle Bob's Ice Cream Emporium. It's open late into the evening. Yuuummm!

Cruisers who want to do a little dry-ground exploration can take advantage of the on-site Budget Rent A Car office. Ask any of the friendly marina staff to make contact for you.

Speaking of the trolley, visiting cruisers may very well want to take a ride to the complex's southern gate. Just beyond, you will find a nice strip shopping area with a host of gift shops and CW's Market and Deli (941-472-5111), a most useful specialty grocery store. A walk of four or five additional blocks holds even more promise.

If you don't take heed to any of this writer's other dining recommendations in this guide, please listen to this one. The (no kidding) Mucky Duck Restaurant (941-472-3434) fronts onto the Gulf side beach, just a quick walk from South Seas Plantation's southern gateway. Ask any local for directions. The hamburgers are absolutely scrumptious and the fried grouper sandwiches, well—words just fail me. There is nothing on the menu that isn't good and the atmosphere is wonderful—sort of a British-style pub with the waves crashing in the background. Every time we visit Captiva, we feel it is mandatory to re-review this restaurant, just to be sure the quality hasn't suffered, you understand.

Another superb Captiva Island dining attraction is the Bubble Room Restaurant (15001 Captiva Drive, 941-472-5558). Visitors up for a walk of three blocks or so from the South Seas gate can track their way to this memorable restaurant. The name is derived from the old-style Christmas bubble lights that are sprinkled throughout the dining room. There are no bubbles in the cuisine, however. It's first rate!

With the possible exceptions of the two inns on Cabbage Key and Gasparilla Island, there is simply no better place on Pine Island Sound than the South Seas Plantation Marina to coil your lines and rest from your travels a bit. Cruisers can rely on a warm and knowledgeable welcome, and the amenities are truly world class.

South Seas Plantation Marina (941) 472-5111

Approach depth—6 feet minimum (low tide)
Dockside depth—5-8 feet
Accepts transients—yes

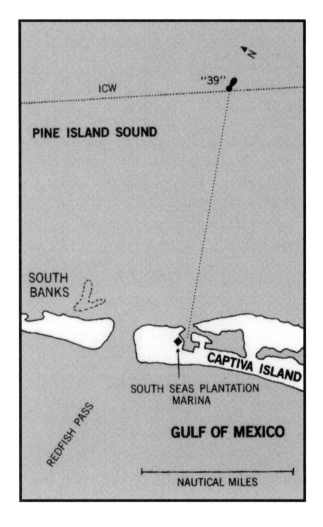

Wooden and concrete fixed piers—yes
Dockside power connections—up to 100 amp
Dockside water connections—yes
Waste pump-out—yes
Showers—yes
Laundromat—yes
Gasoline—yes
Diesel fuel—yes
Ship's and variety store—yes
Restaurant—three in complex and others nearby

Redfish Pass (Standard Mile 13.5)

After traversing the channel leading to South Seas Plantation Marina as far west as unlighted daybeacons #19 and #20, it is possible to break off to the north and follow a fairly broad, but mostly unmarked track to the inlet known as Redfish Pass. By paralleling the western shoreline, 6-foot depths can be carried into the interior reaches of the pass.

This inlet separates Captiva Island to the south from North Captiva Island. No bridge as yet crosses the pass, and it is hoped none ever will.

During the last year or so, with the closure of Blind Pass just to the south, tidal currents seem to have strengthened in Refish Pass. This has resulted, at least temporarily, in a deeper channel than was available in times past. County sponsored markings now outline Redfish Pass's seaward channel, and currently minimum 8 foot depths can be expected. Of course, on-the-water conditions may be very different by the time of your arrival. Most of the channel markers are not charted, and they are frequently shifted and changed to follow the ever-moving sands. Nevertheless, for the moment at least, local captains seem to be making good use of this outlet to the briny blue.

North Captiva Island

North Captiva still enjoys what one writer has termed as "true island status." You must still travel by water to reach its shores, and landlubbers can only look longingly across the waters of Redfish Pass.

Once upon a day, intrepid Pine Island fishermen maintained an on-again, off-again occupancy in a small village set on the shores of North Captiva's Safety Harbor. With the demise of large-scale commercial fishing on the sound, the old buildings fell into disrepair. Until just a few years ago, cruisers with shallow-draft vessels could anchor abeam of the one-time settlement and dinghy ashore for exploration.

The last remnants of the Safety Harbor village were destroyed with the development of a private club around the shores of the harbor. Today's visitors will find only modern buildings overlooking the water, with one interesting exception. One of the old stilted fishing houses remains on the northeastern point of Safety Harbor. This historic structure has now been restored as a private home, and speaks to passing mariners of those rugged, simple days of the Pine Island Sound commercial fisherman, which are now gone forever.

Safety Harbor & Anchorage (BAIL-Suggested) (Standard Mile 17)

During fair weather (only!), cruisers might choose to anchor off the southern flank of Captiva Pass, north of the charted channel leading to Safety Harbor and behind the easterly banks of the northernmost point of North Captiva Island. The channel leading from the ICW's unlighted daybeacon #48 to Safety Harbor and this anchorage is more than slightly confusing and sometimes frustrating (see below), but many navigators will be able to track their way to this overnight haven and maintain minimum 6-foot depths.

Once behind North Captiva's northerly

point, cruisers can anchor in some 6 to 12 feet of water. There is good protection to the west and southwest and some minimal shelter for light breezes blowing from the northwest. Otherwise, this anchorage is wide open. It is most definitely not the place to spend the evening in high winds or thunderstormy conditions. The adjacent North Captiva shoreline exhibits moderate residential development.

Safety Harbor itself is accessed by way of an indifferently marked, but charted, channel that leads south from the deep water abutting the southeasterly reaches of Captiva Pass to a large, almost landlocked lagoon. This once secret refuge used to house an abandoned fishing village. Those times are unfortunately in the past and the land is now intensively developed as a housing and condo complex known as the Safety Harbour Club.

The channel itself is tricky and currently exhibits minimum 4- to 4½-foot depths. We do not recommend this passage for any craft larger than 36 feet, and most certainly it is not for vessels drawing 4½ feet or more.

At one point, just when making the turn into the main body of Safety Harbor, you will pass one of the old stilted fishing houses. Captains straying just a mite too far to the east will find themselves in 1 to 2 feet of water.

If you do find your way through the Safety Harbor channel, you can tie off temporarily to a fixed wooden pier, abeam of unlighted daybeacon #17. This dock is associated with the adjacent Barnacle Phil's Restaurant. Dining patrons are free to moor here while sampling the restaurant's delights, but overnight stays are not allowed. Judging from the huge crowds we witnessed at Barnacle Phil's during a recent visit, this place must be doing something right. Many dining patrons were seated at long, family-style tables in the open air and

within easy sight of the water. A very good time seemed to be had by all.

While docked at the Barnacle Phil's pier, you might also ask directions for the Island Market Place Deli and Groceries. Galley restocking was never so easy.

There is no transient dockage available in Safety Harbor at the current time. All the many piers and slips you will spy are part of the very private Safety Harbor Club. So, except for the restaurant dock and its culinary attractions, visiting cruisers need only traverse the difficult Safety Harbor channel for sightseeing purposes.

Captiva Pass & Anchorage (BAIL-Suggested) (Standard Mile 18.5)

The inlet cutting between North Captiva Island and Cayo Costa (island) is a mixed bag for cruisers. On the one hand, the pass's seaward passage is anything but straightforward. Even the channel from the ICW is flanked by unmarked shoals. On the other hand, the interior reaches of Captiva Pass are deep and provide one of the most delightful fair-weather anchorages in Pine Island Sound. During weekends a fleet of local craft about the size of the Spanish Armada descend on the pass and anchor just behind (east of) the southern tip of Cayo Costa. This island is part of a state park (see below) and is almost entirely in its natural state. The inlet is overlooked by tall Australian pines from the shores of Cayo Costa, with a beautiful beach a short step away to the northwest.

Minimum 8-foot depths run to within 50 yards (or sometimes closer) of the eastern side of Cayo Costa's southern tip (just where you would expect good depths from a study of chart 11427). For best shelter, try anchoring amidst the charted 10- to 11-foot depths just

Barnacle Phil's Restaurant, Safety Harbor

north of the pass. Here you will be sheltered from western and northwestern winds. Strong breezes from any other quarter call for a different choice of overnight stops.

Tidal currents, as you would expect, run quite swiftly through the pass. Be sure the hook is well set before breaking out the dinghy and heading ashore.

The Stilted Fish Houses of Pine Island Sound

East of flashing daybeacon #52, passing cruisers can still see some of the houses built on stilts which are so much part and parcel of Pine Island Sound's colorful history. While some of these structures have sadly fallen victim to the passage of the years, many have survived and some have now been renovated as private vacation homes and even permanent residences.

The history of Pine Island Sound's stilted houses began in 1897 with the development of the Punta Gorda Fish Company. To accommodate the booming trade in commercial fishing which soon materialized on the sound's waters, the company built a whole series of houses raised atop stilts directly on the water. The intrepid Pine Island anglers would live for weeks at a time in these primitive structures while harvesting mullet from the sound. Other stilted buildings were used as "ice houses." Writing in the April 1989 issue of *Southern Boating* magazine, Jane T. Adams described something of the life of the Pine Island fisherpeople:

> The fisherman's job was arduous. . . . The gill netters and seine fishermen often worked together. Mr. Quednau recalls that he . . . and two crew members caught 33,000 pounds of mullet in 10 days. . . . On occasion, 40,000 to 60,000 pounds were caught at a time. The gill netters would then take their catches to the ice houses to be kept cold until the run boats could transport them to the Punta Gorda wharf. . . . Since refrigeration was so important to the welfare of the industry, it was quickly discovered that the ice houses could be moved. . . . Two barges would flank the building at low tide and slide large beams underneath it. At high tide, the barges and beams lifted the building off its pilings. The barges then moved the structure to another location.

While, tragically, some of the old stilted houses have been wantonly destroyed, others are now being preserved as a reminder of those early days of Florida's commercial fishing trade. Boaters should take every opportunity to observe these vanishing pieces of Americana for themselves.

Alternate Pine Island Sound Channel (Standard Mile 19.5)

A wide channel strikes north-northeast from flashing daybeacon #52 (on the ICW) and eventually leads past Useppa Island until finally passing into Charlotte Harbor hard by the northwestern tip of Pine Island (charted as Bokeelia Island). While the southerly portion of this route is unmarked, the broad width of the channel allows most navigators to keep to good depths with careful attention to the surrounding landmarks. Minimum depths run

around 6 feet on this passage, but most soundings are better than 8 feet.

Nervy skippers might consider working their way carefully to the east from a position north of flashing daybeacon #52 on the alternate channel, towards the charted stilted houses. Be on guard against the charted shallows.

South of unlighted daybeacons #5 and #6, the alternate channel skirts Useppa Island to the west. This island, its facilities, and its adjacent anchorage will be reviewed below in the discussion concerning the Pine Island Section of the ICW.

A reliable, marked channel north of Useppa Island allows mariners ready access from the ICW to the alternate Pine Island Sound channel and vice versa. Minimum depths are 7 feet in this cut, with most sections boasting at least 8 feet of water.

As you are traversing this connecting cut, look north to charted Mondondo Island. This body of land features a beautiful private home. Boy, talk about getting away from it all.

Back on the alternate Pine Island Sound Channel, it would be possible in fair weather (only) for captains to anchor off the southeastern shores of Patricio Island, between unlighted daybeacons #6 and #7. You will be protected only from western breezes, but in light airs this is a delightful place to spend an evening, overlooked by the isle's wild shores.

Jug Creek Facilities

The alternate Pine Island Sound channel eventually intersects a marked cut leading into Jug Creek, southwest of flashing daybeacon #8. Jug Creek lies between Pine Island to the south and Bokeelia Island to the (you guessed it) north. The stream winds through a series of mangrove stands, and after much twisting and turning eventually leads to a marina facility. The channel is shallow, with low-tide depths of only 3½ feet. Clearly, this limits the passage and its associated facilities to boats drawing less than 3½ feet.

Four Winds Marina is found on the most upstream section of the Bokeelia Island channel, past unlighted daybeacon #39. This is a surprisingly complete and extra-friendly, down-home type marina. The facility's obvious drawback is its 3½-foot entrance depth on the Jug Creek channel. If your draft can squeak through this thin water (and the 4-foot low-water dockside depths at the marina), then you should not hesitate to make use of this fine facility.

Four Winds gladly accepts transients and provides overnight berths at fixed wooden piers replete with water and 30-amp (or less) power connections. The harbor is extremely well sheltered and would be a good spot to ride out heavy weather. Gasoline and diesel fuel are on hand, as are clean showers and a full-line ship's and variety store. Mechanical repairs are available for both gasoline- and diesel-powered craft, and boats up to 30 feet can be hauled out via a forklift. The marina also features dry stack storage for smaller powercraft. An on-site restaurant, the Lazy Flamingo (941-283-5959), makes for convenient dining. Seperate boat slips are available for restaurant customers (while dining), without the necessity of obtaining a berth at the marina.

All in all, this writer could not help but like Four Winds Marina in spite of its skimpy water and the long cruise necessary to reach its docks from the ICW. If you're not in a hurry, and your craft draws less than 4 feet, give this facility a try for a different cruising experience.

Four Winds Marina (941) 283-0250

Approach depth—3½ feet (minimum, low-water)

Dockside depth—4 feet (minimum, low-water)
Accepts transients—yes
Fixed wooden piers—yes
Dockside power connections—30 amp
Dockside water connections—yes
Showers—yes
Gasoline—yes
Diesel fuel—yes
Mechanical repairs—yes
Ship's and variety store—yes
Restaurant—on site

Cabbage Key (Standard Mile 21.5)

Let us now return to the ICW route and review the Pine Island Sound facilities and anchorages between flashing daybeacon #52, where our discussion of the alternate channel (above) began, and Gasparilla Island.

North of flashing daybeacon #60, a charted channel cuts sharply west to an interesting port of call. Cabbage Key is home to an inn of the same name, and its history is more than fascinating. The rambling, venerable house that today houses Cabbage Key Inn was built in 1938 as a winter home for Alan Rinehart, son of American mystery writer Mary Roberts Rinehart. It is said that Ms. Rinehart actually penned some of her most famous stories while visiting with her son, possibly including the famous *The Circular Staircase*.

Alan bought Cabbage Key for $2,500 and spent another $125,000 on his house. The walls are painted a cool white with green trim, and guests are cooled by large ceiling fans. The private-home-turned-inn sits perched atop a huge shell mound left over from the days of the Caloosa Indians.

The house was first opened as an inn in 1942 and has been operated continuously as a hostelry and restaurant ever since. It does not require any imagination on this writer's part to understand why patrons are attracted to this lovely, peaceful isle. Oh, yes—the inn's

Cabbage Key Inn (rear view)

"nature walk" among the island's tropical blend of palms, royal poincianas, and cabbage palms is not to be missed, either.

Another unique aspect of Cabbage Key Inn is the wallpaper adorning its dining room. This room is papered with genuine one-dollar bills donated and autographed by the inn's guests. According to Laura Stewart and Suzanne Hupp, writing in their absolutely fascinating book, *Florida Historic Homes*, "the practice began years ago when a pessimistic patron tacked a dollar on the wall with his name on it. That way, or so the story goes, even if he lost everything, he could still come back to the pleasant island for a drink."

Unfortunately, we must report that the interior of Cabbage Key Inn seems darker and a bit dingier to us than in times past. It looked as if the whole place could use a good cleaning.

It should also be noted that the luncheon crowd carried out to Cabbage Key from the mainland has grown considerably. The midday meal has, quite frankly, become rather touristy in character. To experience the full charms of Cabbage Key dining, this writer now suggests that you pay the inn an evening visit.

Cabbage Key can only be reached by water. Cruisers can, of course, find their way to the inn's docks with ease.

The marina associated with Cabbage Key Inn is found at the western terminus of the marked channel. While transients are readily accepted, be prepared to be greeted by an abrupt dockmaster who will likely inquire forcibly whether you are there to stay overnight or to have a meal. If the answer is no to both questions, you will be asked to move along immediately.

Visiting vessels will find berths at somewhat sparse fixed wooden piers with full water and power connections. Dockage for boats larger than 40 feet is somewhat limited. All skippers would be well advised to make advance dockage reservations. Entrance depths are an impressive 6 to 8 feet, with similar soundings dockside. While no fuel or repairs are available, the marina does feature fair showers and a laundromat.

Cabbage Key Inn Marina (941) 283-2278
  http://www.cabbage-key.com/index2.asp

Approach depth—6-8 feet
Dockside depth—6½-8 feet
Accepts transients—yes
Fixed wooden piers—yes
Dockside power connections—30 and 50 amp
Dockside water connections—yes
Showers—yes
Laundromat—yes
Restaurant—on site

Useppa Island and Associated Anchorages (one, BAIL-Suggested) (Standard Mile 21.5)

Like Cabbage Key, Useppa Island can only be reached by water. This body of land is now home to an ultra-exclusive resort known as the Useppa Club. The development's fine homes set on huge lots can be seen peeping out from the well-vegetated shores of Useppa Island from the water. The houses make for an attractive view, to say the least. The club's marina (941-283-0290) is found at the eastern terminus of the marked channel that heads off from the Waterway's eastern flank between flashing daybeacons #63 and #64. Sadly enough, transients are not accepted at this facility, though the dockmaster has informed this writer that "prospective members" are allowed a trial visit. Better hold on to your wallet.

Even those of us who do not qualify financially to be considered "prospective members" can visit Useppa's waters courtesy of two good anchorages adjacent to the island shores. The

Useppa Club, Useppa Island

most easily accessible (and the only BAIL-suggested) of the two is found just off the ICW, east and northeast of unlighted daybeacon #61 and opposite the Cabbage Key Inn Channel. Here boats can get off the Waterway and hold minimum 6-foot depths to within 75 yards of the island shoreline. A bit farther out from shore, soundings improve to 9 feet or so. Protection is excellent from eastern, northeastern, and southeastern breezes and there is even some shelter from westerly airs. Strong winds from the south or (particularly) the north would be a problem.

In fair weather, it's a quick dinghy trip from this anchorage across the ICW to the docks of Cabbage Key Inn. Unless you have some fresh Florida lobster in the galley, I would suggest taking this dinghy ride for your evening's repast.

Useppa Island's other anchorage is accessed by first traveling the deep, marked channel north of the island that we met in our discussion of the Pine Island alternate channel. At unlighted daybeacon #4, you can curve around to the south and follow the correctly charted band of deep water abutting the island's eastern beaches. Here boats can anchor in 7- to 8-foot depths with plenty of protection from westerly winds. There is

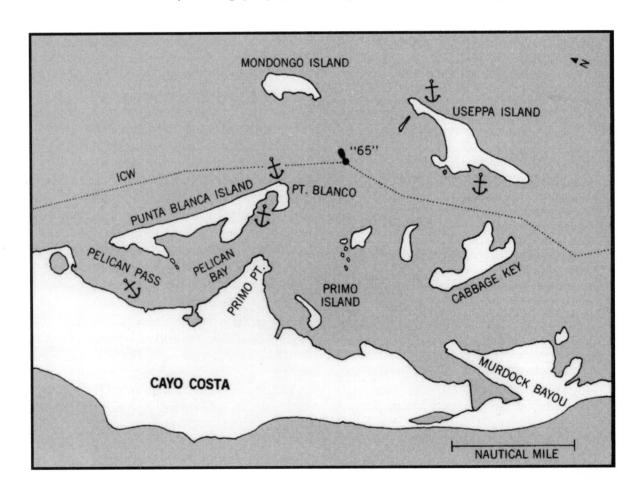

little protection from strong breezes blowing from any other direction. While this is certainly a fair-weather anchorage, Useppa's attractive shoreline may well draw many skippers to this spot during appropriate weather conditions.

Of course, it goes almost without saying that you should not attempt to dinghy ashore from either of the Useppa Island anchorages described above. The entire island is *very* private.

Point Blanco Anchorage (BAIL-Suggested) (Standard Mile 23)

In westerly winds cruising craft of any description can anchor just off the ICW in 8-foot depths along the deep waters off Point Blanco, north of flashing daybeacon #64. Drop the hook off the point's eastern flank. Here the beautifully green shore is overlooked by tall Australian pines which sigh in the wind and lull you to sleep. You will be open to the wake of vessels passing by on the ICW, and protection is minimal for heavy weather.

Wild-eyed captains piloting vessels that can stand some 4-foot soundings may carefully follow a difficult, unmarked channel to the charted deeper water behind Point Blanco. By following the shores as they cut first north, then east behind the point, you can find your way into a super-sheltered basin with wonderful protection from even the most foul weather. Depths in the basin itself run 5 to 9 feet, but, again, you will have to plow through some thin 4-foot waters to get there. The encompassing shores are well wooded and completely in their natural state. *Be sure* to read the navigational account of this anchorage in the next section of this chapter before attempting entry. Even with

these specific instructions, you may need a touch of luck to stay off the bottom.

Pelican Bay Anchorage (BAIL-Suggested) and Cayo Costa State Park (Standard Mile 25)

The last refuge adjacent to the ICW on Pine Island Sound south of Boca Grande Pass is found on the waters of broad Pelican Bay, west of unlighted daybeacon #72. If you can stand the 4- to 4½-foot MLW entrance depths, this is one of the best anchorages on Pine Island Sound. The bay is surrounded by the magnificently undeveloped shores of Punta Blanca Island to the east and Cayo Costa to the west. Cayo Costa State Park maintains a fixed wooden dock on the bay's western shore. While overnight slips (lacking any power and water connections) can be rented for $10, these berths are really only appropriate for small craft. Depths at the outer piers run 5 to 6 feet, while only 3 to 4 feet of water is found at the inner slips. Most boats should anchor in the bay and dinghy in to the docks.

This park dock is a very fortunate find for cruisers, as it provides ready access to the island and its park. Cayo Costa is owned entirely by the state of Florida and it remains the largest undeveloped barrier island along the western shores of the Sunshine State. The park rangers run a shuttle from time to time between the docks and the Gulf-side beaches. Here, visitors will discover a campground, picnic area, and bathrooms. Please note that trash collection at the park docks is no longer offered as it was in years past.

For the truly adventurous among us, it's possible to take a long, long dinghy ride south to charted Murdock Bayou (south of charted Primo Island). Study chart 11427 and note that the westerly branch of the bayou cuts back to the north and eventually leads to a shallow, lakelike body of water. The passage from the main bayou to the lake cuts between (and under) dense, overhanging mangroves. It resembles nothing so much as a tunnel set amidst lush vegetation. This is one of the most unique cruising experiences in Western Florida, but please remember that approach depths are quite shallow. Perform your explorations strictly by dinghy.

Cayo Costa was once inhabited by the Caloosa Indians, as is evidenced by the many shell mounds archeologists have identified on the island. In later years there was a small fishing village on the isle's shores, but today the only human residents are the park rangers.

Well, they may be the only human residents, but Cayo Costa is a treasure chest of local wildlife. The island features such diverse terrain as pine forests, oak-palm hammocks, and mangrove swamps. Amidst this varied landscape, quiet visitors may observe ospreys, bald eagles, and the magnificent frigate birds. These creatures have the largest wingspan for their body size of any bird in the world. In addition, one of the state's largest colonies of white and brown pelicans resides on Cayo Costa. If you are into bird watching, it would be easy to linger on this timeless isle for weeks at a time.

An early morning walk on the nearby deserted beaches of Cayo Costa is something that must be experienced to be understood. Walking along the wet sand, with the sun just beginning to peep over the Gulf, it struck this writer that once all of Western Florida was just like this. How fortunate that we in the cruising community plying the waters of this coastline still have the opportunity for such an intensely isolated and personal experience.

The entrance into Pelican Bay is known appropriately enough as Pelican Pass. This passage carries meager depths of 4 feet at low water, though we observed sailcraft drawing better than 4 feet entering and leaving the bay during high and mid-tide. *Be sure* to read the navigational account of Pelican Pass below *before* attempting first-time entry.

Once on Pelican Bay's interior reaches, depths improve to 6 feet or better along a broad band. Consider dropping the hook once abeam of the park docks to the west. While a legion of local craft regularly cruise the waters south of this point, there are many unmarked shoals to worry with.

Pelican Bay is sheltered enough for light to moderate airs, but it is not the sort of spot where this writer would want to ride out a full gale. Check the forecast and pick a sunny day of fair breezes for your visit.

The Meeting of the Waters

North of flashing daybeacon #75, the ICW skirts out into a broad body of water which charts 11427 and 11425 label as Charlotte Harbor. Personally, I think of these waters as the northern reaches of Pine Island Sound, with the foot of broad Charlotte Harbor found to the east and northeast. Whatever you call it, it can be bit of a shock for mariners to find themselves on such an open section of the ICW where the waters seem to go on and on in almost every direction. To the west lies reliable Boca Grande Inlet. The Waterway cuts north into Gasparilla Sound past the island of the same name, with its many facilities and lovely Victorian inn.

Boca Grande Pass (Standard Mile 26.5)

The inlet lying between Cayo Costa and Gasparilla Island boasts the deepest naturally occurring seaward channel in all of Western

Florida. Boca Grande Pass has minimum 18-foot depths, with soundings up to 50 feet in a few spots. The passage is well marked and relatively easy to run during daylight. Clearly, this is the best path to and from the open Gulf between Fort Myers and Venice.

In spite of all these fortunate characteristics, however, cruisers should be aware of several significant shoals flanking the inlet channel. During one of our many visits to Gasparilla Island, we observed a large sailcraft that had tried to enter Boca Grande at night and run aground amidst breaking water on the inlet's southern shoal. Fortunately, the craft was later able to extricate itself without major damage, but that must have been some night to endure on those rolling waters.

Northbound captains can take advantage of

Gasparilla Island shore

the charted swash channel cutting north along the western banks of Gasparilla Island's southerly tip (immediately west of the charted lighthouse). This cut is unmarked, but an old pier will help you to keep to the good water (see below). Currently, this channel holds at least 6 to 7 feet of water at low tide, and, in fair weather, during daylight, it is reasonably easy to run. Don't try it at night or during stormy conditions. Please read the navigation account in the next section of this chapter for additional details.

Passing cruisers cannot help but notice a lovely, cottage-style lighthouse overlooking the nothern banks of Boca Grande Pass. This old sentinel of the sea began operation in 1890. After some years of disuse in the late 1960s and early 1970s, it has now been fully restored and lighted once again. Please check out our account of Gasparilla Island history below for the full story.

Gasparilla Island

What can I say about a Gulf barrier island that has provided some of the best times this writer and his first-rate first mate have ever enjoyed? Well, you might say that if a barrier island is not going to be left in its natural state, Gasparilla is a shining example of how it should be developed. You could also say that the island serves as the home for one of the most beautiful and delightful Victorian inns in all of America, or you might mention the quiet delights of the isle's one village, Boca Grande. Whatever this writer or anyone else says about Gasparilla Island in the way of both cruising and shoreside delights, it will probably fall short of the mark. Perhaps it's not really going too far to say that those who have not visited Gasparilla have not really seen Western Florida. To be certain, Gasparilla

Island deserves a heavy red circle on every cruiser's chart and several days in his or her cruising itinerary.

Gasparilla Island has benefited from the exclusivity of its visitors since the early 1900s. Wealthy Northerners by the hundreds came to Gasparilla during the Roaring Twenties and thereafter to hide from the harsh northeastern winters amidst the rambling confines of the island's famous inn. While a few small condos have been built near the island's northerly tip, most development has taken the form of lovely residential neighborhoods punctuated by beautifully kept lawns and large, clapboard homes painted in pastel shades.

A bike path made from the old roadbed of the Gasparilla railroad runs the length of the island. Bicycles are everywhere for rent. A pedaling excursion down this path from Boca Grande to the old Gasparilla Lighthouse allows visitors an intimate view of the island homes, as well as some of the more undeveloped regions. A stroll along the beaches bordering Boca Grande inlet within sight of the lighthouse is an experience to be savored like a fine, claret wine.

You might also choose to visit the second of Gasparilla Island's lighthouses, a short hop from downtown Boca Grande. A small park around the base of this sentinel is interesting for its plaques with explanations about Boca Grande Inlet and the lighthouses.

A third site well worth your time is Banyan Street. Here a canopy of stately but twisted trees planted by Peter Bradley in 1914 has formed a roof over the street. Biking down the road, it almost appears as if you are cycling through a tunnel.

The quaint village of Boca Grande has long served as the center of activity on Gasparilla Island. Today, visitors will still find brick streets and walking paths flanked by cooling palm and banyan trees. The old train station has been converted into a complex of shops, including an ice cream stand and restaurant. Be sure to the check out the nearby Ruhama's Books in the Sand (5800 Gasparilla Road, 941-964-5800), where you may purchase volumes detailing the history of Gasparilla Island (*Walking Tours on Boca Grande* by Nancy Sokoloff is highly recommended by this writer). Interesting shops and quaint dining attractions pepper Boca Grande like grains of sand on a beach. None of these is large enough to be intrusive upon the idyllic scene. Rather, these gift shops, drugstores, and clothing boutiques add to the island's charm.

Downtown Boca Grande is within easy walking distance of all the marina facilities discussed below. This is indeed fortunate, as all cruising visitors will have the opportunity to experience the delightful atmosphere of this island village for themselves.

Cruisers looking to resupply their larders should track their way to Hudson's Grocery (417 Park Avenue, 941-964-2621) in the heart of downtown Boca Grande. This small but surprisingly full line market is a Gasparilla tradition. Here you will find fresh produce, good meats, and even roasted chickens. It's a five-block walk from Millers Marina or a four-block hike from Inn Marina to Hudson's. If you have trouble with this distance and know exactly what you need, this market does offer dockside delivery for phone orders of $25.00 or more.

For a great breakfast and a memorable evening meal, hike the short distance from Millers Marina (or a much longer walk from the Inn Marina) to Loons on a Limb (corner of Third Street and E Railroad Avenue, 941-964-0155). This is where all the locals go to break their morning fast, and there are few better recommendations for any dining establishment. Take our word for it, both the pancakes and omelets are memorable. Loons on a Limb is not open for lunch, but reports from locals paint an interesting picture for the evening meal served here. For an offbeat dining experience with scads of local color, give it a try.

Come lunchtime (and now in the evening as well), track your way to the Loose Caboose (Fourth Street and Park Avenue, 941-964-0440). This delectable little restaurant is located on the south side of the old depot and features outdoor dining during fair weather. During the last year or so, the bill of fare at the Loose Caboose has become far more sophisticated. The evening meals feature true continental-style cuisine. Fortunately, the good old cheeseburgers and milkshakes for which this dining spot has long been famous are still available at lunch (and as good as they ever were). The Loose Caboose also has its own ice cream stand. Of course, you may hear your arteries stopping up after a lunch like this, but hey, it's only now and then, right?

The best coffee, cappuccino, pastries, and delectable homemade breads on the island are

Loose Caboose restaurant

found at the Boca Grande Bakery (384 E Railroad Avenue). Several outside tables are available for sidewalk dining. You will undoubtedly discover a host of locals taking advantage of this outstanding dining attraction. It also wouldn't be a bad idea to take a fresh-baked loaf of bread back to the galley. Ummm, I can smell the wonderful aroma now.

The Pink Elephant Restaurant (Bayou Avenue, 941-964-0100) overlooks the Gasparilla Island anchorage basin (see below) just to the west. This restaurant is under the same ownership as Gasparilla Inn (see below). It rivals the inn's dining room, and visitors can be assured of finding the highest-quality cuisine while dining in an airy atmosphere of large, plate-glass windows. Downstairs there is a delightful English-style pub, which is a perfect spot to unwind after a long day on the water.

If you are in the market for anything in the way of outdoor clothing, check out Boca Grande Outfitters (375 Park Avenue, 941-964-2445). While there, be sure to visit the real boss of the outfit, Sophie. Of course, any reply to your questions will probably be a bark, as Sophie is a friendly yellow Labrador retriever. Sophie has become such a hit among Boca Grande regulars that the shop has had special T-shirts printed with the pooch's likeness. How's that for a popular pet? Give Sophie a pat for us!

Summertime cruisers should note that activities are curtailed on Gasparilla Island from June through September. Some of the restaurants and shops close, and there is a general exodus of the seasonal population.

Boca Grande is a village built around an inn. Since 1911 faithful visitors have flocked to the pastel-shrouded Victorian mansion known as Gasparilla Inn (941-964-2201). This delightfully rambling behemoth of a hostelry

Gasparilla Inn (main entrance)

is open to guests every year from mid-December to mid-June. Surprisingly enough, the main inn and its dining room (but not the associated marina) are closed during other times of the year, though some of the separate cottages can still be rented.

Several years ago, the inn purchased the nearby Waterway Motel and renamed this facility "The Innlet." While it cannot lay claim to Gasparilla Inn's unforgettable Victorian ambiance, or its fabulous dining, the Innlet is open year round.

The main inn building and its various smaller companions are painted a pale yel-low. The large lobby and common room are decorated with shades of white, green, and pink set atop a natural wood floor. White wicker furniture is everywhere in evidence and tea is served every afternoon at 4:00 P.M. Sitting there sipping our tea, my first mate and I would not have been too surprised to see Zelda and F. Scott Fitzgerald or his favorite character, Jay Gatsby, come strolling by in a white linen suit. Gasparilla Inn is just the sort of place where dreams seem to become reality.

The inn also features a billiard room, a backgammon room, and a lovely bar. All the rooms look as if they have just stepped out of the 1920s.

An eighteen-hole golf course and spectacular clubhouse serve as the inn's backyard. Linksters visiting the golf club will ascend a tall, rounded bridge spanning the island's main canal. Powerboaters may have their first real view of the inn's facilities while cruising under this unique bridge.

Guests of Gasparilla Inn never go wanting for fine dining. Your room fee includes *all three daily meals*. Few who sample the quality of Chef Alfons' cuisine will want to miss any of these repasts. Breakfast and dinner are served in the massive main dining room, just off the lobby. Guests may choose to have their lunch either in the dining room or at the nearby beach club. Lunch at the beach club features an unforgettable buffet line replete with everything from fine hamburgers to an incredible selection of cold salads (the crab and lobster salad is our favorite) to the freshest of crab cakes and other hot, daily specials.

In March of 2000 Gasparilla Inn opened a new health club at the beach facility. This sumptuous addition features a full exercise room, steam room, sauna, massage rooms, and beauty parlor. The feeling of luxury is absolutely pervasive.

Gasparilla Inn offers lodging both in the main building and in separate cottages, many of which have their own porches. While we have stayed in one of these latter units, I would actually suggest a room in the main inn for your first stay. The Victorian ambiance is even more pronounced in this intimate setting.

During our first stay at Gasparilla Inn, none other than the prominent actor Harrison Ford and his entire family occupied the table next to us. The inn's air of sumptuous relaxation must have been a very welcome respite from the hustle, bustle, and daily demands of Hollywood.

To state the obvious, cruisers or landlubbers desiring to stay at Gasparilla Inn should make reservations early! It should also be noted that the rates will never be described as inexpensive, but considering the timeless memories you will take away with you, the price seems reasonable to this writer.

Well, as you have probably surmised, I could go on and on and on singing the praises of Boca Grande and Gasparilla Inn, but for now let us push on to a quick look at the island's fascinating history, followed by an overview of the region's plentiful marine facilities.

Gasparilla Island History   History suggests that Spanish explorers had established a Catholic mission on Gasparilla Island as early as 1565. This small settlement was part of the ongoing Spanish attempt to bring the local Indian population under European sway through religion. Even though hundreds of missions once dotted the Florida landscape from St. Augustine to Key West, the program ended in failure even before Florida was ceded to the English following the Seven Years' War.

Sometime during the 1700s, legend has it that the infamous pirate Jose Gaspar established his headquarters on Gasparilla Island. Tall tales speak of his warehouse of treasures and ill-gotten booty. By all accounts, Gaspar was a real ladies' man. His reputation for the treatment of female prisoners is unsavory, to say the least.

One story often told of Gaspar tells of his capturing a lovely Spanish princess named Josefa in the latter stages of his buccaneering career. For the first time in his life, the pirate was smitten with true love and begged for the young lady's hand in marriage. When she proudly refused, Gaspar was so incensed that he is supposed to have drawn his sword and decapitated her on the spot. Overcome with remorse, Jose buried her body on the island shores but, as a reminder, kept her head preserved in a glass jar on his ship.

In 1890 construction began on a "cottage-style" lighthouse overlooking deep Boca Grande (meaning "Big Mouth") Inlet. Boca Grande Lighthouse shone its light out over the Gulf for the first time December 31, 1890, and storm-tossed sailors breathed a sigh of relief. In 1927 a second lighthouse was built on Gasparilla to serve as a rear range marker for the older light. This tall, white, skeletal structure still sits hard by the Gulf beaches near the village of Boca Grande.

Boca Grande Lighthouse was abandoned by the Coast Guard in 1967 and quickly fell victim to vandals and the salt air. In an effort to save the old light, the local citizens of Gasparilla persuaded the federal government to transfer ownership of the light to the islanders in 1972. The lighthouse was placed on the National Register of Historic places in 1980. Beginning in 1985, a local group, the Gasparilla Island Conservation and Improvement Association, has worked diligently to restore the lighthouse and its various outbuildings. The effort has been an unqualified success and modern visitors will find the venerable lighthouse, once again with its immaculate white clapboard walls, relighted and gazing out over its inlet. The lands about

Boca Grande Lighthouse

the light are now part of the 135-acre Gasparilla Island State Recreation Area.

In 1894 Peter Bradley, a successful Boston business leader, acquired a large interest in the phosphate mining operation on the Peace River to the north. He correctly foresaw that the only way for the company to prosper was the establishment of a deep-water shipping port. The obvious choice was naturally deep Boca Grande Inlet. Within a year, Bradley, along with James Gifford, president of the Charlotte Harbor and Northern Railroad, had successfully completed a railroad running from Punta Gorda to the southern tip of Gasparilla Island. Soon tons and tons of phosphate were being loaded onto oceangoing vessels, and in later years the port was used for the shipping and receiving of oil. (The old terminal has been abandoned. In 1990, plans were announced to remove the oil-storage tanks and subdivide the area into luxury home sites.)

Anyway, Bradley soon began to realize that the true value of Gasparilla lay not so much in phosphate shipping as in tourism. He founded the town of Boca Grande and, as Sara Bird Wright comments in her exemplary book, *Islands of the South and Southeastern United States,* "the town was built with gracious boulevards lined with casuarina (Australian pine) and banyan trees. . . . The Gasparilla Inn was completed in 1912, along with a casino, bathhouse, boat house, and marina. Affluent patrons then began coming down; the island even lured people away from Palm Beach, which was becoming overcrowded."

"Affluent" is certainly the operative word in Ms. Wright's description. None other than the likes of the Morgans, Cabots, and DuPonts journeyed to Gasparilla Inn in their luxurious private railway cars. The famous tycoon J. P. Morgan died while vacationing in Boca Grande, and John Jacob Astor used to go shark fishing here.

The course of Gasparilla Island and the village of Boca Grande had been set. Today, the isle is still mercifully free of high-rise condos, fast-food restaurants, and honky-tonk night clubs. The old inn still brings in the rich and famous, as well as humbler guests. Katharine Hepburn is a frequent visitor and the Levi Strauss family owns a private residence on the island.

The 1,500 year-round residents of Gasparilla Island and Boca Grande are working hard through their island conservation association to preserve their unique corner of paradise from the rampant commercial development which has overtaken so many other regions of Florida. So far, they have succeeded admirably, and it is hoped the future will remain much as the past. With its rich history, ranging from Spanish missions to pirates to phosphate shipping, and its natural beauty, Gasparilla today remains one of the brightest and truest gems on the Western Florida coastline. Perhaps even the old pirate himself would be pleased.

Gasparilla Island Facilities & Anchorage (BAIL-Suggested) (Standard Mile 28.5)

Most of Gasparilla Island's marina facilities are found off the charted passage west of unlighted daybeacon #2. Minimum depths on this channel are about 6 feet, but there are a few unmarked shoals to avoid. After coming abeam of flashing daybeacon #7, visiting cruisers must make a choice. A turn to the southwest will lead you down a broad creek to Gasparilla Island's principal marina and a smaller second facility.

A cut to the north provides access through a narrow passage into a wide basin that serves

Sheltered basin anchorage, Gasparilla Island

as a popular, BAIL-suggested anchorage. Minimum 5- to 5½-foot depths are initially encountered on the passage from the main channel to the anchorage, deepening to 6 feet or better on the basin itself.

This is a superbly protected overnight anchorage that boasts good shelter no matter from which quarter the fickle winds choose to blow. You won't find a better foul-weather hideyhole anywhere.

Gasparilla Inn and the Pink Elephant Restaurant maintain a few docks on this harbor's western shores. The northernmost five slips in this small complex are under county control.

Gasparilla Inn's principal boating facilities are found farther upstream on the canal making off to the north-northwest from the basin anchorage (see below). Smaller craft that can

clear a 13-foot fixed bridge can continue cruising up the canal to these docks. Sailing and other vessels needing more clearance must enter via the canal's northern entrance, near the ICW's unlighted daybeacon #3.

Anchor in the Gasparilla basin near its midline, and then back down towards the easterly banks. To minimize swinging room, consider setting a stern anchor towards this shoreline. Some captains actually tie off their sterns to the mangrove shoreline, but this is a decidedly bad idea as this sort of shoreside growth is protected by law.

When it comes time to break out the dinghy, you can usually find a spot to tie off on one of the five northernmost slips abutting the westerly shoreline, described above. Depths in all these slips run to 4 feet or less at low water. Only dinghies and smaller power vessels need apply. The five southside slips are reserved for patrons of the adjacent Pink Elephant Restaurant.

The one exception to this happy state of dinghy dockage occurs during the tarpon-fishing season in April through July. During this time, all the shoreside slips are reserved for the use of local fishing craft. Tying a dinghy off even for a few moments in any but possibly one of these berths will likely result in a ticket. On the other hand, the northernmost slip is quite shallow (1 foot at MLW), and most local fishermen do not make use of this space. You may be able to temporarily moor your dinghy here during tarpon season, but, then again, you might still be greeted with a ticket.

Let's now turn our attention to the two marinas on the southwestern arm of the entrance channel. The first up is Millers Marina, overlooking the northwestern banks. With the curtailment of transient dockage at the Inn Marina (see below), Millers now boasts the only readily accessible wet-slip space for visitors within walking distance of downtown Boca Grande. That is quite an advantage.

Millers is a medium-sized establishment that happily accepts transients at its fixed wooden piers with all power and water connections. Depths at the outer slips are an impressive 7 to 8 feet, and 5½ feet of water can be carried at the inner docks. Boats up to 100 feet can be accommodated, though there is only room for a few craft at the larger end of this spectrum. Gasoline and diesel fuel are readily available, as is a laundromat. We are happy to report that the marina's showers have recently been rebuilt, and are not only new, but shiny clean. Mechanical repairs are available through on-site mechanics.

Another recent addition to Millers Marina is the location of Bill's Fish Market directly in the on-site ship's and variety store (which doubles as the dockmaster's office). Here visiting cruisers can purchase the very best in the fresh catch of the day, including stone crab claws (in season). It doesn't get any more convenient than this.

The Osprey Boutique gift shop (941-964-0538) is found downstairs, beside the ship's store, while Harpers Seafood Restaurant (941-964-0232) is perched atop the complex and commands an imposing view from its second-story location. Electric and gas golf cart and bicycle rentals are cheerfully provided to facilitate a visit to nearby downtown Boca Grande. This writer found the current incarnation of Millers to be a friendly marina that does all in its power to meet the needs of visiting cruisers and resident boaters alike.

And, if you have any trouble, just take it up with Obo, the marina's black Labrador retriever. It's a secret, but we'll tell you anyway. Obo is the one really in charge.

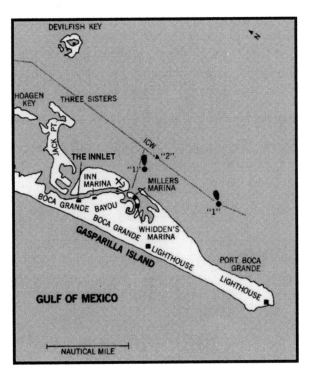

Millers Marina (941) 964-2232

Approach depth—7-9 feet
Dockside depth—7-8 feet (outer slips)
                5½ feet (inner docks)
Accepts transients—yes
Fixed wooden piers—yes
Dockside power connections—up to 50 amp
Dockside water connections—yes
Showers—yes
Laundromat—yes
Gasoline—yes
Diesel fuel—yes
Mechanical repairs—yes
Ship's and variety store—yes
Restaurant—on site

Before leaving our discussion of Millers Marina, it should be noted that this facility has gained the reputation as the "headquarters" for the lively tarpon-fishing season that runs from April through July each year. Several island fishing tournaments for the "silver king" (tarpon) are held during this period.

The few small docks of Whidden's Marina (941-964-2878) are also found on the northwestern banks a bit farther upstream from Millers Marina. This is a truly low key facility. Virtually all of the scanty wet-slip dockage is occupied by rental powercraft. The dingy onsite variety store opens out into a dim-lit pool hall. That should give you some idea of what's going on here. Just behind the docks, visitors will discover a motley collection of caged animals, including Ziggy the pot-bellied pig.

You don't see marinas like this much anymore. That's a good thing!

Moving north-northwest past the basin anchorage discussed above, the charted canal is soon spanned by a bridge leading to the Gasparilla Inn golf club. Powerboats that can clear this span's 13 feet of vertical clearance can continue upstream to the island's other marina facilities. Larger craft and wind-powered vessels must make use of the northside entrance to the canal.

Another several hundred yards of upstream cruising will bring cruisers abeam of the Inn Marina (941-964-2777) on the western banks.

Inn Marina, Gasparilla Island

This facility was acquired by Gasparilla Inn in late 1990. Unfortunately, all this facility's fixed wooden pier slip space is now occupied by long-term, resident craft. Transients are no longer accepted due to the space limitations. Gasoline and diesel fuel can still be purchased dockside, and a small ship's store is located just behind the docks. The Inn Marina also features a newly enlarged dry stack storage building.

The Gasparilla canal eventually passes through a hard turn to the east and heads out for the open water of southern Gasparilla Sound. The passage out to the Waterway is *very* different from that pictured on the current edition of chart 11425. *Be sure* to read the navigational information presented later in this chapter concerning this channel before running this cut.

Study chart 11425 for a moment and notice the broad, semicircular cove northwest of the charted channel leading from the canal's easterly entrance to the ICW (hard by charted Jack Point). Boats drawing less than 4½ feet can anchor on this cove with good protection in northerly and westerly winds. There is absolutely no shelter from southerly breezes and little to be had when winds blow briskly from the east. Depths of 4½ to 6 feet hold to within 150 yards of the northwesterly shoreline.

Peekins Ranch Cove Anchorage (Standard Mile 32)

Let us now return to the ICW as it knifes its way through mostly shallow Gasparilla Sound. In westerly breezes, skippers may choose to anchor in Peekins Ranch Cove, west of flashing daybeacon #13. There are some unmarked shoals to avoid, but careful navigation should see you safely inside the cove and anchored in 6 feet (or better) of

water. The shoreside is partially in its natural state, with several fine-looking homes breaking the landscape here and there. This is definitely not the spot to drop the hook in fresh easterly winds, as my mate and I discovered one fine sunny day in January. It should also be mentioned that there is no opportunity to dinghy ashore from this anchorage to sample the delights of Gasparilla Island.

Gasparilla Marina (Standard Mile 34)

Gasparilla Marina provides superbly sheltered dockage at modern, fixed wooden piers. The charted entrance channel cuts northeast from flashing daybeacon #20, just southeast of the old Gasparilla Island railway bridge. Entrance depths run between 8 and 9 feet, with a good 6 to 6½ feet of low-tide depths at dockside. Transients are welcome at the marina's fixed wooden piers. All berths feature full power and water connections. Cruising visitors will also discover gasoline, diesel fuel, waste pump-out service, extensive dry stack storage, and a well-stocked ship's and variety store. The on-site showers are barely adequate and non-climate controlled. There is also a fair laundromat on the marina grounds.

Gasparilla Marina's harbor is very well protected. You should be able to hunker down snugly in your slip with any but hurricane-force winds in the offing. If that's not enough for you, how about full mechanical and below-waterline, haul-out repairs? The marina's impressive travelift is rated at a 70-ton capacity.

The nearby Fishery Restaurant (see below) is spoken of with longing by local residents. The Fishery now features a seafood market as well. It's ever so nice to just hike a very short distance and then bring the freshest catch of the day back to your galley.

All in all, Gasparilla Marina is a friendly marina facility that this writer recommends to all cruisers who don't need a first-class shore-side shower.

Gasparilla Marina (941) 697-2280

Approach depth—8-9 feet
Dockside depth—6-6½ feet (low-water)
Accepts transients—yes
Fixed wooden piers—yes
Dockside power connections—30 and 50 amp
Dockside water connections—yes
Waste pump-out—yes
Showers—yes
Laundromat—yes
Gasoline—yes
Diesel fuel—yes
Mechanical repairs—yes
Below-waterline repairs—yes
Ship's and variety store—yes
Restaurant—one nearby

Fishery Restaurant (Standard Mile 34)

Study chart 11425 for a moment and note the channel cutting to the north-northeast, between unlighted daybeacon #21 and the old Gasparilla Island railway span. This minimum 6½-foot cut leads to a long, fixed wooden pier associated with the Fishery Restaurant (941-697-2451), mentioned above. Depths alongside run some 6 to 8 feet, but you must be sure to moor only to the dock's southern face. Dining patrons are welcome to tie up while patronizing the adjacent restaurant or seafood market, but no overnight stays are allowed.

The restaurant and fresh seafood market are both wonderful. Now, cruisers can decide whether to stoke up their bellies in the restaurant or take something fresh back to the galley to be prepared aboard. Seldom will cruisers find such a convenient dining attraction, particularly one with such good dockage facilities.

Uncle Henry's Marina Resort (Standard Mile 34)

This large, ultramodern marina is found at the terminus of the long, southward-flowing channel that cuts off from the ICW between the old railway span and the Gasparilla Island causeway bridge. The passage is narrow in places, but it is well marked. Minimum low-water depths seem to be about 6 feet. Meanwhile dockside soundings run at least 6 to 7 feet.

The entrance channel leads to the fixed concrete docks of Uncle Henry's Marina Resort. The dockage basin is well sheltered from all but unusually strong northerly winds. Full dockside power, water, telephone, and cable television hookups are available at every slip. Transients are eagerly accepted for overnight dockage or a longer stay. Gasoline and diesel fuel are available, as are adequate, climate-controlled shoreside showers and a laundromat (with paperback exchange library). The friendly dockmasters can usually make arrangements through local independent technicians for boats that need mechanical servicing. Waste pump-out service is offered dockside.

A shopping and motel complex is located immediately behind the marina. Here visiting cruisers will find Uncle Henry's Marina Resort Motel and the Vineyard Restaurant (941-964-5696). The Vineyard serves breakfast and lunch downstairs, while the evening meal is ready for hungry patrons on the restaurant's second floor. This dining room features a great view of the harbor.

The retail complex also includes a flower shop, a beauty salon, the Gasparilla Island Chamber of Commerce (941-964-5800), and a surprisingly well supplied and sophisticated food store, Gill's Grocery & Deli Market

(941-964-2596). Gill's features imported foods, a full-service deli, and dockside deliveries for phone orders of $25.00 or more. How's that for shoreside amenities?

While Boca Grande is a bit too far for comfortable walking, Uncle Henry's rents golf carts, or the marina can usually arrange for motorized transportation.

All in all, Uncle Henry's offers just about every imaginable service except repairs. Advance reservations are recommended, particularly during the winter and spring tourist seasons.

Uncle Henry's Marina Resort (941) 964-2300
http://www.bocagrande.com/marina.htm

Approach depth—6-15 feet
Dockside depth—6-7 feet (minimum)
Accepts transients—yes
Fixed concrete piers—yes
Dockside power connections—30 and 50 amp

Dockside water connections—yes
Waste pump-out—yes
Showers—yes
Laundromat—yes
Gasoline—yes
Diesel fuel—yes
Mechanical repairs—arranged through local
    independent contractors
Variety store—yes
Restaurant—on site

Gasparilla Pass

The inlet lying north of Gasparilla Island is known, appropriately enough, as Gasparilla Pass. This evil cut is shoal and should not be attempted by any pleasurecraft. Two of its three entrances are cut off by low-level fixed bridges. The third has depths of as little as 3 feet. The passage out into the open Gulf is shoaly and breakers are very much in evidence. Don't let them do any breaking for you.

PINE ISLAND SOUND NAVIGATION

Probably the largest impediment to good navigation on Pine Island Sound is the beautiful scenery. It's not uncommon to become enraptured with the all-natural isles and stilted fishing houses and not watch where you are going. Scraping the barnacles off the bottom of your craft is a time-honored maritime practice, but this writer suggests you have it done in a yard and not on a sandbar.

For the most part, successful fair-weather navigation of Pine Island Sound is a delight. While shallow water is present, the channel is usually fairly broad and forgiving. Sidewaters and the various anchorages along the way require a more cautious approach.

When winds exceed 15 knots and storms are in the forecast, Pine Island Sound can have a decidedly different look. Winds have more than enough fetch to stir up a wicked chop. Skippers of smaller cruising craft should deeply consider waiting for a day of light airs to undertake passage through the sound.

Those used to traversing more open inland waters will find no unusual navigational problems on Pine Island Sound. Captains accustomed to sheltered passages may, on the other hand, be a bit daunted by the wide water. Take heart—with charts 11427 and 11425 in hand, plus the information below, you should come through with no problems.

On the ICW Our account of the passage through Pine Island Sound begins abeam of flashing daybeacon #11 (to its northwesterly side). While some may consider the waters to the west to be a part of San Carlos Bay, for our purposes we will think of this area as the southern foot of the sound.

From #11, the ICW swings sharply west-northwest and passes flashing daybeacon #12 to its southern side. At #12 an underwater power line passes under the ICW. The line reemerges on either side of the Waterway and continues its path set atop *26-foot* towers. Sailcraft that somehow miss the channel on these waters could be in for a shocking experience.

Another swing, this time to the southwest, leads cruisers past flashing daybeacon #13 and unlighted daybeacon #13A. Very shallow water is found south and southeast of #13 and #13A. Be sure to stay to the north and northwest of these aids.

Past #13A, northbound cruisers will follow a lazy turn to the northwest. Unlighted daybeacon #14 and flashing daybeacons #16 and #18 warn of shallows abutting the Waterway's north and northeastern flank.

York Island Anchorage (BAIL-Suggested)
To make good your entrance into the anchorage off the southeastern shores of York Island, depart the ICW about half-way between flashing daybeacon #13 and unlighted daybeacon #13A. Cruise to the northwest, pointing to end up some 100 yards off the island's southeasternmost point.

Be sure to retrace your steps when it comes time to leave. Shoals lie to the west

and south separating this anchorage from the ICW channel.

Ding Darling Anchorage (BAIL-Suggested)
From flashing daybeacon #16, set course for the mid-width of the broad cove to the south. As you cruise into the interior reaches of this water body, watch ahead for some small signs set atop equally petite pilings. These markers denote the boundaries of the Ding Darling Wildlife Refuge. For best depths, be sure to set the hook *north* of the signs.

On the ICW The Waterway flows northwest along a broad path of deep water through the heart of southern Pine Island Sound. Unlighted daybeacons #20 and #22 mark shallows to the northeast. Stay well to the southwest of these aids.

After leaving #22 behind, set course to come abeam of flashing daybeacon #23 to its northeasterly side. A huge power line with 85 feet of vertical clearance spans Pine Island Sound from northeast to southwest near #23. It could certainly lead to confusion during nighttime passages. There is also shoal water west and southwest of #23. Be sure to pass this aid well to its northeastern side. Soon you will come abeam of unlighted daybeacon #24 and another anchorage opportunity.

Chino Island Anchorage (BAIL-Suggested)
Simply cruise northeast from unlighted daybeacon #24 towards the northwest-to-southeast centerline of Chino Island. Good depths persist to within 50 yards of the island's shores. Be sure to drop the hook far

enough from the banks so that you will not swing into the shallows immediately adjacent to the shoreline.

On the ICW   Do not attempt the charted passage west of flashing daybeacon #26. Not only is this cut shoal and treacherous, but Blind Pass has now closed completely.

North of flashing daybeacon #32, the ICW channel passes through an improved cut. Numerous unlighted aids help keep you to the proper course. At unlighted daybeacon #37, good water again broadens out in a wide band to the north.

Captiva   Island—Roosevelt   Channel & Anchorage (BAIL-Suggested)   Cruisers running the Roosevelt Channel, serving two of Captiva Island's marinas and one BAIL anchorage, should set course from unlighted daybeacon #38 for the cut's northeasternmost marker, flashing daybeacon #2. The channel angles southwest from #2. Captains will find many more aids to navigation than those pictured on chart 11427. All you really need do is remember your "red, right, returning."

Jensen's Twin Palms Marina lines the western shores near unlighted daybeacon #13. Tween Waters Marina is considerably farther to the south, also on the western banks.

Be careful if you attempt to drop the hook inside the BAIL anchorage on the eastern side of the channel between unlighted daybeacons #14 and #15. Even though you will most likely find a host of local craft moored here, on-site research shows that it ain't too difficult to wander into 5-foot depths. The best water is found nearer to #15.

Do not cruise south of unlighted daybeacon #21. Depths begin to rise thereafter.

South Seas Plantation & Redfish Pass   The unusually well-outlined channel leading to South Seas Plantation Marina and Redfish Pass cuts sharply west from flashing daybeacon #39. Happily, the latest incarnation of this cut is a far straighter passage than its earlier counterpart, with but a small dogleg at unlighted daybeacon #13. West of #13, it's a pretty straight shot into the South Seas harbor entrance. After making your way into the entrance canal, the fuel dock and the first rank of piers will soon open out to starboard.

Captains making for Redfish Pass from Pine Island Sound should follow the South Seas channel to a point between unlighted daybeacons #18 and #20. At this point, turn to the north and cruise parallel to the eastern shores of Captiva Island's northern tip. Stay some 75 to 100 yards off the beach and you can follow the channel into the inlet's interior reaches.

While the inner portion of Redfish Pass between Captiva and North Captiva islands is quite deep, the passage out to sea is flanked by extensive shoals to the north and south. This seaward cut is now marked and can often be run successfully in fair weather. As always, though, it would be best to investigate local knowledge before attempting the cut. Check with the good people at South Seas Plantation Marina for the latest information.

Pine Island Channel   An indifferently marked channel well east of unlighted daybeacon #42 runs into the western shores of Pine Island. This cut is used regularly by local fishermen piloting small outboard craft. It is much too winding and shallow for safe cruising by larger vessels.

Safety Harbor & Anchorage (BAIL-Suggested)   Skippers bound for either the Safety Harbor channel or the anchorage behind the northern tip of North Captiva Island can depart the ICW at unlighted daybeacon #48. Run a careful compass course from #48 to a point some 100 yards north of flashing daybeacon #1 and unlighted daybeacon #2, the outermost aids to navigation on the Safety Harbor channel.

Once abeam of #1 and #2, captains choosing to drop the hook in the BAIL-suggested anchorage can break off to the northwest. Be mindful of the correctly charted shallows west and northwest of #2. Be sure to keep east of #2 as you work your way to the northwest. Eventually, this shoal will be left behind, and good depths begin to run to within 100 yards of the westerly shoreline. Anchor well before coming abeam of the main Captiva Pass outlet to the Gulf.

The Safety Harbor channel cuts south-southwest between flashing daybeacon #1 and unlighted daybeacon #2. This cut is a bit better marked than in times past, and virtually all the various aids to navigation are now charted. Remember, though, this channel is rather shallow in spots and is not appropriate for vessels drawing more than 4½ feet.

Take all red markers to your starboard side and green beacons to port. After passing between unlighted daybeacons #3 and #4, you will be confronted by one of the old stilted fishing houses dead ahead.

All vessels *must* pass closely by the eastern tip of the old stilted house and then curl around to the west and follow the markers into the interior of Safety Harbor. Hapless navigators who wander even a speck too far to the east when passing the stilted house will find themselves aground in 1 foot of water. Even when passing the old house closely as you should, low-tide depths of 4 feet can be expected.

Soon the single fixed wooden pier of Barnacle Phil's Restaurant will come abeam to starboard. The channel continues on and eventually curls around the rear portion of Safety Harbor. This portion of the passage leads to a large collection of private docks, but no accommodations are available for visitors. Most transient cruisers will want to cease their explorations at the restaurant dock.

Captiva Pass Anchorage (BAIL-Suggested) Captiva Pass offers a fine fair-weather anchorage. The waters east of Captiva Pass are occupied by a huge shoal, with depths running to 3 feet. You must pass either north or south of these shallows to find your way into the inlet's interior.

From the south, set course from unlighted daybeacon #48 to bypass the shoal on its southern flank. Work your way along the broad band of charted deep water abutting the eastern shores of North Captiva Island's northerly tip. Eventually, you can swing to the west and enter the inlet.

Many cruisers choose to enter Captiva Pass via its northerly passage. This cut is nearer and more convenient to the good anchorage off Cayo Costa. Leave the Waterway some 100 yards north of flashing daybeacon #51 by curling back around slowly to the west. This maneuver will help to avoid the charted shoal southwest of #51.

As the eastern banks of southern Cayo Costa come abeam, break off from the inlet channel and track your way north, paralleling the island's easterly shoreline. Stay some 50 to 75 yards off the beach. Good water continues for some distance to the north, but eventually the charted shoals begin to shelve out from the shore. To be on the safe side, drop anchor after proceeding no more than 200 yards north of the inlet's passage.

Alternate Pine Island Channel   At flashing daybeacon #52, the alternate channel leading to the southern reaches of Charlotte Harbor breaks off to the north-northeast. Much of the southerly section of this cut is unmarked, but the channel is quite broad. By using chart 11427 and identifying the various landmarks along the way, most navigators will be able to find their way to a point abeam of Useppa Island with little difficulty.

After cruising north from #52 for some .4 nautical miles, cruisers whose craft draws less than 5 feet can work their way carefully to the east-southeast for another .6 nautical miles for a close view of the stilted fish houses near Captiva Rocks. Don't approach to within less than 300 feet of the houses, as they are anchored in shoal water.

As you cruise the gap between Part Island to the east and Useppa Island to the west, you will soon catch sight of unlighted daybeacon #5. From this point to the end of the channel off Bokeelia Island, northbound craft should pass all green beacons to their (the cruisers') port side and take red markers to starboard.

Unlighted daybeacon #5 serves the dual purpose of marking the western tier of the alternate channel and as the easternmost aid to navigation on the passage connecting with the ICW north of Useppa Island. This cut will be covered in the discussion of Useppa Island below.

Unlighted daybeacons #6 and #7 help skippers run the gap between Patricio and Broken islands. It's then a long run of some 1.5 nautical miles from #7 to flashing daybeacon #8 off Jug Creek. Point to come abeam of #8 to its westerly quarter.

Jug Creek/Bokeelia Island   South of flashing daybeacon #8, the Jug Creek channel begins its twisting and winding path to the east-southeast. The prolific markers follow the usual "red, right, returning" strategy.

The channel has so many hairpin curves that collision with a powercraft traveling at high speed around one of the blind turns is a very real concern. This writer suggests that you proceed at a wary speed while running this cut.

At unlighted daybeacon #30 the channel to Four Winds Marina takes a hard jog to starboard and passes through a narrow cut. Don't miss this turn. It's easy to overlook.

On to Charlotte Harbor   From flashing

daybeacon #8, set course to pass unlighted daybeacons #9 and #11 fairly close to their southeastern sides. This is the shallowest portion of the alternate channel, with some low-tide soundings in the 6-foot range or slightly less. Good water soon opens out again to the north.

If, by some chance, you should be continuing around Pine Island into Matlacha Pass, be aware that beacon colors reverse at unlighted daybeacon #95. Southbound cruisers navigating the pass should now begin to take green beacons to their (the cruisers') starboard side and red to port.

Back to the ICW North of flashing daybeacon #52, the ICW cuts through another dredged cut until finding deeper water at flashing daybeacon #57. At this point, the Waterway darts briefly northeast and then cuts north again between Cabbage Key and Useppa Island. North of flashing daybeacon #60, the easy-to-follow Cabbage Key channel strikes to the west.

Useppa Island and Associated Anchorages (one, BAIL-Suggested) At unlighted daybeacon #61, mariners can cut into the western shores of Useppa Island to the BAIL-suggested anchorage, once abeam of the Cabbage Key channel to the west. Good depths continue to within 100 yards of shore. Cruisers entering the cove may spy a small, marked channel to the north. This cut is used by local property owners on Useppa Island and is of no interest to visiting cruisers.

The channel to the private Useppa Club Marina runs off to the southeast between

flashing daybeacons #63 and #64. The prolific markers are obvious.

Chart 11427 correctly forecasts a small channel running from the Useppa Club harbor around the island's northerly tip. On-site research found this cut passable, but most larger vessels should probably opt for the wider, marked channel discussed below. If you should try this first cut anyway, watch out for a stone jetty abutting the island's shoreline. Give this hazard a wide berth when passing.

The marked channel running east to west between the ICW and the alternate Pine Island Sound channel lies north of Useppa Island. Its westerly entrance is found a short distance south of the Waterway's flashing daybeacon #64. Captains cruising this cut from the ICW to the alternate channel should pass red beacons to their (the markers') northerly sides and green markers to their southern quarter.

You can enter the anchorage bordering on Useppa Island's eastern shores by continuing to cruise east on the connecting channel for some 50 yards past unlighted daybeacon #4. Then, cut sharply to the south and, keeping the island shoreline some 150 yards to your westerly side, you will find good water between #4 and the first point on the island. Farther to the south, depths rise somewhat.

Point Blanco Anchorages (BAIL-Suggested) To access the outer anchorage adjacent to Point Blanco, begin easing west of the Waterway channel as the southeastern portion of the point comes abeam, west of your course, between unlighted daybeacons

#65 and #67. Good water runs to within 75 yards or so of the shores, which are lined by tall Australian pines.

Brave captains who attempt to enter the anchorage behind Point Blanco should follow the charted deeper waters striking west, south of the point. Set a course designed to keep you off the banks by some 25 yards or so. Proceed at idle speed and keep a close watch on the sounder. Soon you will pass between a large patch of old pilings to port and a smaller, motley collection of piles striking out from the Point Blanco shoreline.

Eventually the channel cuts around the western side of Point Blanco. Maintain your 25 yards' clearance with the shoreline until the waters open out to the east behind (north of) the point. This is, without a doubt, the most critical part of this difficult passage, and even careful navigators can come to grief.

For best depths, hug the southerly banks as soon as you swing to the east and begin to enter the sheltered anchorage. Eventually, if you are lucky enough to make it this far, the channel opens out a bit at the rear of the cove. Even so, set the hook so as to favor the southerly shoreline.

On the ICW   Shallow water abuts the eastern side of the ICW between unlighted daybeacons #71 and #72. Favor the westerly side of the channel to avoid this hazard.

Pelican Pass Anchorage (BAIL-Suggested)
Come abeam of unlighted daybeacon #72 and set a careful course which will carry you into the northwestern third of Pelican Pass's northerly mouth, thereby favoring the Cayo Costa shoreline. Be on guard against the correctly charted finger of 3-foot waters stretching out from Punta Blanca Island to the southeast. These shoals seem to be forever building outward.

Curve slowly around to the south and enter the main body of Pelican Bay on its mid-width. Consider dropping the hook as the park service docks come abeam on the western shoreline. Farther to the south, depths become much more uncertain.

On to Boca Grande Pass   Flashing daybeacon #76 is the last aid to navigation on the ICW south of Boca Grande Inlet. Switch from chart 11427 to 11425 at this point for continued detail of the Waterway to points north.

It's a run of slightly better than 2 nautical miles from #76 to flashing daybeacon #1, the first marker north of Boca Grande. While this track does not border on any shoals, you can expect chop and current to pick up as you traverse the waters east of Boca Grande Pass.

Boca Grande Pass and Swash Channel   It truly doesn't get much easier than this on those often unstable tracks between inland waters and the open Gulf. Boca Grande Pass is wide and its seaward passage is well marked. Nevertheless, there are a few potential problems about which cruisers should be informed.

The inlet's waters between Cayo Costa and the southerly tip of Gasparilla Island are deep almost from shore to shore. The situation changes somewhat as you move seaward. Favor the northerly and north-western side of the channel slightly as you move out to sea from the two islands. This maneuver will help to avoid charted Johnson Shoal off Cayo Costa.

A long, thin band of shoals flanks the northern and northwestern side of Boca Grande Pass for a goodly distance out to sea. Use the charted channel markers to avoid this hazard. Come abeam of and pass flashing buoys #12 and #10 close to their northerly sides. Too wide a berth to the north or northwest could land the luckless boater in the aforementioned shallows.

Also be on guard against the charted 4-foot shoal northeast of flashing buoy #5. Favor the southeasterly portion of the channel when passing through this portion of the inlet.

To run the swash channel cutting into Boca Grande's northerly flank, cut to the north after passing the southern tip of Gasparilla Island, defined by its charming cottage-style lighthouse. Keep the easterly banks some 50 yards off your starboard side. Be very, very mindful of the correctly charted shoals to the west. Soon you will spot a long, dilapidated concrete pier striking out from the easterly banks. Pass this old structure by some 20 yards to your starboard side. Eventually, good water will open out to the north and northwest.

Please remember, this swash passage is totally unmarked and borders on very shoal, breaker-tossed water to the west. We specifically do not recommend this passage during foul weather or at night. Even in the bright sunshine and the best of conditions, please proceed with more than the usual caution.

Gasparilla Island & Anchorage (BAIL-Suggested)   The principal entrance to the facilities grouped about the village of Boca Grande on Gasparilla Island will be spied west of unlighted daybeacon #2. The channel is straightforward until coming abeam of flashing daybeacon #7. Be sure to come abeam of #7 to its northern side (your port side). A shoal is building out from the creek's southside entrance point and is beginning to encroach on #7. Once abeam of #7, take a few moments to assess the situation.

The stream to the southwest leads to Millers and Whidden's marinas, while a cut into the canal to the north will bring the visiting cruiser to a basinlike anchorage and the docks just behind the Pink Elephant Restaurant.

All craft should proceed at idle, no-wake speed past #7, no matter which course they may choose. These speed restrictions remain in place throughout the northside canal and southwestern creek.

If you choose to continue down the southwesterly passage to Millers or Whidden's marinas, favor the northwesterly shores heavily as you cruise upstream to the two marinas. Inviting as it may look, the southeastern side of the creek is quite shallow. It might appear as if there's enough room for anchorage, but the shallows are far closer than you might think. While we observed a few small sailcraft swinging on the hook just south of Whidden's Marina, most larger vessels would do better to make use of the marina facilities.

Enter the north-running canal on its centerline. The Gasparilla Inn golf course will be prominent to starboard. Soon you will pass into the broad basin which is a popular, BAIL-suggested anchorage. Remember, swinging room is at a premium, so use a Bahamian moor or a stern anchor. The docks behind the Pink Elephant will be sighted to the north on the western banks.

Boats that can clear a 13-foot fixed bridge can continue on up the canal, holding to the middle. Eventually the docks of the Inn Marina will come abeam to port.

Soon the main body of the canal turns sharply to the east and begins its trek out into the open waters of southern Gasparilla Sound. Don't attempt to enter either of the two coves lining the northerly banks between the easterly turn and the canal's exodus into the sound. Both are quite shoal.

If you would like to anchor in the broad, semicircular cove east of the canal's entrance, continue cruising dead ahead from the mouth of the canal for some 200 yards. You can then turn into the northerly banks and feel your way in with the sounder.

The channel from the Gasparilla canal back to the ICW does not bear any remote resemblance to the passage pictured on the current edition of chart 11425. The improved cut detailed on the chart has apparently long since disappeared.

Fortunately, there is still a good, deep route back to the ICW. After exiting the canal, continue cruising straight ahead (to the east-northeast) for 200 yards or so. Then turn sharply to the southeast and set a compass course directly for unlighted daybeacon #3. Good depths of 6 feet or better are carried by following this procedure.

On the Waterway   The Western Florida ICW knifes its way through Gasparilla Sound via a dredged channel. Shallow water is very much in evidence outside of the Waterway. This is not the place for haphazard exploration. Take your time and stay on course.

Peekins Ranch Cove Anchorage   Entry into this anchorage is complicated by the long tongue of charted but unmarked 3-foot (or less) water that stretches far to the east, north of Peekins Ranch Cove. To avoid these shoals, set a careful compass course from flashing daybeacon #13 into the cove's interior section, bypassing the shallows well north of your course. If depths should start to rise, try giving way to the south and see if your soundings improve.

Once past the shoal, drop anchor before closing to within less than 200 yards of the westerly shores.

On to the Gasparilla Causeway   As you pass unlighted daybeacon #14, you may catch sight of two green, unlighted daybeacons to the west and northwest. Ignore these aids. They mark a shortcut through the old railway bridge. This passage is somewhat shallow and poorly marked. Only shallow-draft outboards and I/O-powered craft should attempt it.

At flashing daybeacon #20, the marked channel to Gasparilla Marina breaks off to the northeast, while the Waterway turns to the northwest and soon passes through the old Gasparilla Railroad bridge. The center span has been removed on this now unused bridge, and it no longer poses a barrier.

The charted channel leading to the Fishery Restaurant runs north-northeast immediately southeast of the Gasparilla Railway bridge. As usual, pass red markers to your starboard side and take green beacons to port. Eventually, the restaurant's one, long face dock will come abeam to port. Be sure to moor to the southern face of this pier only!

The waters between the railway span and the Gasparilla Causeway (highway) bridge can be a busy place. To the north, two deep coves make off from the Waterway. The eastern offshoot is used for the dumping of treated waste water and would be a truly lousy place to anchor. The western stream eventually leads to a huge Mercury outboard and I/O testing facility. No facilities are available for cruising craft, but you can often see the bright yellow Mercury test boats out and about on these waters while cruising by on the ICW.

The well-marked passage to Uncle Henry's Marina cuts in from the south between the two bridges. Keep all red markers to starboard and all green to port. *Stay in the channel.* Shoal water with less than 1-foot depths borders a portion of this cut.

Gasparilla Pass Absolutely no cruising-size craft should attempt to run Gasparilla Pass. The waters are shoal and two of the three entrances into the pass are spanned by fairly low-level fixed bridges.

Charlotte Harbor

Cruisers reading this account who have had occasion to cruise North Carolina's Pamlico Sound will already have a pretty good notion of just what Charlotte Harbor is really like. While it can not lay claim to the Pamlico's breadth, this is also a large body of water with two impressive feeder rivers. Charlotte Harbor has very few protected anchorages and only a couple of marinas servicing cruising craft.

Unlike Pamlico Sound, Charlotte Harbor can boast of one good-sized city along its banks. Punta Gorda, a name for many years synonymous with commercial fishing in Western Florida, is today a quiet, but by no means small, residential community which offers one full-service marina, two yacht clubs, and several anchorages.

The Myakka and Peace rivers feed into Charlotte Harbor's northerly reaches. The Myakka suffers from some shallow depths, and neither stream provides what could really be described as first-rate anchorages, though adventurous captains will discover several spots worthy of consideration.

In spite of these somewhat negative characteristics, this writer could not help but like Charlotte Harbor, and I recommend it to my fellow cruisers. There are few other spots in Western Florida where mariners can experience such wide waters bounded by such little-developed shores. Sailors, in particular, will find Charlotte Harbor well suited for a good day of cruising. So, don't be in such a hurry while passing by on the ICW that you miss the considerable charms of this lovely water.

Lower Charlotte Harbor

For once, the story can be told in a few words. Charlotte Harbor south of Punta Gorda lacks any really protected anchorages and sports only one (albeit a fine one) marina. While it makes for a wonderful sailing ground, when evening approaches, it's time to head for either Burnt Store Marina or one of the marinas or anchorages to the north at Punta Gorda or the Myakka or Peace rivers.

Burnt Store Marina & Country Club

Charlotte Harbor has only one marina facility that is located outside of Punta Gorda, but it is one of the best you will ever find. The charted channel running to the east, east of flashing daybeacon #6, leads to the sheltered dockage basin of Burnt Store Marina. The approach cut carries 6½ feet (more likely 7 feet) of water. Depths in the dockage basin run around 7 feet at low water. The marina is set in the middle of a large condo and resort housing project. In fact, the best way to spot the entrance channel is to watch for a line of three-story condos and/or a six-story condo tower overlooking the shoreline.

Burnt Store harbor is home to an unusually large collection of manatees. In fact, a live manatee birth that took place in the waters of the dockage basin was featured on a local television broadcast in 1998. Power captains should be ultrasure to proceed strictly at idle speed when cruising to and from their slips. This is the sort of place where even a small wake could be a real problem.

Burnt Store offers just about every imaginable service. Transients are gratefully accepted at (mostly) fixed wooden piers. The marina boasts 425 slips in all! Full water and power connections are readily available, as are gasoline, diesel fuel, and waste pump-out services. Full mechanical servicing for both diesel and

Burnt Store Marina, Charlotte Harbor

gasoline power plants is now offered Monday through Friday. Vessels can also be hauled out via the marina's 40-ton hydraulic trailer. Extensive dry stack storage for powercraft is now available at Burnt Store as well.

Shoreside, cruisers will find good, climate-controlled, clean showers and a small but adequate laundromat alongside a full-line ship's, variety, and grocery store (including deli and snack bar). Transients may also make use of the complex's swimming pool, 27-hole golf course, athletic club (with sauna), and tennis courts. Bicycle rentals are also available. Salty's Harborside Restaurant is found immediately adjacent to the docks and offers the freshest in fried and broiled seafood. The Sunday mid-day buffet is really spectacular. Those interested in a before- or after-dinner drink can find their way to the Castaway's Lounge. *Wow!* How's that for full service? Think you just might could fit a visit to this absolutely first-class facility into your schedule?

Incidentally, cruisers looking to charter cruising craft on Florida's western coastline need look no further than Burnt Store Marina. Several charter services make their home in the marina's dockage basin. One of the largest is operated by Southwest Florida Yachts (800-262-7939). While this firm's home offices are found at Marina Town Yacht Club in North Fort Myers, their impressive sailcraft fleet is housed at Burnt Store.

Another well-respected charter operation based at Burnt Store Marina is Yachting Vacations (800-447-0080). Boasting a sailcraft fleet of 16 vessels, this agency was declared (several years ago) the best charter agency *in the world* by *Cruising World* magazine!

Burnt Store Marina (941) 639-4151
    http://www.wcicommunities.com/
    community.cfm?id=bsmcc

Approach depth—6½-7 feet (minimum)
Dockside depth—7 feet (minimum)
Accepts transients—yes

Floating docks—one
Wooden and concrete fixed piers—yes (mostly wooden)
Dockside power connections—30 and 50 amp
Dockside water connections—yes
Waste pump-out—yes
Showers—yes
Laundromat—yes
Gasoline—yes
Diesel fuel—yes
Mechanical repairs—yes
Below-waterline repairs—yes
Ship's and variety store—yes
Restaurant—on site

Cotton Key Channel

The charted channel north of Key Point that cuts east to Pirate Harbor serves a series of private docks built along a huge complex of canals. There are no facilities for visitors, nor is there enough room to anchor. Most cruisers, except those fortunate enough to own a home in this development, will want to continue north to Punta Gorda or the Myakka and Peace rivers.

LOWER CHARLOTTE HARBOR NAVIGATION

Entry into Charlotte Harbor from the northerly reaches of Pine Island Sound is facilitated by good markings at the large bay's southern mouth. These aids are rather widely placed, however, and wise captains will lay out compass and/or GPS courses well ahead of time and follow them religiously while on the water. North of Burnt Store Marina, there are no more aids to navigation short of Punta Gorda and the entrance to the Myakka. Fortunately, there are no shoals save a band of narrows directly abutting the shoreline to worry with.

Entering Charlotte Harbor Come abeam of and pass flashing daybeacon #4, well south of Cape Haze, to its northerly side. You need not be too cautious. There is no shallow water for several miles in either direction.

Set a new, semicircular course to pass between flashing daybeacons #5 and #6. Stay away from #5. This aid marks a large shoal building out from Cape Haze.

The channel cutting east to Burnt Store Marina will be found east of flashing daybeacon #6. You will most likely sight the development's six-story condo tower looking out over the marina entrance long before you are able to pick out the outermost aids to navigation. Remember the good, old "red, right, returning" axiom and you will have no difficulty.

North of flashing daybeacon #6, you need only keep anywhere vaguely near the mid-width of Charlotte Harbor for excellent depths. If your destination is Punta Gorda, point to eventually find flashing daybeacon #1, west of Mangrove Point. If the Myakka is your intended destination, follow a course to meet up with unlighted daybeacon #7, well south of Hog Island.

The Myakka River

Killer turtles swoop from overhanging trees, the Myakka's river people claim, and a sea monster once lurked in the waters near the pit where Jose Gaspar buried his doubloons. But beneath the hype and legend, the amber river flows through some of Florida's most treasured wilderness and through history as real as mastodons, Ponce de Leon and the Indian and Civil Wars.

You will seldom read a better description of the Myakka than the one presented above from Del and Marty Marth's magnificent book, *The Rivers of Florida*. The chapter on the Myakka, written by Tim Dorsey and Rick Barry, is typical of this "must-read" study of the Sunshine State's great waterways.

Indeed, few will ever contest the claim that the Myakka is one of the most beautiful and historic streams in all of Florida. Years ago this writer wandered happily through the confines of Myakka State Park, many miles upstream from Charlotte Harbor, and came away with the memory of breathtaking river banks, tall cypress trees crowned with black ravens, and a bridge to nowhere disappearing into the lush foliage.

There is, unfortunately, some bad news for those of us who pilot cruising craft. While, to be sure, there is still the opportunity to anchor amidst wonderfully natural shores, it must also be noted that depths in the river channel fall to 4-foot levels after cruising a mere 8 miles from the river's juncture with Charlotte Harbor. This is far short of the river's most beautiful sections, many miles farther to the north.

Adding insult to injury, the Myakka is spanned by a fixed bridge with only 24 feet of vertical clearance a mere 3 nautical miles from Charlotte Harbor. Although in fair breezes sailcraft could conceivably anchor below this span, the fair upper reaches of the river are clearly off limits for most wind-powered vessels.

Equally clear is the lack of protected sidewaters along the stretch of the river accessible to cruisers. Those desiring to spend the night swinging on the hook amidst the Myakka's storied waters must anchor in the river itself. While such a strategy is fine in light to lower moderate winds, this is not the place to be caught out in heavy weather.

Some soundings of 5 feet will be encountered along the course of the Myakka channel, well short of the 4-foot region described above. Along with the height restriction imposed by the bridge, this thin water pretty well restricts a river cruise to boats drawing less than 4½ feet.

So check the forecast, assess your boat's draft and vertical clearance requirements, and make your plans accordingly. Even with all its restrictions for larger craft, few will forget a trip up this timeless river where life seems to have ebbed by, much as the river's current, leaving behind little change for the last hundred years.

Myakka River Anchorages

Remember that all the anchorages described below are only appropriate for light winds. During stormy times, head for one of the marinas or anchorages at Punta Gorda or Peace River and visit the Myakka another day.

Any pleasureboat drawing less than 4½ feet may consider anchoring on the charted patch of 7- and 10-foot water south of the small, charted channel leading north to El Jobean. The river waters abeam of the side channel make for a truly wide-open anchorage. Some

development is still apparent along the river's banks, particularly to the north.

Skippers may also consider dropping the hook along the river between unlighted daybeacons #A and #B. These nondescript aids are not easy to spot on the water. This anchorage affords a good view of the Myakka's undisturbed easterly shore. In fair weather, it would be easy to linger here for a day or two just drinking in the magnificent scenery like fine wine.

There is a third, far more protected anchorage a few miles farther upriver, but you must be able to stand some 4-foot depths to reach this haven. North of unlighted daybeacon #22, soundings deteriorate to the 4-, and possibly an occasional 3½-foot mark. There is an unmarked shoal to avoid, but north of unlighted (and uncharted) daybeacon #23, the river narrows and depths deepen to between 5 and 9 feet. Cruising craft can anchor abeam of charted Tarpon Point in about 6 feet of water with good protection from western and eastern breezes. There is even some shelter to the north. With its depth requirements, this anchorage can only be recommended for somewhat wild-eyed captains piloting smaller powercraft.

MYAKKA RIVER NAVIGATION

As delightful as the Myakka truly is, one must acknowledge the presence of shallow water along much of its length. Navigators who wander from their intended track could find themselves in 4-foot waters before they know what is happening. You must pay strict attention to business while cruising this river. When the scenery gets to

be too much for you, drop anchor and kick back for an hour or two. Of course, don't forget you must be able to clear the 24-foot fixed bridge spanning the Myakka at the charted location of El Jobean to even visit the upper portion of the river.

Approach from Charlotte Harbor From

the main body of Charlotte Harbor, point to pass unlighted daybeacon #7, well south of Hog Island and Locust Point, to its fairly immediate easterly side. You can then curve your track to the northwest and set course to pass unlighted daybeacon #8, south of Shoal Point, by at least 100 yards to its westerly quarter. As the name of the point implies, the shoal to the northeast is building out into the river.

From #8, it is a run of 2.5 nautical miles upriver to the next aid, unlighted daybeacon #9. Stick to the river's mid-width. A broad band of shoals extends out from both banks of the river. Come abeam of and pass #9 by at least 100 yards to its eastern side.

Past #9, you must follow a markerless stretch of the river to the 24-foot fixed bridges stretching between Charlotte Beach and El Jobean. Again, stick to the centerline. You can expect some 5-foot depths, possibly even less, between #9 and the bridge.

Upstream on the Myakka River   The Myakka fixed bridge has a vertical clearance of 24 feet. Immediately after passing under this span you will catch sight of an old railroad bridge. This venerable span has been left in place (though it is long since unused) with its center section swung permanently open. The *horizontal* clearance

through the span is only 30 feet, a rather narrow passage for some larger powercraft.

After leaving the two bridges behind, the Myakka begins a long, slow turn to the north. Stick to the centerline and watch carefully for unlighted daybeacon #A. This is a rather nondescript aid to navigation consisting of a small piling with some sort of strange round daymark atop it. Pass #A to its westerly side and continue upriver on the centerline looking for unlighted daybeacon #B. This latter aid is of the same sort as #A. Now, I know it doesn't make sense from the color, but pass #B to its immediate easterly side. From this point, the color scheme returns to the usual pattern. Pass red beacons to your starboard side and green markers to port as you cruise upstream.

Depths begin to fall off to 4 feet, possibly a little less, near unlighted daybeacon #20. If you can take these soundings, it's possible to continue cruising northwest past unlighted daybeacon #22. Upstream of this aid, favor the western banks to avoid the charted shoal abutting the eastern shoreline. Once past this hazard, you can drop the hook in 5- to 6-foot depths.

Don't attempt to cruise upstream past the intersection with Big Slough. The river narrows considerably and depths become much too uncertain for cruising-size craft.

Punta Gorda

Modern Punta Gorda is a prosperous residential/retirement community that guards the intersection of the Peace River and Charlotte Harbor. One cannot visit this thriving city without coming away with the sure and certain conviction that the town is undergoing a boom in housing. The incredible series of charted canals southwest of the principal waterfront serves a growing metropolis of expensive homes, many with their own private docks. If the fishermen of yesteryear could see Punta Gorda today, they would scarcely recognize the town they once knew.

Visiting cruisers will find two yacht clubs, one super marina, and four anchorages to serve their needs in Punta Gorda. Shopping facilities of all descriptions are within walking distance or, at most, a cab ride from all the area facilities. Punta Gorda makes a fine restocking depot for pleasurecraft cruising between Fort Myers and Venice.

The town of Port Charlotte sits across the southerly mouth of the Peace River from Punta Gorda. The two communities are so alike that they can almost be thought of as one town by visiting cruisers.

It doesn't take a genius to see why more and more people are being drawn to Punta Gorda and the town of Port Charlotte during their retirement years. The fine waters set about beautiful shores and quiet, often palatial residential neighborhoods, not to mention the nearly ideal climate, are enough to set anyone to musing on a property purchase in this fortunate community.

Numbers to known in Punta Gorda include:

Astor Cab—941-624-4554
Charlotte Shuttle and Transporation— 941-627-8922
Budget Rent A Car—941-743-1404
Enterprise Rent-A-Car—941-575-4200
West Marine—941-637-0000
Chamber of Commerce—941-639-2222

Punta Gorda History   Punta Gorda was a quiet fishing village until the arrival of the

Florida Southern Railroad in 1886. This new mode of transportation at last provided a ready outlet for Charlotte Harbor and Pine Island Sound's rich seafood bounty. For many years it looked as if the northeastern United States was determined to consume all the aquatic life in these waters.

A large ice plant was soon built and the Punta Gorda Fish Company was formed. Within a few months, this well-organized operation undertook construction of the stilted fishing houses on Pine Island Sound that we considered earlier in this chapter.

By 1897 more than 230 people worked the offshore fisheries, with another several dozen plying the sound and bay. These intrepid fishermen accomplished their hardy tasks aboard 140 different vessels. Gill netting for mullet was the most profitable activity. The northern markets simply could not seem to get enough of this seaborne delicacy. Spanish mackerel, oysters, and channel bass were also harvested in quantity.

As the twentieth century progressed, the phenomenal catches lessened. The boom days of the Punta Gorda commercial fisherman now live only in the memory of the town's older residents. Well, gone they may be, but those who listen carefully along the waterfront during a quiet night may still hear, in their mind's ear at least, the groan of the nets or the cry of the fisherman as he returns from a successful catch. The lore and history of the Punta Gorda fisherpeople are part and parcel of this town, and they will never be entirely forgotten.

Riviera Marina
The charted, *L*-shaped channel south of Mangrove Point provides access to Alligator Creek and what must be described as one of

the seediest marinas that this writer has ever visited. Honestly, folks, you kind of have to see this one to believe it. The fixed wooden docks are not in the best of repair and some of the covered slips are truly dilapidated. Riviera Marina claims to offer both mechanical and haul-out repairs, but the travelift looks as if it may have just been the original experiment in the product. The management has informed this writer that transients are accepted, and it is quite possible that you might find a slip for the evening, assuming you can beat off the seemingly hundreds of stray cats that frequent the piers. Gasoline is available and there is a variety and ship's store on the grounds.

In spite of the seemingly negative characteristics noted above, we did note a large number of hauled craft sitting on cradles undergoing work by their owners. It was also equally obvious that Riviera Marina is used by many local fishermen. For all this though, most visiting cruisers, particularly sailcraft, will probably want to choose one of the other facilities farther to the north.

Surprisingly enough, the adjacent Riviera Oyster Bay Restaurant (941-639-2633) is absolutely first-rate! It is under entirely different management from the marina. I was very taken with my fried seafood platter as was my mate with her deviled crabmeat. By all accounts, this is a memorable dining spot. If you should happen to find a slip in Riviera, then by all means visit the Oyster Bar.

Riviera Marina (941) 639-2008

Approach depth—4½-5 feet (minimum)
Dockside depth—5 feet (low-water)
Accepts transients—limited
Fixed wooden slips—yes (some not in the best of condition)
Dockside power connections—20 amp only

Dockside water connections—yes
Gasoline—yes
Mechanical repairs—limited
Below-waterline repairs—yes
Variety store—yes
Restaurant—on site

Punta Gorda Canals

The charted passage north of Mangrove Point skirts by a small park and public launching ramp, and eventually enters the maze of canals to the east. While good depths of 6 feet or better are carried well into the canals, we could not find enough swinging room anywhere for a vessel over 26 feet to anchor. The local residents might take a dim view of this practice in any case.

Punta Gorda-Port Charlotte Anchorages (BAIL-Suggested)

East of unlighted daybeacon #3, the marked channel leads into the southern mouth of Peace River and directly between the Punta Gorda and Port Charlotte waterfronts. There are at least four spots that visiting cruisers might consider dropping anchor along this populated portion of Peace River.

First up, boats drawing *less* than 5 feet can break off from the main channel just east of unlighted daybeacon #3 and track their way almost due north to the westernmost of the three charted and marked channels, west of Live Oak Point. Point for the gap between the outermost markers, flashing daybeacon #1 and unlighted daybeacon #2. Study chart 11426 for a moment and notice that the canal north of #1 and #2 leads to a fairly large basin known (but not charted) as Edgewater Lake.

The entrance and approach channel carries at least 5 feet of water, while soundings on Edgewater Lake run from 6½ to 8 feet.

Once past the entrance, track your way

directly up the connecting canal to Edgewater Lake. Anchor anywhere near the basin's mid-width. This refuge is wonderfully sheltered from all winds—in fact, it's the only really sheltered anchorage along the Punta Gorda-Port Charlotte waterfronts. The shoreline is, as you would expect, pocked by very heavy residential development. Do not try to dinghy ashore in Edgewater Lake. All the banks are privately owned.

With fair winds or moderate breezes from the north or northwest, you might consider anchoring northeast of #3 in the correctly charted 5- and 6-foot depths southwest of Live Oak Point. This is obviously *not* the place to ride out foul weather, but with fair breezes in the offing, it will serve. Cruisers needing to go ashore can dinghy to the northeastern side of the Peace River bridges (see below) and come ashore on the east side of Live Oak Point at a public beach.

Southeast of unlighted daybeacon #4, just short of the high-rise Peace River bridges, skippers might choose to drop the hook in the 5-foot waters abutting the southeastern banks. Some shelter is afforded from southern and southeastern airs, but this anchorage is wide open to blows from all other quarters. Again, this is *not* the place to hunker down when bad weather shows up in the NOAA forecast. Cruisers visiting this anchorage can dinghy ashore at Gilchrest Park. Watch for a pink gazebo overlooking the southeastern shoreline. Pull your dink up on a sandy beach which you will spot close by.

We are happy to report that the city of Punta Gorda, which used to limit stays in this anchorage to 24 hours, now allows cruising craft to anchor here for 5 days (out of any 30 days). That's quite an improvement!

Finally, cruising craft that can clear the 45-foot fixed twin bridges northeast of unlighted daybeacon #4 can anchor on the charted 7- and 8-foot waters behind (northeast of) Live Oak Point. Depths quickly rise to 4 and 5 feet as you track your way west and northwest towards the shoreline. Boats drawing more than 4 feet should anchor just far enough behind the point for effective shelter and stay well off the southwesterly banks.

Live Oak Point does provide a lee when the fickle breezes are blowing from the west and southwest. Well, you guessed it—this overnight stop is wide open from all other directions. The shores are guarded by a fairly thick collection of commercial development.

The northeasterly banks behind (northwest of) Live Oak Point (adjacent to the just described anchorage) are flanked by two small restaurants with petite docks. One is a raw bar while the other is associated with an adjacent motel. Both the piers are too shallow and small for cruising-size craft, but mariners looking to dine here can tie off their dinghies temporarily while patronizing the restaurants. You may also land your dinghy on the narrow, sandy beach south of the raw bar. This is a publicly owned strip of land.

Isles Yacht Club

One of Punta Gorda's two yacht clubs is found south and east of unlighted daybeacon #3A. The yacht club channel is actually the easternmost of the three marked and charted cuts south of #3A.

After cruising south on the well-marked channel past unlighted daybeacon #11, the passage enters a sheltered, southward-running canal. Cruisers making for Isles Yacht Club should hang a turn to port off this stream onto the first eastward-running canal. The yacht club will come up at the easterly end of this stream. Minimum low-water soundings

Isles Yacht Club, Punta Gorda

on the approach channel and canal are 6½ feet.

Isles Yacht Club is one of the best and friendliest clubs in this land of fine yacht clubs. A member of the staff even took the time to help this writer find a nearby launching ramp during our research and, at a later time, the club membership gave this writer a very warm reception during a luncheon presentation.

Cruisers who are members of clubs with appropriate reciprocal privileges are gladly accepted for guest dockage at mostly fixed wooden piers. Some slips consist of wooden pilings set out from a concrete seawall.

Minimum entrance and dockside depths are a very impressive 8 feet. The harbor is very well sheltered and should be more than sufficient for a snug stay in really nasty weather. Full dockside power and water connections are available, and both gasoline and diesel fuel can be purchased by members and club guests only (except on Mondays, when the club is closed). Guests are limited to a one-week stay unless special arrangements are made. The marina is staffed from 8:30 A.M. to 4:00 P.M., Tuesday through Saturday, and 8:30 A.M. to 3:00 P.M. on Sundays. Shoreside, visitors will find a swimming pool and tennis courts. The club dining room is open for lunch from 11:30 A.M. to 2:00 P.M., and dinner is served from 5:00 P.M. to 9:30 P.M. every day except Sunday and Monday. The club closes on Sundays at noon (after serving breakfast). Visiting cruisers will most definitely want to take advantage of this sumptuous dining opportunity.

Isles Yacht Club (941) 639-1369

Approach depth— 6½-11 feet
Dockside depth—8 feet
Accepts transients—members of yacht clubs
    with reciprocal privileges
Fixed wooden piers—yes
Dockside power connections—30 and 50 amp
Dockside water connections—yes
Gasoline—yes (members and guests only)
Diesel fuel—yes (members and guests only)
Restaurant—on site

Fishermen's Village Yacht Basin

As one local captain put it so succinctly to this writer, "Fishermen's Village is *the* marina in Punta Gorda." The mostly breakwater-enclosed, well-protected harbor of Fishermen's Village Yacht Basin is found at the southeastern foot of the well-buoyed channel near flashing daybeacon #2.

As you cruise into the harbor, you can't miss the huge enclosed shopping and dining complex southwest of the dockage basin. This unique collection includes seven restaurants and 33 shops of all descriptions. For steak and prime rib, you can't beat the Captain's Table (941-637-1177). Those up for the best catch of the day should spare no pains to make their way to the Village Fish Market (941-639-7959). Not only can you dine on the freshest

Fishermen's Village Yacht Basin, Punta Gorda

of seafood here, but there is a retail counter where you can purchase all types of sea creatures and take them back to your own galley for preparation. Finally, for those with a taste of Italy, you simply can't do better than the Bella Luna Italian Restaurant (941-575-4544).

Fishermen's Village itself is superfriendly and does all in its power to meet every need of visiting cruisers. Transients are eagerly accepted at fixed concrete piers with every conceivable power and water connection.

Minimum entrance depths are some 6 to 8 feet with 6½- to 8-foot depths in the well-sheltered dockage basin.

There are adequate, climate-controlled showers to wash away the day's salt and a laundromat for catching up on the dirty clothes. Gasoline, diesel fuel, and waste pump-out service are available and there is a small ship's store just behind the fuel dock. Visiting cruisers may also make use of the swimming pool and tennis courts behind the

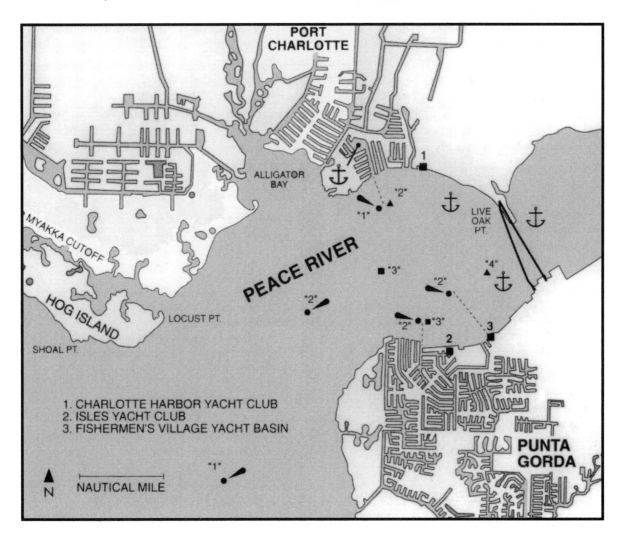

1. CHARLOTTE HARBOR YACHT CLUB
2. ISLES YACHT CLUB
3. FISHERMEN'S VILLAGE YACHT BASIN

N

NAUTICAL MILE

marina complex. The dockmasters can often arrange mechanical repairs through local, independent mechanics but no below-waterline repairs are available.

Bicycles can be "borrowed" from Fishermen's Village to visit the nearby downtown business and historic district. It's an easy one-mile bike ride and a most enjoyable hike into town. Here you will discover a Publix supermarket and a Rexall drugstore. Ask any of the friendly marina staff for directions. Of course, you can also take a taxi (see numbers above).

Fishermen's Village is the headquarters for the International Sailing School (800-824-5040). Those who need to brush up on the necessary skills to sail before the wind should check it out atop the dockmaster's office.

All in all, Fishermen's Village can only be rated as an absolutely first-rate facility from any point of view. It is a must stop for all vessels cruising Charlotte Harbor and/or the Peace River.

Fishermen's Village Yacht Basin (941) 575-3000
  http://www.fishville.com/marina.htm

Approach depth—6-8 feet (low water)
Dockside depth—6½-8 feet (low water)
Accepts transients—yes
Fixed concrete piers—yes
Dockside power connections—30 and 50 amp +
  3 slips with 100 amp
Dockside water connections—yes
Waste pump-out—yes
Showers—yes
Laundromat—yes
Gasoline—yes
Diesel fuel—yes
Mechanical repairs—independent contractors
  only
Ship's store—small
Restaurant—7 on site

Charlotte Harbor Yacht Club

Charlotte Harbor Yacht Club maintains good dockage in a protected basin along the northerly shores of the lower Peace River, directly across from the Punta Gorda waterfront. The yacht club channel is the first charted cut west of Live Oak Point.

Members of other yacht clubs with reciprocal arrangements are accepted for guest dockage at fixed piers and slips. Low-water entrance depths run to 6½ feet, while cruisers will find a good 7 feet of water dockside. The club's dockmaster is on duty from 8:30 A.M. to 4:00 P.M., Tuesday through Saturday. The club is closed on Mondays and there are no dockside attendants on Sunday. Full power and water connections are readily available at every slip and members and guests (only) can purchase gasoline and diesel fuel dockside. Showers are available in the clubhouse. The club dining room is open for lunch and dinner Tuesday through Saturday, with a Sunday brunch from 11:30 A.M. to 2:00 P.M.

Charlotte Harbor Yacht Club (941) 629-5131

Approach depth—6½-8 feet
Dockside depth—7 feet
Accepts transients—members of other yacht
  clubs with reciprocal privileges
Fixed wooden piers—yes
Dockside power connections—30 amp
Dockside water connections—yes
Showers—yes
Gasoline—yes (members and guests only)
Diesel fuel—yes (members and guests only)
Restaurant—on site

Other Punta Gorda and Port Charlotte Facilities

Just northeast of the fixed bridge, the city of Punta Gorda maintains a small launching ramp and a single pier dominated by commercial fishing vessels. Pleasurecraft would do well to look for dockage elsewhere.

On the opposite shore, across from the

small city marina, a restaurant and a motel (with restaurant) maintain two small, low-level docks overlooking the eastern side of Live Oak Point. Both of these piers have very thin water, running to only 3 feet. Also, the piers are so low that they can really only accommodate small, runabout-type power-craft. Again, cruising craft larger than 24 feet should seek dockage and shelter at some more appropriate location.

PUNTA GORDA & CHARLOTTE HARBOR NAVIGATION

Everything is pretty much straightforward in navigating the waters lying about the southerly mouth of the Peace River and the Punta Gorda-Port Charlotte waterfront. Just be sure to take enough time to correctly identify all markers before going ahead. At times, it's easy to confuse the main channel markings with some of the side cuts' aids to navigation.

Alligator Creek and Riviera Marina Vessels cruising to this rather different marina should pass between the first two western-most markers, flashing daybeacon #1 and unlighted daybeacon #2. A host of uncharted markers will then lead you through an *L*-shaped channel into the mouth of Alligator Creek. Pass red markers to your starboard side and green to your port.

Once inside the creek's boundaries, hold to the mid-width as you work your way upstream. The marina will soon come up on the port-side banks.

On to Punta Gorda and Charlotte Harbor Set course to come abeam of flashing day-beacon #2, well east of Locust Point, to its westerly side. While you could actually pass #2 on either side, its color dictates the west and northerly passage as preferred.

Flashing daybeacon #2 marks your entry into the southerly mouth of the Peace River.

The upper reaches of this stream will be covered in the next section of this chapter, but for now, let us review the Punta Gorda and Port Charlotte waterfront and their various facilities.

From #2, set course to come abeam of unlighted daybeacon #3 to its fairly immediate southerly side. While there are no shoals other than a thin strip of shallows abutting the shoreline in the immediate vicinity, the preferred channel takes a turn to the southeast. Look to the southeast and use your binoculars to pick out unlighted daybeacon #3A from the markers leading to Isles Yacht Club. Come abeam of #3A to its immediate southerly side.

Isles Yacht Club At unlighted daybeacon #3A, the channel to Isles Yacht Club will be obvious to the south. There are actually many more markers on this cut than those indicated on chart 11426. Follow the markers into the mouth of the sheltered canal dead ahead. Take the first canal which opens up to your port side. Follow the mid-width of this stream east to the yacht club docks.

Lower Port Charlotte Anchorages (BAIL-Suggested) From unlighted #3, mariners have access to two anchorages on the Port Charlotte (northern) side of Peace River. To reach the sheltered refuge on Edgewater Lake, set a northerly course from a position just east of #3 for the gap between flashing daybeacon #1 and unlighted daybeacon #2. These aids are the outermost (southernmost) markers on the westernmost of the three charted channels west of Live Oak Point. Once between #1 and #2, continue dead ahead for the westernmost of the three canals that you will spy ahead.

Enter the canal on its mid-width and track your way upstream to Edgewater Lake. Drop the hook anywhere within shouting distance of the lake's mid-section.

You might also choose to spend the evening anchored southwest of Live Oak Point. Set course from #3 for the charted 5- and 6-foot waters southeast of the easternmost of the three sets of markers leading into the northern banks. Don't approach to within less than 250 yards of the banks and be on guard against the correctly charted 2- and 3-foot shoals a bit farther to the east. These shallows surround the point and the shoreline just to the north. Be sure to drop the hook well west of this thin water.

Charlotte Harbor Yacht Club You can gain access from unlighted daybeacon #3A to Charlotte Harbor Yacht Club on the northern banks. Set course from #3A for the easternmost of the charted channels, west of Live Oak Point.

Don't be fooled. From the river you can only see a small portion of the dockage harbor. Keep the faith. Follow the markers in and the basin will eventually open out to starboard, while the clubhouse will be prominent to port.

On Peace River Channel From unlighted daybeacon #3A, come abeam of and pass unlighted daybeacon #2X and flashing daybeacon #2 to their northwesterly sides. It's easy to confuse #2 with the markers leading southeast to Fisherman's Village Yacht Basin. This latter cut is easily followed into the marina's sheltered harbor.

Upstream from flashing daybeacon #2, the channel narrows a bit. Pass unlighted daybeacon #4 to its immediate northwesterly side and then point directly for the pass-through of the 45-foot fixed twin bridge dead ahead. After passing under both spans, you should spot the small city marina to the southeast, and a line of power-cable towers breaking the water in a northwest-to-southeast line across the breadth of the river. Chart 11426 warns of submerged ruins on these waters. Continue straight ahead and put this hazard behind you.

Punta Gorda Anchorage (BAIL-Suggested) Depart the main channel at unlighted daybeacon #4, itself a short hop southwest of the twin fixed bridges. Ease your way towards the southeastern banks, feeling your way along with the sounder. For best depths stay at least 200 yards off the shoreline.

Live Oak Point Anchorage (BAIL-Suggested) After passing under the twin, fixed high-rise Peace River bridges, continue straight ahead under the charted 75-foot power lines. After leaving these hazards well behind, curl around to the northwest and point for the charted 7- and 8-foot waters east of Live Oak Point's southeasterly tip. Watch your sounder carefully as you approach a position abeam of the point. If depths start to rise, retreat to the southeast. Drop anchor *as soon as* the point comes abeam southwest of your course line. Stay well off the southwesterly, Live Oak Point shoreline. Depths of 3 and 4 feet await your keel just a stone's throw farther to the west and northwest.

The Peace River

The Peace River is actually named for the wild peas that once grew profusely along its banks. In fact, the stream was originally named "Pease River." The spelling was apparently changed after Florida became a part of the young United States in the 1840s.

Today, while the river suffers to some extent from decades of phosphate mining along its banks, the upper reaches of this river are known as a canoeing paradise. Unfortunately, these idyllic waters are far beyond the practical cruising limits for larger pleasurecraft.

The lower Peace River boasts a shoreline ranging from all-natural terrain to stretches where a few private homes show through here and there. Most of the banks are composed of marsh grass and are, frankly, not as attractive as those of the Peace's sister stream, the Myakka.

Not that the Peace River lacks for gunkholes. There are myriad opportunities to anchor well off the beaten track, sometimes with nary a house or building within sight. The anchorages discussed below are only a portion of the possible havens along the river's lower reaches. Imaginative and adventurous captains can take chart 11426 and carefully cruise to many additional overnight or lunch stops.

There are practically no marina facilities on the course of the Peace River. One boatyard near Punta Gorda offers repairs, but no dockage.

Only boats drawing 5 feet or, preferably, less should attempt to cruise the Peace River. In a few spots, 5-foot depths could be a problem for longer-legged craft.

Sailors must also take the twin Live Oak Point/Punta Gorda and I-75 bridges into account. All these spans have a vertical clearance of 45 feet. Larger sailcraft must forego the cruising charms of the Peace River in light of these height restrictions.

In summation, this writer cannot say that the Peace River was his favorite body of water in Western Florida. Nor was it the worst. I would place the river somewhere in the middle.

Punta Gorda Marina

South of unlighted daybeacon #9, a relatively shallow, poorly charted channel leads through a narrow, tree-enveloped opening to Punta Gorda Marina (941-639-2750). Low-tide entrance and dockside depths of only 4½ feet could be a problem for some boats.

Punta Gorda Marina does not offer any transient dockage, but they do feature full mechanical and below-waterline, haul-out repairs. Their travelift can haul any boat up to 35 tons.

Entrance to Punta Gorda Marina

Cleveland Anchorage

After swinging under the twin I-75 bridges, the Peace River channel cuts over to the southeastern shores near the charted village of Cleveland. Actually, only a few homes over-look the river—not much of a village really, but still quite aesthetically appealing from the water.

Good depths of 6 feet or better run to within 25 yards of the banks. There should be enough swinging room for boats up to 45 feet. Protection is quite good for all but strong southwesterly winds. There is some river current in evidence, so make sure the anchor is well set before heading below.

Long Island Anchorage

North of unlighted daybeacon #21, boats can anchor just off the river channel in the correctly charted 5-foot waters. Protection is good from all winds and vessels up to 38 feet should have enough elbow room. Be *sure* to show an anchor light at night. While there is little in the way of commercial traffic on the Peace River, there is always the possibility that someone could happen along during the evening hours.

Harbor Heights Anchorage

North-northeast of unlighted daybeacon #23, a broad channel of deep water rushes on to a parting of the river below Hunter Creek. This guide's coverage of the Peace River ends at this division of the waters. You can anchor south of the forks in 8 to 12 feet of water with plenty of swinging room and superb protection. Again, it would be a very good idea to show a bright anchor light.

PEACE RIVER NAVIGATION

Trust me when I tell you that the Peace River is not the sort of place to go cruising ahead at full bore with an occasional visual reference to the various aids to navigation along the way. The river channel wanders this way and that, and not all the markers are visible from the preceding aid. Depths do run to 5 feet in one or two spots, but most of the channel is far deeper. Remember that the 45-foot height of the two fixed bridges sets the overhead clearance for boats cruising the Peace River.

On the Peace River After passing under the twin spans of the Live Oak Point/Punta Gorda (Highway 41) fixed bridge (45 feet of vertical clearance), continue straight ahead until you are at least 100 yards northeast of the (75-foot) power line. At this point, the channel swings sharply north, but should you be seeking Punta Gorda Marina, your course will be different.

Punta Gorda Marina Follow the charted deep water off the southeasterly banks. Be sure to stay well away from the 1- and 2-foot shoal lying well off the shoreline. Watch for a series of markers running on a west-to-east line out from the southeastern shore. Ease your way into the channel and expect some 4½-foot depths.

On the Peace River Be sure to use the "Continuation of Peace River" section of chart 11426 for all your upstream navigation on this body of water. This portion of the chart gives excellent detail of the river well upstream past this guide's coverage.

After leaving the power lines behind, turn to the north and point to come abeam of unlighted daybeacon #6 to its westerly side. Curve around #6 and head east. Set your course to come abeam of and pass unlighted daybeacon #8 to its northerly side.

Now the channel follows yet another turn, this time to the southeast. From #8 you must point to come abeam of unlighted daybeacon #9 to its southerly side. Be on

guard against the charted 3-foot shoal lying to the southwest between #8 and #9.

North and east of unlighted daybeacon #9 the channel narrows, but becomes better marked. Vessels bound upstream should pass green markers to their (the cruisers') port side and take red beacons to starboard.

East of unlighted daybeacon #12, the river channel passes under the twin I-75 fixed bridges. Vertical clearance is set at 45 feet.

East of the bridge, be sure to pass unlighted daybeacon #15 to its southerly side. Don't get too close to #15, as a shoal seems to be building around the aid from the north.

Cleveland Anchorage Once abeam of unlighted daybeacon #19 to its easterly side, begin feeling your way to the east with your sounder. Drop the hook before you are less than 25 yards from the shore. Be sure your anchor is set so as not to swing closer to the banks.

On the Peace River At unlighted daybeacon #19, the Peace River channel begins a lazy turn to the north. Point to eventually pass unlighted daybeacon #21 to its easterly side. Between #21 and the next upstream aid, unlighted daybeacon #22, you can drop the hook on the river's midwidth, providing you show a prominent anchor light at night.

The most difficult (and shallowest) portion of the upstream Peace River channel lies between unlighted daybeacons #22 and #23. Even by following the instructions outlined below, you will more than likely find your vessel tracking its way through 5-foot soundings.

To maintain the best depths possible, curve around to the northeast after leaving #22 behind, and point to come abeam of #23 to its immediate southeasterly side. This track will run you close to the marshy southeastern shoreline. As soon as you pass #23, cruise quickly to the northwest out into the mid-width of the river and the correctly charted broad band of deeper water.

North of unlighted daybeacon #23, mariners may again choose to drop the hook on the river's centerline. Don't forget the anchor light.

This guide's coverage of the Peace River ends where Hunter Creek breaks off to the northeast. Farther upstream, unmarked shoals become frequent—not much of a problem for canoes, but a very different situation for cruising vessels.

CHAPTER 3

Placida Harbor to Anna Maria Island

The Western Florida ICW between Placida Harbor and Anna Maria Island comprises some of the most intriguing waters on the Sunshine State's western coast. While the region may lack some of the scope, grandeur, and adventure of Pine Island Sound and Charlotte Harbor, gunkholes and anchorages abound on this stretch of the Waterway.

From Placida Harbor, north of the Gasparilla Island Bridge, the ICW runs between the Western Florida mainland and a whole series of barrier islands to the west. With a few exceptions, this geographic arrangement makes for a sheltered passage which power captains will dearly love. Sailors will be less happy to learn that most of the passage south of Sarasota is relatively narrow. After all those great sails on the wide waters to the south, it's once again time to crank up the iron gennie and join your powered brethren in cruising with the screw.

The Waterway's sheltered nature is most certainly not all bad news, though. It takes really rough weather to churn up a nasty chop along much of this section. Lemon and Sarasota bays are two notable exceptions to this generally forgiving character. Winds over 15 knots can make for a rough ride on these two wider bodies of water, particularly in the Sarasota area.

If you should somehow dislike anchoring off, or just need to spend a night or two moored to a marina's dock, don't be concerned. A host of facilities serves up all the services that cruisers might require. Another rather prolific group of marine firms along this stretch caters mostly to smaller powercraft and their dry-storage needs. Read the data below and make your selection accordingly.

Two major communities demand any cruiser's attention along this stretch. Moving south to north, the first of these is the delightful town of Venice. Boasting first-class marina facilities, Venice is a friendly community with a far slower lifestyle than that of the metropolitan regions farther to the north. Sarasota is a major city with a whole bevy of marinas, yacht clubs, waterside restaurants, and a fine collection of anchorages.

Only two inlets currently offer reliable access to and from the open Gulf north of Gasparilla Island. Venice Inlet can be used with confidence by most craft. At Sarasota, both Big Pass and New Pass have some significant shoaling problems. Big Pass and New Pass cannot be currently recommended without serious reservations.

Moving to the north, the next inlet encountered by cruisers will be Longboat Pass. This seaward cut can now be considered a reasonable navigational risk.

In between these cuts are various other, mostly smaller seaward channels, which some locals use regularly. Unfortunately, without specific up-to-date local knowledge, visiting cruisers must use these passages at their own risk.

Most mariners will find their sojourn between Placida and Anna Maria Island to be a real cruising delight. Few will want to rush blindly north to Tampa Bay without sampling the various gunkholes and other watery delights along the way. This writer strongly suggests that you include plenty of time in your cruising itinerary to fully enjoy these memorable waters.

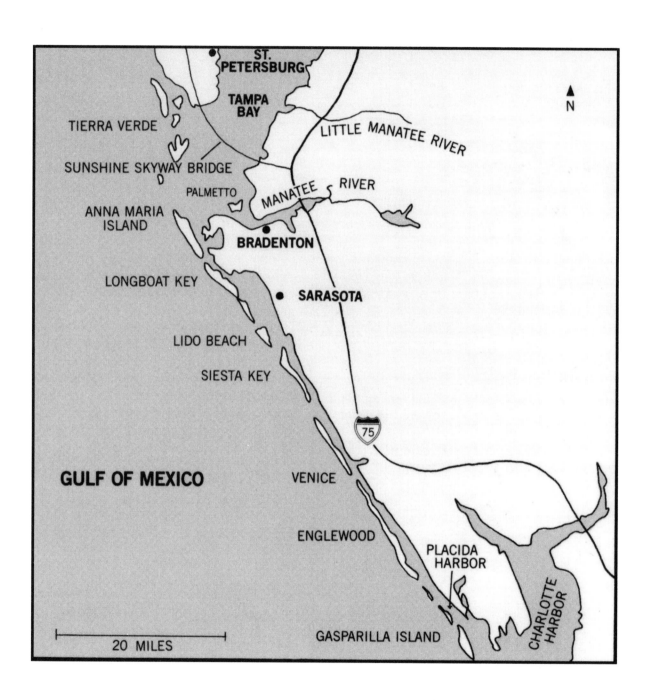

Charts Most navigators can get by with but a single chart along this section of the coastline, though offshore sailors may want a second.

11425—covers all inland waters and inlets between Gasparilla Island Causeway and Placida Harbor to Anna Maria Island and the ICW's southerly entrance into Tampa Bay

11424—offshore chart that covers pretty much he same area as 11425 with considerably less detail; it would be useful for offshore cruisers approaching the coastline

Bridges

Englewood Bridge—crosses ICW at standard mile 43.5, northwest of flashing daybeacon #22—Bascule—26 feet (closed)—opens on demand

Manasota Bridge—crosses ICW at standard mile 50, northwest of flashing daybeacon #42—Bascule—26 feet (closed)—opens on demand

South Venice/Tamiami Trail Bridge—crosses ICW at standard mile 55—Bascule—25 feet (closed)—opens on demand

Venice Avenue Bridge—crosses ICW at standard mile 56.5—Bascule—30 feet (closed)—opens 10, 30, and 50 minutes after the hour weekdays 7:00 A.M. to 4:30 P.M.—does not open at all 4:35 P.M. to 5:35 P.M.—at all other times opens on demand

Hatchett Creek Bridge—crosses ICW at standard mile 57, southwest of flashing daybeacon #5—Bascule—16 feet (closed)—opens on the hour and every 20 minutes thereafter weekdays 7:00 A.M. to 4:20 P.M. but does not open at all 4:25 P.M. to 5:25 P.M.—opens every 15 minutes weekends 7:30 A.M. to 6:00 P.M.—at all other times opens on demand

Casey Key Bridge—crosses ICW at standard mile 59, north of flashing daybeacon #9—Bascule—14 feet (closed)—opens on demand

Blackburn Bridge—crosses ICW at standard mile 63, north of unlighted daybeacon #32—Swing bridge—9 feet (closed)—opens on demand

Stickney Point Bridge—crosses ICW at standard mile 69, northwest of unlighted daybeacon #62—Bascule—18 feet (closed)—opens on demand

Siesta Key Bridge—crosses ICW at standard mile 71.5—Bascule—25 feet (closed)—opens on the hour and every 20 minutes thereafter 11:00 A.M. to 6:00 P.M.

Ringling Bridge—crosses ICW at standard mile 73.5, northwest of flashing daybeacon #10—Bascule—22 feet (closed)—opens on the hour and half-hour 7:00 A.M. to 6:00 P.M.—at all other times opens on demand

New Pass Inlet Bridge—crosses New Pass Inlet west-southwest of unlighted daybeacon #11—Bascule—23 feet (closed)—opens on the hour and every 20 minutes thereafter 7:00 A.M. to 6:00 P.M.

Longboat Pass Bridge—crosses Longboat Pass Inlet west of unlighted daybeacon #4—Bascule—17 feet (closed)—opens on demand 6:00 A.M. to 10:00 P.M.—at all other times requires three hours' notice

Cortez Bridge—crosses ICW at standard mile 87.5, north of unlighted daybeacon #49—Bascule—22 feet (closed)—opens on the hour and every 20 minutes thereafter 7:00 A.M. to 6:00 P.M.

Anna Maria Island Bridge—crosses ICW at standard mile 89, northeast of unlighted daybeacon #52—Bascule—24 feet (closed)—opens on the hour and every 20 minutes thereafter 7:00 A.M. to 6:00 P.M.—at all other times opens on demand

Gasparilla Island Bridge to Alligator Creek

North of the Gasparilla Island causeway, the ICW flows into Placida Harbor. While the harbor is a good-sized body of water in its own right, northbound cruisers leaving Pine Island Sound or Charlotte Harbor behind will quickly note its relatively narrower width. Soon the Waterway follows a canal to Lemon Bay. This impressive body of water runs north for some 10 nautical miles but narrows as it approaches another canal near Alligator Creek, leading to Venice. Lemon Bay's average width is better than half a nautical mile and strong winds can kick up a chop. Most of the bay's waters are shallow and, with a few notable exceptions, cruisers should stick to the Waterway channel. Even this formalized cut is known to be shoaling along its edges.

This portion of the ICW is characterized by beautiful, lightly developed shores. Lemon Bay is absolutely lovely. Seen from the cockpit in the warm sunshine of a late summer afternoon, with the blue waters stretching out to the green, well-wooded shores—well, you'll just have to experience it for yourself to know what I mean.

Marina facilities are adequate on Placida Harbor and Lemon Bay, but they could not be described as prolific. At least four marinas provide good overnight dockage along this 18-statute-mile run. Slow-moving craft should take these distances into account if night is fast approaching.

Excellent anchorages abound and seem to be everywhere. Most offer good shelter for even heavy weather. If you should happen to fall short of a marina and a moonlight cruise is not to your liking, there is almost certainly a good place to drop the hook nearby.

Your cruise south of Venice is typical of the entire run to Anna Marina Island. While there are still great waters ahead, they offer little else save simpler navigation than the cruising grounds on Lemon Bay.

Placida Harbor Anchorage (Standard Mile 34.5)

Captains whose craft draw less than 4½ feet can leave the ICW between unlighted daybeacon #24 and #24A and feel their way west for 100 yards or so in 5-foot low-water depths. This is strictly a fair-weather anchorage. The only real protection is provided by the causeway to the south. Frankly, there are far better refuges close at hand, so unless you just have to stop here, consider one of the anchor-down spots described below.

Cape Haze Anchorage (BAIL-Suggested) (Standard Mile 36)

It's almost as if some omniscient marine architect decided to start things off right just north of Gasparilla with a really first-class anchorage. The large cove cutting into the Waterway's northeastern banks northwest of unlighted daybeacon #30 offers minimum 8-foot depths and super shelter from all winds. The bottom of this cove has been dredged in years past, and the holding ground is a bit suspect, though neither we nor our neighbors had any problems with dragging anchors during our several stays. There is enough swinging room for anything smaller than the *Exxon Valdez*. The shores are overlooked by moderate to heavy residential development. While many among us would prefer a natural shoreline, it must be noted that the homes are not unattractive and the many private docks with vessels lying beside them make for a true nautical atmosphere. Seldom will cruising mariners find such a well-sheltered and easily entered anchorage so close to the ICW.

Cove Anchorage (Standard Mile 36.5)

Note the large cove indenting the northeastern banks at unlighted daybeacon #35. While not as large, nor quite so sheltered, as the Cape Haze anchorage, this water does provide good protection and features minimum 7-foot depths. The main body of the cove provides enough elbow room for a 48-footer to swing comfortably. Cruisers dropping the hook in this cove will again have the opportunity to view the heavy but comely shoreside residential development. The cove eventually leads to a small canal lined with private docks. There are no facilities and no room to anchor along this stream.

Don Pedro Island Anchorage (Standard Mile 37)

North of unlighted daybeacon #2 the Waterway quickly begins its approach to the sheltered canal which provides a conduit into Lemon Bay. There is one additional opportunity for snug overnight anchorage before entering the canal.

This haven is found on the charted 7-foot waters west-southwest of unlighted daybeacon #4. Boats drawing 5 feet or less can leave the ditch and cruise to within 25 yards of the western banks. Minimum depths are in the 5-foot range. Craft needing more water can drop the hook within 25 yards of the Waterway channel in 6 to 7 feet of water. Protection is good for all but the heaviest weather. Strong northerly blows would cause the most problems.

This is a delightful anchorage. The Don Pedro Island shoreline to the southwest is an all-natural collection of leafy green banks with taller trees farther to the west. A few private homes overlook the shoreline northeast of the Waterway. You will have to contend with the wake of any passing powercraft, but otherwise your stay should be one punctuated by peace and security.

Palm Island Marina/Gulfwind Marine (Standard Mile 38)

One of the best marina facilities between Placida Harbor and Venice sits at the southern foot of Lemon Bay, northwest of unlighted daybeacon #7. Since 1998, this marina has undergone a change of ownership, and it is now only vaguely connected to Palm Island Resort. The name has been changed to Palm Island Marina.

The new incarnation of Palm Island Marina is a first-class operation. We were very impressed with the dockmaster and his staff's can-do attitude. Visiting cruisers can now be assured of receiving a warm and knowledgeable welcome.

Good entrance and dockside depths of 6 to 6½ feet will be plenty for most vessels. Transients are accommodated at fixed wooden slips featuring all power, water, and cable television connections. Gasoline or diesel fuel can also be purchased, while shoreside amenities include excellent, air-conditioned showers and a laundromat. Waste pump-out service and extensive dry stack storage for powercraft are available as well.

Palm Island Marina features a refreshing on-site swimming pool where transients are welcome. An adjacent kitchen facility is open for free use by all visiting cruisers.

While a ferry still leaves the Palm Island

Palm Island Marina

Marina docks regularly for Rum Bay Restaurant on nearby Knight Island (see below), we now recommend that cruisers bent on a night of landside dining check out the on-site Johnny Leverocks Seafood House (941-698-6900).

Gulfwind Marine (941-697-2161) leases the rear portion of the Palm Island dockage basin and offers dry storage for small power-craft, mechanical repairs, and a ship's store. Most of this service work seems to be geared to small and medium-sized powerboats.

Palm Island Marina (941) 697-4356
Gulfwind Marine (941) 697-2161
  http://www.palmislandmarina.com
Approach depth—6 feet minimum

Dockside depth—6-6½ feet
Accepts transients—yes
Fixed wooden slips—yes
Dockside power connections—up to 50 amp
Dockside water connections—yes
Waste pump-out—yes
Showers—yes
Laundromat—yes
Gasoline—yes
Diesel fuel—yes
Mechanical repairs—yes (at Gulfwind Marine)
Ship's store—yes (at Gulfwind Marine)
Restaurant—on site

Cape Haze Yacht & Beach Club (Standard Mile 38.5)

An indifferently charted channel cuts east off the ICW, south of unlighted daybeacon #9, to the newest marina lining this portion of the Western Florida ICW. Unfortunately, at the time of this writing, Cape Haze Yacht & Beach Club is going through some financial difficulty. Our last visit seemed to find this firm on the road to recovery, but, to be on the safe side, be sure to call ahead to check on current conditions.

Cape Haze accepts transients at fixed wooden piers set in a fairly sheltered harbor. Minimum entrance and dockside depths run about 5½ feet, with many slips having 6- to 7-foot soundings. Full power and water connections are offered, as are waste pump-out service, extensive dry stack storage, and mechanical repairs for gasoline engines (only). Gasoline and diesel fuel can be purchased at the marina fuel dock. Visiting mariners will also discover first-class, climate-controlled showers, a full laundromat, heated swimming pool, and Jacuzzi. There is even a superb clubhouse (open to visiting cruisers), which includes a kitchen and large-screen color television.

When it comes time to slake a healthy appetite after a long day on the water, we suggest the on-site Ship's Lantern restaurant (941-697-2244). While we have never had the chance to dine here, this restaurant's longevity recommends its cuisine most highly.

The list of services and amenities at Cape Haze certainly speaks well of a visit to this facility. Let's just hope that the parent firm is able to get its financial act together.

Cape Haze Yacht & Beach Club (941) 698-1800 (888) 770-1800

Approach depth—6-6½ feet minimum
Dockside depth—5 ½-7 feet minimum
Accepts transients—yes
Fixed wooden piers—yes
Dockside power connections—up to 50 amp

Dockside water connections—yes
Waste pump-out—yes
Showers—yes
Laundromat—yes
Gasoline—yes
Diesel fuel—yes
Mechanical repairs—gasoline engines only
Restaurant—on site

Lemon Bay

North of unlighted daybeacon #8 the ICW flows out into the wider waters of Lemon Bay. Cruisers lucky enough to sight the bay's waters for the first time during fair weather will never forget the experience. To be succinct, Lemon Bay is gorgeous.

Looking out on Lemon Bay

Lemon Bay often reminds me of author Mike Greenwald's description of the Mediterranean. The bay can be "a bit like the girl with green eyes. There can be a surprise behind her smile." So it is with this body of water. While serving up a true aesthetic feast for the eyes, much of the bay is shallow and the ICW channel itself often shoals along its margins. While there are side trips, gunkholes, and anchorages galore, depths of as little as half a foot wait to greet the keel of the unwary.

So enjoy the sights, take your time, and have a safe cruise. Just remember that most of us can't stay on Lemon Bay forever. I know it's hard, but *c'est la vie.*

Rum Bay Restaurant on Knight Pass (Standard Mile 39.5)

North-northwest of unlighted daybeacon #9, unlighted daybeacon #9A marks the intersection of the Waterway and the passage running west and north into old Knight Pass channel. The inlet that gave rise to this stream has long been closed, but Rum Bay Restaurant maintains a marked and dredged channel from the ICW into the old cut. This passage leads to two sets of wooden piers where Rum Bay patrons are free to tie while dining. The restaurant also operates a ferry from the mainland to allow for visits by landlubbers. Channel and dockside depths are around 5½ to possibly 6 feet. While a sign on the docks advertises slips for boats up to 40 feet, they appeared to this writer to be more appropriate for craft under 36 feet. No overnight accommodations are available.

Stump Pass (Standard Mile 41)

The Stump Pass channel makes into the Waterway's southwestern flank immediately southeast of unlighted daybeacon #17A. The buoyed passage leads to (but not through) a locally controversial inlet. Since the last edition of this guide appeared, both the approach channel and the seaward-cut portion of Stump Pass have shoaled severely. We no longer recommend that any vessel larger than a skiff attempt to make use of any part of this channel or the anchorages that both this writer and BAIL used to recommend adjacent to Thornton Key. Let me be clear about this; barring the completion of some future dredging project, all boats should keep clear of the Stump Pass channel.

The good news is that plans are in the works to dredge Stump Pass, but a late-breaking story that has appeared just as this account is being tapped out on the keyboard suggests that there are some financial and contractual problems with this project. Hopefully, all these difficulties will be cleared up sometime in 2000, and, with luck, perhaps in the next edition of this guide we can once again recommend exploration of Stump Pass, particularly its onetime good anchorages. Let's just hope for the best.

Fish Tail Marina at Stump Pass Standard Mile 41)

The well-marked entry channel leading to Fish Tail Marina (formerly Stump Pass Marina) cuts to the northeast abeam of unlighted daybeacon #17A. You can't miss the marina, courtesy of a lighthouse-like tower perched over the ship's store and fuel dock.

Fish Tail provides limited wet-slip dockage in an enclosed, well-protected harbor. Low-water entrance depths run a somewhat thin 4½ to 5 feet with 5-foot low-water soundings in the enclosed basin. Transients are accepted, but clearly the forte here now runs far more to dry stack storage of smaller power-

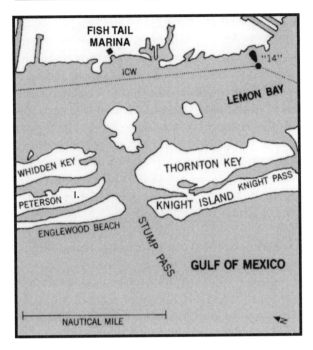

Dockside depth—5 feet (MLW)
Accepts transients—yes (slip space limited)
Fixed wooden slips—yes
Dockside power connections—up to 50 amp
Dockside water connections—yes
Gasoline—yes
Diesel fuel—yes
Mechanical repairs—gasoline engines only
Ship's and variety store—yes
Restaurant—on site

Rock Creek (Standard Mile 43)

Captains cruising north-northwest of unlighted daybeacon #21A on the ICW may notice a locally marked channel cutting east-northeast to charted Rock Creek. Unless you pilot a shallow-draft outboard or I/O-powered craft, don't enter this cut. Low-water depths run to as little as 4 feet. If you should happen to fit these requirements, there are several small-scale marinas on the creek near the 9-foot fixed bridge. Gasoline and some low-key mechanical repairs can usually be had.

Englewood Beach Anchorage (BAIL-Suggested) (Standard Mile 43.5)

Study chart 11425 for a moment and notice the broad ribbon of deep water that stretches southwest, northwest of flashing daybeacon #22 (immediately southeast of the 26-foot bascule bridge). Skippers with a flair for taking a chance can find good anchorage along this stretch of water. The channel (which eventually leads to Englewood Beach) is unmarked and surrounded by shoal water, so enter with caution and be ready for the unexpected. By keeping to the channel, 6-foot minimum depths can be maintained for quite some distance upstream, though not as far as 11425 would lead you to believe.

Cruisers following the Englewood Beach channel south will encounter a side cut running to the west-northwest just as the main

craft rather than overnight dockage. In fact, the dockmaster has informed this writer that the marina usually only sees transients on the weekends. Berths at Fish Tail consist of wooden pilings set out from a concrete sea-wall. Dockside connections run the gamut from 30 to 50 amps. Shoreside, cruisers will find a swimming pool and a hot-tub spa. Other marine services include gasoline, diesel fuel, and mechanical repairs for gasoline-powered craft only.

A ship's and variety store overlooks the entrance cut just behind the fuel dock. This pier fronts directly onto the bay, and is not breakwater protected as are the remainder of the marina's slips. The poolside, semi-open-air Marker 17A Cafe (941-697-0241) is open for lunch daily and serves dinner Tuesday through Saturday.

Fish Tail Marina at Stump Pass (941) 698-2472
Approach depth—4½-5 feet (MLW)

passage swings to the southeast. With a great deal of navigational caution (see below), minimum 6-foot depths can be carried on this side channel. The stream eventually dead ends at a restaurant called The Captain's Club (941-475-3184). This dining spot has its own docks, which patrons are free to use while dining. Low-water depths alongside run around 5 feet.

Englewood Beach's best anchorage is found southeast of the just discussed side channel, on the charted 8-foot waters. This spot has excellent protection, courtesy of the adjoining southwestern (beach-side) banks and the charted shallows and islands to the northeast. It would take some seriously heavy weather to bother you in this haven. As you would expect, the small islands and shoals to the northeast are undeveloped, while the southwestern banks are populated by pleasant residential neighborhoods.

Do not try to continue following the Englewood Beach channel to the southeast. While the stream eventually rejoins Stump Pass, depths run out far sooner than chart 11425 would lead you to believe.

Englewood Anchorage (BAIL-Suggested) (Standard Mile 44.5)

Between unlighted daybeacons #25 and #26, skippers can safely depart the ICW and cruise northeast through 6-foot waters to within 200 yards of the banks. This shoreline is part of the mainland community of Englewood—not to be confused with Englewood Beach, which occupies the barrier island to the southeast. In fair weather, these waters make for a fine anchorage with a super view of Lemon Bay's wide expanse. The northeastern shoreline gives some protection when breezes are blowing from the north or

northeast, but otherwise the anchorage is pretty open. Overnighters must also contend with the wake of any vessels passing by on the Waterway, but hopefully most power captains will be respectful. During one visit, we spotted at least four sailcraft bedded down in this refuge. One can only conclude that it is a popular stopover with the local sailing crowd. Captain and crew stopping in this anchorage can dinghy ashore northeast of unlighted daybeacon #28 at a public park which will be spied along the eastern banks.

Royal Palm Marina (Standard Mile 46.5)

Royal Palm Marina's entrance channel breaks off from the ICW to the east-southeast, just northwest of unlighted daybeacon #30. This facility is friendly to transients, and stays up to 10 days are allowed. Depths on much of the entrance cut run from 5 to 6 feet, but one lump places the minimum MLW soundings at 4½ feet. Dockside, 7-8-foot soundings can be expected. Transients are berthed at fixed concrete piers featuring a full array of power and water connections. With winds blowing directly across Lemon Bay, boats docked at Royal Palm may experience a fair amount of chop. According to the marina management, this effect is minimized by the shallows southwest of the docks.

Gasoline and diesel fuel are readily available, as are full-service mechanical and below-waterline, haul-out repairs. The marina's travelift is rated at a 50-ton capacity. Shoreside amenities include clean, non-climate controlled showers, a small combination ship's and variety store, and a laundromat.

Fideli's Restaurant (60 Indiana Avenue N, 941-475-3414), the Old Englewood Diner (498 Dearborn Street W, 941-473-1858), and

Bubba's BBQ (470 Dearborn Street W, 941-473-2707) are all found within a fairly long walk from the dockage basin. Ask any of the marina staff for directions.

Royal Palm Marina Yacht Basin (941) 474-1420

Approach depth—4½-6 feet
Dockside depth—7-8 feet
Accepts transients—yes

Fixed concrete piers—yes
Dockside power connections—up to 50 amp
Dockside water connections—yes
Showers—yes
Laundromat—yes
Gasoline—yes
Diesel fuel—yes
Mechanical repairs—yes
Below-waterline repairs—yes
Ship's and variety store—yes
Restaurant—several nearby

GASPARILLA ISLAND BRIDGE TO ALLIGATOR CREEK NAVIGATION

Let's make this simple. Except for the side trips outlined below, stick to the Waterway. In most cases, if you make an unplanned deviation from the ditch, it's time to either get out and push or find out what Sea Tow is doing at the moment.

Watch your stern as well as your forward progress to quickly note any leeway. *Stick to the centerline of the ICW channel.* Keep your binoculars handy to help pick out markers in Lemon Bay. For some reason, many of these aids seem to blend in with the shoreline. Stay alert, watch the sounder, and you will reach Venice without scrapes.

Gunkholes and anchorages along this portion of the ICW run the full gamut, ranging from those where you would just about have to be asleep to find the bottom, to others where even the careful mariner can stir some mud.

North through Placida Harbor After leaving the Gasparilla Island Bridge behind, the Western Florida ICW follows a bit of a winding path through the waters of Placida Harbor. At flashing daybeacon #23, the Waterway takes a swing to the north-north-west. Come abeam of unlighted daybeacon

#24 to its westerly side and point to pass unlighted daybeacon #24A to the same quarter. Between #24 and #24A, the Placida Harbor anchorage will come abeam to the southwest.

Placida Harbor Anchorage Leave the Waterway about halfway between unlighted daybeacons #24 and #24A, and feel your way to the west at idle speed for a hundred yards or so. Watch the sounder. Farther to the west and southwest depths deteriorate to 4 feet or even less.

On the ICW At flashing daybeacon #26, the Waterway again changes its track. This time cruisers must follow a bend to the northwest. A minimum-wake zone begins at unlighted daybeacon #28 and runs north to unlighted daybeacon #4. This regulation apparently protects the many private docks that line the Waterway along the northeastern banks.

Just to keep life interesting, you must again cut back to the north-northwest at flashing daybeacon #29. Northwest of unlighted daybeacon #30, one of the best anchorages on the entire run from Placida

Harbor to Venice comes up on the north-eastern banks.

Cape Haze Anchorage (BAIL-Suggested) Simply enter this cove on the mid-width of its broad mouth. Drop anchor anywhere so as not to swing to within less than 25 yards of the surrounding shores and settle down for a night of peace and security. The adjoining canal retains fair depths, but it is too narrow for effective anchorage. Visiting cruisers should probably avoid this stream.

Cove Anchorage Favor the southeastern shoreline slightly as you enter the cove northeast of unlighted daybeacon #35. Anchor anywhere near the cove's mid-width. Don't attempt to enter the canal heading off to the east if your craft is larger than 30 feet.

On the ICW Northwest and north of unlighted daybeacon #2, the Waterway enters a sheltered passage known as "The Cutoff." This ribbon of deep water ushers cruising craft into the bright confines of Lemon Bay.

Don Pedro Island Anchorage Once abeam of unlighted daybeacon #4, swing 90 degrees to the west-southwest and follow the deep waters in towards the shoreline. Good depths of 6 to 7 feet are found within 25 yards of the Waterway channel. Skippers will find 5 feet of water almost to the banks. If you draw 4½ feet or less, it's quite possible to loop the anchorage to the south and east, and rejoin the Waterway just southeast of flashing daybeacon #3.

On the Waterway Boats drawing 3 feet or better should not attempt to enter the

unnamed sidewater northwest of unlighted daybeacon #5. In spite of the "6-foot" soundings shown on chart 11425 at the stream's entrance, on-site research revealed that depths have risen to at least 4-foot levels.

Northwest of unlighted daybeacon #7, powerboaters should slow to no-wake speed to protect the two marinas along the northeastern banks. Both have marked entrances which are visible from the Waterway.

At unlighted daybeacon #8, the ICW at last passes out into the wider waters of Lemon Bay. Unless winds exceed 15 knots, it should be a merry meeting.

Northwest of unlighted daybeacon #9, passing cruisers will note unlighted daybeacon #9A. A marked channel leads west and then northwest from #9A into old Knight Pass and the Rum Bay Restaurant dock. Cruisers continuing north or south on the ICW must take care to separate the Waterway markers from the beacons on this side cut.

Knight Pass/Rum Bay Restaurant Channel The channel is well outlined from #9A and reasonably easy to follow into the old pass's interior reaches. The restaurant docks will come up on the port shore. The first set of piers is used by the ferry running from the mainland to the restaurant. Visiting mariners may want to consider the more upstream set of docks. Here you won't be bothered by the ferry.

Cruising farther upstream past the second set of restaurant docks is not recommended. Depths quickly decline as you begin to approach the now closed pass.

On the ICW The Waterway takes a sharp cut to the north at flashing daybeacon #11 and heads toward Lemon Bay's eastern banks. This can be an unexpected turn for those not following the ICW's track on chart 11425. Be ready for it.

Use your binoculars to help pick out unlighted daybeacon #13 to the north. At #13 the Waterway begins to bend back to the northwest. You will have completed this turn by the time you pass flashing daybeacon #14. North of #14 the ICW channel runs straight for the Venice approach canal, with only a few minor angles here and there.

The charted channel east of unlighted daybeacon #17 leads to a private dockage area. There are no services for transients, nor is there room to anchor.

Take care as you approach unlighted daybeacon #17A. The Stump Pass channel departs from this marker and cuts west. Similarly, the marked route to Fish Tail Marina runs northeast from #17A. Be sure to sort out the bevy of markers and pass #17A to its easterly side. Northbound cruisers should then point to pass unlighted daybeacon #18 to its southwesterly quarter.

Stump Pass As mentioned above, the Stump Pass channel has now shoaled so badly that it is inappropriate for any craft larger than a rowboat. We heartily recommend that all cruising-size vessels not attempt to enter the marked cut leading to the pass. Perhaps future dredging will once again provide access to the pass and its interesting anchorages, but, for now, just keep on trucking up or down the ICW.

On the ICW The Waterway continues to be straight and reasonably easy to follow from the Stump Pass intersection to flashing daybeacon #22. Some of the runs between the various daybeacons are rather lengthy, so you may want to use your binoculars to help pick out the next aid. Just northwest of #22, an anchorage opportunity will come abeam to the west and south.

Englewood Beach Channel & Anchorage (BAIL-Suggested) The channel leading to Englewood Beach is not as simple to traverse as it might appear from a casual study of chart 11425. The route is entirely unmarked and it borders on shoals to the east and west. While the deep water extends south-southwest (and then southeast) in a wide band, it's all too easy to wander away from the good depths. Proceed slowly and detail a crew member to keep a constant watch on the sounder. If depths rise to less than 5½ feet, you are encroaching on the surrounding shallows. Stop and make corrections at once before grounding depths are reached.

Depart the Waterway about halfway between flashing daybeacon #22 and the Englewood Bridge (to the northwest). Cut sharply south-southwest and point to eventually come abeam of (what I call) the "Subm pile" island by some 30 to 50 yards to your port side. A shallow spoil bank shelves out from the westerly shoreline along this portion of the channel, and there is also very shallow water north of the submerged pile island, lying east of your initial passage from the ICW to the waters west of the island. If all this sounds confusing (and I know it does), follow along on chart

11425 with me and all will become clear. Well, clearer.

Continue favoring the island shores as you cruise to the south. Eventually, you will pass by the southern tip of the island, east of your course. Continue holding to the same track until you are within 25 yards or so of the southwestern banks.

You may then choose to cut back to the west-northwest and enter the charted cove, overlooked by the Captain's Club restaurant. Skippers following this cut must heavily favor the southern shoreline to bypass the correctly charted, broad band of shallows to the north.

The main Englewood Beach channel cuts sharply southeast at the intersection with the restaurant cove. Favor the southwestern banks as you cruise along. Eventually, the channel takes a jog to the south. Halt your forward progress before reaching this southerly turn. As suggested by the "Shl rep 1983" designation on chart 11425, our research revealed that depths have risen to 4 feet or less in the body of the southerly turn. Drop the hook well northwest of this unhappy obstruction.

On the ICW   Northwest of flashing daybeacon #22, the ICW passes through the Englewood Beach bascule bridge. This span has a closed vertical clearance of 26 feet and currently opens on demand.

After passing through the bridge, cruisers will spy a collection of boats docked and anchored to the southwest. After a whole series of attempts to find an anchorage on these waters, we hit 4-foot depths every time. Obviously the locals know something

we don't, but, equally obvious, it would be difficult if not impossible for first-time visitors to find the good water without local help. Navigators lacking this sort of specific information are advised to bypass this potential haven entirely.

North of the Englewood Beach span, cruisers will pass flashing daybeacon #24 to its southwestern side. Just northwest of #24, you may spy a channel running into the northeastern banks. This cut serves Travis Boating Center (941-475-7100), a dry stack storage facility for smaller powercraft. No significant transient services are available.

Between the next two (moving north) aids, unlighted daybeacons #25 and #26, captains may choose to enter an open but deep anchorage to the northeast.

Englewood Anchorage (BAIL-Suggested)
Simply depart the Waterway about halfway between unlighted daybeacons #25 and #26, and cruise towards the northeasterly banks. Good depths persist to within 100 to 150 yards of the banks. This good water actually runs well to the southeast and is bounded by the Travis Boating Center channel, described above.

On the ICW   Don't attempt to explore the charted channel southeast of unlighted daybeacon #28A. Our soundings showed that this onetime cut has shoaled to 4-foot depths. There is also no protection to speak of for overnight anchorage.

The marked entrance to Royal Palm Marina will come up just northwest of unlighted daybeacon #30. The passage is well marked and reasonably easy to follow.

North of flashing daybeacon #32, Lemon Bay begins to narrow as it runs on towards its connecting canal near Alligator Creek. Depths outside of the ICW channel rise significantly. Take all precautions to keep to the Waterway.

The small, charted channel northeast of unlighted daybeacon #36 leads to a few private docks. There are no services for transients and no room to anchor.

Similarly, the channel leading to Forked Creek, northeast of unlighted daybeacon #38, holds 5-foot depths, but the stream offers no facilities nor anchorage possibilities.

North of unlighted daybeacon #41, the Waterway markers seem to be a bit easier to pick out from the surrounding shoreline. Perhaps the narrower width of the water helps in these observations. At any rate, you will not need to use your binoculars with quite so much regularity, but keep them close at hand just in case.

The Manasota bascule bridge with 26 feet of closed vertical clearance crosses the Waterway northwest of flashing daybeacon #42 and unlighted daybeacon #43. Wonder of wonders, this span opens on demand for vessels that need more clearance.

Northwest of unlighted daybeacon #50, all boats should slow to idle speed. A pontoon ferry crosses the Waterway here to provide access to the Gulfside beaches. Continue at idle speed until reaching the "Resume Safe Operation" sign.

Flashing daybeacon #51 and the shallow mouth of Alligator Creek (on the northeastern banks) herald the Waterway's entrance into the Venice Canal. Hang on, there is yet more great cruising ahead.

Venice to Little Sarasota Bay

While researching the waters lying about the charming community of Venice, this writer had occasion to spend a bit of time with one of the local marina managers one hot, summer afternoon. After we got to know each other, he inquired as to where my research had taken me before coming to Venice. I related my lengthy cruises on Tampa Bay and the surrounding waters. The manager looked at me for a few moments out of the corner of his eye and finally said, "Please don't tell them we're here."

While it would take the rosiest-colored glasses to look at Venice as if it were a small, backwater village, there is no denying that a calmer, more tranquil lifestyle is found here than at some of the metropolitan centers to the north. Venetians, many of whom are retired folks, seem intent on enjoying their lives in the Florida sunshine and simply taking it easy. They are happy to welcome cruising visitors and their town provides notable facilities and at least one anchorage.

With its fine inlet, wonderful waterside restaurants, and good marinas alone, Venice deserves any cruiser's full attention. Factor in the town's innate friendliness and you have a must stop for every vessel cruising the Western Florida ICW.

North of Venice, the ICW soon tracks through the somewhat wide reaches of Blackburn Bay, and then spills into the larger confines of Little Sarasota Bay. Marina facilities continue to be prolific and there are two decent Gulf-side anchorages on Little Sarasota Bay.

Enough said—let's explore these marvelous waters together. Some of the best cruising in all of Western Florida awaits.

Venice Attractions

Believe it or else, Venice is known as the "shark's tooth capital of the world." These old teeth are remnants of the hundreds of thousands of sharks who have died in the Gulf of Mexico. The teeth survive and some are eventually washed to shore. The local Chamber of Commerce actually gives away a small bag of shark's teeth gathered by local residents to any visitor for the asking.

The week of July 4 brings the Venice downtown festival. An extravaganza of arts, crafts, and food, this notable event also features a fascinating sandcastle-building contest. This sandy competition has attracted the attention of the national press over the last several years and it has been featured on the ABC show "Good Morning America."

The largest special event of the year is the Venice Sun Fiesta in October. This weeklong celebration includes a parade, musical entertainment, and a community fair. Of course, no Floridian festival would be worth its salt without copious quantities of good seafood, not to mention an old-fashioned beauty contest.

A host of other events augments these two major happenings. No matter when you cruise into Venetian waters, there's a good chance that you will find something going on out of the ordinary.

Numbers to know in Venice include:

Midway Taxi—941-426-8749
Yellow Cab—941-480-9222
Avis Rental Cars—941-484-2227
Budget Rent A Car—941-359-5353
Enterprise Rent-A-Car—941-485-2774
Chamber of Commerce—941-488-2236

Venice History   Following the close of the Civil War, the state of Florida made an earnest bid to attract settlers to its western coastline. One hundred and sixty acres were free for the asking to anyone who would agree to settle and develop his tract.

In 1868 a group arrived from Georgia and points north to settle around the inlet that we would one day come to know as Venice Pass. These early pioneers included some of the oldest family names in Venetian history, including Webb, Roberts, Blackburn, and Higel.

The small village's first post office was established by Frank Higel in 1888. The original name given to the new town was "Horse and Chaise."

The modern history of the town we call Venice really began in 1911 when Ms. Potter Palmer purchased 140,000 acres of land in Western Florida, much of which comprised the site of the modern-day town. Ms. Palmer had inherited a sizable fortune from her late husband, who owned the Chicago Palmer House Hotel. With her encouragement, both moral and financial, the railroad reached Venice in 1911. Transportation was further enhanced by the completion of a hard-surface road to Sarasota in 1916.

The Roaring Twenties saw a construction boom that was to transform the village into the town of Venice. Some years earlier a New York physician, Dr. Fred Albee, came to town with the idea of planning a model community. His blueprints languished for a decade but were eventually undertaken by the Brotherhood of Locomotive Engineers as a retirement community for their members. Soon a whole series of canals graced by houses of Northern Italian architecture had been built. Someone suggested that the town change its name to Venice to acknowledge its striking resemblance to that Italian city. The idea took root and today visitors will find a uniquely American version of the city of canals.

With the opening of the Western Florida ICW in the 1960s, pleasureboating traffic increased by leaps and bounds.

Today Venice boasts 78,000 year-round residents, with many more seasonal visitors. The community is still a lovely mix of Italian and American architecture which draws more retirees year after year. Even in these days of rapid change and progress, those gallant pioneers who settled so long ago by the small inlet are not forgotten. Their names are indelibly etched on such landmarks as Roberts Bay, Blackburn Point, and Higel Park. Without their efforts, the bright and shining city that is today's Venice might never have come to pass.

Gulfwind Marine of Venice (Standard Mile 55)

Look at chart 11425 for a moment and notice the *L*-shaped offshoot coming off the Waterway's western shore just north of standard mile 55. This water plays host to the first of Venice's several fine marina facilities.

Gulfwind Marine of Venice

Gulfwind Marine of Venice features full repair services and transient dockage in a well-sheltered harbor as well. Berths are found at fixed wooden piers with full power and water connections. Depths run from 7 to 8 feet. Mechanical repairs for both gasoline and diesel power plants are offered as are gasoline, diesel fuel, and below-waterline repair services (40-ton travelift), along with a bait and tackle shop. Crawdad's restaurant (941-484-3515) is located within the complex as well as a small motel.

Gulfwind Marine of Venice (941) 485-3388

Approach depth—6½-8 feet
Dockside depth—7-8 feet
Accepts transients—yes

Fixed wooden piers—yes
Dockside power connections—up to 50 amp
Dockside water connections—yes
Gasoline—yes
Diesel fuel—yes
Mechanical repairs—yes
Below-waterline repairs—yes
Tackle store—yes
Restaurant—on site

Fisherman's Wharf Marina (Standard Mile 57)

Follow the Venice canal on chart 11425 until it flows out into wider waters just north of the Hatchett Creek Bridge. East of unlighted daybeacon #4, the second of Venice's pleasurecraft stops will come abeam. Fisherman's Wharf is a medium-sized marina that offers

Fisherman's Wharf Marina, Venice

dockage on the southern banks of the creek, east of #4, and on a long wooden face dock that fronts directly onto the Waterway's northern flank. To access the marina's inner slips, an obscurely charted shoal must be avoided. This tongue of shallows has grown over the last several years and it is now more of a problem than once it was. Please read the navigational information on this marina presented below, *before* attempting first-time entry. Your keel will be ever so much happier for the effort.

By successfully avoiding the above-mentioned shoal, 5½ MLW depths can be carried on the approach to Fisherman's Wharf. Dockside there is some 5½ to 6½ feet of water at low tide.

While spaces seem to be at a bit of a premium, transients are accepted at fixed slips which mostly consist of wooden pilings set out from a concrete seawall and a long, fixed wooden face dock that fronts directly onto the ICW. Advance reservations are most definitely recommended. Shelter is quite good for all but the heaviest weather. Complete dockside power and water connections are on hand, as are gasoline, diesel fuel, and waste pump-out service. Showers and an on-site laundromat round out the marina services.

The old, full-service restaurant at Fisherman's Wharf is now closed, but there are still two on-site dining possibilities. Marker 4 Oyster Bar (941-484-0344) is found directly on the southern shores of the marina's creek, a bit farther to the northeast. We found a warm crowd at this establishment in a party-like atmosphere. The music was a trifle loud for this writer's taste, but then my first mate says I'm an old fuddy duddy about this sort of thing. Besides copious quantities of barley and hops and other harder fare, Marker 4

serves seafood and sandwiches. This is not the place to belly up for a really big meal, but the dishes we tried were quite good.

If your sweet tooth is giving you a hard time, don't miss The Little Ice Cream Shop (941-480-9696). This calorie-rich establishment makes its home immediately beside Marker 4. The ice cream and desserts are really, really good!

Fisherman's Wharf Marina (941) 484-9246

Approach depth—5½-8 feet (low-water)
Dockside depth—5½-6½ feet (low-water)
Accepts transients—yes
Fixed wooden slips—yes
Dockside power connections—up to 50 amp
Dockside water connections—yes
Waste pump-out—yes
Showers—yes
Laundromat—yes
Gasoline—yes
Diesel fuel—yes
Restaurant—2 on site

Venice Yacht Club (Standard Mile 58)

After traversing the shallow reaches of Roberts Bay, the ICW turns sharply northwest at flashing daybeacon #13. As you approach the next northerly aid, unlighted daybeacon #14, a very well marked but indifferently charted channel breaks off to the west-southwest and leads to the docks of the Venice Yacht Club. Excellent depths of 7½ feet or better are held in this channel.

The club's formidable dockage basin and clubhouse overlook the western shores of the wide swath of waters spanning the gap between Roberts and Donna bays, near the mouth of the southernmost of the three charted canals. Some additional slips are located on this stream. Dockside soundings range from 7 to 8 feet. Transients who are

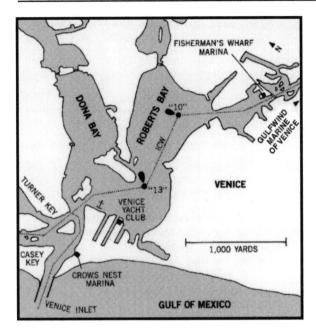

members of yacht clubs with reciprocal privileges are accepted for guest dockage. The club maintains a full-time dockmaster on duty from 8:00 A.M. to 5:00 P.M. The fixed slips feature all power and water connections and (unusual for a yacht club) gasoline and diesel fuel can be purchased at an on-site fuel pier maintained by the club. Shoreside, visiting cruisers will find excellent dining facilities. Lunch and dinner are served seven days a week with a super Sunday brunch. There is a refreshing swimming pool for those needing to cool off after a hot day on the water. Downtown Venice is found within a very long walk, or you might choose to take a taxi. Here you will find several additional restaurants and good shopping.

Venice Yacht Club (941) 488-7708

Approach depth—7½-10 feet
Dockside depth—7-8 feet
Accepts transients—members of yacht clubs
    with reciprocal privileges

Fixed wooden piers—yes
Dockside power and water connections—yes
Gasoline—yes (members and accredited guests
    only)
Diesel fuel—yes (members and accredited
    guests only)
Restaurant—on site

Donna Bay (Standard Mile 58)

The southwestern mouth of Donna Bay fronts onto the ICW's flank between unlighted daybeacon #14 and flashing daybeacon #3. While some local outboarders regularly cruise this body of water, depths of 2 to 4 feet are all too common. There are no markings on the bay, nor any facilities. Cruising captains are advised to avoid this shallow trap.

Venice Anchorages and Higel Park Facilities (BAIL-Suggested) (Standard Mile 58.5)

The best anchorage on the waters lying about Venice is found on the charted ribbon of deep water south of unlighted daybeacon #1. This haven has changed recently. The city of Venice has now marked the channel from #1 to the Venice Yacht Club. None of these new markers is yet reflected on chart 11425. This cut runs hard by the seawall that flanks the channel to the west. There is still space to anchor on the eastern third of the charted deep water, but clearly swinging space has been reduced. Be sure to anchor east of the marked channel. Cruisers dropping the hook in the channel may well be asked to move along by a local water cop.

Many skippers wisely choose a Bahamian-style mooring in this now reduced-space anchorage. Minimum depths run around 7 feet, but you must take care to avoid the correctly charted shoal farther to the east. The westerly banks provide excellent protection when winds are blowing from this quarter and there is also fair shelter for moderate breezes from the north or south. Easterly winds over 15 knots could make for a bumpy evening.

Good water runs all the way from #1 to a position abeam of the Venice Yacht Club. With its new markings, this passage can even be used as an alternate entrance to the club's docks.

Shallow-draft vessels sometimes anchor south of the Venice Yacht Club opposite the charted southernmost, blunt-ended cove which chart 11425 (Venice inset) denotes with a sounding of 6 feet. You can now count on finding 6 feet of water in this haven, but thinner depths lie just to the east. There is good protection from western, southwestern, and northwestern winds, but shelter is nil to the east, northeast, and none too good to the southeast. The flanking shoreside development is prolific, to say the least.

Cruisers dropping anchor in either of these two spots can dinghy ashore at Higel Park. The public park is perched on the southern shores of the blunt-tipped cove, just west of the second anchorage reviewed above. Cruisers will find bathrooms, telephones, and trash disposal in the park. Restaurants (including the Crows Nest—see below) and shopping are within a walk of several blocks. Ask any local for directions.

A new feature at Higel Park is a fixed, wooden face dock that lines the southerly banks of the cove. A public launching ramp guards the innermost reaches. Stays up to 18 hours (once each 10 days) are allowed at this pier, and low-water depths alongside run about 5½ feet. We saw two large sailing vessels moored temporarily here during our last visit in early 2000.

Venice Inlet (Standard Mile 58.5)

At flashing daybeacon #3, the ICW intersects the easterly reaches of reliable Venice Inlet. This well-defined cut is a popular passage to and from the waters of the open Gulf. At the present time, cruisers can expect minimum depths of 10 feet in the channel. Tidal currents do run quite swiftly, however. These swiftly moving waters seem to keep the inlet in optimal condition so, at least for the foreseeable future, cruisers can use this seaward passage with a fair amount of confidence.

Crows Nest Marina (Standard Mile 58.5)

Crows Nest Marina maintains a line of slips on the southern shores of Venice Inlet, southwest of unlighted daybeacon #5. This is yet another of the friendly marinas in Venice which gladly accept transients. Overnight berths are provided at fixed wooden (and, would you believe, recycled plastic) slips featuring all power, water, and cable television connections. Gasoline and diesel fuel are available, as are shoreside showers. Most of Crows Nest's slips have depths of 6 to 7 feet, with 12 to 15 feet of water at the outermost face docks and a few berths with soundings as thin as 4 feet. Swift tidal currents can make docking tricky, so have all hands stand by with your largest fenders. The marina dockmaster is very helpful in minimizing this problem.

While the Crows Nest dockage basin is relatively well sheltered, it must be noted that this would not be a good spot to get caught in a gale. The chop in the inlet could build to prodigious proportions and the marina is bound to get some of this backwash.

The real star at Crows Nest is the on-site restaurant of the same name. A late check in early 2000 once again confirmed that it is, quite simply, one of the best restaurants in Florida.

This dining spot is divided into upper and lower floors, each with its own distinctive character. The first level is a pub-type atmosphere with a nautical raw bar and a grill. The upper story is what we in the South used to call a "sit-down" restaurant, with an expansive view of Venice Inlet from its large, plate-glass windows. The food upstairs is simply superb. The seafood bisque appetizer was some of the best I have ever enjoyed and the broiled red snapper entree was enough to bring this writer back time and time again. Crows Nest Restaurant has also been presented with an "Award of Excellence" by *Wine Spectator* magazine. To be succinct, this is just about as good as it gets.

Crows Nest Marina & Restaurant
(941) 484-7661
(941) 484-9551 (Restaurant)

http://www.crowsnest-venice.com

Approach depth—10-foot minimum
Dockside depth—4-15 feet
Accepts transients—yes
Fixed wooden slips—yes
Dockside power connections—yes
Dockside water connections—yes
Showers—yes
Gasoline—yes
Diesel fuel—yes
Restaurant—on site

Lyons Bay (Standard Mile 59)

A marked channel makes off to the north from the ICW at unlighted daybeacon #4 into the waters of Lyons Bay. Low-water depths on this cut can run to as little as 4 feet. Add to this the lack of swinging room for cruising-size vessels and you have two good reasons to bypass this body of water entirely.

Crows Nest Marina, Venice

Casey Key Bridge Facilities
(Standard Mile 59.5)

North of flashing daybeacon #5, the Waterway leaves the principal Venice waterfront and begins its northward trek to the Casey Key Bridge. Two waterfront restaurants with dockage and a low-key marina line the eastern banks just south of this span (north of unlighted daybeacon #10).

The fixed, wooden face dock associated with Urbaneck's Restaurant and the adjacent Sunset Grill (941-488-2941) comes up first, moving south to north. This pier fronts directly onto the Waterway and features 6 feet of water at low tide. As with all the facilities along this stretch, docking can be tricky as *tidal currents run quite swiftly indeed*. During one visit, it looked as if a 5-knot ebb tide was boiling through the bridge!

Gulf Harbor Marina (941-488-7734) maintains a fuel dock north of Urbaneck's. This facility specializes in dry storage of small powercraft, but it also offers some services of interest to transients. Gasoline and diesel fuel can be purchased at a fuel dock (depths alongside are 5½-6 feet) fronting directly onto the waterway. A ship's and variety store is found just behind the fuel pier. While no transient wet slips are available, the marina does offer covered slips for resident craft. Some mechanical repairs are offered, mostly for outboards and I/O's, and boats can be hauled out on the marina's 20-ton travelift.

Pelican Alley Restaurant (941-485-1893) sits hard by the southern side of the Casey Key Bridge. It has a hundred-foot, fixed face dock with good depths of 7 to 8 feet.

Now, listen up. If you haven't eaten at Pelican Alley, you have missed one of the real treats in Western Florida. Do yourself a big favor and stop here. Everything is wonderful, from the sandwiches to "Shrimp and Scallops Marie," a delightful blend of diced tomatoes, onions, peppers, olives, and mushrooms in a very tasty tomato sauce. Well, there goes my diet again!

Blackburn Bay Anchorage
(Standard Mile 61.5)

North of the Casey Key Bridge the ICW soon enters the marginally wider waters of Blackburn Bay. While much of the bay outside of the Waterway is shallow, there is one pretty good spot to anchor for boats drawing 4½ feet or less. Depths of 5 feet or so swing in towards the bay's southwestern shores between unlighted daybeacons #20 and #21. Good water holds to within 50 yards of shore and there is superior protection from all but strong northerlies. On the negative side, the bottom is mud, so anchoring is not carefree, and you may be rolled around a good deal by the wake of passing vessels. The western shores are populated by heavy residential development, but the landscaped yards alongside the palm and palmetto trees make for an eye-pleasing combination.

Blackburn Bridge Facilities
(Standard Mile 63)

North of unlighted daybeacon #32, the Western Florida ICW takes its leave of Blackburn Bay after passing under a decrepit 9-foot swing bridge. Some marina facilities are found both north and south of this span.

Blackburn Point Marina (941-966-3735) is a small operation guarding the western shores immediately south of the Blackburn Bridge. This marina changed hands in 1999, and while the new owner is friendly to cruisers, he has no plans to offer dockage to transients. On the plus side, the on-site restaurant has now reopened as Casey Key Fish House, and judging from the many patrons who were dining as we cruised by in January of 2000, they must clearly be doing something right. Unfortunately, as alluded to above, plans call for all the available fixed wooden, wet-slip dockage to be rented out on a month-to-month basis, so it is doubtful if there will be any room for those who just want to dock long enough to partake of the restaurant's delights. Of course, you could always secure a slip at nearby Casey Key Marina (see below) and take the short walk back across the Blackburn Bridge. It might just be worth it.

North of the Blackburn span, a channel leading east to no fewer than three pleasure-craft-oriented facilities is outlined by low-level, privately maintained unlighted daybeacons. Entrance depths run between 5 and 6 feet, while 4½ to 6 feet of water is found at most of the interior piers and slips.

First up is Casey Key Marina on the southern banks. While the marina's slips are not terribly numerous, transients are accepted for overnight dockage at fixed wooden piers with good power and water connections. Advance reservations would be a good idea. Gasoline can be purchased at the fuel dock and modest, non-climate controlled showers and a laundromat are on hand as well. There are two gift shops in the marina complex, but no ship's or variety store.

The Flying Bridge restaurant (813-966-7431) is located on the upper floor of the

Casey Key Marina

Casey Key complex. The downstairs location is now occupied by Caroline's on the Bay (941-966-4822) restaurant. While this writer did not have the opportunity to sample the fare at either dining spot, the impressive population of cars in the parking lot for the midday meal certainly gives good cause to believe that these restaurants are popular with the local crowd.

A new dining spot known as Bob's Boathouse (941-312-9111) overlooks the ICW's westerly banks immediately south of Casey Key Marina. We have found the food here to be quite good, and the atmosphere is unique. Both the exterior and interior are decorated with real, full-size, wooden-hulled powerboats. Obviously, someone bought some distressed vessels, slapped on a coat or two of paint, and voila, you have a dining atmosphere that is just about irresistible to those of us who go cruising on the water. The screen-porch dining, overlooking the Waterway, is also ever so nice in fair weather.

Sorry to say, Bob's Boathouse does not currently offer any dockage. However, rumors have reached us that suggest that in the future, the restaurant may well build a pier directly on the ICW for its waterborne patrons. Watch for it, and please send us e-mail at opcom@netpath.net if you discover that this has indeed come to pass.

Casey Key Marina (941) 966-1730

Approach depth—5-6 feet
Dockside depth—4½-6 feet
Accepts transients—yes
Fixed wooden piers—yes
Dockside power connections—up to 50 amp
Dockside water connections—yes
Showers—yes
Laundromat—yes
Gasoline—yes
Restaurant—on site

Mariners in need of repairs should continue cruising east past Casey Key to Lighthouse Boatyard (941-966-2552), formerly John Holmes Boatyard. This impressive facility will be spotted overlooking the northern banks. The Lighthouse yard has a sure and certain reputation among local mariners for providing quality mechanical (gasoline and diesel power plants) and haul-out repair services. The yard boasts an impressive 80-ton travelift. All available wet-slip dockage is reserved for the use of service customers. Skippers needing repairs north of Venice need look no further.

Osprey Marine Center (941-966-5657) lines the eastern terminus of the canal directly across from Lighthouse Boatyard. Osprey's primary concern is small-craft dry storage, but gasoline, a ship's and variety store, and some outboard and I/O mechanical repairs are also offered.

Little Sarasota Bay (Standard Mile 63)

North of Blackburn Bridge, the Western Florida ICW breaks out into the wider waters of Little Sarasota Bay. Your passage should still be reasonably smooth unless some really strong winds are in the offing. Most of the bay is quite shallow, and, as usual, you should stick to the Waterway except for the gunkholes outlined below.

A portion of Little Sarasota Bay's western shoreline is protected as part of the Jim Neville Preserve. The incredibly green, all-natural shores are a striking sight from the water.

Midnight Pass Inlet (Standard Mile 65)

Under present conditions, cruisers should not even consider trying to make a "Midnight run." The channel, such as it ever was, lies west of the ICW's unlighted daybeacon #41A, but it has shoaled and now sports shallow patches with only a few feet of depth.

Midnight Pass Facilities
(Standard Mile 66)

South of unlighted daybeacon #48, a pile-marked channel leads cruisers who can stand some 4½-foot depths west-southwest to a single marina and several restaurants, two of which offer waterside dockage. The channel markings lack any daybeacons, or even arrow markers, so you must approach this cut with care and keep an eye glued to the sounder.

As you begin your approach to the southwesterly banks, the channel divides. The northside fork leads to Midnight Pass Marina, while the southerly branch provides waterborne access to Ophelia's On The Bay restaurant. Let us first review the marina.

Midnight Pass Marina (941-349-9449) is a small facility that does not offer overnight, transient dockage. The marina does have a travelift and can haul pleasurecraft up to at least 40 feet. Some low-key mechanical repairs (to gasoline engines only) and gasoline are available. Low-water approach and dockside depths run in the 4½- to 5-foot range.

Midnight Pass Pub is located just in front of the marina. Free dockage is afforded to patrons of this establishment. The Turtle restaurant sits just beside Midnight Pass Marina, but a sign warns that dockage is not allowed for this eatery's patrons. The Turtle lacks any dockage of its own.

The channel cutting south to Ophelia's On The Bay restaurant (941-349-2212) carries depths of as little as 4 feet. Water levels dockside deepen to 5 and 6 feet. Skippers whose craft draw less than 4 feet can thank their shallow keels for affording them a unique dining experience. If you are about to grow gills

and are just a bit tired of the fresh catch of the day, then Ophelia's On The Bay is just the ticket. Offering Continental-style cuisine, this dining spot is one of the most elegant in the region, and certainly the best of its type available from the water.

Little Sarasota Anchorage
(Standard Mile 67)

Cruising craft can anchor within 100 yards of the southwestern banks at unlighted daybeacon #51 in minimum 5½-foot depths. Typical soundings are around 6 feet. There is little in the way of protection from winds over 10 knots unless the breezes in question are blowing from the west or southwest. The southwestern banks are flanked by heavy and not so attractive residential development. Passing powercraft may throw you a goodly amount of wake.

White Beach Anchorage
(Standard Mile 67.5)

A much-improved anchorage (better than the one reviewed above) is available to cruisers south and west of unlighted daybeacon #57. A sharp point of land to the south forms a sheltered cove. Minimum depths of 5½ feet run to within 100 yards of the banks. There is good protection from southern, southwestern, and western breezes, but very little from northerly or easterly blows. The banks are overlooked by the usual private homes. The houses to the south are particularly attractive. Again, you will have to deal with the wake of passing vessels, but it is hoped that this won't be too much of a problem during the evening hours.

Stickney Point Bridge Facilities
(Standard Mile 69)

Two radically different facilities are located on the northeast and southwest shores of the

ICW, southeast of the Stickney Point Bridge (northwest of unlighted daybeacon #62). Siesta Key Marina (941-349-8880) guards the southwestern banks and offers dry storage. This firm is primarily a dry-stack storage facility for smaller powercraft. No other transient services save a hard-to-reach gas pump and a ship's store are offered.

A large complex of retail shops and one restaurant overlook the northeastern shores. Coasters Restaurant (941-925-0300) fronts directly onto the Waterway, but the other shops border a man-made basin lying to the southeast. Coasters has a few extremely shallow slips fronting onto the Waterway, while additional docks line the northern side of the basin.

Very skimpy entrance and (interior basin) dockside depths of a mere 2½ to 4½ feet will limit the accessibility of this stop for many cruising-size vessels. We ran aground on the docks fronting directly onto the Waterway in a 19-foot I/O-powered craft. These slips are virtually useless at low tide. Obviously the complex's piers were designed with smaller, outboard-powered craft in mind. Dockage by cruising-size vessels is problematical at best.

It might not be worth the effort anyway if you are just seeking a good meal. Recently, we had occasion to sample the fare at Coasters. Not only was the service slow, and the prices anything but inexpensive, but our crab cakes were 95 percent bread crumbs. Barring some major change in its kitchen, we pointedly do not recommend this restaurant.

Coasters Restaurant

VENICE TO LITTLE SARASOTA BAY NAVIGATION

While there are very few navigational concerns in running the Venice Canal portion of the ICW, it's a different story while cruising through the waters about the city of Venice and its inlet. This is most certainly not the place for powercraft to go charging ahead at planing speeds. For one thing, there are many private docks to consider. Even more importantly, the markers on the various Venice-side channels, coupled with more than a few twists and turns in the Waterway channel, demand caution. Have the Venice inset portion of chart 11425 close at hand and be ready to sort out any confusion over aids to navigation before you actually reach the beacons in question.

Tidal currents run swiftly on the Venetian waters, courtesy of the inlet. Sailcraft and single-screw trawlers should be on the alert for leeway. All vessels need to take this rapid water movement into account when docking or anchoring.

North of Venice, the tidal currents continue for a few miles, but eventually the Waterway widens a bit while traversing Blackburn and Little Sarasota bays. Fortunately, it would take a really strong wind to make things uncomfortable on this portion of the Waterway.

While the ICW remains well marked throughout the two bays, most of the waters outside the channel are shoal. As per standard operating procedure along this section of the Western Florida coastline, stick to the marked Waterway channel or risk running aground.

Navigators should also take into account several long, no-wake zones outlined below. Trust me, they will affect your arrival time in Sarasota if you pilot a powercraft.

Venice Canal North-northwest of unlighted daybeacon #52, the ICW enters a protected canal that runs generally north for some 3.8 miles until emptying into wider waters adjoining the Hatchett Creek Bridge. At flashing daybeacon #53, the canal swings sharply to the northeast. All markers cease north of #53 until you leave the Hatchett Creek span behind.

With one exception, there is little development along the canal and powerboaters can make good time. If you happen to meet or overtake a sailor or slower craft, please slow down and watch your wake when passing. Tall wakes can be a real problem in this relatively narrow channel.

Cruisers will pass under the 25-foot South Venice/Tamiami Trail bascule bridge near standard mile 55. This span opens on demand. Future plans call for this bridge to be replaced by a fixed, high-rise structure, and construction is now imminent.

Immediately north of the South Venice bridge (northeast of charted Venice Municipal Airport), powercraft skippers must slow to idle speed when passing Gulfwind Marine of Venice. This facility is found on the L-shaped cove and is designated as facility #17 on chart 11425. Official no-wake signs warn both north- and southbound vessels of this regulation. Please pay attention to this stricture. Unthinking captains who power by at planing speed can severely rock boats docked in the basin.

As you cruise between Gulfwind Marine and the Venice Avenue Bridge, watch the western banks. You will catch sight of the Venice High School football stadium. I can't recall offhand another location on the ICW where you can see such a sports center from the water.

Another 1.4 nautical miles brings northbound boaters to the Venice Avenue bascule bridge, with 30 feet of closed vertical clearance. This span has restricted opening hours. From 7:00 A.M. to 4:30 P.M., Monday through Friday, the bridge opens 10 minutes, 30 minutes, and 50 minutes after the hour, except it does not open at all between 4:35 P.M. and 5:35 P.M. At all other times of the day or night and on weekends, the bridge opens on demand. Sailcraft should do everything possible to coordinate their arrival with this complicated schedule. There is little room to maneuver in the landcut while waiting for the bridge to open.

Switch to the Venice inset section of chart 11425 as you approach the Hatchett Creek Bridge. The minute detail of this inset will give you a much clearer picture of the sometimes complicated Venetian waters.

Adding insult to injury, the Hatchett Creek-U.S. 41 Highway Bridge comes up soon after the Venice Avenue span. With the bridge's closed clearance of only 16 feet, most cruising captains will have to contend with the regulated opening schedule. Currently, the bridge opens on the hour and each 20 minutes thereafter from 7:00 A.M. to 4:20 P.M., Monday through Friday, except that it does not open at all from 4:25 P.M. to 5:25 P.M. On Saturdays, Sundays, and legal holidays, the bridge deigns to open for us peon cruisers on the hour and each quarter hour from 7:30 A.M. to 6:00 P.M. At all other times (if you can figure out when those might be) the bridge opens on demand. Don't look at me, folks. I didn't make up the schedule.

Cruise northwest at idle speed once through the Hatchett Creek span. An official no-wake zone runs from the bridge to flashing daybeacon #10. This prohibition protects Fisherman's Wharf Marina, which will come up to the northeast at unlighted daybeacon #4.

Fisherman's Wharf Marina   Entry into Fisherman's Wharf Marina is complicated by a shoal flanking the Waterway to the northeast, between unlighted daybeacons #4 and #6. This patch of shallows has grown to the southeast a bit over the past several years, and it is now more of a problem. Nevertheless, this hazard can be avoided if you know it's there. The shortest passage for northbound cruisers is a bit more problematic. Leave the Waterway soon after passing under the Hatchett Creek Bridge, and begin hugging the outer face of the marina dock that fronts directly onto the ICW. If you berth here, it's all smooth sailing. On the other hand, if your assigned slip is to be found on the more sheltered berths flanking the southeastern banks of the cove, east of #4, then you must curl around the northwestern end of the outer pier, staying as close to the docks and any vessels you may find moored there as possible. Even by following this procedure, you may land in 5-foot MLW depths. Also, don't maneuver in so close to the outer dock that you are in danger of sideswiping any of the boats that may be tied up there.

Captains cruising south on the ICW or piloting deep-draft vessels should depart the Waterway some 25 yards southeast of unlighted daybeacon #8 and begin heavily favoring the port-side banks as you cruise southeast to the Fisherman's Wharf's inner slips. The trick is to stay well away from the patch of water lying northeast of the gap between #6 and #4.

The dockmaster's office is located just behind the westernmost set of inner docks on the cove's southeastern side. Here you will also find the fuel pier.

On the ICW   Northwest of Fisherman's Wharf, the waters about the ICW spread out and the passage becomes far more complicated. Continue to cruise at idle speed at least until reaching flashing daybeacon #10. There are many private docks in this area, and a large wake could damage any number of vessels. In fact, it would be a good policy to cruise at minimal speed through the entire Venice region. Not only will this wise practice reduce wake, but it will also give you a chance to sort out the markers.

At flashing daybeacon #10, the ICW channel takes a sharp turn to the west. Don't miss this turn! The shallow waters of Roberts Bay lie to the east and north waiting to trap the unwary. Point to pass unlighted daybeacon #11 to its fairly immediate northerly quarter.

At flashing daybeacon #13, the Waterway again swerves sharply, this time to the north-northwest. Make the cut just

before reaching #13 and point to come abeam of unlighted daybeacon #14 to its southwesterly side.

As you are cruising between #13 and #14, you will undoubtedly spot the prolific markers stretching west from #14 to the Venice Yacht Club. Don't let these obscurely charted aids confuse you. Use your binoculars to positively identify #14 before cruising on to this aid.

Venice Yacht Club Channel and Anchorage (BAIL-Suggested)   The Venice Yacht Club channel stretches west-southwest from unlighted daybeacon #14 on a well-marked, slightly curved path to the club's dockage basin. The clubhouse will be obvious.

If you wish to anchor off the yacht club, drop the hook just east of the southernmost, blunt-tipped cove, indenting the westerly banks. Although you will see some boats anchored farther to the south and southeast, on-site research revealed that these vessels were in 6-foot waters. Higel Park is found on the southern shores of the blunt-tipped cove.

On the ICW   From #14, the Waterway continues straight on until coming abeam of flashing daybeacon #16 to its southwesterly side. At #16 the channel cuts farther to the northwest and the daybeacon numbering sequence begins anew. At unlighted daybeacon #1, cruisers can enter the northernmost of the two Venice anchorages.

Venice Anchorage (BAIL-Suggested)   Enter the wide swath of deep waters abutting the western banks by cutting sharply south and passing just east of unlighted daybeacon #1. Look for the new but uncharted markers ahead. These aids define a channel running hard by the west side seawall that eventually leads to the Venice Yacht Club. To anchor, ease a bit to the east of the marked cut, but take care to avoid the correctly charted 1-foot shoal farther to the east.

On to Venice Inlet   Cruisers northbound on the ICW, or those seeking Venice Inlet, should pass unlighted daybeacon #1 to its northeasterly side and point to come abeam of flashing daybeacon #3 to its northeasterly quarter. Daybeacon #3 marks a strategic intersection between the ICW and Venice Inlet.

Venice Inlet   Enter Venice Inlet by turning sharply southwest about halfway between unlighted daybeacon #1 and flashing daybeacon #3. Pass #3 well to your starboard side. This is as it should be. You are now headed *toward* the sea, so take all green markers to your starboard side and red aids to port.

Be on the alert for strong tidal currents as you cruise through Venice Inlet. The surge will surprise you at full ebb tide.

South of Venice Inlet's unlighted daybeacon #5, you will quickly spot Crows Nest Marina in the dimple-shaped cove indenting the port-side banks. With the possible exception of a few problems courtesy of the strong tidal currents, this marina is easily entered.

West of unlighted daybeacons #2A and #3, the inlet channel runs between twin stone jetties. The channel is obvious. Continue straight on out into the Gulf. Next stop . . . Carrabelle?

On the Waterway   Cruisers continuing north on the ICW past Venice Inlet should set their course to come abeam of and pass flashing daybeacon #4 to its southerly side. Just before reaching #4, the marked cut to Lyons Bay heads off to the north. As this side trip is not recommended for strangers, it will not be further reviewed here.

Between unlighted daybeacon #3A and flashing daybeacon #5, the charted shoal flanking the Waterway's southwestern margin is building outward. Favor the northeastern side of the ICW slightly as you cruise between #3A and #5. Hopefully, dredging will soon alleviate this problem.

The Waterway takes its last major turn in the Venice area at flashing daybeacon #5. Come abeam of #5 to its easterly side and turn to the northwest to follow the Waterway.

The route remains straightforward until reaching flashing daybeacon #9. North of this aid, all vessels should slow to idle speed to protect the marina and restaurant docks lining the eastern banks.

Soon the Waterway is spanned by the 14-foot Casey Key/Albee Road bascule bridge. It is fortunate that this bridge opens on demand. The tidal current boiling through this portion of the ICW on the ebb and flood is something to see. We estimated its speed at 5 knots plus. All vessels should proceed at maximum alert when docking or passing through the bridge.

At unlighted daybeacon #14, the

Waterway is pinched between two prominent shoals as it passes out into Blackburn Bay. Favor the western side of the channel slightly between #14 and flashing daybeacon #16. At #16, the channel turns a bit to the north-northwest.

Blackburn Bay is another portion of the Western Florida ICW where it is almost mandatory to keep strictly to the marked channel. For much of its run through Blackburn Bay, the Waterway borders on significant shoals to the east and west.

North-northwest of unlighted daybeacon #20, mariners will encounter the first good anchorage after leaving Venice behind.

Blackburn Bay Anchorage Depart the Waterway some 100 yards southeast of unlighted daybeacon #21. Cut in sharply towards the southwestern banks. Good depths run to within 50 yards of shore. Retrace your steps to the northeast when it's time to leave.

North on the ICW A long slow-speed manatee zone begins at unlighted daybeacon #22 and stretches north to unlighted daybeacon #29. Just grin and bear it.

North of unlighted daybeacon #29A, powerboaters should again slow to minimal speed to protect the docks of South Bay Yacht and Racket Club to the northeast. Continue at idle speed to unlighted daybeacon #35, north of Blackburn Bridge.

North of unlighted daybeacon #32, the Waterway hurries on towards the Blackburn Point swing bridge. You may spot some boats anchored east of the channel, south of the bridge. Don't be tempted! Our

research revealed that these vessels were moored in only 4 feet of water.

The relic known as the Blackburn Point bridge has a closed vertical clearance of only 9 feet, but it does open on demand. Just before passing under the bridge, you will spot Blackburn Point Marina to the west. Similarly, the privately maintained, unlighted daybeacons leading to Casey Key Marina, Lighthouse Boatyard, and Osprey Marine Center cut off to the east, north of the span.

North of the Blackburn Point span, the ICW passes out into the wider waters of Little Sarasota Bay. Chop should still not be a problem unless winds exceed 20 knots. No side trips are available on the bay until reaching flashing daybeacon #41.

Midnight Pass Brave captains whose craft draw no more than 3 feet may consider entering the easterly portion of the Midnight Pass channel as an interesting gunkhole. The passage is unmarked and the seaward channel is unusable by strangers.

If you should make the attempt, leave the ICW north of flashing daybeacon #41 and enter the channel by favoring the port-side banks. Don't get right up next to the beach. Stay some 20 yards off the sands for best depths.

Watch ahead for a sandy beach, also on the port banks. It would be best to drop the hook once abeam of this spot. On weekends, local powerboaters often beach small craft here.

Midnight Pass Marina and Ophelia's On The Bay Channel The pile-marked channel to Midnight Pass Marina and Ophelia's restaurant takes off from the west-south-western flank of the ICW between unlighted daybeacons #47 and #48. Take the first two red-topped piles to starboard. As you approach the third pile, the channel splits. Boats visiting Midnight Pass Marina can follow the northern fork, while diners putting into Ophelia's should follow the channel cutting to the southwest. Remember—depths on both these cuts run as thin as 4 feet.

Little Sarasota Anchorage   The deep waters west of unlighted daybeacon #51 actually present a wide prospect. It is quite possible to leave the Waterway just south-east of #51 and make a broad loop in towards the southwestern banks, rejoining the ICW 200 yards southeast of unlighted daybeacon #53, all with 5-foot minimum depths. Drop the hook anywhere you choose on these waters. Be sure to anchor so as not to swing closer than 100 yards to the southwesterly banks, where depths finally deteriorate.

White Beach Anchorage   Best depths are maintained by cutting in towards the southwestern banks some 100 yards northwest of unlighted daybeacon #57. While boats drawing 4 feet or less can cruise a goodly distance to the southeast, some 5-foot soundings will be encountered on this corner of the cove. Good water runs to within 75 yards or so of shore.

On the ICW   Powerboats should slow down north of flashing daybeacon #60 as they begin their approach to the Stickney Point Bridge in order to protect the craft berthed at the facilities south of the span. If you should decide to dock at the Coasters complex lining the northeastern banks (southeast of the bridge), remember to use the docks fronting onto the southeastern dockage basin. The slips looking out directly onto the Waterway are very shallow.

The Stickney Point Bridge has a closed vertical clearance of 18 feet, but it does open on demand.

North of the Stickney Point span, no-wake regulations are in effect to unlighted daybeacon #72. This is yet another of those seemingly interminable slow-speed zones for powercraft.

Sarasota Bay to Anna Maria Island

Picture a tall, bright city shimmering against the clear waters of a wide bay in the hazy summer sunshine. Now throw in plenty of protected waters glutted with anchorages (albeit restricted ones) and a more than adequate selection of marina facilities and yacht clubs. Add a host of waterside restaurants with their own dockage. Well, my friend, we have just managed to conjure up a mental picture of Sarasota Bay and the city for which it's named. Add all these fortunate qualities to the Gulf-side islands known as St. Armands

Key, Longboat Key, and Anna Maria Island, three of the most popular, though partly unspoiled, barrier islands in Western Florida, and you have the formula that brings cruisers back time and time again to the waters lying about the city of Sarasota.

On the negative side, Sarasota is one of the only cities in Western Florida that has chosen not to cooperate with the BAIL anchorage program. This is much to the city leaders' discredit! Anchorage on the waters surrounding Sarasota is now restricted to no more than 48 hours. Go figure!

Vessels cruising in from the Gulf or sailors ready to make the offshore jump will have to contend with the relatively shallow depths on both inlets serving Sarasota Bay. Even though New Pass was dredged just a few years ago, MLW soundings now run as thin as 5 feet. Big Sarasota Pass continues to display depths of as little as 4½ feet at low tide.

The ICW enters Roberts Bay north of the Stickney Point Bridge and follows this water body's ever-widening shores until it passes through the Ringling Bridge near standard mile 74. Cruisers used to the sheltered waters running north from Fort Myers are in for quite a shock. The wide reaches of Sarasota Bay stretch before you to the north, while the city of Sarasota rears its high-rise buildings to the east and New Pass Inlet eventually makes off to the southwest. After a memorable, though sometimes choppy transit of Sarasota Bay, the Waterway crosses south to north through Anna Maria Sound and finally meets the mighty waters of Tampa Bay.

This is a very pleasant section of the Western Florida ICW, with good anchorages and warm, friendly marinas. Don't be in such a hurry to explore the wonders of Tampa Bay that you pass Sarasota's many charms too quickly.

Phillippi Creek (Standard Mile 70)

North of Stickney Point Bridge, the ICW follows a short landcut into the southern reaches of Roberts Bay. Along the way, mariners will pass the confusing, multiple mouths of Phillippi Creek along the eastern shore near unlighted daybeacon #72. While a few local runabouts sometimes go upstream to a restaurant with a small-craft rental agency, the creek's depths are totally inadequate for cruising-size craft. Cheer up! Better things are not far ahead.

Roberts Bay Anchorage (BAIL-Suggested) (Standard Mile 71)

The first anchorage and yacht club you will encounter north of Stickney Point are absolutely

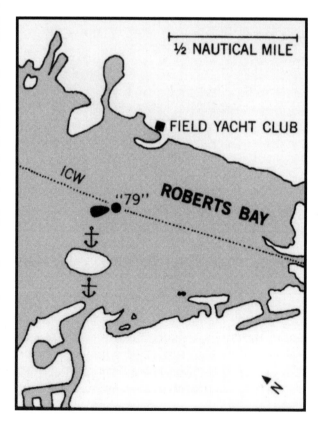

first-rate. Notice the charted "Spoil" west of unlighted daybeacon #78. This feature is actually a rather substantial, well-wooded body of land and it is much more prominent in reality than it appears from a careless study of chart 11425. Boats drawing 4 feet or less can cruise around the entire island keeping some 25 to 30 yards off the (island) shores and rejoin the Waterway near unlighted daybeacon #80. In good weather, you can drop the hook amidst ample swinging room for most pleasureboats between #78 and the island's eastern banks. This spot has 6 to 7 feet of water, but only minimal protection. With strong breezes in the offing, boats as large as 48 feet and drawing 4½ feet or less can go behind the isle, or drop the hook off either of its points, depending on wind direction, for good shelter. As you would expect, the island sports no development, while a few private homes peep out from the Siesta Key shoreline to the west. This is a particularly attractive anchorage and it is still highly recommended by this writer. Unfortunately, during the last several years, local water skiers and jet skis (which we cruisers call "water maggots") have begun using the waters west of the spoil island as a kind of competition course. Hopefully, this won't be a problem during your visit, but at least we've warned you. Be sure to read the navigational information presented later in this chapter before beginning your first circuit around the island.

The Field Club (Standard Mile 71)

Passing cruisers cannot help but note the elegant Field Yacht Club headquarters. Housed in the former Florida homeplace of

The Field Club

Marshall Fields, this is one of the most exclusive yacht clubs in all of Florida. The clubhouse is actually built over an arm of its entrance stream. A moatlike opening allows water to flow under the clubhouse.

The club's marked channel cuts east off the ICW just south of unlighted daybeacon #78 and maintains depths of 5½ to 6 feet. A few docks are found on the southern shore of the creek leading to the clubhouse, but most of the recently refurbished and expanded piers are enclosed in a well-protected basin cutting into the stream's southern banks. Dockside soundings range from 5½ to as much as 8 feet. Members of yacht clubs with appropriate reciprocal arrangements are accepted for guest dockage at the club's fixed wooden piers featuring full power and water connections. The club has a dockmaster on duty from 9:00 A.M. to 5:00 P.M., Tuesday through Friday, and from 8:00 A.M. to 5:00 P.M. weekends. The docks are unattended on Mondays. While the dockmaster is on duty, club members and accredited visitors (only) can purchase gasoline and diesel fuel from the dockmaster.

Upon going ashore, visiting cruisers will find showers, a swimming pool (open from June through Labor Day), and tennis courts. The Field Club offers good dining, with lunch served Tuesday through Saturday; the evening meal, Tuesday through Sunday; and a Sunday brunch. Reservations are required! No other restaurants are within walking distance, but a short taxi ride can take you into nearby Sarasota, where the dining and shopping choices are practically unlimited.

The Field Club has some special rules for cruising visitors, and we quote from the *Florida Council of Yacht Clubs' Guide:* "No outdoor cooking allowed. No laundry or towels to be hung on boats. Leashed pets allowed in marina area only. Owners responsible for clean-up. All food & beverages consumed on club grounds must be purchased on club grounds."

The Field Club is perched amidst a lovely setting with beautifully green shores and palatial homes. Captains and crew who enjoy the quieter side of cruising, as opposed to the bustling facilities along the principal Sarasota waterfront, and have the necessary club affiliation, should give the Field Club their most serious consideration. Call well ahead of time to make advance arrangements.

The Field Club (941) 924-1201

Approach depth—5½-6 feet
Dockside depth—5½-8 feet
Accepts transients—members of clubs with reciprocal agreements
Fixed wooden piers—yes
Dockside power and water connections—yes
Showers—yes
Gasoline—yes (not open to the general public)
Diesel fuel—yes (not open to the general public)
Restaurant—on site

Siesta Key Bridge Anchorages (Standard Mile 71.5)

Two additional anchorages are found east and west of the Waterway respectively, just south of the Siesta Key bascule bridge (north of flashing daybeacon #82). The west-side haven has everything except an all-natural shoreline. Good depths of 6 to (mostly) 8 feet lead you into a lakelike bay where you can drop the hook in 8 to 9 feet of water. Protection is sufficient for anything short of a full gale. There is enough swinging room for Benny Goodman. The surrounding shores are overlooked by an attractive residential neighborhood.

Boats as large as 40 feet and drawing less than 4 feet can find a real hurricane hidey hole on the eastern anchorage. The cove is shaped like an inverted C. Depths at the difficult entrance run a bare 4 feet, but improve to 7- and 9-foot levels at the rear, protected portion of the cove. The shores are bordered by a concrete seawall and are lined by private docks set beside a dense collection of expensive homes. If you need to duck the weather, it doesn't get much better than this.

Spoil Anchorage (Standard Mile 72)

In easterly winds or light airs, boats that are not bothered by a cruise through 4- to 5-foot depths can skirt the charted spoil northeast of flashing daybeacon #2 and anchor within 75 yards of shore in some 6 feet of water. You must be careful to avoid the spoil, which is marked with a concrete pile and sign indicating the presence of an artificial underwater reef. Skippers who successfully leave this hazard behind can drop the hook within 50 yards of the eastern banks in 5 to 6 feet of water. Shelter is good for easterlies and fair for breezes from the north or south. Winds over 10 knots blowing from the west would make this anchorage most uncomfortable.

Big Sarasota Pass (Standard Mile 72.5)

The wide, marked channel cutting southwest to Big Sarasota Pass makes into the Waterway northwest of flashing daybeacon #6 and unlighted daybeacon #7. Low-tide depths near the inlet's entrance into the Gulf have shoaled to 4½- and 5-foot levels, but, at the moment, this isn't much worse than the region's other inlet, New Pass.

The inner portion of the Big Sarasota Pass channel holds good depths of 6 feet, with soundings of 8 to as much as 23 feet being the norm. This portion of the passage leads to one anchorage along the inlet's western shoreline

and allows access to another marked cut. This second channel flows to two other anchorages and the Sarasota Yacht Club. Let us first review the inlet's west-side anchorage and then we will move on to consider the yacht club passage running north between Bird and Lido keys.

Big Sarasota Pass Anchorage

Minimum depths of 7 feet run almost into the western shores southwest of unlighted daybeacon #15 (on the Big Sarasota Pass channel). Typical soundings run in the 10- to 17-foot region. This is a very popular stopover for local pleasurecraft. During weekends, you will undoubtedly be joined by a host of fellow cruisers.

This anchorage is set against a local park and the beautiful, all-natural western shores are overlooked by tall Australian pines. It's terribly tempting to break out the dinghy and head ashore to explore the nearby beaches. In fact, with fair winds in the offing, I recommend it heartily.

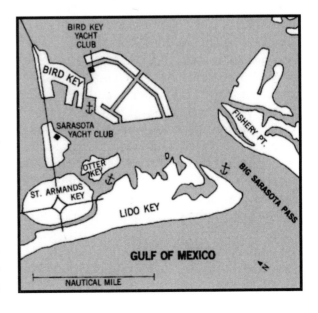

Obviously, this is not an anchorage fit for strong winds. You may even want to think long and hard before committing to an overnight stay. While it's a great spot to while away a warm fall afternoon, the awakening might be rude should an unexpected thunderstorm blow up during the night. Another drawback is the strong currents that regularly sweep through these waters. *Don't* try to swim ashore!

Sarasota Yacht Club Channel and Associated Anchorages

The broad channel running north-northwest to the Sarasota Yacht Club breaks off from the flank of Big Sarasota Pass abeam of unlighted daybeacon #15. The stream runs between Bird Key to the east and the shoals outlying Otter, St. Armands, and Lido keys to the west. The passage is eventually blocked to the north by a 10-foot fixed bridge.

This cut provides access not only to the club's docks, but to two anchorages as well. While fairly well marked, this channel definitely requires caution on the part of visiting cruisers. Be sure to read the navigation data for this passage presented later in this chapter before making your first attempt.

Minimum depths on the channel are about 8 feet. However, the charted marsh flats west of the cut cover at high and mid-tide. It's altogether too easy to wander into 3 feet of water. Cruisers should also be warned that the aids to navigation on this cut are rather small and can be hard to spot from the main body of Big Sarasota Pass.

The first spot that you might consider dropping the hook lies west of unlighted daybeacon #7. A small but relatively deep channel makes in from the west just south of Otter Key. This stream leads to a wonderful, BAIL-suggested, overnight haven which will be reviewed separately below.

North of unlighted daybeacon #10 a difficult, mostly unmarked channel cuts east-northeast and eventually leads through a small canal and a 7-foot fixed bridge to the docks of the Bird Key Yacht Club. As most cruising vessels will use this club's primary entrance off the ICW, we shall review this facility later in this chapter.

For now we need only note that the square cove west of the small Bird Key canal makes a good anchorage. While extra caution must be exercised to bypass several shoals bordering the channel's entrance, once past these hazards, good depths of 7 feet or better are found on the cove's broad interior reaches. Boats anchoring here would be protected from all winds except those blowing west across the main body of the yacht club channel. Vessels as large as 40 feet will find plenty of room to swing gracefully on the hook. *Be sure* to read the navigational account of this anchorage below before trying it for the first time.

The dockage basin adjoining the Sarasota Yacht Club is found on the channel's western shores, just south of the 10-foot fixed bridge, pretty much abeam of unlighted daybeacon #12. This friendly club maintains a full-time dockmaster seven days a week, 8:00 A.M. to 5:00 P.M. Transients from all clubs with appropriate reciprocal privileges are accepted for guest dockage at fixed concrete piers with all power and water connections. Depths at the outer docks are an impressive 10 feet or better. The innermost slips against the seawall have only 5 feet of water, but these soundings are clearly the exception. Most boats will find plenty of water at this club's piers.

The club maintains a fuel dock featuring gasoline and diesel fuel. This service is provided for members and accredited guests only and it's not open to the general public. Ashore, transients will find showers, a swimming pool, and excellent dining facilities. Lunch and dinner are served seven days a week. A host of other nearby restaurants is accessible by foot or a short taxi ride. The St. Armands Key shopping area is also within walking distance, but unfortunately there is not a grocery store in the immediate vicinity.

Sarasota Yacht Club (941) 365-1908

Approach depth—8-18 feet
Dockside depth—5-15 feet (most slips in the deeper part of this range)
Accepts transients—members of clubs with reciprocal privileges
Fixed concrete piers—yes
Dockside power and water connections—yes
Showers—yes
Gasoline—yes (members and guests only)
Diesel fuel—yes (members and guests only)
Restaurant—on site and several others nearby

All cruisers without very specific local knowledge are discouraged from an attempt to explore the waters north of the 10-foot fixed bridge. The numerous shoals are unmarked and it's a cinch to run aground even when you are trying to proceed with care.

Otter-Lido Key Anchorage (BAIL-Suggested)

What must surely be the best, though not the navigationally easiest, anchorage anywhere near the Sarasota Yacht Club and Big Sarasota Pass is found by following the 6-foot (minimum depth) channel south of Otter Key. Even though it is a BAIL-suggested haven, anchorage on these waters is now restricted to a 48-hour stay courtesy of the Sarasota city government. Fortunately, this time period will not bother many mariners, but it is a wholly needless restriction nevertheless.

After you cruise west-southwest from unlighted daybeacon #7, deep waters eventually open out before you in a broad pool. The offshoot directly southwest of the entrance is surrounded by high-class residential development and affords excellent protection from all but strong easterly winds. Unfortunately, there is only enough elbow room for vessels up to 32 feet.

The correctly charted 9- to 13-foot waters southwest of Otter Key are far roomier and still well protected. The dredged bottom strata are a bit suspect for holding, but we have not had any troubles of this type during our several visits. Otherwise, this is a super anchorage and comes highly recommended by this author. There is plenty of swinging room for even the largest pleasurecraft, but the entrance's narrow mouth (from the yacht club channel) might be a bit tricky for vessels exceeding 42 feet in length.

The Otter Key banks to the northeast are undeveloped, but Lido Key's shores to the southwest are lined by what my friend and research assistant Andy Lightbourne termed "millionaire's row." The houses are simply enormous and quite impressive. Surrounded by manicured lawns that look as if each blade of grass has been individually clipped, many have swimming pools and private docks. It is a very special treat to spend an evening tucked snugly amidst such luxury without a single worry about the next mortgage payment.

As the Otter Key channel flows placidly on to the northwest, the stream eventually splits and wraps enfolding arms around St. Armands Key. In spite of depths shown on chart 11425, we found less than 4 feet of water on the northeastern fork. The westerly arm is spanned by a fixed bridge with only 7 feet of vertical clearance. Skippers of all but small craft should confine their explorations to the waters southeast of the split.

St. Armands Key History This delightful island is named in honor of its first permanent European resident, Charles St. Amand. Somehow the extra *r* has appeared over the years with nary an explanation.

According to legend, John Ringling won Lido and St. Armands keys in a poker game before establishing the winter headquarters for his famous circus in Sarasota during the late 1920s. Ringling dreamed of making St. Armands into an exclusive shopping district surrounded by palatial homes. Canals were dredged, rose-colored sidewalks took shape, and roads were pushed this way and that on the island. Hundreds of Australian pines were imported to line the streets.

To allow ready access to his island paradise, Ringling built a causeway across the water from Sarasota. In 1926 the new roadway was opened with great ceremony. A parade marched across the bridge and a band from the circus played on a bandstand in the island's traffic circle. Opening-day sales of lots exceeded one million dollars.

A scant year later Ringling presented the causeway to the city of Sarasota as a gift. Soon the Depression hit, and the once graceful avenues and traffic circle languished in obscurity. The bandstand rotted away and it seemed as if a century had passed since the triumphal opening-day parade.

Finally, development again returned to St. Armands in the 1950s and continued through the 1960s. In 1972, the "circle" was redeveloped as a lavish shopping center with fine

Continental restaurants. While it may have come some fifty years later than planned, Ringling's dream has at last become a reality.

Sarasota (Standard Mile 73)

The modern-day city of Sarasota has grown by leaps and bounds since the days when John Ringling first brought his circus to its winter home in the small town. Today, huge glass-and-steel skyscrapers gaze benevolently over the waters of Sarasota Bay. Traffic is thick on the streets, but there is still something of Old Florida about this city.

There are so many things to see and do in modern Sarasota that it would be a simple task to fill an entire book with activities for visitors. Only a few of the stand-out attractions can be mentioned in the course of this account.

Auto and music buffs will be more than fascinated by the Bellm's Cars & Music Museum of Yesterday (5500 Tamiami Trail N, 941-355-6228). Visitors can examine an unbelievable collection of 175 restored antique automobiles, including Rolls Royces, Pierce Arrows, and many others. The Great Music Hall features 1,200 music boxes, calliopes, and an imported Belgian organ. There is even a penny arcade featuring working antique coin machines for the children. The museum is located at 5500 North U.S. 41. Cruising visitors will need a rental car or a taxi to reach this attraction.

The Sarasota Jungle Gardens (3701 Bayshore Road, 941-355-5305) is a 10-acre extravaganza of lush tropical growth, waterfowl, and beautiful sculpture. A petting zoo, bird show, and a shell and butterfly museum round out the attractions.

One of Sarasota's premier architectural landmarks is the Van Wezel Performing Arts Hall.

Its lavender seashell shape is easily visible from the bay. Many a cruiser has probably passed by and wondered at this unusual structure.

The shoppers among us will want to set their course for the antique shops and art galleries of historic Palm Avenue. During the 1920s Sarasota's most affluent citizens, including the Ringling family, shopped in this district. The area deteriorated during the Great Depression, but it has now been rebuilt. Today, modern buildings sit side by side with restored edifices dating to the Roaring Twenties.

Even though the circus has moved its winter headquarters elsewhere, its one-time owner, John Ringling, left behind a huge art museum and one of the most fascinating houses in the United States. The John and Mable Ringling Museum of Art (5401 Bayshore Road, 941-359-5700) was created in 1927 by John Ringling for the people of Florida. After making millions through his far-flung business enterprises, Ringling "amassed an art collection of over 600 paintings, numerous statues, and decorative arts, including approximately 27 tapestries." Ringling and his wife assembled their amazing collection between 1924 and 1931.

The museum is housed in a whole series of buildings on the former Ringling estate. The entire property, along with all its assembled artwork, was deeded to the state of Florida upon John Ringling's death in 1936. It is now open to the public. The museum is an absolute "must see" for every visitor to Sarasota. You must also be sure to see the circus museum and the Asolo Theater, the "Official State Theater of Florida."

John Ringling and his wife, Mable, did more with their time in Sarasota than just putting together a world-class art collection. They also built one of the most unique homeplaces in America.

The Ringlings originally came to Sarasota seeking a winter home in 1912. The circus's winter headquarters was established in the city much later. In 1924 John and Mable began construction of their winter homeplace. They called it "Ca'd'Zan," which means "House of John." Writing in their wonderful book, *Florida Historic Homes*, Laura Stewart and Susanne Hupp describe Ca'd'Zan as "one of Florida's grandest homes. Completed in 1926 at a cost of about $1.5 million, the structure combined architectural elements drawn from two of Mrs. Ringling's favorites—the facade of the Doge's Palace in Venice and the tower of the old Madison Square Garden in New York, where her husband's circus regularly appeared."

Well, you can understand that this writer could go on and on describing this unbelievable estate. Fortunately for your eyes and my fingers, Ca'd'Zan is also open to the public. Guests by the hundreds gawk and wonder at the Ringling home's almost bizarre opulence daily. Cruisers not only have the opportunity to tour Ca'd'Zan by land—they may also choose to anchor within sight of its tiled walls. Out of the hundreds of points of interest in Sarasota, if I had to pick but one, the magnificent Ringling estate and Ca'd'Zan would most certainly be my choice. Again, cruisers will need some form of motorized transportation to visit the grounds. There are no dockage facilities on the bay.

Phone numbers to know in Sarasota:

Courtesy Cab—941-954-1970
Safeway Taxi—941-921-0012
Alamo Car Rentals—941-359-5540
Avis Rental Cars—941-359-5240

Budget Rent A Car—941-359-5353
Boat/U S Marine Center—941-755-9670
E&B Marine—941-351-3431
West Marine—941-924-6777
Chamber of Commerce—941-955-8187

Marina Operations and Marina Jack's Restaurant (Standard Mile 73)

Returning now to the ICW's principal south-north track, the first of mainland Sarasota's principal facilities comes up on the east-northeastern shores, to the northeast of red, unlighted daybeacon #8A. A marked, deep channel leads the fortunate cruiser to one of the largest marinas in Western Florida, a super restaurant, and a popular anchorage. Think it might just be worth your time?

Study inset 2 on chart 11425 for a quick moment and the locate the facility known as Marina Operations. This marina is designated as facility #43 on 11425 and it is found in the semi-enclosed basin east of Golden Gate Point. Believe you me, on the water, the marina's location will be readily apparent.

While you might expect Marina Operations to be a publicly owned facility, it is actually a friendly commercial operation that eagerly accepts transients for overnight or temporary

Marina Operations, Sarasota

dockage. The marina maintains prolific transient dockage at mostly fixed, concrete piers with every conceivable power, water, and cable television connection. There are also a few wooden and floating piers, but these are the exception. Protection is good for all but the heaviest weather, courtesy of the hook-shaped peninsula to the south. Gasoline, diesel fuel, waste pump-out service, adequate, air-conditioned showers, and a semi-open-air laundromat complete the facility's non-dining amenities. Some mechanical repairs can occasionally be arranged through independent local contractors. Entrance and dockside depths are better than 8 feet, with typical soundings ranging from 10 to as much as 12 feet.

If you happen to arrive at Marina Operations during the lunch or dinner hour, a lucky star must be shining over your vessel. The on-site restaurant, Marina Jack's (941-365-4232), sits out over the piers and provides its patrons with a fine view of the harbor and the western skies at sunset. The interior of Marina Jack's has been completely remodeled during the last several years, and the decor is now quite attractive indeed. Downstairs you will find a large open-air bar, which is great for lunch or evening cocktails. Serious diners will want to head upstairs to the main dining room. Here patrons will find an unbelievably extensive menu ranging from Scallops Elyse to Fillet Florentine to grilled rib-eye steaks served in a Madeira sauce. While not exactly inexpensive, the prices are reasonable for the quality of food you will enjoy at this house of gastronomic pleasure.

As you would imagine, a bevy of shoreside shopping opportunities are available by foot from Marina Operations. This facility is located in the heart of downtown Sarasota. Those needing to reprovision will need a taxi to reach a supermarket or ship's store, but otherwise there is plenty to do and see close at hand. An impressive collection of glass-and-steel high-rise buildings overlook Marina Operations to the east, while idyllic Bayfront Park occupies the tongue of land to the south that helps to enclose the dockage basin.

Marina Operations (941) 955-9488

Approach depth—10-11 feet
Dockside depth—8-11 feet
Accepts transients—yes (extensive)
Fixed concrete piers—yes
Fixed wooden piers—a few
Floating docks—a few
Dockside power connections—up to 100 amp
    (in case you need to run your elevator)
Dockside water connections—yes
Waste pump-out—yes
Showers—yes
Laundromat—yes
Gasoline—yes
Diesel fuel—yes
Mechanical repairs—arranged through independent contractors
Restaurant—on site and several nearby

Sarasota Anchorage (BAIL-Suggested) (Standard Mile 73)

Cruisers who prefer to anchor off have not been forgotten in the scheme of mainland Sarasota. The charted 8- to 12-foot waters west and south of Bayfront Park's hooklike peninsula bordering Marina Operations' southerly flank regularly play host to several dozen anchored vessels. Some local craft are hooked to mooring buoys, but there is plenty of swinging room for almost any craft to drop anchor. There is good protection from easterly breezes and some shelter from northerly or southerly blows. Strong winds blowing across the Waterway from the west could make for a bumpy evening.

This anchorage is quite pleasing to the eye. The all-natural shores of Bayfront Park are backed by Sarasota's high-rise downtown buildings. In the absence of strong westerlies, you could scarcely do better when anchoring in the Sarasota region.

Anchorage is officially limited to a maximum stay of 72 hours in this city-sanctioned haven (as opposed to 48 hours on all other Sarasota area waters). In practice, however, it has been our experience that this 72-hour limit is seldom enforced. Things could have changed by the time of your visit, however.

Dinghies are no longer accommodated at Marina Operations, and dinghy landing at Bayfront Park is now restricted to the beach in front of O'Leary's Water Sports and Grill (941-953-7505). This small facility is located on the southeastern corner of Bayfront Park, on the land hook's southerly shore. Once pulled up on O'Leary's beach, you will find public rest rooms and telephones within walking distance.

Golden Gate Point Anchorage (Standard Mile 73)

Some boats occasionally anchor in the charted 12-foot waters west of Golden Gate Point. Here you will find a cove formed between the arms of the point and the causeway leading to the eastern genesis of the Ringling Bridge. You must be sure to anchor well in towards the rear of the cove to avoid the charted cable area. Boats as large as 40 feet should find plenty of swinging room and good protection from all but strong southerly and westerly winds in 7- to 9-foot depths. The causeway shores play host to a public launching ramp and a jet ski rental shop. The Golden Gate shores are flanked by extremely heavy, high-rise condo development. With the head-

lights and noise of passing automobiles, this could not exactly be described as a particularly peaceful overnight haven.

Bird Key Yacht Club (Standard Mile 73)

West-southwest of flashing daybeacon #10, itself just southeast of the Ringling Bridge, cruising vessels can follow a well-marked channel to the docks of the Bird Key Yacht Club. You will see a sign denoting the club channel near unlighted daybeacon #2, the first aid on the cut. The channel carries 9 to 12 feet of water and dockside depths are a good 8 to 10 feet in the principal basin in front of the clubhouse. A few of the smaller slips located around on the canal carry only 5 to 6 feet of water.

Bird Key Yacht Club accepts cruising visitors who are members of other clubs with reciprocal privileges. Advance reservations are required by the club management. As slip space is somewhat limited, make your arrangements well in advance. Dockage is at fixed wooden piers with full power and water connections. Gasoline and diesel fuel can be purchased by members and guests only—not the public. Showers (but no laundry facilities) are available in the clubhouse to wash away the day's salt. The club is closed Tuesdays. Lunch and dinner are served daily (except Tuesdays) in the on-site dining facilities. The club boasts a swimming pool (also closed on Tuesdays) and several tennis courts.

Bird Key Yacht Club (941) 953-4455
   http://www.birdkeyyc.com

Approach depth—9-12 feet
Dockside depth—8-10 feet (main basin)
**Accepts transients—members of clubs with
   reciprocal privileges. Advance reservations
   required**
Fixed wooden piers—yes

Dockside power and water connections—up to
   50 amp
Showers—yes
Gasoline—yes (members and guests only)
Diesel fuel—yes (members and guests only)
Restaurant—on site

Sarasota Bay

Sarasota Bay (also known as Big Sarasota Bay) stretches for a length of some 9 nautical miles on its southeast-to-northwest axis from the Ringling Bridge to Longboat Pass, west of Tidy Island. The southern two-thirds of the bay is deep and quite broad, with an average width of almost 3 nautical miles. The mainland shores to the east exhibit surprisingly light development north of downtown Sarasota and make for a good view from the water. Some smaller facilities, including one good boatyard and several marinas accepting transients, are available. You also have the opportunity to anchor within sight of one of the most famous houses in all of Florida.

The western banks of Sarasota Bay are comprised of the long, thin island known as Longboat Key. This body of land was actually used by the Timucuan Indians as a vacation spot long before the first Europeans touched the shores of Western Florida. Today, the isle has been intensely developed, but the condos and private homes are still interspaced with some natural stretches. This writer could not help but like Longboat Key, if only for the memory of becoming hopelessly lost on its much less developed roads during my high-school years.

Two large marinas and several other smaller facilities beckon cruisers on Longboat Key. There are also several notable waterside restaurants with their own docks and one particularly good anchorage south of Longboat Pass.

The Quay (Standard Mile 73.5)

The *L*-shaped cove east of flashing daybeacon #12 is definitely worth a look. Most navigators will be able to find their way to the cove's interior reaches with minimum 6½-foot depths. As you enter the cove and follow its sharp turn to the north, a huge, peach-colored building will be prominent on the eastern banks. This complex is known as The Quay. It consists of offices, retail shops, and no fewer than five restaurants. Dockage is plentiful at a privately maintained wooden face pier in front of the complex. Visitors are free to dock here while patronizing any of The Quay's businesses. Depths at the pier run 6 to 7 feet. There are no overnight accommodations.

Among the Quay's restaurants are Michael's Seafood Grill (941-951-2467) and Bart's Bayside (941-954-3839).

Now, as if all that weren't enough, for you cruising diners there is yet another choice in The Quay's cove. The Boathouse Restaurant (941-363-2628), associated with the Sarasota Hyatt, maintains its own docks on the cove's northeastern corner. Depths of 6 to 7 feet can be expected at its fixed wooden face docks. The restaurant is built out over the water and is quite prominent, though the only sign is a very small affair. In good weather outside dining is available.

Payne Terminal (Standard Mile 74.5)

The eastward extension of the New Pass Inlet channel (reviewed below) crosses the southern foot of Sarasota Bay and leads to a rectangular cove on the mainland shore charted as Payne Terminal. Apparently, this stream was once used as an oil loading and offloading terminal. That era has now passed and present-day visitors will find only a public launching ramp and the headquarters of the Sarasota Coast Guard Auxiliary (on the cove's southern banks). There are no services for transients, nor is there enough swinging room to anchor. Most visiting cruisers will wisely choose to bypass this errant sidewater.

Whitaker Bayou (Standard Mile 75)

Whitaker Bayou cuts into the mainland (eastern) shore of Sarasota Bay northeast of flashing daybeacon #13. The bayou plays host to one of Sarasota's premier repair facilities, The Yacht Center (941-365-1770). This facility is located on the stream's southern banks. The yard offers full-service mechanical (gas and diesel) and below-waterline, haul-out repairs. The on-site travelift is rated at 70 tons.

Surprisingly, the entrance to Whitaker Bayou is somewhat indifferently marked with white PVC pipes. Even more surprising, low-water entrance depths are a meager 4 to 4½ feet, and these soundings continue on into the boatyard docks. If you need more water, make your approach at high tide.

New Pass Inlet (Standard Mile 74.5)

The channel leading southwest to New Pass Inlet breaks off from the ICW at unlighted daybeacon #NP, on the southern reaches of Sarasota Bay. Shoaling on this seaward cut has currently lowered low-water soundings to **5** feet in places. This thin water is now present in spite of recent full dredging. Obviously, this cut shoals in just about as fast as the Army Corps can pump out the sand.

Couple the relatively shallow depths with the frequent presence of intimidating rollers and waves abutting both sides of the seaward portion of the New Pass channel, and it's easy to see why no one will ever consider this an easy inlet. Captains not familiar with the two Sarasota seaward passes (Big Sarasota Pass and New Pass) may want to continue tracking their way northward to Longboat Pass (see below) or even the Tampa Bay entrance before making that often difficult jump from inland to offshore waters (or vice versa).

New Pass is spanned by a bascule bridge with 23 feet of closed vertical clearance. I'm sorry to say that this span has a regulated opening schedule. Because of the strong current, this bridge is more than a casual cause for concern.

A few low-key facilities are found on the pass's southeasterly banks, northeast of the 23-foot bridge. None cater to larger cruising craft. First up is the friendly bunch at the Sarasota Sailing Squadron (941-388-2355). A host of small sailing craft belonging to the club's members anchor off the point southeast of flashing daybeacon #13, near the charted WSPB radio tower. The club does not have much in the way of dockage and there does

New Pass dock watchers

not seem to be anything in the way of services for transients.

Moving farther towards the Gulf, Gulfwind Marine (941-388-4411) comes up next. This marina caters almost exclusively to smaller powercraft and there are no services for transients except gasoline and a ship's store. Old Salty Dog Restaurant (941-349-0158) does have a dock adjacent to Gulfwind to which patrons are free to tie while dining. Depths are a very impressive 10 feet at dockside, but the fierce tidal currents can make for a hazardous approach to the pier.

Just short of the bascule bridge, boaters will find a small convenience and tackle store with its own dock guarding the southeastern banks. Dockside depths run 9 to 10 feet and there should be enough room for one 40-footer to tie up temporarily. Again, the current is a cause for genuine concern and caution.

We are sorry to report that the entrance to the once-popular, BAIL-suggested anchorage on the charted cove indenting New Pass's northwestern banks, southwest of the bridge, has now shoaled in entirely. Unlighted nun buoy #4, shown on chart 11425, at the cove's entrance has been removed.

We tried repeatedly to enter this anchorage from many different angles, including passages hard by both shores of its entrance, and found 2½- to 3-foot depths every time. While the interior waters remain deep, no craft larger than a skiff can now enter this sidewater safely.

Quick Point Channel

A marked channel breaks off from the northwestern flank of New Pass and curves around Quick Point. While the initial portion of this passage lacks any beacons, the channel northwest of Quick Point is well outlined with red, unlighted daybeacons. The cut eventually rejoins the deeper waters of Sarasota Bay at unlighted daybeacon #18. The vast majority of this channel holds 10 to 13 feet of water, but there is one exception. Near unlighted daybeacon #2, hard by Quick Point, water depths rise to some 5½ to 6 feet. Deep-draft vessels that might have a problem with these depths can enter and leave the cut by way of its deeper, easier-to-follow northwesterly entrance.

Quick Point channel leads to one friendly facility abeam of unlighted daybeacon #8. Spindrift Yacht Services offers extensive dry-stack storage, gasoline, and a well-stocked ship's store. Add to this a yacht brokerage, the Dry Dock Restaurant (941-383-0102), mechanical repairs (arranged through independent contractors), power and sail charters, and one of the most helpful attitudes in all of Western Florida. Perhaps now you have gained some impression of why local cruisers speak so highly of this facility. Unfortunately, Spindrift's limited wet-slip space does not allow for transient dockage. Oh, well—stop by and say hello anyway.

Spindrift Yacht Services (941) 383-7781

Approach depth—5½-13 feet
Dockside depth—8-10 feet
Gasoline—yes
Mechanical repairs—independent contractors
Ship's store—yes
Restaurant—on site

Ringling Mansion (Standard Mile 77.5)

Let us now turn our attention to the various sidewaters, facilities, and anchorages along Sarasota Bay's northeastern flank between Whitaker Bayou and Long Bar Point (north of the ICW's flashing daybeacon #18). The first point of interest worthy of our attention is the fabulous Ringling mansion, Ca'd'Zan, east of flashing daybeacon #15. This attraction is noted as a "Cupola" on chart 11425.

The old mansion sits directly on the bay's banks and makes a truly striking sight from the water. Depths of 5 feet or better run to within .2 nautical miles of the house. There are no provisions for dockage by pleasurecraft, but in good weather you can anchor abeam of the homeplace for an evening which will not soon be forgotten.

Even if an overnight stop is not in your plans, please take a few minutes to depart from the Waterway for a closer look at this unique attraction. Your voyage will be far richer for the extra effort.

Bowlees Creek Facilities (Standard Mile 78.5)

A pile-lined channel cuts the northeastern shores of Sarasota Bay northeast of unlighted daybeacon #16, and leads to a good facility on Bowlees Creek. Low-water entrance depths on the stream's interior reaches run as little as 4½ to 5 feet. Vessels drawing 4½ feet or less should not have any undue difficulty.

Bowlees Creek splits into two branches some 100 yards upstream from its mouth. The southeasterly fork leads to the Holiday Inn-Sarasota/Bradenton Airport Marina. This facility is nestled in the sheltered upstream terminus of Bowlees Creek and should make a great spot to ride out heavy weather. Transients are readily accepted for dockage at fixed wooden piers. Resident craft are moored to floating concrete piers. Power connections up to 30 amp, water hook-ups, gasoline, and diesel fuel are available. Visiting cruisers can even connect to cable television and the pier-side telephone system. Captains and crew will also discover clean shoreside showers, a laundromat, and a swimming pool perfect for

cooling off in after a hot day on Sarasota Bay. If you should wish to spend a night or two away from the liveaboard routine, the adjacent Holiday Inn is quite convenient. The motel also maintains a restaurant which the dockmaster described to this writer as "elegant." A lunchtime snack bar serving hamburgers and other sandwiches is available poolside. This is the only facility offering transient dockage on the mainland shores of Sarasota Bay north of the Ringling Bridge.

Holiday Inn-Sarasota Airport Marina (941) 355-2781)

Approach depth—4½-5 feet (mean low water)
Dockside depth—4½-5 feet (mean low water)
Accepts transients—yes
Fixed wooden piers—for transient use
Floating concrete docks—for resident boaters
Dockside power connections—up to 30 amp
Dockside water connections—yes
Showers—yes
Laundromat—yes
Gasoline—yes
Diesel fuel—yes
Mechanical repairs—independent contractors
Restaurant—on site

Bayshore Gardens (Standard Mile 78.5)

Northwest of Bowlees Creek, a second channel cuts in to a private condo dock. Skipping a bit farther northwest, we find a marked and charted passage making its way into a creek serving the Bayshore Gardens community. Low-water depths of 4½ to 5 feet could be a bit skimpy for some sailcraft.

The creek eventually splits. The northeasterly arm curls back around and forms a sheltered dockage basin for the residents of Bayshore Gardens. Signs on the creek leave no doubt that this facility is completely private with no transient services.

The opposite shore hosts Trailer Estates Marina (941-756-4912). This is a strictly small-craft facility which offers only gasoline and a small ship's store. Dockside depths are a meager 4½ feet at mean low water.

There is really very little of interest for visiting cruisers on the Bayshore Gardens creek. Unless you happen to be lucky enough to own property nearby and have access to the private marina, it would probably be a better plan to explore elsewhere.

Longboat Key Moorings
(Standard Mile 77.5)

Turning our attention back to Sarasota Bay's southwesterly shoreline, one of the two finest facilities on the bay is found at the foot of the charted channel south of Bishops Point and west of the ICW's flashing daybeacon #15. The dockage basin is denoted as facility designation #54A on chart 11425.

Longboat Key Moorings is a huge dockage facility enclosed in a protected basin and associated with an adjacent housing and condo development. It would take a serious gale to bother pleasurecraft berthed snugly in this harbor.

While it remains uncharted after many years (where are you, NOAA?), the Moorings' entrance channel is quite well marked with a host of unlighted daybeacons. Once you spot this collection of markers, it's an easy task to enter the harbor with good water. Minimum entrance soundings run around 6½ feet with a generous 9 to 20 feet of water dockside.

Transients are accepted at Longboat Key for overnight berths at ultramodern, fixed PVC-decked, concrete pile piers featuring all power, water, and cable television connections. Gasoline and diesel fuel are available, as well as waste pump-out services and a complete laundromat. The marina's large collection of shoreside showers is one of the finest on the Western Florida coastline, and it is fully climated controlled. Mechanical services can be arranged through independent technicians.

Longboat Key Moorings features a most impressive complex of shops and restaurants along the harbor's southerly shores. Housed in these buildings is a well-outfitted ship's store (and harbormaster's office) rubbing elbows with a full-line deli. The friendly staff will even make deliveries from the deli directly to your slip. For larger orders, a Publix supermarket and Eckerd drugstore are found within easy walking distance. Bike rentals are also available and courtesy van transportation can be arranged to the St. Armands shopping center.

When it comes time to slake a healthy appetite ashore, the Cafe on the Bay (941-383-0440), also located in the same complex, is a good choice. This is a sophisticated dining attraction with Continental-style cuisine. Shorts and T-shirts, while tolerated, are not exactly the preferred uniform of the day. If your attitude needs some adjustment beforehand, don't overlook the Marker 15 Lounge.

Other shoreside amenities include a heated swimming pool, tennis court, and a hot tub. A golf course is found a stone's throw from the marina grounds.

Well, if you know of a marina with more complete services, then by all means stay there. For my money, if you are in the market for a large, resort-type marina, then don't miss the chance to berth at Longboat Key Moorings.

Longboat Key Moorings (941) 383-8383
http://www.longboatkeymarina.com

Approach depth—6½+ feet
Dockside depth—9-20 feet

Accepts transients—yes
Fixed concrete and wooden piers—yes
Dockside power connections—up to 50 amp
Dockside water connections—yes
Waste pump-out—yes
Showers—yes
Laundromat—yes
Gasoline—yes
Diesel fuel—yes
Mechanical repairs—yes (independent technicians)
Ship's and variety store—yes (large)
Restaurant—on site and several nearby

Whale Key—Buttonwood Harbor Channel (Standard Mile 81)

South-southwest of unlighted daybeacon #19, cruisers can follow the marked and charted channel to a restaurant with dockage. Most of the cut holds minimum 6½-foot depths, but it climbs to 4½ feet as you approach the restaurant docks.

The Buttonwood Harbor Channel splits at unlighted daybeacon **#12**. Take the right-hand, or northwestern, arm of the channel to visit Pattigeorge's Marina Restaurant (941-383-5111). This fine dining spot has the deserved reputation of serving some of the most imaginative, Oriental-flair cuisine on the Western Florida ICW. Believe you me, if your craft fits the size and draft requirements, this is a must stop for those in search of waterside epicurean pleasures.

Unfortunately, Pattigeorge's docks did not appear adequate to this writer to serve vessels larger than 30 feet. Also, remember those 4½-foot dockside depths.

Whitney Beach Facilities (Standard Mile 83.5)

Northwest of flashing daybeacon #23, Sarasota Bay begins to narrow as the Waterway rushes on to the southern foot of Anna Maria Sound. Along the way cruisers can easily visit the second of the two first-rate marina facilities on Sarasota Bay.

Southeast of unlighted daybeacon #33, the charted channel running west-southwest splits near unlighted daybeacon #11. The marked passage continuing on to the southwest eventually cuts north-northwest to Buccaneer Marina. This establishment provides good transient dockage and a really first rate on-site dining attraction.

Buccaneer's entrance depths run from 6 to 7 feet and dockside soundings seem to range from 6½ to 8 feet. Long- and short-term transients are eagerly accepted at fixed wooden slips set in a semicircle around the inn and swimming pool. All power and water connections are readily available, and visitors will find six good showers and a full laundromat inside an air-conditioned, well-appointed clubhouse. There are also several tennis courts, all available to transients who pay an extra fee.

The on-site restaurant (see below) also houses two interesting gift shops, and some other shopping is accessible via a long walk. There is also a public beach within an easy step of the docks, while the on-site swimming pool welcomes visiting cruisers.

The huge Buccaneer Restaurant serves simply wonderful food, including one of the very best prime ribs that this writer and his ace research partner, Morgan Stinemetz, have ever enjoyed. There is also a full-service bar, poolside dining in fair weather, and live entertainment most nights. That's quite a lineup, I'm sure you will agree. Tell Tom we sent you!

Buccaneer Marina (941) 383-4468

Approach depth—6-7 feet minimum

Buccaneer Marina

Dockside depth—6½-8 feet
Accepts transients—yes
Fixed wooden slips—yes
Dockside power connections—up to 50 amp
Dockside water connections—yes
Showers—yes
Laundromat—yes
Restaurant—on site

A second, small-craft facility can be accessed by cutting southeast at unlighted daybeacon #11, and then turning west into the first canal. After a fairly lengthy cruise down this stream, Cannons Marina (941-383-1311) will be spotted dead ahead. This small facility has gasoline, a ship's store, and mechanical repairs for outboards. There is no overnight dockage and no other services for transients. Depths on the approach channel run 5½ to 7 feet with 5½- to 6-foot soundings dockside.

Longbeach—Jewfish Key Anchorage (BAIL-Suggested) and Associated Restaurants (Standard Mile 85)

One of the best and most popular anchorages between Placida Harbor and Tampa Bay is found on the wide swath of deep water stretching west from the gap between unlighted can buoy #39 and unlighted daybeacon #40. Minimum 9-foot depths, excellent shelter, and easy access to and from the ICW have combined to make this refuge one

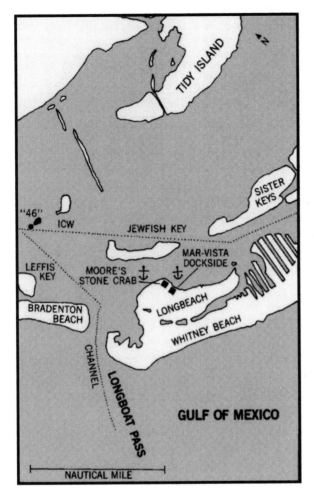

Two spots provide excellent shelter. Choose the one which is best sheltered from the prevailing winds. The first is found on the tongue of charted 13-foot water stretching south into a cove hard by the village of Longbeach. Minimum depths of 9 feet are held to within 75 yards of the western banks and even closer to the northwestern shores. There is some shallow water to the south and southeast, but boats up to 50 feet will find plenty of swinging room with excellent protection from all but northeasterly winds. If you find this anchorage crowded, it might be a good idea to use a Bahamian-style mooring to avoid swinging into your neighbor during the night. The surrounding shores are only lightly developed and are quite attractive.

So, you think the haven described above sounds pretty good. Well, hold on to your captain's hat—the best is yet to come. No fewer than two fine restaurants flank the cove's northwesterly banks. Moore's Stone Crab Restaurant (941-383-1748) is readily visible near the cove's northeasterly point. The docks stretch out well into the water. Vessels as large as 45 feet can tie to the outer pier, where skippers will find 6 to 8 feet of water. Depths on the smaller inner piers run to 5 feet. Restaurant patrons are welcome to spend the night at this dock without further charge, but no power or water connections are available.

Put simply, Moore's is one of this writer's favorite Western Florida restaurants. The atmosphere of simpler days has been preserved here and the pace is delightfully relaxed. Do you like fresh seafood? (If you don't, shame on you.) Moore's has its own fishing fleet. The catch of the day is unloaded out of the boats and straight into the kitchen, which tends to make it fresh. Moore's is open seven days a week.

of the most-used havens on or near Sarasota Bay. As if all that were not quite enough to attract you, consider the presence of not one, but two restaurants with their own docks bordering the southerly portion of the anchorage. This was all enough reason for *me* to tarry here for a while; you do what you want.

The deep-water channel eventually rejoins Longboat Pass (see below) to the west. While boats drawing less than 3 feet can make this journey, most skippers would be well advised to enter and leave the anchorage from the ICW.

Moore's Stone Crab Restaurant, Longbeach

Mar-Vista Dockside Restaurant (941-383-2391) guards the cove's southwesterly corner. The restaurant dock is a rather small affair that has only 4 feet of water at low tide. Cruising-size boats would do well to anchor out and dinghy ashore. Mar-Vista features a warm, convivial atmosphere. The al-fresco dining is *very* popular. My first mate and I enjoyed an idle time over excellent drinks sitting at the long bar and looking out over the many boats anchored in the cove. Sandwiches and fresh seafood are served along with the copious drinks. The local favorite seems to be the grouper.

The second spot where you should consider anchoring, particularly if the winds are blowing strongly from the north or northeast, is found on the deep water behind (to the southwest of) the long, private island southwest of

flashing daybeacon #41 known as Jewfish Key. Minimum depths are again 9 feet, and there is almost enough swinging room for a small freighter. Some tidal current is present in this cut, so make sure the anchor is well set and there is plenty of room between you and your neighbors. The island to the northeast sports a single house and private pier, but is otherwise in its natural state. The mainland shores are lightly developed. This is an attractive anchorage that most cruisers will want to visit time and time again. The two coveside restaurants are still only a short dinghy ride away.

Mariners in need of galley supplies, and up for a very long dinghy ride, can work their way south to the charted mouth of Bishop Bayou. By following this stream as it cuts to the northwest, you will eventually come up behind a shopping center. Here you will find a few cleats set off a concrete seawall where you can tie your dinghy off temporarily.

Longboat Pass (Standard Mile 86)

The channel leading to Longboat Pass breaks off from the ICW between unlighted daybeacons #45 and #47. This is a narrow inlet through which tidal currents often boil. The seaward cut is spanned by a 17-foot bascule bridge which opens on demand from 6:00 A.M. to 10:00 P.M. Minimum depths of 10 feet can now be expected in the marked cut. Of course, future shoaling could and probably will eventually erode these happy soundings. Considering the current and the 17-foot horizontal clearance of the bascule bridge, I would not attempt to bring anything larger than a 45-footer in through this inlet. If you should make the attempt, proceed with caution.

Cortez Bridge Facilities (Standard Mile 87)

Two marinas are ready to serve cruising craft hard by the Cortez Bridge, north of unlighted daybeacon #49. Moving south to north, the first of the two facilities is found at the terminus of its charted, L-shaped channel cutting in from the bridge's southwestern corner. Bradenton Beach Marina is a medium-sized establishment that has undergone a complete remodeling since the last edition of this guide appeared. A huge dry stack storage building has been added, and this structure is more than obvious flanking the harbor's southerly side. The dockmaster's office has

Bradenton Beach Marina

been moved to a point directly behind the principal wet-slip dockage pier, and the marina ship's store has been closed. An on-site restaurant opened just behind the dockage basin, but this operation has been shut down, and the space has not yet been filled by another tenant. All in all, Bradenton Beach Marina has a far more prosperous air these days, and visiting cruisers can use this facility with confidence.

The marina's entrance channel is a little curvy for first timers, but it carries minimum 5½- to 6-foot depths. Check out our navigational account of this facility below for channel advice.

Bradenton Beach gladly accepts transients at its fixed wooden piers equipped with twin 30-amp power and water connections. The outer docks carry some 10 to 11 feet of water, while 5½ to 6 feet is encountered on the innermost slips. Neither this marina nor the Seafood Shack (reviewed below) is particularly well sheltered for really nasty weather. Gasoline, diesel fuel, and full mechanical (gas and diesel engines) and haul-out repairs are available. The on-site travelift is rated at 35 tons and a second, most impressive 70-ton lift should be in operation by the time this account finds its way into your cockpit. Adequate, non air-conditioned showers and a semi-open-air laundromat are found shoreside. Several restaurants, including the redoubtable Bridge Tender Inn (see below), are only a few steps away.

Bradenton Beach Marina (941) 778-2288

Approach depth—5½-6 feet (minimum)
Dockside depth—10-11 feet (outer docks)
                5½-6 feet (innermost slips)
Accepts transients—yes
Fixed wooden piers—yes

Dockside power connections—30 amp
Dockside water connections—yes
Showers—yes
Laundromat—yes
Gasoline—yes
Diesel fuel—yes
Mechanical repairs—yes
Below-waterline repairs—yes
Restaurant—several nearby

While running the approach cut leading to Bradenton Beach Marina, cruisers will be led hard by the outermost tip of the Bradenton Beach Historic Pier. It is quite possible for boats drawing 4 feet or less to break off first to the west and then southwest, and follow a channel outlined by white PVC pipes to a small pier that fronts the Bridge Tender Inn (135 Bay Street, 941-778-4849). Consult the navigational account later in this chapter for more complete navigational instructions.

Slips are for the use of dining patrons only—no overnight stays are allowed. Depths in the white-PVC-pipe-outlined channel run around at least 4½ to 5 feet at mean low water with 5-foot soundings dockside.

The Bridge Tender Inn is a particularly noteworthy dining spot. Housed in the remodeled quarters of historic Bayside Inn, it features dinner entrees that are memorable, to the say the very least. We particularly recommend the "Seafood Melange," a yummy concoction of fresh seafood and mushrooms in a white-wine and garlic sauce served over pasta. Well, this writer's appetite is piqued!

The Seafood Shack Restaurant and Marina is found on the ICW's easterly banks just north of Cortez Bridge. Berths are provided by the friendly dockmaster for both resident and visiting craft at fixed wooden piers with water and 30- to 50-amp power connections. The marina's marked entrance channel has one

Seafood Shack Restaurant & Marina

4½- to 5-foot low-water lump, but otherwise it carries 6 to 12 feet of water. Dockside depths run a very respectable 8 to 10 feet on the outermost piers but fall off to only some 5 feet of water on the inner sections of the harbor. After tying up, cruisers going ashore will find good showers. The adjacent Seafood Shack restaurant serves the freshest of Florida seafood. There is an excellent view of the Waterway from the upstairs dining room. Ask for a table by the large windows. Don't miss the Seafood au Gratin, a tempting combination of shrimp and fresh fish served in a tangy cheddar cheese sauce. Ah, I can taste it now!

Seafood Shack Restaurant & Marina
  (941) 794-1235

Approach depth—4½-12 feet
Dockside depth—8-10 feet (outermost dock)
                      5-6 feet (inner slips)
Accepts transients—yes
Fixed wooden piers—yes
Dockside power connections—up to 30 amp
Dockside water connections—yes
Showers—yes
Mechanical repairs—independent contractors
Restaurant—on site

Anna Maria Sound

North of the Cortez Bridge, the Western

Florida ICW begins its trek through Anna Maria Sound. This body of water can get as rough as a cob when winds are blowing from the north, off Tampa Bay and down the sound's full length. Most of Anna Maria's waters are quite shallow. Stick to the Waterway unless you plan to try one of the somewhat questionable sidewaters reviewed below.

Palma Sola Bay (Standard Mile 87.5)

The marked channel cutting east to Palma Sola Bay intersects the ICW near unlighted daybeacon #50. If you have followed this writer's account from Flamingo, you know that I'm not bashful about recommending gunkholes. However, Palma Sola may be one body of water that you might want to consider bypassing. Depths in the often confusing channel run as little as 4½ feet. There are currently no facilities for cruisers available on the bay. Most of the charted side channels serve condos and private dockage areas. There is certainly no room for anchorage on any of these cuts.

Fearless skippers piloting boats that draw 4 feet or less can, if they are willing to undertake a long cruise, find one anchorage and a restaurant with a dock on upper Palma Sola Bay. Study chart 11425 and notice that the bay's northerly lobe is pinched off by a 10-foot fixed bridge. In spite of the soundings shown on chart 11425, depths of 5 feet or better run quite close to the southerly banks, west of the bridge. You can throw out the hook in 5 to 7 feet of water with good protection from northerly and westerly winds. This anchorage provides little shelter from strong southern breezes. The causeway lying to the north is made up of a white sand beach which the locals often use for fishing. Traffic noise and lights from the adjacent highway could disturb your esteemed repose.

West of the anchorage, Reef Restaurant (941-792-7711) sits perched on the causeway's southwestern flank. This eatery has its own docks with from 5 to 10 feet of water. There are no overnight accommodations.

Anna Maria Island

Anna Maria Island has one of the most delightful climates in Western Florida. The surrounding waters tend to mitigate both very hot or unusually cold weather. It is said that frost has appeared only once in the last ten years.

This writer has come across two accounts of how the island came by its name. The first, found in Sarah Bird Wright's *Islands of the South and Southeastern United States,* asserts that the name is a contraction of "Ana-Maria-Cay," named in honor of Mary, the mother of Christ, and Mary's mother, Ann. An article written by Paul Winder in the November 1988 edition of *Southern Boating* magazine contends that "in the early 1500s, Hernando de Soto named the island for the wife of Charles II of Spain. . . ." Readers may take their pick.

Anna Maria Island has a long history of tourism. At the turn of the century, Rurick Cobb built the isle's first resort, which was known as the Oar House. This venerable hostelry survived until 1980 when, tragically, it burned to the ground.

The residents of Anna Maria remain a close-knit bunch. The local citizens are bound together by the common purpose of preserving those qualities that drew visitors to their isle in the first place. In the past several years the town council has dealt successfully with non-resident parking on the beach and the dumping of toxic wastes by the Army Corps of Engineers.

The island has three communities. Anna Maria City is perched on the shores to the north, with Holmes Beach in the middle and Bradenton Beach to the south.

Amidst much modern construction, many old-style Floridian homes remain on Anna Maria Island. It seems altogether fitting and proper that these structures are still present. In this land where the locals are fighting tooth and nail to preserve the past from the ravages of the present, the old Floridian island dwellers would be proud.

Perico Harbour and Johnny Leverocks Restaurant (Standard Mile 89)

Northeast of flashing daybeacon #51, the ICW flows under the Anna Maria Island Bridge. Immediately after passing through this span, a marked channel leads east and then northeast to a small marina and a restaurant. Entrance depths into Perico Harbour's dockage basin are a scant 4 feet at low tide. Obviously, this facility is confined to vessels drawing less than 4 feet. Gasoline and diesel fuel are available dockside and there is a shoreside ship's store plus extensive dry stack storage. No other transient services are available.

Yet another branch of the fine Johnny Leverocks Restaurant chain (941-342-8865) is located just south of the dockage basin. Patrons of this seafood restaurant can dock in 4 feet of water at a floating pier while dining. Skippers of larger cruising craft will not want to attempt entry into this harbor.

Holmes Beach Facilities (Standard Mile 91)

Boats drawing less than 4 feet may carefully follow a channel with minimum 4½- to 5-foot depths west and southwest of flashing daybeacon #62. This cut leads to two small-craft marinas and one restaurant.

The pile-marked channel is reasonably easy to follow as it skirts first southwest and then west to a split near unlighted daybeacon #18. The south-side branch leads to Holmes Beach Marina (http://www.holmesbeachmarina.com, 941-778-2255). This medium-sized firm is concerned mostly with dry storage of small powercraft. Dockside depths are a meager 4½ feet, and the marina's few wet slips are open to rough water. Gasoline (but no diesel fuel) and mechanical repairs to outboards, I/O's, and some inboard gasoline engines are offered.

The northerly branch of the channel leads careful cruisers to a sheltered canal which again splits on its interior reaches. Approach depths at the canal's entrance run as thin as 4½ feet at low water. The northerly arm is home to Captain's Marina. This facility is yet another of those small powercraft-type marinas so prevalent in this region. One or two slips are sometimes available for small-craft transients, but this writer would certainly not recommend this dockage for any craft larger than 26 feet. Gasoline can be purchased and mechanical repairs to outboards and I/O's are offered. There is a combination ship's and tackle store on the marina grounds.

Captain's Marina (941) 778-1977

Approach depth—4½-5 feet
Dockside depth—4½-5 feet
Accepts transients—limited to smaller powercraft
Fixed wooden piers—yes
Dockside power connections—limited (15 amp only)
Gasoline—yes
Mechanical repairs—mostly outboards and I/O's
Ship's store—yes

The southerly branch of the canal leads

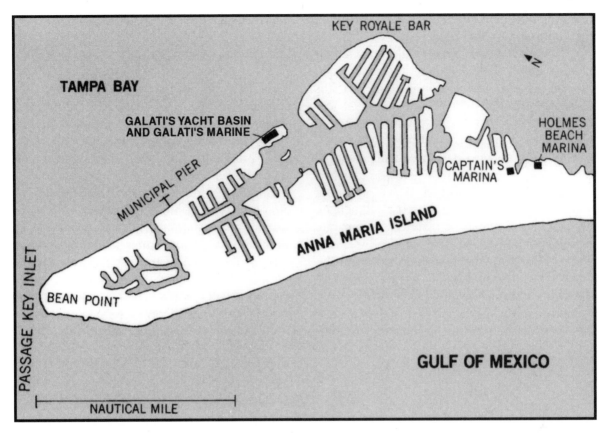

boaters to a restaurant that has seen many changes of name and ownership during the last several years. Currently known as The Marina Bay, this is one waterside dining spot that is probably better bypassed. In any case, the 4-foot dockside depths are not adequate for any but small craft.

Galati's Yacht Basin and Galati's Marine (Standard Mile 92)

North of unlighted daybeacon #63, the ICW cuts to the northeast and follows a dredged cut through "the Bulkhead," which is the shoal blocking the northern mouth of Anna Maria Sound. Just short of the sound's terminus, cruisers have a last opportunity to visit a

combination friendly marina, super-service facility, and great restaurant. Lying west of unlighted daybeacon #63, a marked channel makes its way in from Bimini Bay, home of Galati's Yacht Basin and Galati's Marine. Galati's has always been one of our favorite facilities in this region. In times past, however, there was a bit of a shoaling problem on the marina's entrance cut. We are happy to report that dredging, just completed as this account is being penned, has deepened approach soundings to at least 7 feet. Yea!

Captains cruising between the daybeacons into the inner reaches of Bimini Bay will spot the wet slips associated with Galati's Yacht Basin almost dead ahead. Look for a series of uncharted and unlighted daybeacons marking the channel into the docks.

Galati's is happy to accept transients at their fixed wooden docks featuring fresh water and 30- to 50-amp power connections. Depths alongside run between 4½ and 6 feet at low tide. Some of Galati's slips are covered, while others are left open for wind-powered craft.

The super-friendly dockmaster will be glad to direct you to the fuel dock where you can purchase gasoline or diesel fuel. Waste pump-out service is now available as well. Ultraclean, fully climate controlled showers and a first-rate laundromat are found just behind the basin. There is also an enhanced ship's store on site. Galati's Yacht Basin is highly recommended by this writer to his fellow cruisers.

If you are lucky enough to arrive at Galati's at or even near mealtime, a lucky star is shining over your cruise. The on-site dining attraction at this marina is known (inappropriately enough) as Rotten Ralph's Restaurant (941-778-3953). Let's not mince words with this one—in spite of its somewhat less than appealing name, the seafood is fabulous— some of the best you will enjoy along this coastline. During fair weather, open-air, dockside dining is available with a wonderful view of the harbor and the nearby boat slips. Even during times of a less than ideal climate, the dining room's plate-glass windows usually give a more than satisfactory view of the water. The adjacent bar is a local gathering spot for the cruising and fishing crowd and a great place to meet up with some fellow mariners. What more could you want from a marina restaurant? Don't miss this one!

Unfortunately, we found out the hard way

Rotten Ralph's Restaurant

that wet-slip dockage is not really available for patrons of Rotten Ralph's Restaurant. Don't attempt to moor to the fuel dock or an open slip while dining. Trust me, you'll be asked to move along about halfway through your meal. On the other hand, if you are docked at Galati's overnight, it will be an easy matter to check out Rotten Ralph's.

Skippers in search of service work need look no further than the adjacent Galati's Marine repair yard. To reach the yard facilities, you must first traverse a narrow channel running around a small island, northwest of the yacht basin. Care is needed when rounding this cut. Expect low-water soundings in the channel of only 4½ feet. There is about three inches of water outside of the marked passage. With advance arrangements, the yard personnel will be glad to pilot your vessel through this cut to the repair facilities. That seems like a very good idea indeed to this writer.

Galati's offers extensive mechanical repairs for both gasoline and diesel power plants, and haul-out, below-waterline services by way of a 55-ton travelift. Judging from the number of craft that were hauled up for work during our visit, this yard must enjoy a sure and certain reputation with local skippers.

Galati's Yacht Basin and Galati's Marine
(941) 778-0755
(941) 778-0757

Approach depth—7+
Dockside depth—4½-6 feet (low tide)
Accepts transients—yes
Fixed wooden piers—yes
Dockside power connections—30-50 amp
Dockside water connections—yes
Waste pump-out—yes
Showers—yes
Laundromat—yes
Gasoline—yes
Diesel fuel—yes
Mechanical repairs—yes (extensive)
Below-waterline repairs—yes (extensive)
Ship's store—yes
Restaurant—on site

SARASOTA BAY TO ANNA MARIA SOUND NAVIGATION

Successful navigation of Sarasota Bay and Anna Maria Sound is sometimes complicated by the relative width of these two bodies of water. Winds over 10, and certainly 15, knots have more than enough fetch to raise a teeth-chattering chop. Also, tidal currents in and around Big Sarasota Pass, New Pass, and Longboat Pass can be formidable. On Sarasota Bay, some of the Waterway markers are spaced so widely that it's a good idea to run compass and/or GPS courses between the beacons. In short, this is not a stretch of the ICW to be taken lightly. Make good preparations before-hand, try to pick a sunny day with light airs, and you should eventually find your way to the mighty waters of Tampa Bay.

On to Roberts Bay   North of the Stickney Point Bridge, the ICW runs through a dredged landcut for some 1.7 nautical miles before emptying into the relatively wider waters of Roberts Bay near unlighted daybeacon #75. A substantial portion of this cut is lined by private docks with vessels moored to the piers. No-wake regulations are now in effect from the Stickney Point Bridge to Roberts Bay.

Don't attempt to enter the cove indenting the northeasterly banks at flashing daybeacon #64. It may look inviting, but on-site research revealed depths of 4 feet or less.

Only very shallow-draft boats with specific local knowledge should attempt to enter the southwestern mouth of Phillippi Creek, near unlighted daybeacon #72. We consistently encountered 4-foot depths trying to enter this stream from several different angles.

North of unlighted daybeacon #75, the ICW passes out into Roberts Bay. Continue following the well-marked channel until coming abeam of unlighted daybeacon #78 to its westerly quarter. Two excellent side trips are available from this aid to navigation.

The Field Club   Fortunate cruisers visiting the Field Club, east of unlighted daybeacon #78, should turn into the well-marked channel just south of #78. For best depths, do not try to enter the channel from flashing daybeacon #79 as chart 11425 would tend to suggest.

Roberts Bay Anchorage (BAIL-Suggested) To enter the super anchorage in and around the spoil island west of unlighted daybeacon #78, cut almost due west from #78 and point towards the center of the substantial island dead ahead. In good weather, you can drop the hook some 50 to 75 yards offshore.

For better protection, you can cut to the north and track your way around the spoil island's northerly tip, keeping some 25 to 50 yards offshore. Turn to the south and

cruise behind the island, keeping about the same distance offshore. Drop anchor once the mid-width of the island comes abeam to the east. Vessels drawing 4 feet or less can actually circumnavigate the island.

Siesta Key Bridge Anchorages   The westside anchorage, south of the Siesta Key Bridge, is entered by abandoning the Waterway some 50 yards south of the span and cutting into the broad entrance which you will spot to the west. Favor the seawalled starboard banks as you enter the stream. Soon the cove forks. Don't attempt the left-hand (southerly) branch. It is shoal with 4-foot depths. The principal right-side (northerly) fork leads into a lagoonlike body of water with excellent depths. A canal comes off the northwestern corner of the lagoon, but there is no room for anchorage on this offshoot.

The easterly anchorage has a tricky entrance and should only be attempted by boats drawing less than 4 feet. The best water is found hard by the cove's southerly entrance point. Here you should spy two unadorned pilings. Pass between these piles, favoring the southern side heavily. Even with this procedure, expect some 4- to 4½-foot depths at low tide. After leaving the entrance behind, cruise back into the mid-width and follow the cove as it swings to the south and then back to the north in a classic C-shape. The best depths and protection are found on the wider upstream section of the cove.

On the ICW   North of flashing daybeacon #82, the ICW says hello to the Siesta Key bascule bridge. This bridge has a closed vertical clearance of 25 feet and sports a restricted opening schedule. The bridge opens on the hour and every 20 minutes thereafter from 11:00 A.M. to 6:00 P.M., year round, seven days a week.

Spoil Anchorage Depart the ICW at flashing daybeacon #2 and set course to enter the cove to the northeast, favoring the southerly and easterly banks. As you enter the anchorage, you may spy a concrete piling with a diamond-shaped yellow sign to the north. Don't approach these waters. The sign warns of an artificial reef. After passing this obstacle to your port, you can begin a slow, lazy turn to the north and anchor along the cove's south-to-north centerline. Return to the Waterway by retracing your steps. A straight course back out to the ICW would land the hapless (clueless?) navigator right on the artificial reef.

On the ICW The Waterway cuts a tiny bit farther to the west at flashing daybeacon #2. This is a narrow portion of the channel, and you must be sure to pick out the various aids to navigation before proceeding. Tidal currents pick up markedly, courtesy of nearby Big Sarasota Pass inlet. Watch your stern for excessive leeway. Eventually you will pass between flashing daybeacon #6, to its westerly side, and unlighted daybeacons #5 and #7 to their easterly quarters. North and northwest of #7, the channel broadens and Big Sarasota Pass lies to the southwest.

Big Sarasota Pass Big Sarasota Pass, even with some low-water depths of 4½ feet,

boasts several points of interest on and off the channel inland of the shallower portion of the channel.

To enter Big Pass, continue cruising on the ICW for some 100 yards northwest of unlighted daybeacon #7. Then turn sharply to the southwest and point to come abeam of and pass flashing daybeacon #19 by about 50 yards to its southeasterly quarter. Point to pass unlighted daybeacon #17 to the same side and keep about the same distance off this aid.

Eventually you will pass flashing daybeacon #16 by some 50 yards to its northwesterly side. Opposite #16, unlighted daybeacon #15A has been added to the array of aids to navigation on the Big Pass channel. Pass #15A to its southeasterly quarter.

The charted channel swinging east around Fishery Point near flashing daybeacon #16 carries good 12- to 13-foot depths, but it is a relatively narrow cut that borders on shoal water. There is certainly not enough room for a cruising boat to anchor. This small passage is best left to local small craft.

From #16, set course to come abeam of and pass unlighted daybeacon #15 fairly close to its southeasterly side. From #15, you can enter the Sarasota Yacht Club channel (see below) or visit the delightful anchorage along the southern shores of Lido Key, to the west.

If you decide to anchor off Lido Key, continue following the Big Sarasota Pass channel past #15 for some .1 nautical miles, as if you were putting out to sea. You can then cut directly in towards the western shores with excellent depths almost into the beach. Remember the strong tidal currents that regularly scour this anchorage. Be absolutely sure the hook is well set before you leave the helm.

Big Sarasota Pass continues to track seaward, skirting a huge shoal on its western flank. Good depths continue through this entire run until you leave Sarasota Point behind at flashing daybeacon #6. From #6, the channel soon cuts sharply south-southeast and depths become far more problematical. At the time of this writing, a series of unlighted, green daybeacons outlines the southwestern edge of the channel along this southeasterly run. If these beacons are still in place at the time of your arrival, be sure to stay northeast of them.

Eventually, you will come abeam of unlighted daybeacon #3. At this point, the channel turns back to the southwest and heads for charted flashing buoy #1. Don't cut the corner between #3 and #1. Swing wide for best depths.

Be advised that the outer portion of the Big Pass inlet channel could be *very* different from the scheme depicted above by the time you read this account. Proceed with maximum caution and check with one of the local marinas or yacht clubs about the passage's latest condition and marking before making the attempt.

Sarasota Yacht Club Channel   Navigation of this channel is complicated by two persistent problems. Note the long shoal correctly charted on 11425 striking out from the entrance's northeastern point. This hazard can quickly trap the unwary, particularly at high tide. Also, remember that the mud

flats west and southwest of unlighted daybeacons #2 and #4 are covered at high tide. This stretch of water looks very different than what you might expect from the chart.

Just to make matters a little more interesting, the initial daybeacons on this cut are very hard to spot from the main body of Big Pass. Be sure to use your binoculars to help pick out #1, #2, and #4.

For best depths, cut north some 100 yards southwest of unlighted daybeacon #15 (on the Big Sarasota Pass Channel) and point to pass between the first two aids to navigation on the yacht club channel, unlighted daybeacons #1 and #2.

Once between #1 and #2, you need only pass all the subsequent red markers by some 25 yards to your starboard side for good depths to the yacht club docks. North of unlighted daybeacon #8, the channel swings a bit to the northeast. The deep water still extends in a broad stretch before you. Just be mindful of the charted shoal abutting the eastern banks. Pass unlighted daybeacon #11 to its easterly side and favor the western shores to avoid this hazard.

Extra care must be exercised should you choose to anchor in the cove east of unlighted daybeacon #10. This side cut is mostly unmarked and can only be described as difficult. Very shoal water of 2 feet or even less flanks the entrance channel to the north and, particularly, the south. To find the deeper water, continue on the main yacht club channel, north of #10. Watch for a "Manatee—No Wake" sign east of the channel. Just before coming abeam of this sign, turn sharply east and point to pass the "Manatee" sign to your port side. Soon thereafter, you will spot another "No Wake" sign, which should also be passed to your port side. Once abeam of this second sign, continue more or less straight into the cove, favoring the northerly banks.

Don't venture to the south until you are well into the cove's interior reaches. Only very small craft that can clear the 7-foot fixed bridge may make use of the cut-through to Bird Key Channel.

Otter/Lido Key Anchorage (BAIL-Suggested)

Otter/Lido Key Anchorage (BAIL-Suggested) Watch along the southwestern banks for unlighted daybeacon #7. Depart the main channel immediately south of #7 and point to enter the passage running south of Otter Key by favoring the undeveloped, mangrove-lined northerly banks. Soon the main channel will cut to the northwest, while the smaller, southwesterly-side arm will be spotted almost dead ahead.

Ignore two pilings that you may spy near the shoreline to the southwest, immediately southeast of the smaller (southwesterly) arm of water. These piles are founded in very shallow water.

After you swing northwest on the main cut, good water spreads out almost from shore to shore, but to be on the safe side hold to the waters at least somewhat near the mid-width. Don't attempt to enter the waters surrounding St. Armands Key to the northwest. In spite of soundings shown on chart 11425, shoals are immediately encountered.

Back on the ICW Captains navigating along the Sarasota waterfront between flash-ing daybeacon #6 and the Ringling Bridge (plus the eastern banks of Sarasota Bay, north of the Ringling span) should switch to inset #2 of chart 11425. Its greater detail simpli-fies an understanding of the area.

From flashing daybeacon #6, cruisers northbound on the ICW should set course to come abeam of flashing daybeacon #8 to its westerly side. It's then a simple hop to unlighted daybeacon #8A. The deep channel to Marina Operations and its adjacent anchorage cuts northeast, to the north of #8A.

Marina Operations and Anchorage (BAIL-Suggested) To visit Marina Operations, Marina Jack's Restaurant and/or the BAIL-suggested Bayfront Park anchorage, con-tinue on the Waterway until you are about halfway between #8A and flashing daybea-con #10. Watch to the northeast for un-lighted daybeacons #2 and #3. Once these aids are abeam, simply alter course to the northeast and cruise between #2 and #3. The remainder of the passage into the ma-rina is quite broad and deep.

If you decide to anchor, follow the marina entrance channel past Golden Gate Point. Watch to the southeast and you will undoubtedly observe a host of anchored vessels. Depart the marina cut some 100 yards southwest of the hook-shaped point which encloses the dockage basin. Cruise to the southeast and pick out any likely spot. Remember to leave plenty of room between your craft and any neighbors you might find already secure in the anchorage.

Golden Gate Anchorage From flash-ing daybeacon #10, set course for the northeastern corner of the cove that is west of Golden Gate Point. Be sure you are well past the charted cable area before dropping the hook. Note the correctly charted 5-foot shoal abutting the northwestern banks on the cove's southwesterly reaches.

On the ICW   Northwest of flashing daybeacon #10, the Waterway exchanges greetings with one of the busiest bridges on the entire Western Florida ICW. The Ringling causeway span has a closed vertical clearance of 22 feet and a restrictive opening schedule. Fortunately, plans are on the drawing board to replace the existing bascule bridge with a fixed, high-rise structure. The onset of construction is uncertain at the time of this writing.

Currently, the Ringling Bridge opens only on the hour and half-hour, daily, from 7:00 A.M. to 6:00 P.M, year round. During the evening and nighttime hours the bridge opens on demand. Plan your cruise around these regulations to avoid long delays.

Once through the Ringling span, set course to come abeam of flashing daybeacon #12 by some 50 yards to its westerly quarter. You have now crossed into the southern reaches of broad Sarasota Bay. Expect increased chop courtesy of the long wind fetch. From #12, several side trips are found on the bay's easterly shores.

The Quay   Depart the Waterway some .1 nautical miles southeast of flashing daybeacon #12. Point for the broad opening of the L-shaped cove on the northeastern corner of the causeway leading to the Ringling

Bridge. In spite of soundings shown on 11425, you can expect minimum 5-foot depths between the Waterway and the cove's entrance.

Enter the cove on its centerline and follow it as the water swerves sharply to the north. After making the turn, The Quay will be obvious to starboard and The Boathouse Restaurant will be dead ahead.

Payne Terminal   If for some unexpected reason you should decide to cruise into Payne terminal, cut east-northeast just north of unlighted daybeacon #NP. Several unlighted daybeacons noted (only) on inset 2 of chart 11425 will lead you in. Be aware that unlighted daybeacon #23 is found well north of the stream's entrance and there is shallow water east of this aid. Favor unlighted daybeacon #22 and cruise into the entrance on its mid-width.

Whitaker Bayou and The Yacht Center   Vessels bound for Whitaker Bayou, home of The Yacht Center, should set a course from flashing daybeacon #13 for the stream's westerly mouth. Enter the creek on its mid-width and be ready for some low-tide depths of 4 feet.

New Pass Inlet   Remember that depths on New Pass Inlet have now shoaled to some 5 feet at low water. The seaward side of the channel is also frequently ringed by breakers, and it can be more than slightly intimidating. Lacking the completion of some future dredging project or specific, up-to-date local knowledge, visiting cruisers might do better to make use of Longboat

Pass to the north or even the Tampa Bay entrance channel.

North of flashing daybeacon #12, the ICW quickly rushes on to an intersection with the New Pass Inlet channel at unlighted junction daybeacon #NP. To run the inlet, cut sharply west-southwest at #NP and point to pass between flashing daybeacon #16 and unlighted daybeacon #17. You are now heading *toward* the open sea, so take all green markers to your starboard side and all red beacons to port. Be ready for sharp tidal currents. Watch your stern carefully for lateral leeway.

As you span the gap between unlighted daybeacon #15 and flashing daybeacon #13, watch to the south for anchored sailcraft associated with the Sarasota Sailing Squadron. Larger powercraft should slow to minimum-wake speed when passing.

While many local boats follow the charted belt of 7-foot waters east of the point occupied by the Sailing Squadron's headquarters (and the charted WSPB radio tower) to the south and then back to the west, this trip is not recommended for strangers. The entire passage is unmarked and borders on very shoal water.

West-southwest of flashing daybeacon #13, the inlet channel comes under the lee of Lido Key to the south. Between unlighted daybeacon #11 and the bascule bridge, Gulfwind Marine will be spotted on the southeastern banks, followed by a bait and tackle store with its own dock.

Just before reaching the bascule span, cruisers can cut back to the north and enter the Quick Point channel. This passage will be reviewed in detail below, but for now

we need only note that entry into the cut from this quarter is complicated by the absence of any aids to navigation south of Quick Point. If you do attempt to enter this channel from New Pass, take it slow and glue your eyes to the sounder.

The New Pass bascule bridge, west-southwest of unlighted daybeacon #11, has a closed vertical clearance of only 23 feet and a highly restricted opening schedule. Seven days a week, from 7:00 A.M. to 6:00 P.M., the bridge opens on the hour and then every 20 minutes thereafter. In light of the strong tidal currents which regularly scour the inlet, this span can be a real cause for concern during its regulated waiting periods. If you have to wait, stop well back from the bridge and mark time in the channel as best you can, making sure to leave plenty of room between yourself and any other vessels which happen to be waiting.

Please remember that we no longer recommend entry into the one-time Sands Point-Longboat Key anchorage lining New Pass's northwesterly shore, just southwest of the bascule bridge. The entrance to this cut has now shoaled to MLW soundings of only 2½ feet, even on its eastern and western flanks, where the good water used to be.

Passage west of the New Pass bridge gets a bit more problematic. West of flashing daybeacon #7, the passage cuts out into the Gulf, with a huge shoal flanking the inlet just to the north. Take care; this portion of the channel is treacherous and most definitely not for the faint of heart.

Quick Point Channel   Many captains will wisely choose to enter Quick Point

Channel from its easy-to-follow northerly entrance rather than the passage from New Pass. To reach the northerly entrance, cruise northwest from flashing daybeacon #13 for .9 nautical miles. Then, set a new compass course for unlighted daybeacon #18 on the southwestern banks. This aid marks the northerly entrance to Quick Point Channel. Pass #18 and all the other red daybeacons on this channel to your *port* side.

From #18 the channel runs southwest past unlighted daybeacon #16. At unlighted daybeacon #14, the channel swings sharply to the northeast. Stay well to the west and southwest of all the red markers and you can follow the cut as far as Quick Point with little difficulty. Spindrift Yacht Services will come up on the southwesterly banks at unlighted daybeacon #8.

On the ICW It's a long run between the four daybeacons which mark the Waterway's passage along the southeast-to-northwest axis of Sarasota Bay. It would be a good idea to plot compass and/or GPS courses between these aids to navigation long before your visit to the bay. There is little in the way of shallow water to worry with for almost a mile to either side of the ICW's track. Nevertheless, if you're like this writer, it is always comforting to have some idea of where you are. Follow the courses you have laid out carefully and tick off the markers on 11425 as they come up.

From flashing daybeacon #13, it is a long run of 2.3 nautical miles to the next northerly aid, flashing daybeacon #15. While it makes little difference, officially you're supposed to pass #15 to its north-easterly side. From #15, mariners may choose to cruise to the Ringling Estate on the northeastern shore.

Ringling Estate Anchorage The Ringling Mansion is noted on chart 11425 north of Stephens Point, by the "Cupola" notation. Boats that can stand some 5-foot depths can cruise directly from flashing daybeacon #15 for the charted location. Skippers piloting craft that need a bit more water should approach the estate from the north, thereby bypassing the long, correctly charted shoal stretching out from Stephens Point. If you plan to anchor, be sure to drop the hook before approaching to less than .2 nautical miles of the shore. Closer in, depths rise to 4 feet or less.

On the ICW It's a run of 1 nautical mile between flashing daybeacon #15 and unlighted daybeacon #16 on the ICW. West of #15, one of the finest facilities on Sarasota Bay guards the Gulf-side banks.

Longboat Key Moorings A large collection of (mostly) unlighted and still uncharted daybeacons outlines the entrance to Longboat Key Moorings' sheltered dockage basin, south of charted Bishops Point. Use your binoculars to pick out the various pairs of markers as you approach the westerly shoreline. Be mindful of the shallows stretching well out from Bishops Point to the north as you make your approach.

Cruise between the outermost set of lighted daybeacons, and continue straight ahead between the various markers into the harbor.

After entering the harbor, look towards the basin's southern banks. The dockmaster's office is found in the complex of buildings that overlook this shoreline.

Bowlees Creek Channel Northeast of unlighted daybeacon #16, mariners can cruise to a variety of sidewaters in the Whitfield Estates/Bayshore Gardens region. The only facility catering to cruising craft is found on Bowlees Creek.

The Bowlees Creek entrance channel is outlined by small, privately maintained daybeacons. The channel's southwesterly entrance is denoted by a sign advertising Holiday Inn Marina. Cruise between the various markers until coming abeam of the small, charted island lining the channel's southeastern flank near the creek's mouth. Favor the starboard side of the channel as you pass the island's northeastern tip and enter the creek. Once past the stream's mouth, immediately cruise back to the mid-width.

Soon the creek splits. The southerly (starboard) branch leads directly to Holiday Inn Marina.

Unnamed Channel Cruisers may well spot an uncharted channel between the Bowlees Creek entrance and the cut leading to Bayshore Gardens. This passage serves a very private condo dock and should be avoided by visiting vessels.

Bayshore Gardens Channel Remember, there are no facilities catering to cruising craft, or even room to anchor, on the creek leading north to Bayshore Gardens. If you choose to cruise the stream anyway, follow the well-marked channel as it skirts a small, charted island on its western flank. Soon the creek's mouth will appear dead ahead. Enter on the mid-width and continue holding to the centerline as you cruise upstream. Eventually, you will spot the private Bayshore Gardens dockage basin to port, while Trailer Estates Marina will come up almost dead ahead and a little bit to starboard.

On the ICW From unlighted daybeacon #16, it's a 1.3-nautical-mile run to flashing daybeacon #17. Come abeam of #17 to its northeasterly side. The Waterway takes a sharp turn west at #17. Follow the well-marked channel until it again swings to the north-northwest at flashing daybeacon #23.

After leaving flashing daybeacon #21 behind, northbound cruisers will pass into a stretch of the Waterway where shoal water begins to line a goodly portion of the ICW channel. Gone for the most part are the deep waters of Sarasota Bay. Stick to the Waterway and you should not have any difficulty.

Before entering the stretch reviewed above, captains and crew have a last opportunity for dockside dining on the wider reaches of Sarasota Bay.

Buttonwood Harbor Channel and Pattigeorge's Restaurant Most mariners will want to cruise into the Buttonwood Harbor Channel strictly for dining at Pattigeorge's. The southerly branch of the channel leads only to a condo dock.

Leave the Waterway at unlighted daybeacon #19 and set a compass course for the red-and-white junction daybeacon #A. Pass this aid closely to its northwesterly side. Continue on the same course, pointing to pass between the first two aids on the Buttonwood Harbor Channel, unlighted daybeacons #1 and #2.

Remember your "red, right, returning" rule as the cut skirts to the northwest of Whale Key. At unlighted daybeacon #11, the channel splits. To visit the restaurant, cut to the west-northwest and follow the red markers to the restaurant docks. No-wake regulations are in force throughout these waters.

On the ICW Northbound skippers on the Western Florida ICW will follow an almost arrow-straight track from flashing daybeacon #23, northwest through the shoaling reaches of upper Sarasota Bay. The charted markers southwest of unlighted daybeacon #25 lead to a series of private docks and are of little interest to visiting cruisers. By contrast, at unlighted daybeacon #33, a facility welcoming transients lies just to the west.

Whitney Beach Facilities The well-marked channel leading to the Buccaneer Marina cuts sharply west-southwest immediately to the southeast of unlighted daybeacon #33. Enter the channel by passing between the first two unlighted daybeacons, #1 and #2. The cut remains straightforward until passing between the innermost set of unadorned pilings. A sign hard by these piles directs craft visiting Cannons Marina to go south, while the channel to Buccaneer Marina cuts off to the west.

If you should decide to visit Cannons Marina, depart the marked channel by cutting sharply to port. Follow the southwestern shoreline until you spot the first canal running towards the Gulf. Turn into this stream on its mid-width. Cannons Marina will eventually be encountered on the western terminus of the canal.

Most cruisers will continue on to Buccaneer Marina by turning west and following the marked cut past a series of condos. As the passage begins a turn to the southwest, watch the port shore for the swimming pool. The dockmaster's office is just behind the pool.

On the ICW The ICW stretch between flashing daybeacon #37 and unlighted daybeacon #47 is subject to shoaling and strong tidal currents, courtesy of nearby Longboat Pass. Shallow water is a particular problem between #37 and unlighted daybeacon #40. Here the Waterway darts between two islands, while a broad band of deep water makes in from the west. Be ready for different aids than those pictured on chart 11425 as you cruise through this stretch. Remember—northbound cruisers should pass all red beacons to their (the markers') westerly or southwesterly sides, while green aids to navigation should be taken to their easterly and northeasterly quarters.

Longbeach Anchorage (BAIL-Suggested) Between unlighted can buoy #39 and unlighted daybeacon #40, a wide channel sweeps off to the west and provides wonderful anchorage. To enter this haven, depart the Waterway some 75 yards south of #40. Do not get too close to #39. There is some shoal water west of this aid.

Slowly curl back around to the west-northwest by keeping the undeveloped Jewfish Key shoreline to your starboard side. Soon you will spy the deep cove to the southwest which is lined by the two restaurants described earlier. If you decide to anchor here, favor the western shores. While good depths extend out from this shore in a broad band, notice the charted shallows to the south and southeast.

You may also anchor behind "Jewfish Key." Drop the hook at any likely spot well short of the channel's approach to the Longboat Pass Bridge.

The passage to Longboat Pass via this channel is not recommended. A shoal coming in from the east pins the cut almost directly against the bascule bridge crossing the inlet. Even by hugging the bridge, some 4-foot depths (or possibly less) can be encountered.

On the ICW Slow down after passing between unlighted daybeacons #43 and #44. The markers to the north can be quite confusing. It's all too easy to scramble the aids to navigation denoting the channel to Longboat Pass with the Waterway beacons. Point to pass between flashing daybeacon #46 and unlighted daybeacon #45. If you do not plan to enter Longboat Pass, continue on course, pointing to pass unlighted daybeacon #47 to its easterly side. Southbound captains should observe the same precautions. Use your binoculars to help differentiate the various aids to navigation.

Be prepared for strong tidal currents as you pass through the intersection between the ICW and the Longboat Pass channel. Single-screw trawlers and sailcraft should be particularly alert for side-setting currents.

Longboat Pass The swiftly moving channel leading to Longboat Pass cuts into the ICW's western flank between unlighted daybeacons #45 and #47. The inlet passage cuts back sharply to the south-southwest. Initially you should pass unlighted daybeacon #7 to its fairly immediate southeasterly side. You are now heading seaward, so pass all subsequent red markers to your port side and all green aids to your starboard as you continue towards the inlet. Be ready for a different configuration of aids to navigation than those shown on chart 11425 or discussed below. With the swift current, this is a changeable channel and markers are frequently shifted.

Visiting cruisers can pretty much ignore the side channel cutting back to the northwest from unlighted daybeacon #6 on the Longboat Pass channel. This uninteresting cut leads to a launching ramp and some private docks.

Nonetheless, for purely personal reasons I will never forget this little passage. While performing our original research on these waters, we observed a fisherman "catch a seagull." The angler in question threw out his bait, only to have it snatched up by an alert seagull. Unfortunately, the creature became hooked. The fisherman was able to reel in the bird and detach his hook, apparently without injury to the gull. That was one lucky bird to be able to fly on his way.

At unlighted daybeacon #4, the pass channel turns sharply to the west-south-west and hurries on towards the 17-foot (closed vertical clearance) bascule bridge crossing the inlet. Favor the eastern side of the inlet channel slightly as you approach #4. Some shoaling seems to have encroached on the cut's western quarter in this region.

Fortunately, the bascule bridge spanning Longboat Pass opens on demand during the daylight and evening hours (6:00 A.M. to 10:00 P.M.). During the night and early morning, the span only opens with three hours' notice. Even then, I wouldn't hold my breath.

West of the bascule bridge, follow all markers carefully out into the Gulf. A long shoal extends out from the inlet's northwestern point and flanks the channel for some distance out to sea.

On the ICW   North of unlighted daybeacon #47, it is sometimes hard to pick out the next northward aid to navigation, flashing daybeacon #48. Use your binoculars to identify #48 and set course to come abeam of and pass this aid to its westerly quarter.

North of #48, the ICW begins its approach to the Cortez bascule bridge. North of unlighted daybeacon #49, no-wake regulations are in effect on both sides of the Cortez span. Powercraft take note. Slow to idle speed or risk the gift of a ticket from the Florida Marine Patrol.

Bradenton Beach Marina and Bridge Tender Inn   Directly north of unlighted daybeacon #49, the L-shaped channel leading to Bradenton Beach Marina cuts off to the west. As you cruise the initial stretch of this cut, you will come hard by the outer tip of the Bradenton Beach Historic Pier. This structure has recently been refurbished, and it now makes for a striking sight from the water.

Boats bound for the dining delights of the Bridge Tender Inn should leave the Bradenton Beach Marina channel once abeam of the historic pier and cut to the southwest, passing the long dock to your starboard side. Watch for several white PVC pipes lining the channel. Some have been painted with green tops—obviously you should pass these close by your port side. Eventually, the Bridge Tender Inn pier will be spied dead ahead.

Conversely, the Bradenton Beach Marina channel cuts north past the large pier. Soon the marina docks will be obvious to port.

On the ICW   The Cortez bascule bridge has a closed vertical clearance of 22 feet. It has a restricted opening schedule year round. From 7:00 A.M. to 6:00 P.M. daily, the span opens only on the hour and every 20 minutes thereafter. Oh well, one more delay!

Once through the Cortez Bridge, you will spot the Seafood Shack Marina and Restaurant on the eastern banks. Continue at idle speed until well past this facility.

Favor the eastern side of the channel slightly between the Cortez Bridge and unlighted daybeacon #50. Chart 11425 correctly indicates a wide band of shoal water abutting the western banks. The two small, charted channels opening into the western shores between the Cortez Bridge and #50 serve private docks and are best bypassed by cruising craft.

Just short of unlighted daybeacon #50, especially adventurous boaters may decide to explore Palma Sola Bay to the east.

Palma Sola Bay   Don't forget that there are currently no marina facilities available to visiting cruisers on Palma Sola Bay and the only good bay anchorage requires a long cruise from the Waterway. The channel is also more than slightly confusing. But for those of you who simply have to anchor where no man (or woman, for that matter) has dropped the hook before, a navigational account of the bay is presented below.

Leave the Waterway some .2 nautical miles south of unlighted daybeacon #50 and set course to come abeam of unlighted daybeacon #1, southwest of Prices Key, by some 20 yards to its southerly side. Be mindful of the tongue of 3-foot shallows east of #50 and the shelf of 2-foot water flanking the Cortez peninsula. Unlighted daybeacons #3, #5, and #7 lead east to a very confusing intersection.

Near unlighted daybeacon #9, three channels converge and the markers are as mixed up a collection of aids to navigation as you will ever see. The southern channel leads to some private docks. Depths are more than slightly suspect. The north-side cut is far deeper, but it serves a series of private docks associated with a condo development on the bay's northern banks. Unless you happen to have a friend in this development, there are no services to be had.

All but local skippers will want to continue east on the main Palma Sola Bay channel. To achieve this objective, find unlighted daybeacons #9 and #10 amidst all the clutter, and continue cruising east by passing between these two aids.

The channel then becomes much easier to follow. East and north of unlighted daybeacon #24, a broad section of deeper water opens out before you. Ignore the charted channel on the easterly shores at Palma Sola Park. This small stream is crossed by a low-level fixed bridge and leads to a small-craft launching ramp.

Instead, set course for the westerly end of the 10-foot bridge which pinches off the bay's northerly reaches. As you approach the bridge, break off to the west. By staying some 25 to 30 yards off the beach, you can follow the shoreline west to the Reef Restaurant.

On the ICW   Aids to navigation are a bit few and far between from unlighted daybeacon #50 to the Anna Maria Island Bridge. The Waterway is not particularly narrow along this stretch, but it does border on shoal water to the east and west. Observe all aids carefully and watch for leeway.

Be sure to come abeam of and pass unlighted daybeacon #52 to its westerly side. Only after passing #52 should you adjust course to the north-northeast and point for the Anna Maria Island Bridge's pass-through. This bascule bridge has a closed vertical clearance of 24 feet and restricted opening times. The span is regulated year round, seven days a week, 7:00 A.M. to

6:00 P.M. During these times the bridge opens only on the hour and every 20 minutes thereafter. At all other times of the day, the span opens on demand. Look, don't blame me—write your congressman.

North of the Anna Maria span, a C-shaped channel cuts to the west. This small cut serves a small-craft launching area. Besides the fact that it is hard to follow, there are no facilities nor anchorage opportunities for cruising-size vessels.

The shallow channel to Perico Harbour and Johnny Leverocks Restaurant makes off to the east, just north of the bridge. If you decide to make the attempt, proceed with the greatest caution.

From the Anna Maria bridge, the ICW cuts to the northeast. Be sure to pick up the markers. The hapless navigator cruising due north will land in 2 to 3 feet of water. Set course to pass flashing daybeacon #54 to its westerly side. Continue on course, pointing to pass between flashing daybeacon #56 and unlighted daybeacon #55.

The channel now begins a slow turn back to the north-northwest. Again, take care to pick out the markers. Very shoal water flanks both sides of the Waterway. Near unlighted daybeacon #59, a charted range helps southbound vessels keep to the Waterway from flashing daybeacon #62 to #59. The channel is quite narrow in this section. Keep an eagle eye on the sounder. If depths start to rise, make corrections at once before grounding depths are reached. At flashing daybeacon #62, skippers whose craft can stand 4½-foot depths can break off to the southwest and visit Holmes Beach Marina and Captain's Marina.

Holmes Beach Channel and Facilities

South of flashing daybeacon #62, a sign advertises Captain's Marina. The channel is outlined by small but fairly numerous green and red unlighted daybeacons as well as unadorned pilings. The channel winds quite a bit, and you must take great care to keep to the marked cut. Eventually the channel splits near unlighted daybeacon #18. To visit Holmes Beach Marina, cut south after passing #18. Follow the markers in to the dock.

The canal to Captain's Marina and The Marina Bay restaurant is entered by striking north immediately after passing #18 and setting a course to cruise between #20 and #21. Once between these aids, curve your course around to the west and enter the canal on its mid-width. As you enter the stream, watch for a single upright piling. Be sure to stay away from this faceless marker and pass it to your port side.

Soon the canal splits. Cruisers seeking Captain's Marina should follow the northerly fork.

On the ICW The charted spoil island east-northeast of unlighted daybeacon #59 will appear far closer to the channel than might be expected by northbound navigators. After making the turn at flashing daybeacon #58 (the forward, red, flashing range marker), it will be obvious that this is an optical illusion.

From flashing daybeacon #62, the Waterway skips along to unlighted daybeacons #62A and #63 and flashing daybeacon #64. Study chart 11425 for a moment. Notice the 4-foot shoal south of #64. These shallows are for real and are now marked by #62A. Be sure to pass #62A to its westerly quarter, and come abeam of #63 to its immediate easterly side. From #63, the ICW cuts to the north-northeast. Point to pass flashing daybeacon #64 to its fairly immediate northwesterly side.

Just before making your final run from Anna Maria Sound into Tampa Bay, you may decide to visit one last facility to the west.

Galati's Yacht Basin and Galati's Marine Cruisers may enter Bimini Bay to visit Galati's Yacht Basin and Galati's Marine by either of two different routes. The deeper approach is by way of Tampa Bay. From the bay's deeper waters, you must point to pass flashing daybeacon #1, west of the Bulkhead, to its westerly quarter. Then, set a course to pass between unlighted daybeacons #1 and #2, the northeasternmost aids to navigation on the Bimini Bay entrance channel.

Mariners cruising north on the ICW will find the passage described above to be a bit out of their way. All but especially deep draft vessels can cut sharply west-northwest at a point about halfway between unlighted daybeacon #63 and flashing daybeacon #64 and point to come abeam of flashing daybeacon #1 by some 25 yards to its southerly side. Be mindful of the 2- and 4-foot depths found on the Bulkhead to the north during this run and, equally daunting, correctly charted 4- to 5-foot waters west of #63. Once abeam of flashing daybeacon

#1, turn again, this time to the south, and point to pass between unlighted daybeacons #1 and #2.

South of #1 and #2, a series of uncharted but nevertheless prolific markers leads cruisers into Bimini Bay. The newly dredged channel eventually turns to the northwest towards the marina. As you would expect, pass red markers to your starboard side and green aids to your port.

Soon you will spy Galati's Yacht Basin dead ahead. Cruise between several pairs of markers straight into the wet slips.

Captains in search of Galati's Marine's repair yard must continue following the marked channel around a small island. Eventually, as you cut back to the northeast, the yard's docks will be sighted dead ahead. *Hug the piers!* Even a small deviation to port could land you in a couple of inches of water.

On to Tampa Bay Flashing daybeacon #64 marks the southerly genesis of a dredged channel running through the formidable shoal known as "the Bulkhead" that lies along the northern mouth of Anna Maria Sound. This stretch of the Waterway is subject to shoaling. Don't be surprised to find different markers than those shown on chart 11425.

For the moment, the channel seems to be holding good depths and it is well marked. North of flashing daybeacon #67 and unlighted daybeacon #68, the wide and deep waters of mighty Tampa Bay beckon.

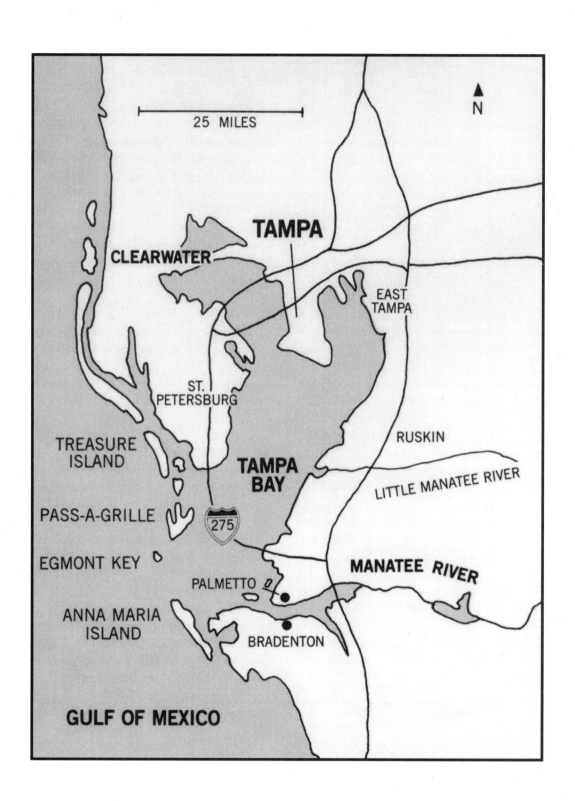

CHAPTER 4

Tampa Bay

Look at any map of Florida's western coastline and you will undoubtedly note that the most prominent geographic feature on the chart is a body of water which resembles a short, fat-bodied alligator with a curved tail and wide, gaping jaws. This imposing landmark is none other than Tampa Bay, described by some as the liquid heart of Western Florida. Since the times of earliest European colonization (and before that vis-à-vis the local native Americans), ships and boats of every size and description have set their course to this vast bay. Modern-day pleasurecraft skippers are following in the footsteps of their nautical ancestors by the thousands. This writer's heart is with that happy horde. The beautifully natural shores set amidst bright, shining cities and isolated anchorages comprise a siren's call which mariners can not and must not ignore.

Tampa Bay's yawning mouth thrusts west into the Gulf of Mexico. Several small barrier islands bisect the entrance, principal among them being Egmont Key. In fair weather, this magnificently undeveloped island beckons to be explored and enjoyed.

A host of channels darts between these various land masses and allows for ready access to and from the open Gulf. The extremely well marked large ship's channel cuts between Egmont and Mullet keys. Heavily used by oceangoing ships, this passage can be confidently relied upon by pleasureboat skippers.

The Western Florida ICW cuts across the bay's mouth south to north. While some extra-large, deep-draft pleasurecraft may want to follow the magenta line and turn east into the bay before tracking back to the north, most

cruisers will be able to follow the Sunshine Skyway Channel straight across the lower bay. This memorable route parallels the huge Sunshine Skyway Bridge. Believe you me, this colossal structure makes for a sight from the water which you will not soon forget.

The Manatee River (the "alligator's" curved tail) cuts into Tampa Bay's southeastern flank. This deep stream is easily navigated to a host of anchorages and marina facilities, most of which are associated with the thriving cities of Bradenton and Palmetto.

The two shorelines of lower Tampa Bay exhibit strikingly different characters and must be considered separately in any discussion of cruising on the bay. To the west, the magnificent city of St. Petersburg guards the shoreline, with its wealth of beautiful green parks, a successfully restored downtown section, and one of the largest municipal marinas that this writer has ever visited. The lower bay's eastern banks are only lightly developed, and are quite eye-pleasing from the water. Several small rivers and lesser streams lead to an adequate selection of marinas and more than a few anchorages.

Farther to the north, Tampa Bay is bisected by the so-called Interbay Peninsula. The large lobe of water striking to the northwest is known as Old Tampa Bay, while the smaller body of water to the east is named Hillsborough Bay. While much of Old Tampa Bay is off limits to larger sailcraft, there are still several marinas and some intriguing, off-the-beaten-path anchorages for power cruisers to consider.

Hillsborough Bay is dominated by the city of Tampa. This metropolitan area seems bent on moving into the twenty-first century with a real bang. Sadly, marina facilities catering to pleasure craft in Tampa are now rather scarce. Fortunately, two absolutely first rate yacht clubs are ready to serve Tampa's cruising visitors who have the appropriate reciprocal agreements.

In our review of Tampa Bay, we will first explore the Manatee River, followed by a discussion of the bay's western mouth and the ICW passage across this body of water. This account will be followed by a detailing of lower Tampa Bay's western shoreline, then the eastern banks. Finally, we will explore Old Tampa and Hillsborough bays. There's a lot of water to cover, so bend on the jib and let's forge ahead.

Charts   Most captains will find the second and third charts listed below sufficient for navigational coverage of Tampa Bay. Those who want to see everything may choose to acquire all five.

11425—provides somewhat more detailed coverage of the Manatee River (over much of its track) than is available on 11414

11414—large-scale chart giving good coverage of Lower Tampa Bay, including the inlet channels and passages through the Sunshine Skyway; also details a portion of the upper Manatee River not covered on 11425; this chart is a must have for anyone cruising Tampa Bay, as is the one listed below

11413—covers upper Tampa Bay, Old Tampa Bay, and Hillsborough Bay, including the channels and approaches to Tampa

11412—a general, small-scale chart whose chief purpose for many cruisers may be to give a good overview of the coastal waters between the Manatee River and Tarpon Springs

11411—detailed ICW chart that follows the Waterway across the mouth of Tampa Bay into Boca Ciega Bay; it includes detailed coverage of the Sunshine Skyway Channel; oddly enough, if you follow the magenta line course of the ICW, which briefly darts east of the Sunshine Skyway, you will need chart 11414 in addition to 11411 in order to follow the Tampa Bay portion of the Waterway

Bridges

Sunshine Skyway Bridge, central span— crosses mouth of Tampa Bay, east of flashing buoy #1A—Fixed—175 feet

Sunshine Skyway Bridge, northern, ICW span—crosses mouth of Tampa Bay hard by ICW-Sunshine Skyway Channel intersection, east of unlighted daybeacon #13A—Fixed—65 feet

Snead Island Bridge—crosses small canal connecting Manatee River and Terra Ceia Bay—Fixed—13 feet

Bradenton/Highway 41 Business Bridge— crosses Manatee River hard by Bradenton waterfront, east of unlighted daybeacons #21A and #22A—Fixed—41 feet

Bradenton/Palmetto Railway Bridge—crosses Manatee River hard by Bradenton waterfront—Bascule—5 feet (closed)—usually open unless a train is due

Bradenton/Highway 41 Bypass Bridge— crosses Manatee River west of unlighted daybeacons #23 and #24—Fixed—40 feet

Interstate 75/Manatee River Bridges—cross Manatee River northeast of unlighted daybeacon #31, near Ellenton—Fixed—40 feet

Alafia River/Highway 41 Bridge—crosses

Alafia River east of turning basin and unlighted daybeacon #18—Fixed—28 feet

22nd Street Causeway Bridge—crosses passage between East Bay and McKay Bay near commercial port of Tampa—Fixed—40 feet

Platt Street Bridge—crosses Hillsborough River in downtown Tampa—Bascule—15 feet (closed)—opens only on the hour and half-hour 9:00 A.M. to 4:30 P.M. weekdays and 8:00 A.M. to 6:00 P.M. weekends and legal holidays

Leroy Selman/Highway 618 Bridge—crosses Hillsborough River in downtown Tampa—Fixed—40 feet

Brorein Bridge—crosses Hillsborough River in downtown Tampa—Bascule—15 feet (closed)—opens only on the hour and half-hour 9:00 A.M. to 4:30 P.M. weekdays and 8:00 A.M. to 6:00 P.M. weekends and legal holidays

John F. Kennedy Boulevard Bridge—crosses Hillsborough River in downtown Tampa—Bascule—11 feet (closed)—opens only on the hour and half-hour 9:00 A.M. to 4:30 P.M. weekdays and 8:00 A.M. to 6:00 P.M. weekends and legal holidays

Gandy Bridge—crosses southerly mouth of Old Tampa Bay, well north of unlighted can buoy #11K—Fixed—43 feet

W. Howard Franklin/Interstate 275 Bridge—crosses Old Tampa Bay north of Gandy Bridge—Fixed—44 feet

Courtney Campbell Parkway Bridge—crosses Old Tampa Bay north-northeast of flashing daybeacon #A—Fixed—40 feet

The Manatee River

Mariners making the 5-nautical-mile upstream cruise to Bradenton and Palmetto on the Manatee River will experience one of the most delightful waterborne treks in Western Florida. Much of the shoreline is undeveloped and begs to be explored by dinghy. Good overnight anchorages abound, though most must be chosen with a ready ear to the forecast wind speed and direction. Marina facilities are available along the river's entire course, but the best spots are found adjacent to Bradenton.

While there are certainly some shoals to watch for, most sailors can cruise a goodly portion of the waters between the river's westerly reaches and Bradenton. The entrance channel itself is narrow and usually calls for firing up the auxiliary.

Farther upstream, a marked channel continues east and northeast for another 3 nautical miles to the twin Interstate 75 bridges near Ellenton. This stretch of the river is completely without marina facilities and is much too open for anchorage in all but the lightest of airs.

Legend of the "Singing River"

While researching the Manatee River, this writer was already aware of the local lore which speaks of the Manatee as a "singing river." What took me by surprise were the many sober residents who informed me that after living by the river's banks for many years, "you get so used to hearing the singing that it doesn't bother you anymore." Even on a warm summer morning that statement left a bit of chill in the air.

The so-called singing has been described as an "intense, melodic humming." Several tall tales purport to explain the unearthly melody that wafts its way down the river banks from time to time. One story speaks of two competing

Indian tribes that lived on opposite shores of the Manatee River. The son of one tribal chief fell in love with the daughter of the opposing band's leader. Forbidden to marry or even meet, the couple stole away one night and rendezvoused at modern-day DeSoto Point. When the lovers met face to face at last, they heard a ghostly singing on the water. Soon, the two tribes were united following a great battle. The estranged couple were then allowed to marry and their off-spring became the tribe's future leaders.

Another tale tells of the ghost of a woman who was imprisoned by a pirate, and forever after would wail for her freedom. Others believe that the sounds come from the ghost of a dog who was mysteriously killed with his owner while walking along the river's banks.

Whatever the cause may be, natural or supernatural, don't be overly concerned should you hear the "humming" while anchored along the quiet river shores. The spirits, whoever they are, seem to be friendly.

Boca Del Rio Marina

Navigators studying charts 11425 or 11414 will note the partially breakwater-enclosed harbor of Boca Del Rio Marina (941-792-9610), south of unlighted daybeacon #9. This is perhaps the funkiest little marina and repair yard operation left on this portion of the Western Florida coastline. Don't try to find your way to Boca Del Rio by land. It is stuck smack in a residential neighborhood, just where you would least expect to find any sort of pleasurecraft facility.

Boca Del Rio features a *U*-shaped harbor, which is sheltered only on its western flank. Strong northerly or easterly blows funnel directly into the harbor and can make for a bumpy evening. Entrance depths run from 7

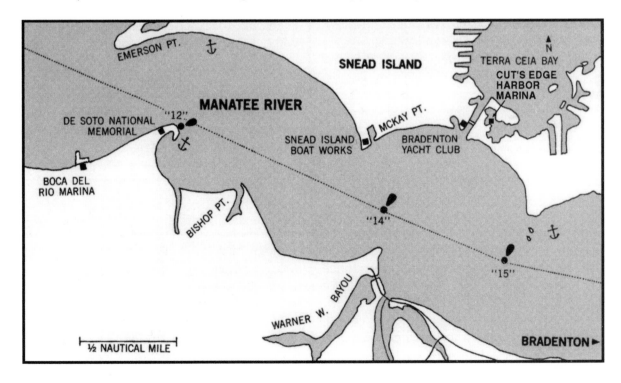

to 9 feet, while 6 to 7½ feet of water can be expected dockside. All wet-slip dockage at Boca Del Rio is now rented out on a month-to-month basis (plus service customers), with no provisions for overnight transients.

The repair yard here features a 35-ton travelift and full mechanical repairs for both gasoline and diesel power plants. More than a few local captains seem to take advantage of these services. While clearly not offering the resources of Snead Island Boat Works (see below), Boca Del Rio is one of those vanishing breed of mom and pop yards. Give them a look-see if your servicing problems are not too broad ranging.

DeSoto Point Anchorage
(BAIL-Suggested)

While it's certainly not the simplest anchorage on Manatee River, local cruisers often choose to drop anchor in the pocket of 6-foot water just inside the shelter of DeSoto Point, south and east of flashing daybeacon #12. Great care must be taken to avoid the correctly charted shoals to the south, and a similar patch of 4-foot shallows guarding the point. Captains circumventing these hazards will find themselves in a cove protected from western and southerly blows. The very best spot to anchor is found on the waters west of the charted 4-foot shallows, but, of course, you must avoid all the surrounding thin water to get there safely. There is scant shelter for winds blowing from the east or north. The surrounding shores are almost entirely in their natural state and are generally quite attractive. The rear of the cove is now overlooked by a huge, white cross, a part of the national memorial (see below).

It is quite possible to dinghy in to shore and leave your tender pulled up on the beach while visiting the highly recommended DeSoto National Memorial. The park offers a 20-minute orientation film, which describes the landing of Hernando DeSoto (supposedly) on the waters of Manatee River in 1539. There is also a museum and a nature walk for visitors to enjoy. Every spring DeSoto's landing is reenacted as part of a weeklong festival.

Snead Island Anchorage

One of the finest anchorages on the Manatee River is easily found along the broad band of deep water northeast of unlighted daybeacon #11. Good minimum depths of 6 feet or more run to within 75 yards of the northern banks. The shoreline is entirely undeveloped and challenges the angler to try out his rod and reel. The banks are well wooded, with many trees set out into the water. This setting reminded me of a coastal river along my native North Carolina shores.

In northerly winds, the protection is excellent, though the anchorage is wide open to blows across the river from the south. There is some shelter to the east and west courtesy of Emerson and McKay points. For this writer's money, mariners cruising on the Manatee's friendly waters should give this anchorage their most serious consideration.

Snead Island Boat Works

One of the biggest surprises on the Manatee River comes up just to the east of McKay Point (north of flashing daybeacon #14) on the charted harbor indenting the northern banks. What would appear when first seen from the river to be only a large repair operation turns out to be a marina as well, with a full-blown dockage basin. Snead Island Boat Works' deep-water harbor is actually far larger and more sheltered than a quick study of chart

Snead Island Boat Works, Manatee River

11425 would lead you to believe. Covered slips are very much in evidence, though there is open dockage as well. While transients are sometimes accepted for overnight berths, the management has informed this writer that most of the available fixed wooden dockage is taken up by resident vessels and service customers. Cruisers who do successfully arrange for overnight berths will find dockside water and power connections up to 50 amps. Dockside depths in the basin range from 7½ to 10 feet, while some 6 to 7 feet of water will be found at the fuel dock. Gasoline and diesel fuel are readily available at a separate fuel pier fronting directly onto the river's banks. Snead Island Boat Works (including the fuel pier) is closed Saturdays and Sundays.

As you would expect, the firm's mechanical and haul-out repair capability is quite extensive, to say the least. Snead Island's marine railway is complemented by two travelifts (50 and 60 tons, respectively). If you can't get it fixed here, better find out how new boat sales have been doing lately. The yard also maintains a well-stocked ship's store just behind the fuel dock. One of the truly fine marine firms on the Manatee River, Snead Island Boat Works is most certainly an integral cog in the region's excellent pleasurecraft-oriented facilities.

Snead Island Boat Works (941) 722-2400

Approach depth—7-9 feet
Dockside depth—6-7 feet (fuel dock)
                    7½-10 feet (dockage basin)
Accepts transients—limited
Fixed wooden piers—yes (some covered)
Dockside power connections—up to
  50 amp
Dockside water connections—yes
Showers—yes
Gasoline—yes
Diesel fuel—yes
Mechanical repairs—extensive
Below-waterline repairs—extensive
Ship's store—yes

Bradenton Yacht Club

Between flashing daybeacons #14 and #15, passing cruisers will observe the charted channel along the northern banks leading to Terra Ceia Bay. Bradenton Yacht Club guards the western banks of this small cut's southerly mouth and is readily recognized by the bright blue roof of its mammoth clubhouse. This large, obviously well financed operation accepts members of other accredited yacht clubs with reciprocal agreements. Most of the club's fixed wooden piers (with all power and water connections) are found in a concrete breakwater-protected harbor immediately adjacent to the clubhouse. There is a small charge for electric service. A few additional berths are found on a face dock fronting onto the canal. The club dockmaster is on duty Wednesday through Sunday.

Ashore, fortunate visitors will find full dining and bar services from Tuesday through Sunday. The club is closed on Mondays. There is also a large swimming pool and two tennis courts. Invigorating shoreside showers are also available.

Of the many fine yacht clubs in Western Florida, Bradenton is clearly one of the best. This writer is more than happy to recommend it.

Bradenton Yacht Club (941) 748-7930
(941) 722-5936

Approach depth—7½-9 feet
Dockside depth—7-9 feet
Accepts transients—members of clubs with
**   reciprocal agreements**
Fixed wooden piers—yes
Dockside power and water connections—up to
**   50 amp**
Showers—yes
Restaurant—on site

Bradenton Yacht Club

McKay Point Anchorage
(BAIL-Suggested)

Study chart 11425 or 11414 for a moment and notice the "Special Anchorage" north-northeast of flashing daybeacon #14. Pleasurecraft skippers are welcome to make use of this BAIL-suggested haven. Depths of 5 to 9 feet can be held to within 100 yards of shore along a (more or less) centerline between McKay Point to the west and the docks of Bradenton Yacht Club to the east. There is good shelter from northern, north-easterly, and northwesterly blows, but the anchorage is wide open to winds from the south, southeast, or southwest. The surrounding shores are interspaced with sparse and very attractive residential development.

Terra Ceia Bay

The small canal leading northeast from Bradenton Yacht Club to Terra Ceia Bay plays host to several other interesting pleasurecraft facilities. However, to reach these yards and marinas directly from the Manatee River, cruisers would need to pass under a 13-foot fixed bridge. On the other hand, it is quite possible to make a bridgeless approach from Terra Ceia Bay. Thus, we shall review these facilities as part of our look at Terra Ceia in the next section of this chapter.

Hooker Point Anchorage
(BAIL-Suggested)

On many occasions, this writer has found anchorages on the water which are far better than they first appear on a nautical chart. The patch of deeper water east of Hooker Point (northeast of flashing daybeacon #15) is a study in the opposite case. During our several visits to these waters, we have consistently discovered that you can only cruise a short distance behind the actual land mass of the point before the shallower water to the north intrudes upon your course. The charted marsh south of the point was barely visible and gives no protection to speak about. Nevertheless, careful skippers can pilot their way into mini-mum 6-foot waters just east of the point with good protection from western and northern winds. This is definitely not the place to spend the night if breezes are blowing from the south unless you want to imitate a Mexican jumping bean. The surrounding shores are overlooked by light to moderate residential development. Be sure to read the navigational information presented later in this chapter before making your first attempt to enter this haven.

Wares Creek Anchorage

Skippers who mind their navigational p's and q's (or, better yet, have a GPS interfaced with a laptop computer containing the latest digitized charts) can take advantage of the patch of charted deep water north and west of Wares Creek, well southwest of unlighted daybeacon #16. In southerly winds, this is a good anchorage, and there is also some pro-tection from easterly blows, courtesy of nearby Point Pleasant. Minimum depths of 6 feet can be maintained by staying in the unmarked cut. Two sets of dilapidated pilings actually help you to keep to the good water, but there are no formal aids to navigation. Be sure to read the Wares Creek navigational information presented later in this chapter before attempting your first entry.

The best spot to drop the hook is found northeast of a private dock which you will spot at the southern foot of the entrance channel, where chart 11425 indicates that the deep water swings to the southeast and heads for the creek's mouth. On-the-water research revealed that, in spite of what 11425 indicates, good depths deteriorate soon thereafter. There should be enough swinging room for boats as large as 36 feet, short of the shallower water. The southerly shoreline is overlooked by moderate residential development.

Bradenton and Palmetto

Bradenton is the dominant city on the Manatee River. It is only appropriate that a river as beautiful as the Manatee should have a community such as Bradenton, which seems to exude an atmosphere of class and graciousness. This writer found Bradenton to be one of the most likable cities in Western Florida. To be sure, this is no village, but the atmosphere of a smaller town has somehow been preserved. Life clearly moves a bit slower in Bradenton than the frenzied pace of Tampa or Clearwater to the north. Cruising visitors are the delighted beneficiaries of this genteel atmosphere.

The city of Palmetto, on the other hand, guards the Manatee's northerly banks opposite Bradenton and offers one fascinating historical attraction and good provisioning. Cruisers berthing at Regatta Pointe Marina will want to make the acquaintance of this community.

Cruisers docking at either Twin Dolphin Marina or Regatta Pointe (or anchoring nearby) can easily walk to a potpourri of local sights and attractions. The Manatee County Chamber of Commerce (222 10th Street, 941-748-3411) is only a quick two-block walk from Twin Dolphin Marina. This is a great place to begin your visit in Bradenton. The chamber provides several excellent pamphlets and maps which will help to ensure that you get the most from your time in the city.

After leaving the chamber, your next stop should probably be the South Florida Museum and Bishop Planetarium (201 10th Street W, 941-746-4131). Fabulous starshows are presented at the planetarium daily (except Mondays). A laser light show is usually in the offing on weekends as well.

Housed in the same building as the planetarium, the South Florida Museum gives a thorough overview of southwestern Florida's natural history.

However, as wonderful as the naturalistic exhibits at the museum are, the star attraction is "Snooty," the oldest living manatee in captivity. He was born in captivity and transported from the Miami Seaquarium to Bradenton in 1949. He has been delighting crowds of children and adults alike for the last half-century.

This manatee has it made. He is fed a huge quantity of the finest lettuce, carrots, and apples every day, which probably contributes to his weight, which is currently 1,100 pounds.

If he thinks someone is watching, this ham disguised as a manatee will roll over on his back and lie just below the surface of the water. His keeper will then throw the food on his stomach, and he will sweep it into his mouth via his flippers.

In 1999, Snooty was joined by a "teenage" manatee (five years of age) named Mo. Mo weighs better than 900 pounds, and we have been told by their handler that the two manatees are now eating almost 200 pounds of food a day. Boy, that's some serious groceries.

Another Bradenton attraction worthy of your attention is the Manatee Historical Park (604 15th Street E, 941-741-4075). The park features a restored historical courthouse, church, general shore, and furnished "cracker-style" house. The park is open 9:00 A.M. to 5:00 P.M., Monday through Friday, and 2:00 P.M. to 5:00 P.M. on Sunday. Cruisers will need a taxi to get there.

The Gamble Plantation Mansion, located in nearby Ellenton (3708 Patton Avenue, 941-723-4536), is the only surviving antebellum mansion in Western Florida. Constructed between 1843 and 1850, it was built by Maj. Robert Gamble, a member of an Old Virginia plantation family and veteran of the Seminole Indian Wars. The house features Greek Revival architecture and walls of tabby and brick that are two feet thick. The front verandah is adorned with eighteen 25-foot columns. The house originally presided over a 3,500-acre estate where massive quantities of sugarcane were grown. Over 1,500 acres of this land were under cultivation in 1851, worked by 151 slaves.

During the last sad days of the War Between the States, Confederate secretary of state Judah P. Benjamin fled south on an odyssey that would eventually take him to England. Major Gamble hid the Confederate official for several weeks on his plantation until transportation to Cuba could be arranged.

Today, the Gamble mansion has been restored and outfitted with period furnishings. It is open to the public from 9:00 A.M. to 4:00 P.M. daily, except Tuesday and Wednesday. Again, you will need a taxi or rental car to reach the plantation. Don't miss this example of Floridian plantation life.

Bradenton features many other attractions and points of interest, but we must hurry on to take a quick look at this community's colorful history and then return to our account of the Manatee River. Check in at the Chamber of Commerce for more touring suggestions.

Numbers to know in Bradenton include:

Bruce's Taxi Service—941-755-6070
Checker Cab of Bradenton—941-755-9339
Yellow Cab—941-748-4800

Avis Rental Cars—941-359-5240
Hertz Rent A Car—941-355-8848
Boat/U S Marine Center—941-925-7361

Bradenton History   Sometime during 1521, Ponce de Leon explored the central section of Florida's western coastline. It is likely that he visited the Manatee River, but hostile Indian attacks soon forced his withdrawal.

The Manatee enjoyed almost 300 years of isolation until the arrival of Josiah Gates in 1842. He was followed by two brothers, Hector and Joseph Braden. These two successful professional men came south after the 1837 collapse of Union Bank in Tallahassee. They eventually settled much of the land around present-day Braden Creek.

Bradenton was largely spared the pains of battle during the Civil War, but it struggled through Reconstruction, as did the rest of the South. The first post office was founded in 1878 and named "Braidentown." The spelling was later changed to conform to the pioneer brothers' family name.

By the early 1900s, Bradenton's future had been assured by the arrival of the Seaboard Railroad. A bridge was built across the river to the community of Manatee, and Bradenton was incorporated in 1903.

Following World War II, tourists and people seeking a warmer climate have been arriving by droves. It seems likely that this bright picture will continue in the future.

Regatta Pointe Marina

Northeast of flashing daybeacon #19, one of the finest marinas in Western Florida graces the Manatee River's northerly banks. A marked channel leads visiting cruisers and resident captains alike to fabulous Regatta Pointe Marina. Anyone visiting this facility is sure to

Regatta Pointe Marina

agree that here is a first-class operation that simply exudes friendliness and competency.

The marina's dockage basin is almost completely enclosed by a concrete riprap breakwater that gives good protection from all but the strongest storms. Transient dockage is eagerly provided at fixed wooden piers with water and power connections to 100 amps. The central pier is concrete, which provides for electric trams to ferry landlubber diners to and from the parking lot. This novel aspect of the marina may give you some idea of the facility's very special nature.

Entrance depths fall between 6½ and 9 feet. While the approach cut is well marked, there can be some confusion for first-timers attempting to reach the easternmost piers. Dockside depths run from 6 to 8 feet.

Visiting cruisers have access to eight first-class, fully climate controlled showers and an air-conditioned laundromat on site. A small paperback exchange library is found in the laundromat. Gasoline and diesel fuel are readily available at a fuel dock which is accessed through the central entrance channel. Mechanical repairs can be arranged through a plentiful supply of independent contractors. A small ship's and variety store is located in the dockmaster's office just behind the fuel pier. Dockmaster Tom has done a commendable job in stocking this relatively small space with an impressive assortment of marine essentials.

One of the most impressive features at Regatta Pointe is the presence of waste pump-out connections *at every slip*. According to my experience, there are only a handful of marinas

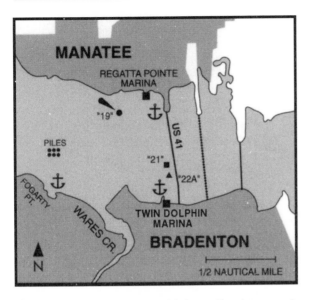

anywhere else in the world that offer this novel and most useful service.

Regatta Pointe features a refreshing swimming pool and hot tub that are open to all waterborne visitors. The adjacent "Tiki Hut" bar serves basic sandwiches, a few salads, and cold beverages.

Regatta Pointe boasts 350 wet slips. Several years ago, the available dockage was vastly expanded. With all the additional berths this already impressive facility is now a real nautical showplace.

Dining will never become boring at Regatta Pointe. The large restaurant set out over the docks has been reopened as TKO Shea's Sports Cafe (941-721-9172). As the name implies, TKO Shea's is now more of sports bar than a restaurant. This dining spot has gone through a whole series of managers and owners over the last several years, and it may very well be something else again by the time of your visit.

In our opinion, the number-one on-site dining choice at Regatta Pointe is the Riverside Cafe (941-729-4402). This medium sized restaurant is located on the harbor's northeastern corner. Open for all three meals of the day, Tuesday through Saturday (Sunday and Monday breakfast and lunch only till 3:00 P.M.), the cafe offers food that can only be described as wonderful. This writer and his first-rate first mate are forever dreaming of the excellent grouper sandwiches and Bleu cheese burgers at Riverside. In 1999 I was lucky enough to host Morgan Stinemetz, sailing columnist for the *Sarasota Herald,* my research assistant, and cruising writer extraordinaire, at an evening meal at Riverside. My broiled red snapper was out of this world and Morgan was equally taken with his shrimp parmigiana. Trust me, don't miss this one!

Cruisers who are in need of galley restocking will find a convenience store within two blocks and a supermarket about one-half mile away. You may want to take a taxi to the grocery store. Ask one of the friendly dockmasters to call a cab for you.

If you happen to be in the market for a new boat, several brokerage firms are based in the office complex flanking Regatta Pointe to the north. Be sure to stop by Massey Yacht Sales (941-723-1610) and say hello to Ed Massey, one of the largest yacht dealers in Western Florida. Tell him we sent you. My good friend Andy Lightbourne, to whom my *Cruising Guide to the Northern Gulf Coast* is dedicated, purchased his proud Pearson 35 here.

Regatta Pointe Marina (941) 729-6021
  http://www.americaholdings.com/regatta.htm

Approach depth—6½-9 feet
Dockside depth—6-8 feet
Accepts transients—yes
Fixed wooden piers—yes
Floating docks—a few in the outer area

Dockside power connections—up to 100 amp
Dockside water connections—yes
Waste pump-out—yes (at every slip)
Showers—yes
Laundromat—yes
Gasoline—yes
Diesel fuel—yes
Mechanical repairs—independent local contractors
Ship's and variety store—yes
Restaurant—2 on site

J. A. Lamb House

Just a stone's throw west of Regatta Pointe Marina, the venerable J. A. Lamb House (circa 1899) looks out proudly over the Manatee River's northern banks. Constructed for Julius Lamb, the son of Palmetto's founder, S. S. Lamb, the house was extensively renovated and restored in 1996. It now presents a peaceful, snow-white, but striking facade to Riverside Drive. While privately owned and not open to the public, the house is nevertheless well worth the two-block walk from your slip at Regatta Pointe. Take the camera along.

The J. A. Lamb House consists of three floors with heart pine as the major construction timber. The most notable features are the octagonal turret towers and handsome

J. A. Lamb House, Manatee River

columned porches. Leaded, beveled-glass windows are placed throughout the residence. The interior is arranged on a classic central-hall plan with 20 major rooms and four fire-places. The woodwork is highly detailed with deep stepped baseboards and casings. Tidewater red cypress was utilized for the solid doors and heart pine for the flooring. How's that for impressive construction?

Twin Dolphin Marina

One of the most exciting new marinas on the entire Western Florida coastline now over-looks the Bradenton waterfront along the Manatee River's southerly banks, south of unlighted daybeacon #22A. Twin Dolphin Marina occupies the old location of the Bradenton City Yacht Basin, but, believe me, this new, privately managed facility is light years ahead of the old city dockage basin.

Twin Dolphin Marina is absolutely first rate in all respects. Upon taking over the old city facility, the new owners completely rebuilt all the docks, dredged the harbor, and, most recently, opened a second dockage basin on the western side of the the on-site restaurant.

Still not enough for you? Well, check on the marina swimming pool, open to all visiting cruisers. It is perched above the eastern dock-age basin with a commanding view of the river. There is also a twin gas grill adjacent to the pool, free for the use of all mariners, and a Jacuzzi.

As you've probably guessed by now, transients are eagerly accepted in both breakwa-ter-protected dockage basins. Berths in the older east-side basin consist of fixed concrete piers, with new concrete decked floating piers in the newer, western harbor. All slips feature full 30-50-amp power and freshwater hookups. Approach and dockside depths are at least 8 feet MLW, and we found many soundings in the 10+-foot region.

Gasoline and diesel fuel can be purchased dockside. Some mechanical repairs can be arranged through local, independent techni-cians. Waste pump-out service is offered as well.

The dockmaster's building is located imme-diately behind the swimming pool, itself just to the rear of the east-side dockage basin. Housed here is a good ship's and variety store plus very good, air-conditioned showers and a full laundromat. During our last visit, we were impressed to observe paperback exchange libraries in the laundromat and outside the shower facilties.

When it comes time to slake a healthy appetite, your choices are many. The on-site Twin Dolphin Marina Grill (941-748-8087) is worth considering, but it is a bit pricey. The restored downtown Bradenton business dis-trict on 12th Street is within walking distance, or you might choose to get there by way of Twin Dolphin's convenient bike rentals. On 12th Street you will discover Fisherman Joe's Restaurant (440 12th Street W, 941-746-3077), open for lunch and dinner, as well as Robin's Restaurant (428 12th Street W, 941-747-8899), where you can get a good breakfast or lunch. Of course, you could always take a quick taxi ride over the bridge and visit the Riverside Cafe at Regatta Pointe (see above). That would be a good choice indeed!

Twin Dolphin Marina is located hard by the Bradenton library. The South Florida Museum and Bishop Planetarium (reviewed above) is only a short step from the marina docks. The hits just keep on coming!

Wow, are you as tired out from reading about all Twin Dolphin has to offer as I am from typing? If so, put a red circle around the

Bradenton waterfront and be *sure* to check out Twin Dolphin Marina the very next time your waterborne travels take you to the Manatee River.

With the cross-river presence of Regatta Pointe and Twin Dolphin, Bradenton and the Manatee River can now claim two world-class marina facilities second to none. See you there!

Twin Dolphin Marina (941) 747-8300
http://www.twindolphinmarina.com

Approach depth—8-14 feet
Dockside depth—8-12 feet
Accepts transients—yes
Concrete fixed piers—yes (east basin)
Concrete floating piers—yes (west basin)
Dockside power connections—30 and 50 amp
Dockside water connections—yes
Waste pump-out—yes
Showers—yes
Laundromat—yes
Gasoline—yes
Diesel fuel—yes
Mechanical repairs—independent local contractors
Ship's and variety store—yes
Restaurant—one on site and several nearby

Bradenton-Palmetto Anchorages (BAIL-Suggested)

With no major storms in the forecast, there are two anchorages just short of the Bradenton-Palmetto (Highway 41 Business) bridge that cruisers might consider. If winds are blowing from the north, northeast, or northwest, captains whose craft draws less than 5 feet and is no more than 38 feet in length might drop the hook northeast of unlighted daybeacon #20, in the shelter of the east-side point jutting out to the bridge. This 5-foot haven is found between the Regatta Pointe dockage basin and the point. Care must be taken to avoid the charted, but unmarked 3-foot patch of shallows south of

Regatta Pointe Marina when entering this anchorage. Skippers visiting this refuge for the first time may be surprised to discover an unlighted daybeacon #1, seemingly in the middle of the anchorage. This aid marks a small channel leading to a local launching area and Regatta Pointe's northeastern slips. Anchor well south of #1 for best protection and depths. Closer to shore, the correctly charted 3-foot shallows wait to trap deeper draft vessels. The bridge automobile traffic can be a bit of an annoyance during the evening and early morning. The eastern point of land comprises a small, but highly restful local park. Visiting cruisers can probably find a place to moor temporarily at the adjacent launching ramp. Bathrooms are found in the park and a walk of several blocks north into Palmetto will lead you to grocery stores and several restaurants. You might also consider the short hike to nearby Regatta Pointe for dining at one of their two fine restaurants.

Be warned that space in this anchorage can be a bit cramped courtesy of Regatta Pointe's dockage complex to the west. There's still room for a few boats but not nearly so much as once there was. Many veteran cruisers are now anchoring farther to the south (out into the main body of the river) for increased swinging room. Of course, there is less shelter, but you also won't have to worry about bumping into your neighbor during the night. Be sure to show an anchor light!

A slightly deeper but more open anchorage is found on the opposite shore of Manatee River, south of unlighted daybeacon #22. Visiting cruisers can anchor off the prominent point of land, occupied by Twin Dolphin Marina Grill restaurant, just west of Twin Dolphin Marina. Depths run to some 6 feet and protection is fair for southern and southwesterly breezes, but the anchorage is open on all other sides. This is most definitely not a spot for foul weather. The adjacent shoreline is surprisingly pleasant, flanked by a developing riverfront park. Dinghy landing is not allowed at Twin Dolphin Marina, and getting ashore from this anchorage can be more than slightly challenging.

The Upper Manatee River

The upper reaches of the Manatee River, east of the Bradenton-Palmetto (Highway 41 Business) bridge, makes for an interesting and aesthetically pleasing cruise, but there are no further marina facilities nor any good anchorages. Minimum depths of 6½ feet, with most soundings showing better water, can be held on the river's marked channel to a point just short of the I-75 bridges.

The various coves are uniformly shallow and your only anchoring option is to drop the hook almost in mid-river. While this might be fine for light airs, you wouldn't catch this writer swinging out there in any breeze of 10 knots or better.

Much of the shoreline on the Manatee's upper reaches is less developed than the banks to the west. Private homes peep out here and there, while heavier residential development is in evidence near the charted site of Ellenton on the northern banks.

Eventually, mariners will encounter the twin, high-rise I-75 bridges. East of these spans, depths quickly rise and cruising craft are advised to stay clear.

The Braden River

The wide but shallow mouth of the Braden River makes into the Manatee's southern flank south-southeast of unlighted daybeacon #26. While chart 11414 indicates a shallow channel, on-site research failed to discover this cut. All but small, shallow-draft outboard-powered boats are advised to bypass this stream.

MANATEE RIVER NAVIGATION

With the exception of its entrance, the Manatee River is a joy to navigate. Good markings are amply supplemented with usually deep water. The few exceptions to this forgiving nature are noted below.

As mentioned, the Manatee's entrance is one of these exceptions. While well marked, it is a narrow cut where navigators must watch carefully for leeway and pay close attention to business. Sailcraft should proceed under auxiliary power, and all captains should affix an eye to the sounder.

The various sidewaters and anchorages noted below are also of a generally forgiving nature. While shallows do abut a goodly portion of the river's shoreline, this shoal band is rather narrow and is usually easily avoided.

Take your time, keep charts 11414 and 11425 at hand, and review the information below. These simple precautions will allow you to enjoy this magnificent river as it should be appreciated, cruising gaily up and down its track rather than heeled over on a sandbar.

Entrance into the Manatee River   As discussed above, the Manatee River's westerly mouth is the most complicated portion of the stream's passage. Study chart 11425 carefully and coordinate it with the information below before making your attempt. This cartographical aid gives much better resolution than its sister, 11414.

Northbound cruisers on the Western Florida ICW can set their course from unlighted daybeacon #68, immediately north of "the Bulkhead," to flashing daybeacon #2, the westernmost aid on the Manatee River channel. Some 1.3 nautical miles of deep and open water separate #68 and #2. Cruisers voyaging south on the Waterway can set course from flashing daybeacon #70, the first ICW aid south of Mullet Key Channel, for #2. This is a longer run of some 1.9 nautical miles. Intrepid skippers entering Tampa Bay from the open Gulf should probably also use #70 as a point of reference. Be sure to read the navigational information on the bay's various inlets and the ICW's passage across its mouth in the next section of this chapter for more details.

Come abeam of flashing daybeacon #2 to its fairly immediate northeasterly side and look southeast to catch sight of a pair of range markers. Line up on this range and begin cruising towards the forward marker. Some 30 yards before reaching this beacon, alter course slightly to pass it to your starboard side. As you pass, you may well be surprised to see that this forward range marker is actually flashing daybeacon #4. In a very unusual arrangement, there is a sign pointing northwest on the aid that designates it as "#A," while the "#4" sign points to the southeast. At any rate, abandon the range before reaching #4 (or #A) and set course to come abeam of flashing daybeacon

#6 to its fairly immediate northeasterly side. Be sure to pick out #6 with your binoculars. Do not mistake the tall, rear range markers as #6. Flashing daybeacon #6 is only 17 feet tall and it will be found a bit farther to the east. Be on guard against the correctly charted shallows north of your course. At low water this hazard is quite visible, but during rough conditions or higher water levels, it can take you by surprise.

At #6 the Manatee River entrance channel takes a jog to the east. Set a careful compass course to come between flashing daybeacon #7 and unlighted daybeacon #8. Again, you must guard against the large shoal to the north. The run between #6 and #8 is the narrowest in the entrance channel. Take your time, watch for leeway, and have the chart ready to quickly resolve questions which might arise.

Once between #7 and #8, bend your course to the southeast and point to pass unlighted daybeacon #9 to its immediate southwesterly side. There is shallow water of 4 feet or less east-northeast of #9, but otherwise good depths open out before you almost all the way to Bradenton. There is still one other trouble spot to worry with, though.

Skippers choosing to visit Boca Del Rio Marina will want to depart the river entrance channel at #9 and set a careful compass course for the harbor's entrance to the south. If you pilot a fixed-keel, deep-draft sailcraft, watch out for the finger of 5-foot water to the west.

From #9, point to pass unlighted daybeacon #10 to starboard and unlighted daybeacon #11 to port, soon followed by flashing daybeacon #12, hard by DeSoto Point. Take #12 by some 15 to 20 yards to your starboard side.

Unlighted daybeacon #10 marks a patch of 3-foot shoals building northwest from DeSoto Point. Favor the northeastern side of the channel when passing #10. From flashing daybeacon #12, pleasureboats of most drafts will find excellent water all the way east to the Bradenton-Palmetto (Highway 41 Business) bridge. The few hazards along the way are noted below.

DeSoto Point Anchorage (BAIL-Suggested)

The anchorage east of DeSoto Point is not recommended for boats drawing more than 4½ feet due to the surrounding shallows. While 6-foot minimum depths can be maintained, it's a breeze to wander into 4-foot soundings.

To enter the anchorage, continue past flashing daybeacon #12 for another 100 yards as if you were heading for Bradenton. Then turn sharply south and come behind DeSoto Point, leaving the land 100 yards or so to your northwestern side. The trick is to avoid the 2-foot shoals surrounding the point and stay west of the charted 4-foot shoal. This can be a whole lot easier said than done. Eventually, though, if you successfully avoid both hazards, you can drop the hook in the bubble of deep water west of the 4-foot patch of shallows.

To say the least, it would be hazardous for strangers to attempt to find the narrow, unmarked channel between the point shoals and the 4-foot shallows.

A far easier passage, particularly for deep-draft vessels, is to continue cruising on the main river channel until you are east of the charted 4-foot shoal. You can then cut in toward the southerly banks and drop the hook well short of (north of) the correctly charted band of shallows abutting the shoreline. Then, you can explore the waters to the west behind DeSoto Point by dinghy.

Snead Island Anchorage

From either unlighted daybeacon #11 or flashing daybeacon #12, you can set course for the deeper water running to within 75 yards of the northeastern banks. Simply stay at least 75 yards from shore and avoid the charted shallows well to the east and west for minimum depths of 6 feet. Boats needing 7 or 8 feet of water need only drop the hook a bit farther out into the river.

East on the Manatee River

The charted sidewater east of Bishop Point holds 5-foot depths, but it is too narrow for anchorage by cruising-size boats. While the stream plays host to any number of local craft docked at private piers, visiting cruisers would be well advised to avoid this stream.

Be sure to pass well to the north of flashing daybeacon #14. This aid marks a large shoal building out into the river's flank from McNeil Point.

As you pass #14, Snead Island Boat Works will be visible to the north. Remember that you can only see the fuel dock and a small portion of the available dockage from the river.

Both Warner West Bayou and Warner East Bayou, southeast of #14, are crossed by low-level fixed bridges. This, coupled with some relatively shallow soundings, means that these streams are off limits for larger boats.

McKay Point Anchorage (BAIL-Suggested)
To enter the anchorage north-northeast of flashing daybeacon #14, cut in towards the northerly banks, pointing for the waters west of the Bradenton Yacht Club dockage basin. Drop the hook before approaching to within less than 100 yards of the shoreline. You can depend on 6-foot depths in this area, dropping off to 4½ to 5 feet moving east closer to the yacht club.

Passage to Bradenton Yacht Club
Cruisers making for the Bradenton Yacht Club should set course from the main channel as if they intend to enter the small canal leading from the Manatee River to Terra Ceia Bay. Set course from a position abeam of flashing daybeacon #14 to come abeam of unlighted #2 to its immediate westerly side. From this point, you need only cruise dead ahead into the mid-width of the canal's southerly entrance. Be ready for the swift tidal currents which regularly plague this cut.

As you enter the canal, Bradenton Yacht Club's entrance will be obvious to port.

Additional navigational information on Terra Ceia Bay will be presented later in this chapter as a part of our review of lower Tampa Bay's eastern shores.

On the Manatee River
Flashing daybeacon #15 marks another long, building shoal that runs southwest from Hooker Point. Be sure to pass well south of #15 to avoid these shallows. East of #15, captains may decide to take a stab at the anchorage upstream from Hooker Point.

Hooker Point Anchorage (BAIL-Suggested)
Remember that you cannot actually get in very far behind the protection of Hooker Point (to the west) before depths begin to deteriorate. Set your course for the first of the several private homes you will spot fronting onto the western shores north of the point. As the main body of Hooker Point comes abeam to the west, drop the hooker. Farther to the north, 4-foot depths are soon encountered.

Wares Creek Anchorage
Entry into the charted deep water leading to the mouth of otherwise shallow Wares Creek is facilitated by the presence of two dilapidated groups of pilings. There are unmarked shoals with 1- and 2-foot depths on both sides of the cut, so this haven is pretty well relegated to the adventurous among us.

The first set of pilings is well charted and serves to mark the shallows on the entrance's eastern flank. Pass the piles by some 15 yards to their westerly sides, and head straight in towards the southern banks.

The second group of pilings is charted as a single "pile" on 11425, but there are actually quite a few just visible above the water's surface. Stay about the same distance to the east of these derelicts and point for a private dock you will see on the shore.

You can drop the hook some 30 yards before reaching the private dock, or more devil-may-care captains can feel their way carefully to the southeast for a short distance. Be warned that the good depths do not extend as far southeast as chart 11425 would lead you to believe. Those who push their luck a bit too far will wind up in 4-foot waters.

On to Bradenton and Palmetto   A series of shoals, most likely spoil islands, pepper the mid-width of the Manatee River just west of the Bradenton and Palmetto waterfront. To avoid these traps, simply follow the prolific markers.

Swing a bit to the north and point to pass unlighted daybeacons #16 and #18 to their fairly immediate northerly sides, and come abeam of flashing daybeacon #19 to its southerly quarter. Your course then shifts sharply to the south. Point to come abeam of and pass unlighted daybeacon #20 to its easterly side and continue on course until you pass between unlighted daybeacons #22 and #21. Another sharp turn, this time to the east, leads you between unlighted daybeacons #21A and #22A. The pass-through of the Bradenton/Highway 41 Business Bridge will then be dead ahead.

Regatta Pointe Marina   Wise captains who decide to do themselves a big favor and visit Regatta Pointe Marina should depart the track outlined above at flashing daybeacon #19. Two sets of unlighted, privately maintained daybeacons lead you into the central entrance without undue difficulty.

The easternmost slips at Regatta Pointe are not accessible via the main entrance after you have passed through the breakwater. Instead, skippers looking to find these

(eastern) slips should depart the approach channel shortly before passing through the main entrance and follow the breakwater to the east. The restaurant will be to your port side. Don't slip too far to the south. The charted bubble of 3- and 4-foot waters awaits cruisers who make this unhappy maneuver. Curl around the easternmost tip of the piers and follow the boat ramp markers (beginning with unlighted daybeacon #1) to the northeastern slips.

Bradenton-Palmetto Anchorages (BAIL-Suggested)   Mariners choosing to drop anchor in the refuge adjacent to Regatta Pointe, along the river's northerly shoreline, should depart the marked channel at unlighted daybeacon #20. Cut towards the northeast, giving the waters fronting onto Regatta Pointe a wide berth. This maneuver will serve to avoid the correctly charted bubble of 3- to 4-foot waters just south of the dockage basin. Eventually you will slip into the gap between Regatta Pointe and the eastern point of land. Watch for unlighted daybeacon #1 dead ahead. Anchor well south of this aid for best depths.

The anchorage along the opposite shoreline is found by continuing to follow the Manatee River's well-marked channel until passing unlighted daybeacon #22. You can then cut almost due south towards the large building and point of land that will be so obvious along the shoreline. Drop anchor before approaching to within less than 50 yards of the point. Chart 11425 and 11414 warn of a sunken wreck immediately adjacent to the banks.

On the Manatee River East of unlighted daybeacons #21A and #22A, the river's track soon flows under the Highway 41 Business fixed bridge. Twin Dolphin Marina is easily accessible south of #21A and #22A.

Many skippers will choose to discontinue their upstream explorations at this point, but for those who must forge ahead, a navigational account of the Manatee's upper reaches is presented below.

The first span has a vertical clearance of 41 feet, followed closely by a railway bridge with only 5 feet of closed vertical height. Fortunately, this span is usually open unless a train is due.

From the railway span, head straight for the third bridge's pass-through (vertical clearance 40 feet). Shallow water impinges on the channel to the north and south, east of the third span. Be on guard for leeway.

Once through this bridge, you need only follow the markers to unlighted daybeacon #31, abeam of Ellenton. Farther upstream, there are no additional aids to navigation and depths drop off quickly east of the twin I-75 bridges.

Tampa Bay Entrance and the ICW

The gaping westerly mouth of Tampa Bay reaches out into the open waters of the Gulf of Mexico by way of three deep passages. To the south, the bay's mouth is bordered by Anna Maria Island, while to the north a whole series of sandspits and barrier islands associated with Mullet Key make up an often indistinct barrier where it is all too easy for the visiting cruiser to become confused and disoriented. Don't commit this error; the waters around Mullet Key and its lovely county park are mostly cheats and blinds waiting quietly to trap the unwary mariner.

Southernmost of Tampa Bay's three seaward cuts is Passage Key Inlet. This passage, along with Southwest Channel to the north, are deep but not well marked. The principal inlet is known as Egmont Channel on its westward reaches and Mullet Key Channel farther inland. This route is used by large, oceangoing ships which regularly ply the bay to Tampa's commercial docks. It is, as you would expect, extensively marked with lighted aids to navigation. Strangers are advised to make this passage their inlet of choice.

Two barrier islands divide Tampa Bay's three inlets. Passage Key is a small, uninhabited sandspit lying between Anna Maria Island and Egmont Key. Egmont Key, farther to the north, is a more substantial body of land and boasts a lighthouse alongside several good anchorages.

The Western Florida ICW leaves the protected reaches of Anna Maria Sound and darts north via a sparsely marked passage to Mullet Key Channel. From this point the magenta line cuts eastward under the magnificent Sunshine Skyway fixed bridge. The Waterway follows a *C*-shaped path and eventually crosses back under the northerly spans of the Sunshine Skyway on the southern reaches of Boca Ciega Bay. Cruisers who plan to forego a visit to the interior reaches of Tampa Bay, including the waterfronts of St. Petersburg and Tampa, may ignore this complicated route and follow the well-marked Sunshine Skyway Channel directly north to Boca Ciega.

It is only fair to observe that Tampa Bay's entrance can become more than slightly choppy with even moderate breezes. Many a captain and crew have breathed a sigh of relief when coming under the welcome protection of the shallows east of Mullet Key.

It is unfortunate that this reputation for wind and wicked wave has blinded many visiting cruisers to the fair-weather charms of this most westerly region of Tampa Bay. In appropriate conditions, mariners should seriously consider leaving a bit of time in their schedules to appreciate this unique region. A Native American evidently felt long ago that there could not be a fairer place than Egmont Key anywhere else in the world. This writer urges his fellow cruisers to experience these delights for themselves.

Passage Key Inlet

Passage Key Inlet lies between Anna Maria Island and Passage Key. While it is mostly deep, the pass lacks any aids to navigation and is surrounded by unmarked shoals. It is the least desirable of the three inlets serving Tampa Bay. Although fair-weather daylight navigation of the pass is possible, most cruising visitors will wisely choose either Southwest or Egmont channels to the north.

Passage Key

Passage Key is a small, oblong island guarding the waters north of Bean Point. From the cockpit, this isle appears to be little more than a sandbar at high tide. In light breezes and fair weather, cruisers may consider anchoring in the 7- and 8-foot waters east of the key. Do not approach to within less than 300 yards of the shores for best depths. If a thunderstorm appears over the horizon, all anchored craft should skedaddle as soon as possible.

Passage Key is a bird sanctuary and is home to gulls, skimmers, terns, and mallard ducks. Landings are strictly prohibited. Numerous signs posted on the island shores reinforce this prohibition.

Southwest Channel

The Tampa Bay inlet known as Southwest Channel consists of a broad ribbon of deep water lying between Passage and Egmont keys. While there are really only two aids to navigation along the cut, this inlet is actually quite simple to run in all but foul-weather, low-visibility conditions. Minimum depths are currently an impressive 15 feet, with soundings up to 30 feet in evidence.

Egmont Key

During the 1840s Florida became a new territory of the young United States and Americans began streaming south to this new land with a tropical climate. It was not long before these vigorous settlers came into conflict with the Seminole Indians, ushering in one of the saddest chapters in American history.

The Seminoles were actually not native to the Florida peninsula. The original Timucuan and Calusa Indians had mostly died out by the mid-1800s from disease. Several branches of the Creek Indian nation began moving into Florida during the early 1800s and took on the name of Seminoles.

There were actually three Seminole Indian wars. The first two were inconclusive conflicts which were destined from the start to be repeated. The third war saw a change in the strategy of government forces. Rather than try

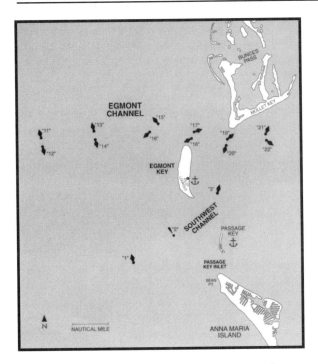

to exterminate the Seminoles, the emphasis shifted to capturing and then deporting them to Oklahoma, which was then known as Indian territory.

As the third Seminole Indian war drew to an unhappy close, a host of the Native Americans were temporarily imprisoned on Egmont Key before being sent west. One of the Seminole chieftains, Tigertail, looked about at the lovely cabbage palms and sea oats set amidst the sugar white beaches of Egmont Key and decided to remain forever in his beloved land. According to legend, Tigertail swallowed powdered glass and lay down one last time upon his blanket set under the swaying palms. The young chief could not have picked a more beautiful place for his bones to rest.

Egmont Key retains its haunting loveliness to this very day. The 300-acre island is now a state park and it is protected from development. Tall

palm trees reflect in the clear, glistening waters, and cruising couples stroll along the white beaches without a care. The old lighthouse guarding the key's northerly tip still winks at passing vessels as it has for the last 140 years. Truly, Egmont is a wondrous place that every cruiser should visit without fail.

Unfortunately, during the last several years, the county park authorities have seen fit to close more and more of Egmont Key to protect nesting birds. As it currently stands, the southern two-thirds of the island is now closed to landside visits. Fortunately, the northern section, including Egmont's fascinating lighthouse, remains friendly to human visitors. Numerous signs warn cruisers away from the closed portion of the key. Be sure to land your dinghy on a signless portion of the shoreline.

Besides the solitary beaches and swaying palms, cruisers also land on Egmont for its shelling. There are far fewer shell hunters here than on Sanibel or Captiva islands to the south. This writer's conversations with local cruisers indicates that Egmont now boasts the best shelling in all of Western Florida.

Snorkelers and scuba divers may want to explore the ruins of old Fort Dade, which once guarded Egmont Channel on the island's northern tip. This old stockade was built in the late 1800s during the Spanish-American War and, as far as this writer has been able to learn, never fired a shot in anger. Today, the fort's ruins are quickly being washed away into the waters of Egmont Channel.

Don't overlook the old lighthouse near the island's northeastern point. After checking at the Coast Guard station, visitors can climb up to the top of the 85-foot lighthouse for a breathtaking view of Tampa Bay and Egmont Key.

The best place to anchor is found off the charted pilot boat dock along the isle's easterly

Egmont Key Lighthouse

point is known as the "coal dock." At the turn of the century, coal and other supplies were offloaded at Egmont from ocean freighters and temporarily stored before being ferried to the mainland by shallow-draft vessels. A ferry boat carries passengers from the mainland to this pier. As far as I have been able to learn, pleasurecraft are still not allowed to tie up here, but, again, you could anchor off in good weather and dinghy ashore.

Egmont Channel

This cut is also known as Tampa Bay Channel, and rightly so. It is through this channel that dozens and dozens of oceangoing ships enter and leave Tampa Bay every week. With this sort of deep-draft traffic, it's not difficult to imagine that the passage is exceedingly well marked with lighted aids to navigation. While, as with all inlets, the chop can be more than a bit daunting at times, you

Pilot boat dock, Egmont Key

shores. This location is noted as "Pilot Lookout" on the current edition of chart 11411. The pier has been leased by the Tampa Bay Pilot Association since 1912. Pleasurecraft are not allowed to moor here, but you can certainly drop the hook east and south of the dock. Minimum depths of 10 feet run within 50 yards of the beach. This anchorage is well protected from westerlies, and the hooked southside tip of the island gives some protection when winds are blowing from this quarter. Strong blows from the east or northeast call for a delay in your visit.

A second pier lying off Egmont's northerly

would have a tough time getting lost in Egmont Channel. By all accounts, this is the best passage into and from Tampa Bay, particularly during inclement weather.

Mullet Key and Fort DeSoto Park

Mullet Key guards the northerly flank of Egmont and Mullet channels. Along with its sister islands, Madelaine, St. Jean, St. Christopher, and Bonne Fortune keys, Mullet Key remains one of the only undeveloped pieces of land left on the barrier islands lying off St. Petersburg and Clearwater. This region has been designated a county park and named after the old fort which has been partially preserved on Mullet Key's southwestern point.

Mullet Key is a historically significant body of land. It is thought that Ponce de Leon anchored off the isle in 1513 while exploring Western Florida. Indian attacks forced him to use his ship's cannon for defense. During this engagement one of the Spanish sailors was killed. His was the first known death of a European soldier in North America.

Ponce returned to Mullet Key in 1521 and again fought with the local Indians. The old explorer received a mortal wound and died upon returning to Havana.

In February of 1849 a young army engineer named Lt. Col. Robert E. Lee visited Mullet Key. After surveying both Mullet and Egmont keys, Lee recommended that forts be established on both islands.

It was not until long after the Civil War, in 1898, that Lee's plans were put into practice. Construction of Fort DeSoto began in the fall of that year and was completed some twenty-four months later. The fort was armed with 12-inch mortars which, as at Fort Dade, were never actually put to use in military action.

During World War II, Mullet Key was used as an Air Force gunnery and bombing training center. In 1948 Pinellas County took possession of the island and its surroundings fellows with the express intention of creating a county recreational park. A road was finally completed in 1962 and the park officially opened in 1963.

Unfortunately, there are no *reliable* means for larger cruising vessels to visit the county park and historic fort. Consult the review of Bunces Pass Channel below for more information.

Sunshine Skyway Bridge

The mammoth Sunshine Skyway Bridge and causeway stretch across the mouth of Tampa Bay for almost 11 statute miles. This huge span is one of the longest bridges and causeways in the world, and it is certainly one of the most impressive.

The bridge cruisers see today spanning Tampa Bay is actually the second Sunshine Skyway. The original bridge was struck by a ship in 1980 during foul weather. The center portion of the west-side span was completely swept away and several vehicles, including one tourist bus, tragically plummeted into the waters below.

It was decided not to rebuild the old bridge but to construct an entirely new span. This newer structure was in use for several years before the older bridge was removed completely. Small, shallow, spoil islands have been placed around the new bridge's central supporting pillars. Now barges and ships should run aground before striking the bridge a death blow.

Sunshine Skyway Channel

At flashing buoy #26 chart 11411 shows the magenta-line ICW passage cutting east-northeast under the Sunshine Skyway.

Sunshine Skyway Bridge over Tampa Bay, photo courtesy Florida Department of Commerce

Eventually this passage curls back around to the west and rejoins the Waterway's trek to the north, just off the northernmost section of the Sunshine Skyway. While this route is fine (but lengthy), any boat drawing less than 8 feet should not have a problem following the more direct Sunshine Skyway Channel paralleling the bridge's (and causeway's) western flank. This cut rejoins the official Waterway channel on Boca Ciega Bay. The Skyway Channel holds minimum 9-foot depths and is quite well marked. It is also more sheltered than the official ICW passage. Unless your plans call for a cruise on Tampa Bay to St. Petersburg or the Tampa waterfront, chances

are the Sunshine Skyway cut will serve you better.

Bunces Pass

Bunces Pass breaks off to the west between unlighted daybeacons #11 and #13 (on the Sunshine Skyway Channel). This cut theoretically holds minimum depths of 6 feet to the 19-foot fixed bridge connecting Cabbage and Madelaine keys. This passage is rather broad and it is now marked by unlighted daybeacons. Nevertheless, it's not the sort of place that we would suggest taking boats larger than 35 feet. The cut borders on shoal water, with only 1- to 2-foot depths along much of its length, and the markings are none too numerous.

The best spot to anchor would be abeam of Mullets Key's northerly point, between unlighted daybeacons #1 and #3, in 10 to 20 feet of water. Here, in good weather, you could dinghy ashore and visit the county park. Of course, you must be able to clear the 19-foot fixed bridge to reach this refuge. There is not enough protection for anything approach-

ing a heavy blow, but you should be all right if winds do not exceed 10 knots.

I specifically do not recommend trying to enter Bunces Pass from the Gulf of Mexico. In spite of some reports to the contrary, the best low-water depths you can hope for on this passage are 4 feet, and it's an elementary matter to wander into even shallower, breaker-tossed waters.

TAMPA BAY ENTRANCE AND ICW NAVIGATION

Many sailors rejoice when leaving the more constricted waters of Anna Maria Sound behind and passing out into the wide mouth of Tampa Bay. At last, you can cut the iron gennie and let out the sails. Just remember that this region can become exceedingly rough when wind speeds exceed 10 knots from any quarter. In really heavy weather, it would be far wiser to put back into port for a day or two and await fair breezes before crossing the bay.

Cruisers interested in running one of Tampa Bay's three inlets, or anchoring off either Passage or Egmont keys, can safely abandon the Waterway and approach either of these islands from the deep waters off their easterly shores.

Aids to navigation on the ICW's southerly run across Tampa Bay are very widely spaced. Be sure to pre-plot your compass/GPS courses and follow them faithfully on the water.

At flashing buoy #26, especially large, long-legged vessels can cut east-northeast through the Sunshine Skyway into the heart of lower Tampa Bay. You must then follow a 10-nautical-mile semicircular route to

rejoin the Waterway's trek to the north in Boca Ciega Bay. As mentioned above, most pleasurecraft skippers will opt for the shorter, sheltered Sunshine Skyway Channel. The prolific markers along this cut make navigation a delight.

The Bulkhead to Mullet Channel From flashing daybeacon #67 and unlighted daybeacon #68, set a careful compass course for flashing daybeacon #70 to the north-northeast. It's a run of 2.4 nautical miles between #68 and #70. Fortunately, the track does not stray near any shoals.

Come abeam of #70 to its westerly quarter and continue on, pointing to come abeam of flashing buoy #26 to its westerly side. At #26, you must choose whether to turn east into lower Tampa Bay, west into Egmont Channel and the Gulf of Mexico, or follow the Sunshine Skyway Channel to the north.

As you approach #70, the tilted, round top of the St. Petersburg Thunder Dome will be visible on the Pinellas peninsula to the north. We shall learn more about this unusual entertainment facility in our discussion of St.

Petersburg. Let's pause for a moment in our account of the ICW to address navigating Tampa Bay's three inlets and its two barrier islands.

Passage Key Inlet   Successful navigation of Passage Key Inlet, the narrowest of Tampa Bay's three seaward passages, is complicated by the long, unmarked shoal building out from Passage Key's (the island's) southwesterly point. To avoid this hazard, favor the Bean Point (southerly) side of the channel slightly when passing out into the Gulf. Notice that there are also significant shoals lying southwest of Bean Point. These shallows are equally unmarked. My best advice is to continue cruising to the west between these two shoals and hope for the best (or make use of a GPS interfaced with a laptop computer). Frankly, this writer suggests using the Southwest or Egmont channels instead, but so many local captains seem to make use of Passage Key Inlet that I felt obligated to present the navigational information above.

Passage Key Anchorage   Approach Passage Key off its eastern shores from the deeper waters of Tampa Bay. Drop the hook before approaching to within less than 300 yards of the beach. Remember that Passage Key is a nesting bird sanctuary and landing is not permitted.

Southwest Channel   All you need do to find your way through Southwest Channel is to avoid the small shoals off southern Egmont Key and stay well north of flashing daybeacon #2.

To enter the channel, come abeam of flashing buoy #3, well off Egmont Key's southeastern point, by .3 nautical miles to its southerly side. Set course to pass out into the Gulf, leaving Egmont's southern tip at least .3 nautical miles to your northerly side.

Keep a watch for flashing daybeacon #2 and stay several hundred yards (at least) north of this aid. It marks the long shoals running west from Passage Key.

Egmont Key   Approach Egmont Key on its eastern banks from Tampa Bay. Use your binoculars to pick out the charted pilot boat dock on the southern half of the eastside beaches. Head directly for this pier.

As you approach to within 100 yards of the pilot boat dock, break off to the south and select your anchorage. Good depths run to within 50 yards of shore.

Alternately, you can follow the deep water north, keeping at least 200 yards off Egmont Key, to Egmont Channel. Deep water runs hard by Egmont's northerly point. You should spot the coal dock and lighthouse as this point comes abeam.

Egmont Channel   Flashing buoy #26 marks the intersection of the Western Florida ICW and Mullet Key Channel. This latter cut leads west to Egmont Channel which, in turn, provides super-reliable access to the open Gulf. It doesn't get much simpler than this, gang. Both Mullet Key and Egmont channels are lit up like Christmas trees.

As you pass by Egmont Key's northerly point, use your binoculars to try and pick out the ruins of Fort Dade. They may have already washed away by the time you arrive.

ICW Route through Lower Tampa Bay If for some reason you should choose to follow the semicircular, *C*-shaped ICW passage through lower Tampa Bay rather than the Sunshine Skyway Channel, turn east-northeast at flashing buoy #26 and head under the Sunshine Skyway's central pass-through. Vertical clearance is set at 175 feet, so most masts should clear it.

Once past the span, follow the well-marked Cut A Channel to flashing buoy #3B on the Cut B Channel. Between #3B and the next northeasterly aid to navigation, flashing buoy #6B, the ICW track breaks off to the north. Abandon the Cut B Channel about halfway between #3B and #6B and set course to pass between flashing daybeacon #1 and unlighted daybeacon #2.

Let's pause for a moment to mention the potential confusion about the numbering system on the aids to navigation in these waters. As will be seen in the discussion below, there are two flashing daybeacon #1's along this stretch of the Waterway and another on the Sunshine Skyway Channel. Follow along carefully on charts 11414 and 11411 to avoid confusion.

Once between the (first) #1 and #2, continue almost due north, pointing to pass between flashing daybeacon #4 and unlighted daybeacon #3. Hold your course for another hundred yards or so, and then cut sharply west and point to pass the second flashing daybeacon #1 to its fairly immediate northerly side. A well-outlined track will now open out before you, leading west to the Sunshine Skyway's northerly span. Consult the discussion of Tampa Bay's western shore presented later in this chapter for a review of facilities along this portion of the channel.

West of unlighted daybeacon #13, the Waterway meets up with twin fixed spans that have 65 feet of vertical clearance. The channel is narrow between #13 and the bridge. Come abeam of #13 to its fairly immediate northerly side and continue straight ahead to the span's pass-through. Watch for leeway.

After leaving the twin bridges behind, point to pass unlighted daybeacon #13A to its northerly side. You will now find yourself at a critical intersection. The Sunshine Skyway Channel makes in from the south, while the Waterway sweeps to the west and an alternate channel cuts to the north. These various passages will be covered in the next chapter.

Sunshine Skyway Channel From flashing buoy #26, turn east-northeast as if you were going to pass under the Sunshine Skyway. Pass flashing buoy #1A to its southerly side and continue on towards the bridge for another hundred yards or so. Then, cut sharply to the north-northwest and point to come abeam of the Sunshine Skyway's southernmost aid to navigation, flashing daybeacon #1, to its easterly quarter. Again, don't confuse this flashing daybeacon #1 with the two other flashing daybeacons bearing the same number on the ICW passage through lower Tampa Bay discussed above.

From #1, the Sunshine Skyway Channel is unusually well marked all the way into Boca Ciega Bay. You will intersect the Waterway immediately after passing flashing daybeacon #26. Slow down. All the markers can be quite confusing. Be sure to correctly identify your intended track before forging ahead.

Bunces Pass Well, what can I say? Local powerboaters may think me a bit lily-livered if I say too many bad things about this cut. These skippers use Bunces Pass regularly without mishap. On the other hand, we have never considered this to be a reliable channel, and only bold visitors will make the attempt. Remember that to reach the cut's best anchorage, you must be able to clear a 19-foot fixed bridge.

If you decide to make the attempt, abandon the Sunshine Skyway Channel about halfway between unlighted daybeacons #11 and #13. Set your course to the west, pointing to pass between unlighted daybeacons #15 and #16, favoring #15 slightly. Once between these two markers, continue on to the west-southwest by passing all red, even-numbered aids to navigation to your port side and taking all green markers to starboard. Don't approach unlighted daybeacons #12 and #10 too closely. They seem to be founded in shoal water.

After you pass between unlighted daybeacons #9 and #10, the 19-foot fixed bridge spanning the channel will appear dead ahead. Pass under the span and continue to follow the markers on the main Bunces channel until your course takes you between "The Reefs" to the north and Mullet Key to the south. Here, east of unlighted daybeacons #1 and #2, you can anchor in fair weather. Further passage out to sea is definitely not recommended.

West-southwest of the 19-foot fixed bridge, a small indifferently marked channel intersects the main cut's southerly flank between unlighted daybeacons #8 and #5. Similarly, another small passage runs south between #5 and unlighted daybeacon #3. While these two cuts are fine for local outboarders, cruising-size vessels are advised to keep clear.

Lower Tampa Bay—Western Shore

The western shoreline of Tampa Bay, south of Interbay Peninsula, can be summed up by two words: "St. Petersburg." This shining city dominates the banks with its beautifully restored downtown, excellent marina facilities, and myriad green parks. Cruisers may be surprised to learn that there are also any number of opportunities to anchor, often within sight of attractive residential neighborhoods. Vessels in need of repairs are not forgotten, either. The yards on Salt Creek are second to none. In short, mariners will find everything and anything they might ever need for an enjoyable and productive stay in this region of Tampa Bay, no matter what their cruising tastes.

While lower Tampa Bay's easterly banks may be a bit less developed, there is no denying this writer's fondness for the western shoreline. St. Petersburg simply seems to radiate a warm welcome for the visiting cruiser and I, for one, advise my fellow skippers to pack it in.

Sunshine Skyway Anchorage

Some mariners occasionally anchor in the lee of the northernmost section of the Sunshine Skyway causeway, north-northwest of unlighted daybeacon #13. In all but light airs or westerly winds, this is a very open haven and it is certainly not recommended for anything approaching heavy weather. Minimum depths are around 7 feet, but there is one shoal which must be avoided. The surrounding shoreline is overlooked by heavy, high-rise condo development that is not particularly attractive.

Holiday Inn/Annapolis Sailing School Marina

Cruisers will discover a sheltered harbor and dockage basin just north of the anchorage discussed above in the charted, water-tank-shaped bay. This marina is associated with an adjacent Holiday Inn and is home to the Annapolis Sailing School (727-867-8102), which also uses the docks for its vessels. Let me say here and now that if you are looking for a good introduction to sailing, you simply can't go wrong by selecting this school of instruction.

The marina itself is a somewhat low key but friendly operation that welcomes transients at its well-sheltered, fixed wooden and concrete piers. One gains the impression that not too many transients have stayed here in the past, but there is certainly no good reason

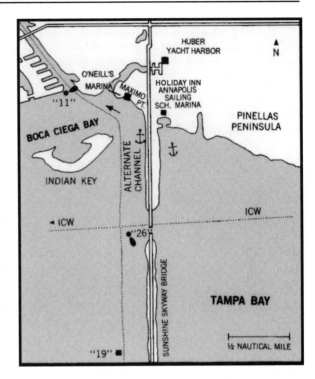

to recommend against this facility for overnighters. Mean low-water entrance depths are about 5 feet and dockside soundings range from 6 to as much as 8 feet. Full dockside power, freshwater, and cable television connections are complemented by shoreside showers and a laundromat. The Holiday Inn features a very simple restaurant.

Holiday Inn/Annapolis Sailing School Marina
   (727) 867-1151 (Ext. 562)

Approach depth—5 feet (mean low water)
Dockside depth—6-8 feet
Accepts transients—yes
Fixed concrete and wooden piers—yes
Dockside power connections—30 and 50 amp
Dockside water connections—yes
Showers—yes
Laundromat—yes
Restaurant—on site

Little Bayou

North of unlighted daybeacon #3 and flashing daybeacon #4, the official ICW passage cuts sharply west, as outlined in the preceding section of this chapter. A second, well-marked channel runs on to the north and provides reliable access to Little Bayou, Big Bayou, Salt Creek, and the various St. Petersburg marina facilities. We shall call this passage the western Tampa Bay channel.

The marked cut leading to Little Bayou lies west of the mid-point between the western Tampa Bay channel's unlighted can buoys #5 and #7. The Little Bayou cut maintains minimum 6-foot depths and eventually leads to a good anchorage for boats that draw 4½ feet or less. While you must follow several bends and twists in the channel, navigators can feel their way west from unlighted daybeacon #17 for a hundred yards or so in the main body of Little Bayou. Depths on this portion of the stream run between 5½ and 6 feet. There is good protection for all winds and tons of swinging room. The westerly banks exhibit somewhat sparse residential development, while the eastern shores are flanked by a whole bevy of condos and private homes. Be sure to read the navigational account of Little Bayou presented later in this chapter before attempting the cut.

Little Bayou is joined to Big Bayou (see below) by a mostly deep canal which, at one point near the mid-point of its passage between the two bayous, opens out into a deep sheltered bay. Unfortunately, both the northern and southern ends of the connecting canal are crossed by 9-foot (vertical clearance) fixed bridges which bar this useful short-cut for all but small powercraft. If you should happen to power one of these feisty run-abouts, don't overlook the opportunity to drop anchor in the interim bay west of Coquina Key.

Big Bayou

While a host of what this writer assumes to be local sailcraft regularly anchors in Big Bayou, visiting cruisers should take account of the twisting, sometimes torturous channel. Minimum depths in the cut run as thin as 5½ feet, but most of the channel carries 8 to 10 feet of water. If you should become confused by the myriad markers and wander out of the channel, 4-foot depths wait to say hello to your keel.

The best anchorage on Big Bayou (such as it is) is found south of unlighted daybeacon #14. Depths in this region run around 4½ to 5 feet. If your draft can stand this somewhat thin water, you may consider dropping the hook here.

Protection is excellent from all but very strong easterly breezes blowing directly up the bayou. The shoreline alternates from almost natural patches to shores with heavy residential and condo development.

A public launching ramp overlooks Big Bayou's western banks, near unlighted daybeacon #16. You can dinghy in to the piers associated with this facility, tie off temporarily, and walk one block south to Munch's Restaurant (727-896-5972). Both breakfast and lunch (open 7:00 a.m. to 3:00 p.m.) are terrific.

All in all, there are certainly other anchorages along lower Tampa Bay's westerly shoreline that are far less complicated than Big Bayou. Perhaps first-timers may want to consider one of these more accessible havens. But, for those who must see it all, a navigational account is presented later in this chapter.

St. Petersburg

North of Big Bayou, the western shores of lower Tampa Bay border upon the central St.

Petersburg waterfront, which hosts the city's many marinas and repair yards. St. Petersburg was quite a surprise for this writer when I performed my original research on these waters. At the time, for some reason I expected a carbon copy of Clearwater, to the north, and I could not have been more mistaken. What this writer found instead was a vital, active city that has not forgotten what drew people to it in the first place. While, to be sure, the St. Petersburg waterfront is highly developed, the various buildings are now part of a rehabilitated downtown with impressive architecture and many, many attractions for residents and visitors alike. The number of city parks is quite impressive and long, luscious green grass is everywhere in evidence. Frankly, this writer was startled by the delightful contrast between this lovely community and its neighbors to the north.

In the space of this account, we can only begin to enumerate St. Petersburg's many attractions. You should make use of the material below as a starting point in coming to know this impressive community. If you plan a longer stay, it might be a good idea to contact the St. Petersburg—Clearwater Convention and Visitors Bureau at (727) 464-7200 or the St. Petersburg Chamber of Commerce at (727) 821-4069. Either of these fine organizations can provide enough information to fill weeks of your time with fresh new activities.

Every visitor to St. Petersburg should begin his or her stay with a trip to the St. Petersburg Historical Museum (727-894-1052). This fascinating collection of St. Petersburg memorabilia is found at the entrance to The Pier (see below). Such things as the nation's first commercial flight, the Orange Belt Railroad, and the famous "Green Bench" of St. Petersburg are recalled in the museum's display. The

museum is within an easy walk of the large St. Pete municipal marina (see below).

Also within walking distance is the Bayfront Center, at 400 First Street S. The Bayfront Center is the site for numerous concerts, opera, and local theater. Check at the ticket office (727-892-5700) for the latest offerings.

The Museum of Fine Arts (255 Beach Drive NE, 727-896-2667) boasts a most impressive collection of French impressionist paintings as well as European, American, Pre-Columbian, and Far Eastern art. Anyone interested in art will find the displays well worth his or her time. You will need a taxi to find your way comfortably to this attraction.

For a more offbeat look at the world of art, try the Salvador Dali Museum at 1000 Third Street S (727-823-3767) next door to the Harborage at Bayboro Marina. Here you will find the world's largest display of the controversial artist's paintings and graphics. As the museum's own pamphlet states, "Salvador Dali created images which will captivate the mind and imagination of the world forever. The images he created perplex, confound, enlighten, and intrigue everyone who encounters them." There is really nothing else to add to that.

Every March sees the appearance of the St. Louis Cardinals baseball team in St. Petersburg's Al Lang Stadium. Fans thrill to open practices and exhibition games. A Cardinal minor league team is in residence throughout the remainder of the regular season and the St. Petersburg Pelicans (Senior Professional League) play from November through January. Again, the stadium is a quick walk from the municipal marina.

More recently, the Tampa Bay Devil Rays major league baseball team has taken up residence in the St. Petersburg Thunder Dome.

The launch of this franchise finally brings to fruition the region's long-fought battle to attract major league baseball to the shores of Tampa Bay.

Only in a city such as St. Petersburg which is so sensitive to its natural environment will you find a park like the Boyd Hill Nature Trail (1101 Country Club Way). Six trails wind peacefully through 216 acres of all-natural forests, marshes, and swamps. A multitude of wildlife is always present.

St. Petersburg, as you can readily imagine, plays host to an impressive group of seasonal activities that ought to provide something for just about everybody. March brings the SPIFFS International Folk Festival to town, with traditional ethnic foods, costumes, entertainment, and crafts from more than 40 countries, as well as The Festival of States, in which marching bands from throughout the United States compete.

Well, if by now you've decided that there's more to do and see in St. Petersburg than could be accounted for in an entire book, you are on the right track. Cruising and landlubber visitors alike should plan to give this rare jewel sitting beside Tampa Bay a hefty slice of their time.

Numbers to know in St. Petersburg include:

Independence Taxi—727-327-3444
Yellow Cab—727-821-7777
Avis Rental Cars—727-536-8026
Budget Rent A Car—727-878-245
E&B Marine—727-327-0072
West Marine—727-895-3098
Chamber of Commerce—727-955-8187
St. Petersburg—Clearwater Convention and
    Visitors Bureau—727-464-7200

St. Petersburg History The modern city of St. Petersburg sits perched on the southern tip of what has come be known as the Pinellas Peninsula. Recent archaeological evidence suggests that Pinellas was visited by both Narvaez and DeSoto during their explorations of Western Florida.

The first settler on the peninsula is thought to have been Antonio Maximo, who arrived in 1823. By this time Florida had passed from its second era of Spanish rule and was now a part of the young United States. Maximo had fought in the Seminole wars and secured a land grant in recognition of this service. He was joined by another individual named William Bunce, and the two partners established a "fish ranche" which did a lively business in supplying seafood to Cuba. A strong hurricane in 1848 completely obliterated the enterprise and both Maximo and Bunce left the area, never to be heard from again.

Within the next several years other pioneers began to filter into the Pinellas peninsula and establish small farms and orange groves near the stream we now know as Big Bayou. The first house was erected in 1856 by James R. Hay.

The small village suffered disaster during the Civil War. Union troops invaded the peninsula and stole practically all the livestock and crops to be found. Every single house was burned to the ground and the orange trees were wantonly hewn down and left to rot. When the inhabitants returned, they took one look at the devastation and stole away in a rowboat that the troops had left behind.

Dr. James Hackney was the first to settle on the site of St. Petersburg. The good doctor bought six hundred acres of land from the state in 1873 for twenty-five cents an acre.

In 1875 one of the two men credited with being the founders of St. Petersburg arrived.

Gen. John C. Williams of Detroit first visited Pinellas in 1875. Over the next four years he acquired some 1,600 acres of land and returned for good in 1879. After an unsuccessful attempt at farming, Williams conceived the idea of establishing a town, complete with rail service. At about the same time, Peter Demens, an emigrant from Russia, had just completed a narrow-gauge railway from Lake Monroe (near the modern city of Sanford) to Lake Apopka. This was the beginning of the famous "Orange Belt Railroad."

Through shrewd business dealings, Williams convinced Demens to extend the railroad to his settlement rather than his next intended choice. Construction was hampered by lack of funds, heavy rains, and yellow fever, but the line was finally completed in 1888. It wasn't long before tons and tons of oranges were being shipped to and from Lake Monroe and Pinellas via this new mode of transportation.

St. Petersburg acquired its present-day name sometime during this period. There have been many stories which purport to tell how the moniker was acquired. The tale usually given the most credence relates the desire of both Williams and Demens to name their new settlement. Agreement seemed to be impossible, so the two played a poker game for the privilege and Demens won. He selected the name of his native Russian city, St. Petersburg.

Citrus cultivation in St. Petersburg received a tremendous boost during the winter of 1894-95. Two hard freezes struck Florida within as many weeks and orange trees all over the state were laid waste. Due to the mitigating effects of the warm Gulf of Mexico, the orange groves in St. Petersburg survived. When word of this reached orange growers in other parts of the state, many moved to St. Petersburg to found new groves.

Since those days the growth of St. Petersburg has been phenomenal, and yet not at the total expense of the natural environment. Perhaps this is because many of St. Petersburg's citizens settled here during the

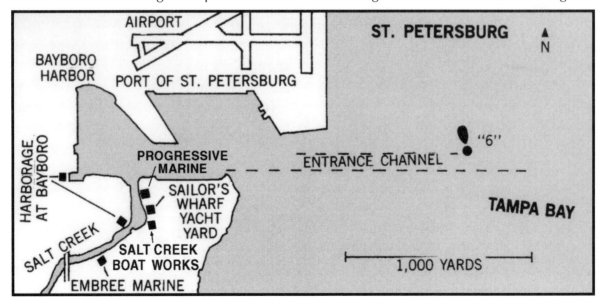

twentieth century for the healthful climate and beautiful waters. An 1885 paper delivered to the New Orleans medical convention stated flatly, "Those who have carefully surveyed the entire state think it (St. Petersburg) offers the best climate in Florida."

The Harborage at Bayboro and Salt Creek Facilities

North of Big Bayou, cruisers following the marked channel along the bay's western shoreline will come upon flashing daybeacon #S. This aid signals the intersection with the important, well-marked, westward-flowing Bayboro Channel, which leads pleasurecraft into the charted deep water south of Albert Whitted Airport. Some of the finest facilities in St. Petersburg are accessed through this fortunate cut and the adjacent Salt Creek.

The first charted cove on the northern banks serves the St. Petersburg commercial shipping port. While the various oceangoing ships that dock there make for a fascinating sight from the water, there are no services for pleasurecraft. The situation is very different just to the west.

Mariners cruising down Bayboro Channel for the first time will be amazed by the huge

The Harborage at Bayboro

collection of yachts which they will spy at the western terminus of the cut. This partially breakwater-enclosed harbor is part of The Harborage at Bayboro, one of the largest privately owned marinas in western Florida. This writer has always found that the staff and management of The Harborage, unlike many huge marina complexes, are friendly and ready to do all in their power to make your stay a pleasure. A full 500 feet of all-concrete floating docks are set aside for transient vessels. Even so, advance reservations would be a wise precaution. Dockside depths of 11 to 14 feet are ready to serve even the deepest-draft sailcraft. The breakwater which fronts the harbor to its eastern side deflects rough water when winds are blowing strongly from this quarter.

Every conceivable power, water, and communication connection, plus waste pump-out service, is readily available dockside. Behind the dockage basin, visitors will discover the dockmaster's building, which contains somewhat small but air-conditioned showers and a laundromat. There is also an attractive cruisers' lounge, with a color television, VCR, and microwave oven, located on the second floor. This is a great place to gather and share cruising stories with your fellow skippers after a long day on the water. If it's a bit warm, don't overlook the marina swimming pool just behind the main dockage basin.

Currently, the Old Key West Deli restaurant (727-894-4363) is located behind the dockage basin. This popular dining spot has just changed hands for the second time in as many years. Only time will tell what the future will hold here. In the past, the sandwiches have been super.

In 1994 and again in 1998, I had the pleasure of addressing the Bayboro Yacht Club at Key West Deli's outside dining area. On both occasions the food and drink were all that the heart (and palate) could desire. I hope I'll be invited back soon.

Since 1998 we have been told that the entire landside portion of The Harborage dockage basin is slated for renovation. If these plans should ever come to fruition, it is likely that the building containing the Key West Deli will be razed to make room for a far more expansive retail/dining/office complex. Even more recently, The Harborage has been sold. Just what impact this new ownership will have on The Harborage renovation plans is more than uncertain at the time of this writing.

Many other restaurants in downtown St. Petersburg are only a short taxi ride away. Check out our account of this district attached to our review of the large St. Pete Municipal Marina below.

The building that plays host to the Key West Deli is also the current St. Petersburg headquarters for the Steve Colgate Offshore Sailing School (800-221-4326). This is one of the most prestigious organizations of its type in the world.

Would you believe that only covers about half of The Harborage's services? The firm also maintains a second set of facilities on the western shores of Salt Creek, to the south. Here cruisers will find a ship's and variety store, the marina fuel dock, a well-supplied parts store, dry storage for literally hundreds of craft, and complete repair and somewhat limited haul-out facilities (crane rated at 5.5 tons). Shazam! If there is a better-equipped marina operation anywhere, this writer has yet to find it. As an added incentive, the Salvador Dali Museum, described earlier, is next door to the docks.

The Harborage at Bayboro (727) 821-6347

Approach depth—15 feet plus
Dockside depth—11-14 feet
Accepts transients—yes
Floating concrete docks—yes
Dockside power connections—up to 50 amp
Dockside water connections—yes
Waste pump-out—yes
Showers—yes
Laundromat—yes
Gasoline—yes (Salt Creek facility)
Diesel fuel—yes (Salt Creek facility)
Mechanical repairs—yes (Salt Creek facility)
Below-waterline repairs—yes (Salt Creek facility)
Ship's and variety store—yes (Salt Creek facility)
Snack bar—on site
Restaurant—several nearby

Deep Salt Creek breaks off from the southwestern corner of the Bayboro Harbor Channel and leads to an incredible selection of repair facilities. Minimum 10-foot depths allow pleasurecraft of most descriptions to visit the yard of their choice.

Captains and crew cruising into the northern mouth of Salt Creek will first catch sight of a commercial shrimper dock to port, followed by Progressive Marine (727-822-2886), also on the eastern banks. This outstanding repair firm features a newly renovated 35-ton travelift, which is outfitted with a crane to facilitate mast stepping and unstepping. Full-service mechanical repairs for gasoline and diesel power plants are offered, as is fiberglass servicing and marine painting. As Joe, the owner, put it to me, "if we can't do it, we know who can." Trust me when I tell you that this yard is truly "full service."

Next up, also to port, are the docks and extensive yards of Sailor's Wharf Yacht Yard (http://www.sailorswharf.com, 727-823-1155). As its name implies, this firm specializes in haul-out (60-ton travelift) and full service

Sailor's Wharf Yacht Yard, Salt Creek

mechanical repairs for sailcraft. There is also an on-site ship's and parts store as well as an extensive sailcraft brokerage associated with this operation. If you happen to be in the market for a new boat, give Jopie or one of his fine staff a call. One look at this yard will clue you in to the fact that this is a first-class operation that does quite a business with local sailors.

BYC Charters (800-879-2244), also known as Sailing Florida, makes its home at Sailor's Wharf as well. In addition to offering extensive sailcraft charters, this operation includes an ASA-certified sailing school.

Opposite Sailor's Wharf, on the western shores of Salt Creek, passing cruisers will observe the dry stack storage, fuel dock, and repair facilities associated with The Harborage at Bayboro. As these facilities are extensively described above, we need only note here that you would have to be blind to miss them.

Salt Creek Boat Works (727-821-5482) overlooks the stream's easterly banks. This firm has a huge repair yard, which offers both full service and do-it-yourself repairs. This is a real rarity in modern-day Florida. Salt Creek features a 40-ton travelift and full mechanical servicing for both diesel and gasoline engines.

Also on site at Salt Creek Boat Works is Advanced Sails (727-896-7245). This "local sailing loft" is very popular with the local wind-powered crowd.

Finally the docks and travelifts of Embree Marine (727-896-0671) will come up on the southern shores. Again, complete haul-out (35-ton travelift) and mechanical services are readily available. This writer found the yard management especially friendly and ready to go that extra mile to do the job right.

Salt Creek is blocked by a low-level fixed bridge just upstream from Embree Marine. This is the end of the line for all but very small powercraft.

St. Petersburg Municipal Marina and St. Petersburg Yacht Club

You may think that you've seen large city marinas before, but just wait until you lay eyes upon the St. Petersburg Municipal

A portion of the St. Petersburg Municipal Marina

Marina. Consisting of two large dockage basins bisected by a parklike tongue of land, this facility frequently plays host to more than one thousand transient cruisers annually. All dockage is at modern, fixed, concrete piers featuring recently updated power, water, cable television, and telephone connections. Entrance depths range widely from as little as 7 to as much as 20 feet. Soundings at the piers run from 20 feet at the outer slips to 7 feet against the concrete seawall. Transient berths are provided in the "Central Yacht Basin" (the northernmost of the two municipal harbors). One of the staff of dockmasters will direct you upon arrival. Be sure to call ahead of time on VHF channel 16 for dockage availability and arrival instructions. Advance reservations are not accepted, but even during the season most boats can usually be accommodated.

Gasoline, diesel fuel, and full mechanical repairs (for both diesel and gasoline engines), are available at the adjacent Marina Point Ship's Store—St. Petersburg Yacht Charters (727-823-2555). Recently, Marina Point has moved into a new, ultramodern headquarters and vastly expanded its ship's store. The new building is most impressive and makes for quite a sight from the water. We were very impressed with the store's many offerings.

Marina Point is found at the entrance to the central harbor basin. Charters of both sail and powercraft are also available. Marina Point

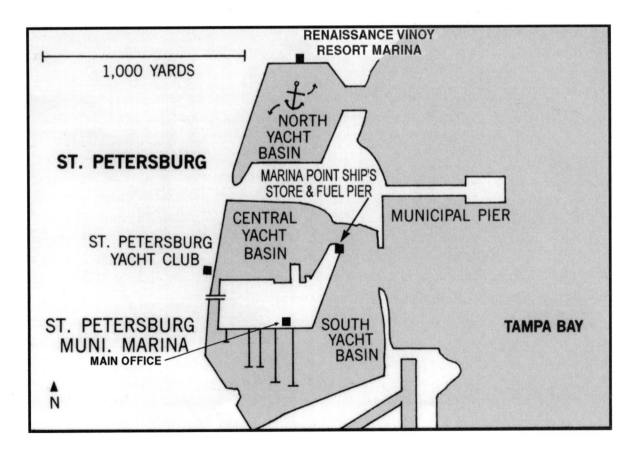

provides first-class mobile marine service as well, including mechanical and sailcraft rigging repairs.

Waste pump-out service is available in the central dockage basin, just beside the public launching ramps. Make arrangements in advance with the dockmaster for this service, as the pump-out station is not regularly manned.

Adequate, air-conditioned showers and a nice laundromat are found at the dockmaster's building adjacent to the south basin, as is a skipper's lounge, with color television (provided by local cruisers). Other, non-climate controlled shower buildings are spread about the marina's extensive grounds.

The beautifully restored St. Petersburg downtown section is but a short step away from the municipal piers. Among other attractions, visitors might consider the Bayfront Center and Al Lang Stadium, both quite visible from the south dockage basin. All in all, it's unlikely that you will exhaust the list of things to do, see, and places to dine while docked along the St. Petersburg waterfront.

Downtown St. Petersburg can now lay claim to many more dining attractions than in years past. We only have space to mention three restaurants that are worthy of any cruiser's attention and within an easy step of the municipal marina, the St. Petersburg Yacht Club (see below), and the Renaissance Vinoy Resort Marina (see below). The Moon Under Water (332 Beach Drive, 727-896-6160) is housed in an extremely attractive building overlooking the water. It features an English-style menu, including some notable curry dishes. Indoor and outdoor seating is available. Midtown Sundries (200 First Avenue S, 727-502-0222) has a mixed menu and a sports-bar feel, but it's not too noisy. There are separate no-smoking areas, pool tables, and, most importantly, good food at moderate prices. Finally, Tangelo's Grill (226 First Avenue N, 727-894-1695) serves outstanding Cuban-style cuisine. The streetside seating is our personal favorite.

So, you prefer to cook up the evening meal in your own galley? Well, downtown St. Petersburg is ready for you too. While you will need to take a taxi to access a full supermarket, don't overlook the Marketplace Express (284 Beach Drive NE, 727-894-3330) gourmet market and deli. Located near the Moon Under Water restaurant, and within walking distance of all the St. Pete waterfront marinas, this is a real find!

To be sure, there are many other places to eat, things to see, and places to go in the downtown St. Petersburg business district. Many more attractions are just a short taxi ride away. Few will become bored with a stay in St. Pete, even if it stretches over several weeks.

St. Petersburg Municipal Marina (727) 893-7329
(800) 782-8350
http://www.stpete.org/marina.htm

Approach depth—7-20 feet
Dockside depth—7-20 feet
Accepts transients—yes
Fixed concrete piers—yes
Dockside power connections—up to 50 amp
Dockside water connections—yes
Waste pump-out—yes
Showers—yes
Laundromat—yes
Gasoline—yes (Marina Point Ship's Store)
Diesel fuel—yes (Marina Point Ship's Store)
Mechanical repairs—yes (Marina Point Ship's Store)
Ship's store—yes (Marina Point Ship's Store)
Restaurant—several more nearby

Now, just in case you are not quite motivated to check out the municipal dockage basin, let it be known that this harbor is also home to the prestigious St. Petersburg Yacht Club. This organization maintains its piers in the southwestern corner of the central dockage basin. Cruisers entering the central harbor can quickly identify the docks by the "SPYC" sign at the eastern end of the club's piers. Members of other yacht clubs with reciprocal privileges are accepted for overnight or temporary dockage at fixed piers with power and water connections. The clubhouse overlooks the docks from across the street to the west. Here guests will find full dining services in both formal and informal settings, as well as showers. Bicycles are also available from the yacht club, which certainly facilitates a cycle tour of downtown St. Petersburg.

St. Petersburg Yacht Club has a regular dockmaster from 8:30 A.M. to 5:00 P.M. daily. Gasoline and diesel fuel can be purchased by club members and guests when the dockmaster is on duty. As is true with the city marina, all of downtown St. Petersburg's charms and The Pier are but moments away.

St. Petersburg Yacht Club (727) 822-3873

Approach depth—7-20 feet
Dockside depth—8-16 feet
Accepts transients—members of clubs with reciprocal privileges
Fixed piers—yes
Dockside power and water connections—yes
Showers—yes
Gasoline—yes (members and club guests only)
Diesel fuel—yes (members and club guests only)
Restaurant—on site

The Pier

One of the most exciting attractions on the St. Petersburg waterfront is the retail and dining complex known, appropriately enough, as "The Pier." Look at the inset on chart 11413 for a moment and notice the label "Municipal Pier" north of the city marina. The long finger of land extending to the east serves as means of access to what will appear from the water to be a huge, inverted pyramid.

It's a long walk from the mainland to The Pier, but trams run regularly from the shoreside parking lot to the outer building for those who are weary of foot. Even before beginning your journey out to The Pier, there is an attraction you should not miss. The St. Petersburg Historical Museum (727-894-1052) guards the northern side of The Pier's entrance. This most worthwhile attraction is open Monday through Saturday, 10:00 A.M. to 5:00 P.M. and on Sundays from 1:00 P.M. to 5:00 P.M.

The Pier's main building, the aforementioned inverted pyramid, contains an incredi-

The Pier, St. Petersburg

ble collection of retail and gift shops, restaurants, and even an aquarium. This latter attraction features a wide variety of tropical and saltwater fish in large, glass tanks. A visit is almost mandatory.

To visit The Pier, dock at either the St. Petersburg Municipal Marina or the yacht club and walk over. While The Pier was originally designed to have boats dock directly against its sides, this practice has apparently very much fallen out of use, possibly due to the strong winds and wicked waves which sometimes batter the docks. Sea gulls and pelicans seem to be the only current dockside residents.

North Yacht Basin Anchorage and Renaissance Vinoy Resort Marina

Refer to the inset on chart 11413 yet again and notice the deep basin north of The Pier, designated as "North Yacht Basin." Most locals call this harbor the Vinoy Basin. Besides making for a wonderfully sheltered overnight anchorage, these waters also play host to St. Peterburg's most prestigious marina facility.

The harbor derives its local name from the pink, stuccoed Renaissance Vinoy Resort Hotel which overlooks the northwestern corner of the cove and is noted on 11413 as "Hotel Cupola." This venerably hostelry has been magnificently restored and is now one

Renaissance Vinoy Resort Marina, St. Petersburg

of the great showplaces in St. Petersburg. If you want to really blow the old wallet, try spending a night or two (that's all most of us could afford) in this unforgettable hotel. I can't think of a better way to take a break from the live-aboard routine.

Along with the Vinoy's renovation several years ago, a full-service pleasurecraft facility, the sumptuous Renaissance Vinoy Resort Marina, was constructed on the adjoining banks of the basin. Besides offering just about any service you might ever require (except repairs), visiting cruisers can be readily assured of an unusually warm and knowledgeable welcome, somewhat unusual for a marina of this size. Transients are cheerfully accepted at the ultramodern concrete decked floating docks which feature every conceivable water, power (now including some 100-amp hookups), and telephone connection. First-class showers and dry cleaning-laundry services are available across the street in the resort hotel. Mechanical repairs can be arranged by the dockmaster or his accommodating staff with a nearby independent service firm.

Visiting cruisers are given full resort privileges at the Vinoy. These services include access to the health club with sauna, steam room, and spa with two hot tubs, as well as an on-site swimming pool. Complimentary transportation is provided to an 18-hole golf course a scant one mile away where visitors may also make use of a clubhouse and a second swimming pool. Still not enough for you? Well, how about 12 clay-surfaced tennis courts within walking distance of the docks and free ice for all nautical visitors?

Within the elegant arms of the Vinoy Resort, visitors will find five wonderful restaurants. The Terrace Room and Marchand's Bar and Grill specialize in luscious Mediterranean cuisine. Give them a try, but check the price list first.

Renaissance Vinoy Resort Marina
   (727) 824-8022 http://www.renaissancehotels.com/TPASR/

Approach depth—9-11 feet
Dockside depth—11 feet
Accepts transients—yes
Concrete floating docks—yes
Dockside power connections—up to 100 amp
Dockside water connections—yes
Showers—yes (across street in resort)
Dry cleaning-laundry service—yes
Mechanical repairs—independent technicians
Restaurant—five on site and others nearby

Anchorage is still allowed in the Vinoy Basin for stays up to one week in duration. After 24 hours, visiting cruisers are required to check in with the dockmaster at the St. Petersburg Municipal Marina. Protection is excellent from all winds save easterly breezes over 20 knots, which would blow directly into the harbor. Even in this circumstance, you could favor the southern shores for some protection.

The surrounding shores are mostly comprised of a delightful waterside park, with St. Petersburg's usual lush Bermuda grass very much in evidence. This is certainly a great spot to spend an evening or two in pleasant surroundings, just where you might least expect to find such a haven. Of course, you must expect some lights and traffic noise from the main road to the west.

Coffeepot Bayou

If my boat drew no more than 5 feet, you would find this writer anchored in Coffeepot Bayou whenever he was in the St. Petersburg region and wanted to spend a night away from the marina docks. This fortunate stream is found north of Vinoy Basin (northwest of flashing buoy #1).

An absolutely gorgeous home overlooks the northeasterly entrance point, and the houses to the south aren't too shabby either. Entrance depths run between 5½ and 8 feet, with most soundings being on the deeper end of that range. The best spot to drop the hook is found in the first bay of the bayou, just northwest of the charted marsh island. Between the island and the 6-foot fixed bridge, cruising boats can anchor in 5½ to 6 feet of water with superb protection from all winds. It doesn't get much better than this, gang, so put a red circle around Coffeepot Bayou.

Smacks Bayou

The crescent-shaped channel leading to Smacks Bayou makes into Tampa Bay's westerly flank north-northwest of flashing buoy #1, north of Coffeepot Bayou. This sidewater also makes a good anchorage, though it can not lay claim to the aesthetic qualities of its sister to the south.

The entrance cut is outlined by small, privately maintained (unlighted) daybeacons and carries a good 6 to 7 feet of water. The bayou itself soon splits into two branches. The northerly track is quickly blocked by a fixed bridge and is too narrow for anchorage by all but small craft.

There is plenty of swinging room for even larger pleasurecraft to anchor just short of the split in the stream. Here you will find depths ranging from 11 to 15 feet and good protection from all but easterly winds. The shores are bounded by heavy residential development.

For even more shelter, follow the southerly branch of Smacks Bayou into the charted lake known as Snell Island Harbor. This deep passage can be relied upon to hold at least 10-foot soundings. You can anchor anywhere on the lake's mid-width in 7 to 10 feet of water with plenty of protection for any weather short of a full gale. In this case, the lake is so large that it might produce its own severe chop. The lake's shores are crowded with one of the densest collections of homes that we observed in the St. Petersburg area.

Bayou Grande

The marked but indifferently charted channel leading to the interior reaches of Bayou Grande strikes to the west, west of flashing buoy #15J. This aid is found on the charted "Cut J-2 Channel." While the initial passage into Bayou Grande holds minimum depths of 6 feet, soundings rise to the 4½-foot region as the channel swings to the north on its way to Riviera Bay. There is really not enough room to anchor in the deeper section of the passage. Considering these less-than-desirable characteristics, most cruising captains would be wise to forego exploration of this sidewater.

LOWER TAMPA BAY—WESTERN SHORE NAVIGATION

Navigation on any portion of Tampa Bay cannot be taken for granted. This is a *large* body of water and captains used to the more protected confines of the ICW can find the breadth daunting and occasionally downright dangerous. Always plan your cruise on Tampa Bay with an ear to the latest NOAA weather forecasts. With winds above 10 knots, be prepared for chop. If the forecast calls for breezes blowing 25 knots or more, it would be far wiser to stay at the dock and play a few more rounds of checkers.

Successful navigation of lower Tampa Bay's western shoreline is facilitated by the presence of a deep, well-marked channel paralleling the banks. While it is certainly possible for skippers to follow the big ship's channel up the bay, this passage favors the easterly shoreline. Almost all cruisers will want to choose the westerly route. It is convenient to all the various side trips on this portion of the bay, including St. Petersburg's excellent marine facilities.

Approaches to the Western Shore Captains northbound on the Western Florida ICW or those entering from the open Gulf via any of the bay's three entrance cuts will find it convenient to follow the Waterway's official passage through the central span of the Sunshine Skyway Bridge. This route was reviewed in the last section of this chapter.

Cut north between flashing buoys #3B and #6B and follow the ICW until you pass between flashing daybeacon #4 and unlighted daybeacon #3. At this point the Waterway route turns sharply to the west, but, to reach the various ports of call along the western shore (except Little Bayou and the Annapolis Sailing School), continue due north, pointing to pass between flashing daybeacon #6 and unlighted can buoy #5.

Southbound ICW skippers (and northbound cruisers making for the Holiday Inn/Annapolis Sailing School Marina or the adjacent anchorage on Little Bayou) should follow the Waterway to the intersection with the Sunshine Skyway Channel, south of Indian Key at flashing daybeacon #26. You can then turn east and pass north of unlighted daybeacon #13A on your way to 65-foot twin fixed bridges. Once through the span, set course to come abeam of unlighted daybeacon #13 to its northerly quarter. As you approach #13, you will most likely spy a sign advertising the "Holiday Inn Marina Beach Resort." From this marker, skippers may choose to cruise north to this facility or anchor in the lee of the Sunshine Skyway Causeway.

Holiday Inn/Annapolis Sailing School Marina & Sunshine Skyway Anchorage For best depths continue to follow the Waterway channel east past unlighted daybeacon #13 for 100 yards or so. Then, turn back sharply to the northwest and set course for the water tank-shaped basin at the northwesterly corner of the cove. If you choose to visit the marina, watch for a single unlighted red daybeacon at the entrance. Take this aid to your starboard side, as you would expect from the "red, right, returning" rule. This maneuver will run you hard by the port-side banks, but, believe it or else, this is where the best depths are located. A shoal has built across a goodly portion of the basin's entrance to the east (starboard side).

Those who decide to anchor off in the shelter of the causeway leading to the Sunshine Skyway can drop the hook at any convenient spot short of the marina basin. Good depths run to within 50 yards of shore. Remember, this anchorage is only sheltered in westerly winds and could be a real bear when breezes are blowing from any other direction.

On to Point Pinellas   If your destination is found elsewhere on the western shoreline, continue following the well-outlined Waterway channel to the east. Review the preceding section of this chapter outlining the ICW route across Tampa Bay for more details. As you come abeam of flashing daybeacon #6 to its southerly side (south of Point Pinellas), the western shoreline's first good sidewater opportunity beckons to the north.

Little Bayou   North of flashing daybeacon #6, two channels veer in towards Tampa Bay's westerly shoreline. The shorter, southerly cut leads only to a public launching ramp and is of little use to cruising craft.

The northerly passage follows a track covering some 1.4 nautical miles from the ICW to the mouth of Little Bayou. As you are traversing this portion of the channel be ready to discover different aids to navigation than those pictured on chart 11414. During our last visit, we found a new unlighted daybeacon #9. Whatever aids you find, just keep red markers to your starboard side and green beacons to port in the usual pattern. North of unlighted daybeacon #12, watch for uncharted and unlighted junction daybeacon #A. The channel running to the north-northeast from #A leads to a private condo dock with no transient services. The main Little Bayou passage cuts to the northwest. This channel

will take you hard by a concrete seawall to starboard and a small mangrove to port. Continue following the markers until you come abeam of unlighted daybeacon #17. You can then cut to the west and feel your way out into the bay's mid-width for 100 yards or so in good water. Don't continue cruising to the west or 4-foot depths will be encountered.

All but very small, outboard-powered boats should discontinue their explorations of Little Bayou at #17. Farther upstream, the waters narrow and a fixed bridge with only 9 feet of vertical clearance blocks the passage.

As you prepare to leave Little Bayou, be *sure* to retrace your steps to the south. The seemingly inviting waters of Tampa Bay to the east are shoal, with depths of as little as 2 feet.

On the Western Shore Channel   To reach the main western shore channel serving lower Tampa Bay, cruise due east for another .2 nautical miles after passing flashing daybeacon #1. Watch to the south for unlighted daybeacon #3 and flashing daybeacon #4. As these aids come abeam to starboard, swing to the north and point to pass between flashing daybeacon #6 and unlighted can buoy #5. The southerly and northerly approaches join at this point and we need only concern ourselves with a single, well-marked channel as we work our way to the north along the western shoreline.

From a position between #5 and #6, the channel runs almost due north. While the track is well outlined, the various aids to navigation are rather widely placed. It might be a good idea to run compass/GPS courses, particularly as you approach un-lighted can buoy #7. Some shoal water is found to the west along this stretch of the channel.

Eventually, navigators will find them-selves abeam of unlighted nun buoy #10 to its westerly side. While the straight course to St. Petersburg's primary marine facilities runs due north from #10, there is a ques-tionable anchorage to the west.

Big Bayou   Please remember that Big Bayou is not the most easily navigated of Tampa Bay's western shore sidewaters. Only experienced captains with a sense of adventure should attempt to drop the hook on this stream.

Those who make the attempt should continue on the main channel for some .4 nautical miles north of unlighted nun buoy #10. Then, turn 90 degrees to the west and use your binoculars to pick out the eastern-most aids of the Big Bayou channel, unlighted daybeacons #1 and #2, as you cruise towards the stream's mouth. Past this point, this writer would not begin to try and describe all the channel's twists and turns. Simply pass all red beacons to your star-board side and take green to port as usual and hope for the best. The best place to drop the hook is found south of unlighted daybeacon #14. Even then, don't approach the shoreline too closely.

Only boats drawing less than 4 feet should attempt to follow the Big Bayou Channel past unlighted daybeacons #17 and #18. Depths become much more uncertain to the southwest and another fixed bridge with only 9 feet of vertical

clearance eventually blocks further progress to the south.

On the Western Shore Channel   North of unlighted nun buoy #10, it's a straightfor-ward run to flashing daybeacon #S. Switch to the St. Petersburg inset section of chart 11413 for navigation on these waters. To the west, Bayboro Harbor Channel and Salt Creek offer the first of St. Petersburg's myr-iad marina facilities.

Bayboro Harbor and Salt Creek   It doesn't get much simpler than this cut. If you run aground here, better break out the old *Chapman's* and have a refresher course in basic coastal navigation. Come abeam of flashing daybeacon #S to its westerly side and turn almost due west into the Bayboro Harbor entrance channel. As you come abeam of flashing daybeacon #10, look north and you will spot the St. Petersburg Coast Guard station.

West of #10, powercraft should proceed at no-wake speed. Soon you will sight the huge dockage complex of The Harborage at Bayboro dead ahead. Enter this facility by cruising around to the northern side of the harbor.

Enter Salt Creek on its mid-width and, for best depths, continue on the centerline as you work your way upstream towards the low-level fixed bridge.

St. Petersburg Municipal Marina   Again, the channels to the St. Petersburg Municipal Marina and St. Petersburg Yacht Club are deep and obvious. From flashing daybeacon #S continue cruising north by passing well to the west of flashing buoy #3. Watch the western banks for twin stone breakwaters. As the gap between these two barriers comes abeam to the west, cut in straight toward this entrance and pass through its mid-width. Be on guard against the charted spoil area to the south, running northeast then south from Albert Whitted Airport.

Both ends of the breakwaters flanking the marina's entrance are delineated by flashing aids. These are fixed to the jetties themselves and should be avoided. While this is obvious during daylight, it's good to know for nighttime entries.

Once past the breakwater, simply follow the docking instructions you should have already received over your VHF from the municipal dockmaster's office. For best depths, stay away from the banks west of the entrance. Some shoal water runs out from this shoreline. Turn either north or south and head for your assigned slip.

Marina Point Ship's Store and fuel dock are found at the entrance to the central basin. The docks belonging to St. Petersburg Yacht Club are also found in this harbor's southwesterly corner.

North Yacht Basin and Anchorage While the entrance to North Yacht (or Vinoy) Basin is not marked, it's still relatively easy to enter. Cruise north past the easterly limits of The Pier and watch to the west for the basin's entrance. As it comes abeam, cut sharply west, pointing to avoid the charted shoals immediately north of the entrance. A sign at the bay's mouth warns powerboats to proceed at idle, no-wake speed.

Once past the entrance, simply select a likely spot anywhere near the mid-width and drop the hook. The pink-stuccoed Renaissance Vinoy Resort Hotel and its marina will be readily visible to the northwest.

North along the Western Shore From a position to the west of flashing buoy #3, east of the St. Petersburg Municipal Marina basin, consider setting a course to come abeam of flashing buoy #1, east-southeast of Coffeepot Bayou, to its western side. Both Coffeepot and Smacks bayous can be accessed from this aid.

Coffeepot Bayou To enter Coffeepot Bayou from Tampa Bay, set course to the west-northwest from flashing buoy #1. Use your binoculars to pick out the easternmost pair of small, privately maintained unlighted daybeacons marking the stream's mouth. Cruise between the various aids and do not wander from the marked passage. Eventually you will enter a wide bay where you will spot the charted marsh island to the northwest. Pass this body of land to your starboard side. Depths fall off to the 5- to 5½-foot region as you pass the small island, but improve to 6-foot soundings a bit farther upstream. Consider dropping the hook some 50 to 100 yards after passing the small island. Farther upstream, passage is barred by a 6-foot fixed bridge.

Smacks Bayou Successful navigation of Smacks Bayou calls for a traversal of the crescent-shaped channel rounding the hook-shaped point east of Snell Island

Harbor. From flashing buoy #1, set a compass course for the charted, easternmost entrance channel aids, unlighted daybeacons #1 and #2. Be sure to avoid the charted fish haven, which you will pass just north of your course.

Follow the various other uncharted marks past #1 and #2 as they curve to the north and eventually cut to the west at the stream's mouth. Remember "red, right, returning," and you should not have any undue difficulty. As you enter the stream, favor the south-side banks slightly.

Shortly after entering the mouth of Smacks Bayou, the stream splits. This is a no-wake area and all boats should proceed at idle speed during their explorations of the stream. Larger craft can anchor immediately southeast of the forks in good water.

If you need better shelter, turn south and follow the mid-width of the deep stream into the charted lake known as Snell Island

Harbor. Favor the western shores slightly as you enter the lake to avoid the charted underwater wreck. Anchor anywhere you choose. Good water runs to within 100 yards (or sometimes closer) of the banks.

On to Old Tampa Bay North of flashing buoy #1, cruisers should probably rejoin the large ship's channel leading into Old Tampa Bay at flashing buoy #10J. It's a fairly lengthy run of 1.8 nautical miles between #1 and #10J. Use your compass and watch for excessive leeway.

From #10J, you can follow the Cut G big ship's channel to the east, or turn north for Old Tampa Bay. This latter route will be reviewed later in this chapter.

Those few brave souls who should decide to visit Bayou Grande will find its entrance channel west of flashing buoy #15J, north of #10J. All I can say is, good luck!

Lower Tampa Bay—Eastern Shore

The eastern banks of lower Tampa Bay could not show a greater contrast to their westerly counterpart. For one thing, while deep water often runs almost up to the west-side banks, a considerable shelf of shoal water extends out for a goodly distance from the eastern shores. To reach the various side-waters along the coast, cruisers usually must traverse dredged channels.

Perhaps even more disparate is the amount of development on this region of Tampa Bay. Large sections of all-natural shoreline are

interspaced with small coastal developments backed by tiny towns and villages.

There are several marinas that serve transients, but it is often a long run between stops. Similarly, while you can certainly find some of the most enchanting overnight anchorages available anywhere, these refuges could not exactly be described as numerous.

In spite of these seemingly negative characteristics, this writer could not help but like this coastline. The lack of heavy development and the opportunity to drop the hook in an isolated haven, often within a few hour's sail of St. Petersburg, are qualities which should not be dismissed out of hand. I recommend you give lower Tampa Bay's eastern shores a try. Captains and crew who treasure a bit of seclusion now and then may just discover this to be their favorite cruising grounds on Tampa Bay.

Terra Ceia Bay & Anchorage (BAIL-Suggested)

The channel leading from Tampa Bay to Terra Ceia Bay lies east of flashing daybeacon #TC (itself northwest of Snead Island). The marked entrance cut exhibits minimum depths of 5½ to 6 feet, but a navigational error could stick the unfortunate cruiser in 3-foot soundings.

While the main entrance to Terra Ceia Bay, outlined above, makes off from Tampa Bay just north of the Manatee River's westerly mouth, there is, as we learned earlier in this chapter, also a passage directly from the Manatee River, near Bradenton Yacht Club. This small stream is, unfortunately, crossed by a 13-foot fixed bridge and most cruising-size craft must gain access to Terra by the main channel making in directly from Tampa Bay.

Immediately north of the 13-foot fixed bridge, one repair yard, a huge trawler dealer, and a small marina offer some services for cruising craft. Cut's Edge Harbor Marina, in particular, seems to be popular with the do-it-yourself crowd.

The principal Terra Ceia entrance channel is marked but, to be frank, additional beacons would be a welcome improvement. Be sure to read the navigational data on Terra Ceia presented later in this chapter before attempting to visit the bay.

Chief among Terra Ceia Bay's attractions are its generally undeveloped character and the possibility for secluded overnight anchorage. The banks support only a few homes and some portions of the shoreline are well wooded. It can be a very special treat to drop the hook where you are likely to be the only pleasurecraft within sight. None of these overnight havens is well sheltered, however. Be sure to keep the weather forecast in mind.

The main body of Terra Ceia Bay is actually far larger than it would appear from a cursory study of chart 11414. Anchoring on the bay's deep mid-width is not a practical possibility except in almost windless conditions. Fortunately, there are at least three more sheltered havens to consider (one of which is a BAIL-suggested anchorage).

The first spot where you might drop the hook is found along the band of deep water south of unlighted daybeacon #9. Minimum depths of 5½ feet can be carried to within 250 yards of the southerly banks. While there is some protection from southerly and northerly winds, this spot is clearly a good-weather anchorage. Blows of as much as 10 knots from the east or west would make for a very bouncy evening. The surrounding shores are almost completely in their natural state, and a real treat for the eyes. In short, this is a beautiful anchorage with plenty of swinging room. In good weather, with no strong breezes forecast, this is probably the spot that I would choose on Terra Ceia. But wait—there are more sheltered havens on the main portion of the bay.

In northerly (or light to moderate southerly) winds, skippers of most sizes of pleasurecraft may well consider dropping the hook on the BAIL-suggested tongue of deep water north-northeast of Bird Key (north of unlighted daybeacon #13). Moving west from Beville Point to a point where you are just short of coming abeam of Bird Key to the south, 5½-foot minimum depths can be held to within 200 yards of the northerly banks. A few homes peep out amidst the tall trees overlooking this shoreline, but these serve to add to the anchorage's appeal, rather than detract from its character.

Finally, for those willing to make a somewhat lengthy trek from Tampa Bay, you can drop anchor on the extreme northwesterly corner of Terra Ceia Bay, short of the charted sunken wreck. Depths of 6 to 8 feet can be held to within 150 yards of the lightly developed banks, and there is fair to good shelter from all winds save southerly breezes. This is the most sheltered refuge on the bay, and it has plenty of elbow room for a 50-footer.

Turning our attention to the pleasurecraft facilities of southern Terra Ceia Bay, first up is Cut's Edge Harbor Marina (941-729-4878). The channel leading to Cut's Edge strikes off to the east, south of unlighted daybeacon #4. Eventually, the passage hooks back around to the west and enters the charted lagoon-shaped body of water almost due south of #4. The harbor is well sheltered but virtually all of the available wet-slip dockage is rented out strictly on a month-to-month basis. Low-water entrance and dockside depths of as little as 4½ feet could be a problem for especially long legged vessels. Plans are under way to add extensive dry stack storage on site.

Clearly the forte at Cut's Edge is service work. Boats are hauled out by way of a 40-ton travelift, and full mechanical repairs for both gasoline and diesel engines are offered as well. There is some do-it-yourself work allowed.

While it will never live up to the class of a Snead Island Boat Works, Cut's Edge is clearly popular, as evidenced by the large number of hauled craft we witnessed during our last visit.

So, if you are up for a somewhat offbeat yard, don't fail to give Cut's Edge your consideration.

The face piers and protected harbor of Marlow Marine Sales (941-729-3370) line the charted canal's western flank, south of unlighted daybeacon #4. This firm is a huge trawler dealership. Cruisers will undoubtedly note any number of impressive Grand Banks and other trawlers while passing by. You may also observe several large work barns and other repair facilities. However, my discussion with this facility's management strongly suggests that service work is now confined to vessels sold or awaiting sale at Marlow Marine.

Lastly, low-key Marsh Harbor Marina (941-722-2858) guards the canal's westerly banks immediately north of the 13-foot fixed bridge. We have never found anyone to talk with here save fellow boat owners. It seems as if Marsh Harbor is pretty much relegated to those docking here on a more or less regular basis. During our last visit, a fellow captain informed us that the "owner has been gone for three days." Clearly, there's not much in the way of services for visitors at Marsh Harbor.

Bishop Harbor

Bishop Harbor is a rather controversial body of water lying between the Sunshine Skyway and the Port Manatee Channel. Another well-respected guide to anchorages and stops along Western Florida's coastline highly recommends the harbor. Indeed, one of this writer's good friends, who once called Tampa Bay his home waters, asserts that he prefers this anchorage over any other along the bay.

However, despite these rave reviews, all captains should know that the entrance channel is narrow, winding, unmarked, and surrounded by water running as shallow as ½ foot. I think it not only possible, but likely, that any cruising craft visiting Bishop Harbor for the first, second, or possibly even the third time is going to run aground.

So, if you want to visit Bishop Harbor for its natural beauty, fine—but you will have to do it without my help. In spite of all the sentiment to the contrary, this writer recommends that you pass by and continue cruising on to Bahia Beach or Little Manatee River.

Port Manatee Channel

The deep, well-marked cut leading to Port Manatee breaks off from the main Tampa Bay big ship's channel between flashing buoys #6B and #8B. This channel serves the large commercial vessels which frequently visit the commercial center at Port Manatee. The shipping of phosphate and other agricultural chemicals are a primary concern at this complex. There are no services or anchorage possibilities for pleasureboaters, and most cruisers will only want to give a quick wave as they pass.

Little Manatee River

The Little Manatee River, just south of Bahia Beach and Mangrove Point, is named, like its bigger sister to the south, for the gentle manatee or sea cow. The creature's name is apparently derived from a Spanish word that refers to the handlike use of the sea cow's front flippers.

Frankly, this stream remains something of a disappointment. On the plus side, Little Manatee River is known as one of the most unspoiled bodies of water on Tampa Bay. Writing in Del and Marty Marth's *The Rivers of Florida*, Greg Lamm comments, "The area is considered the most important nursery ground for marine life in the bay. River marsh and uplands provide habitats for a number of endangered species, including the American bald eagle." Unfortunately, cruising reality intruded and has led this writer to believe Little Manatee would be a difficult gunkhole for most cruising-size craft.

The river's list of detriments is led off by an extremely confusing array of markers on the stream's entrance channel. What really happens is that the river beacons are in close proximity to, and initially almost indistinguishable from, the aids to navigation leading to the three Bahia Beach marinas reviewed below. Even if you can sort out this confusing mess, low-water entrance depths range to as little as 4½ feet. Similarly, while portions of the river's interior reaches boast 8 and 9 feet of water, there are also patches of low-tide 4½-foot soundings as well.

Little Manatee's channel is marked by a series of informal pilings, some lacking any daybeacon boards. Even the daybeacons you will find could most certainly use some paint.

Shell Point Marina overlooks the river's northern banks between the 6- and 7-foot soundings noted on chart 11414, well north of Whiskey Key. This facility keeps 2 or 3 slips open for transients with fresh water and modern 30-amp power connections. Dockage is mostly found at fixed, wooden piers, though there is now one floating wooden dock as well. One shower is located on the marina grounds. Complete mechanical repair services are offered and haulouts are accomplished by a 25-ton travelift. Extensive outside dry stack storage is available for smaller powercraft as is a well-stocked ship's store featuring full electronics sales and service. Dockside depths are in the 6- to 8-foot region.

Recently, a full-fledged restaurant known as the Deck of Shell Point has opened within a very few steps of the marina docks. Screened-porch dining is available in the main building, and a semi-open-air bar overlooks the river. We did not have a chance to dine here, but both the restaurant and bar were doing a brisk business during our last visit.

Shell Point Marina (813) 645-1313

Approach depth—4½-6 feet
Dockside depth—6-8 feet
Accepts transients—yes (2 or 3 slips usually open)
Fixed wooden piers—yes
Dockside power connections—up to 30 amp
Dockside water connections—yes
Showers—outside only
Mechanical repairs—yes
Below-waterline repairs—yes
Ship's store—yes
Restaurant—on site

Skippers can also feel their way carefully to the south off the main river channel, a short distance upstream past Shell Point Marina, and hold 6 feet of water. You must be careful to stop before reaching the shallows to the south and drop the hook in such a way as to preclude swinging into these shoals. There should be room enough for a competent 34-footer to perform this feat. Protection is at least adequate for all winds and really superb when breezes are blowing from the north or east. This anchorage does require caution and the reader is advised to review the navigational information on Little Manatee River presented later in this chapter.

Bahia Beach Facilities and Anchorage

The largest set of marina facilities on lower Tampa Bay's eastern shoreline and one surprising anchorage are gathered about the resort community of Bahia Beach, well east of

flashing buoy #1E on the big ship's channel. No fewer than three marinas wait to greet the cruising boater.

As with Little Manatee River channel, reviewed above, the entrance channel markers can be a bit confusing, but they are soon sorted out after reviewing the navigational information below. Careful captains piloting craft that draw 5 feet or less should not encounter any undue difficulty.

The southernmost facility is Bahia Del Sol Marina, located on the upper reaches of the rectangular cove northeast of charted Sand Island. You must follow a twisting channel with some 5-foot depths to reach the facility, but you will find 6 to 8 feet of water dockside. Transients are accepted by the friendly dockmaster at fixed wooden piers with all power and water connections. Shoreside showers

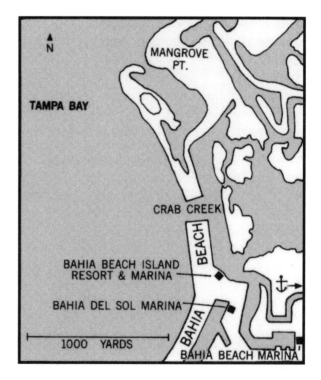

and a laundromat are available at an extranice cruisers' lounge with a color, cable television. Waste pump-out service is also available. Bahia Del Sol is the only marina in the Bahia Beach area that offers this service. Meals can be had at the nearby Bahia Beach Island Resort complex.

Bahia Del Sol Marina (813) 645-0884

Approach depth—5-7 feet
Dockside depth—6-8 feet
Accepts transients—yes
Fixed wooden piers—yes
Dockside power connections—up to 30 amp (a
    few 50 amp available)
Dockside water connections—yes
Waste pump-out—yes
Showers—yes
Laundromat—yes
Restaurant—nearby

Study chart 11414 for a moment and note the middle of the three Bahia Beach channels, north of Bahia Del Sol. This cut leads almost straight into the eastern banks where Bahia Beach Island Resort maintains a fishing pier. Few, if any, cruising-size craft will want to berth here. The channel does, however, provide access to Bahia Del Sol and serves as an alternate route to the northward marked passage.

Two marinas and one secluded anchorage are available to cruising craft on Crab Creek. The marked Crab Creek channel (the northernmost of the three Bahia Beach channels) carries low-water depths of 5½ feet. In times past, it was possible to carry another foot or so by making use of the Bahia Beach Island Resort fishing pier channel (the middle of the three). Now the Crab Creek and Bahia Beach Island Resort fishing pier channels have come to display more or less similar soundings.

After traversing the marked entrance cut,

captains will cruise through a sharp turn to the south on Crab Creek. As you follow this turn in the stream, the large Bahia Beach Island Resort & Marina complex will be very much in evidence on the western banks. Soon thereafter the resort's wet-slip dockage will come abeam along the western banks near unlighted daybeacon #5. During the last several years, this facility has changed hands and been considerably refurbished. The adjacent motel features excellent lodging, and the marina showers are brand new and air conditioned. There are also two swimming pools, a laundromat, five tennis courts, two shuffleboard courts, and a new hot tub. Still not enough for you? Well, check out the three on-site restaurants, the Sunset Lounge, the Captain's Quarters, and the Tropics. This latter dining attraction is open for all three meals of the day.

The marina portion of Bahia Beach Island Resort features berths at fixed wooden piers with all power and water connections (including telephone hook-ups). The dockage basin is well sheltered and makes for a good spot to ride out inclement weather.

**Bahia Beach Island Resort & Marina
    (813) 645-9269**

Approach depth—5½-8 feet (direct channel)
                6-8 feet (fishing pier channel)
Dockside depth— 6½-8 feet
Accepts transients—yes
Fixed wooden piers—yes
Dockside power connections—up to 50 amp
Dockside water connections—yes
Showers—yes
Laundromat—yes
Restaurant—3 on site

The third Bahia Beach marina facility is accessed by continuing to follow the course of Crab Creek as it cuts sharply east and then back to the south. Eventually, the stream will take a final turn to the east and Bahia Beach Marina will be sighted dead ahead. This firm's dockage basin is extremely well sheltered and the management is unusually knowledgeable and friendly.

Many improvements have taken place at this facility since the last edition of this guide went to press. One of the most important is the decision to begin accepting transients on a space-available basis. In times past, overnighters were not readily accommodated at Bahia Beach. Call ahead of time to check on slip availability. A new, huge dry stack storage building has been constructed, and the adjacent repair yard's haul-out business has obviously taken a turn for the better. The yard's travelift is rated at 25 tons. We observed literally dozens of pleasurecraft on the dry, waiting for various service tasks to be performed. There are few better recommendations for any repair yard. Full mechanical service work for both diesel and gasoline power plants is also offered.

Transient and resident craft alike will find berths at newly renovated, fixed wooden piers in the ultra-well-sheltered dockage basin. All slips feature full power and water hook-ups. Gasoline and diesel fuel are readily available dockside. Currently, this is the only facility in Bahia Beach offering fuel.

Shoreside, visiting cruisers will discover adequate, climate-controlled showers, a laundromat, and a small but well-stocked ship's store.

Cruisers wanting to dine out can walk the short stretch to any of the three restaurants at Bahia Beach Island Resort (see above). Unfortunately, there is no provisioning stop nearby.

All in all, we heartily recommend a visit to Bahia Beach Marina, whether you are in the market for secure dockage or full service repairs. Just don't forget to call ahead and check on the latest transient space situation.

Bahia Beach Marina (813) 645-2411
Approach depth—5½-8 feet (direct channel)
**   6-8 feet (fishing pier channel)**
Dockside depth—6-7 feet
Accepts transients—yes (space-available basis)
Fixed wooden piers—yes
Dockside power connections—30 amp
Dockside water connections—yes
Showers—yes
Laundromat—yes
Gasoline—yes
Diesel fuel—yes
Mechanical repairs—yes
Below-waterline repairs—yes
Ship's store—yes
Restaurant—nearby

Cruisers visiting Bahia Beach Marina will note the clubhouse of the Bahia Beach Yacht Club on the basin's northerly banks. This facility leases one pier from the marina, but no guest dockage is currently available.

Well, do you prefer to anchor off rather than spend your evening hours whiling away the time at a marina dock? Fear not—Bahia Beach is ready for you. Just where you might least expect to find it, there is a wonderfully isolated anchorage with heavily vegetated, completely undeveloped shores and excellent depths. This refuge does not even appear on chart 11414, but it is still easy to enter.

Look at 11414 for a moment and notice the stream that comes off Crab Creek just upstream from Bahia Beach Island Resort & Marina where the main creek takes a 90-degree turn to the south. You can follow this sidewater through a whole series of twists and turns, holding minimum 6-foot depths, to a lake-like basin well east of chart 11414's limits. Here you can anchor in 6 to 8 feet of water, with excellent protection from even the heaviest weather and enough swinging room for boats as large as 50 feet. Be warned that the bottom is black, oozy mud which may require some washing of the anchor rode next morning.

Mangrove Point Channel

Study chart 11414 for a moment and you will note an obscurely charted cut running north from the Crab Creek (Bahia Beach) Channel. This former passage has now shoaled in entirely and all the markers have been removed. No craft, not even of the outboard variety, should attempt to venture on this lost channel. Your prop or keel is sure to find the bottom in short order.

Apollo Beach

North of flashing buoys #7F and #8F, the large ship's channel traversing lower Tampa Bay splits into eastern and western passages. The east-side fork hurries on towards the southern mouth of Hillsborough Bay, but there is one additional stop along the eastern shoreline associated with lower Tampa Bay.

The charted and well-marked entrance channel to Apollo Beach is found southeast of flashing buoy #8. Even though you must cross a charted spoil to reach the cut, on-site research revealed that minimum 6-foot depths can be carried, with most soundings showing considerably better water.

The Apollo Beach entrance channel carries minimum low-water soundings of 6 feet. Actually, most of the cut displays soundings of 7 to 8 feet, but there is one 6-foot spot near flashing daybeacon #2 that establishes the minimum depth. Eventually the channel leads to the Tampa Sailing Squadron, a good anchorage, and a fine restaurant with dockage. After passing unlighted daybeacon #12, a wide bay sweeps to the northeast. Pleasureboats of almost any size can drop the hook here in 7 to 15 feet of water with excellent protection from all but gale-force winds. The shores are overlooked by fairly heavy, but not unattractive, residential development.

The Tampa Sailing Squadron (a private yacht club) maintains piers on the northwestern corner of the cove. You will readily spy this facility courtesy of the many local sailcraft anchored at mooring buoys south of the docks. Visitors who choose to anchor in the bay would do well to avoid the club's anchorage and drop their hook farther to the southwest.

Tampa Sailing Squadron (813-645-8377) sometimes accepts members of other yacht clubs with reciprocal privileges for overnight or temporary dockage. This is a superfriendly but somewhat informal organization without a full-time dockmaster, so advance arrangements are definitely in order. Good depths of 6 to 10 feet are set against fixed wooden piers with water and simple power connections.

Tampa Sailing Squadron (813) 645-8377

Approach depth—6-15 feet
Dockside depth—10-15 feet
Accepts transients—members of clubs with reciprocal privileges with special permission only
Fixed wooden piers—yes
Dockside power connections—up to 20 amp only
Dockside water connections—yes
Showers—yes
Restaurant—nearby

Just southeast of Tampa Sailing Squadron, Land's End Marina (813-645-5594) overlooks the waters of Apollo Beach. This facility is more or less a high-dry marina, with little else in the way of services for transients save gasoline. Hold on for a moment, though; Land's End may be worth a second look.

Circles Bar and Grill is located just behind Land's End's fixed, wooden piers. Depths alongside seem to run at least 6 feet. Morgan Stinemetz, ace researcher and cruising writer extraordinaire, has informed this writer that cruising craft can tie up to the fuel dock and patronize the restaurant.

Circles has "a full menu, good selections, a liquor license, wine, and good service," according to Morgan. "I had beef tournedos with wild mushroom sauce. It was great! My buddy had grouper with a glazed peanut sauce, and he said that was also very good." How's that for a great review—is your mouth watering?

LOWER TAMPA BAY—EASTERN SHORE NAVIGATION

Navigation of lower Tampa Bay's eastern shoreline is facilitated by the relative proximity of the large ship's channel traversing the bay from south to north. The various sidewaters along the way have marked channels knifing through the substantial shelf of shoal water extending well outward from a goodly portion of this coastline. Most are reasonably simple to follow, though all require caution, particularly Terra Ceia Bay and Little Manatee River. Take your time, have charts 11414 and 11413 in your hands, study the information presented below, and, in fair weather, you should be all right. Let the wind get up, though, and you could remember this passage for an altogether different reason.

Sailors can easily abandon the ship's channel and follow the mostly deep waters to the north. The few shoals are well charted and larger shallows are marked. Avoid these problem stretches and you should have a wonderful cruise.

Terra Ceia Bay & Anchorages (one, BAIL-Suggested) Mariners traveling north or south on the Western Florida ICW can enter Terra Ceia Bay by abandoning the Waterway some .6 nautical miles south of flashing daybeacon #70 and setting course to come abeam of flashing daybeacon #TC (at the western mouth of Terra Ceia) fairly close to its southerly side.

East of #TC the entrance channel is not nearly so straightforward as you might expect from a casual inspection of chart 11414. The channel wanders a bit, and you cannot always depend on the markers to keep you to the good water.

From #TC, set course to come abeam of and pass unlighted daybeacons #1 and #3 to their fairly immediate southerly sides. From #3, set course to pass just north of unlighted daybeacon #4, and then point to come abeam of unlighted daybeacon #5 to its southerly quarter. Shallow water encroaches on the south side of the channel between #3 and #5. A straight course between these two aids could land you in these shallows. Therefore, bend your course slightly to the north after passing #3 and point to favor the Terra Ceia Point side of the channel somewhat. Of course, don't approach the point too closely, as it is surrounded by a thinner strip of shallows. As #4 comes abeam, south of your track, adjust course to come abeam of unlighted daybeacon #5 to its immediate southerly side.

From #5, the channel takes a sharp turn to the southeast and heads for unlighted daybeacon #7. At #7, the cut turns again, this time back to the east. Remember your "red, right, returning" rule and you should be in good shape until coming abeam of unlighted daybeacon #10 to its northerly side.

If you decide to anchor in the deep water south of unlighted daybeacon #9, feel your way carefully due south from this aid with your sounder. Be sure to drop the hook before approaching to within less than 250 yards of the southerly banks. Closer to shore, depths quickly rise to grounding levels.

Past #10, the next aid to the east, unlighted daybeacon #12, guards a patch of very shallow water to the southwest. Set course to come abeam of #12 by about 20 yards to its northerly side. Don't allow leeway or a navigational miscue to lead you south of this course line.

Once abeam of #12, turn sharply to the southeast and follow the wide ribbon of deep water south of Bird Key past unlighted daybeacon #13 into the deeper portion of the bay.

To reach the anchorage on the northwestern corner of the bay, simply follow the deep mid-width of the bay and avoid the shoreline. As you sight the low-level fixed bridge blocking the northeasterly portion of the bay, begin working your way carefully towards the north-northwestern banks. Be sure to drop the hook at least 150 yards from shore. Be on guard against the correctly charted shallows to the east and northeast adjacent to the fixed bridge.

Boaters desiring to anchor in the BAIL-suggested haven north of Bird Key should turn off the main body of the bay as the centerline of the waters lying between the key and Beville Point comes abeam to the west. For best depths, favor the northern shores slightly. Good depths continue west to a point just before coming abeam of the eastern tip of Bird Key, to the south. Farther to the west, soundings come up to 4-foot levels. Avoid Bird Key itself. The charted ½-foot shoal building east from the isle is for real.

To access the marine facilities on southern Terra Ceia Bay, follow the centerline south, pointing to eventually come abeam of unlighted daybeacon #4 to its fairly immediate westerly side. From #4, point directly for the mid-width of the canal, which will be obvious to the south-southwest. Just before entering the canal, the marked but uncharted channel to Cut's Edge Harbor Marina will open out to the east. After you enter the canal, Marlow Marine Sales followed by Marsh Harbor Marina will come abeam on the westerly banks.

On Tampa Bay   All other ports of call on lower Tampa Bay's eastern shore can be gained by crossing under the main pass-through of the Sunshine Skyway, east of flashing buoy #1A. This truly monstrous span has a vertical clearance of 175 feet.

North of the Sunshine Skyway, it is navigationally simple to follow the big ship's channel all the way to either Hillsborough or Old Tampa bays. There are several ranges along the way, but pleasurecraft can almost always depend on the prolific flashing buoys to show them the way.

On-site research revealed that 8-foot minimum depths can be found over most of the charted spoil areas adjacent to the main channel on lower Tampa Bay. Many soundings were considerably deeper. The same can not always be said of the spoil banks bordering some of the side channels, so proceed with caution.

Farther north, some of the spoil banks lining the channel near Hillsborough and Old Tampa bays can be truly shallow. Obviously, mariners must give these hazards considerably more respect on these waters.

Notice that chart 11413 correctly forecasts some depths in the 4- to 6-foot range south of the Gadsden Point and Cut A channels. This branch of the large ship's channel strikes northeast towards Hillsborough Bay. Study chart 11413 carefully and give these hazards the respect they deserve.

As you might well expect, when winds exceed 10 knots, this otherwise easy passage can become more than slightly rough. As always on Tampa Bay, it would be best to choose a day of fair winds for your sojourn.

Little Manatee River The most logical place to leave the Tampa Bay large ship's channel when cruising into either Little Manatee River or the facilities at Bahia Beach is at flashing buoy #1E. From #1E set course across the charted spoil bank to come abeam of flashing daybeacon #1 by at least 50 yards to its southerly side. Do not make a close approach to #1. The shoal marked by this aid is building to the south.

East of #1, the channel is complicated by the presence of two unlighted daybeacons that are both labeled as #2. Ignore the more western of these two aids. This #2 is the lone marker on a highly questionable channel coming north from Sand Point. Cruising craft are strongly advised to keep clear.

As if that weren't cause enough for confusion, there is also an unlighted daybeacon to the east of flashing daybeacon #1 that is also designated as #1. Whew!

From a position abeam of *flashing* daybeacon #1, set course to come between *unlighted* daybeacon #1 and (the eastern) unlighted daybeacon #2. Favor *unlighted* #1 slightly.

Continue almost due east after passing between unlighted #1 and #2. Soon you will sight the two pairs of *unlighted* daybeacons leading to the Bahia Beach Island Resort fishing pier almost dead ahead. Point for the gap between the first pair of aids, unlighted daybeacons #4 and #5, as if you were going to run this cut. Some 20 yards before reaching #4 and #5, cut sharply south and carefully set course to come abeam of unlighted daybeacon #3 to its immediate westerly quarter.

The above procedure is not as simple as it might sound. First of all, the charted markers southeast of #3, leading to Bahia Del Sol Marina, are easy to confuse with #3. Use your binoculars before leaving the fishing pier channel west of #4 and #5 to positively identify #3 before proceeding. If you mistake the marina markers for #3, your track will lead you into very shoal water.

Even after you've managed to pick out unlighted daybeacon #3, your problems aren't over. Notice the tongue of charted shallows (on 11414) north of the unlighted daybeacon. You must be careful to skirt this shoal to its westerly side as you approach #3. Curl your course around so that you eventually come abeam of #3 to its fairly immediate westerly side.

Well, you've finally made it to #3. Wasn't that fun? Now you must be extremely careful to pick out the small markers to the south-southwest marking the Little Manatee River entrance channel. *Do not* attempt to follow the marina markers to the southeast. Again, this mistake will undoubtedly lead to a rapid and abrupt grounding.

Once you pick out the various Little Manatee River markers, cruise between the various aids to navigation, and try not to say too many unhappy things about their lack of painted daymarkers. Keep faithfully to the marked channel as it curves slowly to the east. Soon, you will sight Shell Point Marina on the northern banks.

If you decide to anchor in the deep water just upstream from the marina, continue following the markers past Shell Point Marina for a short distance until you are some 150 to 200 yards to the west of the island that flanks the south side of the river. Begin feeling your way off the main track with your sounder for a short distance to the south.

Continued exploration on the river's track to the east past this anchorage is not recommended for cruising craft without very specific local knowledge.

Bahia Beach Channels Newcomers should approach the various Bahia Beach channels with respect. Take your time, and read this account thoroughly before making your attempt.

Cruisers voyaging to Bahia Del Sol Marina (the southernmost of Bahia's three marinas) should follow the course outlined in the Little Manatee River section to the western head of the Bahia Beach Island Resort fishing pier channel. Instead of turning to the south as you would to enter Little Manatee River, follow the various daybeacons until you pass between unlighted daybeacons #6 and #7, some 25 yards short of the fishing pier, which will appear dead ahead. Only then should you turn 90 degrees to the south and follow the shoreline as you cruise along. Watch for two uncharted and unnumbered red daybeacons, which mark the westerly limits of the channel. Pass these aids to their easterly sides. Eventually the well-marked marina channel will come abeam to port.

As you approach the marina's aids to navigation, slow down. It is *extremely important* to identify the unlighted daybeacon #3 to the west, marking Little Manatee River channel discussed above. This identification is made even trickier by another unlighted daybeacon #3 at the head of the marina entrance channel. Little Manatee #3 will be by itself and will be spotted north and slightly west of the marina markers. *Ignore Little Manatee #3.* Heading for this aid from the track described above will result in an instantaneous grounding.

Instead, continue cruising south until the first two marina aids, unlighted daybeacons

#2 and #3, come abeam to the southeast. Turn into the well-marked channel and cruise between the various aids into the deep rectangular cove. Don't cut the corner as you turn to the north-northeast to head for the marina docks.

As noted above, the direct Crab Creek approach channel now carries almost as much water as the alternate route via the Bahia Beach Island Resort fishing pier cut. Skippers with vessels drawing 5½ feet or less who are bound for either of the two marinas or the secluded anchorage on Crab Creek can make use of the well-marked direct channel. After coming between unlighted daybeacons #1 and #2 (east of flashing daybeacon #1), simply set course to pass between the various markers leading into Crab Creek.

To reach the harder-to-follow but perhaps slighly deeper alternate route, follow the Bahia Beach Island Resort fishing pier channel until you are some 20 yards west of the pier. Then turn sharply north and point to intersect the marked Crab Creek Channel immediately east of unlighted daybeacons #6 and #7. Cut 90 degrees to the east just before reaching #7 and follow the markers into the mouth of Crab Creek.

Once past the entrance, the Crab Creek Channel takes a definite swerve to the south. Favor the westerly banks. A surprisingly large shelf of shoals is found flanking the eastern shore.

Soon after leaving the Bahia Beach Island Resort & Marina docks behind, the creek swings sharply east and then back to the south. Those cruisers who are headed to Bahia Beach Marina need only follow the stream's centerline all the way there.

If you are inclined to try the fine Bahia Beach overnight anchorage, watch for a sign advertising Bahia Beach Marina just as the creek swings sharply back to the south. You will spy the eastward-running stream leading to the anchorage just beside the sign. Follow the mid-width of the twisting, but deep, creek through its various turns. At one point it may look as if the channel dead ends, but keep the faith—it cuts back to port.

Eventually, you will enter a deep lake. Some sort of concrete storage building and a set of power lines will be spied over the eastern banks. There is also a small marsh island near the entrance into the lake. Leave the marsh island to port and curl around into the open northerly portion of the anchorage. Drop the hook anywhere that will allow your craft to swing clear of the shoreline and settle in for an evening of peace and security.

On Tampa Bay   North of flashing buoy #7F, Tampa Bay's large ship's channel (Cut F Channel section) divides. The so-called Cut G Channel flows on to Old Tampa Bay. This route will be considered later in this chapter. Captains and crew making for Apollo Beach, Hillsborough Bay (Tampa), or any other points of interest on the lower bay's eastern banks should cut northeast and follow the prolifically marked Gadsden Point and Cut A channels.

Avoid the marked channel north of flashing buoy #5 (on the Gadsden Point Channel). This small cut makes into the southern shores of Interbay Peninsula and is associated with MacDill Air Force Base.

Apollo Beach   Entry into Apollo Beach is complicated somewhat by the presence of some of the few shoals directly adjacent to Tampa Bay's large ship's channel. To avoid these shallows, cruise south-southwest from flashing buoy #8 for .7 nautical miles. This maneuver will bypass the charted 4- to 6-foot patches south and southeast of #8.

Once the shallows are well behind you, set a new compass/GPS course in order to come abeam of flashing daybeacon #2 to its northeasterly side. This is a long run of 1.9 nautical miles or so. Use your binoculars to help locate #2.

From #2, the channel stretches its well-defined way to the southeast. Cruisers can now expect minimum low-water depths of 6 feet near flashing daybeacon #2. Farther along, soundings deepen even more after you pass between unlighted daybeacons #3 and #4. Pass all red markers to your starboard side (what else?) and take green beacons to port. As you pass unlighted daybeacon #10, the cut runs hard beside the port-side banks. After passing unlighted daybeacon #12, turn northeast into the mid-width of the broad, baylike cove. If you plan to anchor, be sure to drop the hook southwest of the yacht club's special anchorage charted on 11413.

On Tampa Bay The portion of Cut A Channel that is northeast of flashing buoy #8 borders on some shoals well south of its track. While it would take a whopper of a navigational error to land in these 4- and 5-foot shallows, stranger things have happened, so stay alert.

Northeast of flashing buoys #10 and #11, the large ship's channel takes a sharp swing to the north and enters the foot of Hillsborough Bay.

Hillsborough Bay

Any discussion of Hillsborough Bay is inextricably interwoven with the sprawling metropolitan city known as Tampa. This behemoth community's tall skyline dominates Hillsborough's northerly reaches. The bay's main feeder stream, the Hillsborough River, cuts directly through the heart of Tampa and serves the many commercial vessels which regularly call at the commercial port. For good or ill, the city and Hillsborough Bay are bound together.

We are sorry to report that the pleasurecraft dockage situation has drastically degraded recently. In times past, visiting cruisers could pretty well count on finding a slip at the Harbour Island complex in the heart of Tampa. Sadly, those days are gone. In fact, as this account is being tapped out on the keyboard, there are only two (that's right, two) non-yacht-club transient slips available in all of Tampa. That's not what one could accurately describe as a welcoming state of affairs for the cruising community.

South of Tampa the bay's shoreline is less developed, though a number of large industrial facilities line the eastern banks. The western shores are a part of the so-called Interbay Peninsula. The southern half of this land is occupied by MacDill Air Force Base. Several anchorages are available along the bay's eastern banks and adjacent to the spoil banks lining the large ship's channel.

Hillsborough Bay's shoreline is a study in striking contrasts. It ranges from the incredibly impressive Tampa skyline to the lesser developed lower easterly shores and the glass-and-concrete-shrouded track of the Hillsborough River. Few cruisers will forget their first visit to this fascinating body of water.

The Alafia River

The deep, well-buoyed Alafia River (translated as "oleander") channel strikes east to the south of flashing buoy #22 of the "Cut C" (large ship's) Channel, well northeast of Gadsden Point. This cut is used regularly by the barges and commercial vessels calling upon the Gardinier Phosphate Plant, which dominates the river's northern banks to the west of the fixed bridge that crosses the stream some 1.1 nautical miles east of its mouth. Indeed, you will unquestionably be able to see a huge hill of waste earth piled up beside this plant, just north of the river, long before the entrance actually comes into sight. During our first visit, we were amazed by this man-made geographical feature and wondered where this mountain had come from.

As Greg Lamm again comments in *The Rivers of Florida*, "Once a paradise for fishermen and hunters, the Alafia River in recent decades has lost its fishing and recreational significance because of voluminous pollution. Nearby phosphate mining has degraded the Alafia into an industrial stream, but state agencies and private preservation groups are struggling to reestablish the river as a natural attraction."

As you might expect with this sort of commercial traffic coming to and from the Gardinier phosphate facility, the river channel is deep as far as the plant, with at least 20 feet of water. The upstream waters between the commercial wharves and the river's fixed

bridge have minimum depths of 5½ feet, with soundings of 6 to 8 feet being more the norm.

In spite of the Alafia's commercial character, there are several intriguing anchorage possibilities and one marina facility to consider. One fair-weather haven sometimes employed by local captains lies off the southeastern tip of the large spoil island north of (the Alafia channel's) flashing daybeacon #6. Skippers piloting craft no more than 45 feet in length can cut off from the channel abeam of flashing daybeacon #7 and cruise through minimum 7-foot depths to within 150 yards of the island's southeastern point. Closer to shore, depths fall off to 4 and 5 feet.

In light airs, or when winds are blowing from the west or northwest, this refuge provides fair shelter. It's not the spot for foul weather, though. During inclement times, I would suggest the anchorage outlined below on the Alafia's interior reaches. The spoil island exhibits low, scrubby growth which is not particularly appealing. To the east, the huge waste earth hill described above is quite prominent.

It is also possible to continue cruising north off the eastern shores of the spoil island, keeping well off the beach. Minimum 7-foot depths can be held to a point some 200 yards off the spoil island's northeasterly tip. Here you may also drop the hook in appropriate wind conditions. This refuge does provide shelter from southeasterly winds that is lacking on the spoil island anchorage to the south.

Do not try to cruise around the spoil island's northerly tip and rejoin the large ship's/Cut C channel. Unmarked (but charted)

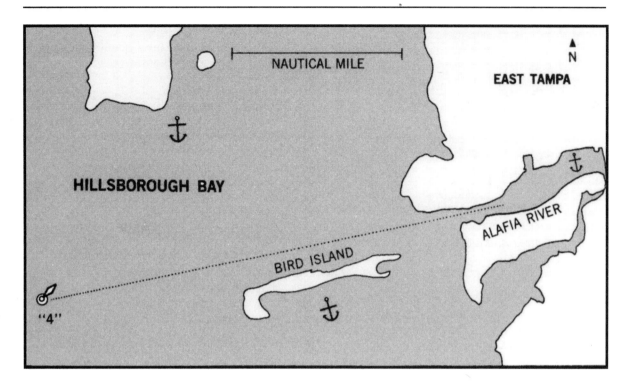

shoals with less than 4 feet of depth are waiting for you.

In northerly blows, vessels can find good shelter south of charted Bird Island. To reach this haven, you must abandon the Alafia Channel between flashing daybeacons #6 and #8 and find an unmarked passage leading across the southerly spoil banks. On sunny days when the water is clear, it's often possible to navigate by eye, but at other times you just have to take your best guess. With this sort of unpredictability, the anchorage can only be recommended for boats drawing less than 5 feet and piloted by die-hard explorers. Minimum depths of 6 feet are carried in the unmarked channel until reaching a point south of Bird Island's westerly tip. Good water then opens out in a broad swath before you and it's a simple matter to swing around to the east and drop your hook off Bird Island's

southerly shores. Minimum depths of 6 feet are held *only* to within 100 yards of the beach. Closer in, soundings deteriorate rapidly. This anchorage offers some protection in moderate easterly winds courtesy of the mainland shores. Of course, the body of the island itself provides super shelter from northerly breezes. With winds out of the south or west, head for the river or points north.

This is a particularly attractive anchorage with some special treats. The beautifully undeveloped banks of Bird Island are part of an official Audubon Society sanctuary. While landing is prohibited, there is nothing to stop us cruisers from anchoring and enjoying the many birds usually in view, often including quite a flock of giant, white ibises.

Boats drawing less than 5½ feet can follow the river's interior track past the phosphate plant with minimum 5½-foot depths (typically

7 to 8 feet) and anchor short of the fixed bridge. There is excellent protection from all but particularly strong easterly winds. While it is possible to get away from the phosphate plant a bit, there might still be some noise during the evening hours (not to mention the chemical smells), particularly if a barge loading is in progress. The nearby Highway 41 bridge is also apt to throw in its share of automobile lights. Fortunately, the shoreline in this area is more attractive. The northern banks are part of a small park with a public launching ramp, while the southerly counterparts are mostly undeveloped.

Boats that can clear the 28-foot fixed bridge (and the charted 33-foot power lines) may consider tracking their way upstream on Alafia River through mostly 5-foot depths to Inter Bay Boat Moorings. This facility flanks the Alafia's southerly banks a short distance east of the fixed bridge. Inter Bay accepts transients at their fixed wooden slips with fresh water and 30- to 50-amp power connections. Depths alongside range from 4½ to 6 feet. Gasoline and diesel fuel plus shoreside showers are available as well. Cruisers in need of repair work will find that Inter Bay offers full mechanical servicing and haul-outs. The yard's 70-ton travelift is most impressive. Do-it-yourself work is also allowed. There is even a nice ship's and variety store in the complex and a "country store" is within walking distance. All in all, Inter Bay Boat Moorings can be described as a decent facility for cruising craft that can stand some 5-foot depths and clear the 28-foot bridge.

Inter Bay Boat Moorings (813) 677-2739

Approach depth—5-6 feet
Dockside depth—4½-6 feet
Accepts transients—yes

Fixed wooden piers—yes
Dockside power connections—30-50 amp
Dockside water connections—yes
Showers—yes
Gasoline—yes (planned)
Diesel fuel—yes (planned)
Mechanical repairs—yes
Below-waterline repairs—yes
Ship's and variety store—yes

Tampa Yacht & Country Club

Moving south to north, the first facility on Hillsborough Bay comes up on the western banks, well west of flashing buoy #25. Tampa Yacht & Country Club accepts transients who are members of clubs with appropriate reciprocal agreements. Berths are provided at fixed wooden piers with a full set of power and water connections. The harbor is partially breakwater enclosed and well protected from all winds. There is even a fuel dock offering both diesel and gasoline for members and club guests. The club docks are attended 24 hours a day, seven days a week. This welcome service is a real rarity when it comes to private yacht clubs. Call ahead of time to make your slip reservations.

Shoreside amenities include showers, a swimming pool, two dining rooms, tennis courts, and extensive horseback-riding facilities. Lunch and dinner are served seven days a week, while breakfast is offered Saturday and Sunday only. Dining reservations are recommended by the management.

The yacht club's entrance channel holds minimum depths of 7 feet, with soundings of 8 to 11 feet as the norm. The channel skirts north of a small island of concrete riprap set out from the harbor's entrance for extra protection from easterly breezes. While there is nothing complicated about the entrance, first-time visitors may want to read the navigational account of the club channel before their first stopover.

Tampa Yacht & Country Club (813) 839-1311

Approach depth—7-11 feet
Dockside depth—7-10 feet
Accepts transients—members of clubs with reciprocal agreements
Fixed wooden piers—yes
Dockside power connections—up to 50 amp
Dockside water connections—yes
Showers—yes
Gasoline—yes
Diesel fuel—yes
Mechanical repairs—independent contractors
Ship's store—small
Restaurant—on site

East Bay/McKay Bay

The Cut C/large ship's channel serving Hillsborough Bay splits at Pendola Point. The passage angling to the northwest, known as Seddon Channel, allows access to downtown Tampa and the Hillsborough River. The wide cut to the northeast quickly leads to East Bay. This deep bay and its various side passages are perhaps the most commercial bodies of water that you will ever visit. Oceangoing freighters, tankers, and the huge wharves to serve them are everywhere in evidence. All this maritime paraphernalia makes for fascinating viewing from the water. Unfortunately, the rank smell of diesel fumes and other chemicals permeates the air everywhere. There is certainly no place to anchor, nor are there any real marina facilities on East Bay.

East Bay is eventually blocked by a 40-foot fixed bridge and a power line with 32 feet of vertical clearance. The waters northeast of this span are known as McKay Bay. On-site research revealed that, in spite of soundings shown on chart 11413, minimum 6-foot depths can be held on a broad band between the fixed bridge and a point just short of the charted overhead power cables. There is little in the way of shelter, but in light airs it would be possible to anchor here. The westerly banks exhibit some low-key residential development, while the shallow easterly shores are guarded by scrub growth. Frankly, I wouldn't anchor here unless there were no other choice. One sniff of the commercial odors wafting on the wind will put you in touch with the reason for my opinion.

Davis Island Yacht Club

Study the Tampa area inset on chart 11413 for a moment and notice the "Seaplane Basin" on the southeastern tip of Davis Island. This sheltered harbor, no longer used by pontoon-equipped aircraft, is now the home of Davis Island Yacht Club. This organization has the reputation of being "the sailingest club on the Gulf coast." The club docks are found on the basin's southern shores. This friendly group tries to keep the ends of each pier open for transients. Members of yacht clubs with reciprocal privileges are accepted for overnight or temporary dockage at fixed wooden piers with power and water connections. The club does not have a regular dockmaster, so be sure to make arrangements in advance.

Davis Island Yacht Club has a shoreside swimming pool, showers, and lounge, but no dining room. Visitors can take a taxi into Tampa to sample its multitude of restaurants and shoreside businesses of all descriptions.

Davis Island Yacht Club (813) 251-1158
http://www.dicy.org

Approach depth—10 feet
Dockside depth—9-10 feet
Accepts transients—members of clubs with reciprocal privileges
Fixed wooden piers—yes

Dockside power and water connections—up to 50 amp
Showers—yes

It is also possible for any cruiser to anchor in the basin north of the yacht club docks in 8 to 10 feet of water. Much of this space is already taken up by boats belonging to members of the Davis Island Yacht Club tied to mooring buoys. You may be able to find enough swinging room amidst this throng, but be sure to set the hook carefully to avoid bumping into your neighbor at night when the wind or tide shifts. The basin bottom is composed of soft mud. Watch for a dragging anchor.

Northwestern Hillsborough Bay

The northwestern lobe of Hillsborough Bay, west of Davis Island, is an area that most cruising skippers should think seriously about avoiding. A broad band of shallows flanks almost all of the surrounding shoreline, and the creeks making into the bay from Davis Island are all small and mostly shallow. Additionally, there are several unmarked shoals in the bay itself to contend with. The charted cut-through between the bay's northernmost reaches and Seddon Channel is spanned by two low-level fixed bridges. One has only 9 feet of vertical clearance. Obviously, cruising-size craft cannot make use of this passage.

So, here is one of the few places where this writer concludes that the cruising effort is not worth the reward. However, for those captains who just have to poke their bow into *everything*, a brief navigational sketch is provided in the next section of this chapter.

Tampa

The so-called Cut D Channel cuts to the northwest at Pendola Point and quickly runs on towards the Tampa metropolitan area. Let us pause a moment in our waterborne coverage to reflect on this successful city.

Tampa is a city that seems bent on entering the twenty-first century with a real boom. Population-wise, Tampa is now the state's second largest city. New, high-rise development is everywhere in evidence. The tall glass-and-steel towers make for an awe-inspiring site from the water.

High-tech and research development firms have flocked to Tampa since the 1990s. One draw is the Tampa International airport, considered to be one of the finest and safest air terminals in the world. Another good reason for all this business interest is the University of South Florida. Founded in Tampa in just the 1960s, the school has grown to be the state's second largest state-supported university.

Tampa is a city that loves its sports. The NFL Super Bowl came to town in 1984 and 1991. This writer was on hand for the latter event, and I can tell you from personal experience that the place was buzzing! Of course, Tampa has its own NFL football team with the Tampa Bay Buccaneers.

Tampa has a whole bevy of attractions for (mostly) landlubber visitors. Cruisers moving up the Hillsborough River past Harbour Island will be astounded by the Tampa Bay Performing Arts Center (1010 W. C. Macinnes Place, 813-229-7827). The building looks impressive, to say the least. Automobile traffic has been routed directly under the building in an arrangement that this writer has never before witnessed. The center contains three theaters designed to handle specific types of entertainment. Be sure to check on events that may be in progress during your visit.

Franklin Street Mall is found just north of Harbour Island and the Performing Arts Center. This development was part of Tampa's downtown revitalization program, which has been in full swing since the 1990s. Now only pedestrian traffic is allowed on the avenue amidst the many retail shops and frequent sidewalk entertainment.

A few steps farther to the north will bring the interested visitor to the Old Tampa Theater (711 N Franklin, 813-274-8286). Originally opened in 1926 by John Eberson, this facility earned the nickname of "Opera House John." Eberson chose a Hispanic architectural theme for his theater which has survived down through the years and still evokes "oohs" and "ahhs" from first-time patrons with its intricate detail. Some of the world's finest art treasures still grace the lobby and halls. The theater was donated to the city of Tampa in 1976 and since then it has become a cultural center. Shows and exhibitions are constantly in progress.

The Tampa Art Museum (600 N Ashley Drive, 813-274-8130) and the $134 million Curtis Hixon Convention Center overlook the Hillsborough River two blocks west of the Tampa Theater. The center regularly features the country's top talent and the museum houses an impressive collection of paintings and sculpture.

Ybor City, a suburb of Tampa, has been closely linked with the American manufacture of cigars since Don Vicente Martinez moved his factory from Key West to Ybor City in 1886. While only one cigar plant today remains in Ybor City, the industry has left an indelible print on the town.

The unique heritage of the Ybor City cigar workers, an eclectic mix of Cubans, Germans, Spaniards, Italians, and Jews, has been painstakingly preserved in the Ybor City State Museum. Among many fascinating exhibits, four of the original cigar workers homes have been moved to the museum site and restored.

Ybor City itself has been undergoing a tasteful renaissance over the past several years. While there is still much work to do, many of the long-vacant buildings have been restored as both retail businesses and fine restaurants.

Finally, if you are interested in a more modern mode of entertainment, take a taxi or public transportation to the nearby Busch Gardens theme park. Renowned for its exotic birds and animals, the park is a potpourri of rides and demonstrations that will thrill the whole family.

Now for the bad news. Where once transient dockage was available in downtown Tampa at the Harbour Island complex (see below), the waterside portion of this facility is now all but shut down. Adding insult to injury, one of Tampa's downtown hotels, which used to be friendly to cruisers, no longer offers overnight dockage. In fact, unless you can secure a berth at one of the Tampa yacht clubs described above, your only recourse for an overnight on-the-water stay in Tampa is the paltry two slips set aside for visitors at tiny Marjorie Park Yacht Basin (see below). This lack of readily available slip space is a real impediment for cruisers who want to visit the vital, active city that is modern-day Tampa. It is to be hoped that the city, or some private entity, will get on the proverbial ball in the near future and secure far more slip space for overnight cruising visitors. Until that happy occasion comes to pass, many of those who arrive by water will be forced to visit Tampa strictly by way of motorized land transportation.

Numbers to know in Tampa include:

Tampa Bay Cab—813-253-2235
United Cab—813-253-2424
Yellow Cab—813-229-2454

Avis Rental Cars—813-396-3505
Budget Rent A Car—813-878-2451
West Marine—813-348-0521

Henry B. Plant and the Fabulous Tampa Bay Hotel

The silver minarets of the world-famous Tampa Bay Hotel still gaze unwinkingly out over the shores of Hillsborough Bay as they have since 1891. This totally astounding edifice was actually modeled in part after the Alhambra Palace in Granada, Spain. An example of Moorish and Turkish architecture, it cost over $2 million to build and $500,000 to furnish.

University of Tampa, formerly the Tampa Bay Hotel

Henry Bradley Plant, one of the two most influential men in Florida's history, came to the Sunshine State during the aftermath of the War Between the States. Plant was a great financier and he is often considered to be the father of the modern American railroad system and of Tampa itself. Much as Henry Flagler pushed his railroad down Florida's east coast, bringing tourism to such diverse towns as St. Augustine and Palm Beach, Plant brought his competing west-coast railway line to Tampa, and the city's future as a major port was assured. At the time of the line's completion in 1884, the city had a mere 700 inhabitants. When the hotel was completed a scant seven years later, the city's population was nearly 6,000. Tampa has seemingly never looked back.

Stories persist that Plant's motivation to build the Tampa Bay Hotel in such a grand fashion was to outdo Henry Flagler's Ponce de Leon Hotel in St. Augustine. Both structures still display an opulence the likes of which will probably never be seen again.

Tampa Bay Hotel first opened its doors on January 31, 1891. Fifteen thousand written invitations were extended. The ladies were presented fans and brass crumb trays, and shaving mugs and ash trays were given to the men. Chinese lanterns and candles lit the grounds and the Albert Opera Company performed Faust. The hotel was filled to capacity and guests slept in the public rooms, bunking on tapestried couches.

Over the years famous guests included the Russian ballerina, Anna Pavlova; John Drew, the famous actor uncle of the Barrymores; and Minnie Maddern Fiske, a leading American actress for 60 years. Theodore Roosevelt, Clara Barton, and Stephen Crane were also guests there. Crane, who died at 28, was author of

Red Badge of Courage. He drafted *The Price of the Harness* while staying at the hotel.

The hotel was a focal point for the invasion of Cuba by American forces during the Spanish-American War in 1898. The war with Spain brought a concentration of 30,000 troops bound for Cuba to Tampa. Theodore Roosevelt camped with his Rough Riders about a mile from the hotel.

Following Mr. Plant's death in 1899, the old hostelry passed through a succession of owners, including the city of Tampa, until it became home to the University of Tampa in 1933. Today, the University of Tampa has become a bustling institution of higher education with almost 3,000 students.

The splendor of Tampa Bay Hotel and Mr. Plant's invaluable contribution to the development of Western Florida are remembered in the Henry B. Plant Museum (813-254-1891), which is now housed in the southern wing of the old hotel. The museum is open Tuesday through Saturday from 10:00 A.M. to 4:00 P.M. If you see nothing else in Tampa, be sure to visit this outstanding attraction!

Tampa History   The first mention of Tampa is found in the sixteenth-century memoirs of Fountaneda. A shipwrecked Spanish lad, he spent seventeen years among the Indians of Tampa Bay. One of many villages he wrote of was one called "Tanpa." Early mapmakers changed the spelling to "Tampa."

S. T. Walker and C. B. Moore mapped more than 75 mound sites in the Tampa region in 1879. Their map shows Indian mounds present at the time of the DeSoto expedition. These locations are now the neighboring cities of Ruskin, Tarpon Springs, Crystal River, Clearwater, Safety Harbor, St. Petersburg, Pass-a-Grille, Gibsonton, Palmetto, Bradenton, and Terra Ceia.

Robert Hackley, Tampa's first settler, arrived at the mound on the northeast side of the Hillsborough River in 1823. He cleared land around it and started his plantation near it.

In 1824 Col. George Mercer Brooke saw the shell mound near the clearing of Hackley's plantation and confiscated the property and mound for the U.S. Army and his namesake, Fort Brooke. Early drawings of Fort Brooke show the Indian shell mound still intact in the 1840s.

After the army withdrew, early settlers expanded the settlement of Fort Brooke by hauling shells from the mound in ox carts for road beds. The last mound in this area (Bullfrog Creek) was used as a foundation in building the Tampa Bay Hotel (now the University of Tampa).

Sparkman and Ybor Channels

North of the charted Peter O'Knight Municipal Airport on Davis Island, the Sparkman Channel breaks off to the north and runs along its deep way to Ybor Turning Basin and Ybor Channel. All these waters are extremely commercial and are very reminiscent of East Bay, discussed above. Again, while the commercial shipping makes for some unforgettable sights from your cockpit, there are no facilities nor anchorage possibilities for pleasurecraft.

Marjorie Park Yacht Basin

The small marina known as Marjorie Park Yacht Basin occupies the tadpole-shaped cove making into the eastern banks of Davis Island off Seddon Channel. Two slips at the fuel dock are usually available for transients, and additional space is sometimes offered when resident craft are away from their home slips.

Would you believe that this meager ration is now the only non-yacht-club, transient dockage currently available in all of Tampa? Things can sure change in a few years.

Marjorie Park's slips are well sheltered and feature fixed, concrete piers with 7- to 10-foot depths alongside. Most slips for resident craft have freshwater and power connections up to 50 amps, but sometimes power hook-ups can be a bit hard to come by in the transient spaces. Gasoline (only) can be purchased at the fuel pier.

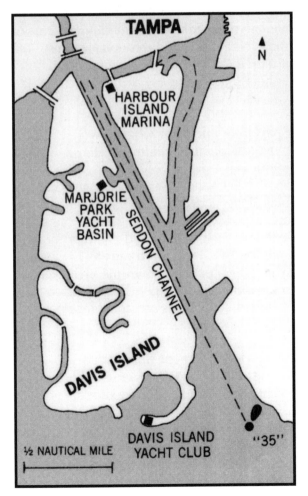

Shoreside, visiting cruisers will not find any showers or a laundromat. On the plus side, a whole host of businesses on charming Davis Island is within walking distance. Patrons of these firms will quickly discover that this community has a far more small-town atmosphere than nearby Tampa.

Cruisers interested in dining ashore will find a host of choices. Rick's Italian Restaurant (214 E Davis Boulevard, 813-253-3310) is excellent, and Pink Flamingo Cafe (210 E Davis Boulevard, 813-251-2928) is open for breakfast and lunch. Other good choices are Estela's Mexican Restaurant (209 E Davis Boulevard, 813-251-0558) and 220 East (220 E Davis Boulevard, 813-259-1220). Galley restocking is made ever so convenient by the close proximity of Davis Island Grocery (304 E Davis Boulevard, 813-251-1928). There is also a convenience store nearby.

Future plans call for the expansion of Marjorie Park Yacht Basin by the city of Tampa. If and when these schemes come to fruition the harbor will be enlarged and a ship's store, showers, laundromat, diesel fuel, and on-site restaurant will be added. The onset of new construction is uncertain at the moment, but our information suggests that the improvements are some time off.

Marjorie Park Yacht Basin (813) 259-1604

Approach depth—8-20 feet
Dockside depth—7-10 feet
Accepts transients—yes (2 slips usually open)
Fixed concrete piers—yes
Dockside power connections—30-50 amp
Dockside water connections—yes
Gasoline—yes
Restaurant—several nearby

Harbour Island Marina

Until recently, transient dockage in

downtown Tampa was reasonably easy to come by, courtesy of the huge Harbour Island development. Located at the southeastern corner of the intersection between Seddon and Garrison channels, this complex has now fallen on hard times. The dockmaster's office has been closed, all the furniture removed, and the phone disconnected. My ace researcher, Morgan Stinemetz, looked in vain for the better part of a day for someone (anyone!) who could give any information whatsoever about the complex's wet slips. Both of us have struck out in this regard. For all practical purposes, Harbour Island Marina is now closed, and even though there are plenty of open slips, it is likely that no one is currently repsonsible for this dockage.

Adding insult to injury, the impressive monorail that used to connect Harbour Island to downtown Tampa is being destroyed at the time of this writing. Many of the shops in the adjacent retail complex have closed, and the three remaining restaurants can only be described as "low end."

It is always sad for us to note the passing of any marina facility, but the demise of Harbour Island is particularly unfortunate. As it now stands, a visit to downtown Tampa by water-borne tourists is really rather difficult. Until the marina portion of the Harbour Island development can enjoy some sort of renaissance, we no longer recommend that visiting cruisers attempt to berth here. Let's hope the future brings on better times.

Garrison Channel

The Garrison Channel cuts north of Harbour Island and spans the gap between the Seddon and Sparkman channels. Unfortunately this deep cut is spanned by two low-level fixed bridges and is unusable by all but very small powercraft.

Upper Hillsborough River

While dockage facilities are at a minimum and there is no opportunity to anchor, a cruise on the Hillsborough River north of Harbour Island is accessible to boats that can clear a 40-foot fixed bridge. There are also several other spans with restricted opening schedules with which you must contend. The huge skyscrapers are a sight indeed, but you may just think you have been transported back to the times of the Arabian Nights after passing under the John F. Kennedy Boulevard (Highway 60) Bridge. The famed thirteen silver minarets of the Tampa Hotel (now the University of Tampa) overlooking the western banks are a sight you will never forget.

The Radisson Riverside Hotel maintains a face dock between the 15-foot Brorein bascule span and the John F. Kennedy Boulevard Bridge along the eastern shore. Depths at dockside run 5 to 7 feet. No overnight stays are currently allowed, but it is possible to moor here temporarily while dining at one of the hotel's several fine restaurants.

North of the 15-foot bascule bridge, downtown Tampa's skyscrapers are a mammoth presence overlooking the eastern banks. The architecture is striking, to say the very least.

Mariners cruising down the course of the upper Hillsborough River will spy a host of hand-painted college logos along the concrete seawalls. Before long you will divine that these have been painted by crew racing teams from colleges all over the country. Apparently the University of Tampa uses this portion of the river for its crew races. If one of these contests should happen to be scheduled during your visit, you should make every effort to attend this exciting event.

North of the John F. Kennedy Boulevard Bridge, passing cruisers can't miss the minarets of the old Tampa Bay Hotel/ University of Tampa to the west. Of all the sights and attractions in downtown Tampa, this massive building was the most unforgettable for this writer.

This guide's coverage of upper Hillsborough River ends at the railroad bridge upstream from the university. The river is now dammed at 30th Street and all boating traffic is barred from the stream's upper reaches.

HILLSBOROUGH BAY NAVIGATION

As with the eastern shoreline of lower Tampa Bay, successful navigation of Hillsborough Bay is very much facilitated by the presence of the large ship's channel. Pleasurecraft of any size and draft can easily follow this waterborne interstate highway to Tampa and the Hillsborough River. Then, it's only a matter of keeping anywhere near the mid-width for good depths.

Outside of the ship's channel, Hillsborough Bay is mostly deep, though some shoals are in evidence. Not all of these shallows are marked and fixed-keel sailcraft must keep a current position at all times through dead-reckoning or whatever means available. There are also some shallows abutting the eastern flank of the ship's channel. Most of these are north of the Alafia River. Be sure to keep well away from these hazards.

On to the Alafia River Follow the Cut C Channel north from its intersection with Cut A. Pass flashing buoy #13 to its easterly quarter and continue north by passing between flashing buoys #15 and #16.

North of #15 and #16, the channel runs near the first of the hollow spoil islands east of the marked track. This body of land will appear much more substantial from the water than you might think from a cursory examination of chart 11413.

After passing unlighted nun buoy #20 to its westerly quarter, the Alafia River Channel makes in from the east.

The Alafia River The main Alafia River Channel is child's play to navigate as far as the phosphate factory perched on the stream's northerly shores. The 20-plus feet of water and numerous beacons have been erected to guide the considerable commercial shipping that serves the plant. Pleasureboaters can take advantage of these excellent aids to navigation as well. Shallow water does border a portion of the deep cut, particularly near the river's entrance, so stay alert and follow the markers unless you intend to make one of the side trips detailed below.

The north-side anchorage behind the large spoil island can be reached by abandoning the river's entrance channel at flashing daybeacon #7. Cut to the north and set course to come abeam of the spoil island's southeasterly tip some 150 yards off the point. Drop anchor well short of the charted circular island to the north. This small land mass is surrounded by shoal water.

Cruisers who continue cruising north behind the spoil island should stay at least 150 yards to the east of both the large spoil island and the smaller (charted) round island just north of the anchorage reviewed above.

Should you decide to do so, good water can be held all the way to a point abeam of the island's northeastern tip. *Don't* attempt to cut to the west and rejoin the big ship's channel, north of the spoil island. In spite of some reports you may have heard to the contrary, depths of 4 feet or less block this passage.

Cruisers choosing the delightful Bird Island anchorage should depart the main channel about halfway between flashing daybeacons #6 and #8. Slow to idle speed and feel your way carefully south with your sounder. You will be trying to discover a dredged but unmarked (and uncharted) channel across the bar south of the main cut. On sunny, clear days, the deeper depths can be spotted from the darker color of the water. In low-light or poor visibility conditions, proceed with the greatest caution.

Once past the unmarked bar channel, continue almost due south until you are at least 100 yards past the southwestern tip of Bird Island, well east of your course line. Carefully curve your track around to the east and point to come behind the western half of Bird Island, at least 100 yards to your northerly side. Don't approach the island more closely or proceed too far to the east into the charted 2-foot waters.

Skippers continuing east into the interior reaches of the Alafia River should proceed at slow speed. The river channel east of flashing daybeacon #7 is a manatee zone. Please do your part to help preserve this unique creature of Floridian waters.

Very shallow water abuts both sides of the main channel east of unlighted daybeacons #9 and #10. Stay strictly in the channel and keep a careful watch over your stern to make sure lateral leeway is not easing you onto the surrounding shoals.

You will enter the westerly mouth of the Alafia River after passing between unlighted daybeacons #13 and #14. Daybeacon #13 is located hard by the northern banks, but depths seem more than adequate.

East of flashing daybeacon #15 your course will take you into the deeply dredged turning basin associated with the phosphate plant. Not that you would, but don't even think about anchoring here.

Instead, look east and find unlighted daybeacons #16 and #18. You will spy #16 almost on the southerly banks. For best depths, pass almost midway between these two aids, favoring #18 slightly. In spite of the 3-foot sounding shown on chart 11413, on-site research revealed that 5½ feet of water can be carried over this bar. Farther to the east, the waters deepen to 7- and 9-foot levels. As the small park and public launching ramp come abeam to the north, consider dropping the hook well short of the fixed bridge and the charted power line. It goes almost without saying that this is the end of the line for sailcraft.

A stone's throw to the east, Alafia River is spanned by a fixed bridge with 28 feet of vertical clearance. There is also a power line set 33 feet above the water. East of the bridge, expect typical 5-foot depths. Mariners who make it this far will spot Inter Bay Boat Moorings on the southern shoreline.

On Hillsborough Bay Captains cruising north past the Alafia River Channel should pass between flashing buoys #21 and #22.

Ignore the charted channel to the west. This cut serves as a crash channel for MacDill Air Force Base. Ponder *that* for a second as you pass. A second was about as long as this writer could stand to think about it.

Tampa Yacht & Country Club   Mariners visiting the Tampa Yacht Club's well-sheltered basin must take into account the presence of a concrete riprap breakwater just east of the harbor's entrance. While this man-made feature serves to blunt sharp chop that might otherwise enter the club's basin, woe to the navigator who tries to go straight into the harbor entrance from Hillsborough Bay. Instead, set course from flashing buoy #25 to bring your craft to a point 100 yards north of the Ballast Point harbor. As you approach the shore, you will see a long pier jutting out into the river. Do not approach this dock. It is founded in shoal water. Instead, look for the yacht club's markers making off to the southwest. These markers will lead you easily into the sheltered basin.

Long Shoal   Sailors leaving the large ship's channel and cruising the mostly deep waters to the north and west must take great care to avoid Long Shoal. This clearly charted hazard is located due north of the MacDill crash channel (see above). Its limits are outlined by two aids to navigation, unlighted daybeacons #1 and #2. Stay away from #1 at all costs. It is founded in extremely shallow water, with oysters lining the bottom.

Davis Island Yacht Club   Captains and crew visiting this fine club and its sheltered basin can depart the ship's channel at flashing buoy #23. Set a careful compass course to pass between Long Shoal to the west and the charted spoil bank west of flashing buoy #31. You must eventually follow a long, slow curve to the northeast to come around the spoil zone and cruise towards the basin's entrance. Enter the "Seaplane Basin" by avoiding the starboard-side point. From here on, you need only avoid the water immediately adjacent to the shoreline for good depths.

Northwestern Hillsborough Bay Remember that cruising on this shoal-plagued stretch of the bay is not particularly recommended for cruising-size craft. If you should choose to ignore this advice, be mindful of the large shoal southwest of Davis Island. On-site research revealed that this hazard is correctly charted on 11413. Also, note the shoals west of Davis Island's southwesterly reaches.

Farther to the north, depths decline to 5-foot levels. While some good water continues to flank Davis Island's western banks, there are a multitude of uncharted shallows farther to the west. Two low-level fixed bridges span the charted passage to Seddon Channel above Davis Island. These bridges have 13 feet and 9 feet of vertical clearance, respectively.

North on Hillsborough Bay   As you approach flashing buoy #28 on the Cut C Channel, switch to the Tampa Inset section of chart 11413. The blown-up scale of this inset gives far better details of East Bay and the channels leading north to the Hillsborough River and Tampa.

East Bay   North of flashing buoy #28, the Tampa large ship's channel divides. The Port Sutton Channel leads northeast into East Bay. Shallow water abuts Hookers Point to the north. Be sure to stay well south of flashing daybeacons #1 and #3 to avoid this shoal. Flashing buoy #5 should be passed well to its southeasterly quarter. Continue to avoid the northwesterly banks as the bay sweeps around to the north. From this point very deep water stretches out almost from shore to shore as far as the 40-foot fixed bridge. Don't forget to hold your nose.

Wild-eyed captains who insist on entering McKay Bay *must* remember the power lines with only 32 feet of vertical clearance immediately northeast of the fixed spans. If (and only if) you can clear the 40-foot bridge and the lines, cruise straight out into McKay Bay, setting course for the water body's mid-width. Cease your forward progress at least 100 yards short of the second set of charted power lines.

Cut D Channel   The Cut D Channel swings to the northwest from its intersection with the Cut C and Port Sutton channels towards Tampa. This channel initially borders on a small park and the Peter O'Knight Municipal Airport along its southwesterly banks. There is a public boat-launching ramp along this track. Larger power vessels should slow to idle speed when passing.

While you would just about have to be asleep at the helm to run aground on Cut D, tidal currents do run quite swiftly through this section. Sailcraft should proceed under auxiliary power and single-screw trawlers should be ready for quick course changes.

Cut D soon leads to a fork. The Sparkman Channel strikes to the north and leads to the Ybor turning basin and channel. A small band of shallows flanks the eastern shores of Harbour Island along the Sparkman Channel, but otherwise the waters are quite deep until Ybor Channel comes to a dead end well to the north.

Seddon Channel flows to the northwest and is the straight course to downtown Tampa. No-wake regulations are in effect from the Sparkman Channel intersection to Marjorie Park Yacht Basin. This small facility will come up on the southwestern banks of Seddon Channel at the charted "CG" (Coast Guard) station. Cruise into the marina on the centerline of its entrance.

Mariners who continue following the Seddon Channel will soon spy the condos and private docks associated with the Harbour Island development on the northeastern banks. Powercraft must again slow to idle speed.

Garrison Channel   Two fixed spans having only 10 feet of vertical clearance cross the Garrison Channel, north of Harbour Island. Only small powercraft can use this cut-through as a short cut between the Harbour Island facilities and Ybor Turning Basin.

The Hillsborough River   Those skippers who choose to continue north on the Hillsborough River and visit downtown Tampa must contend with a bevy of bridges. There is also a charted shoal abutting the northeastern corner of Davis Island. Stay away from this point or you could land in three feet of water.

After passing the Garrison Channel intersection, look towards the northeastern shore for a close view of downtown Tampa's performing arts center. You can scarcely ignore its mammoth, columned facade.

The charted channel striking back to the southwest, north of Davis Island, plays host to some slips for resident craft, but no transient services are available. On-site research failed to reveal the charted bubble of 3-foot water on this stream's mid-width. Apparently, dredging has now removed this obstacle. The passage is soon blocked by a fixed bridge with 9 feet of vertical clearance.

Moving north on the Hillsborough River, the first bridge encountered will be a bascule span with 15 feet of closed vertical clearance. All the non-fixed bridges on the Hillsborough River have the same restrictive opening schedule. From 9:00 A.M. to 4:30 P.M., Monday through Friday, and from 8:00 A.M. to 6:00 P.M., Saturdays, Sundays, and legal holidays the spans open only on the hour and half-hour.

Next up are twin fixed bridges with 40 feet of vertical clearance. These spans are followed closely by a second 15-foot bascule bridge. Past this span, the river crooks to the northwest and moves on towards the 11-foot (closed clearance) John F. Kennedy Boulevard bascule bridge. Once under this bridge, passing cruisers will spy the famous minarets of the old Tampa Bay Hotel to port.

The track is eventually blocked by a 7-foot railway bridge. Our account of the Hillsborough River ends here, though small powercraft can continue upstream for quite some distance.

Old Tampa Bay

Even though it is several times larger than Hillsborough Bay, Old Tampa Bay is certainly the least desirable body of water in the Tampa region for cruising purposes. The upper 75 percent of the bay is spanned by three long, fixed bridges which have vertical clearances ranging from 40 to 44 feet. Obviously, many sailcraft will have to forego cruising the majority of Old Tampa Bay due to these height restrictions. While two marinas south of the southernmost span do cater to cruising craft, there are no other significant facilities on the bay. There are a few anchorages to be found on some of the sidewaters along the way, but none of these was particularly appealing, at least to this writer. For these reasons, Old Tampa Bay is rarely frequented by visiting cruisers.

It should be noted that the shoreline is, for the most part, less developed than that of upper Hillsborough Bay and, if you can clear the bridges, the bay can make for a good afternoon sail. Nevertheless, one can only conclude that Old Tampa Bay is not Western Florida's most cruising-rich body of water.

Our discussion of Old Tampa Bay will begin with a review of the marinas and anchorages south of Gandy Bridge (the southernmost span), covering both shorelines. We will then begin a travelogue north of Gandy

Bridge and follow the western shoreline around to the bay's northerly reaches and descend south again by way of the eastern banks.

Industrial Canal

North of flashing buoy #2K, the large ship's channel running north to Old Tampa Bay splits. The northeasterly fork is known as Cut K Channel and provides the best access for cruising-size craft to the bay's upper reaches.

Cut K leads directly to a deep, charted canal that strikes east into Interbay Peninsula. While this cut has excellent 25-foot-plus depths, it is quite commercial in nature and more than slightly noisy. It might be possible for pleasurecraft to anchor here overnight (if you should have enough anchor rode for a proper scope), but this writer does not recommend it. If you prefer to drop the hook, I suggest the Snug Harbor anchorage reviewed below.

Power Plant Channel

The well-outlined channel cutting to the northwest north of flashing buoy #2K leads to a coal-fired power plant. The plant can be located by its bevy of charted stacks east of Masters Bayou. While, as you would expect, there are no facilities for pleasurecraft, nor even anchorage possibilities, a portion of this cut does make a good approach to South Gandy Channel and Masters Bayou, reviewed below.

South Gandy Channel & Masters Bayou Facilities and Anchorage

The South Gandy Channel runs hard by the southern flank of the long causeway leading from the western shores of Old Tampa Bay to Gandy Bridge. This fairly well marked cut leads to Masters Bayou, home of a couple of repair yards catering to pleasurecraft. There is also one sheltered spot to anchor for those cruisers with a bit of risk taking in their blood.

Gandy Channel holds minimum depths of 6 to 6½ feet, with typical soundings in the 10- to 19-foot range. While most of Masters Bayou is quite shallow, a deep cut (for the most part) follows the western and northern banks well upstream. A series of private markers helps keep you to the good water. Shallow water abounds on both sides of Gandy Channel and the Masters Bayou cut. Caution is certainly called for.

West of unlighted daybeacon #5, the first of Masters Bayou's facilities will come up along the northerly banks. Gandy Bridge Marina (727-576-5117) is a mostly small-craft facility that does offer bait, tackle, gasoline, and a small variety store. The adjoining docks are rented out on a month-to-month basis, and are not appropriate for larger, cruising craft.

Next up is NOA Marine (727-576-9315). This repair yard offers complete mechanical and below-waterline repairs. The firm's travelift is rated at a 60-ton capacity. All wet-slip dockage is reserved for service customers.

First Chance Marine (727-725-8600, formerly Cruising World Marina) guards the northern banks in the crook of Masters Bayou (just as the stream's channel turns sharply to the south). This facility no longer offers any services for transients. It is now primarily a small powercraft sales agency.

South of First Chance, the Masters Bayou Channel meanders to the south and eventually cuts back to the west. Soon after you traverse this westward bend, you will see the docks of Viking Boatworks (727-576-1094) overlooking the northern shore. Depths alongside run around 8 feet. This friendly yard offers full-service mechanical (gas and diesel), electrical, and below-waterline, haul-out repairs. Twenty-four-hour emergency servicing is also available. Viking's travelift can lift up to 70 tons. There is a large parts department in the yard as well. Talk about a can-do attitude, the management at Viking has informed this writer that there "isn't anything we can't do." All wet-slip dockage is reserved for service customers.

After leaving the Viking yard behind, Masters Bayou opens out into a baylike body of water known as Snug Harbor. Most of the bay's waters are quite shallow, but there is one fortunate exception. Notice the charted bubble of 12-foot water (on 11413) just west of the point where the channel is briefly squeezed between a peninsula to the south and the mainland to the north. On-site research reveals there is enough swinging room for boats up to 38 feet to anchor in 11-foot depths. Protection is superb from all winds except westerly blows exceeding thirty knots. The bay's northern shores are bordered by private docks and attractive homes. You will sight several sunken derelicts sitting on the charted shoals to the south. Be *sure* to anchor well north of the old wrecks.

Interbay Peninsula Facilities

North of unlighted can buoy #11K (an aid on the Cut K Channel), cruisers can follow a broad band of deep water running roughly parallel to Interbay Peninsula. This passage eventually leads to the Gandy Bridge pass-through, but two facilities of note are found south of the span.

Study chart 11413 for a moment and notice the large Y-shaped canal cutting east into Interbay Peninsula, south of Gandy Bridge.

A new facility known as Tampa Bayside Marina (813-831-5757) is set to open at the time of this writing, on the waters south of the peninsula, which lines the southern banks of the Y-shaped canal. Even though chart 11413 shows only 3 feet of water adjacent to this shoreline, there is actually a deep channel here that was used, until recently, by deep-draft tugs.

Initially Tampa Bayside Marina will be pretty much a high-dry storage operation with sales of gasoline and diesel fuel. Future plans call for the construction of transient wet slips, a waste pump-out station, showers, ship's store, bait and tackle shop, and on-site restaurant. We wish this new pleasurecraft marina well and hope that we will be able to report on its many new services available to cruising craft in the next edition of this guide.

The northern fork of the Y stream plays host to Imperial Yacht Center. This facility boasts row upon row of covered slips in a very well protected harbor. Obviously, these berths are only suited for powercraft, unless some sailor were to go through the arduous job of mast removal.

According to our conversation with the marina's manager, "transients are very welcome." Berths are found at fixed wooden piers featuring water and 30-50-amp power connections. Dockside depths at the northern slips are an impressive 8 to 10 feet, while some 5-foot soundings are found on their southerly counterparts. Entrance depths in the canal are 15 feet or better.

Gasoline, diesel fuel, and waste pump-out are all readily available. As a matter of fact, Imperial claims to have "the cheapest fuel in the area." A well-stocked ship's and parts store is located in the complex, and a newly refurbished convenience-type variety store is now found in the dockmaster's office just behind the dockage basin. There is also a fairly large powercraft sales operation on the premises, featuring small- to medium-sized vessels. Full mechanical and haul-out repairs (75-ton travelift) are offered.

Jimmy Mac's restaurant (813-839-3449) is found just south of the Imperial Yacht Center dockage basin, within easy walking distance. It is set in an old Florida style building with a metal roof, and outside dining overlooking the water is available on the wraparound porch. The menu is heavy into sandwiches and seafood. You might also consider taking a taxi ride into nearby Tampa for many additional dining options. In short, Imperial Yacht Center is a large, full-service operation that can meet just about any conceivable need of the powercruiser.

Imperial Yacht Center (813) 832-2628
http://www.ij.net/yacht

Approach depth—15 feet minimum
Dockside depth—8-10 feet (northern slips)
                        5-8 feet (southern slips)
Accepts transients—yes
Fixed _covered_ slips—yes
Dockside power connections—up to 50 amp
Dockside water connections—yes
Waste pump-out—yes
Gasoline—yes
Diesel fuel—yes
Mechanical repairs—yes
Below-waterline repairs—yes
Ship's store—yes
Restaurant—nearby

Cross Bayou Canal

The smallish stream known as Cross Bayou Canal cuts into the southwestern shores of Old Tampa Bay above the W. Howard Franklin Bridge, west of the charted St. Petersburg/Clearwater Airport. This stream features minimum depths of 6 feet along its poorly marked entrance channel to a point

abeam of the squared-off, charted harbor on the eastern banks. You must also be able to clear a 45-foot, charted power line spanning the creek's entrance to reach this harbor. _Sailors take note!_ Be sure to read the Cross Bayou Canal navigational section presented later in this chapter before attempting the creek for the first time.

The square cove harbor is the surprising home of a good-size dining and retail complex lining the northern banks. Boat Yard Village has been built to resemble an old commercial fishing community, with rusty tin roofs and graying timbers. A number of restaurants are complemented by a host of gift shops and other businesses.

Boat Yard Village does not offer much in the way of dockage. The few fixed wooden piers in evidence were mostly occupied by several resident craft during our visit. There might be room for one thirty-footer amidst the 7- to 8-foot dockside depths, but many larger craft will want to anchor off and dinghy in to the complex.

Low-water depths at the harbor's entrance run from 4½ to 5 feet, but 6 to 8 feet of water is found on the cove's interior reaches. Protection should be first-rate from all winds. This wouldn't be a bad place to ride out heavy weather, except that it's well off the beaten path.

Allen Creek

The small and winding stream known as Allen Creek makes off from Old Tampa Bay's westernmost reaches northwest of Cross Bayou, and almost due south of the charted "Penthouse," which is actually only one of the many high-rise condos overlooking the banks along this portion of the bay. To reach this body of water, your craft must be able to clear the charted bridge spanning the westerly lobe of Old Tampa Bay west of Cross Bayou. Vertical clearance is set at 47 feet for this fixed bridge.

Allen Creek features some markings and minimum depths of 6 feet, with typical soundings running from 7 to 8 feet. Care is still necessary to keep to the deep water and avoid the surrounding shoals. The stream eventually wanders to the west and meets up with the docks and dry stack storage building of Gulfwind Marine of Clearwater (727-536-2628). This is a boat sales facility, which made it very clear to this writer that no transient services are available. This lack of dockage, plus the absence of room for anchorage, will probably relegate this creek to those captains doing business with Gulfwind.

Safety Harbor Anchorage

Only the wild-eyed captains among us will be drawn to the possible anchorage on the northernmost section of Old Tampa Bay known as Safety Harbor. Unmarked shoals are everywhere in evidence, and it's all too easy to wander into 1 to 2 feet of water, even when you are trying to be cautious.

The entrance to Safety Harbor is spanned by a charted power line with 98 feet of vertical clearance. For once, this particular electrical conduit is useful. It can serve as one of the only navigational points of reference on upper Old Tampa Bay.

If you somehow bypass all the shoals, boats of most sizes can anchor off Philippe Point in 7 to 10 feet of water. Depths are shallower than those shown on the current edition of chart 11413, but still more than adequate, at least outside of the shoals. Shelter is good for light to moderate winds only. Strong blows from the north or south would be particularly uncomfortable.

Philippe Point is the site of a park bearing the same name. Its green shores are attractive and restful, and one of the old Indian mounds has been preserved in the park. Its position is actually noted on chart 11413. You may catch sight of a large church from the water, sitting just behind the park. The east-side banks are overlooked by moderate residential development.

North of Philippe Point, depths begin to rise markedly, in spite of the soundings noted on 11413. The stream is soon blocked by a low-level fixed bridge. This writer suggests that cruising boaters discontinue their explorations once abeam of Philippe Point.

Safety Harbor History   Philippe Park is named for Count Philippe, a doctor in the French Navy who was captured during Colonial times by pirates. The outlook for the Count's longevity was dim indeed until an epidemic of yellow fever struck the band of marauders. His ministrations were so appreciated by the pirates that they give him a map of Tampa Bay, describing it as "the most beautiful body of water in the world." Count Philippe established a large plantation on the shores of Safety Harbor on the site of the park that today bears his name. It is said that he later introduced the first grapefruit to Florida here. This writer has also heard that claim for a plantation on the St. Johns River, however. In any case, it is fitting that the modern-day name of Philippe Park commemorates the name of this early Floridian pioneer.

Culbreath Bayou

The charted U-shaped channel southeast of the W. Howard Franklin Bridge, on the bay's eastern banks, is actually much more obscure than it appears on 11413. On-site research found that many of the markers were missing and those that were in place were low and hard to spot. As we have grown to expect, this channel leads only to small canals lined by private homes and docks, with one exception. East of unlighted daybeacon #12, the eastward-flowing creek divides into two northern branches. The westernmost of these two streams hosts a series of docks that are used by local sailcraft and are under the management of Imperial Yacht Center. No transient services of any type are available and the docks are unattended. Cruisers would do far better to call on the main site of Imperial Yacht Center south of Gandy Bridge.

Four Finger Creeks

Southwest of charted Sunset Park (on Interbay Peninsula), four creeks comprise what appears to be a four-fingered hand cutting east into the shoreline. Our on-site research discovered two pilings marking an entrance channel into these creeks with minimum 6½-foot depths. Unfortunately even the two middle streams, the largest of the quartet, are too small for anchorage by all but petite power vessels under 28 feet. All four of the streams are lined by heavy residential development and private docks. So, for all their promise on chart 11413, these four creeks are probably best avoided by the visiting cruiser.

OLD TAMPA BAY NAVIGATION

Navigation of Old Tampa Bay is, shall we say, interesting. North of Gandy Bridge, there are essentially *no* aids to navigation outlining the preferred channel, or the surrounding shoals, for that matter. While a few side channels display some low-key markers, you must often hunt carefully for these with your binoculars. Captains cruising on Old Tampa Bay must practice sound navigation and keep a running check of their position at all times.

South of the Gandy span, the situation is very different. Two big ship and barge channels allow pleasurecraft reliable access to the marina facilities on Masters Bayou and Interbay Peninsula.

As mentioned at the beginning of this section, skippers who choose to cruise the upper reaches of Old Tampa Bay must be able to clear three fixed bridges with vertical clearances of as little as 40 feet. Transiting southernmost Gandy Bridge is

not too complicated, but both the W. Howard Franklin and the Courtney Campbell Parkway spans are quite long and often require a lengthy cruise just to reach the raised pass-throughs.

A broad shelf of shoal water extends out for a goodly distance from most of Old Tampa Bay's shoreline. Navigators who lose track of their current position are all too likely to meet up with this underwater obstruction.

Strong northerly winds that blow for several days can lower water levels on Old Tampa Bay below charted levels and those soundings discussed below. While this is not too likely, it might be best to check on conditions at Imperial Yacht Center if breezes are blowing strongly from the north upon your arrival.

The various creeks and sidewaters reviewed below can only be described as fair to prohibitive. This is quite simply not the place to take your 55-foot Hatteras, or even a 35-foot Pearson.

Entrance into Old Tampa Bay Cruisers following the Cut F, big ship's channel should take the westward-running Cut G Channel north of flashing buoys #7F and #8F. At flashing buoy #10J, the marked passage takes a 90-degree turn to the north and becomes the Cut J Channel. Avoid the charted spoil banks east of the channel between flashing daybeacon #12J and flashing buoy #4K. These are some of the few spoils on Tampa Bay which are shallow. On-site research revealed that depths can run to as little as 4 feet.

North of flashing buoy #2K, the channel splits. The northwesterly fork runs on to a coal-fired power plant and can be used by pleasurecraft bound for the facilities or anchorage on Masters Bayou and the South Gandy Channel. The northeasterly passage is known as the Cut K Channel. This passage provides access to Tampa Bayside Marina, Imperial Yacht Center, and the pass-through on Gandy Bridge. This is the route to take if you are bound for the bay's northerly reaches. We shall first review the power plant channel, followed by a discussion of Cut K and points north.

Masters Bayou/South Gandy Channel
From flashing buoy #2K, cut northwest into the power plant channel, pointing to pass between flashing buoys #1 and #2. Continue following the well-marked track until you are just short of passing between flashing buoys #9 and #10. Leave the power plant channel at this point and set a careful course to come abeam of the easternmost aid on the South Gandy Channel, unlighted daybeacon #1, by some 100 yards to its easterly quarter. Be on guard against the correctly charted tongue of 3- and 4-foot water extending south from #1. Also note the shoals well east of #1.

As you make your approach to #1, the two charted radio towers will be quite visible on the causeway leading to Gandy Bridge. These huge antennae make excellent landmarks, but remember that they are well west of #1.

Once abeam of #1, turn sharply west and point to pass #1 by some 15 yards to its northerly side. Past #1 the channel remains well marked to unlighted daybeacon #5. There is shallow water *both* north and south of the marked cut, so watch your stern in order to quickly note any leeway.

Once abeam of #5 (to its northerly side), there are no further markers short of the Masters Bayou entrance. It is still a fairly lengthy run between #5 and the creek's mouth. This portion of the channel certainly calls for caution. Believe it or else, on-site research revealed that best depths are maintained by favoring the southern side of the channel *slightly* between #5 and the bayou's entrance. While there is certainly shallow water to the south, there seems to be a broad shelf of shoals extending out from the northern banks.

After coming abeam of the south-side entrance point, begin immediately favoring the *northern banks* as you head into the stream's interior reaches. You will first pass the small docks of Gandy Bridge Marina, followed by NOA Marine and First Chance

Marine. Soon thereafter the creek cuts sharply south.

Moving upstream on Masters Bayou, the channel is outlined by pilings with arrow pointers. For the most part, the deep water runs along the western and then northern banks, though there is one spot where an oyster bank runs off the western shore. A piling with an arrow marker warns cruising craft away from this hazard.

Eventually the stream turns back to the west. You will spot Viking Boatyard at this point. West of the yard, favor the northern banks as the stream is squeezed between an undeveloped island to the south and the mainland to the north. Soon the water opens out into a bay. Continue cruising west for 50 to 75 yards past the island. You should spot several sunken boats just west of the island and south of the channel. Be sure to cruise past (upstream and to the west of) these old wrecks before attempting to turn south and anchor. Feel your way south carefully with your sounder. Be sure to drop the hook well before coming abeam of the sunken vessels to your eastern side. The trick is to cruise only as far from the northern banks as is necessary to leave enough swinging room to comfortably anchor. Cruising farther to the south invites a nighttime session on the southern shoals.

Imperial Yacht Center and Passage to Northern Old Tampa Bay From flashing buoy #2K on the Cut J-2 Channel, bend your course to the northeast and point to pass between flashing buoys #3K and #4K on the Cut K Channel. This passage is easy to follow as far as flashing buoy #10K. At this point, the deep industrial canal runs east into Interbay Peninsula. If you should make the questionable decision to enter this highly commercial area, do so on the stream's mid-width.

To continue north, point to pass unlighted can buoy #11K to its immediate easterly side. You can then set course to pass the forward, lighted Cut K range marker to its fairly immediate westerly side. This maneuver will avoid the shallows to the east. While they do not come too close to your track, be aware of the charted shoals to the west as well.

From the forward range marker, set course to come abeam of the rear lighted range marker by some .3 nautical miles to its westerly quarter. This course will lead you away from the charted "subm piles" (submerged pilings).

Once abeam of the rear range marker, you can either set course for the mid-width of the eastward-running canal leading to Imperial Yacht Center (on the southeast side of Gandy Bridge), or point for the Gandy twin span pass-through. The Gandy Bridge passage has a vertical clearance of 43 feet. Sometimes sustained northerly winds can increase this clearance, but it's best not to count on more than 43 feet.

On Old Tampa Bay As there are no real anchorage opportunities or viable gunkholes for cruising-size craft on either shore between Gandy and W. Howard Franklin bridges, most captains will want to set course for the charted pass-through of the Franklin span. This track does not really lead near any water shallower than 10 feet.

The closest shoal water is found on the charted tongue of shallows running north-northeast from the northern quadrant of the west-side causeway, leading to Gandy Bridge. It would take a big-time course error to find the bottom here.

The W. Howard Franklin Bridge has a vertical clearance of 44 feet. Sailors who happen to tack a bit to the east or west on the broad bubble of deep water south of this span may be in for a long trek back to the raised section of the bridge.

After leaving the W. Howard Franklin Bridge behind, navigators must begin to concern themselves with the huge tongue of shallow water to the west. Those bound for Safety Harbor can set a direct course for the 40-foot pass-through of the Courtney Campbell Parkway Bridge to the north-northwest. Even small, outboard craft should avoid the charted 10-foot span on this bridge's western reaches. On-site research revealed that depths can run to 2 feet just north of this opening.

Cruisers headed for either Cross Bayou Canal or Allen Creek may want to set course for the privately maintained but charted (16-foot) flashing daybeacon #A. From #A you can cut west to either stream.

Cross Bayou Canal Set course to come abeam of the northerly tip of the charted jetty running out from the St. Petersburg/Clearwater Airport by some 100 yards to your southerly side. Once this point is abeam, cut south and aim to keep the point of land some 50 yards off your port side. A series of charted, unlighted daybeacons will help you keep to the good water. Pass between these aids and then head directly for the mouth of the creek.

The bridge crossing this portion of Old Tampa Bay has its southerly terminus along the shoreline several hundred yards west of Cross Bayou's entrance.

Sailors are again reminded of the 45-foot power line crossing the northerly portion of Cross Bayou Canal. Compare your mast height and make your decision accordingly.

Continue holding to the mid-width as you cruise into Cross Bayou Canal. Begin watching the easterly banks for the entrance to the harbor, overlooked by the fishing village complex. Cruise into the harbor on the centerline of its entrance as well. The best water is found abeam of the complex's docks, with somewhat shallower depths abutting the southerly shores.

Further upstream exploration on Cross Bayou Canal past the harbor junction is not recommended for larger vessels. Our prop found the bottom while trying to explore the stream's southerly reaches.

Allen Creek There is one problem in cruising to Allen Creek. The charted tongue of shoal water running south from the westerly limits of Courtney Campbell Causeway is apparently building out. We noticed that it seems to have thrust its way much farther south than you might think. One nondescript pile is the sole aid marking this hazard. Set your course so as to stay well south of these shallows.

Captains must cruise under the fixed, high-rise bridge, east of the creek. Vertical clearance is set at 47 feet.

After leaving the long shoal and the bridge behind, work your way west to the Allen Creek Channel. Approach the entrance carefully, watching for two small, triangular markers. Pass these aids to your *starboard* side and an unadorned piling to your port. Continue cruising down the centerline of the creek. Soon you will spy an old, semisunken barge to port which sports a goodly growth of bushes and small trees.

Eventually the stream takes a hard jog to starboard. The piers and buildings of Gulfwind Marine will then be visible dead ahead, while a huge concrete-and-glass office building will be prominent to starboard.

On to Safety Harbor The entrance to Safety Harbor is flanked by huge shoals to the east and west. The shallows running south from Booth Point, east of the harbor's entrance, are particularly impressive. To avoid these potential grounding zones, slant your course to the northwest after passing through the Courtney Campbell Parkway Bridge and point to eventually pass between unlighted can buoy #1 and unlighted nun buoy #2. Be mindful of the shallows extending well south from Booth Point north of your course track.

Once between #1 and #2 cut back to the north-northeast just a bit and set course to come abeam and pass unlighted nun buoy #4 to its fairly immediate westerly quarter. You can then point for the middle of the five huge power poles marching across Safety Harbor's southerly entrance. These lines have a 98-foot vertical clearance.

Watch the depth finder as you cruise along. If your soundings start to rise above 8 feet, slow down and make corrections before grounding depths are reached.

Cruise past the center power pole and hold scrupulously to the centerline of the bay as you move along to the north. Drop anchor as Philippe Point comes abeam to the west. Farther passge to the north is not particularly recommended in light of the extensive charted but unmarked shoals abutting both shorelines and extending far out into the bay.

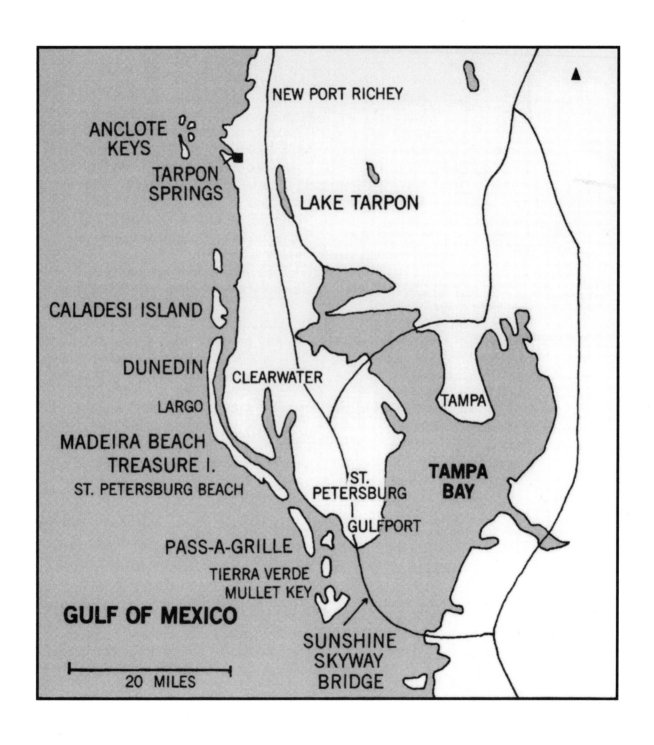

NEW PORT RICHEY

ANCLOTE KEYS

TARPON SPRINGS

LAKE TARPON

CALADESI ISLAND

DUNEDIN

CLEARWATER

TAMPA

LARGO

MADEIRA BEACH
TREASURE I.
ST. PETERSBURG BEACH

ST. PETERSBURG

TAMPA BAY

GULFPORT

PASS-A-GRILLE

TIERRA VERDE
MULLET KEY

GULF OF MEXICO

SUNSHINE SKYWAY BRIDGE

20 MILES

CHAPTER 5

Boca Ciega Bay to Tarpon Springs

Okay, class, now listen up. It's time for your weekly nautical pop quiz. What 36-statute-mile section of the Western Florida ICW plays host to almost 50 marinas and boatyards sitting side by side with more anchorages than you can imagine? Well, if you guessed the heavily developed section of the Waterway between the northern reaches of Tampa Bay's entrance and Anclote Key, then go to the head of the class.

This is truly an amazing section of the Waterway. If you have not traveled this stretch before, you are in for an unforgettable experience. Never before have we seen such an incredible selection of pleasurecraft facilities crowded into such relatively few miles. With the exception of isolation, if you can't find it here, better give up.

The ICW leaves Tampa Bay and the Sunshine Skyway behind and enters the southerly reaches of broad Boca Ciega Bay. Two alternate passages lead cruisers north past the lower bay's complicated islands and peninsulas. To the west, Pass-A-Grille Inlet offers a reliable passage to the Gulf of Mexico.

Farther to the north, the Waterway runs between beach-side barrier islands displaying a level of development which can only be described as a concrete jungle, and the far more attractive mainland St. Petersburg shoreline. A host of marinas waits to greet cruising craft along the St. Petersburg waterfront. Johns Pass Inlet, near the city's northerly limits, provides another dependable seaward access point.

After transiting a canal-like passage known, appropriately enough, as "The Narrows," the ICW spills into broad Clearwater Harbor. Now the heaviest development shifts to the mainland shores. If there is a more built-up community anywhere than Clearwater, I haven't found it. Of course, the Gulf barrier islands also support a heavy population. Facilities run the full gamut and are available on both shorelines. Yet a third Gulf passage, Clearwater Pass, is reliable and convenient for all types of pleasurecraft.

Finally the ICW begins to leave all the heavy development behind as it enters the broad waters of St. Joseph Sound. Some portions of the ICW channel through St. Joseph Sound display low-water depths of as little as 6 feet, or sometimes slightly less. Deep-draft vessels take note.

Anclote Key heralds the northerly terminus of the Western Florida ICW. The nearby Anclote River and the absolutely delightful village of Tarpon Springs make a great jumping-off point or port of arrival from the wide-open waters of the Big Bend to the north.

With the exception of the overnight refuges around Anclote Key and one haven near Tierra Verde, almost all the ICW anchorages north of Tampa Bay are overlooked by a variety of developed shores. While some may yearn for the peace and serenity of Pine Island Sound, there are still plenty of sheltered spots to ride out even the nastiest weather for those who prefer to swing on the hook rather than tie up to the dock.

In short, while those among us who enjoy backwater cruising may not be totally taken with this stretch of the Western Florida ICW, there is no denying that it has more to offer than can be imagined. Take your time, watch out for all the restricted bridges and no-wake zones, and enjoy your cruise.

Charts Most navigators will need only one chart for the complicated waters between northern Tampa Bay and Tarpon Springs. A few cruisers will also want the offshore chart detailing these waters.

11411—large-scale chart providing excellent detail of the Waterway route and the various inlets along the way from Boca Ciega Bay to Anclote Key; also includes the Anclote River to Tarpon Springs

11412—covers all the offshore waters between Tampa Bay and Anclote Key

Bridges

Isla Del Sol/Alternate Channel Bridge—crosses alternate Boca Ciega Bay channel north-northwest of flashing daybeacon #11 and Frenchman Creek—Fixed—18 feet

Pinellas Bayway southern "E" span—crosses ICW at standard mile 113, northwest of unlighted daybeacon #39—Bascule—25 feet (closed)—opens on the hour and every 20 minutes thereafter 9:00 A.M. to 5:00 P.M.—at all other times opens on demand

Pinellas Bayway northern "C" span—crosses ICW at standard mile 114, north of unlighted daybeacon #25—Bascule—25 feet (closed)—opens on the hour and every 20 minutes thereafter 7:00 A.M. to 7:00 P.M.

Mud Key Channel Bridge—crosses Mud Key Channel immediately south of the Pass-A-Grille Yacht Club—Fixed—14 feet

Corey Causeway Bridge—crosses ICW at standard mile 118, northwest of unlighted daybeacon #39—Bascule—23 feet (closed)—opens on the hour and every 20 minutes thereafter 8:00 A.M. to 7:00 P.M. weekdays and 10:00 A.M. to 7:00 P.M. weekends and holidays

Treasure Island Causeway Bridge—crosses ICW at standard mile 119, north of flashing daybeacon #14—Bascule—8 feet (closed)—opens on the hour and every 15 minutes thereafter 7:00 A.M. to 7:00 P.M.—11:00 P.M. to 7:00 A.M., only opens with 10 minutes' notice

Long Bayou/Seminole Bridge—crosses Long Bayou north of unlighted daybeacon #31—Fixed—20 feet

Johns Pass Bridge—crosses interior reaches of Johns Pass, west-southwest of flashing daybeacon #6—Bascule—25 feet (closed)—opens on demand

Welch Causeway Bridge—crosses ICW at standard mile 123—Bascule—25 feet (closed)—opens on the hour and every 20 minutes thereafter 9:30 A.M. to 6:00 P.M. weekends and holidays—at all other times opens on demand

Park Boulevard Bridge—crosses ICW at standard mile 126, north of unlighted daybeacon #12 in the heart of "The Narrows—Bascule—25 feet (closed)—opens on demand

Indian Rocks Beach Bridge—crosses ICW at standard mile 129, northwest of flashing daybeacon #33—Bascule—25 feet (closed)—opens on demand

Belleair Bridge—crosses ICW at standard mile 132, north-northeast of flashing daybeacon #47—Bascule—21 feet (closed)—opens on the hour and every 15 minutes thereafter noon to 6:00 P.M. weekends and holidays—at all other times opens on demand

Clearwater Pass Bridge—crosses Clearwater Pass west of flashing daybeacon #14—Fixed—74 feet

Clearwater Memorial Causeway Bridge—crosses ICW at standard mile 136, north-

northeast of unlighted daybeacon #13—Bascule—25 feet (closed)—opens on the hour and every 20 minutes thereafter 9:00 A.M. to 6:00 P.M. weekdays and on the hour and half-hour 2:00 P.M. to 6:00 P.M. weekends and holidays—at all other times opends on demand

Mandalay Channel Bridge—crosses Mandalay Channel just north of the Clearwater Municipal Marina—Fixed—14 feet

Dunedin/Honeymoon Island Bridge—crosses ICW at standard mile 142—Bascule—24 feet (closed)—opens on demand

Boca Ciega Bay to Treasure Island

The Western Florida ICW splits into two alternate branches near the northern tip of the causeway leading to the Sunshine Skyway Bridge. Both routes soon lead into the broad southerly mouth of Boca Ciega Bay. This large body of water is split, fractured, and subdivided by bridges, causeways, man-made islands, and islets. It's all too easy to become confused, so take your time and keep chart 11411 at hand.

The mainland shores of Boca Ciega are part of St. Petersburg, while the Gulf-side barrier islands consist of the abundant beach development so typical of the entire run from Tampa Bay to Anclote Key. All this variable landscape is not necessarily bad news for cruisers. Anchorages abound, even if few are of the isolated variety. Marinas are dotted here and there all along the way. Many are large, first-rate operations which cruisers can make use of with full confidence that they will find every imaginable service.

All in all, we enjoyed this section of the ICW. Even with its copious development, there are a host of opportunities to get off the Waterway and explore. What better recommendation can there be for any true cruiser?

The Split (Standard Mile 111)

At flashing daybeacon #26, skippers northbound on the Western Florida ICW meet a very definite parting of the ways. The primary Waterway channel cuts west and then northwest through the broad mid-width of southern Boca Ciega Bay. An alternate passage for those boats which can clear an 18-foot fixed bridge swings to the north. Assess your craft's requirements and the on-the-water conditions carefully before choosing your route.

We shall first review the many cruising opportunities of the alternate channel, followed by the side trips, anchorages, and marinas of the principal Waterway passage via Pass-A-Grille and Tierra Verde. After the two routes rejoin, we will follow the ICW to Treasure Island Causeway.

Alternate ICW Channel (Standard Mile 111)

Powercraft that can ease under an 18-foot fixed bridge without scraping their flybridge might well choose the alternate route running north, east of Indian Key. Not only is this passage far more sheltered than the primary Waterway channel, it also offers easy access to several first-rate marinas and two anchorages. Even sailors can take advantage of the anchorages and one marina, as these points of interest are both thankfully located well south of the fixed span.

The first and possibly the best anchorage on the alternate route is found on the correctly charted ribbon of deep water east of unlighted daybeacon #4. This channel skirts between the mainland shores to the east and a patch of shallow water to the west. Minimum depths of 10 feet are held in the unmarked channel. The banks to the east give excellent protection when winds are blowing from this quarter, while Indian Key to the west gives some protection from moderate westerly breezes. There is even some shelter to the north, courtesy of Maximo Point. A strong southerly wind clearly calls for an ongoing search elsewhere. Swinging room should be sufficient for most sizes and types of pleasurecraft. The shores to the north are only lightly developed, but you may be bothered by traffic entering and leaving the Sunshine Skyway during the night.

The marked passage to O'Neill's Marina will be spied on the eastern banks, east of flashing daybeacon #6. This facility accepts transients on a space-available basis. Call ahead of time to check on slip availability. Low-water entrance depths are in the 5- to 6-foot range, while dockside soundings run from 5½ to 7 feet. Berths are provided at fixed, wooden piers with 30-amp power and freshwater hook-ups. The harbor is well sheltered from inclement weather. Mechanical repairs are available for gas-powered engines only. Smaller vesssels can be hauled out by way of a new 8-ton powerlift. Gasoline (no diesel fuel) can be purchased and there is a combination variety store and bait and tackle shop on the premises. The one on-site shower is adequate but not climate controlled.

O'Neill's Marina (813) 867-2585

Approach depth—5-6 feet (minimum)
Dockside depth—5½-7 feet

Accepts transients—space-available basis
Fixed wooden piers—yes
Dockside power connections—up to 30 amp
Dockside water connections—yes
Shower—yes
Gasoline—yes
Mechanical repairs—gas engines only
Variety store—yes

Frenchman Creek cuts the northeastern banks of the alternate channel between unlighted daybeacons #7 and #9. This stream leads under two fixed bridges with 18 feet of vertical clearance to Huber Yacht Harbor (727-867-2117). Approach depths run some 6½ to 8 feet with 5½ to 8 feet of water dockside. While this facility does not take transients for overnight dockage, complete repair and fueling services are readily available. Haul-outs are accomplished by a 70-ton travelift.

The northern shores of Frenchman Creek below (before reaching) the fixed bridges and Huber Yacht Harbor play host to a collection of docks associated with nearby Eckerd College. While there are no services for visitors, cruisers will be interested to observe the bevy of small craft pulled up on the shore. Powercraft should be alert for small boats in the creek.

Some boats occasionally anchor in the charted deep water west-southwest of unlighted daybeacon #9. While minimum depths run in the 5- to 6-foot region, there is absolutely no protection from fresh westerly breezes, and strong easterly winds are none too welcome either. In northerly and southerly breezes, Indian Key to the south and the islets to the north do give some protection, but even so you wouldn't catch this writer here if winds were forecast to exceed 10 knots. If the weather chooses to cooperate, there is plenty of swinging room for most craft. The undeveloped sands of Indian Key to the south make a delightful backdrop.

North of the 18-foot fixed bridge, the alternate channel follows a well-marked passage out into a wide and mostly deep eastward-striking lobe of Boca Ciega Bay. No fewer than two first-class marinas and one yacht club are found on the easterly reaches of this body of water.

Before we go on to discuss these facilities in depth, let us take a moment to note that southbound cruisers on the ICW can easily reach these marinas via the northern leg of the alternate channel, *without having to suffer the 18-foot bridge.* Thus, the facilities described below are readily accessible to sailcraft as well as to their powered brethren.

It is quite possible to follow the broad path of deep water north and west of flashing day-beacon #15 to a large yacht club guarding the northern shores of Isla del Sol. The passage features minimum 8-foot depths at least as far as the marina, with most soundings being considerably deeper. This facility will be detailed in the discussion of the main Waterway channel later in this chapter.

The charted canal cutting into Boca Ciega's southeastern shores leads fortunate cruisers to Maximo Marina. This facility's location can be identified by the "Boathouses" designation on chart 11411. If you are looking for a marina that satisfies most needs that might arise for cruising craft (and who isn't?), then your search is finished. Set your course for Maximo Marina, sit back, and enjoy.

Minimum entrance depths of 8 feet are coupled with very impressive dockside readings of 10 to 15 feet, surely enough for even the longest-legged sailcraft. Transients are enthusiastically accepted at both fixed wooden and (somewhat older) floating docks.

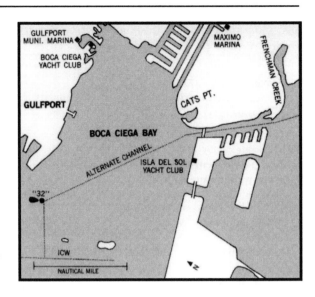

The harbor is extremely well sheltered and would make an excellent haven to ride out heavy weather. The marina features 330 wet slips (with both fixed, wooden and some new floating wooden decked piers) and 320 dry-storage slots. The management claims to offer the largest selection of covered slips on the Sunshine State's western coastline. We would certainly not argue with that contention. Every conceivable dockside power and water connection is readily available, as are diesel fuel, gasoline, and waste pump-out service. Full mechanical repairs are featured and haul-outs are quickly accomplished by a 50-ton trav-elift. There are three sets of shoreside showers, with the central unit featuring air conditioning. There is also an on-site laundromat with a small paperback exchange library, and a new bait and tackle shop. A branch of the impressive Johnny Leverocks Restaurant chain (727-864-3883) is close at hand and the marina has a small ship's store. A "West Marine" store (727-895-3098) is also found within easy walking distance of the dockage basin. All in all Maximo must be rated as a good find for visiting cruisers, and one you will want to check out.

Maximo Marina (727) 867-1102
    http://www.maximomarina.com/maximo-marina.htm

Approach depth—8½-11 feet
Dockside depth—10-15 feet
Accepts transients—yes
Fixed wooden and floating docks—yes
Dockside power connections—up to 50 amp
Dockside water connections—yes
Waste pump-out—yes
Showers—yes
Laundromat—yes
Gasoline—yes
Diesel fuel—yes
Mechanical repairs—yes
Below-waterline repairs—yes
Ship's store—small
Restaurant—on site

Now, just in case that's not quite enough to attract you to Boca Ciega's easterly reaches, there is yet another notable marina and yacht club to be found on the upper reaches of the charted channel entering the bay's northeasterly reaches (near Clam Bayou). As you cruise through the marked channel with minimum depths of 7½ feet, the protected harbor of Boca Ciega Yacht Club will come abeam to port. Believe me, you can't miss it. The clubhouse is also quickly spotted, just east of the harbor. We found one 5½- to 6-foot lump at the entrance to the club harbor, but otherwise dockside depths range between 7 and 9 feet. The docks are of the fixed wooden variety and feature modern power and water connections. Groceries, supplies, and several restaurants are found within a mile of the clubhouse. This friendly club is glad to accept overnighters if (and only if) prior arrangements have been made. Longer term

dockage is not available. Transient slip space is limited and is usually at a premium during weekends. Be sure to call the club's dockmaster at the number listed below well ahead of time. If there is any way that the club can accommodate you, it will do all in its power to meet your needs.

Boca Ciega Yacht Club (727) 321-7295
    http://www.sailbcyc.org

Approach depth—5½-6 feet (minimum)
Dockside depth—7-9 feet
Accepts transients—limited (prior arrangements necessary)
Fixed wooden piers—yes
Dockside power connections—up to 30 amp
Dockside water connections—yes
Restaurant—several within walking distance

Gulfport Municipal Marina occupies the well-sheltered dockage basin at the channel's northeasterly limits. This fine and friendly municipal marina welcomes overnighters and provides berths at new, fixed concrete piers. The city dockmaster suggests that visiting captains call ahead and make advance arrangements. Cruisers will find the harbor crowded with a beautiful collection of sleek sailcraft and a few powerboats to round out the bill. Depths alongside run 8 feet or better. Since the last edition of this guide went to press, the dockage basin has been completely rebuilt, and the new berths are better than ever. Waste pump-out service has also been added.

Fresh water, 30-50-amp power, cable television, and telephone connections are found at each berth. Shoreside amenities include new, air-conditioned showers and a well-stocked ship's and variety store. Gasoline and diesel fuel can be purchased, and some mechanical repairs can be arranged through independent local contractors. Five restaurants are located within a long, long walk of the docks. One of the best choices is La Cote Basque (727-321-6888), a French-style dining spot.

Gulfport Municipal Marina (727) 893-1071

Approach depth—7½-8 feet (minimum)
Dockside depth—8-10 feet
Accepts transients—yes
Fixed concrete piers—yes
Dockside power connections—up to 50 amp
Dockside water connections—yes
Waste pump-out—yes
Showers—yes
Gasoline—yes
Diesel fuel—yes
Mechanical repairs—yes (independent local
  contractors)
Ship's and variety store—yes
Restaurant—long walk

Mariner's Cove Marina (727-321-5792) guards the bay's northern shores at facility designation #9 on chart 11411. This small operation is engaged exclusively in the dry storage of smaller powercraft and no facilities except gasoline are available to the cruising boater. Meager entrance depths of only 4 to 4½ feet will restrict even gasoline purchases to small, shallow-draft vessels.

North of the bay's marinas, the alternate channel eventually cuts to the west and rejoins the principal ICW route at flashing daybeacon #32. Our discussion will now return to the official ICW passage, beginning at the split with the alternate channel on the southerly reaches of Boca Ciega Bay.

ICW to Pass-A-Grille

The ICW channel sweeps sharply west from its intersection with the western Tampa Bay and alternate Boca Ciega Bay channels on its way to the Pinellas Bayway "E" Bridge. This is an open passage where fresh winds have more than enough fetch to foster an unwelcome chop.

Shortly after you pass through the Pinellas span, northwest of flashing daybeacon #21, the extensive piers of Tierra Verde Marina (Standard Mile 113) will come abeam to the southwest. This (yet again) friendly marina has an impressive array of convenient dockside and shoreside services. Tierra Verde Marina gladly accepts transients at its modern, fixed wooden piers. There are currently 84 wet slips, and a dry-storage building housing 343 powercraft is also available. Depths alongside are an impressive 9 to 10 feet or better. As you would expect, all dockside power and water connections are provided, as are gasoline, diesel fuel, and waste pump-out service. The pump-out charge is $5.00. One adequate, non-climate controlled shower is available shoreside. Cruisers will also be happy to learn that the retail complex sitting just behind the piers contains a convenience variety store, a large boat-rental agency, and the Island Oasis Restaurant (727-867-0100). There is also a bait and tackle shop among the offerings. A tiki-style, open-air bar overlooks the dockage basin. Full mechanical repairs for both gasoline and diesel engines are available through Tierra Verde Marina. Boats as large as 35 feet can be hauled via the dry-storage facility's forklift. In addition to the on-site restaurant, several other dining choices are within walking distance. Ask the friendly dockmaster or his staff for a recommendation.

About the only negative aspect of Tierra Verde Marina is its relative openness to wind, wave, and strong tidal currents. Strong northerly and southerly blows, in particular, can be a problem at the piers, which lack breakwaters. During normal weather, this aspect of the marina should not be too great a problem.

Tierra Verde Marina (727) 866-0255
http://www.lakewaymarina.com/tierraverde/

Approach depth—15+ feet
Dockside depth—10-25 feet (10 feet directly against seawall)
Accepts transients—yes
Fixed wooden piers—yes
Dockside power connections—up to 50 amp
Dockside water connections—yes
Waste pump-out—yes
Shower—yes
Gasoline—yes
Diesel fuel—yes
Mechanical repairs—yes
Restaurant—on site and several nearby

Pass-A-Grille Inlet and Associated Channels (Standard Mile 113.5)

Southwest of flashing daybeacon #24, a broad swath of deep water leaves the ICW and runs south and west towards reliable Pass-A-Grille Inlet. This cut is used on a regular basis by a host of local pleasurecraft and it can be relied upon to provide reliable access to and from the open waters of the Gulf of Mexico. Most markers are clearly charted, a sure sign of a stable seaward cut.

Marina and repair yard facilities are available on the tongue of deep water cutting north from flashing daybeacon #11, and a marina of note is found on the Tierra Verde Canal, south of flashing daybeacon #10. Oh, so you prefer to anchor out? Well, the most isolated (but navigationally difficult) haven short of Clearwater Harbor is to be found on the so-called South Channel, south of #10. Does that whet your appetite? Then read on.

Pass-A-Grille Beach and Facilities

The southerly tip of the barrier island flanking Pass-A-Grille Inlet's northerly flank is known as Pass-A-Grille Beach. We felt a noticeable change for the better when visiting this community. A far less frenzied, small-town atmosphere is coupled with these shaded, quiet neighborhoods than that found in boisterous St. Petersburg Beach to the north. Most cruisers will welcome this change and will want to spend some time in this community which thankfully has been overlooked by the minions of concrete and steel.

North of flashing daybeacon #11, deep water runs along the westerly banks to a fixed bridge with 14 feet of vertical clearance. Two small marinas and a boatyard overlook the westerly shores between #11 and the bridge. The first of these is found near the 8-foot sounding designation north of #11.

Merry Pier Marina consists of a single fixed wooden T-shaped dock which sits in an exposed position near Pass-A-Grille Beach Channel's southern foot. Overnighters are accepted, but if winds are forecast to exceed 10 knots (particularly from the south), this writer advises you to seek shelter elsewhere. During one of our on-site research trips, a moderate southerly breeze was enough to raise a chop at the pier which would not only disturb your evening's rest, but make docking hazardous as well. I suspect that most of the local captains use this pier as a fuel and supply stop and berth their craft at another marina.

Gasoline, diesel fuel, and a medium-size ship's and variety store are available on the pier.

Probably the best reason to tie up to Merry Pier is found just across the street, at the notable Sea Horse Restaurant (727-360-1734). The bill of fare is a bit on the simple side, but we have consistently found everything on the menu to be superb. The grouper sandwiches, by any account, are wonderful.

Merry Pier Marina (727) 360-6606

Approach depth—8-15 feet
Dockside depth—8-16 feet
Accepts transients—limited
Fixed wooden piers—yes
Dockside power and water connections—yes
Gasoline—yes
Diesel fuel—yes
Ship's and variety store—yes
Restaurant—across the street

Next up is the small dockage basin of Pass-A-Grille Marina (727-360-0100). This facility features a large, metal dry-storage building which is highly visible from the water. There are also 15 wet slips on site, but the marina management has informed this writer that these berths are filled "99 percent of the time" by resident craft. Besides fuel (gas and diesel) and small-craft mechanical (outboard and I/O) repairs, visitors will find few services here.

Tiny Warren's Marina flanks the westerly banks, immediately south of the 14-foot fixed bridge. This small but friendly establishment occasionally (read that as "rarely") takes overnight dockers at its very low, fixed wooden piers. Clearly service work is the forte here. Full mechanical repairs are supplemented by a do-it-yourself or leave it to be done (your choice) haul-out yard. The facility's travelift is rated at a 12-ton capacity. Warren's is a family-owned business, and we found the staff to be in touch with the needs of cruising craft.

If you should happen to obtain dockage, some low-key power and water connections are available. Several restaurants are within an easy jaunt.

Warren's Marina (727) 360-1784

Approach depth—8-15 feet
Dockside depth—7-8 feet
Accepts transients—very limited

Fixed wooden piers—yes (unusually low)
Dockside power and water connections—limited
Mechanical repairs—yes
Below-waterline repairs—yes
Restaurant—several nearby

Captains cruising north from Warren's are soon greeted by a fixed bridge with only 14 feet of vertical clearance. Pass-A-Grille Yacht Club is found north of this span. Sailboats and taller powercraft can reach this facility via Mud Key Channel to the north (reviewed later in this chapter).

While this club does not employ a regular dockmaster, members of other clubs with reciprocal agreements are accommodated for a maximum three-day stay. Advance reservations are required. Lunch and dinner are served Tuesday through Sunday (lunch only on Sunday) in the well-appointed dining room (reservations requested).

The docks consist of modern, fixed wooden piers which feature impressive depths of 9 to 10 feet at the outer slips, while 6 to 7 feet of water can be held alongside the inner harbor docks. Power connections up to 50 amps and water outlets are ready at hand. Retail and grocery stores are within walking distance, as are several additional restaurants. The harbor is well sheltered from all but the heaviest weather.

Pass-A-Grille Yacht Club (727) 360-1646
  http://www.pagyc.com

Approach depth—8-15 feet
  (via Pass-A-Grille Beach Channel)
        5½-11 feet
  (via Mud Key Channel)
Dockside depth—6-10 feet (deeper depths on outer face dock)
Accepts transients—members of clubs with reciprocal agreements

Fixed wooden piers—yes
Dockside power and water connections—yes
Showers—yes
Restaurant—on site (and several others nearby)

Tierra Verde Resort Marina and Canal

Another excellent marina is found on the northeasterly terminus of the Tierra Verde canal, whose entrance cuts the island southeast of flashing daybeacon #10 (on the Pass-A-Grille Inlet channel). This stream can also be accessed by the smaller charted canal southeast of unlighted daybeacon #14 (near Tierra Verde Island's northwesterly tip), but this passage is crossed by a low-level fixed bridge. Most cruising-size craft will need to make use of the unencumbered stream southeast of #10.

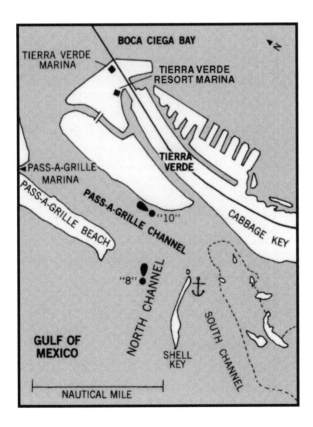

The canal's entrance from the Pass-A-Grille Channel is well marked. Minimum depths at the entrance are some 6-8 feet, improving to 10-19 feet on the stream's interior reaches. Heavy residential development overlooks both shores. This is obviously the high-rent district. Many of the houses have swimming pools and private docks. The *huge* powercraft usually moored at these piers are incredibly impressive. Yards look as if the yardman lives on the premises. But wait—the best is yet to come.

Northeast of the canal's intersection with its small, northwesterly sister, cruisers will soon catch sight of a mammoth collection of both power and sail yachts ahead. This is your first sight of Tierra Verde Resort Marina.

First of all, it doesn't take a nautical genius to quickly discern that this is one of the most sheltered harbors you will ever find. If really nasty weather is in the forecast, you couldn't do better than quickly coil your lines at this marina and batten down the hatches.

The marina itself is associated with a low-rise hotel, condo complex, and an on-site restaurant plus bar. Transients of every description are accepted for overnight or temporary dockage at fixed concrete (and some wooden) piers set atop wooden pilings. Every conceivable power, water, telephone, and cablevision connection is to be found at all slips. Dockside depths of 8 to 12 feet are enough for even the deepest-draft sailboat. Gasoline, diesel fuel, and waste pump-out services are readily available, and mechanical repairs can be arranged through nearby Tierra Verde Marina. For those who want to take a break from the live-aboard routine, shoreside lodging is close at hand. The on-site Waterside Sports Bar and Grill and Fort DeSoto Joe's Restaurant is excellent, if a bit pricey. Both indoor and outdoor dining are featured.

Transients are afforded the use of the large swimming pool, tennis courts, and hot tub. Good, air-conditioned showers are found at two different locations in the marina complex. A recently refurbished laundromat is, as you would expect, part of the package. A tiny ship's and variety store is found in the dockmaster's office. The grounds are immaculately manicured. The green, green grass and waving palms are definitely recommended for those who have seen one too many steep waves.

Tierra Verde Resort Marina (727) 866-1487
http://www.tvresortmarina.com

Approach depth—8½-19 feet
Dockside depth—8-12 feet
Accepts transients—yes
Fixed concrete and wooden piers—yes
Dockside power connections—up to 50 amp
Dockside water connections—yes
Waste pump-out—yes
Showers—yes
Laundromat—yes
Gasoline—yes
Diesel fuel—yes
Mechanical repairs—yes
Ship's and variety store—yes
Restaurant—on site

South Channel Anchorage

Many local cruisers make frequent use of the unexpected anchorage on the charted south channel running (would you believe) south from the principal Pass-A-Grille Inlet cut (south of flashing daybeacon #10). While a study of chart 11411 would probably discourage most strangers from entering this seemingly wayward passage, on-site research revealed a very different picture *for boats that draw 4 feet or preferably less.*

In the first place, the charted marsh designated as "The Reefs" on 11411 is actually much more substantial than it would appear.

Visitors will discover a large grass savanna, punctuated here and there by some higher ground. This combination of earth and greenery actually gives pretty good protection from southerly winds.

Even more promising is the anchorage found off the crescent-shaped beach, just inside the easterly tip of the long, thin sand island known as Shell Key, well southwest of flashing daybeacon #10. While (in spite of soundings shown on 11411) you must run through one patch of 4½-foot waters when rounding the point, it is quite possible to anchor some 25 yards off the beach in 6- to 8-foot depths. Protection is good from northerly winds and fair from southern breezes. Nevertheless, this is clearly not a heavy-weather anchorage and if a hard blow is in the forecast, retreat to one of the nearby marinas and wait for fair winds.

Once the anchor is down, it's then a simple matter to imitate the locals and dinghy ashore to explore the beautifully unspoiled white sand beaches.

Cautious skippers can explore South Channel past the anchorage. Many local anglers apparently fish this stretch regularly. While the channel is broad and deep for a goodly distance to the south and southwest, please remember that the unmarked cut is surrounded by shoal water, and it eventually peters out entirely.

Mud Key Channel (Standard Mile 114)

Let us now return our attention to the principal ICW passage as it begins its approach to the northern leg of the Pinellas Bayway Bridge (also known as the Pinellas Bayway "C" bridge), well north of flashing daybeacon #24. Immediately south of the span, cruisers can easily enter charted Mud Key Channel. While offering an anchorage possibility in its own right, this cut allows access to Pass-A-Grille Yacht Club for craft which cannot clear the 14-foot fixed bridge at the channel's southern foot.

Minimum depths on the channel are around 6 feet, with typical soundings in the 8- to 11-foot region. The entire passage is surrounded by heavy, but not visually displeasing residential development. There are one or two tricky spots along the way, so be sure to read the navigational information presented later in this chapter before making your first entry.

As you cruise down the main body of Mud Key Channel, the tall, pink tower of the beautifully restored Don CeSar Hotel (727-360-1881) will be readily spotted to the northwest.

Recalling the days of Florida's golden age, when only the rich and powerful regularly visited the Sunshine State, this edifice has been a mariner's landmark for many a year. The tall building is noted on chart 11411 as "Hotel." While the Don CeSar does not have any dockage of its own for cruising visitors, a close approach to the structure is described in the next subsection below.

Boats up to 38 feet and drawing no more than 4 feet can drop the hook at the mouth of the first southward-striking canal near Mud Key Channel's entrance from the ICW. As you ease into this sidewater, one patch of 5-foot depths will be encountered, followed by 6- to 11-foot soundings. Farther to the south, the side canal narrows far too much for anchorage, and depths become uncertain. This haven has excellent protection from all winds save exceptionally strong easterly blows.

Big McPherson Bayou (Standard Mile 114)

For my money, the best anchorage short of Clearwater Harbor is found on the channel cutting into the Waterway's western banks, just north of the Pinellas Bayway Bridge (northern "C" half). Big McPherson Bayou leads to not one, but two magnificent havens with a plenitude of shelter from any weather short of a hurricane.

The entrance portion of the channel is unmarked and somewhat tricky, but elementary caution should see you into the deeper interior reaches with minimum 8-foot depths.

The first and best spot to anchor is found at the mouth of the first stream that comes abeam to the northeast. Boats of most sizes will find plenty of elbow room. Just be sure to pick your spot carefully to avoid swinging into the correctly charted shallows to the south

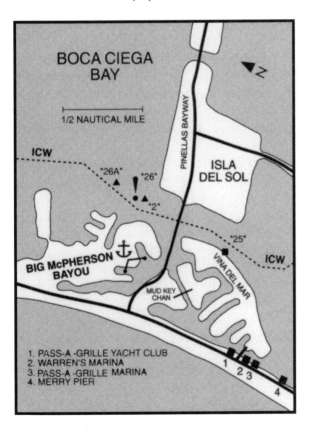

and southwest. The starboard shore of this offshoot has fairly heavy, but attractive residential development, while the port-side banks are only sparsely built up at this time. All in all, this is one of the most superb anchorages you will find along this developed portion of the Waterway.

Boats up to 34 feet may also choose to drop the hook in the charted 7- and 9-foot cove farther to the northwest. This delightful sidewater is surrounded by attractive homes and features almost perfect shelter.

From both anchorages, the tall, pink tower of the Don CeSar Hotel looms over the shallow western banks. No dockage facilities are available for pleasurecraft, but if you are of a mind, break out the dinghy and go ashore at one of the undeveloped portions of the western shoreline. Please don't trespass! It would be a memorable experience indeed to dine ashore at the Don CeSar. Reservations are most certainly recommended and this would definitely be the time to dig out the old navy blazer. Just be sure to brush off the mold and mildew first.

Isla del Sol Yacht and Country Club (Standard Mile 114.5)

A wide and deep channel runs east from unlighted daybeacon #2 (south of flashing daybeacon #26) and skirts the northern shores of artificial Isla del Sol. This cut eventually intersects the alternate ICW channel, discussed earlier in this chapter, near flashing daybeacon #15. While minimum 8-foot depths, with soundings running as deep as 25 feet, can be held all the way from the ICW to the alternate channel, the passage is unmarked and should be run with care.

The extensive piers of Isla del Sol Yacht and Country Club will come abeam to the south

about halfway between the ICW and flashing daybeacon #15. This facility has reverted to its former status as a private yacht club which only accepts visitors who are members of other clubs with appropriate reciprocal privileges. Advance reservations are definitely recommended by this writer. The Isla del Sol Yacht Club is associated with a large country club, golf course, and condo development. Visitors will find berths at fixed wooden piers featuring all power and water connections. The harbor is mostly breakwater-enclosed, a definite plus in this area, and dockside depths are an unusually deep 10 to 20 feet. Shoreside facilities include showers, a laundromat, and an attractive boaters' lounge. There is a small strip-type retail shopping center within walking distance. Visitors can use the tennis courts, swimming pool, golf course, and club dining room. Several other alternate restaurants are within walking distance.

Isla del Sol Yacht and Country Club (727) 867-3625

Approach depth—8-25 feet
Dockside depth—10-20 feet
Accepts transients—members of yacht clubs with reciprocal privileges only
Fixed wooden piers—yes
Dockside power connections—up to 50 amp
Dockside water connections—yes
Showers—yes
Laundromat—yes
Variety store—nearby
Restaurant—on site and several nearby

St. Petersburg Beach Anchorage

The charted deep water between the two artificial islets, southwest of unlighted daybeacon #33, offers a sheltered overnight anchorage unless winds of over 15 knots are blowing from the east. Minimum depths of 6 feet can be held by scrupulously holding to the mid-width at the entrance to the cove. East of the charted shallow water at the rear of the cove, typical soundings range from 6 to 10 feet. There is plenty of swinging room for even the largest pleasurecraft. Surprise, surprise—the surrounding shores feature heavy development with barely a space between the various buildings and houses.

Corey Causeway Facilities
(Standard Mile 117.5)

Southeast of Corey Causeway Bridge (northwest of unlighted daybeacon #39), a few low-key facilities are available along the westerly banks. The most promising is yet another branch of Johnny Leverocks Seafood Restaurant (727-367-4588). This dining spot maintains a face dock fronting onto the Waterway's southwestern banks, just southeast of the bridge. There should be room for a boat as large as 50 feet to moor alongside. Dockside depths range from 10 feet at the outer pier to some 6 feet nearer the seawall. Visiting cruisers are welcome to tie up while dining, but no overnight dockage or other marine services are available.

One small hotel offers a few low-level docks on the charted branch of deep water sweeping south, on the western shores of the large cove that is southeast of Corey Causeway. While Bay Palms Motel (727-360-1754) allows guests to dock their boats here, the piers are obviously only appropriate for smaller craft. Cruising captains would do well to look elsewhere.

Blind Pass Marina and Inlet
(Standard Mile 118)

Blind Pass Marina is screened off from the Waterway by a high-rise condo building

southwest of flashing daybeacon #9. It is a simple matter nevertheless to follow the deep water around the northern point of the peninsula southwest of #9 and work your way back towards the low-level fixed bridge to the south. Soon the extensive fixed wooden piers of Blind Pass Marina will come abeam on the eastern banks. This facility offers transient dockage, though there are currently only 3 to 4 slips open for this purpose, and these can only handle certain sizes and drafts of pleasureboats. The dockmaster suggests calling ahead of time and checking on availability.

Dockside power and water connections are very much in evidence, and the docks are well sheltered from all but strong southerly winds. One adequate, non-climate controlled shower and an air-conditioned laundromat with a large paperback exchange library are

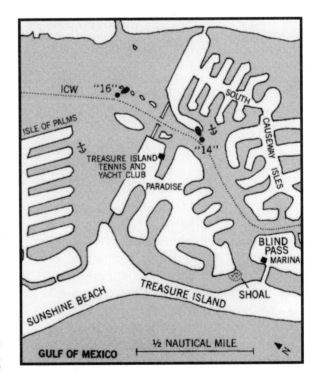

available shoreside. Waste pump-out service (scheduled for an upgrade in early 2001) is also offered.

The on-site restaurant at Blind Pass is now closed. A hunt is currently under way for a new tenant. In the meantime, cruisers docking at this marina can walk across the street to Groupers Restaurant (9524 Blind Pass Road, 727-367-9000). Our conversation with several fellow cruisers seemed to indicate that the food here "is not half-bad."

Further passage south past the marina to Blind Pass Inlet is blocked by a low-level fixed bridge with only 11 feet of vertical clearance. This is not really objectionable as the inlet is shoal and quite unsafe.

Blind Pass Marina (727) 360-4281

Approach depth—9-11 feet
Dockside depth—6-8 feet
Accepts transients—yes (somewhat limited)
Fixed wooden piers—yes
Dockside power and water connections—yes
Waste pump-out—yes
Shower—yes
Laundromat—yes
Restaurant—nearby

Waterway Anchorage

Boats in immediate need of getting off the ICW may consider anchoring in the deep water east of flashing daybeacon #14. You must drop the hook before journeying too far to the east, or you could land in 5-foot depths. Probably your best bet is to set course for the westerly point of the peninsula separating the first and second coves (moving south to north) and drop the hook before getting closer than 100 yards of this promontory.

You will be exposed to the wake of all passing vessels and there is minimal shelter from inclement weather. Frankly, there are much better anchorages not far to the north or south, so this spot should probably be considered strictly for emergencies or in fair weather.

Treasure Island Tennis & Yacht Club (Standard Mile 119)

The docks of Treasure Island Tennis & Yacht Club sit perched on the northern banks of the rectangular cove making into the Waterway's western shoreline between flashing daybeacon #14 and the Treasure Island Causeway bascule bridge. This club accepts transient guests for overnight or temporary dockage who are members of yacht clubs with appropriate reciprocal privileges. Visitors are required to give at least 24 hours' notice before arrival. The club employs a full-time dockmaster who is very accommodating to visitors. The fixed wooden slips feature full power and water connections and showers are available in the clubhouse. Entrance and dockside depths are a very impressive 12 feet. Shoreside, visitors will find a cooling swimming pool, 14 clay tennis courts, a Nautilus room, and full dining facilities. Dinner and lunch are served Tuesday through Saturday and breakfast is offered Saturday and Sunday beginning at 9:00 A.M. Several other restaurants and a shopping center are found a half-mile from the clubhouse in downtown Treasure Island.

Treasure Island Tennis & Yacht Club
(727) 367-4511

Approach depth—12 feet
Dockside depth—12 feet
Accepts transients—member of yacht clubs with
appropriate reciprocal privileges
Dockside power connections—up to 50 amp
Dockside water connections—yes
Showers—yes
Restaurant—on site

BOCA CIEGA BAY TO TREASURE ISLAND NAVIGATION

Successful navigation of the Western Florida ICW and its various auxiliary channels between the southerly reaches of Boca Ciega Bay and Treasure Island is not a matter to be taken lightly. Dozens of channels crisscross the Waterway as it works its way to the north and the various aids to navigation on these conflicting tracks can be confusing, to say the least. Then, just to make matters a bit more interesting, there are three bridges with restricted opening schedules.

Most sidewaters have unmarked entrances. While many are deep enough for most craft, they do warrant cautious navigation to avoid the surrounding shallows.

Large portions of this run are open to wind and wave. While the islands and causeways give some shelter, winds over fifteen knots (and sometimes less) can make for a spray-filled voyage. If possible, pick a day of fair breezes for your transit across the bay.

So, keep chart 11411 at hand. Read the information below carefully and make advance plans to avoid any likely trouble spots. With these precautions, you should enjoy your cruise and not meet up with Boca Ciega's bottom.

Approaching the Split   As mentioned earlier, the convergence of three channels at flashing daybeacon #26 can bring on more than a spot of confusion. The track to the east runs under the fixed high-rise northerly span of the Sunshine Skyway and allows access to Tampa Bay's western shoreline. This route was covered in the last chapter. The ICW sweeps sharply to the west, while the alternate channel between Isla del Sol and the mainland strikes to the north. This latter route will be reviewed first, followed by a discussion of the ICW and the various side passages along its northward run.

Slow down as you approach flashing daybeacon #26 and use your binoculars to pick out unlighted daybeacon #25 and flashing daybeacon #26. You should pass directly between these two aids. There is shoal water to the east and west, so don't become confused by the various other markers. Be sure to positively identify #25 and #26 before making your final approach to the intersection.

Alternate Channel   Power cruisers not making for the excellent marinas at Pass-A-Grille and Tierra Verde may wisely choose the sheltered alternate passage east of Indian Key and Isla del Sol. Just remember that you must be able to clear a fixed bridge with a scant 18 feet of vertical clearance to rejoin the ICW.

After passing between unlighted daybeacon #25 and flashing daybeacon #26, continue almost straight ahead, pointing to pass unlighted daybeacon #2 to its westerly side. From this point, northbound mariners should take all red aids to their (the cruisers') starboard side and pass all green beacons to port until rejoining the ICW at flashing daybeacon #32.

Maximo Point Anchorage   To reach the somewhat open anchorage east of Indian Key, depart the alternate channel some .1 nautical miles south of unlighted daybeacon

#4. Head directly for the easterly shore. Some 50 yards before reaching the banks, swing sharply to the north and maintain the same distance from the shoreline as you cruise along. Be mindful of the charted patch of shallows to the west, marked by #4. Stay well east of this hazard.

Consider dropping the hook shortly after #4 comes abeam well to the west. It is quite possible to rejoin the alternate channel by continuing to cruise north along the shoreline. The entrance canal leading to O'Neill's Marina will soon come abeam to the east. Change course immediately and point to rejoin the main channel just northwest of flashing daybeacon #6. Again, be on guard against the very shallow water just south of #6.

On the Alternate Channel Those cruisers who bypass the Maximo Point Anchorage will want to set a course to pass unlighted daybeacon #4 by some 15 yards to its westerly quarter. Don't allow leeway to ease you to the east. As chart 11411 clearly and correctly indicates, there is shoal water with depths rising to a mere ½ foot east of this aid.

Once #4 is behind you, point for the gap between flashing daybeacon #6 and unlighted daybeacon #7. At this point the channel takes a jog to the northwest and hurries on towards a canal-like passage between the artificial islands east of Isla del Sol and the mainland banks. You will enter this passage immediately after passing flashing daybeacon #11 to its easterly side.

Eventually, the 18-foot fixed bridge crossing the canal will be spotted dead ahead. Once through this span, point to pass flashing daybeacon #12 to its westerly side. The channel takes a small jog farther to the west at #12 and continues on its well-marked way into the deeper waters of eastern Boca Ciega Bay.

Northwest of unlighted daybeacon #14 and flashing daybeacon #15, good depths spread out in a wide swath before you. It is now a simple matter to visit the marinas to the east.

Eastern Boca Ciega Marinas To enter the long canal leading to Maximo Marina, continue on the principal alternate channel for several hundred yards past (northwest of) #14 and #15. You can then safely curl back around to the east and set course for the southernmost of the charted canals cutting the bay's easterly limits. A whole series of uncharted markers leads you safely into the canal's mouth. Simply stick to the centerline as you cruise up the canal, and the marina docks will soon appear dead ahead.

Use your binoculars to pick out the bevy of unlighted daybeacons outlining the channel to Gulfport Municipal Marina and Boca Ciega Yacht Club to the northeast. Remember your "red, right, returning" rule.

Passage West to Isla del Sol Yacht and Country Club Captains traveling the alternate channel who choose to make use of the large yacht club on Isla del Sol's northerly shores need not cruise all the way back to the ICW and then follow the Waterway south to this facility. Instead, abandon the alternate channel some 100 yards northwest of unlighted daybeacon

#14 and flashing daybeacon #15 and follow the wide channel of deep water to the southwest. Simply by staying several hundred yards off the southeasterly shores and to the southeast of unlighted daybeacon #3, minimum 8-foot depths should be held all the way to the enclosed harbor.

You may also choose to continue following this channel west to the ICW. Point to pass just south of unlighted daybeacon #2 and minimum 8-foot depths can be maintained into the Waterway's deeper tract.

Alternate Channel to the ICW   After passing between flashing daybeacon #15 and unlighted daybeacon #14, the alternate channel skirts across a wide and deep section of eastern Boca Ciega Bay. No further aids mark the northwest-flowing cut for almost 1.3 nautical miles. Set a careful compass/GPS course to come abeam of flashing daybeacon #16 to its southerly side. From #16, the channel turns west-southwest and heads directly towards an intersection with the ICW at flashing daybeacon #32. Pass between #32 and unlighted daybeacon #17 and then immediately turn either north or south on the Waterway.

Back on the Western Florida ICW   From the infamous split where our discussion of the alternate channel began, the ICW sweeps west through a broad, deep passage on its way to the southern leg of the Pinellas Bayway Bridge. This is an open run with shoal water of 1 and 2 feet flanking the cut to the north and south. While the channel is certainly broad, you must make

sure to pick out the somewhat sparsely placed aids to navigation before forging ahead at speed.

Pass between unlighted daybeacon #25 and flashing daybeacon #26 and remain on course for some 50 yards. Then, cut sharply west, point to pass unlighted daybeacon #16 to its fairly immediate southerly side, and take flashing daybeacon #15 to its northerly quarter. Watch out for the charted shallows to the south during this run. Continue on course, pointing to come abeam of flashing daybeacon #17 to its northerly quarter.

Only four aids mark the long, slowly curving run from #17 to the Pinellas Bayway Bridge. Stay at least 50 yards (or even a bit more) to the south of unlighted daybeacons #18 and #20. Past #20, the Waterway begins a slow bend to the northwest. Pass between unlighted daybeacon #22 (well to its southerly side) and flashing daybeacon #21 (to its northerly quarter). Head straight for the central pass-through of the Pinellas Bayway Bridge once these aids are left behind.

If you like bridges with restricted opening schedules, boy, are you in luck. The southern half of the Pinellas Bayway Bridge, also known as the Pinellas Bayway "E" bridge, is the first in a host of restricted spans plaguing cruisers between Boca Ciega Bay and Anclote Key. By the way, don't become confused—there is another bridge north of flashing daybeacon #24 which is referred to as the Pinellas Bayway "C" bridge. Hence my designation of a northern ("C") and southern leg ("E") of the bayway. This particular bridge (closed vertical clearance 25 feet) features a regulated schedule daily, year round. From 9:00 A.M. to 5:00 P.M., the span opens only on the hour and each 20 minutes thereafter. At all other times, the bridge opens on demand.

Northwest of the southern Pinellas Bayway Bridge, the Waterway continues to follow a very broad and deep passage until passing between unlighted daybeacon #14 and flashing daybeacon #24. Don't approach either of these aids closely. The good water lies in the broad mid-width between the two markers.

From #24, the ICW channel swings sharply to the north and heads for Isla del Sol and the northern half of the Pinellas Bayway. To the south and west skippers may choose to put to sea on Pass-A-Grille Inlet or visit one of the several marinas (and one isolated anchorage) along the way.

Pass-A-Grille Channel & Facilities

Another wide channel strikes first west (from the ICW), then southwest, and then west again to Pass-A-Grille Inlet. To enter this passage, depart the Waterway some 100 yards south of flashing daybeacon #24 and cut sharply west. Pass unlighted daybeacon #14 well to its northerly side. This aid marks the channel's southeastern limits and sits hard by the northwestern corner of Tierra Verde Island. Study chart 11411 for a moment and you will note the small canal running southeast from #14. Small powercraft can use this stream to reach the principal Tierra Verde canal and Tierra Verde Resort Marina. A low, fixed bridge bars larger craft from this stream.

Continue on the Pass-A-Grille Channel

by passing well to the northwest of unlighted daybeacon #12. Follow the channel as it bends to the south past #12. Be prepared to find additional uncharted markers on these waters. As you can imagine, being this close to an inlet, aids to navigation are frequently moved, added to, and deleted. Just remember than you are now "going to sea" and all red marks should be taken to your port side, and green beacons to starboard.

The Pass-A-Grille Inlet channel remains well marked and reasonably easy to run all the way to its westernmost aid, flashing buoy #2. Between unlighted daybeacon #14 and flashing daybeacon #11, avoid the northwestern banks. Similarly, don't encroach upon the shallows abutting the western banks of Tierra Verde between unlighted daybeacon #12 and flashing daybeacon #10. Take your time, and be sure to pick out all aids correctly.

Before reaching the actual seaward cut, skippers can turn north to the facilities at Pass-A-Grille Beach, southeast to Tierra Verde Resort Marina, or south for the anchorage in South Channel.

Pass-A-Grille Beach Channel and Facilities

Captains making for Pass-A-Grille Beach should continue cruising on the Pass-A-Grille Inlet channel, as if you were putting out to sea, until flashing daybeacon #11 comes abeam to the northwest. Then turn in towards the westerly banks until #11 comes abeam to the north. Continue towards shore for another 50 yards or so and then turn north and parallel the shoreline as you cruise along. *Be sure to stay well to the west of flashing daybeacon #11.* Very shallow water is found north of this aid, stretching out from the southerly point of charted Vina del Mar. Heed this warning. Strangers sometimes attempt to pass on the wrong side of #11. A hard grounding is the inevitable and potentially expensive result!

Continue cruising north, keeping about the same distance from the westerly banks. You will first sight Merry Pier to the west, followed farther upstream by Pass-A-Grille Marina and Warren's Marina. Another hop to the north will lead you to a fixed bridge with only 14 feet of vertical clearance. The piers of Pass-A-Grille Yacht Club are located just north of this span. If you need more clearance, enter by way of Mud Key Channel, outlined below.

Tierra Verde Resort Marina   Knowledgeable captains who choose to visit Tierra Verde Resort Marina, guarding the northern terminus of Tierra Verde canal, should continue cruising south past flashing daybeacon #10. This aid should be passed well east of your course line. Watch to the southeast and you should spy a whole series of unlighted markers leading into the canal's mouth. Daytime entry is an elementary matter of cruising between the various marks, favoring the northeasterly side of the channel slightly. A nighttime arrival is tricky and calls for caution by strangers.

Once into the canal, good depths stretch out almost from shore to shore. Simply follow the stream as it flows north to the marina complex. The dockmaster's office is found adjacent to the northernmost piers. Try and raise the office on VHF and the attendant will probably meet you on the piers and direct you to your slip.

South Channel Anchorage   Only vessels drawing less than 4½ feet and piloted by skippers with a sense of adventure should attempt to enter South Channel and its associated anchorage adjacent to Shell Key. While most of the route is deep, there is one spot with 4½-foot depths that seemingly cannot be avoided.

If your craft and temperament fit these requirements, come abeam of flashing daybeacon #10 by at least 100 yards to its westerly side. Once abeam of this aid, set a new course to come abeam of the easterly tip of Shell Key Shoal (sandspit), well west of charted Cabbage Key, by about 15 to 20 yards to your westerly side. This point is building out, but, in spite of soundings shown on chart 11411, there is also shoal water farther to the east. This is the most critical part of the South Channel passage. Even if you hit the right point, chances are that you will encounter some 4½-foot low-water soundings. During our original on-site research, we saw one local sailcraft run aground just off this point, but the skipper was able to quickly extract himself by gunning the auxiliary.

Once past the troublesome point, turn sharply to the south-southwest. Almost immediately, you will spy a crescent-shaped cove backed by a white sand beach to starboard. Again, in spite of the soundings shown on the chart, you can drop the hook within 25 yards of this beach in good water.

The wild-eyed explorers among us can continue following unmarked South

Channel to the southwest. If you happen to be an angler, this can be a most rewarding trip. Follow the southeastern (grassy) shoreline and keep some 25 to 35 yards off the banks. Be sure to discontinue your cruise long before reaching the charted terminus of the channel, well to the southwest. As a rule of thumb, do not approach to within less than 100 yards of The Reef's southwesterly tip.

On the ICW At flashing daybeacon #24, the Waterway swerves to the north and flows on towards the northern leg of the Pinellas Bayway Bridge, also known as the Pinellas Bayway "C" bridge. This span (closed vertical clearance 25 feet) has an even more severe regulated opening schedule than its southern sister. The bridge opens on the hour and every 20 minutes thereafter from 7:00 A.M. to 7:00 P.M., seven days a week. South of this bridge, cruisers can cut west into Mud Key Channel for anchorage or to visit Pass-A-Grille Yacht Club.

Mud Key Channel Depart the Waterway some 25 yards before reaching the southern face of the Pinellas Bayway "C" bridge (northern leg). Cruise west on the centerline of the passage between the bridge and the high ground to the south. Soon the entrance to a canal will come abeam to the south. Mariners seeking anchorage close to the ICW can feel their way into the midwidth of this opening and drop the hook. You must pass through some 5- to 6-foot depths, but soundings quickly deepen again to 6 and 11 feet. Anchor well away

from the point where the canal begins to narrow.

Eventually Mud Key Channel curves sharply to the southwest and runs through a canal. There are no depth problems on this stream, but the same cannot be said of the wide water beyond. As correctly indicated on chart 11411, a shoal has built out on the northwestern flank of the canal's southwestern limits. As you exit the canal, heavily favor the port (southeastern) shore to avoid this hazard. Continue favoring this bank while passing the points of the first two charted peninsulas to the southeast. Good water again spreads out almost from shore to shore as the shorter, third peninsula comes abeam. The docks of Pass-A-Grille Yacht Club will be spotted a short distance downstream on the western shores.

Big McPherson Bayou Anchorage The entrance to what would otherwise be one the best anchorages between Tampa Bay and Clearwater Harbor is complicated by the presence of a large patch of shoal water crossing most of Big McPherson Bayou's eastern mouth. As chart 11411 correctly forecasts, the shallows run from the bridge completely across the entrance's midwidth. In fact, on-site soundings indicate this shoal has built out even farther than shown on the chart.

Fortunately, it is still quite possible to enter the bayou's interior reaches by closely hugging the starboard-side (northwestern) banks. Continue cruising north on the Waterway until the northern portion of the bayou's mouth comes abeam to the west. Then, curl around to the west-southwest and enter the bayou hugging the north-westerly banks.

Soon the bayou takes a 90-degree turn to the north-northwest. Cruise around this sharp point by heavily favoring the eastern banks. Shallows abut the western and southern shoreline on this portion of the creek. You may or may not spot a no-wake sign as you make your turn to the north. If this sign is still present by the time you arrive, be sure to pass to its easterly side.

The best anchorage is found abeam of the first charted offshoot striking northeast. Cruise into the mouth of this sidewater far enough for good shelter and settle down for a night of peace and security.

To cruise upstream to the second side-water, continue to heavily favor the eastern banks. Enter this body of water on its centerline.

Don't attempt to reach the northerly limits of the bayou. Depths become more than suspect past the second cove described above.

Isla del Sol Channel   Skippers desiring to visit Isla del Sol Yacht and Country Club, or even those simply needing a good shortcut to the alternate channel, can follow the deep waters north of Isla del Sol. Depart the ICW at unlighted daybeacon #2. Keep 100 yards or so from the southern banks as you cruise east-northeast, and the marina harbor will come eventually abeam to the south.

If you continue on to the alternate channel, point to eventually join up with this cut about .1 nautical miles northwest of flashing daybeacon #15. This passage is not recommended for strangers at night.

On the ICW   Shoal water abuts the Waterway's eastern flank between the northern Pinellas Bayway Bridge and unlighted daybeacon #30. Be sure to identify all aids carefully along this stretch and proceed with caution.

As you approach flashing daybeacon #32, another potential trouble spot is encountered. The various aids marking the alternate channel to the east are sometimes mistaken for the Waterway beacons. Be sure to pass west of #32 in order to stay in the ICW channel.

The charted deep water west of #32 may look good as a potential anchorage on the chart, but it is actually very much open to wind and wave. Unless you are in need of an emergency stop, far better havens are found to the north and south.

St. Petersburg Beach Anchorage   For best depths, hold scrupulously to the mid-width when entering the cove southwest of unlighted daybeacon #33. Deep water actually extends much farther west than you would expect from studying chart 11411. Nevertheless, depths eventually do rise dramatically. For safety's sake, it would be better to drop the hook on the eastern third of the cove.

On the ICW   Don't attempt to enter the cove west of unlighted daybeacon #35. Depths of 4½ feet or less are encountered soon after leaving the ICW.

At unlighted daybeacon #37 the Waterway begins a lazy turn to the northwest as it runs on towards the Corey Causeway Bridge.

Northwest of unlighted daybeacon #39, the ICW soon exchanges greetings with the Corey Causeway Bridge. Yes, friends, we can all enjoy yet another restricted bridge. What can I say except, "Enjoy the scenery."

The Corey Causeway span has a closed vertical clearance of 23 feet and opens every 20 minutes weekdays from 8:00 A.M. to 7:00 P.M. and from 10:00 A.M. to 7:00 P.M. on weekends and holidays.

North of Corey Causeway, the waters about the ICW begin to narrow and depths outside of the marked cut are very questionable. Take your time and identify the markers as you cruise along.

Blind Pass Marina   Cruise into the wide channel west of flashing daybeacon #9 by favoring the southerly point slightly. To continue on to the marina, simply follow the good water as it turns sharply south. The docks will be quite obvious on the eastern banks. Apparently some of the piers on the northern side of the complex belong to the high-rise condo overlooking the shoreline. Farther to the south, the channel to virtually impassable Blind Pass Inlet is blocked by a low-level fixed bridge.

Please note that we no longer recommend that any cruising-size craft attempt to enter the passage flowing north-northwest from the main Blind Pass channel. A shoal has now built completely across the entrance to this errant stream.

On to Treasure Island on the ICW   North of flashing daybeacon #14, northbound cruisers will sight Treasure Island Causeway Bridge. This span, with a meager closed vertical clearance of only 8 feet, also has a regulated opening schedule. It opens on the hour and every quarter of the hour seven days a week from 7:00 A.M. to 7:00 P.M. During the night, between the hours of 11:00 P.M. and 7:00 A.M., the bridge operator requires 10 minutes' notice before an opening.

Treasure Island Causeway to Belleair Causeway

The waters in and about the Gulf Coast ICW between Treasure Island Causeway and the Belleair Bridge continue the trend towards narrower widths that began near Corey Causeway Bridge. From Treasure Island the Waterway follows the northerly reaches of Boca Ciega Bay to a canal-like passage known, appropriately enough, as "The Narrows." This cut leads in turn to Belleair Causeway, the southern boundary of the bay-like body of water known as Clearwater Harbor.

The passage from Treasure Island to Belleair is spanned by a few bridges, two of which (surprise, surprise) currently open on demand. Don't rejoice prematurely. This stretch of the ICW also features a host of minimum- and idle-speed zones with which you must contend. This is not a stretch of the Gulf Coast ICW where powercraft can expect to charge through at double-digit speed. Allow plenty of time in your cruising plans to span this gap.

There are several excellent marinas that offer transient dockage between Treasure

Island and Belleair. Nevertheless, your choices, at least compared to those in St. Petersburg and Clearwater, are somewhat limited. Conversely, there are many opportunities to anchor for the evening. None of these overnight refuges can be described as undeveloped. Almost invariably, you will be riding the hook in close proximity to prolific residential and sometimes commercial development.

Much of this passage is overlooked by coastal towns and cities rubbing elbows with one another. This is particularly true on the barrier islands to the west. If it were not for the city limits signs, it would be difficult to tell where one community ends and another begins.

A single inlet provides reliable access to and from the open waters of the Gulf along this stretch of the ICW. Johns Pass is uniformly deep, well marked and charted, and relatively easy to run. Currents do run swiftly though, so have an eye for leeway and maneuvering room.

Although it can scarcely be compared to a cruise up the beautifully undeveloped Little Shark River, the run from Treasure Island to Belleair is nevertheless pleasant, with several opportunities for gunkholing and side trips. While a few sections are best left behind as soon as possible, many mariners will want to take advantage of this region's cruising delights.

Isle of Palms Anchorage (Standard Mile 119.5)

Good depths of 8 feet or better are held just south of the two easternmost fingers of land on the charted Isle of Palms, west-northwest of unlighted daybeacon #17. While you must be careful to avoid the charted spoil shoal farther to the south, cautious skippers can break off from the ICW between unlighted daybeacons #17 and #19 and drop the hook off the

second tip of land (moving east to west) in 8 to 13 feet of water. Swinging room is sufficient for boats at least as large as 48 feet. Protection from northerly blows is quite good and is acceptable in light to moderate southerly and westerly breezes. Strong winds from the east could make for a most uncomfortable evening. The anchorage is overlooked by heavy residential development on the Isle of Palms. Traffic noise from nearby Treasure Island Causeway Bridge could also be an annoyance on quiet nights.

Long Bayou Facilities (Standard Mile 120.5)

A long and complex series of privately maintained daybeacons outlines a long channel striking north from the ICW just north-northwest of unlighted daybeacon #23. This cut leads into the interior reaches of mostly shallow Long Bayou. The marked channel has minimum low-water depths of 6 feet. However, a trip outside of the buoyed passage can quickly land careless navigators in 4 feet of water or less. Obviously, captains must exercise more than the usual care when running this cut.

Two marinas are found on the shores of Long Bayou. The first guards the eastern banks just northeast of unlighted daybeacon #29. Lighthouse Point Marina is primarily a power-craft facility, but there are usually three slips set aside for transients. Berths consist of wooden, fixed piers featuring freshwater and 30-amp power connections. Low-tide approach and dockside depths are in the 5-foot region, plenty for most powerboats, even if a bit skimpy for many fixed-keel sailcraft. Gasoline (only) is distributed through an independently operated tackle/ship's store/baithouse near the marina's entrance. Mechanical repairs to gasoline engines are available and boats up to 42 feet can be hauled out via a very large forklift. The Waterfront Lodge (727-345-3000) restaurant is found just across the street.

Lighthouse Point Marina (727) 384-3625

Approach depth—5-11 feet
Dockside depth—5 feet (low water)
Accepts transients—yes (three slips)
Fixed wooden piers—yes
Dockside power connections—up to 30 amp
Dockside water connections—yes
Gasoline—yes
Mechanical repairs—yes (gasoline engines only)
Below-waterline repairs—haul-out up to 42 feet
Restaurant—nearby

A visit to the second of Long Bayou's facilities, Bay Pines Marine (727-392-4922, http://www.baypinesmarine.com), calls for a cruise under the 20-foot fixed highway bridge north of unlighted daybeacon #31. As this facility does not accept transients, many visitors will choose to forego this passage. The channel leading north from the bridge to Bay Pines Marine can be confusing to strangers. Be sure to read the navigational information on Long Bayou presented later in this chapter before making the attempt.

Once the troublesome entrance cut is left behind, visitors will find a collection of wet slips associated with Bay Pines on the western shore of the bayou, followed by a large dry-storage building a bit farther to the north.

Bay Pines Marine requires a minimum two-month stay to rent a wet slip. Dry storage, gasoline, and mechanical repairs are available courtesy of an on-site, independent service firm. Boats up to 28 feet can be hauled out by forklift.

The waters of Long Bayou outside of its improved channel are almost universally shallow. Thus, while the shores are less developed than most in this region, there is little opportunity for overnight anchorage by any but the smallest outboard craft. Even skippers of these petite boats had better proceed with caution or a bent prop could be the result.

Johns Pass (Standard Mile 121.5)

Reliable Johns Pass Inlet strikes into the waters of the open Gulf southwest of the ICW's flashing daybeacon #4, itself west of Turtlecrawl Point. While the charted channel leading to the inlet from #4 is the best-marked and most straightforward route to the seaward cut, adventurous skippers can also reach the pass via the charted deep waters north of Capri Isle. The former channel has minimum 7- to 8-foot depths, while the cut skirting Capri Island has some 5-foot soundings, but most readings are in the 6- to 20-foot region.

With one major exception, Johns Pass is about the most easily run inlet that you will ever find in Western Florida. The channel is straightforward, well marked and charted, and reasonably easy to run for most pleasurecraft. Minimum depths are currently around 12 feet, with many soundings showing much better water. The only fly in the ointment is the strong tidal currents that regularly boil through this cut. Low-powered trawlers and sailcraft must be on maximum alert for these swift waters.

Johns Pass is spanned by a bascule bridge with 25 feet of closed vertical clearance. Fortunately, this bridge opens on demand and does not present too much of an obstruction for pleasureboats.

Johns Pass Marina (727-360-6907) guards the northeastern tip of the land mass flanking the southeastern side of the inlet. The facility

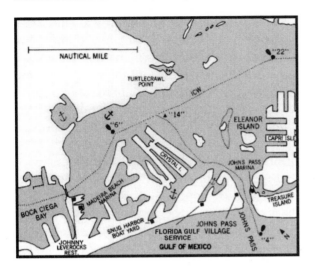

is easily spotted by its large, powder blue dry-storage building. As you might expect, this marina specializes in dry storage of small powercraft and there is no wet-slip dockage available for transients. A fuel pier and a few wooden-decked wet slips front onto the point and all cruisers can readily purchase gasoline and diesel fuel. Dockside depths range from 8 to 10 feet. Mechanical repairs are available for outboard and I/O powercraft. The marina also features a large bait/tackle store and boat sales department.

Johns Pass's northwestern shoreline is over-looked by a huge retail and dining complex known as Johns Pass Village and Boardwalk. Apparently the center was originally designed to have a rustic look but, at least to my eyes, the glitz has overtaken any rural character that might ever have been present. Today, the waterborne visitor usually finds a complex teeming with tourists in search of something to do. Several restaurants are found on the grounds and some certainly serve good seafood. However, cruising visitors may be hard put to find a berth which will allow for a ready visit to the complex.

While a tour ship and a boat rental agency grace the village's waterfront, there is practically nothing in the way of dockage for larger pleasurecraft. Skippers will spy a small fuel dock at the northeastern (ICW side) end of the complex. Boats up to 34 feet can probably battle the current and tie up for a time and purchase gas, diesel fuel, bait, beer, and ice. You may be able to negotiate a stay while dining at one of the on-site restaurants, but don't count on it.

All in all, Johns Pass Inlet provides reliable access to the open Gulf and features the added bonus of a fuel stop and the village complex. Only one other inlet in this region can lay claim to so many positive attributes.

Mitchell Beach Sidewater

The cove that is shaped like a piece of a jig-saw puzzle, cutting into the western banks between flashing daybeacons #6 and #7 on the principal Johns Pass channel (leading from the ICW), offers 6-foot minimum depths and enough swinging room for boats as large as 34 feet. The best spot to drop the hook is at the intersection of the two westerly arms of the offshoot. Here boats can drop the hook in some 7 to 8 feet of water with excellent pro-tection from all winds. Even so, swinging room is a bit skimpy and some captains may want to consider a Bahamian mooring or even a stern anchor. The shores are flanked by heavy residential development. This is not what one would call an isolated refuge.

The northwesterly branch of this cove leads to Florida Gulf Service (727-319-0594). This facility is a low-key repair yard that, rumor has it, is undergoing financial difficulties. Mechanical repairs for both gasoline and diesel engines are still offered, and haul-outs can be accomplished by way of a 40-ton travelift.

Madeira Beach Anchorage

The large, charted offshoot striking west from flashing daybeacon #7 (on the Johns Pass approach channel) makes an ideal anchorage for boats drawing 4½ feet or less. While 6-foot low-tide depths can be maintained by the careful navigator, it's likely that boats swinging on the hook will ease into some 5-foot waters before the night is over. The shores are surrounded by dense residential development and afford excellent protection from all winds. This is not the most attractive overnight anchorage that you will ever encounter, but it would be a good spot to ride out a heavy blow.

Farther to the west, the sidewater splits into two branches. The northern fork leads to the docks of Snug Harbor Boat Yard (727-398-7470). This friendly firm offers complete mechanical repairs for both gasoline and diesel engines, and haul-out repairs via a 25-ton travelift. Additionally, marine carpentry, electrical, and even canvas service is available. Approach depths run 5 to 8 feet with 8- to 9-foot soundings dockside. This writer found the staff at Snug Harbor to be exceptionally affable and willing to go that extra mile to satisfy all the visiting cruiser's needs. No transient dockage or fuel is available on the premises.

Veterans Hospital Anchorages (Standard Mile 122)

Study chart 11411 for a moment and you will quickly spy the designation "Veterans Hospital" northeast of the ICW's flashing daybeacon #6. The old hospital is a striking edifice

Veterans Hospital

and makes for a readily recognized landmark from the water. Two anchorages are available to cruising craft in and about the waters around this center of healing.

The first is located on the charted patch of 6-foot water north and northeast of #6. Careful captains can ease in towards the northeastern banks and drop the hook before reaching the ½-foot shoal clearly shown on 11411. This rather open refuge is only appropriate in light to moderate northerly and southern breezes. A forecast calling for winds from the west or east over 15 knots nixes this spot. You will also be open to any wake raised by passing powercraft. While this is not too likely during the later evening hours, it can make for a rough awakening in the morning if a 55-foot Hatteras should happen by at full bore. The anchorage is overlooked by the old hospital and the beautifully green grounds surrounding the building.

Boats drawing less than 3½ feet can carefully feel their way into the pondlike body of water, just west of the Veterans Hospital's charted position. Chart 11411 shows only 3½ feet of water at the entrance to the pond, but on-site research revealed 4-foot low-tide depths.

Those who can stand this thin water will glide into a beautifully protected anchorage surrounded by mostly undeveloped and, to the southeast, parklike shores. Of course, the old hospital gazing benignly over the water only adds to the haven's appeal. Protection is absolutely super from all winds. During our visit to the pond, we observed several sailcraft (presumably with retractable keels) snugly anchored in the harbor. Always assuming that you can stand the depths, there is simply not a better foul-weather hidey-hole between Tampa Bay and Anclote Key.

Madeira Beach Facilities (Standard Mile 122.5)

Madeira Beach Marina is found on the northwestern banks of the cove southwest of unlighted daybeacon #10, itself just southeast of the Welch Causeway Bridge. Some care must be exercised to avoid the charted shoal southeast of the marina, but several pilings outlining this hazard help visiting cruisers avoid the shallows with minimal difficulty.

Madeira Beach Marina is now a privately leased facility. It used to be city owned, and, quite frankly, it looked to us as if the private incarnation of Madeira Beach Marina is not as well managed as its predecessor.

Well, with that being said, this facility does still accept transients at its well-constructed, fixed wooden piers with power (a few 50, but mostly 30 amp) and water connections. Gasoline and commercial diesel fuel are at hand, as are adequate, non-air conditioned showers, a laundromat, and waste pump-out services. Mechanical repairs can occasionally be arranged through local, independent contractors. A small ship's and variety store is located on the premises. Famished cruisers can easily visit the nearby Johnny Leverocks Restaurant or the Santa Madeira on the mainland side of the causeway (see below for more details). Both a Publix and a Winn Dixie supermarket are located within a five-block walk, and a convenience store is only a short step away.

Madeira Beach Marina (727) 399-2631

Approach depth—6-9 feet
Dockside depth—6-8 feet
Accepts transients—yes
Fixed wooden piers—yes
Dockside power connections—mostly 30 amp
Dockside water connections—yes

Waste pump-out—yes
Showers—yes
Laundromat—yes
Gasoline—yes
Diesel fuel—yes (commercial only)
Mechanical repairs—limited (independent technicians)
Ship's and variety store—yes
Restaurant—several nearby

The notable Johnny Leverocks Restaurant (727-393-0459) flanks the ICW's southwestern banks just southeast of the Welch Causeway Bridge. This dining chain seems to be adding more and more locations all up and down the waterfront between Tampa Bay and Dunedin.

This particular Leverocks maintains its own dock fronting directly onto the ICW. While the pier's southeastern side is reserved for a resident charter sportfisherman, visiting cruisers are welcome to tie up while dining on the northwestern face. There should be enough room for one 34-footer. Dockside depths run around 6 to 7 feet.

The small, charted cove cutting into the northeastern banks just northwest of the Welch Causeway Bridge offers two very different opportunities for epicurean delight. First up is the Santa Madeira restaurant (727-397-0020), which occupies the cove's northwestern point. This imposing dining spot is shaped like a giant sailing craft of old and is an unmistakable landmark. The Santa Madeira is one of the most popular restaurants in Madeira Beach.

The Santa Madeira maintains several slips for the use of its patrons. These consist of wooden pilings that form slips backdropped by a concrete seawall. While care must be taken to avoid scraping the gel-coat on your bow or stern, an alert crew should be able to tie off with few problems. Dockside depths

immediately adjacent to the seawall are only 4½ feet, but 6-foot soundings are found just a short way farther out into the slip. No overnight dockage is permitted.

Opposite the Santa Madeira docks, visiting cruisers may be surprised to spy a metal floating dock flying the "McDonald's" flag. Yes, that's right. Captains and crew who yearn for a Big Mac or a Quarter Pounder with Cheese and those inimitable french fries can feed their faces after a quick tie-up at the floating pier. Dockside depths of 5 feet can be expected, plenty for most powercraft, although a bit skimpy for particularly deep draft sailboats.

Redington Shores Anchorage (Standard Mile 125.5)

The charted cove south of unlighted daybeacon #1 at Redington Shores makes for a protected overnight anchorage set amidst a heavily developed shoreline. Care must be exercised to avoid the correctly charted ½-foot shoal occupying the center portion of the cove, but elementary navigation should see you by these shallows. Since the best anchorage in the cove is found south of the shoal, most cruisers will not even have to worry with this trouble spot. Minimum depths of 7 feet are found in the unmarked channel, ranging up to 11 feet of water in the southwestern corner of the bay. Just to be on the safe side, be sure to read the navigational information presented in the next section of this chapter before visiting this bay for the first time.

Captains seeking overnight shelter should consider dropping anchor near the cove's southwesterly corner. Chart 11411 currently indicates 18-foot depths on these waters, but on-site research revealed that 11-foot soundings are now the norm. Protection is excellent from all winds, but particularly good for strong blows from the south and west. The nearby highway and residential districts may produce a considerable quantity of light and noise during your evening's rest, but that, unhappily, is the norm along this stretch of Western Florida's coastline.

The Narrows and Associated Facilities (Standard Mile 126)

Northwest of flashing daybeacon #2, the northbound ICW cruiser enters a long, skinny stretch of the Waterway known as The Narrows. The run from #2 to the southern foot of Clearwater Harbor is plagued by several long, minimum-wake zones. Mariners, particularly those of the powered ilk, should leave plenty of time in their cruising itinerary to put this stretch legally behind them.

Tidal currents can also run swiftly in The Narrows, but at least rough water won't be a problem. It would take near hurricane-force winds to raise a menacing chop in these confined waters. Cruisers will also be happy to learn that the two bridges spanning The Narrows currently both open on demand.

The Narrows is overlooked by heavy residential development dominated by high-rise condos to the west. The mainland shores are surprisingly only lightly developed and provide a refreshing change from the concrete jungle so evident elsewhere.

Immediately north of flashing daybeacon #27, captains piloting vessels drawing less than 5 feet may choose to visit Green Street Restaurant (727-593-2077). The face dock of this facility sits at the southern terminus of the long minimum-wake zone stretching south from Indian Rocks Beach Bridge. Some skippers who are a bit quick on the trigger could send a prodigious wake your way while

docked here. A sign on the restaurant pier warns boaters that dockage is at their own risk.

The Green Street Restaurant pier has low-tide depths of 5 feet and enough room for boats as large as 50 feet. Discounting the wake problem, this would be an ideal dinner stop before cruising on to a nearby marina or anchorage.

The charted harbor east of flashing daybeacon #31 is home to Indian Springs Marina (standard mile 129, 727-595-2956). This writer originally visited the marina on a January morning with a temperature of some 50 degrees. Having just left the cold North Carolina winter behind a few days before, the weather was warm to me, and I was decked out in shirt-sleeves for my day of on-the-water research. Upon entering the junk-filled but homey office, I observed the marina owner amongst a group of the yard regulars sitting close-packed around a flaming wood stove. They were all dressed in jackets and looked at me as if they wondered whether I had a screw loose as I strolled up *sans* warm clothing. Nevertheless, after explaining my mission, I was courteously shown about.

This rather comical incident, which will always remain with this writer as a fond memory, seems to somehow tell the tale of Indian Springs Marina. It is one of the last of its breed in Western Florida—a small, independently owned boatyard primarily concerned with service work that just barely seems to eke out a living from day to day. In a pinch, though, you couldn't find a better friend on the Waterway.

Indian Springs Marina does not offer transient dockage or fuel, but complete mechanical and below-waterline, haul-out repairs are very much available. Their travelift is rated at 30 tons. The marina also features dry storage in the large, metal building that will quickly be spotted from the Waterway. Entrance and dockside depths of only some 5 feet at low water will be limiting for long-legged craft. Deeper-draft boats can still be hauled during high tide.

As limited as its services may be, this writer cannot help but recommend Indian Springs, if only because it represents a last vanishing glimpse of old Florida that may soon be gone forever. And I think you'll find that these folks can cure what ails you.

Between flashing daybeacon #33 and the Indian Rocks Beach Bridge, first-time cruisers on the Western Florida ICW will be astonished to observe a towering complex on the northwestern shoreline. This was once a combination retail-dining-hotel complex, but the entire space is now occupied by a huge Holiday Inn. The marina portion of the development (standard mile 129.5), formerly known as Hamlin's Landing Marina, has now been renamed Holiday Inn Harbourside Marina. Fortunately, this facility is friendly to transients.

Visiting craft are accommodated at the marina's modern, fixed wooden piers with 30-50-amp power and freshwater connections. Very respectable dockside depths of 6½ to 8 feet are enough for all but the deepest-draft vessels. The docks are sheltered and make a good spot to ride out a heavy blow. As is true all along The Narrows, tidal currents do move swiftly. Practice your best docking technique. Any potential difficulty should be readily solved by the dockmaster. Gasoline and diesel fuel are available, and both showers and a laundromat are located hard by one of the hotel's two swimming pools. A new open-air bar overlooks this pool as well. During fair weather, this wateringhole is usually very crowded by late afternoon.

An on-site variety store is very convenient for light restocking, and both an Eckerd Drug and another convenience store are found within 1½ blocks of the dockage basin. Ask the dockmaster for directions.

There are several restaurants located within the Holiday Inn Harbourside complex. We have not had a chance to sample any of their fare. Again, ask the dockmaster for recommendations.

Holiday Inn Harbourside Marina (727) 595-9484

Approach depth—9-13 feet
Dockside depth—6-8 feet
Accepts transients—yes
Fixed wooden piers—yes
Dockside power connections—30-50 amp
Dockside water connections—yes
Showers—yes
Laundromat—yes
Gasoline—yes
Diesel fuel—yes
Variety store—yes
Restaurant—several on site

Largo Intracoastal Marine (727-595-3592) guards the easterly banks of the ICW near the northern terminus of The Narrows, north of flashing daybeacon #36. The marina's entrance channel (5-foot depths) is vaguely outlined by white PVC pipes. Soundings alongside run 4½ to 5 feet. This low-key firm is primarily in the business of dry-storing smaller powercraft. Gasoline and mechanical repairs for outboards and I/O's are available, but there are no other services for transients and cruising-size craft.

Sand Key Anchorage (Standard Mile 130)

Cruisers who decide to wait for the morning's light before entering Clearwater Harbor, north of Belleair Causeway, can anchor in the charted deep water west of unlighted daybeacon #40. Minimum depths of 7 feet or better can be held from #40 until coming abeam of the entrance's northerly point. Farther to the west soundings rise to 5-foot levels. Caution must be exercised to avoid several unmarked shoals, and captains piloting vessels drawing more than 4½ feet must be sure to discontinue their forward progress before cruising into the shallower western waters. Otherwise, this is a fair overnight refuge with good protection in northern winds and adequate shelter from easterly or westerly blows. Strong winds from the south could call for a quick cruise to one of the nearby marina facilities.

The entire anchorage is surrounded by heavy residential development. The houses on the northerly banks sport a whole series of private docks, many with their own resident craft. Powercraft should enter and leave the anchorage at idle speed.

TREASURE ISLAND TO BELLEAIR CAUSEWAY NAVIGATION

Successful navigation of the ICW between Treasure Island Causeway and Belleair Bridge is complicated by a number of lengthy minimum-wake zones and several bridges with restricted opening schedules. Add to these impediments the presence of fairly swift tidal currents and mariners can readily understand why it's not the time to take a snooze at the helm.

Most of the various sidewaters along the way are reasonably simple to enter, though safe access is usually gained by favoring one shoreline or another. Make no mistake about it, some shallow water is present, and the unwary navigator could find it without having to work too hard.

During our various on-site research trips we have discovered that all the restrictive bridges now monitor VHF. While channel 13 is the stated working frequency, the operators can sometimes be raised on old, reliable 16.

On the ICW   As you leave Treasure Island Causeway behind, set course to come abeam of and pass unlighted daybeacon #15 to its easterly quarter. Chart 11411 correctly indicates shallow water west of this aid.

From #15, it is a quick hop to a position abeam of unlighted daybeacon #17. Northwest of this marker, cruisers have access to the first anchorage north of the Treasure Island bridge.

Isle of Palms Anchorage   If you choose to drop the hook in the somewhat open anchorage off the Isle of Palms' southeastern corner, set a course from a position some 100 yards north-northwest of unlighted daybeacon #17 to come abeam of the island's first charted offshoot of land lying to the west-northwest by some 50 yards to your starboard side. Once abeam of this tip of land, alter course to the west-southwest and point to come alongside of the next point of land by about the same distance to starboard. You can drop the hook in about 10 to 13 feet of water once abeam of the second point.

Study chart 11411 for a moment and you will see that the procedure described above helps to avoid the charted shoal southeast of the anchorage. Depths of less than 2 feet are quickly encountered by cruisers who accidentally encroach upon this hazard. Be mindful of the shallows as you enter and leave the refuge and stay well north and northwest of the shoal.

Do not attempt to cruise west past the Isle of Palms' second offshoot, or towards the southern side of the cove. Shallow water of 4 feet or less waits to greet the foolhardy.

On the ICW The charted channel striking east from unlighted daybeacon #21 leads to a small-craft launching ramp and is of little interest to passing cruisers.

Two intertwined channels leave the ICW's northeastern flank northwest of unlighted daybeacon #23. The more southerly of these two marked tracks points towards a beautiful private residence that is almost large enough to be a clubhouse. The northerly fork leads captains and crew up a well-buoyed passage into Long Bayou and its two marinas.

Long Bayou Much of the interior reaches of upper Boca Ciega Bay, leading to Long Bayou, are quite shallow, with depths of less than 4 feet being the norm. The prolifically marked channel has typical minimum depths of 6 feet, though an occasional lesser sounding might slip in when strong northerly winds have lowered water levels.

To enter the Long Bayou cut, continue cruising on the ICW until the channel leading east, to the northwest of unlighted daybeacon #23, is directly abeam. Then, cut off the Waterway and point to pass between unlighted daybeacons #1 and #2.

Once these aids are left behind, the markers leading to the shoreside house will be directly in front of you, while the Long Bayou cut will be spotted to the north. Turn sharply north some 25 yards east of #1 and #2 and point to come abeam of Long Bayou's most southerly aid, unlighted daybeacon #1, to its fairly immediate easterly side. You can then follow the numerous beacons into the bay's interior reaches, always remembering your "red, right, returning" rule.

Eventually, unlighted daybeacon #29 will come abeam to your port side. The docks associated with Lighthouse Point Marina will then be spied to the northeast. You can cruise directly from #29 to the marina, but be ready for some 5-foot (or slightly less) depths.

North of #29, upstream navigation on Long Bayou is complicated by the charted channel striking west from unlighted daybeacon #31. This cut serves a public launching area and is best avoided by cruising-size craft. Also, there is an uncharted shoal west of #31.

Many visiting cruisers will wisely choose to discontinue their upstream explorations at #29. Bay Pines Marine, north of the bridge spanning Long Bayou, does not offer any services for transients other than gasoline and limited mechanical repairs.

For those who choose to continue on, set course from #29 to bring unlighted daybeacon #31 abeam to your fairly immediate port side. Do not slip west of #31. Very shallow water waits to greet your keel.

From #31, point for the central passthrough of the fixed bridge dead ahead.

This span has a vertical clearance of only 20 feet, much too low for most sailcraft.

Once through the bridge, you will be met by a confusing series of privately maintained daybeacons. All the aids, green or red, are rectangular in shape, an unusual arrangement to say the least. The best advice this writer can give cruisers who make it this far without local knowledge is to pass all red beacons to starboard and all green markers to port, as usual. Good luck!

Johns Pass Inlet Johns Pass Inlet is plagued by swift tidal currents and it is spanned by a bascule bridge with 25 feet of closed vertical clearance. Fortunately, this span does open on demand but sailcraft and single-engine trawlers can still have a few anxious moments while waiting for an opening. Otherwise, Johns Pass is a navigational delight and visiting cruisers can make use of the cut with confidence.

Two routes lead from the Waterway to Johns Pass. The southernmost of the two skirts the northerly reaches of Capri Isle and is marked by only a single aid to navigation, unlighted daybeacon #1. While local captains use this route safely week in and week out, strangers are advised to choose the well-marked entry channel leading south from the ICW's flashing daybeacon #4.

Enter this latter passage by continuing northwest on the ICW until the pass-through between unlighted daybeacons #13 and #14 is immediately abeam to the south-southwest. Then, cruise between these aids and point to come abeam of unlighted daybeacon #11 to its southeasterly

side. Set course to pass the next two red daybeacons to your fairly immediate port side.

South of flashing daybeacon #10, a minimum-wake zone is in effect throughout the remainder of Johns Pass. All boats should proceed at reduced speed until well past the inlet bridge.

At unlighted daybeacon #8, the channel takes a sharp jog to the south-southeast. If your plan is to continue on to the inlet, point to pass flashing daybeacon #7 to its easterly quarter. A good anchorage and several facilities can be found to the west and southwest of #7. These havens will be covered below.

Getting back to the inlet channel, skippers should next point to come abeam of flashing daybeacon #6 to its westerly side. Be mindful of the charted shoal waters to the northeast.

At #6 the inlet channel swings to the southwest and becomes a straight shot to the open Gulf. Simply point for the bridge's central pass-through and leave yourself plenty of maneuvering room if you need to wait for an opening.

As you cruise towards the bridge, the fuel dock and powder blue dry-storage building of Johns Pass Marina will be visible to the southeast. Cruisers would have a hard time missing Johns Pass Village and Boardwalk, lining the opposite banks.

Once the pesky Johns Pass bascule bridge is behind you, a series of easily followed markers leads you well out into the Gulf's deeper waters. Be prepared to find more and different markers than those shown on chart 11411.

Mitchell Beach Sidewater The forked sidewater making into the western banks southeast of flashing daybeacon #7 on the principal Johns Pass entrance channel can be easily entered on its mid-width. Good depths of 6 to 9 feet continue on the centerline throughout both branches of the stream. Skippers looking to drop anchor will probably want to choose the confluence of the two forks. This spot affords maximum swinging room. Florida Gulf Service will be found on the western terminus of the north-side branch.

Madeira Beach Anchorage To enter the super anchorage west of flashing daybeacon #7 (on the Johns Pass entrance channel), continue on the inlet cut past #7 as if you were putting out to sea. After cruising south for some 25 yards from #7, curl back around to the northwest and enter the stream by heavily favoring the port-side shore. By following this procedure, you can expect 6-foot depths, while a slip to the east will land you in 5-foot soundings. Drop the hook anywhere you choose, but be aware that a southerly wind might swing you into the somewhat shallower water abutting the northerly banks.

To cruise farther upstream, continue favoring the port shore until coming abeam of the third, short cove to the north. Work your way back to the mid-width as you cruise past this point. Soon the wide stream splits into two branches. If Snug Harbor Boat Yard is your destination, cruise down the centerline of the northerly fork. You will spy the yard at the westerly end of the stream.

Veterans Hospital Anchorages Two anchorages are available to cruising craft near the ICW's flashing daybeacon #6. Boats drawing 4 feet or more should probably drop the hook in the charted patch of deep water east of #6. Those cruisers making use of this anchorage should leave the Waterway abeam of unlighted daybeacon #5 and cruise carefully to the northeast. Be mindful of the shallows to the northwest that are marked by #6. Stay well away from #6 and avoid the charted ½-foot shoal along the shoreline. Pick any likely spot and settle in for the evening.

Shallow-draft cruising vessels (only!) can make use of the pool-like bay northwest of the charted Veterans Hospital. Hold to the centerline of the shallow entrance stream. Be ready for depths as shallow as 4 feet, or occasionally less. For best depths, drop anchor well away from the shoreline. Leave plenty of swinging room to avoid any vessels which happen to be tied to the permanent mooring buoys on the little bay.

On the ICW Northwest of unlighted daybeacon #5, the ICW follows a sharp turn to the west. This change of course is marked by flashing daybeacon #6, which is itself founded in shallow water. Make the turn, pointing to stay well away from #6. Come abeam of unlighted daybeacon #7 to its fairly immediate northerly side. Shallow water of 2 feet or less guards the channel to the north along this stretch.

Northwest of unlighted daybeacon #10, the Waterway hurries on to the Welch Causeway (also known as the Madeira Beach) Bridge. This span has a closed vertical clearance of 25 feet and still opens on demand except on weekends and holidays. During these times, the bridge opens for us annoying pleasurecruisers every 20 minutes from 9:30 A.M. to 6:00 P.M. Weekend sailors must take these hours into account to avoid a long and frustrating delay.

Before you reach Welch Causeway, a marina and a restaurant with dockage are available to all passing cruisers on the southwestern banks.

Madeira Beach Facilities The docks of Madeira Beach Marina front onto the northwestern banks of the large cove southwest of unlighted daybeacon #10. Successful entry into this facility is somewhat complicated by the large, charted shoal occupying the cove's mid-width, just southeast of the marina.

To avoid this shoal, continue cruising on the Waterway until you are northwest of #10, and the point of land to the southwest is abeam. Depart the ICW and heavily favor the northwesterly banks as you track your way southwest to the marina. As you work your way along the shoreline, you may catch sight of three unsigned pilings to port. These informal aids to navigation mark the shoal water to the southeast. Stay well away from the piles. You will first pass a series of covered slips. Continue on and the marina's principal dockage basin will soon be readily apparent.

On the ICW North of the Welch Causeway (Madeira Beach) Bridge, the ICW follows a dredged channel through a shallow portion of Boca Ciega Bay. Be sure to stick strictly to the marked cut. Depths outside of the Waterway quickly rise to grounding levels.

Do not attempt to enter the charted patch of deep water west of unlighted daybeacon #19. On-site research revealed that the unmarked channel is too obscure and unsafe for larger boats.

At unlighted daybeacon #25, the ICW channel follows a jog to the northwest and moves on towards the last anchorage available to the cruisers short of The Narrows. Northwest of unlighted daybeacon #27, the Waterway markers begin a new series of numbers. The next northerly aid past #27 is unlighted daybeacon #1.

Redington Shores Anchorage In a situation similar to the small bay guarded by Madeira Beach Marina, the cove striking south from unlighted daybeacon #1 features very shoal water on its mid-width, though a good channel hugs the southern banks. Additionally, there is a smaller 1-foot shoal near the rear of the cove which can cause problems.

Most skippers will enter this cove for anchorage. The southwestern corner of the bay makes a super overnight refuge. To enter, depart the Waterway at unlighted daybeacon #1 and heavily favor the portside shores as you cruise through the bay's mouth. If depths start to rise, you are probably encroaching on the shoal to starboard. Give way to the southeast for better depths. Drop the hook anywhere that strikes your fancy as you approach the southwestern corner and settle down for a night of security, even if the nearby automobile traffic does not grant you the most peaceful of evenings.

On the ICW West of flashing daybeacon #2, the ICW enters The Narrows and rough water drops away. Tidal currents do run quite swiftly, however, so stay alert.

A minimum-wake zone begins at #2 and runs north through the Park Boulevard Bridge to unlighted daybeacon #18. This would be a particularly good zone in which to obey the restrictive regulations. The county sheriff's dock is located on the western shores just south of #18.

Just north of unlighted daybeacon #12, cruisers will be greeted by the Park Boulevard Bridge. This fortunate span features a closed vertical clearance of 25 feet and opens on demand—great news indeed for sailors and skippers of single-screw vessels.

North of Park Boulevard, unlighted daybeacon #14 marks a series of semisubmerged stones flanking the easterly banks. Stay well clear of this aid to avoid a rocky experience.

At unlighted daybeacon #21, the Waterway takes a brief northward run through a shallow slough. Stick to the channel. Be sure to watch your stern as well as your progress ahead to quickly note any lateral slippage.

Flashing daybeacon #27 heralds the beginning of a long, long minimum-wake zone stretching north past the Indian Rocks Beach Bridge. Take your time and enjoy the sights.

Unlighted daybeacon #27A marks a small spoil island or shoal fronting onto the western banks. Between unlighted daybeacons #28 and #30, rocks again line the eastern shores. Favor the westerly side of the channel slightly to give this threat a wide margin.

Northwest of flashing daybeacon #33, the ICW extends greetings to the Indian Rocks Beach Bridge. With its closed vertical clearance of 25 feet, sailors will be glad to learn that this span does open on demand.

At unlighted daybeacon #40, northbound cruisers will begin to notice an increase in the breadth of the surrounding water. You are now beginning your approach to Clearwater Harbor and the Belleair Bridge. Daybeacon #40 also heralds the last good anchorage south of Belleair.

Sand Key Anchorage To enter the Sand Key anchorage, west of unlighted daybeacon #40, depart the Waterway some 100 yards north of this aid. Set course to come abeam of the northside entrance point by some 75 yards to your starboard quarter. Avoid the southerly point. It is actually a spoil island and is surrounded by shoal water. Drop the hook either just before or immediately after the northern point comes abeam. Farther to the west, depths of 5 feet or possibly less are encountered.

On to Clearwater Harbor The ICW continues to follow a well-marked, dredged passage set amidst otherwise shoal water to flashing daybeacon #47. The Belleair Bridge spans the Waterway just north of this aid. From this point and for several miles to the north, depths outside of the ICW improve somewhat. There are still shallow spots, however, so depart the marked track only with the greatest care.

The Belleair Bridge has restrictive weekend opening times. With a closed vertical clearance of 21 feet, this span can be another impediment for tall ships. On Saturdays, Sundays, and legal holidays, the bridge opens every 15 minutes, beginning at the top of the hour, from noon to 6:00 P.M. At all other times, it opens on demand.

Clearwater Harbor to Dunedin

Cruisers leaving Belleair Causeway behind are immediately introduced to the oblong, baylike body of water known as Clearwater Harbor. If ever there was a portion of the Western Florida coastline that could be described as overdeveloped, the shores about Clearwater Harbor is it. Yet, even amidst this "progress," there is still at least one opportunity to get off the beaten path and visit lands still in their natural state.

To the east, the mainland ports of call are dominated by the city of Clearwater, which is set atop the highest point of land on the Western Florida coastline. The city's waters spread out in a breathtaking view from the vantage of any of the many high-rise office buildings or condos. Clearwater clearly has its problems, but it is nevertheless a vital, flourishing community which boasts an array of services for cruisers and just about every shoreside business or convenience that can be imagined.

The beach-side barrier islands are a morass of high-rise condos, rubbing shoulders with extensive residential development and commercial shopping centers. The honk of frustrated automobile horns is a far more frequent sound to the visiting ear than the call of the breaker.

North of Clearwater, the eastern shores are graced by the once very Scottish town of Dunedin. Settled in 1870, the city now sports a well-protected harbor. Several outstanding restaurants are located nearby.

Clearwater Pass Inlet, near the midline of Clearwater Bay's north-to-south axis, provides dependable access to the Gulf of Mexico. Clearwater Pass can be used with a fair amount of confidence.

The ICW's passage through Clearwater Harbor is one of the shallowest runs on the entire Western Florida Waterway. Low-water soundings between the Clearwater Causeway and flashing daybeacon #4 (near Dunedin) can run as thin as 6½ feet.

As you might imagine amidst so much development, marina facilities are more than adequate. Both the Clearwater (Beach) and Dunedin Municipal marinas are outstanding. The commercial marina operations in the area are ably supplemented by two yacht clubs.

Anchorages directly off the ICW are somewhat slim, but the same cannot be said of the waters in and around Clearwater Beach. Several excellent overnight refuges are available to most pleasurecraft near the charted Mandalay Channel.

So, while, to be frank, they're not really this writer's cup of tea, the waters about Clearwater and its adjacent beach communities offer many services for cruising vessels. My opinion notwithstanding, many Western Florida mariners set their course for the waters of Clearwater Bay year after year with no complaint.

City of Clearwater

The sprawling city of Clearwater lies about the mainland shores of the like-named harbor for almost 10 nautical miles. In times past this city was known as one of the most beautiful in Western Florida. Even its name recalls the crystal clear waters which once lapped its shores.

This writer had the good fortune one evening to glimpse the beauty which Clearwater can still claim. Due to the vagaries of motel hunting in the city, we found ourselves on the seventh floor of a high-rise condo with a clear view of the harbor. I was able to watch the sun set over the water, and as the golden light slowly faded, we could still pick out the daybeacons and spoil island (backdropped by many high-rise condos). It was easy to understand what drew so many to this land in the first place.

Sadly, it must now be noted that this huge influx of people has led to the worst of heavy, heavy strip-type retail and office development which long ago shrouded much of southeastern Florida. I felt as if the Clearwater of old was not to be found.

However, there is still much to see and do in Clearwater, and with good dockage facilities nearby, visitors can rent a car or take a taxi and explore a number of fascinating attractions.

Many visitors will want to explore the Clearwater Marine Science Center (727-447-0980), located just off the causeway connecting Clearwater and Clearwater Beach. Here you can see "Sunset Sam," an Atlantic bottlenose dolphin who has been in residence since 1984. The staff swears that Sam is actually helpful in acclimating animals new to the facility. Another popular creature is "Big Mo," a 500-pound Loggerhead sea turtle, and Max, a very rare Kemp's Ridley sea turtle. In short, if you are interested in creatures from the sea, then by all means set your course to the Marine Science Center. Cruisers docking at Clearwater Beach Municipal Marina can reach this attraction by foot.

Visiting cruisers interested in architectural history may want to take a ride to the Belleview Biltmore Resort Hotel. Built in 1896, the Belleview is "reputed to be the largest still-occupied wooden structure in the world." In its heyday, it was known as the "White Queen of the Gulf." The grand hostelry played host to millionaires, railroad magnates, and industrial barons.

Among other striking features are the dining room's sunburst windows and priceless skylight of Tiffany stained glass. Completely renovated in 1986, the hotel has reopened to the public. You need not stay at the hotel to experience the historic structure. Historic tours are offered for non-guests. Call 727-442-6171 for more information.

The Suncoast Seabird Sanctuary (18328 Gulf Boulevard, 727-391-6211) is a fascinating facility that is dedicated to the rehabilitation and hopefully re-release of injured sea birds. Since its inception in 1971, more than 15,000 patients have been returned to their natural environment, with an average of 20 or more sick birds being brought in every day. Visitors are always welcome and cameras are definitely recommended.

Two Clearwater events are worthy of all visitors' attention. The Clearwater Jazz Festival, held the third weekend in October, is, according to the local Chamber of Commerce, "one of the top 20 events in the southeast . . . the finest and fastest-growing jazz festival in the nation."

November brings on the famous Kahlua Cup Regatta, one of the top events in the Southern Ocean Racing Conference. The race begins just off the Clearwater Beach pier and is a colorful sight indeed as all the tall ships jockey for position near the starting line. Cruisers will be especially interested in watching the various racing skippers' techniques.

Numbers to know in Clearwater include:

Payless Cab—727-442-9999
Yellow Cab—727-799-2222
Avis Rental Cars—727-530-1406
Enterprise Rent-A-Car—727-796-3442
Hertz Rent A Car—727-531-3774
Boat/U S Marine Center—727-573-2678
West Marine—727-442-2280
Chamber of Commerce—727-461-0011

Belleair Anchorage

While it can most certainly not be described as a quiet, isolated haven, captains desiring to drop the hook for the evening near the ICW can follow the charted deep water striking east just north of Belleair Causeway. Automobile traffic and headlights may disturb your evening's peace, and this should be factored into your decision whether to stay or move on. Minimum depths of 6 feet, with most soundings showing much better water, can be held well in towards the rear of the cove by avoiding the southern banks. This shoreline hosts a large public launching ramp facility, and the rearward banks are over-

looked by a tall, white office building. The anchorage affords excellent protection from southern and eastern winds. There is also some shelter from northerly breezes courtesy of the tongue of land east of unlighted daybeacon #2. Strong westerly winds could make for a very bumpy night.

Waterway Anchorage (Standard Mile 133.5)

In easterly winds, captains seeking an overnight refuge near the ICW might consider dropping anchor in the 6-foot charted waters east of unlighted daybeacon #6, itself southwest of Belleview Island. Good water of 6 feet or better extends to within 100 yards of the eastern shore. Swinging room is ample for any size or shape of pleasureboat and there is good shelter from easterly breezes. Belleview Island also affords a break when winds are blowing from the north and northeast. Protection from other winds is minimal and anchored craft will be exposed to the wake of all passing vessels. The easterly banks are overlooked by extremely heavy commercial development (what else?).

Clearwater Causeway Anchorage (Standard Mile 136)

Study chart 11411 for a moment and note the square cove sandwiched between the southeastern corner of Clearwater Causeway and the peninsula of land to the south. This small body of water provides protected overnight anchorage in all but strong westerly blows. Minimum depths are in the 7-foot region, and boats as large as 60 feet will find plenty of elbow room.

Now for the bad news. The surrounding shores are buffered by not-so-attractive concrete seawalls and are guarded by massive development. Automobile traffic crossing the adjacent bridge produces enough noise and light to rouse Dracula from his coffin. Nevertheless, if you can put up with the racket, there are few more secure places to drop the hook in Clearwater Harbor.

Clearwater Pass Inlet
(Standard Mile 135.5)

I keep waiting for the easily run inlet to be invented. As any skipper who has spent more than a few moments on the water knows, the often unstable threads between offshore and inland waters can produce more than their share of white-knuckle experiences. Well, the bad news is that the problemless seaward cut has yet to come along, but the good news is that Clearwater Pass is about as close as you are likely to get in Western Florida. While waves can still kick up when wind and tides oppose one another, the channel is well marked, consistently deeper than 10 feet, and the cut is carefully maintained. A new 74-foot fixed, high-rise span now crosses the inlet. This bridge is a major improvement over its old bascule predecessor.

The direct route from the ICW to Clearwater Pass departs the Waterway west-northwest of flashing daybeacon #12. A second cut running south from the Clearwater Beach Channel intersects the inlet route near flashing daybeacon #14, just east of the inlet's bridge. This cut will be reviewed in the next section below.

After you leave the inlet bridge in your wake, chart 11411 correctly forecasts a bubble of 7- to 8-foot water abutting the southern banks near flashing daybeacon #8. The adjacent shores host some sort of barge-loading facility, but during calm conditions, passing cruisers should be able to throw out the lunch hook here for an hour or so. It would take a captain far braver (or more foolhardy) than myself to attempt an overnight stay.

Large, high-rise condos gaze benignly over the northern shores west of the inlet bridge, while the southern banks are delightfully undeveloped and sport a parklike atmosphere.

All in all, if you are planning to put to sea or gain access to the ICW from the Gulf, you could scarcely do better than Clearwater Pass.

Clearwater Beach Channel and Facilities
(Standard Mile 136)

Minimum 7-foot depths lead you northwest off the ICW on the well-marked Clearwater Beach Channel just southwest of the Clearwater Memorial Causeway Bridge. This fortunate cut provides ready access to one of the finest facilities in the Clearwater region. A short side trip can also lead you to a quality yacht club with reciprocal privileges. Veteran cruisers in Western Florida make the turn time after time to visit Clearwater Beach's notable facilities.

While, as noted above, the Clearwater Beach cut is deep and boasts good markings, there are still a few tricks which could trap the first-time visitor. Be sure to read the navigational information presented later in this chapter before running the cut for the first time.

At flashing daybeacon #10, a second channel cuts south and eventually runs to Clearwater Pass. Minimum 8- to 9-foot depths make successful navigation of this channel a simple joy. But wait—there's more.

North of unlighted daybeacon #7, the large, westward-running cove leads to the fabulous Clearwater Yacht Club, and anchorage possibilities as well. Two privately maintained but uncharted daybeacons help you to maintain minimum 6-foot depths as you enter this offshoot. Moving east to west, the yacht club's docks will be spotted about halfway down the cove, guarding the southerly banks. This notable facility offers transient dockage (eight guest slips) for members of yacht clubs with reciprocal privileges at modern, fixed wooden piers featuring the latest power and water connections. Dockside depths are 8 feet or thereabouts. The club dockmaster is on duty Tuesday through Sunday, 9:00 A.M. to 4:00 P.M. Advance reservations are strongly suggested. Shoreside amenities include a swimming pool, bar, showers, and a full dining room that serves both lunch and the evening meal Tuesday through Saturday. Reservations are required and a dress code is in effect. Several additional restaurants, including the notable Heilman's Beachcomber (447 Mandalay Avenue, 727-442-4144), are only a walk away. This writer found the club members to be some of the friendliest souls in Western Florida. This stopover is highly recommended for those who meet the visiting requirements.

> **Clearwater Yacht Club (727) 447-6000**
> http://www.clwyc.org
>
> **Approach depth—6-14 feet**
> **Dockside depth—8 feet**
> **Accepts transients—members of clubs with reciprocal privileges**
> **Fixed wooden piers—yes**
> **Dockside power connections—30-50 amp**
> **Dockside water connections—yes**
> **Showers—yes**
> **Restaurant—on site and several others nearby**

Cruisers looking for a secure spot to drop the hook can easily anchor abeam or just to the west of the yacht club docks in 7 to 14 feet of water. There is plenty of swinging room and excellent protection from all winds except strong easterly breezes, which would blow straight up the cove. In fresh westerly winds, you may want to sound your way farther in towards the cove's western terminus for increased shelter. The surrounding shores are lined by heavy residential development but, even so, they are more attractive than those of the two anchorages directly adjacent to the ICW discussed above.

Returning our attention to the primary Clearwater Beach Channel, the cut continues running west-northwest from flashing daybeacon #10 to an intersection with the Mandalay Channel. This passage leads through a fixed bridge to additional facilities and anchorages and will be addressed separately below.

West of unlighted daybeacon #11, mariners may choose to visit one of the nicest city-owned boating facilities that this writer has ever reviewed. Clearwater Municipal Marina offers a host of transient slips for the visiting cruiser. Dockage is at fixed wooden piers with water and power connections up to 50 amp, plus telephone and cable television hook-ups as well. Gasoline and diesel fuel are readily available, as are shoreside showers and waste pump-out service.

Clearwater Municipal Marina is the only pleasurecraft facility, to my knowledge, that supplies an "ADA"-approved lift device to safely transfer handicapped cruisers to and from their vessels. It is only to be hoped that many more marinas will follow the fine facility's lead in this innovative move.

A host of restaurants is only a short step away. Krazy Bill's Restaurant (727-442-2163), located in the shopping complex lining the harbor's northern shores, is famous for its grouper sandwiches. Galley chefs looking to restock their onboard stores will find a convenience store within easy walking distance.

Clearwater Municipal Marina

For more substantial galley supplies, it is a long 1½-mile walk across Clearwater Memorial Causeway to a Publix Supermarket on the mainland. Many visitors will be able to make use of the "Jolley Trolley," a mode of public transportation provided by the city of Clearwater Beach at a mere 50-cent cost. To be succinct, Clearwater Municipal Marina is a first-rate city-sponsored marina that visiting cruisers can use with confidence.

Clearwater Municipal Marina (727) 462-6954
http://www.199.227.224.50/
marine/marina.html

Approach depth—7-17 feet
Dockside depth—9-13 feet
Accepts transients—yes (extensive)

Fixed wooden piers—yes
Dockside power connections—30-50 amp
Dockside water connections—yes
Waste pump-out—yes
Showers—yes
Gasoline—yes
Diesel fuel—yes
Restaurant—several nearby

If the urge strikes to try a meal ashore while docking at Clearwater Municipal Marina, there are two dining spots amid the myriad restaurants within walking distance of the piers that demand your attention. Frenchy's (41 Baymont Street, 727-446-3607) and its nearby brother, Frenchy's Saltwater Cafe (419 Poinsetta, 727-461-6295), are probably places that most first-time visitors would pass by without a single thought. Located on small side streets several blocks north of the municipal dockage basin, these combination bar-and-restaurants attract warm and convivial crowds evening after evening. After you've sampled the stone crab claws, conch fritters, and buffalo shrimp, not to mention the amazing burgers, you won't need to ask from whence comes the attraction. This is a "must taste" spot in Clearwater for all who, like this writer, go looking for new and different dining experiences.

Mandalay Channel and Facilities (Standard Mile 136.5)

A large side channel strikes northwest from the ICW's flashing daybeacon #15 and eventually cuts into a wide passage running just behind Clearwater Beach known as Mandalay Channel. This cut can lead cruisers to several fine anchorages, a yacht club, and a few other casual pleasurecraft facilities. Those power captains who can clear a fixed bridge with 14 feet of vertical clearance can follow the Mandalay Channel all the way south to the Clearwater Municipal Marina.

Minimum depths are 6 feet, with soundings of 7 to a much as 13 feet being more typical on Mandalay Channel. Aids to navigation are well placed, but there are a few gaps which do call for slightly more caution than usual.

West of the Mandalay Channel's unlighted daybeacon #14, cruisers whose craft draw 5½ feet or less can curl back around to the northeast and anchor in the lee of Moonshine Island. While it may have served as the onetime location of an illegal still, today the island is a wonderfully undeveloped mangrove. If the fickle wind chooses to cooperate, this is one of the most attractive overnight havens on these waters. Minimum depths of 6 feet can be carried

well in towards the island's southwesterly banks. Swinging room is sufficient for boats as large as 55 feet, but good shelter is only available from winds blowing generally from the north. There is some protection from southerly breezes courtesy of the land mass to the south, but blows of more than 12 knots from the east or west call for another plan.

West of unlighted daybeacon #14, the principal branch of the Mandalay Channel takes a sharp jog to the south. Another marked cut makes off to the north and northwest towards impassable Dunedin Pass. Depths of 7 to 9 feet can be carried as far north as a position abeam of unlighted daybeacon #20. Shortly thereafter, soundings drop off to 4½ feet or less.

Under no circumstances should even small craft attempt to run Dunedin Pass. To say that it is dangerous comprises a mammoth understatement.

West of unlighted daybeacon #20, Carlouel Yacht Club offers one or two minimal guest slips for members of clubs with reciprocal privileges. The adjacent clubhouse features showers, a swimming pool, and tennis courts (reservation only). The on-site dining room offers luncheon and dinner Wednesday through Sunday and, as usual with yacht clubs, reservations are required. The club does not employ a regular dockmaster, so advance mooring reservations are even more important than usual.

Carlouel Yacht Club (727) 446-9162

Approach depth—7-9 feet
Dockside depth—5-7 feet
**Accepts transients—members of clubs with
    reciprocal privileges (limited)**
**Fixed wooden piers—yes (also some dockage
    along seawall)**
Dockside power and water connections—yes
Restaurant—on site

The principal Mandalay Channel runs south from unlighted daybeacon #14 to a fixed bridge with 14 feet of vertical clearance. In anything short of stormy conditions, pleasure-craft of any size, type, or draft can easily anchor in the channel itself. Just be sure to drop the hook a bit away from the mid-width and show an anchor light in case any nighttime traffic happens along. The surrounding shores sport heavy, but not completely unattractive residential development. High-rise condos are very much in evidence to the south.

Captains and crew cruising south on Mandalay Channel towards the fixed bridge will spot a whole bevy of covered slips to the southeast. This facility is pictured as a black *L* and a straight bar on chart 11411. These piers belong to Island Yacht Club, which is actually a boataminium. No services of any type are available for visitors.

Just behind Island Yacht Club (on the southern shore of the southeastward-running cove), High & Dry Marina (727-443-0637) offers dry storage, a small ship's store, and gasoline. No dockage or diesel fuel can be had. Depths on the approach channel are in the 6- to 13-foot range with 7 to 9 feet of water dockside. Some small-scale mechanical repairs are available for outboard- and I/O-powered vessels.

Immediately north of the 14-foot fixed bridge, a deep (7½ to 9 feet) channel strikes southeast and leads to a first-rate boatyard. Cruisers traversing this cut will first spot (on the northeastern banks) some slips rented on a monthly basis to pleasureboaters by the city of Clearwater. These docks are clustered around the Clearwater Marine Science Center. Continue cruising upstream and Ross Yacht Service (727-446-8191) will come abeam on the northeastern banks. This facility offers full-service mechanical and haul-out

(50-ton travelift), below-waterline repairs to all types of pleasurecraft. The facility has a long-standing tradition of excellence with local cruisers.

Anyone studying chart 11411 would not realize it, but the canal leading southeast to Ross Yacht Service actually dead ends just past this facility. Some local sailcraft seem to regularly tie up to mooring buoys near the canal's eastern terminus. There is very little additional room for transients and visiting cruisers might do well to look elsewhere.

Clearwater Bay Marina (Standard Mile 136.5)

We must unhappily report that the facility known as Clearwater Bay Marina, found in the

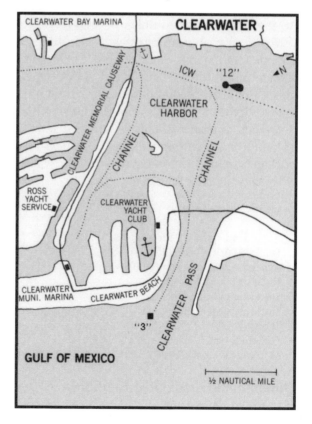

charted harbor just east-southeast of the ICW's unlighted daybeacon #16, has taken a definite turn for the worse recently. Unfortunately, a large gambling ship now makes its home at this facility, and it's clear to us that many of the resources are now slanted in that direction.

The former full-service repair yard has been discontinued, and its headquarters has been flattened. Some mechanical service work is still available by way of a small, on-site repair firm known as Dockside Doctors (727-443-2167). Minimal haul-outs by way of a forklift are also offered.

The marina portion of this operation currently has two slips open for transients. Berths are found at fixed wooden slips in fair condition. Dockside depths of 5 feet at low water could be a problem for deeper-draft vessels. At the present time, only 30-amp electric service is available (and freshwater hook-ups), but the marina hopes to update to 50-amp service in the future. Gasoline, but no longer diesel fuel, can be purchased dockside. One, low-key unisex shower is found on the premises. There are no restaurants, grocery stores, or laundromats within walking distance of the dockage basin. Those in need of these services will need to call a taxi (see above).

Clearwater Bay Marina (727) 443-3207

Approach depth—12 feet
Dockside depth—5 feet
Accepts transients—limited (two slips)
Fixed wooden slips—yes
Dockside power connections—30 amp
Dockside water connections—yes
Shower—yes
Gasoline—yes
Mechanical repairs—yes

Dunedin and Associated Facilities (Standard Mile 139)

East of flashing daybeacon #4, a marked and charted channel leads the fortunate cruiser to Dunedin's enclosed harbor. Of all the various mainland and beach communities between Tampa Bay and the waters south of the Anclote River, Dunedin remains this writer's personal favorite.

Dunedin seems to slumber along at a far more relaxed pace than its robust neighbors to the south. During one visit, we discovered a weekly art and craft show on the harbor park grounds. How many times do you run across an event like that? If you enjoy relaxed, small-town life, then by all means affix a red circle to Dunedin on your chart.

According to locals, this downtown Dunedin's tasteful renaissance began when the former railroad bed was paved over and converted to a hiking trail. Soon, new construction brought a host of quaint and varied shops (not to mention more than a few restaurants) to the downtown business district. The town has obviously not looked back ever since, while still maintaining the atmosphere of a small village.

Visitors to Dunedin should also be acquainted with the local Springfest/Seafood Festival held early in May. This wonderful event features some of the finest seafood you will every enjoy along with street entertainment and arts and crafts exhibitions.

Dunedin's yacht basin is very well sheltered and boasts a city marina which gladly accepts transients. Low-tide minimum entrance and dockside depths of 5 feet could be a concern for deep-draft, fixed-keel sailcraft. Dockage is at fixed wooden piers with water connections and power connections up to 50 amp. The piers along the protecting seawall are being upgraded as this account goes to press. Shoreside showers are available, and a laundromat is located three blocks away. The marina does not offer a fuel dock, but waste pump-out service is available.

A supermarket is found within a 1½-mile taxi or bicycle ride east up Main Street. For taxi service call Yellow Cab at (727) 799-2222.

Meanwhile, the dockmaster's office is found at the northeastern corner of the harbor. Visiting cruisers should check in here for slip assignments. A fresh seafood market offering a wide range of selections is now located on the first floor of the dockmaster's building. It doesn't get any more convenient than this.

As for what to do when it comes time to dine ashore, let me assure you that eating out will never be dull in Dunedin. You don't believe it? Well, just read on!

Dunedin Marina (727) 738-1909
http://www.ci.dunedin.fl.us/
dunedin/marina.htm

Approach depth—5-7 feet
Dockside depth—5 feet
Accepts transients—yes
Fixed wooden slips—yes
Dockside power connections—30 and 50 amp
Dockside water connections—yes
Waste pump-out—yes
Showers—yes
Laundromat—within three blocks
Restaurant—many nearby

The Best Western Jamaica Inn (727-733-4121) overlooks the northern corner of Dunedin Harbor's entrance. This facility no longer offers any dockage, but the restaurant is still worth your attention. The inn's Bon Appétit Restaurant is renowned among cruisers who have an acute interest in their palates. This very refined dining establishment has received the coveted four-star rating from the Mobil

Best Western Jamaica Inn/Bon Appétit Restaurant, Dunedin

Travel Guide. We found the dining room to be incredibly impressive, the service exemplary, and the Continental-style cuisine all one could ask for. If you have a tie and sport coat on board, this is certainly one of the few restaurants in Western Florida where you will want to don this attire. Prices cannot be described in any way, shape, or form as inexpensive. Bon Appétit comprises one of those "nights out to remember" that comes along once in a cruise. Reservations are mandatory and should be made at the earliest possible date.

Dunedin's yacht harbor is bordered to the east by an attractive park which is highly recommended for cruisers who have acquired a serious case of sailor's stride. Once you get your land legs back, it's only a short stroll to the downtown section from the park. Supplementing the four-star restaurant directly on the harbor, there are two other dining spots within two blocks which *must not be missed.*

First up is the cleverly named Sea Sea Rider's Restaurant (221 Main Street, 727-734-1445), quickly spotted on the southern side of the street leading almost due east from the dockage basin. Housed in a historic Florida "conch house" and specializing in the best seafood you will ever enjoy, the restaurant delights diners with the broiled catch of the day and fabulous crab claws. When it comes time to finish the meal, their Key Lime Pie will make a memory which will linger on and on.

An additional block farther to the east, and also on the southern side of the street, you will find Kelly's (319 Main Street, 727-736-5284) nestled between several other buildings. This restaurant receives my vote as one of the finest in all of Florida. The atmosphere is as unexpected as it is delightful. It's like someone dropped a New York-style bistro into Dunedin and added a touch of Florida. The

walls are decorated with such diverse touches as old bicycles hung from the ceiling and modern art prints. The pace is unhurried and seems to encourage slow sipping of your last cup of cappuccino or espresso, an attitude that is too rare in these hurried times.

Even if it were not for the atmosphere, Kelly's would still attract an ultraloyal clientele with its food alone. Some of the most imaginative dishes that I have ever enjoyed have been served up in this rarefied atmosphere. Shrimp set amidst cumin-infused olive oil and chicken breast stuffed with provolone cheese, crumbled bacon and chives, and grilled with basil-infused olive oil are only two of the unforgettable entrees. You may be assured that appetizers, desserts, and the cocktails and wine all bear the same unmistakable mark of Kelly's' constant attention to the smallest details of quality and culinary delight.

Incidentally, for those readers interested in learning more about what to see, where to go, and even where to dine in the Tampa, St. Petersburg, Clearwater metropolitan area, this writer highly recommends *Tampa Bay Magazine.* Its quality level is among the very elite regional magazines that I have reviewed. Subscriptions can be obtained by calling 727-791-4800.

Dunedin History Seven years after Florida entered the Union in 1845, Richard Leroy Garrison filed the first recorded deed on Curlew Creek. He was given 160 acres under the Bounty Land Act of 1850 for service in the Seminole Indian Wars. Following the Civil War in 1865, settlers came from Europe, the British Isles, and the eastern United States.

John Ogilvie Douglas and Hugh Somerville came to the shores of Sarasota Bay from Edinburgh, Scotland, around 1870 and opened a general store on the waterfront. Ships from Cedar Key, bound for Tampa around Pinellas Point, stopped for items including groceries, hardware, dry goods, saddlebags, and good water.

Rival George L. Jones of Marietta, Georgia, established a general store east across the dirt road, putting up a sign that read "Jonesboro." In 1878 the Scots answered this with a sign reading "Dunedin," which is Gaelic for Edinburgh. Apparently the persistent Scots won out, as they often do.

Dunedin was the trading center of the Pinellas Peninsula into the 1900s. It was also the social center. People came from miles around in horse-drawn buggies for waltzes on Saturday nights at the Dunedin Yacht Club Inn. Tourists viewed 40-foot sailboat races and took picnics to the island.

Pioneers struggled with freezes, hurricanes, mosquitoes, roaches, and poverty. There was no electricity, running water, or ice. The community was literally carved out of a wilderness.

With the coming of the Orange Belt Railroad in 1888, waterborne shipping became obsolete. Dunedin slipped back into the guise of a charming village. Incorporated in 1899, Dunedin was nine blocks long and three blocks wide, with a population of one hundred. The town became the City of Dunedin in 1926. To this day, the community retains its small-town flair as a striking contrast to its southerly neighbors.

Visitors to Dunedin should be sure to experience the Dunedin Historical Museum, housed in the 1888 railway station. It will be found on the southern side of Main Street, one block east of Kelly's.

Additional Clearwater Harbor Facilities

One other marina and a park dock beckon for passing cruisers to stop and while away a few hours on the waters north of Dunedin.

The amply marked and easily followed channel flowing east to invigorated Marker One Marina (standard mile 142) breaks off from the ICW just south of the Dunedin/Honeymoon Island Bridge. To be succinct, this is a noteworthy marina. Boasting a breakwater-protected harbor, Marker One has some of the finest services between the Anclote River and Tampa Bay. Excellent entrance and dockside depths of 6 to 8 feet provide plenty of margin for most craft. Transients are readily accepted at the most modern of fixed wooden piers with every conceivable power and water connection. Gasoline, diesel fuel, an adjacent swimming pool, waste pump-out service, and full mechanical repairs are supplemented by shoreside showers. Mechanical services are provided courtesy of the on-site repair firm known as Chuck Dillon's Marine Repairs (727-733-4047). Marker One boasts an on-site ship's and variety store. The adjacent Jesse's Dockside Restaurant (345 Causeway Boulevard, 727-736-2611) is a large, impressive dining spot which seems to be well frequented by the local crowd. Wow! How's that for services? If you are looking for a large marina with every conceivable amenity, then your search is finished. Coil your lines at Marker One for a memorable stay.

Marker One Marina (727) 733-9324

Approach depth—6-8 feet
Dockside depth—7-8 feet
Accepts transients—yes
Dockside power connections—up to 50 amp
Dockside water connections—yes
Waste pump-out—yes
Showers—yes
Gasoline—yes

Diesel fuel—yes
Mechanical repairs—yes
Ship's and variety store—yes
Restaurant—on site

Caladesi Island (Standard Mile 142)

Skippers piloting craft that draw less than 4½ feet can track their way to the west and southwest from the Waterway just south of the Dunedin Bridge (north of unlighted daybeacon #15) to the well-marked and charted Seven Mouth Creek Channel. This cut allows access to the marina at Caladesi Island State Park, one of the few undeveloped barrier islands along the central portion of Western Florida. No bridge connects Caladesi to the mainland and access is only by boat. A park service ferry does provide transportation for landlubbers.

The park features tall sand dunes, exotic shell hunting, and more than 2 miles of snow white, sandy beaches. The park nature trail offers a fascinating glimpse of pine flatwoods, oak hammocks, and mangrove swamps.

Visiting cruisers are welcome at the park service's metal-decked, floating docks. There are 100 slips on the well-sheltered harbor. No power or water connections are available, but there are bathrooms, showers, and a park service snack bar. Minimum entrance depths are only 4 feet, though you will find soundings of 4½ to 5 feet quite common on the inner part of the channel, with 5 to 8 feet of water on the cut's outer section. Dockside soundings range from 4½ to 6 feet. With the relatively shallow depths, and the channel's twists and turns, this side trip will probably appeal more to the power captain than the sailor, but the swing-keel skipper can also take a crack at it, if he or she so chooses.

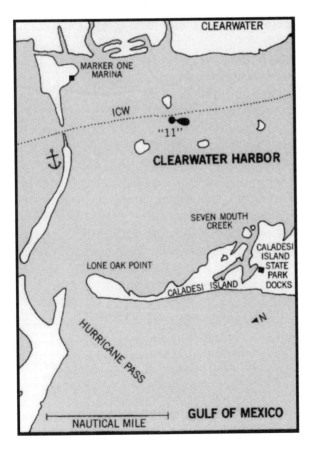

Hurricane Pass

Hurricane Pass was formed by a violent hurricane which struck the coast in 1921. The seaward cut divides what is now called Honeymoon Island to the north and Caladesi Island to the south.

Cruisers studying chart 11411 may note several charted marks leading west from unlighted daybeacon #15 to Hurricane Pass. Don't be fooled. Depths in this errant seaward cut run to 4 feet or less. All craft should avoid this inlet like the plague.

CLEARWATER HARBOR NAVIGATION

Navigation of the ICW through Clearwater Harbor is an unexpected study in caution. Shallow water (as little as 6½ feet in the ICW channel) and confusing markers are two trademark problems along this stretch of the Waterway. This is clearly not the place to go running along at full throttle. All craft should proceed with caution and keep an eye on the sounder. Always have your binoculars and chart 11411 at hand to help sort out the confusing markers and be ready for quick course changes should the need arise.

Belleair Anchorage   Enter the large pool of deep water to the east, just north of Belleair Causeway, by staying some 75 to 100 yards off the southside shore. Watch these banks and you will spot a large, public launching area. Larger, deep-draft vessels should consider dropping the hook before coming abeam of the easternmost portion of this facility. Farther to the east, shoal water extends out for some distance from all the surrounding shores.

Waterway Anchorage   Well, it doesn't get much easier than this. If you choose to drop the hook in the deep water east of unlighted daybeacon #6, simply feel your way east-southeast or northeast from this aid and avoid the narrow strip of shoals abutting the shoreline. Drop the hook and settle in for a secure evening, but remember that a large powercraft might just happen by and give you a good roll.

Clearwater Pass   The direct route from the ICW to Clearwater Pass departs the Waterway west-northwest of flashing daybeacon #12. An additional channel leading from Clearwater Memorial Causeway will be reviewed in the next section.

While this inlet is consistently deep and well marked, tidal currents do run swiftly. Sailcraft and single-screw trawlers should be on guard against excessive leeway. Watch your course over the stern as well as the track ahead to quickly note any slippage.

Leave the Waterway once abeam of #12 and set course to pass between unlighted daybeacons #19 and #20. From a position between #19 and #20 to the bridge spanning the inlet, you need only pass (as you would expect) red, even-numbered aids to your port side and green markers to starboard. This is in marked contrast to the next channel reviewed below.

The fixed high-rise Clearwater Pass Bridge (vertical clearance 74 feet) spans the inlet west of flashing daybeacon #14. This bridge is a welcome replacement for the old 24-foot bascule structure that crossed the pass until several years ago.

Once the bridge is behind, captains who are so inclined can visit the lunch anchorage on the south side of the inlet cut by striking south from flashing daybeacon #8. Good water runs almost into the southern banks, but prudent cruisers will drop the hook long before nearing the charted 2-foot shoal to the southeast. This procedure will also help to remove you from the direct path of any traffic to and from the barge-loading facility on the south shore.

Clearwater Causeway Channel The channel leading west-northwest from the ICW (just southwest of the Clearwater Causeway Bridge pass-through) to Clearwater Municipal Marina is deep and well marked, but the cut is surrounded by shoal water. Some visiting navigators become confused by the markers and this has led to groundings just where you might least expect such an embarrassing event to occur. Read the information below and watch the sounder as you cruise to the marina. Your overnight stay will be ever so much more peaceful for the extra effort.

Markers on the Clearwater Causeway Channel are the opposite of what you might expect if you were looking at this cut as part of the Clearwater Pass Inlet cut. Moving east to west, red beacons should be taken to your starboard side, while green markers can be waved at to port.

To enter the channel, depart the Waterway as unlighted daybeacon #1 comes abeam to the west-northwest. Pass this aid to its northerly side and point to come abeam of the next marker, unlighted daybeacon #2, to its southerly quarter.

From #2 to unlighted daybeacon #6, the cut is reasonably easy to follow, but conditions change between #6 and the next marker, flashing daybeacon #10. It's all too easy to mistakenly identify the "Sign," obscurely charted on the alternate channel running to Clearwater Pass Inlet, as #10. A quick study of chart 11411 correctly reveals that such an error would land you and yours square on the grassy shoal south of the channel. Use your binoculars to make a *positive* ID of #10

before proceeding. Point to come between flashing daybeacon #10 and unlighted daybeacon #9.

At #10, a second channel cuts south to Clearwater Pass. This cut will be reviewed next, but for just a moment, let's push on to Clearwater Municipal Marina. From your position between #9 and #10, point to come abeam of unlighted daybeacon #11 to its northerly side. At this point, the marina docks will be quickly spied to the west. For best water, take a fairly broad turn around #11 before altering course a bit to the west in order to reach the piers.

Returning now to the alternate cut leading to Clearwater Pass, navigators should know that marker colors reverse again. Southbound craft (headed towards the inlet) should take red markers to their (the cruisers') port side and the more prolific green beacons to starboard.

Just before coming between flashing daybeacon #10 and unlighted daybeacon #9 on the main Clearwater Causeway Channel, turn sharply to the south and point to pass unlighted daybeacon #8A to its fairly immediate westerly side. Continue on by coming abeam and passing unlighted daybeacon #7 to its easterly side, and then pointing for the gap between unlighted daybeacons #5 and #6. You can then follow the markers to the Clearwater Pass Channel near flashing daybeacon #14.

To enter the cove northwest of unlighted daybeacon #7, home of Clearwater Yacht Club, depart the north-to-south channel, some 100 yards north of #7, and point to pass the two privately maintained, unlighted daybeacons #1 and #3 to your immediate port side. This route will cause you to heavily favor the southern shore, which is exactly as it should be for best depths at the cove's entrance. Do not wander from this track by easing to the north. This is a sure way to land in depths of 5 feet or considerably less.

Once the entrance is some 50 yards behind you, good depths spread out almost from shore to shore. Clearwater Yacht Club is readily visible on the south banks near the midline of the cove's east-to-west axis. Those who choose to anchor off can select any likely spot and settle in for a secure evening.

On the ICW Mariners cruising north past the ICW's intersection with the Clearwater Causeway Channel will soon approach the Waterway's intersection with the causeway. Just before reaching the span, the sheltered but highly developed anchorage discussed earlier will come abeam to the east. This haven is easily entered almost anywhere along its broad mouth.

As you make your approach to the causeway, the old, low-level bridge, left in place for local fishing, will be spotted. Of course, the central span has been removed, leaving a broad passage for traffic on the ICW.

The Clearwater Memorial Causeway bascule bridge has a closed vertical clearance of 25 feet and, yes (grimace), a restricted opening schedule. For sailcraft that need more height (and that's most of us), the span opens weekdays only on the hour and every 20 minutes thereafter from 9:00 A.M. to 6:00 P.M. On weekends and legal holidays the bridge deigns to open on the hour

and half-hour from 2:00 P.M. to 6:00 P.M. At all other times, the span supposedly opens on demand.

As is often the case on the entire run from Tampa Bay to Anclote Key, a minimum-wake zone is in effect on both sides of the bridge. Power captains had best slow down and enjoy the sights.

North of the Clearwater Causeway, cruisers will begin their approach to the first of several confusing sets of markers along the track of the ICW. North of flashing daybeacon #14A all captains should slow to minimal speed and sort out the mess. The outcropping of land you will see ahead shelters Clearwater Bay Marina's dockage basin. Just south of the land, a few charted markers lead east to a public launching ramp. Obviously, this small cut is of little interest to cruising-size craft. Similarly, the Mandalay Approach Channel (detailed below) breaks off to the northwest. All the markers for these various passages, set so close to the Waterway beacons, can be quite confusing. Use your binoculars to pick out flashing daybeacon #15, unlighted daybeacon #15A, and unlighted daybeacon #16. Pass just to the east of #15 and #15A and (you guessed it) close by the western side of #16. This passage will lead you hard by the point of land stretching out from the yacht basin. This is not a cause for worry. If you stay between the proper set of markers, depths remain good. Pick out the wrong aids to navigation and you will most likely make the local prop repair shops very happy.

Mandalay Channel and Approaches While the Mandalay Channel is well marked and charted, skippers must enter this cut with the understanding that it is surrounded by shoal water. A mistake can quickly lead to that sad sound of a keel crunching along the bottom. So, read the information below carefully, proceed at idle speed, and be sure to positively identify the next marker. Be prepared to find new and different aids to navigation than those pictured on chart 11411, or in the account presented below. This seems to be a changeable area that requires periodic remarking.

Leave the ICW just south of flashing daybeacon #15 and point to pass between the Mandalay Approach Channel's first two aids, unlighted daybeacons #2 and #3. Be sure to pass to the south and west of #2. Some sort of concrete riprap can be seen jutting out of the water north of this aid to navigation.

Continue on, pointing to pass all green markers to port side until coming between unlighted daybeacons #9 and #8. It is a long run between #8 and #9 and the next marker to the northwest, unlighted daybeacon #10. Both sides of the channel along this stretch border on shallows, but the shoal to the northeast is particularly dangerous, with depths of less than 1 foot. Use your binoculars to pick out #10 and set course to pass this aid by some 15 yards to your starboard side.

Pass unlighted daybeacon #12 by about the same distance to starboard and then break out the binoculars again and pick out unlighted daybeacon #12A to the northwest. This aid marks a westward bend in the channel which allows cruisers to bypass the charted shoal bisecting the Mandalay approach cut. Come abeam of #12A to your immediate starboard side and immediately set a course to come abeam of unlighted daybeacon #14 by some 25 yards to your starboard side. Shallows border both sides of the channel between #12A and #14. Keep a close watch on the sounder and be vigilant against excessive leeway. Continue on the same course for some 25 yards past #14. Soon good water again extends out on a broad swath before you.

Captains opting for the anchorage adjacent to the south-southwestern shores of Moonshine Island should depart the marked route leading to Mandalay Channel about halfway between #14 and unlighted daybeacon #16. Cut to the northeast and point directly for the mid-width of the island's shores. Don't stray too close to either #14 or #16, as both aids are somewhat surrounded by shoals. Drop the hook within about 25 yards of shore. Don't attempt to cruise towards the island's southeastern point, where you might see a sign. The placard in question merely warns of a grass shoal (where anchoring is illegal) and is itself founded in shallows.

After passing unlighted daybeacon #14, visiting cruisers must decide whether to continue down the marked cut (to the northwest) to Carlouel Yacht Club or turn sharply south and enter the main body of Mandalay Channel. Remember that Dunedin Pass Inlet is impassable, even for small craft. Thus, only those cruisers heading for Carlouel need enter the northside channel for any but sight-seeing purposes.

If you do decide to enter the northward-flowing cut, point to pass between unlighted daybeacons #15 and #16. Farther to the northwest, you need only pass all red marks to their westerly sides and all green beacons to their easterly quarters until reaching unlighted daybeacon #20. At #20, you will spot the docks of Carlouel Yacht Club on the western banks. Do not attempt to cruise past #20. Depths quickly deteriorate to 4-foot levels or considerably less.

The main body of Mandalay Channel, leading almost due south from its intersection with the Carlouel cut, is easily entered by favoring the western shores slightly. This will help to avoid the clearly charted shoal south of unlighted daybeacon #14. Soon good water envelops the broad channel almost from bank to bank. Skippers can easily follow the cut south to the 14-foot fixed bridge by observing the markers along the way.

On the ICW   The Waterway stretch between flashing daybeacon #18 and (moving north) unlighted daybeacon #2 may just hold the honor of being the shallowest section of the ICW along this coastline of the Sunshine State. During low water, depths of as little as 6½ feet are common. This should not be a problem for boats drawing 6 feet or less, but if you need more, better wait until high water.

Dunedin Harbor   The somewhat indifferently marked channel leading to Dunedin Harbor strikes off to the northeast at flashing daybeacon #4. As you would expect from the "red, right, returning" rule, pass all red markers to your starboard side and all green beacons to port.

Some of the charted aids on the Dunedin Harbor channel are not exactly regulation. The first green beacon is denoted by a tiny daymark set atop a sign advertising the Dunedin dockage basin. Similarly, flashing daybeacon #5 is found set atop the Jamaica Inn dock to port, and flashing daybeacon #4 is actually perched on the rocks just south of the breakwater's entrance. In spite of these vagaries, it's really easy to enter the harbor in daylight and few visiting cruisers will experience any difficulty whatsoever. Just be sure to stay well away from #4. Obviously, visitors should make every effort to arrive before dark and to continue this practice until becoming familiar with the channel.

On the ICW   The ICW channel between unlighted daybeacon #9 and the Dunedin bascule bridge (north of unlighted daybeacon #15) is another problem-plagued stretch of the Waterway. The cut is narrow and closely bordered by shallows with only 2-and 3-foot soundings. Again, these are waters where you can't be in a hurry. Powercraft should slow to nonplaning speed and all captains should keep their binoculars close by. Detail a crew member to keep a watch on the sounder. If depths rise above 6½ feet, you are doing something wrong. Stop and make corrections at once before you give Sea Tow some business.

Cruising north from unlighted daybeacon #9, set course to come abeam of unlighted daybeacon #10 close by its western side. There seems to be a tendency to wander onto the shallows to the west during this run. Watch your course behind as well as ahead to quickly note any lateral slippage.

From #10, point to pass between flashing daybeacon #12 and flashing daybeacon #11. Flashing #12 is located hard by the western shores of a small spoil island.

The worst part of the passage is found between #12 and the Dunedin (Honeymoon Island) Bridge. While you would never guess it, the Waterway aids just to the north, unlighted daybeacons #13 and #15, and flashing daybeacon #14 are hard to spot from a position between #11 and #12. Just to make matters a bit worse, the charted channel cutting east to Marker One Marina and the markers pointing west towards impassable Hurricane Pass can be easily mistaken for the Waterway daybeacons. Be *sure* to pick out #13, #14, and #15 before cruising on to the bridge.

As always in changeable waters such as these, captains should be prepared to find different markers than those discussed above. Occasionally the Army Corps of Engineers decides to completely change the configuration of aids to navigation during their yearly maintenance in a channel of this nature. There's no way to know if this will someday happen here, but *be ready!*

Seven Mouth Creek and Caladesi Island Remember that low-water depths on the channel leading to the marina at Caladesi Island State Park run as skimpy as 4 feet. If you can stand those sorts of depths, depart the Waterway north of unlighted daybeacon #15 and cut west on the marked Hurricane Pass Channel, pointing to eventually come abeam of unlighted daybeacon

#8 (part of the errant Hurricane Pass Channel) to its fairly immediate northerly side. Continue cruising past #8 for 100 yards or so, and then turn sharply south-southwest, setting course to come between flashing daybeacon #2 and unlighted daybeacon #1, the first two aids on the Seven Mouth Creek entrance channel. Don't slip to the east between #8 and #2. The charted patch of 2-foot water is a real hazard on this quarter.

Continue tracking your way to the south on the channel, keeping all red markers to your starboard side and all green beacons to port. Stick to the marked cut. Depths outside of the channel immediately rise to 1 foot or less, and some of the shoals are foul with stumps and other underwater obstructions.

After passing unlighted daybeacon #8, the channel cuts hard to starboard, and depths fall off a bit. At unlighted daybeacons #11 and #12, the passage turns back to port a bit and no-wake regulations begin. The park service docks and ranger office will then be obvious dead ahead.

Hurricane Pass Channel A series of mostly uncharted daybeacons that are nevertheless prominent on the water strikes west just north of unlighted daybeacon #15. The first part of this cut carries depths of 7 to 11 feet, but west of unlighted daybeacon #4, all markers cease and depths rise to 4 feet or less. While cruising craft may safely use the easterly portion of this channel as an approach to Seven Mouth Creek, this writer strictly advises his fellow mariners to avoid the remainder of the cut and the inlet itself.

On the ICW North of unlighted daybeacon #15, the Waterway soon approaches the Dunedin bascule bridge. South of the span, the well-outlined Marker One Channel cuts east. This passage is easily tracked by simply passing between the sets of prolific markers and remembering your "red, right, returning" maxim.

The Dunedin Bridge has a closed vertical clearance of 24 feet and, wonder of wonders, the span actually opens on demand. A minimum-wake zone is in effect for a short distance both north and south of the bridge. On-the-water signs clearly outline the restricted area.

Once the bridge is behind, the broad waters of St. Joseph Sound sweep out before you. The delightful cruising about Anclote Key and river is but a short hop to the north.

Honeymoon Island to Anclote Key

The northernmost leg of the Western Florida ICW stretches for some 7 nautical miles from the Dunedin-Honeymoon Island Bridge to Anclote Key and the mouth of the Anclote River. Farther to the north, cruisers face a long and sometimes troublesome voyage of better than 140 nautical miles across Florida's "Big Bend" to the easterly genesis of the Northern Gulf ICW near the village of Carrabelle. This daunting passage will be covered in the last chapter of this guide.

North of Dunedin Bridge the Waterway knifes through the open reaches of St. Joseph Sound. With a channel featuring low-tide depths of as little as 6 to 6½ feet, boats drawing 6 feet or better might want to think long and hard, or at least consult the tide tables, before beginning this journey. Fortunately, the shallower water is found mostly on the southern leg of this run. If you should decide the depths are too skimpy for your craft, you can always sail into the Gulf's deep waters from Clearwater Pass and then visit Anclote Key and river by reentering the more inland waters via the inlet north of Three Rooker Bar.

From this vantage point, you may choose to anchor next to gorgeous Anclote Key or ease up the Anclote River, with its numerous facilities, and visit the absolutely charming village of Tarpon Springs.

Much of St. Joseph Sound's westerly reaches are wide open to the waters of the Gulf of Mexico. It doesn't require too much nautical prowess to realize that the shallow depths, coupled with a long wind fetch in westerly breezes, can raise a most uncomfortable and occasionally dangerous chop. Small craft in particular had better plan their departure with the latest NOAA weather forecast in mind.

A few marinas line St. Joseph Sound's mainland shores south of the Anclote River, but none offers much in the way of services for transients. Also, all of these facilities require captains to transit long, sometimes rather shallow channels running east from the ICW. Boats drawing more than 5 feet should read the various accounts below carefully before committing themselves to a particular port of call.

The Anclote River itself and Tarpon Springs feature a host of marinas and yards waiting to greet the visiting cruiser. This wonderful cruising ground will be covered in the last section of this chapter.

Anchorages between the Dunedin Bridge and the mouth of the Anclote River are fairly few and far between. Even these are not particularly sheltered and call for an accurate appraisal of the evening winds.

Finally, all mariners who, like this writer, enjoy cruising through less crowded waters will be glad to learn that shoreside development falls away more and more as you cruise to the north. Anclote Key, in particular, is protected from commercial exploitation and is absolutely beautiful. A trip ashore by dinghy is a must!

Dunedin Bridge Anchorage (Standard Mile 142)

Some boats occasionally anchor along the Waterway's western flank, just north of the Dunedin bascule bridge. Depths of 5 to 5½ feet can be carried for several hundred yards west of the bridge by staying 75 yards or so north of the causeway shores. Farther to the west, depths rise to 4-foot levels. Protection is good from southerly winds, but minimal for blows exceeding 15 knots from any other direction. The nearby highway could bring on a fair amount of noise and passing headlights during the evening hours.

Minnow Creek Marinas (Standard Mile 142.5)

A charted channel leads east from the ICW at flashing daybeacon #18 to three facilities on Minnow Creek. The cut carries typical low-tide depths of 5 to 7 feet and is outlined by pilings with arrow markers, but no daybeacon

signs. In strong northerly winds, soundings occasionally rise to 4½-foot levels.

Cruisers nearing the easterly reaches of the Minnow Creek Channel will quickly spy Home Port Marina's large collection of covered slips and dry-storage building ahead and a little to the northeast. At this point, the channel branches out into three different forks. Visiting skippers must take care to properly identify their chosen passage. The northernmost of the three leads to a small boatyard on the creek's northerly banks. This is a tricky run and is best avoided by visitors. The middle channel strikes east-northeast to Home Port, while the most southerly cut leads to two smaller marinas on the southern shores of Minnow Creek.

Home Port Marina (727-781-1443) no longer accepts transients for overnight dockage. The (mostly) fixed wooden piers with water and 30- to 50-amp power connections are now rented out strictly on a month-to-month basis. Many of these slips are covered, ideal for long-term storage of powercraft. Full mechanical repairs of the gasoline variety can be had and your craft can by hauled out via a 35-ton travelift. Strangely enough, though, the management of Home Port has informed this writer that "bottom jobs" are no longer available. Gasoline can be purchased at a floating pier, just north of the main dockage basin. A ship's and variety store is found on the grounds, along with a swimming pool and open-air tiki bar. Dry storage is featured for resident craft. The harbor is a bit open to strong westerly winds, but otherwise is well sheltered.

Two additional marinas are accessed via the southernmost of the three Minnow Creek channels. First up is Island Harbor Marina (727-784-3014), which is almost exclusively a dry-storage facility for smaller powercraft. No fuel is available.

A short trek south will lead you to the two ranks of covered slips belonging to Prior Boat Builders (727-784-1396). This small but friendly facility occasionally accepts power-boats for overnight dockage, but this practice is clearly more the exception than the rule. Pleasurecraft of most sizes can be hauled out courtesy of an on-site marine railway. Mechanical repairs, geared mostly towards outboards and I/O's, are available. Gasoline, but no diesel fuel, can be purchased. Prior maintains a parts store with a good selection of Chris Craft hardware.

Ozona Channel (Standard Mile 143.5)

The forgettable Ozona Channel strikes east from the Waterway between flashing daybeacon #23 and unlighted daybeacon #26. This cut eventually leads to two small marinas near its eastern terminus. After having left the last daybeacon behind, this writer tried to reach the docks from three separate angles. Each attempt led to a grounding and occasioned assorted blue language and a jump over the side to push the boat off while wading in chilly January waters. The boats docked at this marina most certainly know where the channel is from trial and error. Cruisers not familiar with this cut would do very well to salute as they continue on by.

Klosterman Bayou

Study chart 11411 for a moment and you will note a well-marked channel running east-northeast between flashing daybeacon #31 and unlighted daybeacon #34. This minimum-5-foot cut now leads to a private condo dock, and there are no services available to visiting craft nor room to anchor. Just keep on trucking up the ICW.

Three Rooker Bar Anchorage (Standard Mile 147)

In good weather with winds of less than 10 knots (preferably blowing from the west), local captains often drop the hook in the correctly charted 5- and 6-foot waters near the northern tip of Three Rooker Bar. To reach this haven successfully, you must follow a long, markerless passage from the ICW's unlighted daybeacon #35 (or #36) and feel your way carefully with the sounder into the sheltered water just behind the sand spit's northern tip. Great care must be exercised to avoid the 1-foot shallows to the south.

If you are lucky enough to catch the weather right and can find the anchorage without meeting up with the bottom, this is an absolutely enchanting spot. The nearby Three Rooker Bar is, as you would expect, completely in its natural state. Landing on this small landmass is now prohibited to help protect the many nesting birds there. Leave the dinghy on the davits.

Route to the Gulf

Cruisers anxious to begin their sail on open water (and willing to forego the charms of Anclote Key and Tarpon Springs) can put out to sea by using the marked and charted channel running between Anclote Key and Three Rooker Bar, west of unlighted daybeacon #37. This seaward cut currently carries minimum depths of 7 feet, with typical soundings in the 8- to 11-foot region. Of course, with these depths, the chop can be wicked when winds and tide oppose but, then again, when isn't that true of inlets?

Anclote Key and Associated Anchorages (Standard Mile 150)

Northbound cruisers will spy the proud

Anclote Key Lighthouse topping the horizon by the time they reach flashing daybeacon #31. This now abandoned sentinel heralds one of the most beautiful barrier islands in Western Florida. Roughly translated, Anclote means "fair harbor." The Spaniards, who originally gave this designation to the isle, knew whereof they spoke. Whether by good fortune or careful planning, Anclote Key has remained almost completely undeveloped. You will have to experience for yourself its virgin maritime forests, white sand beaches, and clear waters to understand what a special place this really is for visitors. Every single cruiser should set aside a day or so in his or her travel itinerary to enjoy Anclote as one of the last, vanishing reminders of what barrier islands were once all like in Western Florida.

Unfortunately, Anclote Key is surrounded by a broad shelf of shoal water on all sides. The anchorages described below all require a long dinghy trip ashore over very shoal water.

During the winter months, the prevailing winds blow from the north through most of Western Florida. With the passage of bad weather fronts, these blows can reach alarming proportions. None of the Anclote anchorages offer any real protection from these winds. Be sure to check the latest NOAA forecast before committing to an overnight stay.

Do not attempt to enter the channel noted on chart 11411, south and west of unlighted daybeacon #7X (near the island's southerly tip). This cut has shoaled in completely and even a small outboard is likely to match prop against sand.

If you are careful to avoid the shoal water just north of #7X, you can anchor in 7- to 10-foot depths in the charted tongue of deep water some .4 nautical miles north of the daybeacon. Holding ground is good and the key gives some protection from westerly winds.

This writer's favorite anchorage is found on the charted 8-foot waters, east of Dutchman Key's southern tip. You can approach to within .2 nautical miles of this smaller island and stay in good water. This relatively tight access renders this anchorage the closest to Anclote Key, which, of course, also heralds the best

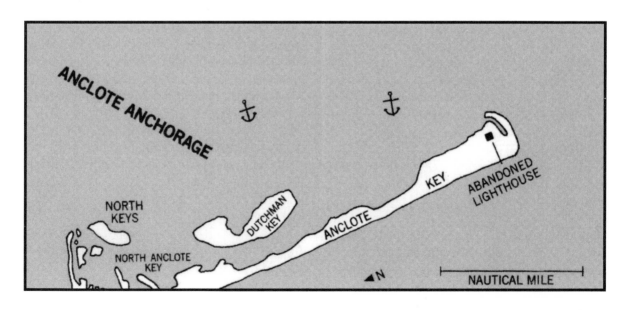

shelter in brisk western breezes. Offsetting this advantage to some extent is the longer dinghy ride necessary to reach the main body of Anclote Key. It would also be a prodigious walk to the lighthouse from this locale.

Wherever you choose to anchor, Anclote Key is well worth your time. Pause for a moment and, if you look with your mind's eye, you may still see an old, sail-powered sponge boat headed for Tarpon Springs, or a sprightly clipper bound for the bustling port of Tampa. Few places in all of Florida can give the sensitive visitor such a sense of this state's bygone days.

HONEYMOON ISLAND TO ANCLOTE KEY NAVIGATION

While it is a feast for the eyes, cruising the ICW through St. Joseph Sound to Anclote Key is certainly no navigational walk in the park. Low-tide depths of as little as 6 (occasionally 5½) feet on the southern portion of this run are a real concern for skippers piloting sailcraft with deep, fixed keels. If you draw better than 5½ feet, it would be far wiser to either put out into the Gulf and cruise back into St. Joseph Sound via the marked inlet between Anclote Key and Three Rooker Bar, or (at the least) cruise through on a rising tide.

As if that weren't cause enough for worry, most of the passage through St. Joseph Sound is very much open to wind and wave from the deeper Gulf waters to the west. Winds over 10, and certainly 15 knots, can be uncomfortable and stronger blows are sometimes downright dangerous. Be sure to schedule your cruise only after consultation with the latest NOAA prognostication.

The Waterway route is well marked all the way to Anclote Key. The side channels are another affair entirely. All these cuts call for caution and a steady hand on the helm.

Cruisers studying chart 11411 will note a series of spoil islands marking the easterly side of the ICW between the Minnow Creek Channel and unlighted daybeacon #42. These bodies of land seemed a bit larger on the water to this writer than they appear on the chart. Most are covered with scrub growth and a few even have some low-lying trees. All are surrounded by shoal water, but shallow-draft vessels can usually anchor some 50 to 75 yards offshore in 4 to 5 feet of water and dinghy in for a closer look. This is a popular weekend pastime for small-craft skippers plying these waters.

On a day of fair weather, most mariners will thoroughly enjoy their passage north to Anclote Key. Those forced to make the trip in less than ideal conditions may have a different story to tell.

Dunedin Bridge Anchorage To access the anchorage north of the Dunedin/Honeymoon Island bascule bridge, depart the Waterway channel soon after passing through the span. Set course to stay at least 75 yards north of the causeway to the west. Consider dropping anchor soon after coming under the lee of the land (causeway) west of the bridge. Depths rise to 4 feet after you cruise 100 yards or so to the west past this point.

Minnow Creek Channel Remember that the channel leading east from flashing daybeacon #18 to Home Port Marina and the other facilities on Minnow Creek is outlined by low-level, privately maintained aids with arrow markers. These markers lack any daybeacon signs and could be more than slightly difficult for strangers to locate at night. During daylight, this will not be a problem.

As the large dry-storage buildings of Homeport come into sight, watch for an uncharted, three-way split in the channel. As explained earlier, the northernmost cut leads to a small yard and is not recommended for visitors. The middle of the three provides access to Homeport Marina, while the southern branch escorts cruising craft to Prior Boat Builders and Island Harbor Marina.

Be sure to stay within the channel markers. Depths outside of the marked passage are 3 feet or less. If you become confused by the numerous beacons, be sure to stop and sort out the situation before moving ahead. Your keel will be ever so much happier for the extra effort.

On the ICW The Waterway channel between Dunedin Bridge and flashing daybeacon #31 is the shallowest portion of the entire Western Florida ICW. Mean low-water depths of only 6 feet are common and if tides are below normal levels, soundings can rise to 5½ feet. Stick strictly to the marked cut and watch your course astern as well as the track ahead to quickly note any leeway.

Ozona Channel The charted cut leading to the two small marinas at Ozona strikes east between flashing daybeacon #23 and unlighted daybeacon #26. This writer suggests that visiting cruisers pass this channel by with hardly a thought. The unmarked easterly reaches of the cut are rife with shoal water.

On the ICW Between flashing daybeacon #31 and unlighted daybeacon #34, the channel markers outlining the passage to Klosterman Bayou flank the easterly portion of the Waterway. The close proximity of unlighted daybeacons #1 and #2 (the westernmost aids of the Klosterman cut) allows these aids to be easily misidentified as the Waterway markers, particularly for southbound cruisers. Such a mistake could land you in the shallower water east of the ICW. As you approach this intersection, break out the spyglass and be sure to pick out the correct markers.

The Klosterman Bayou channel now leads only to a private condo dock. The restaurant that used to overlook the creek's banks is now a distant memory. Passing cruisers should keep on trucking up or down the ICW.

Three Rooker Bar Anchorage To visit this popular anchor-down spot, leave the Waterway at either unlighted daybeacon #35 or #36. Set a careful compass course for the northerly tip of Three Rooker Bar. Expect some 5-foot soundings as you approach the land.

Once the island is in sight, head directly for the northern point. Some 100 yards before reaching the point, begin altering your course slightly to the south and point to drop the hook within 75 yards or so of the crescent-shaped beach south of the point.

All captains *must* be mindful of the 1-foot shallows south of this anchorage. Also, note the correctly charted patch of 3-foot shoals northwest of Three Rooker Bar. It would also be a good idea to avoid the sunken wreck to the north-northeast.

Seaward Cut   Those who can't wait to sail those beautifully blue offshore waters may depart the ICW by using the marked passage between Three Rooker Bar and Anclote Key. To make use of this cut, depart the Waterway at unlighted daybeacon #37 and set course to come abeam of flashing daybeacon #7 by some 25 yards or so to its southerly side. Set a new course to come abeam of and pass flashing daybeacon #1 to the same quarter. To the west, the deeper Gulf waters now spread out before you.

On the ICW   Once between unlighted daybeacons #42 and #41, the old, reliable magenta line vanishes. We must bid a fond goodbye to the Western Florida ICW in our passage to the north. From #42, cruisers must choose whether to continue north and visit the anchorages adjacent to Anclote Key or cut northeast into beautiful Anclote River, home of many marina facilities and the wonderful village of Tarpon Springs.

Anclote Key   Remember that the charted channel south and west of unlighted daybeacon #7X no longer exists. Take my bent prop's word for it, even small craft should desist from trying to find this wayward cut.

To access the anchorage on the patch of deep water north and west of #7X, cruise north, passing #7X by at least 200 yards to your westerly side. This maneuver will allow you to avoid the clearly charted 2- to 4-foot shoal water north and east of #7X. Continue on course to the north for .4 nautical miles and then turn 90 degrees to the west and slow to idle speed. Use your sounder to feel your way in towards the shore. As #7X comes abeam to the south, you can continue cruising west towards the banks for another .1 nautical miles in good water. Closer in, depths rise markedly.

If you should choose to anchor abeam of Dutchman Key instead, follow the deep water north of #7X. Be on guard against the charted tongue of 2-foot water southeast of Dutchman Key. Use your binoculars to identify the smaller island. Once the southern tip of the key is abeam to the west, continue on for some 50 yards to the north. Then, cut sharply west and use your sounder to feel your way in. Be sure to drop the hook before approaching to within less than .2 nautical miles of shore.

Out through Anclote Anchorage   Cruisers anchoring along Anclote Key or leaving Tarpon Springs bound for points north can easily use the northerly reaches of the waters around the island to reach the Gulf. Simply follow the broad tongue of deep water as it sweeps to the northeast. Stay well to the northwest of unlighted daybeacon #3 and well to the south and east of flashing daybeacon #6. These two aids mark the outer limits of the shallows bordering Anclote Anchorage to the east and west. Typical depths will be 7 to 10 feet along this run. Next stop—the Big Bend!

Anclote River and Tarpon Springs

What would you call a river with an absolutely enchanting shoreline interspaced with all-natural stretches and light, attractive residential development? Don't answer yet—we still need to throw in one of the most unique and colorful villages in all of Florida. How about if we also add at least one super anchorage, a whole host of marina facilities, and minimum 8-foot channel depths, with most soundings being deeper? Well, I don't know what *you* call it, but I term this body of water the Anclote River, with the town of Tarpon Springs perched along its banks to the east. It's not going too far to say that those few mariners who have not experienced the climes of the Anclote River will have missed what are undoubtedly some of the finest cruising waters between Flamingo and Carrabelle.

Besides all of the Anclote's many fortunate qualities described above, the river is also well positioned for those ready to make the jump across the Big Bend, or those just arriving from the open waters to the north. Captains can wait for good weather or rest from their travels at the many transient slips available along the stream's course. When it comes time for dinner, the fabled Tarpon Springs restaurants could make you forget to come home.

On the negative side, depths outside of the marked Anclote River Channel rise quickly and dramatically. This is not the place to go exploring off the beaten path. With the sole exception of the anchorage described below, cruising craft are pretty much restricted to the marked track and the various marina channels.

It's not too hard to understand why the Anclote River and Tarpon Springs have become one of the most popular ports of call in northwestern Florida. These cruising grounds certainly deserve a heavy, red circle on every cruiser's chart. Read on and discover why for yourself.

Power Plant Anchorage

North of unlighted daybeacon #18, cruisers will find the Anclote River's only deep, well-sheltered anchorage that lacks heavy local traffic. The charted stream skirts to the west of a small park and eventually leads to the huge power plant readily visible to the northwest. A floating barrier crossing this sidewater several hundred yards north of its intersection with the Anclote River blocks upstream passage for all vessels. There is plenty of room for boats up to 45 feet in length to drop the hook south of this obstruction. Minimum depths are 5½ to 6 feet, with some 7-foot soundings also in evidence. During our many visits to the cove, we have often observed multiple vessels anchored here. There are even a few permanent mooring buoys, but not so many as to obstruct anchorage by visitors.

Strong tidal currents seem to flow through this anchorage at times. Be sure the anchor is well set before heading below for a toddy!

The nearby park makes a nice landside stop for those cruisers willing to break out the dinghy. Picnic tables are well shaded by tall pines, and restroom facilities are available. A small restaurant (open only for breakfast and lunch) is within walking distance, but there is not a grocery store or full-service dining spot nearby. You might be able to phone for a taxi

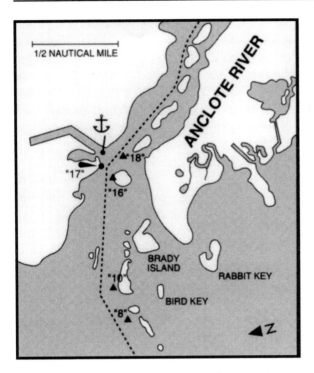

from nearby Tarpon Springs and motor in to this village's many dining spots.

Lower Anclote River Marinas

A host of marinas and boatyards lines the banks of the Anclote River below Tarpon Springs and offers a wide variety of services.

Mariners cruising east of unlighted daybeacon #25 will quickly spot the docks of Sun Marina (727-934-4474) to the north. This firm is now comprised of a dockside cafe and semi-open-air bar with a few fixed, wooden wet slips fronting the facility. No repairs or transient dockage are now available. Enterprising captains and crew might be able to find a berth for tying off temporarily while sampling the restaurant's bill of fare, but don't count on it.

Between unlighted daybeacons #32 and #34, visiting cruisers will find Flaherty

Marine. This friendly facility occasionally accepts transients, but the marina is primarily a full-service repair yard which also allows some do-it-yourself bottom work. Most of the yard's patrons take advantage of Flaherty's professional mechanical and haul-out services. Mechanical repairs are offered for both gasoline and diesel engines. Flaherty's travelift is rated at 35 tons. Awlgrip and Imron painting services are also among this yard's services.

Most of Flaherty's dockage is covered, but there are a few open slips as well. One sailcraft was docked in these open berths when last we visited. Dockside power (30-amp) and water connections are found at each berth. Good entrance and dockside depths of 6 feet or so will be welcomed by sailors and deep-draft power vessels.

Flaherty Marina (727) 934-9394

Approach depth—6 feet
Dockside depth—6 feet
Accepts transients—occasionally
Fixed wooden piers—yes (most covered, but a few open)
Dockside power connections—30 amp
Dockside water connections—yes
Mechanical repairs—yes (gas and diesel)
Below-waterline repairs—yes
Parts store—yes

A no-wake sign attached to unlighted daybeacon #38 heralds one of the densest concentrations of marina facilities on the whole of the Anclote River. No fewer than three large marinas, two of which cater to transient craft, line the northern and northeastern banks as the river follows a slow turn to the south. While shoreside restaurants within walking distance of these three are minimal, transportation to downtown Tarpon Springs, with its sponge markets and many fine restaurants, can usually be arranged.

The first of the three is Port Tarpon Marina, easily recognized by its large, metal, dry-storage buildings. Port Tarpon is the largest facility on the Anclote River and the structures of its associated repair firms testify to the wide array of services available. The marina itself offers transient dockage (though advance reservations are definitely recommended) at fixed concrete piers perched atop wooden pilings. Every conceivable power, water, and communication connection is at hand, as is a fuel dock dispensing gasoline and diesel fuel. Many of the slips are covered and would only be appropriate for powercraft, but there are plenty of open berths as well for sailboats. Showers are available shoreside.

Captains of deep-draft vessels should be on guard against an underwater rock ledge, with low-water depths of 5½ feet or so, stretching from the Port Tarpon fuel dock towards the eastern side of the harbor. Skippers whose craft draws more than 5 feet should take careful note of this obstruction. Call Port Tarpon Marina on VHF 16 before approaching the docks and ask for instructions about how to avoid the ledge while entering the harbor. Otherwise, (except for the ledge) Port Tarpon's outer docks have impressive depths of 8 to 9 feet, while the innermost slips exhibit soundings of 6½ to 7 feet.

If you are in need of service, you've certainly come to the right place. Port Tarpon leases out its repair facilities, and the list is impressive indeed. Cleveland's Diesel and Yacht Services (727-942-2967) provides full mechanical repairs (gasoline and diesel engines) and below-waterline, haul-out services courtesy of a 50-ton travelift. Cleveland's also boasts a well-stocked parts department.

Brown's Marine Service (727-938-3322) features a ship's store and repairs to smaller powercraft. Seebird Canvas (727-938-7152) offers the most up-to-date marine canvas fabrication and repair. The on-site Pelican Landing Restaurant serves breakfast and lunch but it closes at 3:00 P.M weekdays and 4:00 P.M. weekends. A small dock adjacent to the restaurant allows cruisers (with craft up to 35 feet) to dock temporarily while dining. Visiting mariners wishing to dine out during the evening will find it necessary to take a taxi into nearby Tarpon Springs (call Yellow Cab at 727-848-1707). There you will find a host of dining choices.

Port Tarpon Marina (727) 937-2200

Approach depth—5-10 feet
Dockside depth—6½-9 feet
Accepts transients—yes
Concrete-decked fixed piers—yes
Dockside power connections—30 and 50 amp
Dockside water connections—yes
Showers—yes
Gasoline—yes
Diesel fuel—yes
Mechanical repairs—yes
Below-waterline repairs—yes
Ship's store—yes
Restaurant—on site (breakfast and lunch only)

Sandwiched between its two sisters, genial Anclote Harbors Marina also offers transient dockage at fixed wooden piers with water and twin 30-amp power connections. Dockside depths at the outer piers are an impressive 7 to 8 feet, with some 6½ feet of water alongside the inner docks. Live-aboards are also welcomed at Anclote Harbors. Shoreside amenities include good, air-conditioned showers and an adjacent laundromat. No fuel is available. Breakfast and lunch can be eaten at the restaurant associated with Port Tarpon Marina next door. Otherwise, you will have to find ground transportation into Tarpon Springs (call Yellow Cab at 727-848-1707).

Anclote Harbors Marina offers an impressive repair-yard operation. Cruisers can expect to find full mechanical repairs and haul-outs by way of a 40-ton travelift. Do-it-yourself bottom work is allowed, or you may choose to have the yard professionals perform all necessary work.

The staff and management of Anclote Harbors Marina have always been unusually helpful to this writer during my research. It is my sincere belief that visiting cruisers will receive a warm and knowledgeable welcome at this well-appointed facility.

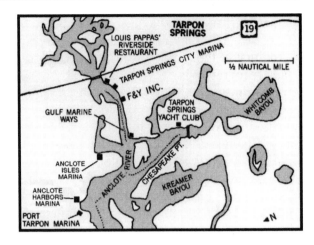

Anclote Harbors Marina (727) 934-7616
  http://gulfside.com/anclote-
  harbors/index.html

Approach depth—8-10 feet
Dockside depth—6½-8 feet
Accepts transients—yes
Fixed wooden piers—yes
Dockside power connections—yes (dual 30 amp)
Dockside water connections—yes
Showers—yes
Laundromat—yes
Mechanical repairs—yes
Below-waterline repairs—yes
Restaurant—nearby (breakfast and lunch only)

Easternmost of the three related facilities, Sail Harbor Marina has undergone an unfortunate transition over the past several years. A large offshore gambling ship now makes its home at this facility. While the marina's wet slips are still in place, the old marina office has now been transformed into a ticket booth. Clearly the emphasis at Sail Harbor is now on gambling rather than pleasurecraft. We suggest that you choose another of the Anclote River's many fine marinas for your stay.

The most exciting new marina to open on the Anclote River in many a year guards the stream's northerly banks, opposite unlighted daybeacon #50. Not only does newly minted Anclote Isles Marina offer a super welcome for visiting cruisers, but it also plays host to what just may be the best charter operation on the northern portion of the Western Florida coastline.

The dockage basin features excellent shelter from foul weather and new, fixed wooden piers. Mean low-water approach and dockside depths run 6 feet or better. Transients are eagerly accepted, and visitors will discover modern 30- and 50-amp power, freshwater, cable television, and telephone hook-ups. How's that for a well-wired marina

Waste pump-out service is offered, but the marina does not have a fuel dock. Some mechanical repairs can be arranged through local, independent technicians. Ask the friendly dockmaster or any of his staff for assistance.

Anclote Isles' shoreside showers are first rate and completely air conditioned. No laundromat is readily available, however.

It's a quick taxi ride into Tarpon Springs for some really first class dining and intriguing attractions (see below). Call Yellow Cab at (727) 848-1707. If you happen to be cruising with bicycles aboard, it's an enjoyable ride into Tarpon Springs as well.

So, you want to cruise the waters of northwestern Florida but don't have your own boat. Well, don't waste any time calling Seacoast Yacht Charters (727-934-5503, 800-322-6070, http://www.seacoastcharters.com). Besides their base of operations at Anclote Isles, these good people also maintain an office and a second charter fleet at the Caloosahatchee's Tarpon Point Marina (see chapter 2). Seacoast offers an outstanding fleet of power- and sailcraft at both locations. Bareboat and captained charters are available. To be succinct, these people simply can't seem to do enough for their customers. We feel confident that anyone wanting to charter a boat in these waters can't possibly do himself a bigger favor than calling Seacoast Yacht Charters. Tell them we sent you!

Anclote Isles Marina (727) 939-0100

Approach depth—6+ feet (MLW)
Dockside depth—6+ feet (MLW)
Accepts transients—yes
Fixed wooden piers—yes
Dockside power connections—30 and 50 amp
Dockside water connections—yes
Waste pump-out—yes
Showers—yes
Mechanical repairs—independent technicians
Restaurant—taxi ride needed

Tarpon Springs

When I was originally researching *Cruising Guide to Eastern Florida,* my first travels through the Okeechobee Waterway were nothing short of amazing. The huge ranches, thousands upon thousands of grazing cattle, the cowboys, and tiny towns caused me to wonder if this could really be the same state which hosts the condo caverns of Fort Lauderdale, Hollywood, and Clearwater. Well, the village of Tarpon Springs is no less unexpected than the backwaters of Okeechobee. As you cruise up the Anclote River, your arrival at Tarpon Springs will be heralded by a fleet of incredibly colorful sponge boats spread along the town waterfront. These docks, along with numerous sponge markets and a vast array of wonderful restaurants, are set amidst a small-town atmosphere which would be very much at home in New England or along the North Carolina coastline. Tarpon Springs, quite simply, is charming.

Among Tarpon Springs' many and varied attractions are its annual festivals. Nowhere outside the country of Greece is the Feast of Epiphany, a Greek Holy Day, celebrated as elaborately as it is in Tarpon Springs. January 6, one of the oldest festival days of the Christian Church, commemorates the baptism of Christ and marks the end of the Christmas season. Originating in the Eastern Orthodox Church as early as the third century, it is still known in the Greek Orthodox Church by its ancient name, *Theophany* (manifestation of God).

Each year the Epiphany ceremony begins at the Greek Orthodox Church of St. Nicholas. Mass is performed at an altar surrounded by a half circle of striking, gold-framed icons. When the last chants of liturgy subside, the archbishop performs the traditional custom of the Blessing of the Waters, praying for calm seas and the safety of all sailors.

Ecclesiastics from archbishop to altar boy, resplendently gowned in embroidered robes of crimson and gold and carrying jeweled crosses and croziers, lead the procession to the beautiful waters of Spring Bayou. The archbishop casts a white cross into the waters at the edge of the bayou, and some fifty youths dive from a semicircle of small boats to retrieve it. The one who can retrieve the cross will be blessed with good luck for one year.

Every year, the Chamber of Commerce hosts the annual "Seafood Festival," where visitors can sample everything from alligator and oysters to shrimp and squid. Check with the Greater Tarpon Springs Chamber of Commerce (727-937-6109) about the dates. It has been held in May of each year in the past, but that date may change.

Modern-day Tarpon Springs really began in 1890, when diving for natural sponges came to be the dominant local industry. The technology and technique for this colorful enterprise was imported from Greece and the Mediterranean isles. As the industry grew, many a native Helene emigrated to Florida to seek his fortune in the sponge-rich Gulf waters off Anclote Key. To this very day, you are just as likely to hear Greek as English spoken along the quiet streets of Tarpon Springs or in the streetside sponge markets. The bonhomie is often a tangible quality. Few, if any, other ports of call can lay claim to such a friendly atmosphere in such unexpected surroundings.

If you happen to be in the market for a natural sponge or two, then you have certainly set your course for the right port of call. Far more durable and economical than their synthetic counterparts, natural sponges are enjoying a modern-day renaissance and are very much in demand. You will find no better prices anywhere. Even if you don't need a sponge, please take the time to stroll through the markets. They are like nothing you will see anywhere else in all of Florida.

Of course, people of Greek extraction are known for something besides sponges— namely, wonderful food. Tarpon Springs sports an incredible collection of wonderful restaurants serving everything from authentic Greek fare to the freshest in American-style fried seafood. You can certainly suit your own palate, but this writer recommends the so-called combination dishes that seem to mix the best of both Greek and American cuisine. The "Greek-style shrimp" served at many of the town's best dining spots is a shining example of this cuisine.

It would probably require a short book on its own to adequately review all the many Tarpon Springs restaurants. It's really hard to go wrong. For now, let's just mention a few standouts among the crowd.

Any discussion of dining in Tarpon Springs simply must begin with Louis Pappas' Riverside Restaurant (10 Dodecanese Boulevard, 727-937-5101). This mammoth dining institution is a three-story affair which overlooks the Anclote River's southeastern banks just upstream from the Tarpon Springs city marina. Louis Pappas and his brothers have been serving seafood—Greek, American, and mixed styles—for many a year along with a multitude of other fare. Be sure to make reservations ahead of time to avoid a long wait.

Some dockage used to be available at Louis Pappas' for its waterborne patrons. At the present time, all the available wet-slip space is pretty much filled by local craft.

Diners seeking a more informal menu will want to check out Mr. Souvlaki Restaurant (510 Dodecanese Boulevard, 727-937-2795). The Greek-style sandwiches and salads are to die for.

Don't overlook visits to the Hellas Restaurant (785 Dodecanese Boulevard, 727-943-2400), Mykonos Restaurant (628 Dodecanese Boulevard, 727-934-4306),

Louis Pappas' Riverside Restaurant, Tarpon Springs

and/or Santorini Restaurant (698 Dodecanese Boulevard, 727-945-9400). All serve outstanding Greek/American cuisine. You simply can't go wrong with any of these choices.

If the current special in "sea creatures" trips your culinary trigger, check out Paul's Shrimp House (530 Athens, 727-937-1239). The "peel and eat" steamed shrimp and Paul's famous potatoes are not to be missed.

For something entirely different, pay a visit to Ballyhoo Grill (900 Pinellas Avenue N, 727-944-2252). The forte here is Key West style seafood, just where you would least expect to find it.

To break your morning fast, find your way to either the Plaka Restaurant (769 Dodecanese Boulevard W, 727-934-4752) or Taste of Greece (709 Dodecanese Boulevard, 727-938-0088). Try the feta cheese omelets at either dining attraction. Yuuummm!

Numbers to know in Tarpon Springs include:

Golden Nugget Taxi—727-938-5353
T. S. Yellow Cab—727-799-2222
Yellow Cab—727-848-1707
Avis Rental Cars—727-367-2847
Enterprise Rent-A-Car—727-942-3155
West Marine—727-846-1903

Tarpon Springs History   Tarpon Springs was first settled by A. W. Ormond and his daughter, Mary. Coming to Florida from Ninety-Six, South Carolina, in 1876, they built a cabin near Spring Bayou when there were still no other homes in sight. A year later, J. C. Boyer, an adventurer from Nassau, sailed into the bayou. He and Mary were married and started the first family where Tarpon Springs now stands.

In 1877 George Inness, a foremost American artist, discovered the scenic beauty of the Anclote River, which he and his son, George, Jr., would depict in their famous paintings.

Mary found her new home to be a never-ending wonder. Thinking that the fish she saw inhabiting the bayou were tarpon, she named the small settlement Tarpon Springs in 1879. (The fish she saw were in fact mullet and not tarpon.)

The village of Tarpon Springs was founded in 1882 by Anson P. K. Safford, the first territorial governor of Arizona. In the meantime, John K. Cheyney from Philadelphia was building a development concern called the Lake Butler Villa Company and, after Safford's death, Cheyney began promoting the region as an exclusive winter resort. This early Tarpon Springs land boom was to see its share of wealthy and famous customers. Lake Tarpon (formerly Lake Butler) still looks much as it did when the Duke of Sutherland fell in love with its lush vegetation, bought 30 acres, and built an estate overlooking the water where he could peacefully fish and hunt.

Tarpon Springs waterfront

The Tarpon Springs townsite was laid out by Mayor W. J. Marks and surveyed by John C. Jones. In 1884, a post office was established, and the railroad was soon to follow. Eleven years after it was first settled, Tarpon Springs was incorporated on February 12, 1887.

Sponge harvesting soon became the community's most important industry. In 1890, Cheyney discovered money could be made by harvesting sponges growing in the waters of the Gulf. John Cocoris, the first Greek to settle in Tarpon Springs, brought sponge divers from the islands of Greece to harvest the beds. Tarpon Springs still maintains its reputation as the largest natural sponge market in the world, with an annual revenue in excess of $5,000,000.

Sponges can be found in every ocean of the world, from the tropics to the arctic. Although there are some 5,000 varieties, only a few are suitable for commerce, and four of these are found in the Gulf of Mexico.

The part of the sponge that is used is the skeleton. This is a network of connecting passages built up of a unique fiber called spongin. Tough, compressible, and resilient, it can absorb twenty-five times its own weight in water, and be quickly squeezed almost dry. Sponges vary in size from less than an inch to over three feet in diameter.

When alive, the sponges are covered with a black, fleshy, rubbery skin, and filled with soft, gray matter called gurry. To be used the sponge skeleton must be freed from all organic matter and foreign bodies. It must be thoroughly cleaned, dried, and usually trimmed.

The sponge markets are still very much in evidence amidst modern-day Tarpon Springs. As you stroll the quiet streets of this enchanting village, take a few moments to reflect on

all those who have gone before you, as well as on the city leaders who have had the foresight to preserve their vision of Tarpon Springs.

Tarpon Springs Marina Facilities & Anchorages

Anchorages are all but nonexistent on the Anclote River upstream of the power plant haven described earlier in this chapter. Cruisers preferring to spend the evening swinging on the hook would do well to make use of this haven.

Transient dockage in downtown Tarpon Springs is now ever so much easier to come by, courtesy of the revitalized Tarpon Springs City Marina. You simply can't pick a better spot to coil your lines to experience the color and character of the unique village that is Tarpon Springs. This fortunate facility is found on the principal town waterfront, south of unlighted daybeacon #51, in the heart of the friendly hustle and bustle of the business district and its sponge markets.

After a flirtation with becoming a resident-only facility, Tarpon Springs City Marina is once again ready, eager, and waiting to serve visiting cruisers. Transient dockage is afforded at newly refurbished, fixed wooden piers. There are usually four to five slips kept open just for visitors. Call ahead for reservations during the winter season.

The dockage basin is well sheltered and features mean low water soundings of 6 feet or so. Dockside power connections of the 30- and 50-amp variety are offered as are freshwater hook-ups at each slip. Good, but somewhat petite (one per sex), air-conditioned showers are available in the dockmaster building immediately adjacent to the piers. It's a long walk of some 1½ miles to the nearest laundromat. Many cruisers may want to take a taxi (see above).

It's a very quick step from the municipal marina to the restaurants described above (plus many additional choices) and the colorful sponge markets.

A convenience store is found within walking distance, but it's a 1½-mile hike to the nearest supermarket. Fortunately, another grocery store (some 2 miles from the marina) is accessible by way of the city bus service. Ask the city dockmaster or his fine staff for directions and assistance.

So, with the exception of repairs and fuel, I'm sure you will agree that the newly enhanced version Tarpon Springs City Marina has just about everything a visiting cruiser could desire. We suggest you pay dockmaster Bob a visit. You won't be sorry!

Tarpon Springs City Marina (727) 937-9165

Approach depth—6 to 10 feet
Dockside depth—6 feet (MLW)
Accepts transients—yes
Fixed wooden piers—yes
Dockside power connections—30 and 50 amp
Dockside water connections—yes
Showers—yes
Laundromat—1½ miles away
Restaurant—many nearby

One additional, privately owned marina is located upstream of the city marina. Unfortunately, to make your way to this facility successfully, you must negotiate an unmarked passage around a very large shoal that occupies most of the river north and northeast of the Tarpon Springs waterfront. Until this situation improves, we suggest that you leave The Landing at Tarpon Springs (727-937-1100) to local captains.

Gulf Marine Ways (727-937-4401) occupies the Anclote River's southern banks near the heart of Tarpon Springs, east of unlighted daybeacon #50. This friendly yard features full haul-out repairs (via a marine railway), while mechanical services can be arranged through independent local contractors.

Set amidst the sponge boat docks between Gulf Marine Ways and Tarpon Springs City Marina, the large fueling pier of F&Y, Inc. (727-937-4351) guards the southern banks. This firm wholesales gasoline and diesel fuel to local retail outlets. Direct fuel sales to pleasurecraft are usually confined to larger vessels who need a prodigious load of fuel. We did find the management very friendly, so if you need to fill up your Hatteras, don't fail to stop by and say hello to the manager, John Young (surely one of this writer's long-lost cousins).

Spring Bayou and Tarpon Springs Yacht Club

The small but affable Tarpon Springs Yacht Club is found at the southeastern terminus of the charted channel leading from the main Anclote River track into Spring Bayou. *However,* captains should *not* run the marked cut. Instead, navigators must follow the charted but mostly unmarked cut-through just south of the former Reis Boat Yard. Even so, depths run as thin as 4 feet on this cut. *Be sure* to read the navigational information on this questionable passage presented below before attempting to reach the yacht club docks.

Tarpon Springs Yacht Club accepts members of other yacht clubs with appropriate reciprocal privileges for temporary dockage. Be sure to call ahead of time and reserve space with the dockmaster. The club does not usually have anyone in attendance at the docks unless advance arrangements have been made.

This club is open *only* on Wednesday, Friday, and Saturday from noon into the evening hours, when dining and bar facilities are available. Dockage is at rather smallish fixed wooden slips with only 20-amp power and water connections. As you might expect, no fuel or repairs are to be had.

Tarpon Springs Yacht Club (727) 934-2136

Approach depth—4 feet
Dockside depth—4-5 feet
Accepts transients—members of clubs with
    reciprocal privileges—advance arrangements
    necessary
Fixed wooden piers—yes
Dockside power connections—20 amp
Dockside water connections—yes
Restaurant—on site (open Wednesday, Friday,
    and Saturday only) and many others nearby

ANCLOTE RIVER NAVIGATION

Successful navigation of the Anclote River Channel could almost be summed up by saying, "Stay in the marked channel and remember 'red-right-returning.'" The few exceptions to this general rule will be noted below.

To facilitate passage by Tarpon Springs deep-draft commercial fishing vessels, the entire Anclote River channel is slated for maintenance dredging as this account goes to press. When complete, the cut will be even more a proverbial piece of cake for pleasurecraft.

Depths outside of the buoyed Anclote River channel quickly rise to grounding levels. Stay in the marked passage and do not attempt to explore any likely looking coves. The noted anchorage near the power station is the only truly safe haven on the river.

Entrance from Anclote Key The entrance channel into Anclote River from the deeper water of St. Joseph Sound and the Anclote Anchorage lies east of Anclote Key. A huge power plant with the charted stack guards the river's northern mouth and makes an excellent landmark. The channel is sandwiched between very shoal water to the north and south. At unusually low tide, these shallows bare

completely and it can look as if the mud flats stretch on forever. You may be getting tired of me saying it, but stick to the marked cut and you should find nothing less than 6 feet of water, with many soundings substantially deeper.

Cruise into the entrance channel by passing between flashing daybeacon #1 to its southerly quarter and unlighted daybeacon #2 to its northerly side. After passing between #1 and #2, continue cruising on the same course to the east-northeast, passing between three additional pairs of markers along the way. Eventually, you will come abeam of unlighted daybeacon #8 to its northerly side. Upstream of #8, the passage turns to the east-southeast. Point to pass south of flashing daybeacon #9 and north of unlighted daybeacon #10.

Do not attempt to enter the charted channel north-northwest of unlighted daybeacon #8. This errant cut is mostly unmarked and is much too tricky for cruising-size craft.

East-southeast of unlighted daybeacon #10, the channel continues on an arrow-straight course to flashing daybeacon #17. From #17 the channel follows another bend, this time to the southeast. Between

#17 and unlighted daybeacon #18, the river's best anchorage will come abeam to the northeast.

Power Plant Anchorage   Enter this broad sidewater northeast of flashing daybeacon #17 on its mid-width and continue upstream past the public launching ramp, which will be passed to starboard. Drop the hook anywhere short of the floating barrier.

Tidal currents do run somewhat swiftly in this anchorage, so be sure the anchor is well set. It would be a good idea to stay topside and watch a fixed point on shore for at least 10 minutes before beginning your galley preparations.

On the Anclote River   As you approach unlighted daybeacon #21, the channel hugs the southern banks. Depths seem to be more than adequate.

After passing unlighted daybeacon #30, watch for a significant shoal off to the north side of the channel. During our last visit, it was covered with pelicans and smaller waterfowl.

At unlighted daybeacon #38 an official no-wake zone begins to protect the three large marinas on the northern and northeastern banks. As you leave the easternmost marina behind and follow the river through its turn to the south, watch the eastern banks for a beautiful house overlooking the water. It's one of the most magnificent homes on the river.

Don't attempt to enter the charted Chesapeake Point Channel, which cuts to the south between flashing daybeacons #39 and #43. This cut is now shoal and even outboard craft can find the bottom.

The entrance to the new Anclote Isles Marina lies north of unlighted daybeacon #50. Cruise straight into the dockage basin on the mid-width of the approach passage.

The Anclote River Channel remains easy to follow all the way upstream to Tarpon Springs City Marina. Be sure to proceed at idle speed along the town waterfront.

At the present time a large patch of shallows has built across a goodly portion of Anclote River north and northeast of the downtown Tarpon Springs waterfront. There is a way around this shoal, but the passage is unmarked and tricky. This is one time where it would probably be better to leave these upstream waters to the local captains who know what the bottom is doing this week. Visiting cruisers will therefore find it prudent to discontinue their upstream explorations at Tarpon Springs City Marina.

Tarpon Springs Yacht Club Channel   Remember that the mostly unmarked channel to Tarpon Springs Yacht Club carries low-tide depths of a meager 4 feet, or sometimes less. If your boat can stand these soundings, leave the main Anclote River Channel at unlighted daybeacon #50. Turn due south and heavily favor the easterly banks as you work your way carefully along. Your course will lead you under the stern of the boats docked along the waterfront.

As you leave the moored boats behind, point directly for the small opening dead ahead. As you pass out into the main body of Spring Bayou, head directly for the red, unlighted daybeacon you will see ahead. Shortly before reaching this aid, cut sharply to port and point for the low-level bridge which you will sight ahead. Be on guard against some uncharted shoal water to the east. Soon the yacht club's docks will come abeam to port.

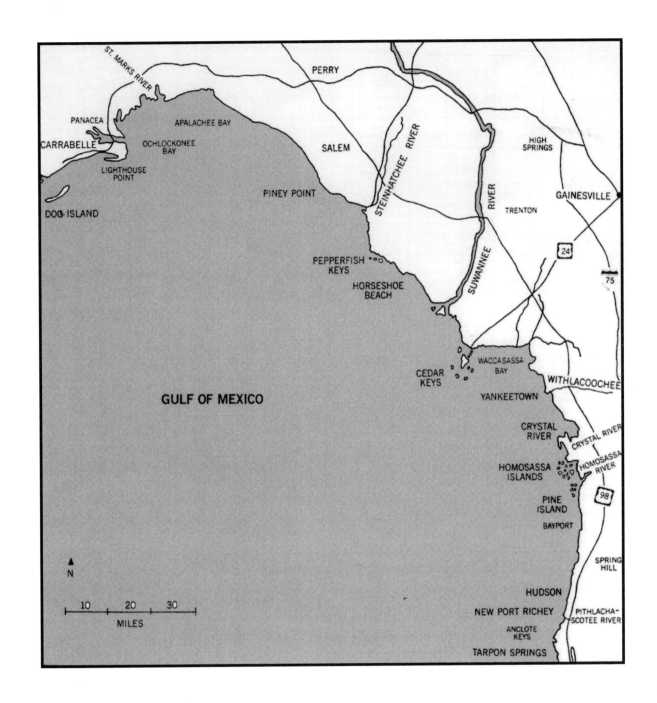

CHAPTER 6

The Big Bend

What can one say about the coastline of Florida's Big Bend? Frankly, this writer finds himself rather perplexed as to whether the lands and waters between Anclote Key and the St. Marks River are a cruising and nature lover's paradise, a region beginning to undergo destructive development, or a whole collection of shoaly, sometimes rocky waters lacking any protected intracoastal waterway lying in wait for your keel. The reality is that the Big Bend is probably some of all these and much more.

Perhaps the first thing we should note is that most of the Big Bend's immediate coastline has been preserved in its natural state for the foreseeable future thanks to timely and prolific land purchases by the Nature Conservancy. (As you may have noticed, we try to avoid blatant plugging of any organization other than restaurants and the occasional marina, but if you are looking for a worthy recipient of those tax-deductible dollars, this group is a goodie!) Much of the Nature Conservancy's land has been turned over to the U.S. Fish & Wildlife Service and set up as official wildlife refuges. Writing in the April 1988 issue of *Southern Living* magazine, Harry Middleton gives a haunting portrait of these lands and their waters:

> The Nature Conservancy has really saved . . . the wild pine and hardwood hammocks . . . the miles and miles of clear, clear estuarine creeks; the rich fishing and oyster beds . . . the cool, shady ravines . . . deep blue rivers; . . . unspoiled islands; . . . everywhere the sound of birds . . . the simple, unpretentious traditions and culture

of the old mullet fishing villages and hard luck timber towns; and the oyster men in their armada of small boats, working the bay from dawn till dusk, scraping the oyster beds with their long-handled tongs. . . . And this is a crude sketch, a hasty outline of the Big Bend's seemingly limitless beauty and abundance. There is so much more.

Mr. Middleton's description is entirely apt for the westerly reaches of the many rivers and bays indenting the Big Bend here and there. Indeed, the beauty of the Big Bend's rivers and streams is at times almost dreamlike. The fortunate cruiser in these climes can still experience the same sort of landscape that must have greeted Native Americans hundreds of years ago.

Unfortunately, however, the Nature Conservancy does not have the power to preserve the small towns and villages which lie a few miles to the east along the various streams. While, to be sure, some of these communities remain as quaint and delightful as ever, others have been "discovered." New, sometimes garish construction can only be a grief to those who value the unique character of this region. Yet, other communities remain very much as they have been for the past fifty years. The sensitive visitor must now pick and choose his or her ports of call with care to experience the Big Bend of yesterday.

From a cruising navigator's point of view, the one colossal word which comes to mind when discussing the Big Bend is "shallow." There is no other section of Florida's eastern, western, or panhandle coastline which sports such consistently shallow depths. Except for the marked river channels, the shores can only be approached by small, flat-bottomed craft. Adding insult to injury, many of the buoyed approaches to the Big Bend rivers are themselves quite shoal. Low-water soundings of 4 feet might even be considered the norm. While there are several fortunate exceptions to this rule, skippers piloting craft that draw 5 feet or better may well consider setting course directly from Anclote Key to the St. Marks River or Carrabelle and Dog Island. Sailors with fixed keels who yearn for an uninterrupted offshore passage may want to opt for this plan in any case, but perhaps you should think twice.

In spite of our reservations about recent development, we really can't recommend that you bypass the Big Bend rivers. Their natural beauty will be a part of your cruising stories for many years to come. If time allows, this writer highly recommends that you give them a try. Just read the information presented in this chapter completely and critically, and make your selection of stops along the way accordingly.

As mentioned in the last chapter, there is no protected intracoastal waterway north of Anclote Key. Mariners will be cruising the waters of the open Gulf all the way to Carrabelle and St. George Sound before picking up the sheltered reaches of the Northern Gulf ICW. This is a run of better than 140 nautical miles in a straight line. If you decide to follow the Big Bend buoyage system, the track is considerably longer. Obviously, this is not the sort of passage to be undertaken lightly. Fuel, supplies, and, of course, the weather forecast must all be planned for and taken into account in order to ensure a safe voyage.

Two fundamentally different strategies are available to cruising captains journeying north or south across the Big Bend's waters. Those who choose to forego the delights of the region's rivers or who are in a hurry can set a straight course from Anclote Key to the St. Marks River or Dog Island (bordering St. George Sound and the village of Carrabelle). This is a wide-open passage which will appeal to many sailors, particularly during times of fair weather with good winds. Powercraft had better be sure their fuel supply is up to the task before undertaking this route. A well-functioning GPS interfaced with a laptop computer would be a real advantage for navigators following this passage.

The real disadvantage of this offshore cruising plan is that you will often be as much as 40 to 60 miles from the nearest coastline, far too great a distance to run for cover if an unexpected storm should come running up the Gulf. Of course, visits to the Big Bend rivers are also impractical for those following the offshore route. On the other hand, this is clearly the fastest and most direct approach to crossing the Big Bend.

Cruisers of a more conservative bent can follow the series of offshore markers known as the Big Bend buoy system. These aids to navigation will lead you up the coastline, keeping some 5 to 10 nautical miles offshore. Because of the bend in the land, this route is lengthier, but the buoys and daybeacons along the way will serve to fix your position and keep you on course. The various river channels are readily accessible via this route, though, again, you will have to pick and choose (not to mention consult the tide tables) to make sure a particular passage is deep enough for you.

So there it is, with all its glory and faults. Florida's Big Bend is something different for everyone who visits its singular shores. And just in case we haven't quite yet enticed you to include these unique cruising grounds in your travel plans, let's listen to a bit more of Harry Middleton's description of the Big Bend:

> Just below the water's surface, oyster bars glow white as bone, appearing to snake through the shallow water like enormous sea snakes, even though they are fixed in time and place. In the diminishing light, beds of aquatic grass and wetlands give off a startling range of colors: yellows and golds and soft browns. The wetlands look like a work of art: an etching on stained glass.

Charts Cruisers will need quite a few charts to cover the Big Bend. All but the southernmost and northernmost charts are large-format cartographical aids, which are not always the easiest to use on the water. Unfortunately, short of using digitized, computer charts, there is no choice in the matter.

11411—small-format ICW chart that provides good detail of the coastline from Anclote Key to the Pithlachascotee River

11409—the first of the small-scale, large-format Big Bend charts; covers the coast and offshore waters from Anclote Anchorage to the Crystal River; also includes Gulf Harbors, the Pithlachascotee River, Hudson, Hernando Beach, and the Homosassa River

11408—details the Big Bend from just north of the Crystal River to Horseshoe Point; includes the Withlacoochee River, Cedar Key, and the Suwannee River

11407—yet another large-format chart; details the waters from Horseshoe Point to Rock Islands; includes the Steinhatchee

11405—an important large chart, showing the waters of the northernmost section of the Big Bend and the easterly reaches of the Florida Panhandle; it is valuable for navigating the St. Marks River, Shell Point, Alligator Harbor, and the easterly entrance into St. George Sound

11406—ultradetailed chart of the St. Marks and Wakulla rivers

11404—detailed, small-format chart showing the easterly tip of the Northern Gulf ICW; also gives good detail of the anchorages on Dog Island and the village of Carrabelle and its like-named river

Bridges

Pithlachascotee River/Highway 19 Bridge—crosses Pithlachascotee River southeast of unlighted daybeacon #41—Fixed—12 feet

Steinhatchee River Bridge—crosses Steinhatchee River well east of unlighted daybeacon #24—Fixed—officially 25 feet but local reports say 30

Anclote Key to the Homosassa River

The southernmost 20 nautical miles of the Big Bend shoreline between Anclote Anchorage and the Homosassa River is perhaps the shallowest portion of the entire passage south of the St. Marks River. With one important exception, the entrance channels at Gulf Harbors, Hudson, Aripeka, Hernando Beach, Bayport, and the Homosassa River have low-water depths of 4 feet, or sometimes less. The Pithlachascotee (locally known as the Cotee) River boasts a 6½-foot entrance channel. While almost all of these streams feature some marina facilities, they are mostly oriented to smaller, outboard and I/O craft. As depths rise quickly and dramatically outside of the marked channels, anchorages are practically nonexistent. One significant exception is found near Gulf Harbors.

Frankly, with the possible exception of the Pithlachascotee River, this is a portion of the Big Bend that many skippers of larger cruising craft will choose to put behind them. If you should need shelter, of course, and catch the tide high enough, it is possible to duck inside and visit with the few marinas catering to cruising craft.

Gulf Harbors Channel

The two marked channels serving the resort community of Gulf Harbors lie almost due east from flashing daybeacon #4, north of Anclote Key. The southernmost cut holds minimum depths of 4½ to 5 feet, but it leads only to some private docks along the southern banks of Gulf Harbors.

The northside passage parallels a long shoal to the north and eventually leads to a deeper, eastward-striking canal. This stream is surrounded by heavy residential and some commercial development. Craft of most sizes can follow this stream east-southeast to its terminus at U.S. 19.

The northside entrance cut carries a mere 3½ to 4 feet of water at low tide. Depths on the interior portion of the canal improve to a minimum 5½ feet of water, with soundings up to 10 feet in places. This channel, like the remainder of the Big Bend, has a tidal range of approximately 3 feet, so if you need more

than 4 feet of water it is quite possible to carry 6 feet or better at high tide in the entrance channel into the deeper canal.

As you cruise east-southeast on the northern Gulf Harbors Canal, watch to starboard for the first cutoff running south. This offshoot quickly leads to a wide, baylike body of water with minimum 8-foot depths which can serve as one of the few protected anchorages between Anclote Key and the Homosassa River. Most boats should find plenty of elbow room and excellent protection when anchoring here. The shores are overlooked by voluminous residential development. Do not attempt to dinghy ashore!

Moving back now to the main canal, the docks of Gulf Harbors Yacht Club will be spotted on the northerly banks. This club sometimes accepts visitors from certain clubs that have reciprocal agreements. The members have suggested contacting the club well ahead of time at 727-849-4559 to make dockage arrangements. Cruisers who are able to secure a berth will tie their lines to fixed wooden piers featuring water and 30-amp power connections. Low-water dockside depths are around 5 feet.

At the canal's eastern tip, captains and crew will spy a Ramada Inn to port, a Leverocks Restaurant to starboard, and a series of floating slips dead ahead and lining the north side of the canal. This was once the home of A-B Sea Sailing Charters, but that business is now only a distant memory. Currently, there are no facilities for visiting cruisers on these waters.

The Pithlachascotee River

Let's get this cleared up right away. Don't even try to pronounce the name of this river. Even the locals don't make the attempt.

Rather, they call this stream the "Cotee River," and that is how we shall refer to it hereafter.

The Cotee is one of the deepest rivers on Florida's Big Bend. Its well-marked entrance channel will be spied some 2.5 nautical miles north of the (northern) Gulf Harbors passage. Minimum low-tide entrance and interior depths of 6½ feet drop to 12-foot soundings in a few spots. The river flows east to the town of Port Richey and several small marinas which now offer more transient dockage than in times past. Good anchorages are totally lacking. The shoreline is overlooked by a goodly collection of private homes and some condos.

Even before entering the river's mouth, cruisers are in for a real treat. Study chart 11411 for a moment and note all the charted "Shacks" north and south of the Cotee entrance channel. These houses are actually far more prolific than the chart would lead you to believe. On the water, they dot the seascape like spots on a leopard.

In a situation very similar to the one we encountered to the south on Pine Island Sound, these so-called shacks, or houses built on stilts, were originally constructed to serve commercial fishermen. As this salty trade dropped off during the 1950s, many of these structures were bought and redone as private weekend residences. Larry Korman of Korman's Sunset Landing has informed this writer that today the Who's Who of Port Richey own the old stilt houses. It was obvious from our on-the-water inspection that these weekend homes were universally well cared for and highly prized. Don't attempt too close an approach, however, as they are all founded in shoal water.

The first of the Cotee's facilities comes up on the southern shores between unlighted daybeacons #25 and #26. A well-marked channel leads through minimum 5-foot entrance depths to the well-sheltered fixed wooden and metal decked floating piers of American Marina (727-842-4065). Low-tide soundings at the docks run from 4½ to 5 feet. This medium-sized facility is obviously most interested in the dry stack storage of smaller powercraft. The available wet slips are pretty much rented out on an annual basis. Don't look for anything in the way of transient dockage here. In fact, except for gasoline, a tiny ship's store, and mechanical repairs for outboards and I/O's, there is very little to interest visitors at this facility.

Korman's Sunset Landing marina (727-849-5092) comes up, also on the southern banks, between unlighted daybeacon #33 and flashing daybeacon #35. This ultrafriendly establishment does not have the facilities to accommodate overnight transients, but if you need any advice about the Cotee or about cruising the Big Bend in general, be sure to stop and ask for Larry or his son Buddy. They are some of the nicest and most helpful individuals you will ever find under the Florida sun. Korman's offers gasoline and a fine ship's and variety store. Some mechanical repairs to outboards and I/O's are also available.

The Port Richey version of the infamous Hooters Restaurant (727-841-0801) gazes out over the Cotee's eastern banks opposite flashing daybeacon #35. This dining spot offers dockage for its clients and features open-air dining overlooking the river. Of course, interior tables are also available in air-conditioned comfort. Entrance depths can easily run as thin as 4½ feet of water, while 5- to 6-foot depths will be encountered dockside.

The Cotee's newest marina facility gazes out proudly over the easterly banks near flashing daybeacon #35. For best entrance depths, though, it's best to continue cruising upstream

Joshua's Landing Marina, Pithlachascotee River

to unlighted daybeacon #41. Check out our entry instructions in the next section of this chapter.

Joshua's Landing Marina welcomes both transients and live-aboards in a well-sheltered, *U*-shaped harbor that features first-class, fixed wooden piers. High-tide entrance depths run about 5 feet, with 3½-foot soundings at mean low water. Dockside depths are in the 5-foot range. The marina management hopes to dredge in 2001, but, for now, captains piloting boats drawing 3½ feet or more must time their entry and egress to coincide with high tide. Freshwater, 30-50-amp power,

and cable television hook-ups are available at all berths. Waste pump-out service is also offered.

The dockage basin is overlooked by a two-story dockmaster's building. The second floor of this structure boasts nice, air-conditioned showers and a full laundromat with paperback exchange library. A gas BBQ grill is kept under the building and is available without charge to both resident and visiting cruisers.

The nearest convenience store can be reached by way of a half-mile trek on Highway 19. By the time you read this account, a "super Wal-Mart," with an extensive grocery section, will have opened about a mile north of the marina.

Catches Seafood and More (7811 Bayview Street, 727-849-2121) and Seaside Inn and Restaurant (5330 Treadway Drive, 727-848-4628)

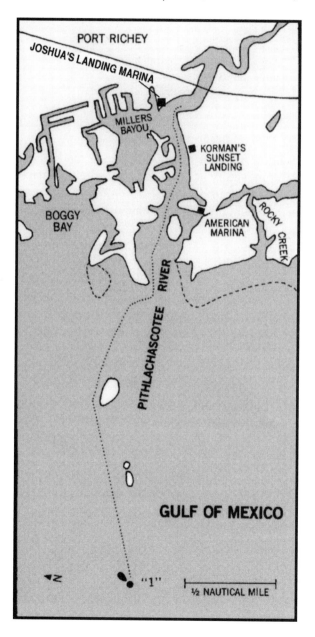

are both within walking distance. We have not had a chance to personally check out either of these dining spots, but both are recommended by the owner of Joshua's Landing.

Over and above these dry statistics, we found a community atmosphere among the happy patrons at Joshua's Landing that is all too frequently lacking at larger, more commercially oriented facilities. We are glad to see this spirit alive and well.

Joshua's Landing (727) 841-8566

Approach depth—3½ feet (MLW)
                    5 feet (MHW)
Dockside depth—5 feet (MLW)
Accepts transients—yes
Fixed wooden piers—yes
Dockside power connections—30 and 50 amp
Dockside water connections—yes
Waste pump-out—yes
Showers—yes
Laundromat—yes
Restaurant—two nearby

Southeast of unlighted daybeacon #41, the Cotee is crossed by the fixed Highway 19 Bridge. Just before you reach the span, the small Port Richey city pier overlooks the southwestern bank. This quaint dock is obviously designed for fishermen and it is seldom frequented by boats of any description.

This guide's coverage of the Cotee River ends at the Highway 19 Bridge. Boats that can clear the span may continue cruising east for some distance in good depths, but there are no more marinas nor opportunities to anchor.

Hudson

The three channels serving the resort community of Hudson lie 9 to 10 nautical miles southeast of flashing daybeacon #10, designated as "St. Martins" on chart 11409. The town's location can be readily spotted from the water, courtesy of the three snow-white, high-rise condos overlooking the point just south of the middle channel. The southernmost cut serves several private dockage basins and is mostly uninteresting to visiting cruisers. The middle channel leads to at least one marina with good dockside depths but, as is the usual case along this southernmost stretch of the Big Bend, low-tide entrance depths run to 4½ feet. Of course, to repeat, you could wait for high tide and hold 6 to 7 feet of water all the way in.

At unlighted daybeacon #22, a side channel cuts to the south and curls around the adjacent point. This passage provides access to the sheltered harbor serving Skeleton Key Marina. The owner of this facility informed this writer that few transients have heretofore visited his marina, but he certainly would not turn them down. Berths consist of tiny, floating wooden decked finger piers stretching out from a concrete seawall. Larger cruising craft will find these finger docks to be of minimal use. Dockside depths are a nice 6 to 10 feet. Freshwater and 20-30-amp power hook-ups are available at all slips. Mechanical repairs for gasoline engines are complemented by gasoline, open-air dry stack storage, clean but non-climate controlled showers, and a minimal ship's and variety store. Two restaurants are close by. Sam's Hudson Beach Snack Bar (727-868-1971) is an open-air, sandwich-type establishment whose patrons dine while looking out onto the Hudson Channel. Many cruisers will prefer the restaurant at Inn on the Gulf (727-868-5623); all reports paint a sure picture of enjoyment. Ask the friendly marina owner or his staff for directions.

Skeleton Key Marina (727) 868-3411

Approach depth—4-4½ feet (low water)
Dockside depth—6-10 feet
Accepts transients—yes
Floating wooden finger piers—yes
Dockside power connections—up to 30 amp
Dockside water connections—yes
Showers—yes
Gasoline—yes
Mechanical repairs—gasoline engines only
Ship's and variety store—small
Restaurant—two nearby

The northernmost of the three charted Hudson channels has always heretofore led to nothing but a commercial fishing craft harbor. All that is now about to change. The extensive dockage basin and its surrounding 10.5 acres of land have been purchased, and plans are going forward to convert this facility into a first-class, pleasurecraft-oriented marina. It will probably be known as Port Hudson Marina. The entrance channel, which is now rather shallow, will be dredged. When complete, and the completion date is uncertain at the time of this writing, Port Hudson will make an ideal jumping-off point for those heading across the Big Bend, or a first port of call for cruisers arriving from points north. Watch our *Salty Southeast* newsletter for updates on the construction progress at this facility.

Aripeka

It's a shame that the channel leading to the old fishing village of Aripeka (4 nautical miles north of the northernmost Hudson Channel) is so shallow. There may be no better preserved example of a tiny fishing community in all of the Big Bend. Unfortunately, low-tide depths rising to as little as 2 feet relegate this cut to flat-bottomed, outboard-powered craft exclusively.

Hernando Beach

The shallow channel leading to Hernando Beach lies some 4.5 nautical miles north of the Aripeka cut. Clearly Hernando Beach is a questionable stop that will only interest those cruisers who are willing to risk an arduous channel and some thin water. On the plus side, two marinas of medium size wait to greet visiting cruisers with some services. On the negative side (are you tired of hearing this?), the entrance channel carries a bare 3 to 4 feet of water at low tide. Additionally, the access cut is surrounded by shoals which sport a few thousand rocks. A member of the local Coast Guard Auxiliary warned this writer to stay "strictly in the middle of the channel." He related that boats deviating just slightly from the midline have been known to have a rocky encounter, and we don't mean a meeting with a boxer from Philadelphia. Of course, depths at high water are a good 6 feet or better.

There are *many* more aids to navigation in the Hernando Channel than those shown on the current edition of chart 11409. The prudent and cautious mariner may be able to run the channel during daylight without problems, always assuming that you can stand those low-tide depths. You will simply have to evaluate your draft, the weather, and the time of day to decide whether to try this cut or move on to the Homosassa River.

The town of Hernando Beach is delightfully still more of a fishing village than a resort town. No high-rise condos mar the landscape and, particularly during weekends, the local anglers are out in force. While it may lack some of the old, quaint homes of Apalachicola, there is no denying that Hernando Beach will appeal to those who cherish small-town America.

At unlighted daybeacon #24, a somewhat confusing channel cuts south, then east, and eventually leads up a long canal to two marinas. First up is Gulfstar Marina, overlooking the eastern banks just as the canal takes a sharp turn to the south. This operation struck us as being a bit on the rough side.

Gulfstar is very much into haul-out repairs. A host of boats was sitting on cradles during our visit. A couple of the fixed wooden slips (with low-key power and water connections) are usually open for transients, with low-tide depths of 5½ to 7½ feet. Full mechanical repairs, along with a ship's and variety store, are also offered. The nearby Gators restaurant (352-596-7160) is highly recommended by the locals.

Gulfstar Marina (352) 596-5079

Approach depth—3-4 feet (low tide)
Dockside depth—5½-7½ feet
Accepts transients—yes
Fixed wooden piers—yes
Dockside power connections—up to 30 amp
Dockside water connections—yes
Mechanical repairs—yes
Below-waterline repairs—yes
Ship's and variety store—yes
Restaurant—one nearby

Hernando Beach Yacht Club maintains a few docks with 7 feet or so of depths just south of Gulfstar. This is a small club that probably does not have room enough for cruising visitors.

Snappers Marina sits just south of the yacht club and offers good facilities for cruisers. Transients are accepted at wooden decked floating piers featuring good depths of 5 to 8 feet. Dockside power and water connections are available, as is one unisex, non-climate controlled shower, gasoline, full mechanical repairs, and a 25-ton travelift for haul-outs. There is also a small ship's and variety store on the premises. Future plans call for the availability of diesel fuel at Snappers, but we could not verify a definite date for the onset of this service. Gators restaurant (352-596-7160) is a short step away.

> **Snappers Marina (352) 596-2952**
> **http://www.wide-world.com/motor/**
>
> **Approach depth—3-4 feet (low tide)**
> **Dockside depth—5-8 feet**
> **Accepts transients—yes**
> **Floating wooden docks—yes**
> **Dockside power connections—up to 30 amp**
> **Dockside water connections—yes**
> **Shower—yes**
> **Gasoline—yes**
> **Mechanical repairs—yes**
> **Below-waterline repairs—yes**
> **Ship's and variety store—small**
> **Restaurant—nearby**

The Homosassa River

Since the time when Europeans first began exploring the shores of *la Florida,* or "the land of flowers," the Homosassa River has had the reputation of being one of the loveliest streams in the Sunshine State. Happily, that air of beauty continues to this day on the river's lower reaches. Indeed, the Homosassa's banks, west of unlighted daybeacon #57, are idyllic. Here the hardwoods so reminiscent of the Big Bend begin to appear and often stretch right down to the water's edge.

In the 1930s Babe Ruth used to come here for the quail hunting. The river's waters were some of Pres. Grover Cleveland's favorite fishing grounds. In 1880 he built a hunting and fishing lodge, which used to occupy the site of present-day Riverhaven Marina. The painter Winslow Homer came to Homosassa in 1904

and completed some of his most noted works here. Obviously, this lovely river has been attracting admirers for some time. Today's cruising visitors benefit from many of the same qualities that once drew so many famous Americans to these waters.

On a less happy note, the river's channel has shoaled to low-water depths of only 2½ to 3 feet near unlighted daybeacons #57A and #58. The locals have dubbed these waters "Hell's Gate." Obviously, cruising-size craft will have to enter and exit the Homosassa at high tide only.

An equally unfortunate note is sounded in the town of Homosassa, east of unlighted daybeacon #74. This small community has begun to develop as a tourist center. On weekends, small craft dot the river's waters in a passable imitation of a swarm of killer bees. A host of private homes and low-level town houses now overlooks the banks here and there. Yet, something of the old fishing village that was once Homosassa survives, and this writer could not help but like this friendly community.

Homosassa boasts its own state historic site, the Yulee Sugar Mill Ruins. This 5,100-acre sugar plantation on the Homosassa River became productive about 1851. In those early days, the manufacture of sugarcane products was an exacting and expensive business, requiring a boiler, steam engine, horizontal mill, and kettles.

Operating for thirteen years, the mill supplied sugar products for Southern troops during the Civil War. In May 1864, a Union naval force captured ammunition and supplies at the plantation and burned it to the ground.

Made of native limestone, the mill has been partially restored. It consists of a large chimney about nine feet square with an extending structure about forty feet long that housed the boiler. Beside the mill are parts of the grinding machinery.

Homosassa River Facilities

Flashing daybeacon #2, the westernmost aid on the Homosassa entrance channel, is found better than 10 nautical miles southeast of flashing buoy #2, itself many miles west of St. Martins Keys. The channel is more than slightly twisty and turny. Depths outside of the marked cut, even on the river's interior reaches, rise dramatically. This is not the place to go exploring. Stick to the buoyed route.

Unlighted daybeacons #37 and #38 mark the Homosassa's westerly entrance. Northeast of these aids, there was once a very neat, water-access-only restaurant known as the Crow's Nest. Sad to say, this restaurant is gone now, and the buildings that remain are a private fishing club.

A heavy concentration of small-craft facilities lines the river along the town waterfront farther to the east. Cruising-size craft may find a few available slips, but clearly the emphasis here is again on smaller outboard- and I/O-powered vessels. Dry stack storage of runabouts seems to be big business.

West of unlighted daybeacon #81, Riverhaven Marina (352-628-5545) will come up on the northern banks. This well-managed facility is clearly numbered among the small-craft, dry stack oriented marinas so dominant on the Homosassa. Riverhaven has practically no wet-slip dockage to speak of. Its few floating piers serve the drystack storage. Gasoline and mechanical repairs are offered.

A bit farther upstream, passing cruisers will

Atlantic Fishing Club, Homosassa River

be amazed by K. C. Crump Restaurant (352-628-1500) on the northern banks. This establishment consists of a huge restaurant, featuring outdoor dining, built to resemble an antebellum plantation house. A wide swath of green grass runs down to the river and the restaurant's extensive fixed wooden piers. While no overnight dockage is allowed and no other marine services are offered, dining patrons are welcome to tie up while feeding their faces. Depths alongside run 6 to 9 feet.

Opposite K. C. Crump, MacRae's Marina (352-628-2602) consists of a host of smaller, fixed wooden slips, a waterside variety, bait, and tackle store, and a motel set back from the water. No transient dockage is available, but gasoline can be purchased in front of the dockside bait and tackle store. Of course, the rustic motel would be a good bet for taking a break from the live-aboard routine, and the notable Charlie Brown's Crab House restaurant is immediately adjacent.

Homosassa Riverside Resort graces the southern banks of the Homosassa River a short distance upstream from MacRae's. This combination marina, motel, and restaurant sports the largest (fixed wooden) slips on the river. As many as 25 berths are usually open for transients. Dockside power (up to 50 amp) and water connections are available, and the firm maintains a shoreside ship's and variety store. Gasoline (but no diesel) can be purchased dockside. While Riverside Resort does not offer mechanical repairs, they will be glad to call in local, independent technicians should you need service work preformed on your vessel.

The adjacent motel is extensive and convenient, but the real shoreside attraction is Charlie Brown's Crab House (352-621-5080). As its name implies, this dining spot is famous for its live crabs, which are stored in large glass tanks on the restaurant's porch. As my ace research assistant Morgan Stinemetz describes it, the bill of fare is "seafood, seafood, and more seafood." Prices are moderate, and, by all accounts, the "seafood, seafood, and more seafood" is excellent.

Upstairs, the Yardarm Lounge and the "Monkey Bar" overlook the Homosassa and a small body of land that has come to be known as "Monkey Island." It seems a whole collection of monkeys was placed on this island around 1990 "because they kept escaping from a local zoo." Most were killed off during the great 1993 "Storm of the Century," but the island has now been repopulated by what one local resident described as "those mean little creatures." The monkeys are fed oranges, grapes, and Purina Monkey Chow by the locals.

Homosassa Riverside Resort (352) 628-2474
   http://www.homosassariverside.com

Approach depth—2½-5 feet (minimum)
Dockside depth—4-5 feet
Accepts transients—yes
Fixed wooden piers—yes
Dockside power connections—up to 50 amp
Dockside water connections—yes
Gasoline—yes
Ship's and variety store—yes
Restaurant—on site

East of Riverside, the Homosassa becomes somewhat shallower and a new series of markings begins. Magic Manatee Marina (352-628-7334) flanks the northern banks opposite unlighted daybeacon #5. This facility is strictly concerned with the dry stack storage of smaller powercraft. Gasoline and some mechanical repairs to outboards and I/O's, as well as a small ship's and variety store, are the only marine services available.

The Homosassa continues upstream for many miles, often frequented by canoes and smaller powercraft. The zoo up at the main spring features an underwater viewing room where visitors can watch the fish and manatees that frequent the locale. Depths become much too unreliable for cruising craft, however, and most larger boats will probably want to discontinue their explorations at the Homosassa village waterfront.

ANCLOTE KEY TO HOMOSASSA RIVER NAVIGATION

If you have opted for the direct route from Anclote Key to Carrabelle, St. George Sound, and Dog Island, there's not a whole lot more that we can add except set the Loran or GPS and keep a careful DR plot. Obviously, the various ports of call and channels discussed below will be of minimal interest to mariners choosing this straight path.

Cruisers following the Big Bend buoyage system and remaining within 5 nautical miles or so of shore can pick and choose among the passages outlined below. Just remember that most of these cuts are rather shallow and several have the added benefit of adjacent rocks! On the other hand, almost all of the cuts have many more markings than those shown on the charts. Always remember your faithful "red, right, returning" rule, take your time, and, if your draft allows, you may come through with nothing more than a few jangled nerves.

North from Anclote Flashing daybeacon #6 marks the northerly exit from Anclote Anchorage. This aid can actually be passed on either side, but for best depths, leave it off your westerly flank (its easterly quarter). From #6, consider setting a course for flashing daybeacon #4, north of Anclote Key. Come abeam of this aid to its easterly quarter. Once abeam of #4, captains can choose to visit Gulf Harbors to the east.

Gulf Harbors Channel Remember that the southern Gulf Harbors Channel leads only to a collection of private docks. Visiting cruisers will almost certainly want to pick the northerly cut.

The westernmost aids on the northerly channel are unlighted daybeacon #1 and flashing daybeacon #2. Obviously, you should pass between these two aids and follow the remaining markers into the mouth of the eastward-running canal.

The tongue of land shown on chart 11411 lining this passage's northerly reaches is actually a rocky body of land, almost a jetty, which is partially covered at high tide. At all costs, stay well away from this hazard. *Be sure* to watch over your stern for excessive lateral leeway.

Local navigators have warned this writer of a rock abutting the south side of the northern Gulf Harbors Channel between the two easternmost sets of markers. *Be sure* to keep strictly to the channel's centerline when passing between unlighted daybeacons #8 and #7, and unlighted daybeacons #10 and #9!

Enter the canal on its mid-width. Watch the southerly shore for the first offshoot. If you are looking for anchorage, this is the place to be. Drop the hook anywhere near the center of this surprisingly large bay.

To continue on to the canal's easterly terminus, simply follow the centerline to the east-southeast. You will eventually spy Highway 19 dead ahead.

The Pithlachascotee River Captains can also cruise northeast from flashing daybeacon #4 to flashing daybeacon #1 and unlighted daybeacon #2, marking the western tip of the Pithlachascotee (Cotee) River Channel. For best depths, we suggest that you do not cruise directly from #4 to #1 and #2. Rather, set your course farther to the north and come abeam of #1 and #2 by some .5 nautical miles to their westerly quarter. You can then turn directly into the channel, passing between flashing daybeacon #1 and unlighted daybeacon #2.

The Cotee River channel remains well outlined and easy to follow as far as unlighted daybeacon #12 and flashing daybeacon #13. At this point, the cut takes a hard jog to the south. Point to come abeam of flashing daybeacon #16 to its immediate easterly side. Once abeam of #16, immediately cut hard to the east again, and point to pass between unlighted daybeacons #17 and #18. Take your time through this stretch of the channel and identify all your markers carefully. Hapless navigators who miss the channel will be in 4 feet of water.

The marked channel to American Marina cuts to the south between unlighted daybeacons #25 and #26. Korman's Sunset Landing is readily accessible south of flashing daybeacon #35.

Cruisers bound for the docks of Hooters Restaurant should watch for a white-PVC-pipe-outlined channel cutting east, just before reaching flashing daybeacon #35.

Enter this small channel on its mid-width. Soon it will lead you towards a commercial dockage area. Break off to starboard some 20 yards before reaching the commercial craft and cruise to Hooters' docks.

Joshua's Landing Marina guards the river's easterly banks near flashing daybeacon #35. For best depths, don't turn directly in to the marina from #35. Instead, continue following the main channel to unlighted daybeacon #41. Depart the principal cut at #41 and cut in towards the easterly banks. Some 25 yards short of the shoreline, swing sharply to port and cruise to the north, heavily favoring the starboard side (easterly) banks. Soon the entrance to the marina's U-shaped harbor will came abeam to starboard.

Southeast of unlighted daybeacon #41, the fixed Highway 19 Bridge soon spans the river. The city fishing pier will be spotted on the southwestern shores. Our coverage of the Cotee ends at the fixed bridge.

On to Hudson North of the Cotee Channel, cruisers must bid good-bye to their old friend chart 11411 and switch to 11409. Throughout the remainder of the Big Bend, navigators must contend with large-format charts. The more detailed, small-craft charts do not resume until reaching St. George Sound, Dog Island, and Carrabelle.

The charted channel leading to Double Hammock Creek, just north of the Cotee River cut, is quite shallow and does not lead to any marina facilities or anchorages. It is highly recommended that you keep on trucking.

The next possible port of call is Skeleton Key Marina at the village of Hudson.

Remember that this facility is accessed via the center of the three channels serving the Hudson waterfront. The channel to the south is one more of those passages serving local boats and is best avoided by visiting cruisers.

It is tempting to set a direct course from flashing daybeacon #4 for flashing daybeacon #2, the first aid to navigation of the center Hudson Channel. Notice, however, that such a course would lead you perilously close to the shallow water northwest of the Cotee Channel *and* the 1-foot depths off South St. Martins Reef. Be sure to pass both these shoals well to their westerly sides.

While it is a bit longer, cautious navigators might consider setting course from #4 for flashing daybeacon #10 off St. Martins reef. After traveling 7.4 nautical miles along this route, you can break off due east and cruise some 6.9 nautical miles to the center Hudson Channel's westerly genesis. Granted, this is the longer way to do it, but it's certainly the safest.

Hudson Channel The center Hudson Channel is exceedingly well marked and easy to run in daylight for most boats that can stand the low-water depths of 4 to 4½ feet. As is usually the case along this section of the Big Bend, you will find many more markers than what is shown on the current edition of chart 11409.

The only tricky spot on the Hudson Channel is found as you approach its easterly limits. After passing between unlighted daybeacons #22 and #23, cruisers bound for Skeleton Key Marina should curl their course around to the south and point for the gap between unlighted daybeacons #1

and #2, the first two aids to navigation on the marina entrance channel. After passing between unlighted daybeacons #6 and #7, turn back to the east and round the northside entrance point. Soon the marina docks will come abeam to starboard, perched on the western shores.

North along the Big Bend Cruisers interested in following the Big Bend buoyage system will want to set a course from flashing daybeacon #4 to flashing daybeacon #10 off St. Martins reef. It is a lengthy run of 12.2 nautical miles between #4 and #10. Be sure to come abeam of #10 to its westerly side. East of this daybeacon, depths run to as little as 5 feet on the reef.

Of course, captains who are confident of their navigation can cut north inside of the reef and save several miles of cruising. Should you follow this adventurous strategy, let me again remind you of the 1-foot depths of South St. Martins Reef, west-southwest of the Hudson channels.

Captains bound for the Homosassa River may want to consider setting course from #10 for flashing daybeacon #2, southwest of the river's entrance. Some 16.6 nautical miles of open water separate #10 and #2. Minimum depths on this straight run are about 6 feet, with most soundings ranging from 8 to 10 feet.

Cruisers choosing to enter the relatively shallow channel leading to Hernando Beach should set course from #10 for flashing daybeacon #2, but break off from this run after cruising about 5.9 nautical miles from #10. You can then set a new course for flashing daybeacon #HB at the head of the Hernando Beach Channel, to the east-southeast. *Be sure* to pass north of the charted "Ruins" clearly noted on 11409.

Those bypassing both Hernando Beach and Homosassa will probably want to ignore flashing daybeacon #2 and make the 21.5-nautical-mile run to flashing buoy #2, *well* west of Homosassa Bay.

Hernando Beach   The Hernando Beach Channel is one of the shallowest and trickiest of the passable cuts between Anclote Key and the Homosassa River. It is quite well marked, though, and in fair weather during daylight, boats up to 38 feet (with appropriate draft and tide) may be able to make a successful but cautious approach.

Be warned, however, that the passage is very twisty in places, and it is flanked to the north by rocky islets. There are even a few reports of rocks impinging upon the channel's edge. Fortunately, our keel did not meet up with any of these obstructions, but it is certain that you will want to hold *strictly* to the middle of the channel.

As you approach tripod-shaped flashing daybeacon #HB, two signs designating "Shoal" water will be observed to the north and south. Don't approach either of these makers. Incidentally, while #HB is labeled properly, there is also a sign on the markers designating it as the "Bill Watts Tripod."

Pass #HB to its fairly immediate northerly side and continue following the various markers east, always remembering your "red, right, returning."

Contrary to what you might expect from studying chart 11409, rocky shoal water lines the northern flank of the channel all the way in to shore. More shallows lie to the south, so stay to the channel's centerline.

During low water, the rocky shoals to the north uncover and appear as small, oblong islets. Believe it or else, it's actually easier to cruise this cut during low tide. The shallows are far more obvious.

Follow the marked cut carefully as it twists and turns around the various rocky islands. If you meet another craft, stay as close to the channel's center as possible when passing.

As you approach the channel's easterly end, the situation is confused by a side channel running south to the marina facilities. Just to make matters a little more juicy, there are two unlighted daybeacon #40s in close proximity to each other.

Our best advice is to carefully stay on the main cut as it runs on to the northeast past the first #40 and then continue on to unlighted daybeacon #38. Only after coming abeam of #38 should you curl around to the south and enter the south-running passage by passing the second unlighted daybeacon #40 to your starboard side. If all this sounds confusing, it is, and we can only advise you to take extra care.

Anyway, once you are on the southerly side cut, continue following the prolific markers on to the south until the channel leads you around a point and you enter an eastward-running canal. Don't be tempted to enter any of the canals to the east short of the turn around the point. While they have somewhat respectable depths, they do not lead to any facilities.

Once on the canal that you have been led to by the markers, cruise to the east until the stream dead ends. Turn to starboard. Both marinas and the Hernando Beach Yacht Club will then be quite obvious on the eastern banks.

The Homosassa River It is an unfortunate reality that low-water depths of 2½ to 3 feet have built across the main Homosassa River channel in the vicinity of unlighted daybeacons #57A and #58. Clearly, the vast majority of cruising-size vessels will need to navigate the Homosassa channel strictly at high water. Even then, boats drawing more than 4½ feet should probably pick another port of call.

The long Homosassa Channel begins at flashing daybeacon #4 and winds its way to the northeast for some 4.2 nautical miles before turning more to the east at unlighted daybeacon #28. The waters abeam of #28 exhibit low-tide depths of only 5 feet or so.

At unlighted daybeacon #30, the channel takes a turn to starboard and rounds unlighted daybeacon #31. A whole bevy of markers leads into the river's mouth and tidal currents begin to pick up.

Unlighted daybeacons #37 and #38 usher mariners into the mouth of the Homosassa River. To the northeast, passing cruisers will note the old location of Crow's Nest Restaurant. This is now the site of a private fishing club.

East of #38, the undeveloped portion of the Homosassa will open out before you. The shores are absolutely beautiful, particularly around unlighted daybeacon #45.

As mentioned repeatedly above, the Homosassa River channel has shoaled badly between unlighted daybeacons #57A and #58. This region is known locally, and charted on 11409, as "Hell's Gate." Low-water depths run as thin a 2½ to 3 feet. Our only advice is to wait for high water before attempting this portion of the channel.

At unlighted daybeacon #74 development picks up and the marked cut takes a sharp jog to starboard and then cuts back to port at unlighted daybeacon #75. A slow-speed manatee zone begins at #75.

At unlighted daybeacon #76, a year-round, idle-speed, no-wake zone begins. All boats should proceed at minimal speed throughout the developed upstream portion of the river.

By the time you reach unlighted daybeacon #81, the riverbanks will become lined with private homes. A bit farther upstream, the marina facilities described earlier will be obvious on both shorelines.

After passing Homosassa Riverside Resort on the southerly banks, watch for a small island near the southern shoreline sporting a miniature lighthouse. This small body of land plays host to the marooned monkeys described earlier in this chapter.

East of "Monkey Island," the numbering system on the Homosassa begins anew with unlighted daybeacon #2. This portion of the river is far shallower than its westerly counterpart; it's probably best left to smaller craft.

Should you decide to visit Magic Manatee Marina, the dry-storage building and docks will be obvious to port as you come abeam of unlighted daybeacon #5.

Crystal River to Cedar Key

The central section of Florida's Big Bend is a real study in striking contrasts. To the south, Crystal River boasts some of the clearest water to be found anywhere in the world. Yet the stream is overlooked by a huge nuclear power plant to the north and the town of the same name lying about the river's upper reaches is undergoing a steadily expanding tourist economy. The Withlacoochee River lies a few miles north of its sister stream, but it is light years different in character. This is really the first of the beautifully undeveloped rivers of the Big Bend, and visiting cruisers will come away with haunting memories of the stream's loveliness. Cedar Key, another 14 nautical miles or so to the north, was once one of the quaintest villages in all of Florida. While much of the historic downtown section remains, Cedar Key has clearly been "discovered." New construction is very much in evidence and two modern restaurants overlooking the principal waterfront stick out like proverbial sore thumbs.

From the cruiser's point of view, the three ports of call along the central Big Bend have quite a bit to offer. All have deeper entrance channels than most of the streams to the south. The Crystal and Withlacoochee rivers have good marina facilities, while Cedar Key can at least boast one of the few good anchorages along the Big Bend.

So, perhaps there's something for everyone and you may just find waters that demand a return time and time again. By all means, you should give the Withlacoochee your most careful attention.

The Crystal River

The crystal clear waters of Crystal River are fed by more than 30 natural springs, pumping in 300 million gallons of water each day. The river is considered by many to be the most important manatee refuge in Western Florida. Biologists have identified some 200 of the gentle beasts, or about 17 percent of the entire state's manatee population, living along the river. For all these reasons and more, Crystal River is one of the most popular bodies of water for diving and snorkeling in all of Florida.

The lower, undeveloped portion of the Crystal River shoreline is quite appealing to the eye. This area is part of the Chassahowitzka Wildlife Refuge and is protected from strip malls and T-shirt shops. Here the landscape begins to change in response to your northward movement along Western Florida's coastline. Increasingly, visiting cruisers will observe oaks, cedars, and other hardwoods.

Today, the modern age is being felt along the banks of this pristine stream. A huge nuclear power plant overlooks the river to the north, near its westerly mouth. Everywhere you go on land, the nuclear-accident warning sirens are very much in evidence.

The town of Crystal River sits sprawled about the upper cruising limits of the stream. This community sports a whole array of new construction and it is much frequented by tourists during the weekend.

Crystal River's channel can usually be relied upon to hold minimum depths of 5½ feet as far upstream as the charted "Indian Mound." To be on the safe side, skippers piloting vessels drawing better than 4½ feet might want to wait for a rising tide. Some low-water soundings between the Indian mound and the marina at Crystal City run to 5, possibly 4½ feet. As if that weren't cause enough for a bit of worry, chart 11409 also notes several rocks along the river's course. This writer has been assured by several local cruisers that these hazards can be easily avoided by sticking to the river's centerline.

Two marinas provide transient dockage on Crystal River. The best of the two is found in the town of Crystal River itself.

The western limit of the Crystal River entrance channel lies a good 14 nautical miles northeast of flashing buoy #2. The entrance passage twists and turns its way through the surrounding shallows until finding the river's mouth near unlighted daybeacon #21.

In the past, another well-respected cruising guide has recommended anchoring along the Crystal's northern shore between unlighted daybeacons #23 and #24. During original on-site research we hit *rock* while trying to make use of this haven. In a word, *don't* try it! Instead, you can ease a little way off the main channel to the south, immediately east of unlighted daybeacon #23. Boats with as much as 4 feet of draft can anchor in some 5 feet of water, or slightly less, in the lee of undeveloped Shell Island. Drop the hook as you come abeam of a small, sand beach on the island's northeasterly point. Approach the island shores only by dinghy, as they are quite shoal. Protection is good for all winds, but swinging room is probably only sufficient for boats as large as 34 feet. Farther to the south, shallows are soon encountered.

Between unlighted daybeacon #25 and the stretch of river charted as "The Rocks," good depths of 6 feet or better stretch out in a broad band along the river's track. It is quite possible to ease a bit off the river's mid-width and set the hook with excellent protection from all winds. Just be aware that commercial fishing traffic is possible, and even likely, during the evening hours. A bright anchor light is your best defense against a rude awakening.

Twin Rivers Marina sits near the intersection of the small Salt River and the Crystal along the latter stream's southerly shoreline. The old 30-foot power lines crossing the Salt River between Crystal River and the marina docks have been replaced by a new set of wires with 47 feet of vertical clearance. Sailcraft should still take great care. The entrance channel runs between a small island to port and the starboard shores. Low-water entrance depths run between 3½ and 5 feet. An underwater rock ledge lying just off the docks is the shallowest portion of the approach channel and is certainly a cause for concern if your vessel draws better than 3 feet.

Twin Rivers offers well-sheltered transient dockage and full repair services. The marina docks will soon be sighted along the Salt River's southerly banks. Most of the piers are set in a man-made cove cutting back from the riverbanks. Transient and resident craft are berthed at fixed wooden piers with water and power connections up to 30 amp. Low-tide dockside depths run between 4½ and 6½ feet. Twin Rivers features full mechanical repair services and haul-outs via a 35-ton travelift. There is also a fuel dock offering both gasoline and diesel fuel, and a modest ship's and variety store. There is no restaurant nor any provisioning possibilities for miles around. Be sure your galley is well stocked before committing to an overnight stay at Twin Rivers.

Twin Rivers Marina (352) 795-3552

Approach depth—3½-5 feet (low water)
Dockside depth—4½-6½ feet (low water)
Accepts transients—yes
Fixed wooden piers—yes
Dockside power connections—up to 30 amp
Dockside water connections—yes
Gasoline—yes

Diesel fuel—yes
Mechanical repairs—yes
Below-waterline repairs—yes
Ship's store—yes

Farther upstream, the Crystal River flows into King's Bay, source of many of its freshwater springs. Vessels that can stand some 4½-foot low-tide depths can make use of Pete's Pier/King's Bay Marine on the bay's northeastern banks. This facility sits almost in the heart of the town of Crystal River. A host of grocery stores, motels, and retail establishments of all descriptions is a short walk away.

Pete's Pier is glad to accept transients for overnight berths at fixed wooden piers with water and 30-50-amp power connections. The 50-amp hook-ups are only available in certain slips. Many of the piers are covered and therefore only appropriate for powercraft, but there are now a dozen open berths fit for sailcraft. Clean, air-conditioned showers are readily available, as are gasoline, diesel fuel and free waste pump-out service (for dockage patrons). Pete's features full mechanical repairs, but their marine railway was not operational during our last visit. Until this contraption is repaired, below-waterline servicing will not be available. An on-site bait, tackle, and variety store adds to the marina's offerings.

If it's dinnertime, ask any of the marina staff for directions to either Cravings on the Water (614 NW Highway 19, 352-795-2027) or Crackers Bar and Grill (502 NW Sixth Street, 352-795-3999). Both these dining spots are accessible by foot *and* dinghy! We have not had a chance to sample either, but both have been recommended to us by the staff at Pete's Pier.

In addition to many other landside businesses within walking distance, a Publix supermarket can be found some half-mile from the dockage basin. There is also a laundromat in the same shopping center.

Pete's Pier/King's Bay Marine (352) 795-3302

Approach depth—4½-5 feet (low water)
Dockside depth—4½-6 feet
Accepts transients—yes
Fixed wooden piers—yes
Dockside power connections—up to 50 amp
Dockside water connections—yes
Waste pump-out—yes (for dockage patrons)
Showers—yes
Gasoline—yes
Diesel fuel—yes
Mechanical repairs—yes
Ship's and variety store—yes
Restaurant—several nearby

The Withlacoochee River

Okay, no quibbling this time. The Withlacoochee River has almost everything going for it you can possibly imagine. It used to be that the Withlacoochee had minimum entrance depths of 8 feet, making it the deepest of the Big Bend Rivers short of St. Marks. Following the awesome March 1993 "Storm of the Century," typical low-water depths in the entrance channel rose to some 5 to 5½ feet and have stayed pretty much at that level to the present day. Fortunately much of the channel yields considerably better water. Vessels drawing more than 5 feet might wait to plan their entrance and egress of the Withlacoochee to correspond with a rising tide.

The Withlacoochee's banks are a celebration of deep, almost secret cypress swamps, and marina facilities are adequate. Still not convinced? Well, consider Rex Henderson's unforgettable description of the Withlacoochee as he writes in Del and Marty Marth's *The Rivers of Florida:*

The river's name comes from an Indian word meaning "little great water," a contradiction that speaks eloquently of the Withlacoochee. On a quiet canoe trip, the Florida that the Seminoles knew unfolds. The river's flat, glassy surface mirrors thick green tangles of cypress, oak, ash, and cedar boughs overhanging the banks. . . . Turtles sun themselves on logs. An alligator's eyes and snout poke out above the water in the shallows, then sink quietly beneath the surface. . . . The skies are an aviary of beautiful birds. A bird watcher who spies an osprey may then find his attention claimed by great blue and great white herons.

Well, both Mr. Henderson and this writer could go on and on, and have, but perhaps by now you are getting the picture. If you visit only one river between Anclote Key and St. Marks, let it be the Withlacoochee. In an experience similar to the one above, we came motoring quietly along the river on a foggy morning in October. The primeval landscape of tall cypress and cottonwood trees that opened reluctantly before us was absolutely awesome and completely unforgettable. That same experience waits for any fortunate cruiser who makes the Withlacoochee a port of call.

Getting down off cloud nine for a moment, the Withlacoochee's entrance channel lies some 19.5 nautical miles east-northeast of flashing buoy #2, just north of the never-completed Cross-Florida Barge Canal channel. Minimum entrance and interior depths are some 5 to 5½ feet, though 6 feet or better can still be carried along most of the track. The river is somewhat narrow, and this writer would be reluctant to send any craft larger than 50 feet upstream.

East of unlighted daybeacon #40, the river channel passes into the Withlacoochee's interior reaches. At unlighted daybeacon #40A, passing cruisers will be surprised by a huge, old, combination sail- and powercraft moored on a small offshoot to the south. Believe it or else, this is actually a German World War I spy ship that was brought to America following the close of the conflict. It sank a few years ago off the Eastern Florida coast. A new owner raised the vessel and had it towed to the Withlacoochee, where he planned to restore it. It is now abandoned and rotting away.

While depths are certainly adequate along the course of the Withlacoochee for anchorage, this is a fairly narrow river, and swinging

Withlacoochee River shoreline

room is somewhat skimpy. It could become even tighter if one of the river's commercial fishing fleet happens along during the night and fouls your rode.

As the first house associated with the delightful residential community of Yankeetown comes abeam on the northeastern banks, a small offshoot cuts into the shoreline. Depths range from 5 to 7 feet and the protection from all winds is superb, but swinging room is at a premium. We don't recommend this potential haven for boats larger than 30 feet, and even these vessels will want to employ a Bahamian mooring.

The Withlacoochee's marina facilities are small but accommodating. All three are located at the charted location of "Yankeetown" on the river's northeastern banks. First up is Yankeetown Marina. Most of this facility's docks are tucked away in a small cove indenting the banks, while a few piers front directly onto the river. There is a definite flavor of commercial fishing at Yankeetown Marina, but the superfriendly staff and management are glad to take transient pleasurecraft for overnight or temporary dockage. The marina features fixed wooden piers with good dockside depths of 6 to 9 feet. Many of the slips are covered, but there are usually a few open slots available for sailcraft. Freshwater and 30-50-amp power hook-ups are now available at all the marina's slips. Gasoline and diesel fuel are on hand (with *good* prices), as are full mechanical and below-waterline, haul-out repairs (via a marine railway). Shoreside cruisers will find an unusually well supplied ship's and variety store.

It's an easy walk to Izaak Walton Lodge Restaurant (see below). However, there are no grocery stores within walking distance.

Yankeetown Marina has the added attraction of a resident pair of otters. These loveable creatures can often be seen sporting around the docks. Feel free to look or even take pictures, but don't try to touch the otters. They are, after all, wild creatures with sharp teeth.

Yankeetown Marina (352) 447-2529

Approach depth—5-20 feet
Dockside depth—6-9 feet
Accepts transients—yes
Fixed wooden piers—yes (many covered)
Dockside power connections—up to 50 amp
Dockside water connections—yes
Gasoline—yes
Diesel fuel—yes
Mechanical repairs—yes
Below-waterline repairs—yes
Ship's and variety store—yes
Restaurant—nearby

Cypress Marina and Campground guards the northwesterly banks a bit farther upstream. This facility is still somewhat under construction as of this writing, but the fixed wooden piers are finished and open for business. Transients are accepted, and 20-30-amp power and freshwater hook-ups are offered. Depths alongside run around 7 feet. Low-key showers and restrooms (which could be cleaner) are also to be found on site. Future plans call for the construction of a variety store and laundromat. The store will have basic grocery items, ice, and fishing tackle. Gasoline and diesel fuel will also (at least that's the plan) be dispensed from an adjacent fuel pier. Again, the Izaak Walton Lodge is within walking distance but there are no provisioning facilities.

Time will tell whether all this facility's plans come to fruition. If you visit Cypress Marina, we would like to hear about your experience.

Send us e-mail at opcom@netpath.net or "snail mail" to P.O. Box 67, Elon College, NC 27244-0067.

Cypress Marina and Campground (352) 447-5888

Approach depth—5-20 feet
Dockside depth—7 feet (MLW)
Accepts transients—yes
Fixed wooden piers—yes
Dockside power connections—up to 30 amp
Dockside water connections—yes
Showers—yes
Restaurant—nearby

A few more upriver twists and turns will bring you abeam of the wooden face dock of friendly Riverside Marina and Cottages on the northeastern banks. Some additional slips are located in a small cove cutting into the banks. One glance at Riverside will convince you that this is the spot where most of the resident and visiting sailcraft plying the waters of the Withlacoochee find their berths. This facility exudes good management, and the whole ambiance simply cries out, "Stay here!" During our times on the river, we inevitably spot no less than a dozen sailors moored to the piers.

Riverside Marina is happy to accept overnight transients at its fixed wooden piers featuring water and 30-amp power connections. Depths along the pier fronting onto the river run between 6 and 10 feet, while 4 to 6

Riverside Marina and Cottages, Withlacoochee River

feet of low-tide soundings are encountered alongside the cove slips. Considering the popularity of this facility, advance dockage reservations are definitely recommended. Shoreside, cruisers will find a single unisex shower, a laundromat (with ironing board), and, of course, the adjacent rental cottages. No fuel or repairs are available but the Izaak Walton Lodge is adjacent.

Riverside Marina & Cottages (352) 447-2980

Approach depth—5-20 feet
Dockside depth—6-10 feet (outer dock)
**   4-6 feet (inner cove slips)**
Accepts transients—yes
Fixed wooden piers—yes
Dockside power connections—up to 30 amp
Dockside water connections—yes
Shower—yes
Laundromat—yes
Restaurant—nearby

Just a short hop farther upstream, visiting cruisers will discover the newly reopened headquarters of the Withlacoochee's most venerable hostelry and restaurant, the Izaak Walton Lodge. The lodge is surrounded by the delightful residential community of Yankeetown. Quiet lanes shrouded with pines and hardwoods are lined by a pleasant collection of quaint private homes. There is no downtown, and the community seems to center around the lodge.

That is only as it should be. For many years the story of Izaak Walton Lodge was synonymous with the history of Yankeetown. For those of you who don't know, Izaak Walton was a famous English outdoors writer of the 1600s whose classic book, *The Compleat Angler,* extolled the virtues and peace of sport fishing as opposed to the violence of hunting. By 1922 a group known as the Izaak Walton

League had been formed in America. The members were dedicated to the "preservation of clean water and natural resources." One of the league's members, A. F. Knotts, came to the Withlacoochee during this time to try his luck with the river's angling opportunities. He immediately fell in love with the natural splendor of the Withlacoochee and its wonderful banks. Before many months had passed, he had purchased an old Civil War sugar landing site along the river and begun clearing land for a lodge. With this hostelry, he hoped to lure his friends from the northeast to share in the great outdoor beauty that he had discovered.

During the 1920s, the Knotts family ran the lodge and lived there during the winter and spring months. The local mail carrier was often heard to say that he had to trudge miles down the river to deliver the mail to those "damn Yankees." Somehow this designation stuck, and that is how Yankeetown came by its name.

The lodge survived the Great Depression and was later used as a health retreat and a private residence. After falling on hard times, the old structure was purchased in the 1980s by Linda and Wayne Harrington. They undertook a magnificent restoration. In addition to the lodge rooms and river cabins, Izaak Walton's featured what was surely one of the most outstanding restaurants in all of Florida.

Then, in the spring of 1999, tragedy struck. A fire destroyed the historic lodge and restaurant. We first learned about the conflagration at the 1999 St. Petersburg Sail Expo, and it was a lowly day in this writer's life. Now, we are happy to report that reconstruction of a new Izaak Walton Lodge restaurant has gone forward. The new restaurant resembles the historic structure as much as possible, but guestrooms are no longer located in the main building. Instead, there are currently two nearby duplex apartments for rent, and, eventually, the owners hope to construct a separate but connected building that will house additional guestrooms. We have every confidence that the new incarnation of the Izaak Walton Lodge restaurant will have the some outstanding cuisine as its predecessor. This writer hopes to be one of the first to try the new lodge's fare. I'll give you a report in our newsletter, *The Salty Southeast*.

For us cruisers, the Walton lodge still features a small pier fronting onto the river. This structure survived the fire intact. Transients are accepted for overnight dockage, and you do not have to be a guest of the inn to tie up for the night. No power connections, water connections, or other marine services are offered. Dockside depths run about 8 feet and there should be room for two cruising-size craft at the fixed wooden pier.

Less than a mile up from Izaak Walton's, a U.S. Coast Guard Base guards the northern banks. This headquarters serves mariners along the entire Big Bend.

Our coverage of the Withlacoochee sadly ends at the Coast Guard base. While good depths continue for many miles upstream, the river narrows further, and this portion of the timeless river is better left to our canoeing brethren.

The Waccasassa River

The extremely shallow entrance channel of the Waccasassa River makes into the Big Bend shoreline about halfway between the Withlacoochee and Cedar Key. Unfortunately, low-water depths of 3 feet, or occasionally less, relegate this beautifully unspoiled stream to small, outboard-powered craft. If you should ever find yourself piloting one of these shallow-draft boats, then by all means consider giving the Waccasassa a try. If you enjoy nature, your time will be more than well spent.

Cedar Key

The main Seahorse Key Channel, leading to the old port town of Cedar Key, cuts into the Gulf's clear waters 10.8 nautical miles northeast of flashing buoy #2. A second passage known as the Northwest channel allows ready access to and from the Suwannee River and points north from the town waterfront. The Sea Horse Key Channel holds minimum 10-foot depths, and the Northwest passage has similar soundings except for one 6½- to 7-foot lump. Both cuts wind and turn quite a bit. The Sea Horse Key passage has an amazing *S* turn that has to be seen to be believed. Be sure to read the Cedar Key navigation section later in this chapter before making your first entry attempt.

The downtown section of Cedar Key is a very mixed bag for visitors. Dock Street flanks the town waterfront. This road is a menagerie of gaudy tourist shops, less-than-spectacular restaurants, noisy bars, and precious little automobile parking. To be blunt, this is Florida at its worst!

On the other hand, a stroll along Second Street, the main passage through the historic downtown section, is absolutely delightful. Be sure to visit the Cedar Key Historical Museum (352-543-5549) at the corner of Second Street and Florida 24. There is also a host of art galleries, which we found to be absolutely delightful.

When it comes time to slake a healthy appetite in Cedar Key, you have to pick and choose carefully. There is a host of bad choices. One of your best bets is a place called Pat's Red Luck Café (390 Dock Street,

352-543-6840). My ace research assistant Morgan Stinemetz reports that the food here is "excellent." He particularly recommends the fried shrimp, oysters, and "home potatoes."

It goes almost without saying that Cedar Key is becoming increasingly popular with landlubber tourists, particularly on weekends. On every one of our visits here, parking spaces have been about as rare as an easily run inlet.

Cedar Key has very little in the way of real dockage facilities for passing cruisers. The often rebuilt city pier is located in the heart of the downtown waterfront. It does have five slips, with some 6 feet of water alongside. There are no power or water connections, and the adjacent bathrooms would probably be avoided even by buzzards. The Cedar Key pier is not very sheltered either. This fact is verified by the frequent reconstruction necessary to keep this dock from falling into the water. By all accounts, you don't want to be caught dead here in foul weather. Adding insult to injury, fellow cruisers report that boats docking at the city pier are often at odds with local fishermen who seem to think that the pier is their private domain. Are you starting to get the picture?

Perhaps your best bet, if you should choose to ignore this writer's advice and berth at the city pier (and not make use of the good anchorages described below), is to carefully tie off your boat, and then spend the night ashore. Those following this plan should check out either the Dockside Motel (491 Dock Street, 352-543-5432), directly across the street from the city pier, or the Island Hotel (373 Second Street, 352-543-5111). This latter hostelry is a wonderful bed and breakfast inn listed on the National Register of historic buildings. Its walls, constructed of

seashell tabby with oak supports, have withstood the vagaries of storms since the mid-1800s. The inn has 13 guestrooms, all of which are outstanding. It should also be noted that the Island Hotel has its own dining room, at which the food has been reported to be a "knockout."

Thankfully, there are at least two good anchor-down spots within sight of the Cedar Key waterfront. One is located adjacent to historic Atsena Otie Key. While it may look as if you can cruise directly to the key from the town waterfront, an intervening shoal makes this a tricky proposition indeed. Most skippers should enter this anchorage by cruising northeast from unlighted daybeacon #28. Minimum 10-foot depths are held to a point abeam of Atsena Key's northwesterly point. Farther to the east, depths may look good on the chart, but they begin to deteriorate to 5 feet or so. Nevertheless, boats drawing 4 feet or less may consider easing around the point for better shelter in fresh winds.

This anchorage is well protected from southerly blows and shelter is fair from northerly winds. Strong westerlies or easterly winds over 15 knots call for another plan.

During fair weather, skippers can anchor south of the city pier, between unlighted daybeacons #36 and #8. Depths run 12 to 18 feet and there is plenty of swinging room. Show an anchor light to identify yourself to nighttime traffic. Winds blowing over 15 knots from any quarter would bring on a very bumpy evening.

Cedar Key History Cedar Key, established in the 1840s, played a significant role in the Seminole Indian Wars, the development of the first railroad to cross the state of Florida, Gulf coast shipping and trading, fishing, and

Cedar Key waterfront

the manufacture of cedar for America's major pencil companies. Still largely preserved, the town affords an insight into the development of coastal Florida's towns and architecture of yesteryear.

Rich archaeological artifacts remaining in the form of shell middens and mounds certainly indicate that occupancy of the Cedar Keys predates the coming of Europeans to the New World. The first residents may have arrived as early as A.D. 1500.

In 1834 and 1835 John Gilleland and Edmund Bird were searching for sources of cedar for lumbering. They explored the Santa Fe and Suwannee rivers and discovered the Cedar Keys and their associated harbor. Gilleland was killed during the Seminole Indian War in 1837 and Bird returned to Georgia without pursuing plans for settlements on the Suwannee.

It was between 1842 and 1844 that five settlers established homesteads and obtained permits in the region. Thomas H. Parsons and Henry Crane built houses on Way Key, which was probably the first occupation of the present-day site of Cedar Key. In 1843 Augustus Steele secured a permit to settle on Depot Key (now known as Atsena Otie Key). The 168-acre key, which contained a military depot and hospital left over from the Seminole Indian Wars, was purchased for $227. Steele secured the designation of Cedar Key as a new customs district and helped to establish the abandoned military post as a major seaport on the Florida Gulf Coast. Cotton production and lumbering up the Suwannee and the interior of Florida contributed to the emerging role of Cedar Key as a port.

In 1845, the Florida legislature petitioned the U.S. government for the establishment of a lighthouse on Seahorse Key. The petition noted that the Cedar Keys area was the "depot for all the trade and communication up and down" the Suwannee River.

The steamboat business expanded in the 1850s at Cedar Key. In 1854, 3,000 to 4,000 bales of cotton, sugar, tobacco, and lumber were shipped from Depot Key.

A major event for Cedar Key was the establishment of the Eberhard Faber Mill for the production of cedar pencil blanks and pen holders. It was located on Atsena Otie Key (formerly Depot Key) and soon became the major industry in the area.

Between 1851 and 1852 a charter was granted to the Florida Railroad Company for the establishment of a railroad from Fernandina to Cedar Key. This was a joint venture of Augustus Steel and David Levy Yulee, who was also interested in the Keys' shipping potential.

The outbreak of the Civil War created a lull in the development of Cedar Key and the surrounding lands. The Florida Railroad was in financial difficulty and the establishment of a Federal blockade along the Gulf Coast severely limited the use of the port. Following the destructive war, work began anew at the sawmills which had been established before the Civil War and business began to steadily improve. By September of 1868 there were seven steamer lines running out of Cedar Key, touching at Mobile, New Orleans, and Galveston.

In 1869 Way Key was incorporated as the City of Cedar Key. The town continued to improve and grow and by 1870 had a population of 400. The fishing and lumber industries were going great guns.

By 1884 Cedar Key had an impressive main street and several large commercial establishments. A huge wharf was built out over the water with warehouses nearby and the railroad ended there. Hotels and residential structures were begun west of the town high on a large Indian midden.

When the South Florida Railroad was completed to Tampa in 1884 the deep-water port there began to draw shipping interests away from Cedar Key. This had a devastating effect on the economy and mills began to shut down. The last nail in the coffin was the hurricane of 1896. The destruction was so severe that Cedar Key was abandoned for all intents and purposes.

The turn of the century posed a new challenge to the community's survival. All the major industries had relocated from the island and a report in 1913 indicated no waterborne traffic entering the port. The population was reported at 1,000, and the pier was dilapidated. The only industry in the town was fishing, which survives today as part of the local economy. The significant period in the town's history was over around 1900. The 20th century would see a gradual discovery by tourists of the special qualities of the town and the establishment of a rather important artists' colony and resort atmosphere.

CRYSTAL RIVER TO CEDAR KEY NAVIGATION

Successful navigation of the rivers along the central section of the Big Bend from the Crystal River to Cedar Key is generally simpler than that found on the streams to the south. These channels are somewhat deeper and the passages are exceedingly well buoyed. This does not preclude a few interesting and unexpected twists and turns along the way, so read the information presented below carefully.

Passage along the offshore Big Bend buoyage system now becomes comprised of runs of 10 to 20 nautical miles or better. Just to make life a bit more interesting, the Coast Guard has seen fit to label two of the most important aids to navigation both as #2. Study both chart 11408 and 11409 carefully to be sure you understand the different locations of these two flashing buoy #2s.

As with all passages along the Big Bend, fair-weather voyages are pleasant and often memorable, while foul winds can bring about decidedly different memories. Always plan any cruise along the Big Bend with a ready ear to the NOAA weather forecast.

North to Crystal River Well, this subhead should really read "northeast." From the flashing buoy #2, well west of Homosassa Bay, that we met in the last section of this chapter, cruisers bound for the Crystal River should set course for flashing daybeacon #1 and unlighted daybeacon #2, the westernmost aids to navigation on the Crystal River entrance channel. It is a lengthy run of 14 nautical miles between flashing buoy #2 and #1. Run a careful compass/GPS course and watch for leeway. Don't allow any slippage to the south. An error of this nature could possibly land you in the charted 5-foot depths ranging west from Crystal Bay, south of the river's entrance.

From #1 and #2 the Crystal River Channel twists and turns its way first northeast, then east, and finally southeast into the mouth of the Crystal River. Remember "red, right, returning" and proceed with caution, making sure to carefully identify each marker correctly as you move along.

After passing between unlighted daybeacons #21 and #22, you will enter the river's interior reaches. The huge nuclear power plant to the north will be prominently visible. The channel cuts a bit to the southeast at this point and skirts around the northeastern tip of Shell Island. If you choose to try the anchorage east of the island, continue on the main channel for some 75 yards east of unlighted daybeacon #23. You can then carefully curl around to the south and feel your way along with the sounder for some 25 to 30 yards, keeping at least 50 yards off the small beach on Shell Island. Drop the hook before proceeding any farther to the south. Unmarked shoals soon encroach upon the deeper water.

Cruisers bound upstream on the Crystal River will have no trouble identifying unlighted daybeacon #24. However, we noticed that this marker can be hard to spot when you are voyaging downriver towards the Gulf. Use your binoculars, if necessary, to pick it out from the dark background of trees.

Moving upstream, a newly numbered set of aids to navigation begins east of unlighted daybeacon #25. Pass between unlighted daybeacons #1 and #2, and continue upstream by passing all subsequent red, even-numbered aids to navigation to your starboard side while taking green markers to port.

Hold *strictly* to the river's centerline as you cruise through "The Rocks," east of unlighted daybeacons #11 and #12. Careful and repeated soundings in 1999 seemed to indicate that you could safely avoid any rocky underwater obstructions by holding to this plan of action. Local reports also speak of other scattered rocks along the river's path. Again, your best defense is to hold to the mid-width.

Soon after leaving "The Rocks" behind, the intersection with the Salt River, home of Twin Rivers Marina, will come up along the southern banks. If you decide to frequent this facility, turn into the Salt River, favoring the northwestern shores a bit. Set course to pass between the starboard shore and a small island which should be passed to your port side. After leaving the small isle behind, continue down the Salt River's mid-width to the marina docks. Sailcraft skippers are again admonished to remember the 47-foot power lines spanning the Salt River between its intersection with the Crystal and Twin Rivers Marina.

Depths begin to rise on the Crystal River upstream from the Salt River intersection. The charted "Indian Mound" will appear as a tall hill on the northern banks soon after you leave the Salt River behind. Soundings become particularly suspect east of this point. We found that 5-foot depths could be carried into the westerly reaches of King's Bay. Thereafter, low-tide soundings of 4 feet were all too common.

Boats continuing on to Pete's Pier should pass between unlighted daybeacons #29 and #30 and hold to the bay's centerline thereafter. Watch to the east, and you should spy the docks and slips associated with Pete's Pier/King's Bay Marine. Don't turn into the basin until it is directly abeam to your port side. This plan will help to avoid a host of rocks that lines King's Bay's easterly banks.

North along the Big Bend Cruisers continuing north from flashing buoy #2, well west of Homosassa Bay, must make a fundamental choice. If you opt for the enchanting Withlacoochee River, set course almost due north for the westerly limits of the huge Cross-Florida Barge Canal channel. This passage covers a distance of 7.9 nautical miles. It's then a simple matter to cruise east to the Withlacoochee Channel.

Cruisers continuing on to the north will want to set course for *another* flashing buoy #2, this one south of well-charted Seahorse Reef. It is a lengthy run of 14.3 nautical miles between the two #2s.

Before moving on to a discussion of the Withlacoochee's navigational characteristics, let's briefly mention the two large, charted channels lying north of the Crystal River. The southern of the two serves the nuclear power plant north of the Crystal. Need we say more? All cruisers are advised to keep clear.

The second cut is a bit more interesting. It was to be part of a long, long canal allowing for easy movement of barge traffic between the two coastlines of Florida. Plans for this waterway stretch back to 1935 and Franklin Roosevelt's "New Deal." Actual construction did not begin until 1964. Several miles of the canal were completed on both its eastern and western ends before fervent objections by environmentalists and cost-conscious legislators put a stop to this boondoggle in 1971. Now the channel and a few miles of canal sit idly in mute testament to a project that never should have been begun.

The Withlacoochee River Navigation of the Withlacoochee is generally straightforward. After the March 1993 "Storm of the Century," minimum depths rose to some 5 to 5½ feet at typical low water. Skippers whose craft need more than 5 feet of water to stay off the bottom may want to consult the tide tables and time their arrival and departure with the high water mark.

Be warned that the outer portion of the Withlacoochee entrance channel is flanked by semisubmerged rocks. Stay in the marked cut.

Captains putting into the river's mouth have a choice of either following the westerly reaches of the barge canal channel to unlighted daybeacon #25, or tracking their way directly east to flashing daybeacon #1, the first aid on the river's entrance passage.

Those cruisers who do follow the barge canal to #25 can then cut north to flashing daybeacon #1 and pass through at least 14 feet of water. At #1, turn east-northeast and begin following the prolific markers through the 3.8-nautical-mile channel leading to the Withlacoochee's westerly entrance.

After passing between unlighted daybeacons #4 and #5, you will spot the remnants of a large wooden tripod ahead. This aid (or what's left of it after the March 1993 storm) is set directly on the long, rocky barrier

north of the entrance channel. Ignore the lighted but unnumbered tripod and be *sure* to pass south of flashing daybeacon #9. The rocky shoal continues to flank the channel as far east as unlighted daybeacon #13 (at least). Even east of #13, there are still more rocks and we again advise you to keep to the channel.

The shallowest depths of the entrance channel will now be encountered on the portion of the cut stretching between unlighted daybeacons #28 and #32A. This stretch calls for even more strict attention in keeping to the mid-line.

At unlighted daybeacon #40, mariners can breathe a sigh of contentment as they enter the Withlacoochee's mouth. The channel passes between a small island with a launching ramp to the north and an even smaller islet to the south. Continue straight ahead down the marked cut into the river.

Visiting cruisers might be tempted to try their luck outside of the channel on the wider stretches of the river between unlighted daybeacons #40A and #42. Don't try it. Waters with only 4 feet of depth or less will be immediately encountered.

Between unlighted daybeacons #42 and #43, watch out for a rocky outcropping on the southerly banks. Favor the north side of the channel slightly when passing to avoid this hazard.

Unlighted daybeacon #46 is the last aid to navigation you will see on the Withlacoochee. Simply hold to the midwidth as you cruise upstream past #46 and enjoy the scenery.

Eventually, you will spy the first house associated with Yankeetown on the northwestern banks as well as the offshoot where smaller cruising craft might consider anchoring. Remember that swinging room is tight. If you do decide to enter the offshoot, favor the starboard shores as you enter. Drop the hook before proceeding more than 25 yards upstream, as the creek narrows even more to the north.

Powercraft should come down to idle speed as you cruise past the Yankeetown waterfront. All the facilities described earlier will be found on the northwestern banks. Eventually, if you continue upstream, the Coast Guard docks will be prominent to your port side. This guide's coverage of Withlacoochee River reluctantly ends at this point.

On to Cedar Key Probably the easiest way to find the main Cedar Key—Seahorse Key Channel (also known as the "Main Ship Channel") is to set course from flashing daybeacon #3, at the western terminus of the Cross-Florida Barge Canal channel, to a point some .6 nautical miles southwest of flashing daybeacon #1, south of Seahorse Key. A distance of 10.2 nautical miles separates these two aids. Of course, there are several more imaginative and less straightforward, but perhaps shorter, ways to reach #1, but I'll leave that up to you and your GPS.

Skippers continuing on north past Cedar Key should probably set course to flashing daybeacon #12, well west-northwest of North Key and Cedar Key's Northwest Channel. As you probably figured, it is a long trek of 14.7 nautical miles between flashing buoy #2 and #12.

Cedar Key Channels Cruisers arriving from points south will find it most convenient to enter Cedar Key by way of the Main Ship Channel, south of Seahorse Key. Skippers cruising south along the Big Bend will probably want to make use of the Northwest Channel. We will first review the Main Ship Channel, followed by a discussion of Cedar Key's anchorages, and finally outline the Northwest Channel.

Notice in the discussion of the approaches to the Seahorse Key—Main Ship Channel above that this writer advised navigators to set course to come abeam of flashing daybeacon #1, the first aid on this cut, by some .6 nautical miles to its southwesterly side. Only when #1 is directly abeam should you cut northeast into the channel. This set of maneuvers will avoid the correctly charted spoil and dump area southeast of #1.

No mariner that this writer knows of would call the Cedar Key Main Ship Channel a piece of cake. Some of the markers are set a bit far apart for comfort, and there is one *S* turn that you will have to see to believe. Read the account below carefully, and sort out all the markers with care before moving ahead. Be sure to use the "Cedar Keys" inset of chart 11408 for navigating the Main Ship Channel. Its detail is essential.

From #1, point to pass unlighted daybeacon #3 to its southeastern side and continue on to flashing daybeacon #7. We discovered that on the water, the run between #3 and #7 is a bit longer than you might think. You may want to set a compass/GPS course between these two aids.

Very shallow water abuts the northwestern side of the channel at #7. Come abeam of this aid by at least 20 yards to its southeasterly side.

As you approach flashing daybeacon #9, look northwest to Seahorse Key for a good view of its old lighthouse. This structure seems to be in excellent repair and it makes for a truly memorable sight from the water.

At unlighted daybeacon #12, the cut begins a sharp jog to the northeast. Set course so as to pass flashing daybeacon #14 and unlighted daybeacon #16 to their northwesterly sides.

Continue following the markers to the gap between unlighted daybeacons #24 and #25. At this point, *all* cruisers not intimately familiar with the Main Ship Channel should come to a virtual stop and begin sorting out the markers. The confusing array before you is enough to make any cruiser lose his or her religion. Before we try to find our way through this mess, let's take a moment to first consider the anchorage on nearby Atsena Otie Key.

To reach this excellent haven, continue cruising north from #24 and #25, pointing to pass between flashing daybeacon #27 and unlighted daybeacon #26. Continue north for another 20 yards or so toward unlighted daybeacon #28. Break off sharply to the northeast *before* reaching #28 and point to come abeam of Atsena Otie Key's northwesterly tip by some 25 to 30 yards to your starboard side. Avoid the island's shoreline to bypass the charted rock. For best depths, drop the hook as the northwesterly point comes abeam. Boats drawing 4 feet or less can continue around the

point for another 100 yards and anchor some 25 yards off the island's northern beach. Farther to the east, depths rise quickly to grounding levels. Caution—this channel is completely unmarked and borders on shallow (and rocky) waters. Proceed at maximum alert!

Let us now return to the more than confusing entrance channel. North of unlighted daybeacons #24 and #25, the Main Ship Channel passes through a mind-boggling *S* turn. From the gap between #24 and #25, set course to pass between flashing daybeacon #27 and unlighted daybeacon #26. Continue past #26 and #27 for a short distance and then turn sharply southwest, pointing to pass between #27 and unlighted daybeacon #28. Continue following this track until flashing daybeacon #30 comes abeam to the north of your course. Cruise past #30 a bit and then curl 180 degrees back around #30's southwesterly side until your course is set to the northeast. From here, point to pass between unlighted daybeacons #31 and #32.

If all this sounds more than slightly harried, it is. Study the inset on chart 11408 and compare it to the information above. Take your time, sort out the markers, and with luck you'll come through with only a half-dozen curses aimed at the designers of this channel.

East of unlighted daybeacon #36, the Cedar Key pier will come abeam on the northern shore. If the weather is good, anchor abeam of this dock and consider dinghying ashore. Do not approach unlighted daybeacon #8 (to the east) too closely. It is founded in shoal water.

Northwest Channel Northbound cruisers will find Cedar Key's Northwest Channel far simpler than the run in from the Gulf by way of the Seahorse Key—Main Ship Channel. However, for those approaching Cedar Key from points north via the Northwest Channel, the confusing array of markers described above can be a real problem.

Cruisers heading into Cedar Key via the Northwest Channel should slow down after passing between unlighted daybeacons #21 and #22. Continue east for 50 yards or so after leaving these aids behind. Use your binoculars to pick out unlighted daybeacons #31 and #32 to the northeast. Ignore the other markers to the east; they are part of the Main Ship Channel and can cause nothing but grief for those entering Cedar Key from this quarter. However, be *sure* to pass to the northwest of flashing daybeacon #30.

Set course to pass between #31 and #32. You can then follow unlighted daybeacons #34 and #36 (pass them well to your starboard side) to the town waterfront.

Cruising craft departing Cedar Key through the Northwest Channel should conversely set course to pass between unlighted daybeacons #31 and #32 and then point for the gap between unlighted daybeacons #21 and #22. Be *sure* to pass to the northwest of flashing daybeacon #30 as you make your run between the two sets of unlighted daybeacons.

Once between #21 and #22, turn almost due west and point to pass between flashing daybeacon #19 and unlighted daybeacon #20. From this point, northbound craft should pass all red, even-numbered aids to their (the cruisers') port side and take all green markers to starboard. Of course, skippers bound south on the channel will employ the opposite strategy.

This southernmost portion of the Northwest Channel is the shallowest stretch of the passage. Expect some 6½- to 7-foot soundings.

At flashing daybeacon #16, the Northwest Channel cuts sharply north and then curves more slowly back to the west between flashing daybeacons #11 and #9.

North Key will come abeam south of your course near flashing daybeacon #6. Avoid this islet. It is surrounded by shoals. Flashing daybeacon #2 is the westernmost aid to navigation on the Northwest Channel. From #2, most cruisers will probably want to set course for flashing daybeacon #12, part of the Big Bend buoyage system. It is a run of 6 nautical miles between #2 and #12.

The Suwannee River to St. George Sound

North of Cedar Key, the waters of the Big Bend begin to spread out far and wide before you with increasing distances between the various ports of call. Consider these mileage figures based upon the marked Big Bend off-shore route: From flashing daybeacon #12, off Cedar Key's Northwest Channel, it is a quick cruise of 8.8 nautical miles to the Suwannee. The Steinhatchee Channel is found 33 nautical miles from #12, while the entrance to the

St. Marks River is a prodigious 73.3 nautical miles from the same aid. Should you choose to follow the markers and bypass the St. Marks River, heading directly for St. George Sound, you will be dealing with a cruise of 96.9 nautical miles.

Of course, these distances can be shortened *considerably* by abandoning the Big Bend buoyage system and setting a direct course for your destination, but this would negate the navigational checks provided by the aids to navigation along the way. However you slice it, the trek across the waters of the northern Big Bend to the Florida Panhandle is not something to be taken lightly. Powercraft, in particular, had better take a long look at their fuel state before beginning their passage from the Steinhatchee to either the St. Marks River or St. George Sound.

The rivers and other ports of call along the northern Big Bend are absolutely fascinating. The Suwannee River vies with the Withlacoochee for the honor of being the most beautiful stream in Florida. The Suwannee is far broader than the Withlacoochee and has a charm of its own that is not easily quantified. The Steinhatchee leads to an unspoiled fishing village, with much improved dockage for transients. By the time you see the snow-white St. Marks Lighthouse peeping over the horizon, marking the river of the same name, you will have completed your passage across the Big Bend. The St. Marks is, for all intents and purposes, a river of the Florida Panhandle with corresponding deeper depths and heavily wooded shores. At the St. Marks, your passage will turn west towards St. George Sound and the delightful village of Carrabelle, not to mention the anchorages on Dog Island and the easterly genesis of the Northern Gulf ICW.

It has been said by many others, but it bears repeating here, that the Big Bend's northernmost waters hold something for every true cruiser. Just don't forget those long passages through open water, and plan accordingly.

The Suwannee River

> Way down upon the Suwannee River
> Far, far away
> That's where my heart is yearning ever
> That's where the old folks stay

It is to the good fortune of every cruising skipper that the sentiments expressed above in the first verse of Stephen Collins Foster's immortal "Old Folks at Home," now the official song for the state of Florida, are as true today as when he penned the tune so many years ago. Indeed, the vast majority of the Suwannee River shores are part of a huge wildlife refuge and are protected from any development. The deep, densely wooded and overgrown banks set against the wide, light-brown waters simply must be experienced to be understood. Words are not supposed to fail a writer, but we found it difficult to put this river's almost dreamlike charm into simple phrases and sentences. Perhaps we should turn to the words of an unknown earlier writer who observed, "The Suwannee River rises in the highest mountains of the human soul and is fed by the deepest springs in the human heart."

Adding to, rather than detracting from, the Suwannee's enchantments, is the small village of the same name guarding the northerly shoreline at the river's mouth. If you want to see what a fishing village on Florida's Big Bend of yesteryear was like, then by all means visit Suwannee. If you took away the automobiles,

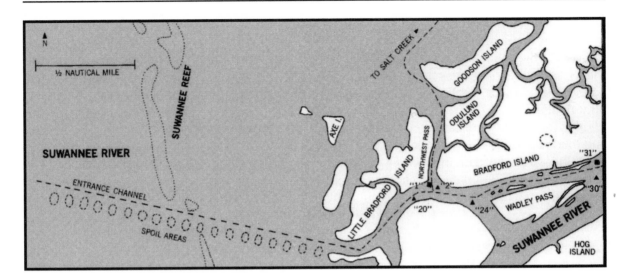

electric lights, and a few other modern conveniences, it would be quite easy to believe that you had somehow traveled back to simpler times. The village offers one marina friendly to visiting cruisers and one restaurant of note.

The marina facilities at the village of Suwannee offer the only dockage for cruising-size craft along the first twenty miles or so of the Suwannee. Anchoring off, though, is a very real option. In fair weather, you can often pitch out the hook just off the river's centerline. When more shelter is needed, the Suwannee offers the largest selection of sheltered coves and refuges of any river along the Big Bend.

Now for the *bad* news! Study chart 11408 for a moment and note the two marked channels leading from the Gulf of Mexico to the Suwannee River. Both are now *quite shallow.* In fact, the southerly of the two, known alternately as West Pass and Alligator Pass, is impassable by any vessel larger than a canoe. Cruising skippers must make use of the northerly passage. This cut, known locally as

the McGriff Channel, darts south of charted Boiler Gap and skirts the southern shores of Bradford Island. Even this channel has low-tide depths of 3 to 4 feet.

But wait, there is some very good news on the horizon. After many years of struggle and agitation by the Suwannee cruising and fishing communities, the McGriff Channel has recently been "federalized," which is to say that it's now the responsibility of the United States Coast Guard. A major dredging project is slated to begin in November of 2000, with the goal of raising the low-water entrance depths to minimum 5- to 8-foot levels. If this project comes to fruition, and there is currently every reason to believe that it will, then the beauty of the Suwannee River will become far, far more accessible to a broad range of cruising craft. If your arrival falls anywhere near the end of 2000 or thereafter, check with the good people at Miller's Marina (see below) about the status of the channel dredging.

In the meantime, cruisers will still have to contend with the thin water at low tide. Again, however, the staff at Miller's Marina comes to the rescue. Just call them up on VHF channel 16, and they will be glad to advise you about current channel conditions and the state of the tide. It is our experience that these fine people can get most any boat drawing 5 feet or less into the river during an appropriate tide level. Just listen to what they say! Incidentally, the tidal range on the Suwannee seems to maintain the Big Bend average of 3 feet.

After leaving the pesky entrance cut behind, depths improve markedly upstream of Bradford Island. Minimum soundings on the river's interior reaches seem to be about 7 feet, with typical depths ranging from 8 to as much as 20 feet.

After traversing the Suwannee's entrance passage, you will meet up with a northward-running side cut northeast of unlighted daybeacon #16. This channel runs first north and then northeast to Salt Creek and a portion of the Suwannee village waterfront. With one major exception, this route serves only local docks, and if it were not for Salt Creek Shellfish Company, cruising captains would probably want to bypass it entirely. Skippers whose craft can't stand this side channel's low-tide depths of 3½ feet may choose to enter at a higher tide to visit the shellfish company. This facility offers a laid-back, informal seafood restaurant that serves some of the best fried shrimp, oysters, scallops, and fish in all of Florida, or anywhere else for that matter. This writer particularly recommends the "Salt Creek Fisherman's Platter." This bounteous combination of softshell crab, shrimp, oysters, and Salt Creek crab roll (and more) is sure to bring a look of glee into the eyes of any true lover of good seafood. Low-tide depths at the restaurant's fixed wooden face pier run 3½ to 4 feet with, of course, more water during high tide. Take note that the Salt Creek Shellfish

Company (352-542-7072) is closed Mondays and Tuesdays and open all other days of the week from 11:00 a.m. to 10:00 p.m.

Markings on the Suwannee River cease east of unlighted daybeacons #30 and #31. Depths soon improve markedly and the Suwannee's first and best marina facility will soon come abeam on the northwestern shoreline. Watch the banks for two yellow signs advertising Miller's Marina. Allow me to pause for a moment to say a special word about the reception you will find at this facility. In all our travels up and down the Western Florida coastline, seldom have we ever encountered any other marina that took as much time and trouble to give this writer all the information that might ever be needed. Visiting cruisers will find a warm welcome upon arriving at this medium-sized, family-operated marina. If you want to know anything about the river, its history, or its people, this is the place to be. The Millers can relate all you care to know, and then some. As far as I'm concerned, Miller's is the place to dock on the Suwannee River, and it is the last word in friendly service.

Miller's Marina is located along the banks of a well-sheltered harbor which is accessed through a small canal leading northwest from the river's banks. Minimum low-tide entrance and dockside depths run around 5 and occasionally 4½ feet. In addition to the amiable reception, Miller's also offers a good array of services. Transients are accepted for overnight or temporary berths at a combination of well-maintained, floating and fixed wooden piers. Freshwater and 30-amp power hook-ups are available at all slips. The showers are squeaky clean, but not climate controlled. Would you believe the Millers has a "full-time housekeep on staff" whose main function is to keep the heads and showers in pristine condition? How's that for full service? Gasoline, diesel fuel, and waste pump-out service are also offered. There is an adjacent ship's store as well, and a complete campground with clubhouse. The Salt Creek Shellfish Company, mentioned above, is a short walk away and is highly recommended.

For many years now, Miller's Marina has been very much in the houseboat rental business. The marina management has informed us that when (notice not "if") the entrance channel dredging project is complete, they plan to sell the houseboat arm of their business, modernize the marina even more, and "cater more to transients." That is a bright and shining prospect indeed!

Miller's Marina (352) 542-7349
http://www.Suwanneehouseboats.com

Approach depth—4½-5 feet (low tide)
Dockside depth—4½-8 feet (low tide)
Accepts transients—yes
Fixed and floating wooden piers—yes
Dockside power connections—30 amp
Dockside water connections—yes
Waste pump-out—yes
Showers—yes
Gasoline—yes
Diesel fuel—yes
Ship's and variety store—yes
Restaurant—nearby

A touch farther upstream, the river takes a jog to the east-southeast. At the beginning of this turn, another canal cuts into the northerly banks. This stream allows access (via its portside fork) to Starling's Suwannee Marine (352-542-9159). Unfortunately, this facility's piers and its shoreside structures are currently in very poor condition. We strongly recommend that you bypass this marina and set your sights on Miller's Marina, reviewed above.

Glance at the Suwannee's outline on chart 11408 again for just a moment. Note the location of Hog Island, lining the river's southern banks, just past the village waterfront. From this point, it is an upriver cruise of 20 *statute* miles to Manatee Springs State Park, the limit of this guide's coverage. In many instances, mariners can simply pitch out the hook on a likely looking part of the river, being sure to show an anchor light. Those wanting a little bit more of an out-of-the-way haven, or seeking better shelter in inclement weather, will want to consider one of the havens outlined below.

First up are the waters off the western tip of the unnamed island (westernmost of two) north of charted Hog Island. Minimum depths of 6 feet can be carried to within 50 yards of the island's northwesterly tip. There should be enough swinging room for boats as large as 38 feet, with plenty of protection from even the heaviest blows. The surrounding shores are the usual extravaganza of natural beauty that is so typical of the Suwannee.

Similarly, cruising craft up to 45 feet should have enough elbow room in 6-foot waters off the westerly tip of the second (moving west to east) unnamed island, north of Hog Island. This body of land lines the Suwannee's northern banks, with the river channel passing to the south of the island. Again, the protection and surrounding shores are all anyone could ask for.

Well, gang, I've saved the best till last. Note the entry of "East Pass" into the southerly banks of the Suwannee River on chart 11408. Captains can choose from two anchorage possibilities (at least) on this sidewater, and the second is about as good as it gets. First, though, you might consider dropping the hook at the northerly mouth of East Pass. Boats as large as 45 feet will find enough swinging room just north of the entrance.

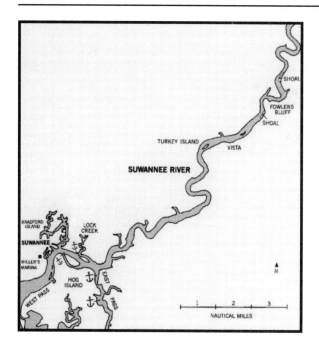

Forget about chart 11408's 4-foot sounding shown on East Pass's interior reaches. We sounded nothing less than 6 feet on the stream's mid-width, with depths running up to as much as 15 feet. We did note a few snags along the way, so watch out for them.

Boats as large as 40 feet may consider tracking their way south on East Pass to the charted knuckle curve where chart 11408 shows a 13-foot sounding. Again, this depth reading must have been taken long ago. We found 8-foot minimum depths along the centerline of this turn. This is, to my mind at least, the best and most beautiful anchorage on the Big Bend. The deep green shores of this isolated haven have an almost mysterious air as one gazes at their brooding cypress and hardwoods. Shelter is sufficient for anything short of a hurricane. Again, be sure to show an anchor light just in case some commercial fishing vessels happen along during the night.

Intrepid cruisers can continue tracking their way upstream on Suwannee for the 20 statute miles to Manatee Springs State Park. Depths remain good and the shoreline remains idyllic. Eventually, you will sight Turkey Island (see map) flanking the southeastern shores. You can anchor off the southwesterly tip of this land body in 6-foot depths with plenty of swinging room. Don't approach the island's northeasterly reaches, however, as shoal water is soon encountered.

You will sight a single house at the charted location of Vista, while a series of fish-camp-type homes overlooks the western banks at Fowlers Bluff. Otherwise, the natural character of the river is undisturbed all the way to Manatee Springs State Park.

As the park comes abeam on the southeastern bank, captains will find a fixed wooden dock fit only for small powercraft. Mariners piloting cruising-size vessels would do well to anchor off and dinghy ashore. Here you will find an amazing fishbowl where crystal-clear waters boil up from springs 50 or more feet below the surface. The waters are so spectacularly clear that you can see all the way to the bottom. As you can imagine, the springs are a very popular site for scuba diving. The surrounding park features a large campground.

Our coverage of the Suwannee River ends at the state park. The river continues to wind its way north and east for better than 200 miles until finding its source in Georgia's great Okefenokee Swamp. Small craft and canoes can continue their upstream journey into this amazing paradise.

The Steinhatchee River

The Steinhatchee is one of the shorter rivers of the Big Bend, but it has very respectable minimum entrance and interior depths of 6 feet. After traversing the well-marked entrance channel, captains and crew will soon find themselves cruising beside the waterfront of the town of Steinhatchee along the river's northern banks. This undiscovered and unspoiled fishing community is one of the most laid-back towns that this writer visited in Western Florida. The chief topic of conversation at all the local gathering places is almost certainly to be about what's been biting lately, rather than the latest world news event. While Steinhatchee cannot lay claim to any quaint buildings or architecture, the town's relaxed atmosphere is most certainly welcome amidst the hustle and bustle of our modern lifestyle.

The Steinhatchee does not boast any deep sidewaters, so the only opportunity to drop the hook is found on the river itself. While the stream is certainly wide enough for plenty of swinging room, and protection is quite good, commercial fishing traffic from the village is likely to pass by during the night. Should you attempt to anchor anyway, squeeze as far off the mid-width as is practical and consider setting two or more anchor lights.

Pleasurecraft facilities along the Steinhatchee have improved markedly over the past several years, though all of the marinas are still unpretentious and of modest size. First up is Wood's Gulf Breeze Marina. This facility guards the Steinhatchee's northerly banks opposite unlighted daybeacon #36. Transients are accepted at Wood's Gulf's fixed wooden piers, but no power connections are to be had. Freshwater tanks can be filled up with a long hose only. Approach depths run around 7 feet at MLW with typical dockside soundings of 5 to 6 feet. Shoreside, new (as of 1999), non-climate controlled showers and a laundromat with new machines are complemented by a small ship's and variety store. Gasoline can be purchased pierside. There are eight adjacent

guestrooms, which are quite convenient for those who want to take a break from the live-aboard routine. The local restaurants (see below) are all within walking distance, and Mason's Market (corner of First Avenue S and Ninth Street E, 352-498-3028), the only grocery in town, is only some three blocks away.

Wood's Gulf Breeze Marina (352) 498-3948

Approach depth—7-20 feet (MLW)
Dockside depth—5-6 feet (MLW)
Accepts transients—yes
Fixed wooden piers—yes
Dockside water connections—long hose
   necessary
Showers—yes
Laundromat—yes
Gasoline—yes
Ship's and variety store—yes
Restaurant—two nearby

Ideal Marina and Fish Camp (352-498-3877) also overlooks the Steinhatchee's northerly shoreline a short hop farther upstream. Low-water entrance and dockside depths of a very scant 1 to 2 feet render this facility unusable by almost all cruising-size craft. Therefore, it is not further reviewed here.

Sea Hag Marina, a far better choice for cruising craft, lies north of flashing daybeacon #47. This facility accepts transients at its modern, floating wooden docks with typical MLW depths alongside of 5-6 feet. At the current time, there are no power or water connections, but these are planned for the future. Shoreside showers are also in the planning stages. Mechanical repairs for gasoline engines are available, mostly of the outboard and I/O variety. The marina also maintains a dry stack storage building.

Sea Hag does offer gasoline, diesel fuel, and a good ship's and variety store, which features a television linked to a 24-hour marine weather broadcast (with doppler radar). The local restaurants are close by, and so is provisioning at Mason's Market (corner of First Avenue S and Ninth Street E, 352-498-3028). Three riverfront rooms are available for rent, two with kitchens, while the third has a Jacuzzi.

Currently, Sea Hag Marina can only offer bare-bones dockage for cruising craft. If all the owner's plans come to pass, however, the picture will be much improved. As my ace research assistant Morgan Stinemetz put it, "these are friendly people who seem to be positioned to do better things with their marina."

Sea Hag Marina (352) 498-3008
   http://www.seahag.com

Approach depth—10+ feet
Dockside depth—5-6 feet (MLW)
Accepts transients—yes
Floating wooden docks—yes
Dockside power and water connections—
   planned for the future
Gasoline—yes
Diesel fuel—yes
Mechanical repairs—gasoline engines only
Ship's and variety store—yes
Restaurant—two nearby

East of the charted 25-foot fixed bridge (which the locals swear has a typical vertical clearance of 30 feet), River Haven Marina (formerly Sportsman's Marine) overlooks the Steinhatchee's northerly banks. Currently this is "the" place for cruising-size craft to berth on the river, always supposing that your boat can clear the bridge. The marina's entrance channel from the main centerline passage is marked by red and green Chlorox bottles. By passing between these informal aids to navigation, minimum 6-foot approach depths can be maintained. Dockside soundings run around 8 feet. Transients are eagerly accepted at River Haven's floating wooden piers. Some slips are covered, while a second set of berths is to be found on an uncovered L-shaped pier. These docks appeared to be in excellent shape as of January 2000, and plans are in the offing to expand the available slip space further. Dockside freshwater and 30-50-amp power connections are provided, as well as gasoline and diesel fuel. Waste pump-out and a new set of showers will hopefully be in place by late 2000. Mechanical repairs for both gasoline and diesel engines can be arranged through a local, independent technician, and some vessels can be hauled out by way of a 15-ton sling lift.

River Haven also maintains four shoreside guestrooms and one efficiency apartment. The rates seemed quite reasonable to us.

When it comes time to visit one of the local restaurants (see below) or stock up the galley at Mason's Market (corner of First Avenue S and Ninth Street E, 352-498-3028), River Haven has an electric golf cart, which they are glad to lend to cruising visitors. How's that for full service?

River Haven Marina (352) 498-0709
   http://www.steinhatchee.com/riverhaven

Approach depth—6-20 feet
Dockside depth—8 feet (MLW)
Accepts transients—yes
Floating wooden piers—yes
Dockside power connections—up to 50 amp
Dockside water connections—yes
Gasoline—yes
Diesel fuel—yes
Mechanical repairs—yes (independent
   technicians)
Below-waterline repairs—yes
Ship's and variety store—yes
Restaurant—two nearby

The village of Steinhatchee has (at least) two dining choices that visiting cruisers can patronize with confidence. Bridge End Café (352-498-2002) is located on the Steinhatchee side of the fixed bridge. This dining spot is open for all three meals of the day. It is located in a homey cottage that somehow seems to reflect the friendly character of Steinhatchee village. The selection of omelets for breakfast is outstanding, and there are seven different styles of burgers to pick from for the midday meal.

Roy's Restaurant (on Highway 51, 352-498-5000), right on the Steinhatchee, features a superb view of the water. Seafood is the specialty here. Satisfied diners pick and choose from a selection of flounder, grouper, catfish, scallops, shrimp, and deviled crab. Prices are bit steeper here than at Bridge End.

Cooey's Restaurant, which we used to recommend highly for visitors to Steinhatchee, is currently closed. We keep hearing about fits and starts to reopen this dining attraction, but no definite information could be found at the time of this writing. Please let us know if you visit and find Cooey's once again in operation. E-mail us at opcom@netpath.net.

St. Marks River

The snow-white crown of the St. Marks Lighthouse signals the end to your passage across Florida's Big Bend. This old sentinel marks the entrance to the St. Marks River. You will only need a quick glance at the marsh grass shores, backed by pines and a few hardwoods, not to mention the good depths shown on your sounder, to know that you have now arrived at the Florida Panhandle, with all its rich cruising opportunities.

Before going on to look at the St. Marks River itself, let's pause for a moment to consider its beautiful lighthouse. Floridians like to say the first lighthouse in North America stood on the banks of the St. Marks River near where Florida begins to bend westward into its panhandle. Local historians claim the Spanish raised a light at the mouth of the river during their early explorations in the 1600s. There's no real evidence to support this claim, and the Boston Harbor Light, built in 1716, remains recognized as America's first lighthouse.

The old Spanish light, if it ever did exist, was gone by the early nineteenth century when control of the area passed from Spain to the United States. Commercial importance of the Spanish settlement at St. Marks was recognized in Washington and in 1828 Congress appropriated $6,000 for a light to mark the harbor's entrance. Unfortunately, builders scrimped on materials so much that the walls were actually left hollow, and the tower had to be demolished.

A new, solid-walled tower erected in its place was well constructed, but the river quickly undercut its foundations. The government was forced to pull it down and rebuild on another, safer location.

This third tower was built much better and raised the lantern to a point seventy-three feet above sea level. Fifteen lamps and fifteen-inch reflectors allowed the light to be seen by ships more than a dozen miles at sea under ideal conditions. The brick-and-mortar tower has endured and still stands proudly to this very day.

Having survived the Seminole Indian Wars, the tower was almost blown up by Confederate soldiers during the Civil War to prevent its use by the Union navy. The blast knocked out a third of its circumference, but the stubborn tower refused to fall. Shortly after the war, the Lighthouse Board managed to repair the lighthouse and, by early 1867, had it back in service.

No longer in use, this old sentinel of the sea still gazes proudly over the waters of the northeastern Gulf of Mexico as a constant reminder of the days of wind, wood, rope, and canvas. The light is often rated as one of the most picturesque sights on the Gulf Coast. Located in a pristine refuge, it's alive with sea birds and other wildlife. Although not open to the public, it is well worth a few moments of gazing time as you enter the river.

The St. Marks River Channel boasts minimum depths of 10 feet, with many soundings showing 15 feet or more of water. The passage is extremely well marked, but it twists and winds first one way and then another. Numerous conversations with local captains, as well as our own soundings and observations, point up the important fact that, while the channel itself is deep, you *must keep to the marked cut.* Outside of the buoys and other aids to navigation, depths quickly rise to grounding levels.

During daylight, most careful cruisers will be able to run the St. Marks entrance channel with few problems. Be advised that it is a long run of almost 8 nautical miles from the outermost marker, flashing buoy #1, to the intersection of the St. Marks and Wakulla rivers. Then it's another mile or so up the former stream to the two regional marinas serving cruising vessels. Sailcraft and slow-moving trawlers should factor these distances into their plans if a late arrival seems to be in the cards. We do not recommend strangers running the long and winding entrance channel after dark.

The St. Marks is an absolutely enchanting river. The riverbanks are almost completely undeveloped as far as the intersection with the Wakulla River. The prevailing marsh grass is backdropped by densely wooded shores, which seem to have changed little since Spanish conquistadors first visited this timeless stream. The village of St. Marks sits at the forks of the St. Marks and Wakulla rivers. Holding to the same theme as the river for which it is named, St. Marks is a delightful, unspoiled fishing town. A stroll along the village's quiet lanes is definitely recommended after a rough Big Bend crossing.

After traversing the entrance channel, cruisers will find themselves at the intersection of the St. Marks and Wakulla rivers near flashing daybeacon #63. Most mariners will want to cut northeast and follow the track of the St. Marks River. While 5-foot depths continue for a mile or so up the Wakulla, unmarked shoals are soon encountered. Our own cruise of this stream taught us that it's easy to wander onto these shallows, even when trying scrupulously to follow the centerline.

One happy exception to the Wakulla's cruising problems is found on its southernmost reaches, well short of the troublesome shoals described above. St. Marks Yacht Club (850-925-6606) flanks the Wakulla's eastern banks just above the St. Marks intersection. This private club is obviously centered around powercraft, as evidenced by its covered slips. Dockside depths are an impressive 8 to 10 feet.

Fort San Marcos De Apalache State Park (850-638-6189) occupies the point of land separating the St. Marks and Wakulla rivers. This must-see point of interest (see history below) features a natural trail, museum, and interpretive outdoor signage. It is a quick walk away from either of the two St. Marks marinas and is highly recommended for all visiting cruisers.

After turning up the St. Marks River past the state historic site, leaving the Wakulla behind, the village waterfront will come abeam on the northern banks. First of the area facilities is Shields Marina, which will come up to the north in the heart of the St. Marks village waterfront. This writer votes Shields the nicest marina in the Big Bend. Finally, cruisers of all descriptions will feel as if they have found an absolutely first class marina more interested in boats of their size, rather than smaller powercraft. Shields Marina is closed on Mondays, so make your plans accordingly. Shields gladly accepts overnight transients at a well-maintained and well-sheltered collection of fixed concrete, floating concrete decked, and floating metal decked piers. Depths alongside run from 4 to 7 feet at mean low water. Long-legged craft drawing more than 4½ feet should check with the marina staff for the deepest slips before tying up. Dockside power connections run the full gamut up to 50 amps, and water connections are also on hand. Gasoline, diesel fuel, waste pump-out service, and full mechanical repairs are available, as is one of the nicest ship's and variety stores on the Big Bend. Plans are under way to expand this store even further. Cruisers will also find new, non-climate controlled showers, a small laundromat, and dry stack storage for smaller powercraft. Come mealtime, you are in luck. All the St. Marks village restaurants, reviewed below, are within easy walking distance. You can reprovision at nearby St. Marks Country Store (859 Port Leon Drive, 850-925-9908).

Are you beginning to get the picture? You simply can't do wrong by coiling your lines at Shields Marina, whether it's just overnight or a weeklong stay. This is a family operation, and Chuck and Brett Shields (father and son) simply can't seem to do enough for both visitors and their resident cruisers. Stop by and spend some time with them, and, oh yes, tell them we sent you!

Shields Marina (850) 925-6158

Approach depth—9-15 feet
Dockside depth—4-7 feet (low water)
Accepts transients—yes
Fixed and floating piers—yes
Dockside power connections—up to 50 amp
Dockside water connections—yes
Waste pump-out—yes
Showers—yes
Laundromat—yes
Gasoline—yes
Diesel fuel—yes
Mechanical repairs—yes
Ship's and variety store—yes
Restaurant—several within walking distance

A short cruise upriver will bring the floating piers of Lynn's Riverside Marina abeam to the northwest. This friendly firm features dockage for transients at several ranks of piers facing onto the river. A surprisingly large collection of covered slips housing resident powercraft is found on a sheltered canal cutting into the marina's banks just southwest of the marine store and fuel dock. Depths at the outer slips run from 5 to 6 feet at low water, while soundings of 6 to 7 feet of water are found at the fuel pier and inner docks. Lynn's also accepts overnighters and offers full power and water connections complemented by gasoline, diesel fuel, and full mechanical repairs. The marina features a nice ship's and variety store. The village restaurants and the local grocery are still only minutes away from the docks.

Lynn's Riverside Marina (850) 925-6157

Approach depth—9-15 feet
Dockside depth—5-7 feet
   (outer slips—low water)

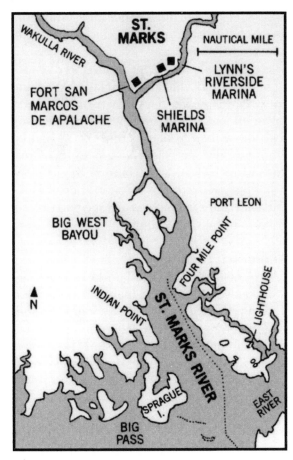

6-7 feet
(fuel pier and inner slips)
Accepts transients—yes
Fixed and floating piers—yes
Dockside power connections—up to 50 amp
Dockside water connections—yes
Gasoline—yes
Diesel fuel—yes
Mechanical repairs—yes
Ship's and variety store—yes
Restaurant—several nearby

As my research assistant Morgan Stinemetz put it so succinctly, dining in St. Marks village is "looking up." All the locals swear by Two Rivers Restaurant (785 Port Leon Drive, 850-925-6732). We have not yet had a chance to check out the bill of fare here, but we keep hearing phrases that are some variation of "the best food in town."

Riverside Café (69 Riverside Drive, 850-925-5668) is open seven days a week (for all three meals of the day) and located right on the St. Marks River. The menu features sandwiches, full dinner entrees, veggie specials, and salads. During the winter months, breakfast is served from 10:30 11:00 A.M.; during the summer from 9:00 to 11:00 A.M. This place has a casual, friendly atmosphere, which most cruisers will cozy right up to.

Posey's Oyster House (55 Riverside Drive, 850-925-6172) has been around forever. It is a large, ultraclean operation with a full bar out back. Posey's is famous for their "topless oysters." If you like raw oysters, be sure to give them a try. Posey's host more than a few "parties," particularly on weekends. Be sure to check out the unique wallpaper composed of genuine one-dollar bills.

As mentioned above, those in search of galley supplies should make their way to the St. Marks Country Store (859 Port Leon Drive, 850-925-9908). Besides basic foodstuffs, the country store also features a bar, deli sandwiches, pizza, and the largest collection of (shall we say) female-oriented beer-company posters that I have ever seen (and I don't want to see any more after this).

St. Marks History For two centuries the St. Marks River has been the site of struggle by Indians, Spanish, British, Spanish again, and Confederate troops.

In 1528, the Spanish explorer Narvaez marched overland with his troops to join ships at Apalachee Bay. His ships never showed, so Narvaez and his men rigged makeshift vessels and set sail, only to perish in a Gulf storm.

Spaniards in 1679 constructed Fort San Marcos de Apalache at the point of land where the Wakulla and St. Marks rivers join. The Spanish were forced to yield the fort to pirates and Indians in the 1700s. The British took San Marcos in 1763, and ceded it back to Spain 20 years later. It is now a state historic site and open to the public.

An international crisis in 1818 was nearly created when Andrew Jackson seized the fort. Ol' Hickory court-martialled two British citizens for aiding Indians and executed them. Fort San Marcos became known from Washington to London to Madrid. The U.S. Congress spent 27 days debating Jackson's conduct, with the House of Representatives voting for censure.

Three years later, Tallahassee became a territorial capital and, to solidify the region's new status, the St. Marks River became a valued transportation route for cotton, slaves, timber, furs, hides, tobacco, alcohol, and mosquito netting. In 1828 the U.S. government built a lighthouse at the St. Marks entrance.

That beacon signaled the channel at which a fourteen-ship flotilla in 1865 disembarked more than 800 Federal soldiers. They marched north to capture Newport, then St. Marks in a rear attack. The ultimate goal was Tallahassee.

Forced to cross the St. Marks River at Natural Bridge because a railroad bridge had burned down, the Union troops were driven back by the Confederates, and Tallahassee was saved. Florida's Confederate capital was the only one east of the Mississippi never captured by the Union.

Today the river is bounded by the St. Marks National Wildlife Refuge, which was founded in 1931. It's the only large parcel of publicly owned land along the St. Marks. An estimated 300 species of birds, including migrating geese, bald eagles, osprey, heron, and egret, inhabit the refuge.

Hunters on the upper St. Marks can still sight bear and wild turkey. Native Wakullan Tony Ward recalls days down on the river's lower end when the town of St. Marks echoed with more than hunters' gunshots. "I had kin who wouldn't dare let the sun set on 'em if they were in St. Marks. During the 1930s it was like 'Gunsmoke' around here. On a Friday or Saturday night you'd see two or three good fights and shootings."

Additional Facilities

Cruisers bypassing the St. Marks River face a voyage of some 40.8 nautical miles from flashing daybeacon #22 to St. George Sound's easterly entrance. Another run of 5.5 nautical miles will bring you to the easterly beginnings of the Northern Gulf ICW. There are two marinas along this lengthy trek to which cruisers might turn for shelter.

The first is found 5.7 nautical miles west-northwest of the St. Marks River's flashing buoy #1 (the St. Marks' outermost marker). Here the residential community of Shell Harbor is perched on the tongue of land lying between Oyster and Goose Creek bays. A fairly well marked channel cuts first north, then northwest, then east, then north, and finally back to the west, at which point a canal leads cruisers into the well-sheltered dockage basin of Shell Point Marina. Depths in the entrance channel run 5½ to 10 feet, while 5½- to 6½-foot soundings are prevalent on the canal leading to the marina. Dockside, cruisers will find 6 to 8 feet of water.

Shell Point Marina is a friendly facility that accepts transients for overnight or temporary dockage. The facility's wooden-decked floating piers are only in fair shape and could stand an overhaul. Water connections and power connections up to 50 amps are found at each slip. Visiting cruisers will find one very low-key shower that could do with a good cleaning and a small laundromat ashore. Gasoline and diesel fuel are readily available, and a small combination ship's, variety, and tackle store overlooks the fuel dock. Mechanical repairs for both gasoline and diesel engines can be arranged. The on-site restaurant was closed as of April of 2000, and no one could seem to tell us definitely if or when it would reopen.

Shell Point Marina (850) 926-7162

Approach depth—5½-10 feet
Dockside depth—6-8 feet
Accepts transients—yes
Floating wooden piers—yes
Dockside power connections—up to 50 amp
Dockside water connections—yes
Shower—yes
Laundromat—yes
Gasoline—yes
Diesel fuel—yes
Mechanical repairs—yes
Ship's and variety store—yes

Shell Point Marina is backed by a surprisingly extensive and attractive "weekend community" of private homes and condos. Nestled among these various structures are the headquarters of my good friends at the Apalachee Bay Yacht Club. This enthusiastic group does not have any facilities for visitors, but you will never find a friendlier bunch of cruisers. This writer had the good fortune to address this group in April of 2000, and a good time was had by all. I hope they invite me back soon!

Finally, cruisers have one last chance to stop short of St. George Sound at Alligator Harbor, north of flashing daybeacon #1, itself hard by the northeastern tip of Dog Island Reef. This is one port of call, though, at least at the current time, that you may want to forego.

The marked Alligator Point Marina (formerly Pride of the Point Marina) entrance channel leads around the northwesterly tip of the shoal guarding the harbor's western reaches. The passage then cuts back to the southeast and leads through minimum 7- to 9-foot depths to the marina's collection of both floating and fixed wooden piers lining the southern banks. Unfortunately, we must report that Alligator Point is experiencing some financial difficulty, and the marina was in "receivership" as of January 2000. These money problems are reflected in the facility's current condition. The fixed wooden docks are in fair shape, but the floating piers rate a C- in our book. Transients are accepted, and most berths feature freshwater and 30-50-amp power hook-ups. These services are complemented by gasoline, diesel fuel, some mechanical repairs, haul-outs via a 40-ton travelift, and a modest bait and tackle shop. The one on-site shower lacks hot water and any shower curtain. Would you believe that the shower head is composed of a thru-hull fitting? This one rates a D- on our scale of shower power. The on-site restaurant is closed, and there are no other restaurants or provisioning depots nearby. Quite frankly, unless you are in a need of immediate dockage, it might be best to continue cruising west to the good marina facilities at Carrabelle.

Alligator Point Marina (850) 349-2511

Approach depth—7-9 feet
Dockside depth—6-9 feet
Accepts transients—yes
Fixed and floating wooden piers—yes
Dockside power connections—up to 50 amp
Dockside water connections—yes

Shower—minimal
Gasoline—yes
Diesel fuel—yes
Mechanical repairs—yes
Below-waterline repairs—yes
Variety store—yes

St. George Sound and the Northern Gulf ICW

West of Alligator Harbor, the weary cruiser can track his or her way through a marked channel to the easterly reaches of St. George Sound. The eastern tip of the Northern Gulf ICW lies just a few miles to the west, while Dog Island to the south offers wonderful anchorage and the village of Carrabelle to the north features delightful marina facilities set amidst a wonderfully unspoiled village. Cruisers wanting to know more about this region and the Northern Gulf ICW between Carrabelle and New Orleans should consult this writer's *Cruising Guide to the Northern Gulf Coast.*

SUWANNEE RIVER TO ST. GEORGE SOUND NAVIGATION

Two terms describe navigation along the northern section of Florida's Big Bend—"wide-open" and "long." Runs between the various aids to navigation become 10 to 15 nautical miles or better, necessitating careful compass courses, good DR tracks, and frequent reference to the GPS (if you're lucky enough to have one).

The passage from the Steinhatchee to the St. Marks River is a cause for special concern. Averaging better than 40 nautical miles by way of the Big Bend markers, this can be as much as an eight-hour run for sailors through wide-open water. Powercraft had better make sure their tanks are topped off before beginning this lengthy run and all skippers should consult the latest NOAA weather forecast.

The three side channels along this portion of the Big Bend run the full range from fairly complicated (the Suwannee cut) to basically simple (the St. Marks River). The Steinhatchee Channel falls somewhere in the middle.

The offshore passages along the northerly Big Bend are really ideal for sailors and trawlers in good weather. Planing powercraft may look at it very differently, particularly if there is a good chop. However you travel it, lay out a good plan, keep a constant update on weather conditions as you go along, and you'll soon be admiring the white serenity of the St. Marks Lighthouse peeping over the horizon.

The Suwannee River Remember that entry into the Suwannee River is possible only by way of the northernmost of the two marked and charted channels (known as the McGriff Channel). In fact, the southerly cut, called alternately West and Alligator Pass, is not really a channel anymore. According to the good people at Miller's Marina, the markers have been placed there by the Coast Guard with no dredging or attempt at depth improvement.

Even the McGriff Channel is none too deep, with low-water soundings of 3½ to 4 feet. Stay strictly to the marked channel. Skippers wandering outside of this passage may well find themselves in but a few inches of water.

It is a run of 8.7 nautical miles from flashing daybeacon #12 off Cedar Key's Northwest Channel to flashing daybeacon #2 and unlighted daybeacon #1, the first aids on the McGriff entrance channel. Fortunately, this passage does not stray near any shallow water, but for maximum safety, set your course so as to come abeam of #1 and #2 a bit to their westerly sides. This plan will ensure a wide berth around the shoal waters south and east of these two aids.

Once #1 and #2 are abeam, cut directly between the pair and begin tracking your way east on the channel. Switch to the Suwannee River inset on chart 11408 for additional detail. East of #1 and #2, pass all subsequent red, even-numbered markers to your starboard side and take green beacons to port.

Extremely shallow water abuts the entrance channel north of unlighted daybeacon #6. Favor the south side of the cut slightly for additional security.

At unlighted daybeacon #15, the channel ducks to the northeast and begins to pass into the river's interior reaches. Northeast of unlighted daybeacon #16, the alternate Salt Creek Channel makes in from the north. The first two aids to navigation on this side cut, unlighted daybeacons #1 and #2, can be confusing to first-timers. Unless you happen to be visiting the Salt Creek Shellfish Company restaurant by way of the side passage, ignore #1 and #2 and point to pass unlighted daybeacon #24, the next upstream marker on the Suwannee, by some 15 yards to its northerly side.

Salt Creek Channel   If you decide to visit Salt Creek and its delightful dining spot, continue on the main channel until the mid-width of the gap between unlighted daybeacons #1 and #2 is directly abeam to the north. Then, cut 90 degrees to port and begin tracking your way north on the cut by keeping red aids to your starboard side and green to port.

At unlighted daybeacon #9, the channel cuts to the northwest. Unlighted daybeacon #12 marks a sharp turn in the channel to the northeast on its way directly into Salt Creek's southwestern mouth. Pass #12 to its fairly immediate northwesterly side and immediately set a new course to cruise between unlighted daybeacons #15 and #16.

The docks of Salt Creek Shellfish Company will come abeam on the southern banks east of unlighted daybeacon #29. Get ready for a gut buster.

Back on the Suwannee   The current edition of chart 11408 shows two aids to navigation, unlighted daybeacons #30 and #31, as the innermost markers on the eastern-flowing channel into the Suwannee River. The waters in and around #30 and #31 are some of the shallowest in the Suwannee (McGriff) entrance channel. At low tide, expect depths as thin as 3½ to 4 feet.

East of #30 and #31, simply follow the mid-width of the deepening channel upstream to the Suwannee village waterfront. Watch for two yellow signs along the northwestern banks marking the entrance to Miller's Marina.

The Suwannee soon passes through a bit of a hairpin turn to the east. Two islands flank the main river channel to the north and south along this section of the stream.

Captains choosing to anchor northwest of the westernmost island (lining the river's southerly banks) should ease their way off the river's centerline towards the entrance to the small passage running south of this body of land. Stop at least 30 to 50 yards short of the entrance and throw out the hook. Don't attempt to actually cruise into the waters behind the island. Depths of 3 feet or less are lurking there for you.

Cruisers passing this island on the main path of the Suwannee will note a sign giving distances for points of interest well upstream. For our purposes, we need only note that the sign correctly indicates a cruise of 20 statute miles to Manatee Springs State Park.

You may also anchor west of the second small island by setting course from the main channel as if you intended to enter the small stream running north of the island. Drop anchor some 25 yards before coming abeam of the small, charted creek on the river's northern banks. Farther to the east, depths rise markedly behind the island.

Soon the deep mouth of East Pass will come abeam on the Suwannee's southern shore. You can anchor easily at this stream's northerly mouth or cruise downstream, holding to the mid-width, until reaching the charted knuckle-like turn shown on chart 11408 as having 13-foot soundings. These waters can be further identified by the small, charted island bisecting the stream in the body of the turn. Watch for snags as you cruise along on East Pass. During daylight, such hazards are easily avoided, but it is a very different story after

dark. Anchor anywhere in the knuckle turn you choose, short of the island, keeping at least 30 yards off any of the banks, and try to remember that you have to come home sometime.

It's a delightful run of some 20 statute miles upstream on the Suwannee River from Hog Island to Manatee Springs State Park. Simply hold to the mid-width. You need only worry with two shoals, which are indicated on the map pictured on page 477.

Mariners may also anchor southwest of Turkey Island (southwest of the charted location of Vista), but don't attempt to approach the island's northeastern tip or cruise the small creek running behind this body of land. Both plans will land you in shallow water.

Eventually, Manatee Springs State Park will come abeam on the starboard shores (moving upriver). Watch for a fixed wooden pier.

Our coverage of this wonderful river ends at the State Park. Cruisers continuing farther upriver should seek that old local knowledge.

North on the Big Bend Captains and crew continuing their northerly trek from Cedar Key's flashing daybeacon #12 (Northwest Channel) can set course directly for flashing daybeacon #14, well southwest of Horseshoe Point. A distance of 11.9 nautical miles separates #12 and #14.

Vessels bound out from the Suwannee River for points north will have to contend with the charted shallows of Red Bank and Hedemon reefs. Set a careful compass course from flashing daybeacon #2 to pass directly between these hazards. After passing well to the west of the shallows, adjust your course to the northwest to find #14.

It's another long run of 10.2 nautical miles from #14 to flashing daybeacon #16, southwest of Pepperfish Keys. Upon reaching #16, lay chart 11408 aside and begin using 11407.

The Steinhatchee Cruisers northbound on the Big Bend buoyage system can set course directly from flashing daybeacon #16 for flashing daybeacon #1, the first (westernmost) aid to navigation on the Steinhatchee entrance channel.

Cruisers voyaging south on the Big Bend are not so lucky. A direct course from flashing daybeacon #18, south-southwest from Big Grass Island, would land you in the charted 3-foot depths. You must cruise south from #18 for at least 1 nautical mile before cutting east to the Steinhatchee's flashing daybeacon #1.

The U.S. Coast Guard added a whole collection of new markers on the Steinhatchee, particularly east of charted unlighted daybeacon #24. These new aids to navigation are not yet reflected on even the latest edition of chart 11407. Their presence is ever so welcome nevertheless.

Don't approach any of the aids to navigation on the westerly section of the Steinhatchee's entrance channel too closely. Local captains suggest that shoaling is beginning to encroach on the various aids. Instead, hold to the channel's centerline when passing between the various markers.

Both flashing daybeacons #1 and #11 are located atop tripods and stand out on the water. At unlighted daybeacon #24 the channel takes a sharp turn. Set course to pass unlighted daybeacon #25 to your port side.

At unlighted daybeacon #30, no-wake restrictions begin and remain in effect throughout the Steinhatchee waterfront. Soon after passing #30, you will see the village's various houses and docks, mostly along the northern banks.

The 25-foot fixed bridge spans the Steinhatchee just upstream from unlighted daybeacon #25. Any number of locals have informed us that this bridge typically carries 30 feet of vertical clearance. Short of getting out the old measuring tape, however, vistiors had better be prepared for only 25 feet of clearance.

Those boats that successfully cruise under the bridge will immediately spot River Haven Marina to port. Farther along, the river cuts to the north. This portion of the stream is not recommended, as the waters soon narrow and depths become quite suspect.

North to the St. Marks River From flashing daybeacon #16, set course for the 13.1-nautical-mile passage to flashing daybeacon #18, south-southwest of Big Grass Island.

If you are journeying north from the Steinhatchee, set course from flashing daybeacon #1, at the western head of the entrance channel, to come abeam of #18 by at least 1 nautical mile to its south side. This will avoid the charted 3-foot shoal due east of #18.

From #18, 10.8 nautical miles separate you from the next Big Bend aid to navigation, flashing daybeacon #20. Another run of 9.9 nautical miles will bring northbound cruisers to flashing daybeacon #22. At #22, it's already time to abandon chart 11407 and dig 11405 out of the chart locker.

From #22 captains must decide whether to cut northwest for the 17.2-nautical-mile journey to the St. Marks River entrance channel (and possibly the marina at Shell Point), or turn due west and head directly for St. George Sound. Let us first turn our attention to the St. Marks, followed by a quick review of the channel leading to Shell Point, and finally our entry into St. George Sound.

St. Marks River The St. Marks River is one of the few bodies of water that is graced with its own special nautical chart, #11406. While this cartographical aid is certainly the last word in detail on the river's passage, many cruisers will be able to follow the prolific markers safely. In case of entry during bad weather, darkness, or other less-than-ideal conditions, 11406 would be invaluable.

The St. Marks Channel is quite deep and most portions of the cut are outlined by a bevy of aids to navigation. Be warned, however, that depths outside of the channel are usually quite shoal.

Quite a few of the St. Marks aids to navigation are small, unlighted, floating buoys. While these show up fairly well during daylight, they are certainly far easier to miss than daybeacons, and finding them at night could be a study in frustration. If possible, time your arrival before dusk.

Take a moment to glance at either chart 11405 or 11406 and notice the unnumbered

flashing marker north of unlighted nun buoy #4. Believe it or not, this aid acts as a forward range marker, paired with the white St. Marks lighthouse to the north. The unnumbered flashing daybeacon does *not* mark the channel and it should be ignored except as part of the range.

From flashing buoy #1, at the southern genesis of the St. Marks entrance channel, to unlighted nun buoy #4, you can follow the above-described range. From #4, cut your course a bit to the northwest and point to pass between unlighted can buoy #5 and unlighted nun buoy #4A.

The run from #5 and #4A to the next set of markers, flashing daybeacon #7 and unlighted nun buoy #6, is a rather lengthy gap of better than 1 nautical mile. One set of markers can be hard to spot from the other. Use your compass to keep you on course.

By the time you reach unlighted nun buoy #8, you will have a wonderful view of the snow-white St. Marks Lighthouse on the point to the northeast. Look all you want, but don't try to approach the light. The waters about the foot of the tower have depths of only 1 to 2 feet.

A charted, semisunken wreck flanks the channel to the east just short of unlighted nun buoy #12. We discovered that a portion of this old derelict is visible during low tide, while it is completely covered at high water.

Northwest of flashing daybeacon #14 the channel remains exceedingly well marked to the intersection with the Wakulla River. The cut does wind quite a bit, so take your time and follow the beacons and buoys carefully.

The intersection of the two rivers is encountered soon after passing between flashing daybeacon #63 and unlighted daybeacon #62. Unless you are visiting the St. Marks Yacht Club, this writer suggests turning up the St. Marks and leaving the Wakulla for small, shallow-draft vessels.

Pass unlighted nun buoy #64 to your starboard side as you enter the St. Marks side of the fork. The old fort and state park will be visible on the northwestern banks. There are no dockage facilities, but there is a launching ramp. Slow to idle speed as you pass.

Soon the village waterfront will become obvious, also on the northerly shoreline. You will soon sight Shields Marina to port. Lynn's Riverside Marina will be spotted on the same side soon after the stream takes a small jog to the north.

Channel to Shell Point Marina   Cruisers journeying to Shell Point Marina will want to use flashing buoy #1, at the southern head of the St. Marks Channel, as a convenient midpoint navigational reference. From #1, you should probably not head directly for the Shell Point entrance cut. Such a course would put you perilously close to the huge shelf of shallow water running south from Goose Creek Bay.

Instead, make your way south from #1 for 1 nautical mile or so, and then set course for the entrance channel. Point to come abeam of flashing daybeacon #2 (the outermost aid to navigation on the Shell Creek Channel) to its southwesterly side. The channel cuts first northwest from #2 and then follows a jog to the northeast.

Eventually the canal leading to Shell Point Marina's dockage basin will come abeam to the west. At this point you will sight a sign advertising Shell Point Marina. Turn 90 degrees to port immediately upon coming abeam of this sign. You can then track your way west through the first of the canals to the marina's dockage basin. The fuel dock and marina office will be spied on the harbor's southern banks.

On to St. George Sound   From flashing daybeacon #22, cruisers bound for St. George Sound should probably set their course for flashing buoy #24, southeast of Ochlockonee Shoal. Stay south of #24 to avoid the shallows. It is a run of some 15.1 nautical miles between #22 and #24.

From #24, those who have not studied chart 11405 might think it possible to track a direct course west to St. George Sound. Such plans would not take into account the long "South Shoal" running (you guessed it) south from Alligator Harbor. To bypass this hazard, set your course from #24 to come abeam of flashing buoy #26, south of South Shoal, by some .2 nautical miles to its southerly side. A distance of 9.7 nautical miles separates #24 and #26.

Continue on the same course for 1.8 nautical miles southwest of #26, and then turn sharply northwest and set a new course to come abeam of flashing daybeacon #1, northeast of Dog Island Reef, by several hundred yards to its northeastern side. Don't slip southwest of #1. The shoal water of Dog Island Reef is waiting for a skipper careless enough to make this mistake.

Cruisers bound for Alligator Point Marina can make their way almost due north from #1 to flashing daybeacon #2, the first aid on this facility's entrance channel. Follow the red markers around Bay Mouth Bar shoal stretching west and northwest from Alligator Point. Stay close to the markers as you pass unlighted daybeacons #4 and #8. There is shallow water to the east and west.

From #8, you can begin to bend your course back to the southeast. The red markers will eventually lead you to the marina docks on the southern banks.

Cruisers continuing directly to St. George Sound can set course from flashing daybeacon #1 to come abeam of flashing daybeacon #2, southeast of charted Lanark Village, by .5 nautical miles to its northerly side. A closer approach might put you in the charted 5-foot waters directly northwest of #2.

From #2, a slight adjustment of your course will bring you abeam of flashing daybeacon #3, also to its northern side. Now the waters of St. George Sound, Dog Island, and Carrabelle lie before you. For more information concerning these delightful waters, please see my *Cruising Guide to the Northern Gulf Coast.*

Well, we made it. It's been quite a journey from Cape Sable and Flamingo to St. George Sound. I hope you will agree that we've seen some wonderful sights and more than interesting waters along the way. I also hope you've had as much fun cruising these waters yourself as this writer has had in bringing them to you. Good luck and good cruising!

Bibliography

Alger, Daniel B. *Two If by Sea: A Guide to Waterway Dining*. Sarasota, Fla.: Siesta Publishing, 1989.

Howard, Robert J. *The Best Small Towns Under the Sun*. McLean, Va.: EPM Publications, Inc., 1989.

Jahoda, Gloria. *Florida: A History*. New York, N.Y.: W. W. Norton and Company, 1984.

Johnson, Capt. Carey. *Boca Grande—The Early Days: Memoirs of an Island Son*. Placida, Fla.: Barrier Island Parks Society, 1990.

Marth, Del and Martha Marth, eds. *The Rivers of Florida*. Sarasota, Fla.: Pineapple Press, 1990.

McCarthy, Kevin, ed. *Florida Stories*. Gainesville, Fla.: University of Florida Press, 1989.

McIver, Stuart. *True Tales of the Everglades*. Miami, Fla.: Florida Flair Books, 1989.

———. *Glimpses of South Florida History*. Miami, Fla.: Florida Flair Books, 1988.

Mulder, Kenneth W. *Tampa Historical Guide*. Tampa, Fla.: Tampa Historical Society, 1983.

Mullen, Harris H. *A History of the Tampa Bay Hotel*. Tampa, Fla.: The University of Tampa Foundation.

Oppel, Frank and Tony Meisel, eds. *Tales of Old Florida*. Secaucus, N.J.: Castle, 1987.

Rinhart, Floyd and Marion Rinhart. *Victorian Florida*. Atlanta, Ga.: Peachtree Publishers, Ltd., 1986.

Roberts, Bruce and Ray Jones. *Southern Lighthouses*. Chester, Ct.: Globe Pequot Press, 1989.

Schueler, Donald G. *Adventuring Along the Gulf of Mexico*. San Francisco, Ca.: Sierra Club Books, 1986.

Sokoloff, Nancy. *Walking Tours on Boca Grande*. Akron, Ohio: Tarpon Press, Inc., 1986.

Stewart, Laura and Susanne Hupp. *Florida Historic Homes*. Orlando, Fla.: The Orlando Sentinel, Sentinel Communications Company, 1988.

Stone, Calvin R. *Forty Years in the Everglades*. Tabor City, N.C.: Atlantic Publishing Company, Inc., 1979.

Tebeau, Charlton W. *A History of Florida*. Coral Gables, Fla.: University of Miami Press, 1971.

———. *The Story of the Chokoloskee Bay Country*. Miami, Fla.: Florida Flair Books, 1991.

Wright, Sara Bird. *Islands of the Southeastern United States*. Atlanta, Ga.: Peachtree Publishers, Ltd., 1989.

Index

POWER CRUISING
The Complete Guide to Selecting, Outfitting, and Maintaining Your Power Boat
By Claiborne S. Young

Boating enthusiast Claiborne S. Young offers sportsmen a complete guide to the selection, outfitting, and maintenance of a power boat. Young has assembled his firsthand experience with power boats into a step-by-step manual, designed particularly with beginners in mind.

Young's guide saves beginners and seasoned boaters, who are stepping up to a larger boat, both time and money. It contains a wealth of research as well as valuable inside tips for avoiding common pitfalls. Young begins with preliminary advice to boaters who are buying their first thirty- to forty-five-foot boat. Explaining how different types of hulls and designs can affect a boat's on-the-water performance, he helps determine the boater's needs of size, power, and style.

While waiting for the boat to be delivered, Young suggests that boaters take care of details such as: acquiring appropriate insurance, choosing a marina, and taking preliminary courses on navigation or safety. Once the boat has arrived, the most exciting part—outfitting—begins. Young lists the basic necessities, as well as practical and optional accessories that can facilitate on-board tasks. His emphasis is on safety as he discusses flotation devices, communication and navigation systems, and the dual importance of reading charts and heeding the warnings of offshore navigational aids.

ABOUT THE AUTHOR

Claiborne S. Young is the author of six books on cruising, including *Cruising Guide to Eastern Florida* ($32.00 pb), *Cruising Guide to the Northern Gulf Coast* ($28.95 pb), *Cruising Guide to Western Florida* ($32.00), and *Coastal NOAA Charts for Cruising Guide to Western Florida* ($50.00 sp), all published by Pelican.

240 pp. 6 x 9 Illus.
Photos Glossary Index 2nd ed.
ISBN: 1-56554-635-0 $17.95 pb

Readers may order toll free from Pelican at 1-800-843-1724 or 1-888-5-PELICAN.

CRUISING GUIDE TO THE NORTHERN GULF COAST:
Florida, Alabama, Mississippi, Louisiana, 3rd Edition
By Claiborne S. Young

"A fine, new guidebook, a bona fide keeper."   *Sailing*

"Young's warm and conversational writing style gives even a landlubber a comfortable trip through the navigational intricacies of sailing the coastal waters enroute to the shoreside attractions that beckon all travelers."   *Touring America*

For the boating enthusiast, this volume is invaluable as an interesting, unique, and thorough guide to the uncommon waters that stretch from Florida to Louisiana.

Boaters will be interested in the Pensacola Lighthouse, both for its value as a tourist attraction and as a navigational reference. Unique restaurants, including Tin Lizzie's on the Tickfaw River, will delight weary, hungry boaters, while thorough marina information will make any scheduled stop a pleasant one with few surprises.

ABOUT THE AUTHOR

Claiborne S. Young is the author of six books on cruising, including **Power Cruising** ($17.95 pb), **Cruising Guide to Eastern Florida** ($32.00 pb), **Cruising Guide to Western Florida** ($32.00 pb), and **Coastal NOAA Charts for Cruising Guide to Western Florida** ($50.00 sp). The newest entry in this series is **Cruising Guide to New York Waterways and Lake Champlain** ($28.95 pb) by Chris W. Brown III. All are published by Pelican.

432 pp. 8 x 9¼ Photos Maps Index 3rd ed.
ISBN: 1-56554-341-6 $28.95 pb

Readers may order toll free from Pelican at 1-800-843-1724 or 1-888-5-PELICAN.

CRUISING GUIDE TO EASTERN FLORIDA
Fourth Edition
By Claiborne S. Young

Boating enthusiasts will welcome this thoroughly researched and comprehensive guide. ***Cruising Guide to Eastern Florida: Fourth Edition*** is the most accurate source of details on the facilities and waters of the Sunshine State's eastern shore. In this updated edition, the reader will discover an overview of bridges at the beginning of each chapter. He will also find firsthand information on current navigation data, anchorage locales along the entire shore, marinas, shoreside dining, and other attractions.

These waters are the most diverse of any U.S. state's coastline. From the broad path of St. John's River to the secret streams of the Okeechobee Waterway to the "condo caverns" of Hollywood and Miami, Florida offers challenges and excitement. As with his other books, Claiborne S. Young furnishes dozens of invaluable maps, photographs, and chart references. Intriguing historical profiles and coastal folklore give visitors a flavor of the region, while sections on unsafe areas help boaters avoid dangerous waters.

ABOUT THE AUTHOR

Claiborne Young's guides have become the gold standard of cruising guides. The author and his navigator wife, Karen, are avid, experienced boaters who have logged countless hours exploring eastern Florida to ensure the accuracy of their descriptions and recommendations. Young also is the author of ***Cruising Guide to Western Florida*** ($32.00 pb), ***Cruising Guide to the Northern Gulf Coast: Florida, Alabama, Mississippi, Louisiana*** ($28.95 pb), and ***Power Cruising: The Complete Guide to Selecting, Outfitting, and Maintaining Your Power Boat*** ($17.95 pb). Additionally, he is the editor of ***Cruising Guide to New York Waterways and Lake Champlain*** ($28.95 pb). All are published by Pelican.

544 pp. 8 x 9¼ Photos Maps Index 4th ed.
ISBN: 1-56554-736-5 $32.00 pb original

Readers may order toll free from Pelican at 1-800-843-1724 or 1-888-5-PELICAN.

CRUISING GUIDE TO NEW YORK WATERWAYS AND LAKE CHAMPLAIN

By Chris W. Brown III

"One of the most complete boating guides to the eastern waterways I have ever seen . . . a top-notch, well-conceived and wonderfully produced book. . . . This one's a winner!"

Great Lakes Cruiser

No serious boater planning a cruise in the area would want to be without **Cruising Guide to New York Waterways and Lake Champlain,** written in the same format as Pelican's other famous cruising guides.

This firsthand account covers everything from more than 1,000 miles of popular waterways (including Lake Champlain, the Hudson River, the Erie Canal, Lake Erie, and Lake Ontario) to less-traveled waters. The Thousand Islands are also explored. The author's personal knowledge perfectly complements the data on the NOAA charts that he suggests for each area. Among the many useful topics covered are

- Current navigational data
- Water depths
- Anchorage locales
- Detailed marina evaluations
- Shoreside dining and other attractions
- Dozens of invaluable maps, photos, and tables
- Intriguing historical profiles

ABOUT THE AUTHOR

Chris W. Brown III, a native of Albany, New York, has owned thirty-seven boats in more than thirty-five years of boating. His most recent adventure was a five-month, 3,300-mile cruise from Miami to the Great Lakes.

Also available in Pelican's cruising-guide series are **Cruising Guide to the Northern Gulf Coast** ($28.95 pb), **Cruising Guide to Western Florida** ($32.00 pb), **Coastal NOAA Charts for Cruising Guide to Western Florida** ($50.00 sp), and **Cruising Guide to Eastern Florida** ($32.00 pb), all written by Claiborne S. Young.

480 pp. 8 x 9¼ Photos Maps Appendixes Biblio. Index
ISBN: 1-56554-250-9 $28.95 pb original

Readers may order toll free from Pelican at 1-800-843-1724, ext. 343.

FLORIDA ALMANAC: 2000-2001

By Del Marth and Martha J. Marth

This is a complete update of the previous edition. Thousands of fascinating facts on Florida are available at your fingertips. A first-rate activities guide, reference manual, atlas, directory, and history book, the *Florida Almanac* contains useful information on everything from government in 1875 to how to get a driver's license.

For those interested in the history and settlement of the Sunshine State, this book covers
- Indian cultures;
- national memorials and monuments;
- landmarks on the national registry;
- the state constitution; and more.

Anyone considering moving to Florida will find
- information on schools;
- descriptions of each county;
- facts on utilities, such as bill comparisons;
- tax and government information; and more.

For the tourist or the Floridian, there are
- maps of each county;
- lists of major festivals, attractions, and art museums;
- charts of rivers and waterways;
- regulations for boating, fishing, and hunting; and more.

488 pp. 5½ x 8½ Ilus. Maps
Charts Index 14th ed.
ISBN: 1-56554-768-3 $23.00 hc
ISBN: 1-56554-769-1 $15.95 pc

Readers may order toll free from Pelican at 1-800-843-1724 or 1-888-5-PELICAN.

THE GARDENS OF FLORIDA

By Steven Brooke and Laura Cerwinske

Florida's environment produces a breathtaking variety of plant life, and nineteen of its most famous and most fabulous gardens are featured in this coffee-table book.

Vivid color photographs-almost two hundred of them-showcase these lovely sanctuaries, small and large. Each garden's focus and history is discussed.

Readers can visit well-known places such as Cypress Gardens and Busch Gardens, tropical fantasies like the Parrot Jungle, and quiet retreats such as the Morikami Japanese Garden. Floral fans, weekend gardeners, and anyone who appreciates beauty will love this book. A list of annual events at Florida gardens is included.

Steven Brooke, an internationally acclaimed architectural photographer, was awarded the Rome Prize in 1991 and is a Fellow of the American Academy in Rome and the Albright Institute in Jerusalem. He received the National Honor Award from the American Institute of Architects and two Graham Foundation grants. Brooke is the author of *Seaside* ($29.95 hc/$19.95 pb), published by Pelican, and *Views of Rome*. A graduate of the University of Michigan, Brooke lives in Miami with his wife, architect Suzanne Martinson, and their son, Miles.

Laura Cerwinske, a native of Miami, was the founding editor of *Florida Home & Garden* magazine and writes articles on garden design for numerous magazines including *Garden Design, Southern Accents,* and *Veranda*. She is the author of *The Book of the Rose* and *A Passion for Roses,* as well as a long list of books on architecture and design. This is her first book with Pelican. She describes her own garden-a wooded acre of exaggerated botany—as a subtropical Giverny.

128 pp. 11 x 8½ Color photos
ISBN: 1-56554-184-7 $29.95 hc
ISBN: 1-56554-179-0 $19.95 pb

Readers may order toll free from Pelican at 1-800-843-1724 or 1-888-5-PELICAN.

VIC KNIGHT'S FLORIDA

By Victor M. Knight

Drawing upon the lore of the true cracker, **Vic Knight's Florida** points out everything you *thought* you knew about Florida. Sit back with the wit and wisdom of a tenth-generation native as he tells the real history of the Sunshine State that you didn't learn in school. Covering five centuries of people and events, plus speculations on the next century as well, **Vic Knight's Florida** spins the yarns that give Florida its unique character.

Knight dispels many historical myths, starting with how the name was chosen. Most people, Floridians and foreigners alike, would claim that "Florida" came from a Spanish word for flowers. Actually, Florida is named for *Pascua de Flores,* the Spanish name for Easter Sunday, the day Ponce de Leon first set foot on Cape Canaveral's sandy shore. Another historical piece of lore describes how the Johnson administration nearly removed five hundred years of history in just thirty minutes when it tried to change the name of Cape Canaveral to Cape Kennedy.

Other points of trivia include the story of the hotel run by the Duchess of Windsor; a single bud of a Japanese plant that created a nightmarish choking of the major waterways; the land boom towns that failed and those that survived when railroads came through; and how for a brief period in time, Florida was its own country.

Vic Knight has compiled his stories from a variety of respected sources, but the telling is all his. He brings a stylish humor to each story with a flair for highlighting the funny, but true, folklore of the state. Knight has owned and operated four radio stations throughout Florida and currently produces his own nationally syndicated Big Band program from his studio at WDBF in Delray Beach. A native of St. Petersburg, he comes from a long line of crackers. Many of Knight's forefathers are the same pioneer settlers who started some of Florida's towns and his grandfather was a state senator. When not on the air, his voice carries across banquet halls, meeting rooms, and sundry locations, where he has entertained thousands with his popular storytelling and particular view of history.

240 pp.   6 x 9¼
Photos Illus. Biblio.
ISBN: 0-88289-964-3 $16.95

Readers may order toll free from Pelican at 1-800-843-1724 or 1-888-5-PELICAN.

FLORIDA SCAMS

By Victor M. Knight

We all know about Florida's sun, surf, and senior citizen population, but what do we know about its seedy underbelly? It is a fact that Florida's loophole-laden tax laws and laissez-faire attitude have attracted all kinds of swindlers, from the garden variety con man to criminals as infamous as Al Capone. It is also a fact that Vic Knight knows virtually all there is to know about every one of them.

As a tenth-generation Floridian, Knight has abundant personal knowledge of Florida history, which augments his wealth of research on scams. Taking the immortal words of his Papa Johnson and Papa Knight, he has compiled a set of Grandaddy's Rules that can help a person see through the "smooth-talking jaspers" who over the years have bamboozled victims out of billions of dollars.

Witty, informal, and sprinkled with down-home Florida vernacular, Knight's tales of the strange educate as they delight. Shady characters like mayor/preacher/convicted felon Oyster King Willie Popham, the fictitious Prince Michael of Austria, and "the mysterious fifty-dollar tipper" carry off a potpourri of scams involving everything from luxury cars to ostrich eggs to phony tax returns. Knight explains how Boca Raton is a city based on the scam, like Treasure Island, whose very name comes from the scam that put it on the map. These cons attract scores of people because they seem fool-proof; but remember Grandaddy's Rule #3: "Nobody ever pulled a rabbit out of a hat without carefully puttin' one in there first."

Victor M. Knight, a successful radio-station owner turned Florida guru, is a busy lecturer and television-show host. His first book, *Vic Knight's Florida* ($16.95), is also published by Pelican.

176 pp. 5½ x 8½ Appendix Biblio.
ISBN: 1-56554-190-1 $9.95 pb

Readers may order toll free from Pelican at 1-800-843-1724 or 1-888-5-PELICAN.